Pluralism or Universalism in International Copyright Law

Information Law Series (INFO)

VOLUME 43

Editor

Objective & Readership

Publications in the Information Law Series focus on current legal issues of information law and are aimed at scholars, practitioners, and policy makers who are active in the rapidly expanding area of information law and policy.

Introduction & Contents

The advent of the information society has put the field of information law squarely on the map. Information law is the law relating to the production, marketing, distribution, and use of information goods and services. The field of information law therefore cuts across traditional legal boundaries, and encompasses a wide set of legal issues at the crossroads of intellectual property, media law, telecommunications law, freedom of expression, and right to privacy. Recent volumes in the Information Law Series deal with copyright enforcement on the Internet, interoperability among computer programs, harmonization of copyright at the European level, intellectual property and human rights, public broadcasting in Europe, the future of the public domain, conditional access in digital broadcasting, and the "three-step test" in copyright.

The titles published in this series are listed at the back of this volume.

Pluralism or Universalism in International Copyright Law

Second Edition

Edited by

Tatiana Eleni Synodinou

Wolters Kluwer

Published by:
Kluwer Law International B.V.
PO Box 316
2400 AH Alphen aan den Rijn
The Netherlands
E-mail: lrs-sales@wolterskluwer.com
Website: www.wolterskluwer.com/en/solutions/kluwerlawinternational

Sold and distributed by:
Wolters Kluwer Legal & Regulatory U.S.
920 Links Avenue
Landisville, PA 17538
United States of America
E-mail: customer.service@wolterskluwer.com

ISBN 978-94-035-2688-1

e-Book: ISBN 978-94-035-2698-0
web-PDF: ISBN 978-94-035-2708-6

Editor

Tatiana Eleni Synodinou is a Professor of Private and Commercial Law at the Law Department of the University of Cyprus.

She has been Principal Project manager/Principal researcher and expert at many EU- and UCY-funded research projects. She is currently the Holder of the Jean Monnet Chair DIGI (Jean Monnet Centre of Excellence DIGIU—Digital Platforms: Under the Scope of the New Era in Digital Services).

She is the author of numerous books, journal articles and chapters in edited books on copyright law, Internet law, private law and commercial law. She has participated as a speaker at numerous conferences and seminars and organized various national and international conferences and study days. She has been an expert in many projects and European Union (EU) studies.

She is a Founding Member and President of the Union of Copyright Law of Cyprus (EDPI) that is the Cypriot affiliate of International Literary and Artistic Association (ALAI) and Member of the European Copyright Society (ECS). She is a contributor to the Kluwer Copyright Blog. She is the Founder and Chief Editor of the student law journal *Nomomacheia*.

Contributors

Orit Fischman Afori, Professor of Law at the Haim Strick School of Law, College of Management, Israel.

Jørgen Blomqvist, Affiliated Professor at the Centre for Information and Innovation Law of the Faculty of Law of the University of Copenhagen, Denmark.

Estelle Derclaye, Professor of Intellectual Property Law at the University of Nottingham, U.K.

Graeme B. Dinwoodie, Global Professor of Intellectual Property Law at Chicago-Kent College of Law, Illinois Institute of Technology, U.S.A.

Séverine Dusollier, Professor of Intellectual Property Law at Sciences Po Law School, Paris, France.

Ysolde Gendreau, Professor at the Faculty of Law of the University of Montreal and Associate Dean for external relations and communications, Canada.

Daniel Gervais, Professor at Vanderbilt Law School, Milton R. Underwood Chair in Law and Director of the Vanderbilt Intellectual Property Program, U.S.A.

Jane C. Ginsburg, Morton L. Janklow Professor of Literary and Artistic Property Law at Columbia Law School, U.S.A.

Jonathan Griffiths, Professor of Intellectual Property Law at the School of Law of Queen Mary University of London, U.K.

Kathryn Hashimoto, Copyright Research Fellow at the Berkeley Center for Law & Technology, University of California, Berkeley, School of Law, U.S.A.

P. Bernt Hugenholtz, Emeritus Professor of Intellectual Property Law at the Institute for Information Law (IViR) of the University of Amsterdam, the Netherlands.

Philippe Jougleux, Professor of Private Law at the Law School of the European University Cyprus, Cyprus.

Dionysia Kallinikou, Emeritus Professor of Law at National and Kapodistrian University of Athens, Greece.

Rudolf Leška, Senior Assistant Professor in copyright and media law at the University of Finance and Administration, Prague (Vysoká škola finanční a správní), Czech Republic.

Agnès Lucas-Schloetter, Professor of Law at Nantes University, France.

Marisella Ouma, Deputy General Counsel at the Central Bank of Kenya, Kenya.

Antoon A. Quaedvlieg, Professor of Private Law, Commercial and Economic Law at Radboud University, Nijmegen, the Netherlands.

Pamela Samuelson is Richard M. Sherman Distinguished Professor of Law and Information at the University of California, Berkeley Law School, U.S.A.

Alain Strowel, Professor at UC Louvain, University Saint-Louis Brussels, KU Leuven and Munich IP Law Center, Belgium.

Tatiana Eleni Synodinou, Professor of Private Law at the Department of Law of the University of Cyprus, Cyprus.

Paul L.C. Torremans, Professor of Intellectual Property Law School of Law at the University of Nottingham, U.K.

Michel M. Walter, Honorary Professor at the University of Vienna and Visiting Prof Danube at University Krems, Austria.

Raquel Xalabarder, Chair of Intellectual Property at Universitat Oberta de Catalunya, School of Law and Political Sciences Barcelona, Spain.

Summary of Contents

Table of Contents

List of Abbreviations

ACTA	Anti-counterfeiting Trade Agreement
AEC	ASEAN Economic Community
AFC	Accessible Format Copies
AfCFTA	African Continental Free Trade Area
AG	Attorney General
AI	Artificial Intelligence
AMU/UMA	Arab Maghreb Union
APA	Administrative Procedure Act
API	Application Program Interface
ARIPO	African Regional Intellectual Property Organization
BC	Berne Convention
BIRPI	Bureaux Internationaux Réunis pour la Protection de la Propriété Intellectuelle
CDPA	Copyright, Designs and Patents Act
CDSM Directive	Directive on Copyright in the Digital Single Market
CELAS	Central European Licensing and Administration Services
CENSAD	Community of Sahel-Saharan States
CESCR	Committee on Economic, Social and Cultural Rights
CETA	Comprehensive Economic and Trade Agreement
Ch.	Chambre (Chamber of the Court)
CISAC	International Confederation of Societies of Authors and Composers
CJEU	Court of Justice of the European Union

CLIP	Conflict of Laws in Intellectual Property
CMI	Copyright Management Information
CMOs	Collective Management Organizations
COMESA	Common Market for Eastern and Southern Africa
CPD	Computer Programs Directive
CPI	Code de la Propriété Intellectuelle
CPP	Copyright Principles Project
CRM	Collective Rights Management
DEAL	Direct European Administration and Licensing
DMCA	Digital Millennium Copyright Act
DRM	Digital Rights Management
DSA	Digital Services Act
DSB	Dispute Settlement Body
DSM	Digital Single Market
E&L	Exceptions and Limitations
EAC	East African Community
EC	European Community
EC Directive	E-Commerce Directive
ECCAS	Economic Community of Central African States
ECHR	European Convention on Human Rights
ECJ	European Court of Justice
ECOWAS	Economic Community of West African States
ECtHR	European Court of Human Right
EEA	European Economic Area
EEC	European Economic Community
EU	European Union
FMLA	Fairness in Music Licensing Act
FTAs	Free Trade Agreements
GATT	General Agreement on Tariffs and Trade
genAI	Generative Artificial Intelligence
ICESCR	International Covenant on Economic, Social, and Cultural Rights
ICT	Information Communication Technologies
IFPI	International Federation of the Phonographic Industry
IGAD	Intergovernmental Authority on Development
ILC	International Law Commission
ILO	International Labour Organization

IMPEL	Independent Music Publishers' European Licensing
InfoSoc Directive	Information Society Directive
IP	Intellectual Property
IPRs	Intellectual Property Rights
ISD	Information Society Directive
ICESCR	International Covenant on Economic, Social and Cultural Rights
ISPs	Internet Service Providers
IViR	Institute for Information Law
LDCs	Least Developed Countries
L&Es	Limitations and Exceptions
ML	Machine Learning
NAFTA	North American Free Trade Agreement
OAPI	Organisation Africaine de la Propriété Intellectuelle
PAECOL	Pan-European Central Online Licensing
PAIPO	Pan African Intellectual Property Organization
PEDL	Pan European Digital Licensing System
PNDCL	Provisional National Defence Council Law
RECs	Regional Economic Communities
RLD Directive	Rental and Lending Directive
RRAs	Reciprocal Representation Agreements
SADC	Southern African Development Community
SatCab Directive	Satellite Broadcasting and Cable Retransmission Directive
SCAPR	Societies' Council for the Collective Management of Performers' Rights
TPB	The Pirate Bay
TDM	Text- and Data-Mining
TFEU	Treaty for the Functioning of the European Union
TPM	Technological Protection Measures
TPP	Trans-Pacific Partnership
TRIPS	Trade-Related Aspects of Intellectual Property Rights
UDHR	Universal Declaration of Human Rights
UGC	User-Generated Content
U.K.	United Kingdom
UN	United Nations

UNESCO	United Nations Educational, Scientific and Cultural Organization
URAA	Uruguay Round Agreements Act
U.S.	United States
USB	Universal Serial Bus
USCA	U.S. Copyright Act
VARA	Visual Artists Rights Act
WCT	WIPO Copyright Treaty
WIPO	World Intellectual Property Organization
WPPT	WIPO Performances and Phonograms Treaty
WTO	World Trade Organization

Acknowledgments

This book marks the second edition of the highly regarded volume Pluralism and Universalism in International Copyright Law, initially published in 2019.

I would like to express my heartfelt gratitude to all the authors contributing to this second edition for their dedication to updating their chapters. Their efforts bring new insights to the ongoing and complex debate surrounding the need for either more or less harmonization—and perhaps even unification—of copyright principles at both regional and international levels, especially as the ideal of universalism faces increasing challenges in today's world.

A special thanks is due to Professor Martin Senftleben, General Editor of the Information Law Series, and to Kluwer Law International for their invaluable collaboration and unwavering support throughout this project.

Dedication

This book is dedicated to an extraordinary man, scholar, and friend, Professor Antoon Quaedvlieg. A contributor to the first edition of this book, Professor Quaedvlieg tragically passed away in 2023, far too soon and unjustly. His profound intellectual contributions, boundless enthusiasm for intellectual property law, and broad scholarly expertise have left an indelible mark on the field. He will forever be remembered not only for his academic legacy but also as a role model of kindness, integrity, and passion for knowledge. We will always cherish his memory with deep affection and respect.

Introduction

Tatiana Eleni Synodinou

1 A HISTORICAL PERSPECTIVE: THE BIRTH OF UNIVERSALISM

After many misadventures as regards the protection of his books in various countries, Mark Twain wrote in 1902 that:

> Only one thing is impossible for God: To find any sense in any copyright law on the planet.[1]

At that point, the cross-border characteristic of cultural dissemination was already an issue and jurists were struggling to solve this legal challenge. The romantic ideal of a "universal" regulation which would harmoniously combine effective protection of intellectual creations with public interest goals[2] has been a dream for creators since the advent of typography.

Current and emerging technological advancements make this claim much stronger. Is there or should there be a single law regulating the protection and dissemination of cultural and information goods in the digital era? The question itself is heretical, as it contradicts the main evolutions in regional, national and international copyright laws since the birth of

1. Mark Twain, *Mark Twain's Notebook, 1902-1903* (Harper & Brothers Publishers, 1935).
2. Anne Latournerie, *Droits d'auteur, droits du public: une approche historique*, L'Économie politique 21-33 (2004). As this author notes: "*L'histoire du droit d'auteur est une histoire politique et culturelle, plus particulièrement celle de la relation entre la défense du créateur comme propriétaire et la défense de la culture comme bien commun de l'humanité.*"

copyright law three centuries ago, such as the well-established principles of copyright territoriality and national autonomy in copyright regulation.[3]

This edited volume gathers together critical approaches adopted by leading copyright scholars on the question of whether pluralism or universalism is the appropriate path to follow for the development of international copyright law, in response to current and emerging technological and societal challenges. Specifically, the aim is to assert that the emergence of a new universalist core in international copyright law (an "international copyright law *acquis*," defined by Dinwoodie and Dreyfuss as "a set of basic principles that form the background norms animating the copyright system")[4] is not a chimera. On the contrary, the foundations of such an approach could be found in the unique way that regional, national and international copyright law instruments (legislation, case law, soft law) interact when responding to current and emerging technologies.

A parallel could be drawn between the fourth industrial revolution[5] and the eighteenth century, which saw the birth of copyright law. In both of these periods, technological advances led to a similar paradoxical situation for creators:[6] the starting point for the birth of national copyright laws, and subsequently, of international copyright law.

The fusion of technologies which blurs the lines between the physical and the digital sphere, and is akin to the beneficial effects of printing technology in the eighteenth century, has led to the democratization of access to copyright-protected content. Furthermore, it has substantially increased the availability of new markets, especially through the accessibility of works in the universal Internet market. However, the technological achievements of the information society, like the devastating effects of unauthorized quick and cheap printing in the eighteenth century, have dramatically increased copyright infringements, especially online.[7] In the same way, international

3. As Dinwoodie and Dreyfuss stress states retain considerable flexibility to fulfill the objectives of IP law in ways that are tailored to their individual conditions; *See*, Graeme Dinwoodie & Rochelle Dreyfuss, *An International Acquis: Integrating Regimes and Restoring Balances,* at International Intellectual Property: A Handbook of Contemporary Research 142 (Daniel Gervais ed., Edward Elgar Publishing, 2015).
4. The idea of an international copyright law *acquis* was first launched by Dinwoodie & Dreyfuss (n. 3).
5. World Economic Forum, *White Paper, Values and the Fourth. Industrial Revolution. Connecting the Dots. Between Value, Values, Profit and Purpose* (Global Agenda Council on Values 2014-2016, September 2016), http://www3.weforum.org/docs/WEF_Values_and_the_Fourth_Industrial_Revolution_WHITEPAPER.pdf (accessed May 24, 2019).
6. Uma Suthersanen, *The First Global Copyright Act,* at A Shifting Empire, 100 Years of the Copyright Act 1911, 4 (Uma Suthersanen & Ysolde Gendreau eds., Edward Elgar, 2013).
7. According to a joint study by the European Union Intellectual Property Office (EUIPO) and the OECD of June 2021, "Global Trade in Fakes: A *Worrying Threat*", the volume of international trade in counterfeit and pirated products amounts to USD 464 billion, or 2.5% of world trade. *See*: https://euipo.europa.eu/tunnel-web/secure/webdav/guest/document_library/observatory/documents/reports/2021_EUIPO_OECD_Report_Fakes/2021_

copyright law was driven by the need of publishers and authors to combat the harsh reality of mass piracy of copyright-protected works in foreign countries. Unauthorized copying of foreign works was for a long time an established feature of European cultural and social life and continued to be so for a considerable period of time after the emergence of national copyright laws. At the same time, unauthorized copying in some countries was considered an honorable practice, contributing to the spread of learning and enlightenment of the local public.

Indeed, in the middle of the nineteenth century, after decades of combating cross-border importation and piracy of books in Europe, major European publishers and authors' societies started to search for a set of coherent and codified international copyright norms.[8] Furthermore, legal uncertainty prevailed as regards the scope and content of copyright protection, since the rights protected under early national copyright laws varied considerably or were variously interpreted.[9] The same uncertainty prevails today, when the borderless reality of the Internet has dramatically increased piracy and unrestricted access to copyright-protected works without the author's permission is often perceived by various Internet communities and digital rights activists to be a harmless practice, justified on public interest grounds, such as the users' rights of access to information, to Internet access, knowledge, education and to take part in cultural life.[10] On a deeper level, copyright—which was originally conceived as a tool to protect the author and to provide incentives for them to create for the benefit of society—is nowadays increasingly perceived as a mechanism working to the advantage of "large, impersonal and unlovable corporations."[11]

In light of this striking parallelism, this book aims to examine whether the rebirth of universalism in international copyright law is a way to respond effectively to pressing and future technological challenges or, on the

---

EUIPO_OECD_Trate_Fakes_Study_FullR_en.pdf (accessed Mar. 18, 2025). *See also*: Commission Staff Working Document, Counterfeit and Piracy Watch List, SWD(2018) 492 final 8, (https://data.consilium.europa.eu/doc/document/ST-15670-2018-INIT/en/pdf, accessed Mar. 18, 2025); Commission Staff Working Document, Counterfeit and Piracy Watch List, Dec. 1, 2022, European Commission (https://policy.trade.ec.europa.eu/news/commission-publishes-latest-counterfeit-and-piracy-watch-list-2022-12-0, accessed Mar. 18, 2025). *See also*, Commission Recommendation of 1.3.2018 on measures to effectively tackle illegal content online, C (2018) 1177 final, https://ec.europa.eu/digital-single-market/en/news/commission-recommendation-measures-effectively-tackle-illegal-content-online (accessed May 24, 2019).

8. Suthersanen (n. 6), 12.
9. Samuel Ricketson, *The Birth of the Berne Union,* 11 Columbia-Volunteer Lawyers for the Arts Journal of Law & the Arts 9 (1986).
10. International Covenant on Economic Social and Cultural Right, Art. 15(1)(a); *See also*, Christophe Geiger, *Freedom of Artistic Creativity and Copyright Law: A Compatible Combination?,* 8(3) UC Irvine Law Review 413-458 (2018); https://ssrn.com/abstract=1617892.
11. Jane C. Ginsburg, *How Copyright Got a Bad Name for Itself,* 26(1) Columbia Journal of Law & the Arts 61 (2002) https://doi.org/10.2139/ssrn.342182.

contrary, whether the decline of universalism is a dominant and irreversible trend.

2 CONFLICTING TRENDS: TOWARDS A REBIRTH OR A DECLINE OF UNIVERSALISM?

The evolution of copyright law, thanks to or due to technological changes, is not something new.[12] Technology has always posed new challenges for copyright law, while copyright law tends to react initially by resisting and subsequently by embracing the new ways of exploiting copyrighted works developed by new technologies. Conversely, copyright law shapes technology by influencing the emergence of certain new technologies and their design and architecture.[13] However, we have reached a unique situation whereby access and communication dogmas give unprecedented dimensions and orientations to the contours of classic copyright concepts. The characteristics of the pre-Internet era society are now replaced by a new way of thinking, which coincides with decentralization, and is based on the common sense of the crowd and the free networking of its members. Communication and access to the content circulating on the information highways are considered to be organic elements of the interactive and connectivity-centered society and of an experience economy.[14] At the same time, the context within which intellectual creations are used has radically changed. The dematerialization and disappearance of the tangible copy is a striking feature of the digital environment. In this context, the need to access a tangible copy of an intellectual creation in the analogue world has been replaced by access to the work itself. Consequently, the intrinsic value of information resides much more in its use than in its acquisition or possession.[15] The options available to copyright users are increased by technological breakthroughs in fields such as 3D printing, artificial intelligence (AI), blockchain and quantum computing. This trend also has

12. Tatiana Synodinou, *Copyright Law: An Ancient History, a Contemporary Challenge,* at Research Handbook in EU Internal Law 81 (Savin & Trzaskowski ed., Edward Elgar, 2014).
13. Maria L. Montagnani, *A New Interface Between Copyright and Technology: How User-Generated Content Will Shape the Future of On-line Distribution* (2008), http://www.cardozoaelj.com/wp-content/uploads/Journal%20Issues/Volume%2026/Issue%203/Montagnani.pdf (accessed May 26, 2019); N. Elkin-Koren, *Making Technology Visible: Liability of Internet Service Providers for Peer-to-Peer Traffic,* 9 New York University Journal of Legislation & Public Policy 15 (2006).
14. Jeremy Rifkin, *Age of Access, Can Civilization Survive when only the Commercial Sphere Is Left as the Primary Mediator of Human Life?*, http://dwij.org/forum/statesperson/rifkin.htm (accessed May 24, 2019).
15. Severine Dusollier, *Incidences et réalités d'un droit de contrôler l'accès en droit européen, in Le Droit d'auteur: un contrôle de l'accès aux œuvres?* 18 CRID 15-52 (2000).

significant repercussions in the field of copyright law, usually in the form of claiming access rights or, more broadly, user rights.[16] This also necessarily pushes copyright law research outside the perimeter of its classical borders. Access to copyright-protected works is becoming part of the democratic claim of access to information[17] since access to knowledge is perceived as a human right that is closely associated with the ability to defend, as well as to advocate for, other rights.[18]

The reality of the creation, production, dissemination and use of copyright-protected works is complex since copyright norms are born out of the multifaceted and often tumultuous interaction of humanist and utilitarian factors and justifications.[19] The intensification of the cross-border flow of intangible assets protected by copyright law and the universal phenomenon of copyright piracy calls for universally harmonized responses in copyright

16. Tatiana Synodinou, *The Lawful User and a Balancing of Interests in European Copyright Law* 41(7) International Review of Intellectual Property and Competition Law 819-843 (2010); Severine Dusollier, *L'utilisation légitime de l'œuvre:un nouveau sésame pour le bénéfice des exceptions en droit d'auteur?* 17 Communication-Commerce électronique (2005); Julie Cohen, *The Place of the User in Copyright Law,* 74 Fordham Law Review 347-374 (2005); Pascale Chapdelaine, *Copyright User Rights and Remedies: An Access to Justice Perspective,* 7(3) Laws 24 (2018), https://doi.org/10.3390/laws7030024.
17. *See*, Christophe Geiger, *Droit d'auteur et droit du public à l'information, Approche de droit comparé* (LexisNexis, 2004); Bernt P. Hugenholtz, *Copyright and Freedom of Expression in Europe,* at Expanding the Boundaries of Intellectual Property: Innovation Policy for the Knowledge Society (Rochelle C. Dreyfuss, Diane L. Zimmerman & Harry First eds., Oxford, Oxford University Press, 2001); Dirk Voorhoof, *Freedom of Expression and the Right to Information: Implications for Copyright,* at Research Handbook on Human Rights and Intellectual Property (Christophe Geiger ed., Cheltenham, UK: Edward Elgar, 2015); Alain Strowel & François Tulkens, *Freedom of Expression and Copyright under Civil Law: Of Balance, Adaptation, and Access,* at Copyright and Free Speech: Comparative and International Analyses 287 (Jonathan Griffiths & Uma Suthersanen eds., Oxford, Oxford University Press, 2006); Masiyakurima Patrick, *The Free Speech Benefit of Fair Dealing Defenses,* at Intellectual Property and Human Rights, Alphen aan den Rijn, The Netherlands (Paul L.C. Torremans ed., Kluwer Law International, 2008); Elena Izyumenko, *The Freedom of Expression Contours of Copyright in the Digital Era: A European Perspective* 119 (3-4) The Journal of World Intellectual Property 115-130 (2016) https://doi.org/10.1111/jwip.12057; Christophe Geiger & Elena Izyumenko, *Copyright on the Human Rights' Trial: Redefining the Boundaries of Exclusivity Through Freedom of Expression* 45(3) International Review of Intellectual Property and Competition Law 316 (2014) https://doi.org/10.1007/s40319-014-0181-3.
18. *See*, John Willinsky, *The Access Principle: The Case for Open Access to Research and Scholarship* (MIT Press, 2006).
19. For a general overview, *see*: Laura Biron, *Creative Works and Communicating Norms, Perspectives from Legal Philosophy,* at The Work of Authorship (Mireille van Eechoud ed., Amsterdam University Press, 2014); Edwin C. Hettinger, *Justifying Intellectual Property,* 18 Philosophy and Public Affairs 31, 36, 45 (1989); Justin Hughes, *The Philosophy of Intellectual Property,* 77 Georgetown Law Journal 287 (1988); Orit Fischman Afori, *Human Rights and Copyright: The Introduction of Natural Law Considerations into American Copyright Law,* 14 Fordham Intellectual Property Media & Entertainment Law Journal 497 (2004).

law. In addition to this technological reality, there is an established and constantly growing societal trend toward new paradigms of copyright law, where copyright users' and consumers' expectations need to be balanced with the interests of content providers (authors, performers and producers).

Furthermore, powerful intermediaries, and more specifically digital platforms have substantially modified the way works are communicated and have become unique de facto private regulators of the communication of copyright-protected works in the international arena.[20] This intermediation is characterized by several issues which emerge at either intermediary or content-provider level (unreliability of automated notice-sending systems and pitfalls of blanket takedown, algorithmic triage and content filtering respectively). The Internet intermediaries' dominant role in shaping the principles which regulate the use of intellectual creations on the Internet is not limited to their function as presumably neutral litigators between content providers and end users.

Faced with these challenges, regional and national copyright systems are in search of elasticity and of drastic reforms. Copyright ecosystems react variously either with the introduction of reforms or by staying inert, depending on their level of technological progress and their development of copyright law and political opportunism. This leads to a labyrinthine mosaic of divergent national responses to universal questions and to a fragmentation at international level.

Regional harmonization efforts and perspectives vary significantly in their degree or scope (such as the European Union (EU) harmonization or codification dilemma), while they often lead to the creation of new sets of rules whose compatibility with the international legal framework is questionable. Furthermore, copyright evolutions in technologically innovative countries or regions (for instance, in the past the intermediaries' safe harbor United States (U.S.) digital copyright regime or Article 17 of the Directive on

20. Primavera De Filippi, *Copyright Law in the Digital Environment: Private Ordering and the Regulation of Digital Works* (Lap Lambert Academic Publishing GmbH, 2012), https://hal.archives-ouvertes.fr/hal-00713403 (May 24, 2019); Luca Belli & Cristiana Sappa, *The Intermediary Conundrum: Cyber-Regulators, Cyber-Police or Both?,* 8 Journal of Intellectual Property, Information Technology and E-Commerce Law 183, para. 1 (2017); Jennifer M. Urban, Joe Karaganis & Brianna L. Schofield, *Notice & Takedown in Everyday Practice*, UC Berkeley Public Law Research Paper No. 2755628 (2017), https://ssrn.com/abstract=2755628; Luca Belli & Jamila Venturini, *Private Ordering and the Rise of Terms of Service as Cyber-Regulation,* 5(4) Internet Policy Review (2016) https://doi.org/10.14763/2016.4.441; Tatiana Synodinou, *Régulation et autorégulation du droit d'auteur sur Internet* at Mélanges en l'honneur du Professeur André Lucas (Jan Pierre Clavier, Carine Bernault, Agnes Lucas Schloetter eds., LexisNexis, 2014); Tatiana Synodinou, *Internet Service Providers' Liability: New Evolutions,* Computer Law and Security Review 57-67 (2015).

Copyright in the Digital Single Market (CDSM Directive)[21] have a strong impact internationally.

Overall, the broader EU approach to acting as an institutionalist protagonist in critical digital domains has had a significant impact on the global regulation of the digital sphere.[22] In this context, the past five years have also seen a resurgence in particularist tendencies within copyright law, driven by divergent regulatory responses to digital challenges. The CDSM Directive is a prominent example, introducing unique obligations for online platforms to address copyright infringement that deviate from the practices in the U.S. and other jurisdictions. These jurisdiction-specific laws reflect a renewed interest in tailoring copyright to local cultural, economic, and political priorities rather than pursuing a one-size-fits-all approach. At the same time, the rapid growth of the global digital economy pressures countries to maintain interoperability and minimize legal fragmentation. This dual movement illustrates a complex balance between universalism and pluralism as recent technological and regulatory developments simultaneously push for a globally cohesive, yet locally adaptable copyright framework.

EU copyright law harmonization is a prominent example of often conflicting regulatory trends. EU copyright law, navigating between unifying and pluralistic approaches, is characterized by significant paradoxes. The often-divergent implementations by Member States of the DSM Directive and especially of Articles 4 (text and data mining exception),[23] 15 (press publishers' right) and 17 (use of protected content by online content-sharing service providers)[24] endanger the vision of uniformity of EU copyright law and will certainly give rise to many preliminary questions that Court of Justice of the European Union (CJEU) will have to answer. Variant approaches also exist regarding the treatment of similar exceptions in different Directives, such as on the disability exception in the Marrakesh and the Information Society Directive, the digital and the general education exception (in the DSM and Information Society Directives), and the parody,

---

21. Directive (EU) 2019/790 of the European Parliament and of the Council of 17 April 2019 on copyright and related rights in the Digital Single Market and amending Directives 96/9/EC and 2001/29/EC (Apr. 17, 2019) Official Journal L 130, 17/5/2019, pp. 92-125.
22. *See*: Elaine Fahey, *The EU as A Global Digital Actor, Institutionalising Global Data Protection, Trade, and Cybersecurity* (Hart Publishing, 2022).
23. Member States have not uniformly interpreted the "machine-readable means" reference in Art. 4(3) CDSM Directive as a mandatory requirement for valid opt-outs for online content. *See*: Teresa Nobre, *The Post-DSM Copyright Report: Research Rights* (Feb. 5, 2024). Available at: https://communia-association.org/2024/02/05/the-post-dsm-copyright-report-research-rights/.
24. Christina Angelopoulos, *Articles 15 & 17 of the Directive on Copyright in the Digital Single Market: Comparative National Implementation Report* (Dec. 12, 2023). University of Cambridge Faculty of Law Research Paper No. 29/2024, Available at SSRN: https://ssrn.com/abstract=4899625 or http://dx.doi.org/10.2139/ssrn.4899625.

quotation and pastiche exceptions in the Information Society Directive and in Article 17 of the DSM Directive.[25]

Furthermore, the regulation of intermediary services and AI by the DSA[26] and the AI Act[27] also raises significant questions. According to Article 53(1)(c) and (d) of the AI Act, providers of general-purpose AI models will have to "put in place a policy to comply with Union copyright law" and "draw up and make publicly available a sufficiently detailed summary about the content used for training" of the AI model. As Peukert notes, it is uncertain what does exactly this obligation means: "*Does the AI Act transform provisions in directives, which are addressed to Member States, into an obligation of AI model providers to introduce a uniform, EU-wide copyright policy? Or do they have to implement 27 territorially limited policies? Does this transformation only concern clear, precise and unconditional provisions of directives or also partially harmonising ones*?"[28] Since the "harmonization by Directive" approach has prevailed in the EU legislative harmonization process, there is no "Union copyright law" and compliance with this obligation depends strongly on the national copyright law of the Member State whose jurisdiction is applicable in the specific case.

At the same time, the CJEU has taken the activist role of promoting the unification that the legislator failed to accomplish. The Court has undertaken a very active role in the completion of the copyright acquis and clarified the meaning and the scope of various concepts found in the EU copyright Directives. In this context, the CJEU has been a significant actor in the building of the EU copyright acquis by relying on various standards and principles: the guarantee of a "high level of protection" for rightholders, the interpretation of concepts found in the EU copyright legislation as "autonomous concepts" of EU law, the principles of effectiveness and proportionality, the need to guarantee a fair balance between copyright and other fundamental rights.[29] Important areas of copyright that had been largely left

25. Caterina Sganga, *Is There Still a Policy Agenda for EU Copyright Law?*, 54 International Review of Intellectual Property and Competition Law 1407-1417 (2023) https://doi.org/10.1007/s40319-023-01365-0.
26. Regulation (EU) 2022/2065 of the European Parliament and of the Council of 19 October 2022 on a Single Market For Digital Services and amending Directive 2000/31/EC (Digital Services Act) (Text with EEA relevance), OJ L 277, 27.10.2022, pp. 1-102.
27. Regulation (EU) 2024/1689 of the European Parliament and of the Council of 13 June 2024 laying down harmonised rules on artificial intelligence and amending Regulations (EC) No 300/2008, (EU) No 167/2013, (EU) No 168/2013, (EU) 2018/858, (EU) 2018/1139 and (EU) 2019/2144 and Directives 2014/90/EU, (EU) 2016/797 and (EU) 2020/1828 (Artificial Intelligence Act) (Text with EEA relevance), OJ L, 2024/1689, 12.7.2024.
28. Alexander Peukert, *Copyright and the Meta-regulation of Intermediary Services and Artificial Intelligence*, *Kluwer Copyright Blog*, Jun. 13, 2024. Available at: https://copyrightblog.kluweriplaw.com/2024/06/13/copyright-and-the-meta-regulation-of-intermediary-services-and-artificial-intelligence/.
29. Eleonora Rosati, *Copyright and the Court of Justice of the European Union* 40 (OUP,

untouched by harmonization directives have been de facto harmonized by the Court.[30] The activism of the Court has often been viewed with skepticism,[31] since the Court has not only answered the questions it has been asked, but sometimes also decided on issues that were not even raised.[32]

The Court's approach also affects the issue of application of international copyright legislation, as has been demonstrated by the CJEU's findings in RAAP[33] and Kwantum.[34] In RAAP, the CJEU held that a Member State may not deny performing artists from third countries outside the European Economic Area (EEA) a right to remuneration by invoking the reciprocity clause of the WIPO Performances and Phonograms Treaty (WPPT). Since the remuneration right is a harmonized one, only the EU legislature can limit that right for nationals of third countries.[35] In Kwantum, the CJEU ruled that Member States cannot apply in national law the criterion of material reciprocity laid down in Article 2(7) of the Berne Convention, since the European copyright acquis does not provide this criterion. Any restriction to the granting of rights provided in the Information Society Directive can be made only through EU legislation alone and not by the laws of individual Member States. As a result, works of applied art of third country nationals are protected in the EU without such a condition.

The tension between regional and universal norms challenges the universalist spirit and legacy of international copyright law instruments, by highlighting its limits and weaknesses. At the same time, pluralist regional or national approaches lead to complexity and fragmentation in relation to questions that have de facto a universal character, such as the digital platform regulation and the copyright law related aspects of AI regulation. In this context, the aim of the book is to answer two interrelated questions: is the

---

2019); Alexandra Bensamoun, *Réflexions sur la jurisprudence de la CJEU: du discours à la méthode,* Propriétés Intellectuelles, Avril 2015, no 55, p. 141.

30. Bernt Hugenholtz, *Is Harmonization a Good Thing? The Case of the Copyright Acquis*, at The Europeanization of Intellectual Property Law: Towards a European Legal Methodology 64 (A. Ohly & J. Pila eds., Oxford: Oxford University Press, 2013).
31. Carine Bernault, *Le droit d'auteur dans la jurisprudence de la CJEU*, Propriétés Intellectuelles, Avril 2015, no 55, p. 120; Jonathan Griffiths, *Infopaq, BSA and the "Europeanisation" of United Kingdom Copyright Law,* Media & Arts Law Review 1 (2011).
32. Agnès Lucas-Schloetter, *Is There a Concept of European Copyright Law? History, Evolutions, Policies and Politics and the Acquis Communautaire,* in *EU Copyright Law, A Commentary* 10 (Irini Stamatoudi & Paul Torremans, eds., 2nd ed. Edward Elgar, 2021).
33. CJEU, Recorded Artists Actors Performers, Case C-265/19, Judgment of the Court, Sep. 8, 2020, ECLI:EU:C:2020:677.
34. CJEU, Kwantum Nederland BV, Kwantum België BV v. Vitra Collections AG, Case C-227/23, Judgment of the Court, Oct. 24, 2024, ECLI:EU:C:2024:914.
35. For an analysis, *see*: Comment of the European Copyright Society on the impact and consequences of the CJEU decision in C-265/19 (RAAP). Available at: https://europeancopyrightsociety.org/wp-content/uploads/2022/05/comment-of-the-european-copyright-society-on-the-impact-and-consequences-of-the-cjeu-decision-in-c-265.19-raap-1.pdf.

Berne Convention's ideological heritage of harmonization of copyright laws in peril? Should this possible plurality of national responses be seen as cause for concern or, should a policy of more profound regionalization of copyright law be adopted?

3 PRESENTATION OF THE BOOK'S STRUCTURE AND SUMMARY OF THE CHAPTERS

The book is divided into five parts. Part I focuses on regional copyright law harmonization efforts. In this context, specific evolutions and emerging trends in national and regional digital copyright laws are analyzed and assessed either as the expression of a necessary diversity or as incompatible with international copyright standards. Part II examines the universalism or pluralism dilemma through the prism of international copyright lawmaking. Part III analyses the "international *acquis*" at the core of copyright law (rights and exceptions) and private international law questions. Part IV explores the gaps in the "international copyright *acquis*" and aims to answer the question of whether these gaps should be filled or not. Finally, Part V focuses on the key question of the balancing of copyright law with fundamental rights from an international and comparative law perspective.

3.1 Part I: Regional Copyright Law Harmonization

Part I focuses on the EU's regional harmonization of copyright law and on the main evolutionary trends in digital copyright law in the US, Canada and Africa.

European copyright harmonization efforts should be viewed as a truthful representation of the multiple and complex challenges posed by modern copyright lawmaking. First, there is a substantial European legacy in relation to the birth of copyright law and to the shaping of international copyright law rules. Second, the European copyright law landscape is typically characterized by a rich diversity of copyright law approaches (authors' rights/*droit d'auteur* and common law copyright traditions, monism and dualism, amalgamation of natural law and utilitarian justifications for copyright protection). Third, individual EU Member States often present quite innovative copyright law responses to specific technological challenges, such as the German and Spanish so-called Google Tax initiatives,[36]

36. *See*: Ley N° 21/2014, de 4 de noviembre, por la que se modifica el texto refundido de la Ley de Propiedad Intelectual aprobado por Real Decreto Legislativo 1/1996, de 12 de abril, y la Ley 1/2000, de 7 de enero, de Enjuiciamiento Civil ; Achtes Gesetz zur Änderung des Urheberrechtsgesetzes vom 7 Mai 2013, Bundesgesetzblat 2013 Teil I Nr 23, 116.

the iconic French "three strikes" system,[37] national regulatory schemes for administrative online copyright enforcement,[38] the Belgian and German additional remuneration rights for on line streaming.[39] Fourth, and more significantly, for more than three decades now, EU law has been making the most laborious and complex efforts internationally to achieve harmonization of copyright law.[40] Since the adoption of the Software Directive in 1991,[41] which was the first piece of EU copyright legislation, EU copyright law harmonization has passed through various phases and forms and can be summed up as a convoluted combination of legislative and judicial rules[42] and principles, which are driven by market priorities and an underlying aspiration to achieve a long-term future EU copyright "unification" or

---

37. *See*, Annemarie Bridy, *Graduated Response and the Turn to Private Ordering in Online Copyright Enforcement,* 89(81) Oregon Law Review (2010) https://doi.org/10.31235/osf.io/bk8w2, https://ssrn.com/abstract=1565038.
38. *See* for instance in Italy, Gianluca Campus, *Italian Public Enforcement of Online Copyright Infringement: New Powers and Procedures for AGCOM*, at: https://copyrightblog.kluweriplaw.com/2018/12/14/italian-public-enforcement-of-online-copyright-infringement-new-powers-and-procedures-for-agcom/: and Greece: Eleonora Rosati, Greece: *New Notice and Take Down Administrative Mechanism for Online Copyright Cases Now in Force*, https://ipkitten.blogspot.com/2018/03/greece-new-notice-and-take-down.html.
39. *See* Arts. 54 and 62 of Law of Jun. 19, 2022 (Loi transposant la directive (UE) 2019/790 du Parlement européen et du Conseil du 17 avril 2019 sur le droit d'auteur et les droits voisins dans le marché unique numérique et modifiant les directives 96/9/CE et 2001/29/CE(1)") and s. 4 of the Act on the Copyright Liability of Online Content Sharing Service Providers of May 31, 2021 (UrhDaG or OCSSP Act 202). On Sep. 26, 2024, the Belgian Constitutional Court referred the issue of fair remuneration of authors and performers on online streaming platforms to the CJEU. *See*: Elena Izyumenko, *Additional Remuneration Rights for Online Streaming on Reference to the CJEU*, https://copyrightblog.kluweriplaw.com/2024/09/30/additional-remuneration-rights-for-online-streaming-on-reference-to-the-cjeu/. *See also*: Senftleben, Martin & Izyumenko, Elena, *Author Remuneration in the Streaming Age: Exploitation Rights and Fair Remuneration Rules in the EU* (2024). Joint PIJIP/TLS Research Paper Series. 137, at https://digitalcommons.wcl.american.edu/research/137.
40. For EU copyright law harmonization, *see*, Bernt Hugenholtz, *Is Harmonisation a Good thing? The Case of the Copyright Acquis* at The Europeanization of Intellectual Property Law: Towards a European Legal Methodology (Justine Pila & Ansgar Ohly eds., Oxford University Press, 2013); Mireille van Eechoud, eds., et al., *Harmonising European Copyright Law, the Challenges of Better Lawmaking* (Kluwer Law International, 2009); Estelle Derclaye ed., *Research Handbook on the Future of EU Copyright* (Edward Elgar, 2009).
41. The first EU Directive on copyright law was the Directive 91/250/EEC of 14 May 1991 on the legal protection of computer programs. The Directive was replaced in 2009 by the Directive 2009/24/EC of the European Parliament and of the Council of 23 April 2009 on the legal protection of computer programs (Codified version).
42. For the jurisprudential evolutions, *see*: Matthias Leistner, *Europe's Copyright Law Decade: Recent Caselaw of the European Court of Justice and policy perspectives,* 51(2) Common Market Law Review 559-560 (2014) https://doi.org/10.54648/cola2014037; Marcella Favale, Martin Kretschmer & Paul L.C. Torremans, *Is There a EU Copyright Jurisprudence? An Empirical Analysis of the Workings on the European Court of Justice,* 79(1) Modern Law Review 31 (2016) https://doi.org/10.1111/1468-2230.12166.

"codification." The EU DSM Copyright Directive renders this regional approach more pronounced. In this context, the compatibility of the EU copyright *acquis* (both legislative and case law based) and of developments in the field of digital copyright law are meticulously analyzed in the light of international copyright law standards.

In Chapter 1, Antoon Quaedvlieg critically analyzes the compatibility of EU regional harmonization with the Berne Convention. Professor Quaedvlieg emphasizes the complementarity of EU and international copyright rules which are always interwoven, while at the same time he refers to the principle of comity, which is the courtesy that is called for in the international community. The application of this principle in the field of EU copyright law means that, against all odds, international law is what obliges the EU to take into account the national copyright traditions of its Member States, especially when these are based on international treaties and shared by a number of states. The author then analyzes the EU Copyright Directives to assess their compliance with the rules of the Berne Convention, Trade-Related Aspects of Intellectual Property (TRIPS) and WIPO Copyright Treaty (WCT), as well as their relationship with national copyright law traditions. He concludes that, above all, EU legislation provides abundant proof of the huge degree of complementarity between EU and international law, extending to elements such as the presumption of authorship and ownership, the concept of work, the structure of exploitation rights and exceptions. In the contributor's view, if the courtship between the EU, the Berne Convention and the WCT can be called eventful, this is something that owes a great deal to the jurisprudence of the European Court of Justice. Indeed, there can be no doubt that the CJEU takes the international *acquis* very seriously. However, there are some examples where the Court followed a radically different interpretation, even to the extent of jeopardizing basic compliance with the Conventions. That may especially happen in cases where the Court pursues goals of economic policy, of a political nature or of consumer protection, such as those of the "new public" criterion in SGAE and the application of the exhaustion doctrine to the licensing of digital users' rights in UsedSoft. In this respect, Antoon Quaedvlieg suggests that European jurisprudence would do well to show greater awareness of copyright "comity." Furthermore, it should also be noted that other decisions made by the Court have provided important building stones for the evolution of international law, such as when the Court of Justice held that the acts of the Pirate Bay platform formed a direct copyright infringement.

In Chapter 2, P. Bernt Hugenholtz explores the creeping unification of copyright in Europe. In his view, even if formal unification in the form of an EU Copyright Regulation still seems to be a long way off, the EU legislator and the Court of Justice are gradually removing or reducing the territoriality of copyright in distinct fields. First, the chapter traces this process of creeping unification of copyright law in the EU. In this context, the author begins by summarizing the process of harmonization that has led to the current copyright *acquis* and highlights the current role played by the Court of Justice as the main promotor of approximation. Professor Hugenholtz emphasizes that as a result of these and other decisions, important areas of copyright law have now been judicially harmonized by the Court and one can only wonder what topics will remain for the EU legislature to tackle in the years to come. Subsequently, the various ways in which EU law has tackled territoriality in copyright law are examined: the exhaustion of the distribution right, the rise of country of origin rules, the less structural solutions that can be found in EU competition law to prevent territorial market fragmentation through the exercise of national copyright and the regulation of multiterritorial licenses for online use of music by the EU Collective Rights Management (CRM) Directive. The author then analyzes the growing role of the EU Charter as a unifying force; in his view, it should be seen as a small revolution that is bolstering the trend toward a unitary European system of copyright. Furthermore, the author adds that primary Union law is also occasionally invoked by the European Court of Justice to protect the internal market from fragmentation by territorial copyright. Nonetheless, a truly unified European copyright has yet to be realized. Overall, a transition from the current, highly harmonized—and increasingly "deterritorialized"—system to a truly unitary copyright system would be evolutionary rather than revolutionary. Professor Hugenholtz proposes that this should be achieved in the form of an EU Copyright Regulation that provides for unitary copyright title and replaces existing national copyright laws. In this respect, in Professor Hugenholtz's view, Brexit may present an unexpected opportunity, since in the absence of the United Kingdom (U.K.), only a few smaller Member States (Ireland, Cyprus and Malta) will represent the British "copyright" tradition inside the EU, and a unified European copyright law that is systematically based on "author's rights" principles will be much easier to accomplish.

Chapter 3 is dedicated to the globalization of CRM and the role of national Collective Management Organizations (CMOs), with an emphasis on EU policy on these issues. For Rudolf Leška, CMOs continue to play a vital and irreplaceable role within the creative ecosystem and in national cultural policies, mainly in continental Europe. The author then denounces the deterioration of traditional features of CRM for the declared sake of competition, global markets and free flow of cultural goods on the Internet.

Rudolf Leška first examines how CMOs responded to the demand for multiterritorial licensing and the latest tendency of supranational licensing hubs and joint ventures, which are no longer based on traditional reciprocal representation agreements but rather on direct licensing. The author criticizes the EU agenda concerning CRM which, despite a long history, has not yet achieved any consistency and remains rather confusing. Unfortunately, it has answered this question by preferring regulatory action rather than market solutions, pointing toward a complex regulation of CRM at EU level. The author criticizes arguments against territorially based licensing schemes, such as the idea that monitoring of illegal use in the online environment can take place from a distance. He also criticizes the European licensing "passport system" under which only those CMOs which possess the necessary capacities (personal, financial, technological) are authorized to grant multiterritorial licenses to users. For now, the true winners are the big publishers and big international users operating online platforms. In his view, as regards EU policies on CMOs, instead of letting the private parties find commercially viable solutions within the realm of private law, the Commission opted for a regulatory solution using public law instruments, disregarding the impact of the regulation on cultural diversity. In the contributor's view, the stated goals of the CRM Directive were not achieved and in all likelihood will not be achieved any time soon if the Commission continues to rely on regulation instead of agreements between the parties concerned. In light of the above, the author argues that the current EU policy in this field and the means chosen for the establishment of the DSM in Europe should not serve as an inspiration for other countries. These measures must be revisited as they lead to a fossilization of the oligopoly of major publishers and global platforms, and ultimately, to less cultural diversity. Instead of creating a supranational borderless market with large corporate-like CMOs, the author asserts that other solutions should be found, based on established licensing standards and the territorial nature of copyright. At the very least, CMOs must be explicitly allowed to insist on obligatory membership for rightholders in respect of their full repertoire in the whole scope of collectively administered rights. As regards the pluralism versus universalism dilemma, the author concludes that for collective management of rights, universalism would lead to less diversity, which should not be a desirable outcome for any copyright policymaker.

Chapters 4 and 5 examine the compatibility of U.S. law with the Berne Convention's standards. The analysis of the compliance of U.S. copyright law with the Berne *acquis* serves as an insightful example of the controversies posed by copyright regulation in technologically driven economies. Indeed, technology players often perceive the standards laid down by the Berne Convention as international constraints, which have contributed to a legitimacy crisis in the current copyright system and impede the construction of a modern U.S. copyright law. Moreover, the U.S. courts continue to shape U.S., and—paradoxically—global copyright law paradigms, since major contemporary copyright issues emerge in disputes related to U.S. technology giants. In this respect, the compatibility of U.S. copyright law with Berne standards is still questionable.

In Chapter 4, Professor Jane Ginsburg analyzes the (non)compliance of the U.S. with its international copyright obligations under Berne, TRIPS and the 1996 WCTs. In her view, the U.S. has not always enthusiastically embraced its international obligations. In this respect, Chapter 4 performs an in-depth examination of the US's shortcomings in respecting the substantive minima laid down by the Berne Convention, with a focus on the protection of moral rights and the prohibition of formalities. In Jane Ginsburg's view, in combining crabbed interpretation of the scope of conventional norms with an overoptimistic assessment of the conformity of U.S. copyright law with these obligations, the U.S. remains out of step with the treaties, in relation to both of these questions. When the U.S. joined the Berne Convention, it did not amend its laws to provide explicit protections for moral rights, instead relying on existing laws. This approach, however, has proven insufficient to meet the standards set by Berne, particularly of Articles 6bis and 10, which require stronger protections for authorship attribution and the integrity of works. The U.S. also passed the Visual Artists Rights Act (VARA), but its scope is limited, only applying to a narrow range of works and not addressing many common uses like mass-market reproductions. Additionally, the U.S. implementation of the WCT deviates from international norms by focusing on false copyright management information and not directly addressing author attribution when it does not involve economic rights. To comply with Berne, the U.S. would need to incorporate a more robust attribution framework, especially within its fair use analysis. Specifically, when dealing with AI-generated content, courts should consider the impact on the moral rights of the artist. AI systems that create works "in the style of" an artist could undermine the artist's market and livelihood, even if they do not directly copy the original works. This market substitution effect may not be captured under the current fair use analysis, which focuses mainly on the specific work being copied rather than the broader effect on an artist's career. Therefore, U.S. courts should expand the fair use framework to account for the broader harm to an artist's legitimate interests.

As regards the fundamental Berne principle of non formalities, the compatibility of measures consisting of rewarding the taking of declaratory measures by offering litigation or remedial enhancements is highly questionable. In this respect, the Berne+ remedies argument rests on a fundamental fallacy, since in the author's view there is no such thing as a Berne+ remedy, and therefore no basis to impose formalities on the availability of some remedies but not others. As a result, the U.S. copyright law provision that makes statutory damages and attorneys' fees available to foreign authors only if they have obtained advance registration violates Article 5(2) of the Berne Convention. It is also unclear whether the U.S. has fully implemented the "making available right" contained in the World Intellectual Property Organization (WIPO) Treaties. Professor Ginsburg first clarifies that compliance with the WCT moreover requires a Member State to cover not only the actual transmissions of streams and downloads but also the offering to communicate the work on demand as a stream or a download. However, the U.S. Copyright Act does not include a right entitled as "making available," or "communication to the public." In this context, the U.S. implementation of the "making available right" reveals the potential shortcomings of relying on multiple exclusive rights collectively to cover the full range of acts comprised within the "making available right": some features of the right may end up being left out. Specifically, U.S. compliance with its WCT obligations turns on whether the U.S. Copyright Act, as interpreted by the courts, confers the exclusive right to offer on demand to the public a work for streaming and for downloading. The author concludes that the relevant case law is inconsistent. Although case law and statutory authority clearly establish that the U.S. distribution right embraces delivery of digital copies, decisions interpreting the scope of the distribution right differ regarding the essential question of coverage of offers to download, while some courts did not accept that the distribution right incorporates the concept of "making available" as reflected in the WIPO Treaties. Furthermore, the coverage of "making available" by public performance and display rights also poses interpretive difficulties. In this respect, the compliance of the U.S. approach with international standards is dubious.

For Pamela Samuelson and Kathryn Hashimoto, however, the flexible fair use mechanism should not be seen as a disturbing national divergence that is incompatible with international copyright law standards. The authors of Chapter 5 pinpoint that the generality of the fair use provision has favored some uses that would have constituted infringements or required compensation in other nations, but that alone does not support the view that the fair use doctrine violates international norms. In this context, Chapter 5 makes two points. First, that the U.S. fair use doctrine was accepted as being consistent with the three-step test when the U.S. joined the Berne Convention in 1989, while the fair use case law has evolved to refine the types of special cases to which it applies, in accordance with the first step of the test. As regards the second and third steps of the test, they are also satisfied, because fair use cases carefully assess harms that challenged uses to markets for protected works and other legitimate interests. The second point is that the U.S. fair use doctrine has remained consistent with the three-step test since the U.S. joined the World Trade Organization (WTO) in 1994. The authors then analyze certain recent court decisions that have taken such an expansive view of fair use as to place the U.S. at odds with its treaty obligations and the argument that U.S. fair quotation decisions do not routinely require source or author attribution. In response to these arguments, Pamela Samuelson and Kathryn Hashimoto conclude that non-compliance with author attribution in fair use cases should be seen as a part of the broader utilitarian U.S. copyright law approach, which has never embraced, and is ill-suited to, moral rights-infused copyright rules. Furthermore, even if a few court rulings interpret fair use in an overly broad way, this does not mean that the fair use doctrine itself violates the TRIPS three-step test. In this context, the fair use mechanism successfully meets the challenge of balancing the legitimate interests of rightholders, subsequent creators and the public, in regulating various uses of copyrighted works that do not have market-destructive effects. Open-ended limitations and exceptions to copyright, such as fair use, allow copyright law to be adapted to a wide range of new uses of protected works made possible by the extraordinary technological advancements in the digital age.

Chapter 6 is dedicated to the compatibility of Canadian copyright law with Berne's standards. In the author's view, the compatibility of Canada's copyright law with the Berne Convention should be analyzed only in light of the history of Canadian copyright law, and this necessarily leads to a division into three stages. The first corresponds to the age of the eager and dutiful beginner. Then comes the time of the pragmatic or realistic international partner who, in the end, develops into a passive-aggressive individualist. As regards the first stage, Professor Gendreau focuses on the introduction of moral rights into Canadian copyright law in 1931 as an obligation stemming from the Berne Convention. The author notes that despite their legislative acknowledgment, the fate of Canadian moral rights in the courts reveals quite a different picture. Indeed, several considerations rendered the provision almost meaningless in practice. The author then critically analyzes later evolutions and specifically the introduction of more detailed provisions on moral rights in 1988. According to Ysolde Gendreau, the compliance of the new provisions with the Berne Convention is not seriously questioned, since a country cannot be faulted for filling in gaps where the Convention has been silent. As regards the second stage, it should be borne in mind that Canada remained at the Rome level of the Berne Convention until signing up to the Paris text became a logical consequence of membership of the TRIPS Agreement within the WTO Agreement of 1994. Indeed, the jump from the Rome text to the Paris text of the Berne Convention required a revision of the Canadian Copyright Act. However, in the author's view, even after the 1997 revision, the present retransmission regime in Canada does not comply with the Berne Convention, due to the requirement of a "new public" criterion which does not exist in the Berne Convention. Such consequences regarding the interpretation of copyright law digress from the observation that, with the advent of intellectual property (IP) rules in trade agreements, actual compliance with the Berne Convention has surprisingly started to be of less importance than might be expected. It is also safe to venture that, when the waters of non-compliance are tested and do not bring about any rebuke, it becomes easier, the next time, to display greater boldness.

The third stage starts with the Copyright Modernization Act of 2012, which has brought Canadian copyright law into the digital era. As Gendreau notes, since the beginning of the century, cases brought before the Supreme Court of Canada gave it the opportunity to enunciate a copyright philosophy that places a greater emphasis on the user of works than on their originators. In this context, the 2012 amendments thus provided the opportunity to create many exceptions—the most famous one surely being the one for user-generated content—that were not directly imposed by the WCTs and can be challenged by the three-step test. Another problem posed by these new exceptions is their relationship with one another. However, the potential incompatibility of the Canadian exceptions with the three-step test has not been judged sufficiently serious to warrant international input. Gendreau critically examines the Canadian Supreme Court's approach to interpreting copyright law in the *SOCAN v. Entertainment Software Association* case, particularly regarding the "making available" right and its alignment with international copyright obligations under the WCT. In this case, the Court emphasized the importance of international conventions for understanding the context of Canadian copyright law but maintained that it is the role of the courts to interpret the will of the legislator, even when this may conflict with treaty obligations. The author concludes that over a period of nearly 90 years, since it started to be an independent member of the Berne Convention, Canada has evolved from a dutiful member of the Union to an increasingly bold individualist, with no consequences to speak of. Depending on one's perspective, Canada may be said to be either paying lip service to the Berne Convention or to be openly defiant. Whichever conclusion is true, it is safe to say that Canada's contribution to international copyright law is that of a country that will look first to its own interests before participating unreservedly in the elaboration of international copyright norms.

In Africa, the evolution of copyright laws has been marked by legal transplantations during the colonial period and by the requirement, during the postindependence period, to comply with international laws on copyright and related rights. In this context, Chapter 7 analyzes the main evolutions in copyright law in Africa, in order to assess their compatibility with international norms and directions.

Marisella Ouma first recalls the history and origins of African copyright laws, highlighting the fact that they were greatly influenced by the colonial era and that they reflect elements of the civil law, the common law and the Roman-Dutch law/common law system. After independence, most African countries retained the copyright laws that they had during the colonial period. Nonetheless, this was a transitional period and not much emphasis was placed on copyright laws.

The author subsequently stresses that copyright laws in Africa have been developed and influenced by various factors over the years. However, the main factor of influence has been the Berne Convention. Each country has developed its copyright laws independently of the other laws within the continent and at different times. Several factors were taken into consideration during the development of new laws or the amendment of existing laws, such as the need to have national laws that reflected the copyright situation in each country, the growth of different copyright industries within and beyond national boundaries and ever-changing technologies, especially in the digital environment.

It is notable that although the laws have been developed along three distinct legal systems, they have similar provisions, which may be attributed to the membership of the Berne Convention as well as the TRIPS Agreement. The contributor notes, however, that at regional level, not much has been done in relation to the formulation of IP policies and laws, and in particular copyright and related rights. Despite the lack of a regional instrument, copyright laws on the African continent have the minimum requirements as provided for under the Berne Convention and this may provide a basis for harmonization of the laws. Certainly, digital technologies have brought several challenges with them. Although several countries have yet to ratify the WCT and the WPPT, some of their provisions have been included in national laws. It remains to be seen whether or not the African Union, the regional and continental IP organizations and the regional economic blocs are working to facilitate the process of merging toward the universal copyright law. As regards the pluralism versus universalism dilemma, the author concludes that universalism has more to do with the approximation of national laws to comply with international copyright law and in particular with the Berne Convention.

3.2 Part II: Pluralism or Universalism in International Copyright Lawmaking

Part II examines the universalism or pluralism dilemma through the prism of international copyright lawmaking. At an international level, the Berne Convention's minimum corpus of rules is the epicenter of universalism in copyright law, and it has evolved under the pressure of technological changes with the 1996 WIPO Internet Treaties.[43] Since then, however, universalist approaches focusing on the Berne legal prototype of setting a minimum level of universal protection have reached an impasse. The impossibility of reaching a general consensus on broad IP issues is leading WIPO to search for alternative ways of promoting international harmonization, with the emphasis on additions to basic IP instruments rather than the classic path of revising the Berne Convention.[44] In this context, linking IP to trade made it possible to bypass the conundrums of the impossible revision of the Berne Convention and led to the TRIPS Agreement.[45] Nonetheless, TRIPS has also

43. WIPO Copyright Treaty (Dec. 20, 1996) TRT/WCT/001; WIPO Performances and Phonograms Treaty (Dec. 20, 1996) TRT/WPPT/001.

44. As Gervais notices, this approach permits the law to evolve selectively for groups of like-minded countries which share common IP policies, since "the risk for the future is that only states that agree with additions to those basic instruments will join them, thus accentuating the tapestry effect and leading to the formation of intellectual property clans"; *See*, Daniel Gervais, *Rethinking the International Intellectual Property System: What Role for WIPO?* at Rethinking International Intellectual Property Law, What Institutional Environment for the Development and Enforcement of IP Law?, Global Perspectives and Challenges for the Intellectual Property System, 1 Center for International Intellectual Property Studies-International Centre for Trade and Sustainable Development Publication Series (2015).

45. *See*: Peter Drahos, *The Universality of Intellectual Property Rights: Origins and Development,* http://www.wipo.int/edocs/mdocs/tk/en/wipo_unhchr_ip_pnl_98/wipo_unhchr_ip_pnl_98_1.pdf (accessed May 24, 2019).

been criticized for not taking sufficient account of the different levels of capacity for innovation and of the interests of the developing and least-developed countries.[46] In this context, the developing countries and user groups resisted multilateral efforts,[47] such as the Anti-counterfeiting Trade Agreement (ACTA) Enforcement Treaty,[48] which failed to progress.[49] At the same time, the view of many developed nations was that TRIPS was incapable of protecting their interests effectively, and consequently they were inclined to seek stronger protection in the form of bilateral or multilateral agreements.[50] As a result, the gentle methodological prototype of "pluralism" replaced the "universalist" or "unitarian" Victor Hugo approach,[51] leading to

46. Ruth L. Okediji, *Reframing International Copyright Limitations and Exceptions as Development Policy* at Copyright Law in an Age of Limitations and Exceptions 429-496 (Ruth L. Okediji ed., Cambridge University Press, 2017).
47. Graeme Dinwoodie & Rochelle Dreyfuss, *An International Acquis: Integrating Regimes and Restoring Balances* at International Intellectual Property: A Handbook of Contemporary Research 126 (Daniel Gervais ed., Edward Elgar Publishing, 2015).
48. ACTA Anti-Counterfeiting Trade Agreement (Oct. 1, 2011), http://en.wikisource.org/wiki/Anti-Counterfeiting_Trade_Agreement (accessed May 24, 2019).
49. *See*, Cristophe Geiger, *The Anti-counterfeiting Trade Agreement (Acta) and Beyond: Towards a Differentiated Approach to Criminal Enforcement of Intellectual Property Rights at Global Level* International Centre for Train and Sustainable Development (2013); Peter K. Yu, *Six Secret (and Now Open) Fears of ACTA,* 64 Southern Methodist University Law Review 975 (2011), https://scholarship.law.tamu.edu/facscholar/438 (accessed May 24, 2019); Annemarie Bridy, *Copyright Policymaking as Procedural Democratic Process: A Discourse-Theoretic Perspective on Acta, Sopa, and Pipa,* 30(2) Cardozo Arts & Entertainment Law Journal 152-164 (2012); Luciano Floridi, *The Anti-counterfeiting Trade Agreement: The Ethical Analysis of a Failure, and Its Lessons,* 17 Ethics and Information Technology 165 (2015), https://doi.org/10.1007/s10676-015-9374-9 (accessed May 24, 2019).
50. *See*, Christophe Geiger, *Multilateralism vs Multilateralism in International IP Law: Lessons to Be Learned from the Failure of the Anti-counterfeiting Trade Agreement at Rethinking International Intellectual Property Law, What Institutional Environment for the Development and Enforcement of IP Law? Global Perspectives and Challenges for the Intellectual Property System* 1 Center for International Intellectual Property Studies-International Centre for Trade and Sustainable Development Publication Series (2015).
51. *See* a relevant extract of Victor Hugo's inauguration speech at the International Literary Congress at 1878 (*Discours d'ouverture du Congrès littéraire international de 1878*): "*Vous et nous, nous sommes les concitoyens de la cité universelle. Tous, la main dans la main, affirmons notre unité et notre alliance. Entrons, tous ensemble, dans la grande patrie sereine, dans l'absolu, qui est la justice, dans l'idéal, qui est la vérité. … Messieurs, votre mission est haute. Vous êtes une sorte d'assemblée constituante de la littérature. Vous avez qualité, sinon pour voter des lois, du moins pour les dicter. Dites des choses justes, énoncez des idées vraies, et si, par impossible, vous n'êtes pas écoutés, eh bien, vous mettrez la législation dans son tort. Vous allez faire une fondation, la propriété littéraire. Elle est dans le droit, vous allez l'introduire dans le code. Car, je l'affirme, il sera tenu compte de vos solutions et de vos conseils. Vous allez faire comprendre aux législateurs qui voudraient réduire la littérature à n'être qu'un fait local, que la littérature est un fait universel. La littérature, c'est le gouvernement du genre humain par l'esprit humain.*"

more fragmentation, greater complexity and to tailored solutions and advancements for countries sharing common approaches.

In the introductory chapter of Part II, Chapter 8, Dionysia Kallinikou focuses on the existential copyright question of whether the Berne Convention should be seen as the epicenter of universalism or the opposite of this, and whether a revision of Berne's principles is necessary in order to respond to technological changes. Professor Kallinikou recalls that the transplantation of international copyright by the method of national treatment and minimum rights permits the national preservation of laws, doctrines and norms. In this context, the Berne Convention should be seen primarily as aiming to preserve pluralist national copyright approaches, since national divergences are tolerated by the Convention. As regards the challenges posed by technological breakthroughs, the author concludes that amending the Berne Convention may be a possibility, but it is unlikely. Despite the digital problems and dilemmas, Berne Convention rules comprise tradition and have secured the international protection of authors, in a balanced way, for a long time. The Berne Convention addresses universal principles and values without interfering in national legal cultures and doctrines. Furthermore, the author emphasizes that cultural diversity is very important within the framework of the digital environment and should be preserved. The Berne Convention is the reference point against which to control the compatibility of national provisions with international norms and represents a worldwide international harmonized system of authors' protection. For all these reasons, the Berne Convention should remain "a uniting force" for the protection of creators and works of literature, art and science.

In Chapter 9, entitled "Universality or Diversity? The WIPO Role and Strategy in International Copyright Lawmaking," Jørgen Blomqvist analyzes the role played in this respect by WIPO in the growing shift away from a general framework allowing a very high degree of freedom regarding the contents of national substantive rules toward a much more thorough international harmonization. By critically appraising the harmonization efforts undertaken by WIPO from the 1970s through to the early 1990s, the author pinpoints that it is fairly obvious that universality in the sense of aiming at identical provision at national level was way beyond what was achievable at that time. However, things changed a little at the time when, at General Agreement on Tariffs and Trades, negotiations were underway which would eventually lead to the establishment of the WTO and the adoption of the TRIPS Agreement, and WIPO undertook an exercise which revealed a shift in focus away from norm-setting at treaty level toward exerting a more targeted influence on national legislation. A period then began where universality was the ideal aim, but the reality of diversity, based on differing interests, had to be factored in, while the intention was to secure as much harmonization as was politically possible, but rather in the form of overall harmonization than outright uniformity of national legislation. Furthermore, WIPO's role in achieving uniformity through the provision of technical assistance to developing, least-developed and transition countries should not be overlooked.

The author then examines later evolutions (such as the Marrakesh Treaty to Facilitate Access to Published Works by Visually Impaired Persons and Persons with Print Disabilities, colloquially MVT (Marrakesh VIP Treaty), which may in principle be interpreted as a step toward unification and the Beijing Treaty). He then critically reflects upon the findings of several WIPO studies on specific topics (such as on the digital environment and the copyright value chain, the impact of digital technology on protected subject matter and on the management of copyright and limitations and exceptions). In Professor Blomqvist's view, despite many years of both norm-setting and technical assistance in the legislative field, a significant degree of diversity exists among national legislations. However, history shows that windows for international norm-setting sometimes open and then close again, and therefore windows for copyright and related rights treaties will certainly open again. Nonetheless, the role and strategy of WIPO is probably best described as that of ensuring an up-to-date, well-functioning system of international copyright and related rights protection, while at the same time safeguarding the highest possible level of autonomy for national legislation.

In Chapter 10, entitled "Toward a New Berne Convention," Professor Daniel Gervais explores the question of whether a revision of the Berne Convention is possible and realistic. In the author's opinion, the argument that Berne can never be revised because of perpetual North-South conflicts or divergences of views among interest groups is unconvincing. In his view, working on a new Berne Convention would open a much-needed discussion on the future of copyright. Since the adoption of the TRIPS Agreement in 1994, WIPO has proceeded to adopt several new treaties based on the foundations of the Berne Convention. What is emerging is a tapestry of standards with a diverse membership. As Gervais notes, it may be time to weave a new agreement on what copyright should be about, as generative AI shakes the foundations of the house built on what were thought to be solid foundations laid in Berne in September 1886. There are several arguments in favor of such an approach, which would lead to a new act to supplement the Berne Convention. This approach is preferable to the adoption of a plurality of discrete instruments, each with a new right of exception, followed by competition to ratify them or not, or even to adopt countermeasures in other fora.

A new act supplementing the Berne Convention would not be a "special agreement" and could thus rewrite the rules more freely. For Gervais, there are a lot of areas where common ground can be found, such as attribution, and some exceptions which seem beyond serious debate, at least as a matter of principle (such as exceptions for print-disabled users). However, the author thinks that more structural changes should be promoted. In this sense, Daniel Gervais criticizes the current artificial fragmentation of authorized uses in order to make each one correspond to one or more legal fragments such as reproduction, public performance, communication, distribution, adaptation and so on. In his view, this type of classical copyright reasoning brings with it a high degree of complexity. Gervais asserts that copyright rights need to be realigned, and he suggests two interconnected mobilizing principles in order to do so. First, he suggests that fragmentation should be done by contract; i.e., the underlying economic right should be a simpler right, which is divisible by contract. Second, he proposes that copyright must focus on uses that markedly restrict the market or the possibilities for exploiting the product, rather than a right to authorize or prohibit technical operations performed on the work or a copy thereof. In this context, it is preferable to have a simpler right incorporating proper limits within the scope of the copyright itself. In order to achieve this aim, the author suggests relying on the flexibility afforded by the three-step test. In the author's view, the economic component of copyright should be a right to authorize or prohibit uses that demonstrably interfere with actual or predictable commercial exploitation. This right would of course be subject to limitations and exceptions, but in keeping with the mobilizing principles articulated above, the objective is to build intrinsic limits within the scope of the right itself and to make it independent of the technical nature of the use made. In order to comply with international norms, the right should be interpreted by defining "use" to encompass current technical uses, but using the three-step test to factor in commercial exploitation. The author then suggests that structuring the right in this way would in many cases imply a temporal component. This would imply that the right would weaken after this initial phase to allow certain uses, some of which could be subject in appropriate cases to a right to remuneration. Daniel Gervais also proposes a number of further changes such as the establishment of a right to prevent first publication and a restructuring of the right of integrity, to limit it to cases when the prejudice to honor and reputation is both significant and demonstrably present. In the case of generative AI, there needs to be a discussion at the international level about the need for a human author to be the cause of the originality required (as implied by the Berne Convention) for a work to be protected by copyright. Furthermore, a new act supplementing the Berne Convention should, *inter alia*: update the text to reflect points on which a consensus is possible with respect to online uses; update the enforcement provisions; and align the Convention with key parts of the WCT and the Marrakesh Treaty. As regards the pluralism or universalism dilemma, for Gervais a new Berne Convention looks like a universalist approach, and thus one that carries not only the two major copyright families but also the rest of the world in its wake. Universal norms provide a framework within which to develop calibrated and therefore arguably pluralist copyright regimes—pluralist but within universalist boundaries.

Professor Graeme Dinwoodie in Chapter 11 explores the role of an international *acquis* in copyright law. As he pinpoints, at its founding, the international copyright system was faced with what might be seen as a binary choice between universalism and pluralism, between a single global code and a range of distinct national rules. He then analyzes how international copyright law instruments have approached the pluralism or universalism dilemma. As regards the Berne Convention, the author notices that the conceptual model embedded in Berne in 1986 was one of national treatment combined with some relatively low-level substantive guarantees of protection. Thus, the choice made in 1886 was motivated both by pluralism and universalism. The drafters opted to pursue a conceptual structure more likely to result in an international copyright system that was universal in reach and ambition, while more pluralist in content. In relation to post-Berne developments, Graeme Dinwoodie highlights that the evolution has sought to accommodate a pluralist approach to copyright law within a system that is universal in reach and which may aspire for increasingly persuasive reasons to install more uniform norms. The content of international copyright system these days is filled far more extensively than in 1886 by norms that derive from regional or international sources, than from national ones. However, the basic structure of an international system reflecting space for the pluralist value of national autonomy persists. Overall, the developments over the last 20 years have shifted the balance of applicable norms within a system of increasingly universal reach in the direction of those norms with an international or regional pedigree. And thus the space for plural national policy choices has shrunk. By the same token, advances in digital communication technologies effect deeper integration in the creation and consumption of creative works. In this context, in some circumstances, pluralism might be dysfunctional. Indeed, the acceleration in social and commercial assimilation might argue not only for a shift toward more extensive global norms but also toward procedural and institutional mechanisms that foreswear the very deliberate internationalization that characterized copyright lawmaking in the twentieth century. So, national autonomy is even more crucial than was formerly the case given the expanded scope of the international system, but so too is the development of global norms. Subsequently, Professor Dinwoodie analyzes the concept of the international copyright *acquis*. A number of challenges require a more detailed international system and one which makes explicit that which formerly was instantiated by autonomous national political processes, institutions and norms. In his view, it is important that the content of such an *acquis* be drawn from national as well as international IP law along with associated jurisprudence and scholarship, including sources such as human rights law that one might not regard as part of copyright. Indeed, an ambitious articulation of universal principles that draws upon plural sources is especially important at this time. A number of challenges requires a more elaborate international system and one which makes explicit that which formerly was instantiated by autonomous national political processes, institutions and norms. A universal system that paid greater respect to pluralism within its confines would match the liberalization of jurisdiction and choice of law in copyright over the last 20 years with a structured international system of jurisdiction and recognition of judgments that allowed an ongoing contest of plural approaches. In this context, he critically assesses Article 17 of the Directive on Copyright in the DSM. The next section of Chapter 11 is dedicated to continuing challenges to the long-standing conceptual model of international copyright law. As he pinpoints, there have been efforts to respond to the realities of plural national approaches in an increasingly interdependent climate. Thus, as the global political economy has pressed hard the formal international copyright model of minimum standards when national political economies are threadbare, scholars and activists have sought to shine a light on the balance embedded in international copyright law. Likewise, one of the principles that would structure the *acquis* would be to articulate principles that reflect the increased interdependence of nation-states and exploit the potential for pooling of resources. In conclusion, Professor Dinwoodie notices that there is a move toward universality and away from pluralism. However, this move occurs within a broader system that seeks to formulate *universal principles* that still validate a *plural* range of national *laws*. A fleshed-out *acquis* would serve various useful functions in the current international copyright climate. But, in his view, the development of an *acquis* does not predetermine any precise reconfiguration of the international copyright system or suggest any preference for universality over pluralism.

In Chapter 12, Michel Walter explores the challenges and opportunities for revising the Berne Convention and proposes reforms to modernize and improve its effectiveness. The Berne Convention has been foundational in establishing international copyright protection. However, it is criticized for its rigidity, particularly its unanimity principle for revisions, and its failure to address the complexities of the digital age.

The author highlights some key obstacles to the revision of the Berne Convention. First, the unanimity principle for revisions makes substantial changes nearly impossible given divergent global perspectives. Second, the fact that the Convention relies on national treatment and minimum standards. In Walter's view, while effective, these principles create tensions with evolving notions of human rights and digital use cases. Indeed, it could be argued that such discrimination against "foreign works" is to be regarded as a violation of copyright seen under the perspective of human rights. However, as Walter notes, the fact that the international copyright system has been in place for decades as well as the fact that the copyright concepts of the various states in detail differ greatly, despite the minimum protection established in the Berne Convention due to the continuing dualism of universalism and pluralism, speaks against such approach for the time being.

Nevertheless, the possibilities of a sensible further development of the existing protection system shall be explored. In the first place, Walter discusses structural issues: points of attachment (extension of protection to electronic publications remains unresolved), the country of origin exception (the rule allowing national legislatures to determine domestic protection disadvantages authors publishing abroad and contradicts equal treatment principles), conflict of Laws (clarification of the "country of protection" principle is needed), national treatment and reciprocity (revisions could simplify reciprocity rules and align protection with the author's home country), and dispute resolution (establishing a specialized WIPO court for copyright disputes, modeled after the EU's preliminary ruling procedure, could ensure consistency and expertise).

Michel Walter, then, focuses on the prospect of a redrafting of the Berne minimum rights, by proposing a series of potential reforms: modernizing moral rights (strengthening authors' rights to claim authorship and protect their works from harmful alterations, particularly in the digital context), expanding exploitation rights (broader rights for digital and traditional works, including flexible protections for emerging uses like AI training), streamlining fragmented rights, such as those for communication to the public, introducing equitable remuneration in areas like digital mass use, library lending, and educational applications, strengthening enforcement and recognizing the importance of CRM organizations to address mass uses of copyrighted works.

At the end of the chapter, Walter presents a draft revision of the Berne Convention, reorganizing its articles and incorporating "plus elements" from treaties like the TRIPS Agreement and the WCT. Proposed changes include expanding the definition of protected works to include new forms like AI outputs, introducing clearer rules for moral rights and equitable remuneration, simplifying the catalogue of rights and introducing open-ended clauses for new use cases. As Michel Walter concludes, while revising the Berne Convention faces significant challenges, including political and legal resistance, such efforts are necessary to address modern realities. The principle of unanimity could be replaced by a qualified majority to facilitate progress. The proposed reforms aim to balance the interests of authors, users, and society, ensuring that the Berne Convention remains relevant in a rapidly evolving world.

3.3 Part III: International Copyright Law *Acquis*

Part III aims to answer the intricate question of whether the knowledge economy and the information society call for a uniform international copyright approach or not, and why. In this context, first the possible core of an international "*acquis*" in copyright law is analyzed. The central question for all the respective authors is whether the pieces of such an *acquis* can be found in the existing sources of international copyright law for each of the topics analyzed or, conversely, whether the response of international copyright law to those questions shows the road to pure pluralism. The chapters also critically reflect on whether or not universalism would be a good way to move forward. Finally, the question of global copyright enforcement, from the perspective of private international law is also discussed.

In Chapter 13, Professor Alain Strowel analyzes the moral interests of authors as universal expressions of the law of autonomy and their plural recognition within or outside copyright law. In the first section of the chapter, the author focuses on the moral right of attribution as a demonstration that moral interests can also be protected by other legal mechanisms or by social norms. Indeed, in his view, the claims that have been translated into the moral rights we know in the author's rights countries are universal, or at least widely shared among humans. However, the interests those rights protect can also be promoted by other legal institutions (within or outside copyright law) or even by social norms (thus outside or beyond the law).

In this sense, there is a plural recognition of personality interests, whether by law or other norms. Even though those norms have probably not achieved the same results as moral rights, one should not fantasize about the effects of our modern moral rights either. Furthermore, today the universal claim to be credited for one's work can be enforced differently because standardized forms of copyright licenses have flourished, and it is easier to make a claim through the choice of a type of license. The interest behind the right of attribution can also be enforced through tort law, a law field that relies heavily on simple moral norms. Furthermore, in countries where the collective management of copyright is well developed, such as in the Nordic countries, the fact that CMOs can and do fight for the moral interests of their members is also a strong factor leading to the effective recognition of moral rights. New technologies can also better serve moral interests, such as Apple's iTunes service which allows the user to find and maintain the accurate attribution of recorded music.

Strowel compares the model of the continental European systems, which have numerous and broad moral rights, with the Anglo-American systems, which have moral rights that are not less developed. As he notes, the differences among civil law countries and among common law countries suggest that there is no universal model for the protection of the moral interests of the authors or even two main models that can be directly compared. The absence of a "universal" model for moral rights also points to a drafting issue and the divergences in formulating the law in different legal systems. As regards this point, in Professor Strowel's view, moral rights should be formulated in broad terms and have broad coverage.

Alain Strowel proposes thinking about moral rights through the prism of two other "ideal types" in the sense of Max Weber—essentially two constructions of abstract models (or two idea-constructs) that help put the chaos of complex realities in order. In this context, the author analyzes copyright law through the prism of the "law of growth," comprising rules favoring the functioning and the expansion of the market, and of the "law of autonomy," which includes all the rules that aim to protect the development of individuals, and in particular their human capabilities. Copyright law

content, like other branches of property law, is a way to control resources for maximizing their use, and it is thus part of the "law of growth." But modern law is also influenced by the superior objective of enhancing the autonomy of persons and their capabilities, i.e., their real opportunities to do and be what they have reason to value. By ensuring that works cannot be marketed without the will of the creator and by allowing the creator to control the fate of his work and to ensure its integrity, the moral rights are also clearly part of this legal dimension. However, overall, in the author's view, copyright mainly belongs to the "right of growth" and only contains some ancillary components that are part of the "law of autonomy." The two legal dimensions of copyright, as the law of growth and the law of autonomy, are mirrored in the two strands that pervade the case law on copyright: most decisions focus on the protection of a thing (property rule) while some, including those on moral rights, tend to protect more against taking (rule of conduct). Other notions and building blocks of copyright, such as originality and the requirements for the establishment of copyright infringement to be established, tend to point toward moral values.

Furthermore, Strowel proposes an EU framework to bring moral rights in line with the law of autonomy, or even unification in this field. The international standard of Article 6bis of the Berne Convention could eventually be literally incorporated in an EU instrument, making it directly applicable and thus more effective. This incorporation into EU law would also allow the CJEU to interpret and apply it in a way that could ensure more convergence between the Member States. One small step further would be to add a provision on the characteristics of the attribution and integrity rights as defined in Article 6bis, making it clear, for instance, that those two rights cannot be assigned, but only waived in special circumstances. One further improvement would be to add the disclosure right (droit de divulgation), while the statutory provisions on moral rights should also define their limitations.

Finally, the role of moral rights is discussed in the context of the massive production of content made possible by generative Artificial Intelligence (genAI) and the spreading of the so-called digital replicas. Whether moral rights as such are the best instrument against digital replicas remains debatable, but at least the fundamental rights behind those rights that are part of the law of autonomy could help to address some issues linked to the spread of digital replicas. If one adopts the lenses of a European lawyer, the justification of a possible right of publicity to address the attribution and integrity issues linked to digital replicas is based on the fundamental rights to dignity and privacy of creators, which are the source of moral rights. As Alain Strowel concludes, this shows that the claims of authorship and integrity are universal, although they can be embedded in plural legal expressions, depending on traditions and cultures.

The next chapter is dedicated to copyright exceptions and limitations. Specifically, Raquel Xalabarder in Chapter 14 explores the question of whether it is possible to promote a common core of exceptions and limitations in international copyright law. The author first analyzes the legal framework of exceptions in the Berne Convention (the mandatory exception of quotation, illustration for teaching, the doctrine of "minor reservations," the three-step test). She then refers to the regime of exceptions in the Rome Convention, the 1976 Tunis Model on Copyright for Developing Countries, the regulation of exceptions in TRIPS and WCT/WPPT, and the Marrakesh Treaty for the Visually Impaired. The author emphasizes that despite these variant sources, exceptions and limitations remain subject to national laws and, unlike exclusive rights, they have hardly been harmonized by international copyright instruments as a "conventional minimum." As a result, acts of exploitation that are exempted (allowed by law) in one country may differ from those allowed in another country and may even lead to the opposite result. She then examines the main differences in the copyright systems in the EU and the US.

As regards the EU acquis on exceptions, the author notes that the need for a deeper harmonization of exceptions and limitations than that provided in Directives had already been identified by the CJEU, which took the opportunity to move forward on this issue, through the preliminary rulings submitted to it by national courts. In addition to applying the principle of strict interpretation of exceptions and limitations, the CJEU has consistently denied it is the only hermeneutical criterion and has turned to several other criteria for the interpretation and application of exceptions and limitations in national laws. The recently approved CDSM Directive may be seen as a pivotal point in harmonizing exceptions and limitations in the EU. This directive introduces mandatory exceptions for text and data mining, digital and online teaching, and cultural heritage preservation, among others, which aim to address the challenges posed by digital and online markets.

She then turns to U.S. law, and specifically to the flexible "fair use" mechanism, which is an equitable rule of reason that can only be examined and decided on the specific facts of each infringing case. Professor Xalabarder then presents a series of examples of how different national laws and courts find different solutions to the same problems, especially in the case of digital and online means. Specifically, she analyzes the divergent legal treatment of search engines and thumbnails, the Google Books project, text and data mining, and user-generated content in U.S. and EU law. She then analyzes the safeguarding of exceptions and limitations against the implementation of technological protection measures and contractual terms. In her assessment, this is another instance of plural solutions in national laws in the field of exceptions and limitations. Exceptions and limitations are being overridden by technological protection measures and contractual terms, and no universal consensus exists as to whether exceptions and limitations are matters of public policy that should not yield to private ordering.

The vulnerability of exceptions and limitations is not really a result of international obligations but rather of their diverse implementation in national laws. In the view of the contributor, national differences create legal uncertainty and unpredictable results, reinforcing the need for licensing and ultimately trumping the very public interests that they are meant to safeguard. In this respect, Professor Xalabarder emphasizes that strict pluralism in exceptions and limitations upsets the internal balance of copyright laws and ultimately delegitimizes the whole copyright system. In this context, she concludes that as we walk toward universal protection of exclusive rights under copyright, we should also aim at stronger uniformity in the area of exceptions and limitations at an international level. How could this be achieved? In her opinion, a uniform code unifying the definitions of work and author, and of exclusive rights, and also defining exceptions and limitations is not only rather unfeasible in practice but also undesirable. This is because exceptions and limitations are a precious tool for public policy and should remain linked to national culture, markets, and ultimately, laws. Subsequently, Professor Xalabarder critically examines other ways to promote an international acquis on exceptions: a Treaty on Exceptions and Limitations, a common "fair use" or three-step test, a common de minimis test, a combination of "strong" reasons that justify exceptions to exclusive rights (such as in the Wittem's European Copyright Code approach) and a two-step test.

Séverine Dusollier in Chapter 15 sheds light on another complex aspect of international copyright law *acquis*: the international fragmentation of copyright duration. In Professor Dusollier's view, a complicated picture lurks behind the set of apparently simple rules to be found at international level and it hides rather well the failure of international copyright legislation to fix a uniform term of protection throughout the world. As a result, it is almost impossible to determine with any certainty or stability the end of copyright over a specific work. Chapter 17 starts by describing how the task of determining copyright duration on a work oscillates between the minimum rules laid down by the Berne Convention and by national copyright laws. The author emphasizes that the most important rule is the minimum duration of 50 years after the author's death and that beyond this threshold, an implicit but key principle is that the term is limited in time. In this context, the establishment of a private property right should be seen only as a limited intrusion into the public domain that should stay as the rule. Certainly, the final determination of the duration is left to national laws, and as a result, this duration actually diverges quite significantly, depending on the country. Most countries then share the rule inspired by the Berne Convention for calculating the term of joint authorship works from the death of the last surviving coauthor and apply a shorter term for photographs or works of applied art, while the rule of *lex loci protectionis* also applies to the duration of copyright protection. The author pinpoints that there is a high degree of variability as to whether and when a specific work has entered the public domain in different countries, which in turn can greatly complicate the task of identifying the composition of the public domain. This is particularly true when the exploitation or use of a public domain work is envisaged simultaneously in many countries. Furthermore, the rule of terms comparison might also complicate the task of determination. According to this rule, if the State has not decided otherwise, the determination of the term of protection will undergo a comparison of the terms laid down in the country of origin and in the country of protection. Section 17.2 explores other reasons for even more fragmentation, by looking at some oddities specific to certain national regimes, such as war-related extensions of protection terms and the intriguing case of Peter Pan in U.K. copyright law. In section 17.3, the variability of the copyright duration resulting from repeated term extensions and transitory provisions is addressed. Séverine Dusollier concludes that the blind spot in which duration is left in international copyright law ought to merit further attention. In her assessment, even if a complete harmonization appears difficult, and maybe undesirable, as it would wipe out cultural differences or national public policies or carry the risk of further extending the protection, some simplification could be beneficial. The international lawmaker could be advised to take more care of the ecology of the copyright system by achieving a greater degree of balance between protection and public domain, and by not letting the former grow wildly to the detriment of the free space left for creation and access to culture.

In Chapter 16, Paul Torremans focuses on the dangers and challenges posed by the segmentation of copyright law in the digital era, from a private international law perspective. The author first demonstrates the complexity of determining the governing law in copyright cases with a digital dimension at a cross-border level. Paul Torremans goes on to critically analyze the approach taken by the Court of Justice of the EU (*Renckhoff and Nintendo v. BigBen* cases), which focuses on a single infringing act, and therefore skips the process of determining the governing law for the other infringing acts. In his view, the question needs to be asked as to how far the Court wants to take this approach, as it may create a revolution in the field of IP. As regards the question of jurisdiction, the author refers to the *Parfummarken* case that was recently decided by the German Bundesgerichtshof. In his view, the approach taken by the courts in those cases is characterized by an inherent tension between, on the one hand, the idea of an overall assessment to identify the infringing act that will lead to the governing law and, on the other hand, the idea that one identifies the initial infringing act. Even more worrying from an IP law perspective is the outcome where the rightholder seems to be left with no means of redress in relation to ancillary acts of As Torremans notes, the CJEU has not significantly addressed non-unitary IP cases since Nintendo, but recent cases like AMS Neve highlight the special jurisdictional rules for unitary rights. The Brussels I Regulation's Article 7(2) provides solutions based on where the act leading to damage occurs, helping avoid the risk of forum shopping in the digital environment. One therefore needs to add a *de minimis* rule that stops this from happening by requiring a minimal link with the jurisdiction. In this respect, the author refers to Conflict of Laws in Intellectual Property (CLIP) principles, primarily focusing on special rules for cases of ubiquitous (copyright) infringement. The CLIP Principles suggest a jurisdictional approach based on where substantial infringement activities occurred or where harm was substantial. This ensures that the applicable law is appropriate and avoids a fragmented approach that fails to reflect the global nature of digital copyright infringement. Although a legislative intervention is necessary in order to put these principles into practice, a flexible approach adopted by the current legal tools can go a long way. Such an approach adheres much more closely to the basic principles of copyright law rather than the approach derived from the *Renckhoff, Nintendo and Parfummarken* cases.

3.4 Part IV: Gaps in the International Copyright Law *Acquis*

Part IV is dedicated to the gaps in the international copyright law "*acquis*," and thus to questions where no universal basis exists. For most of the topics addressed in this part, the emergence of a universal *acquis* could be seen as unorthodoxy, since these are issues where national copyright traditions and philosophies historically prevail. However, should this approach be reversed?

One of the topics where no universal copyright basis exists is the question of authorship. In Chapter 17, I explore the concept of authorship from an international and comparative law perspective in order to derive some common principles which, in my view, should be part of a common universal understanding of authorship. The chapter is divided into two sections. Section 17.1 demonstrates that despite the lack of an official confirmation, a general principle of human intervention as a component of authorship is part of the international copyright *acquis*. In this respect, I first assert that the dominant interpretation of the Berne Convention appears to favor the position that the author should be a natural person, even though some national jurisdictions appear to welcome legal persons as well. Some expressions of this principle are the calculation of the term of copyright protection *post mortem auctoris* and the recognition of moral rights which aim to secure elements of the creator's personhood (the author's "honor and reputation"). This approach is also consistent with the prevailing natural law justification, which inspired the Berne Convention. Furthermore, from a comparative point of view, the principle that the author of the work is primarily a human being also seems to prevail, even though copyright systems based on utilitarian justifications of copyright law accept deemed authorship for legal persons.

However, the depersonalization of authorship through the recognition of legal persons as "authors" and the reality of mass production of artworks by sophisticated AI systems undermine the foundations of this principle. Specifically, as regards AI-generated works, the prevalence of the sacred principle of human authorship requires the existence of a significant level of human intervention in the creative process and consequently renders heretical the recognition of authorship without human input. Indeed, in the case of AI-generated works, the author appears to be another work: the computer program, which acts as the "mind" of the AI system. The only way to award copyright protection would be to attribute the work to the natural person (the computer programmer) who created the software which, in turn, produced the work. This is problematic. The causal link of the work with the software programmer is weak, as he/she sets the rules and parameters under which the software operates but he/she does not define the final form of the work. Furthermore, the software programmer has not deliberately contemplated and conceived his/her contribution as being part of the final form of the work and aimed at the creation of that work. This should be considered as another impediment for the protection by copyright law of AI-generated works. In this respect, the question of whether there is an implicit requirement that creativity must be intentional or purposive is analyzed. Specifically, in the case of AI-generated works, the will of the software programmer is to create the specific software and not the work produced by the AI system. So, if an "intention to create" is really an implicit criterion for authorship, then the software programmer cannot be considered to be the author of the work, but only an author of the software. The question of AI whether users of AI tools should be considered the authors of the output generated by these systems is also explored. The user typically has a closer connection to the final output by setting parameters and making creative choices that influence the results. Such an approach aligns with copyright incentive theories, as it would grant legal protection to AI-generated works, encouraging further use and innovation. However, the level of the user's creative involvement is crucial. If the user's input is minimal or abstract, it might not meet the criteria for authorship, especially when the AI system generates output in ways that are not easily predictable or explainable by the user. The degree of human creativity and decision-making—such as guiding the AI's output in the post-production phase—determines whether the user's involvement is substantial enough to claim authorship. Ultimately, determining authorship of AI-generated works is complex and context-dependent. Different copyright traditions may interpret the issue in various ways, reflecting the challenges of adapting traditional legal principles to modern AI technologies.

Furthermore, the thorny relationship that exists between the concepts of authorship and originality is analysed. In this context, I defend the view that there is a need for a proper, consistent and autonomous definition of the concept of authorship. In my view, making authorship dependent on creativity and on the contrary assimilating authorship with first copyright ownership are both concepts that blur the conceptual core of authorship. Furthermore, defining authorship through originality is a backward approach.

Subsequently, I defend a definition of authorship which does not depend on originality. In this respect, some general principles seem to apply: (1) that an author is a human being; and (2) possibly, an implicit prerequisite of a creative will resulting in the production of the specific form of the work, but not necessarily a will to be an author. Additionally, it could be argued that some aspects of the concept of authorship could be deduced from certain voluntary "omissions" from the Berne Convention, such as the non-inclusion of certain categories of "productions" in protectable subject matter. Furthermore, some useful findings may be extracted from the differentiation between "manufacturers" and "authors." Since a work of the mind is necessarily an intellectual achievement, its expression in the universe of forms which are perceptible by human senses is the result of a process involving its externalization in concrete form. In this context, the author shall be deemed to be the natural person who had the will to create a specific work and expressed this will in the sense that he/she autonomously conceived and probably executed its final form or closely controlled the execution of the work. In conclusion, leaving aside the question of originality, in the absence of a multiplicity of contributors, it would be fairly straightforward to define who the creator of a work is. However, there will still be some cases where it will be difficult to define the creator, such as in relation to AI-generated works (no human author, no creative will), works generated by animals (no human author, no creative will), sports games (no creative will) or purely accidental works (no creative will).

Chapter 18 analyzes the advantages and disadvantages of universalism as opposed to pluralism or state autonomy, how these have played out and are still playing out for the protection of nonoriginal databases and the copyright/design interface and how this analysis can inform the general debate and other copyright topics. Professor Estelle Derclaye first analyzes the disadvantages and the advantages of universalism. The author highlights the fact that universalism entails several negative aspects. First, adopting a universal norm in an international IP treaty is unfair if the parties are not at the same level of development. A second problem with universal rules is that once they are enshrined in a treaty, they are extremely hard to change, as they require unanimity. A third issue is that of the courts. Because treaties are very hard to change, such courts are in fact the "de facto" legislatures when issues are unclear in terms of the law. Finally, universal rules prevent countries from being laboratories and experimenting with different rules. However, universalism also has positive aspects. First, it imposes the same rules, and this creates a level playing field for all parties. Second, private international law vanishes as all parties have the same norms. Third, universal rules also help international trade. Furthermore, having universal rules brings countries and stakeholders together. Overall, universal copyright rules lower costs and increase efficiency, legal certainty and mutual understanding. Professor Estelle Derclaye explores two specific examples, one after the other: nonoriginal databases and works of applied art. As regards the sui generis database right, the author pinpoints that despite several relevant decisions by the CJEU, many questions remain unanswered. The author also pinpoints that it is unclear whether the database right has incentivized the production of databases in the EU compared to elsewhere in the world. Therefore, the database right has spread beyond the EEA and some associated states, and is part of current multilateral negotiations, though its effectiveness is far from proven: its scope is arguably too broad and many of its notions are far from clear. In conclusion, the experience derived from the database right shows that in some cases, i.e., those where a new intellectual property right (IPR) is adopted, it is better to be pluralist. Furthermore, it is unwise to adopt new rules universally outright, without properly testing them. The author then examines the legal protection of works of applied art. She first recalls that the choice as to whether a work of applied art is protectable by copyright is left to countries. In the contributor's view, this is a topic where even the EU has failed, since Article 17 of the Design Directive leaves the copyright/design interface untouched. Consequently, countries have used many criteria to determine whether a work of applied art should be protected by copyright law, with mixed results. In this context, where pluralism has subsisted for so long and legal experiments have yielded results so that one criterion emerges as the best, and there is no cultural diversity problem, adopting a universal rule is warranted. Finally, as regards the central question in the book, Estelle Derclaye concludes that, from a historical perspective, pluralism is good. In her view, when a new problem arises, it is better that countries/regions adopt different rules to see which one(s) work(s) best. In this context, universalism is good ex post facto once these legal experiments have been conducted and little if any controversy remains regarding the rules to adopt.

Chapter 19 is dedicated to copyright contract law. Agnès Lucas-Schloetter first highlights the fact that international copyright conventions do not provide for author-protective rules in contractual matters. At the European level, copyright contract law has not yet been harmonized. However, the Directive 2019/790 on Copyright in the Digital Single Market (CDSM Directive) has introduced harmonized rules, addressing an area traditionally left to Member States. Demands for fairer remuneration for authors and performers have grown louder, particularly in the music industry, where studies show that artists receive a small share of revenues. This is all the more remarkable given that copyright contracts have so far always been regarded as an area of law that would be left to the Member States and could not be harmonized. In fact, the contributor's view is that creative people need support in two respects: first, in order to control the scope of copyright assignments and license agreements and second, to negotiate appropriate remuneration.

As regards the scope of assignments, the author pinpoints that three instruments can be used to protect creative people. First, the interpretation rule in dubio pro auctore. Second, the obligation of specification according to which copyright contracts must expressly indicate which rights are granted, for which types of use, geographical scope, duration, etc. Finally, special provisions for contracts covering future works and/or future types of use. The CDSM Directive introduces a right of revocation for unexploited works, a significant improvement over earlier mechanisms. However, exceptions for collaborative works and sector-specific provisions remain areas of concern. In her view, a prohibition of copyright assignments or licenses covering as yet unknown types of use could also be contemplated at EU level. The author subsequently analyzes the question of termination of the contract due to insufficient exploitation and notes that a right of retraction on the grounds of insufficient exploitation has proven to be rather inefficient in practice. A means of improving the contractual position of creative people might be to introduce a duty to exploit each right granted for each type of use, which could be designated as a "use it or lose it" clause that would have to be enforced before the courts. Additionally, apart from reversion due to insufficient exploitation, creative people could also be granted the right to terminate a copyright contract after a specific period of time. This concept, inspired by the U.S. reversion right, which takes effect 35 years after a copyright assignment or license, is notably absent from the CDSM Directive but remains an area for potential development in Europe.

As regards the central question of the remuneration of creative people, the author notes that there are various mechanisms, ex ante and ex post, in both individual and collective copyright law, which are intended to offset the structural imbalance in bargaining power between creative people on the one hand and publishers and producers on the other. A first solution is to impose a requirement that the remuneration should be proportional to the revenues generated from exploitation of the works or performances. Other solutions could be to require that the remuneration of authors and performers should be fair and to establish a best-seller clause. Furthermore, new collective agreement models should be developed that address the needs of creative people as independent contractors, while the mechanism of "common standards of remuneration" has proven quite ineffective. Article 18 of the CDSM Directive strengthens these efforts by requiring "appropriate and proportionate remuneration" for authors and performers. Transparency obligations introduced under Article 19 of the Directive aim to address the longstanding problem of "information asymmetry" by ensuring that authors and performers receive comprehensive and regular information regarding the exploitation of their works.

A strong copyright contract law also requires certain enforcement mechanisms. Another significant problem is the "asymmetry of information," meaning that authors and performers do not receive adequate information from their contracting partners, especially regarding the revenues generated by use or performance of their works. In this context, the transparency obligation established by the new Copyright Directive is a step toward greater accountability. Finally, copyright contract law should include some mandatory provisions. In Agnès Lucas-Schloetter's view, the key question here is how to avoid circumvention of protective national copyright contract law at international level. According to a basic rule of private international law, the law applicable to contractual obligations may be freely chosen by the parties. However, the freedom of the parties to choose the applicable law is not absolute. For structurally weaker parties, such as consumers and employees, protective mandatory provisions often override choice-of-law clauses. A similar approach should be considered for authors and performers, ensuring fair treatment in international contracts. In this context, a rule protecting authors and performers against disadvantageous choice-of-law clauses would merit serious consideration.

3.5 Part V: Human Rights and International Copyright Law

Finally, Part V explores the topical question of balancing copyright protection with human rights from an international copyright law perspective. The focus in the next three chapters is on the dynamically emerging regulatory force of freedom of expression for the delimitation of copyright monopoly. In this respect, recent case law and trends are analyzed, such as the inherent copyright law antagonism between the right to control access to works and the user's right to obtain access to the work. A focus is given to specific evolutions in the EU and Israel, while the central question is whether there can or should be a common basis for understanding on the question.

In Chapter 20, Professor Jonathan Griffiths analyses the relationship between authors' rights under copyright law and creators' rights as recognized in international human rights law. Specifically, the chapter highlights how authors' rights, grounded in international copyright treaties such as the Berne Convention, differ from creators' rights, defined under Article 27(2) of the Universal Declaration of Human Rights (UDHR) and Article 15(1)(c) of the International Covenant on Economic, Social, and Cultural Rights (ICESCR). The chapter identifies overlaps, particularly in moral rights, but emphasizes key distinctions. Creators' rights prioritize the individual and cultural aspects of creativity over corporate interests, diverging from the economic focus of copyright law. This is underscored by interpretations from the United Nations (UN) Committee on Economic, Social and Cultural Rights (CESCR) and the Human Rights Council's Special Rapporteur on cultural rights, which frame creators' rights as fundamental human rights with broader social obligations, such as ensuring equitable access to culture and protecting marginalized groups.

Specifically, if authors' rights, as established in international copyright law, were indeed human rights, claims to the universalism of copyright norms would be reinforced. In this context, he explores whether the authors' rights protected under copyright laws are synonymous with the creators' rights protected in human rights law. First, the argument that author's rights are protected as human rights is outlined. The analysis focuses on creators' rights but touches also on arguments that authors' rights are encompassed within other generally recognized human rights, such as the right of freedom of expression and the right of property. The chapter then moves on to examine the scope of creators' rights within international human rights law. In Professor Griffiths' view, this comparison shows significant distinctions between authors' rights and creators' rights and, as a consequence, deal a blow to the universalist claim that human rights law provides fundamental reinforcement for the norms established in copyright law. Subsequently, it is suggested that, while it would appear to be very difficult to argue that the copyright system as a whole is supported by the international obligation to protect creators' rights, there are some aspects of the current system which are based on human rights norms. Similarly, there are aspects of copyright law, at international and national level, which sit uneasily with the obligations assumed by states under Article 27(2), UDHR and Article 15(1)(c), ICESCR.

The chapter concludes by arguing that there is an important (if unresolved) relationship between authors' rights and creators' rights, but that we do not have a mutually supportive, pluralist copyright *acquis* in which the international copyright system is underpinned by the human rights of creators. Rather, the two systems operate in relative isolation from one another. Meaningful integration of creators' rights into copyright systems requires clearer definitions, broader consensus, and a recalibrated balance between authors' interests and public access. However, political and institutional obstacles continue to hinder this convergence.

In Chapter 21, Professor Philippe Jougleux provides insights into two mutually antagonistic developments in European copyright law concerning the topic of access to the work of the mind. On the one hand, we are witnessing the progressive recognition of a rightholder's control over access to the protected work in the context of its digital use, either through technical control over the protected work or through interpretation of the existing rightholder's prerogatives in the digital sphere. On the other hand, the user's right to obtain access to it is becoming a societal imperative. The author shows that both aspects are currently emerging through jurisprudential and legislative developments. To summarize, three main arguments work in favor of the right to control access: the scope of the rightholder's prerogatives, the possibility of inserting Digital Rights Management (DRM) mechanisms into digital assets and the recent extension of the economic prerogative into the online environment in order to cover access. It is remarkable that each of these three arguments faces a counterargument in favor of the right to obtain access: the content-mining exception encounters the idea of access control and the case law that emphasizes human rights puts into perspective both DRM protection and the current broad interpretation of online economic rights. He concludes that neither part of this dichotomy should be seen as a revolution but instead as belonging to a long tradition of copyright law that combines rights and freedom in a fair balance perspective. Indeed, in the contributor's view, it would be simplistic to conclude that access has become a new battlefield in a struggle between proponents of a strong copyright law and activists arguing in favor of more user-friendly mechanisms. Instead, it shows that ultimately, a compromise could be reached between these two positions, with the ultimate goal of achieving a fair balance of rights. The right to control access and the right to obtain access have their own objective application and can therefore coexist with one other. However, a number of fundamental issues remain as regards whether this balance can be achieved by using intrinsic elements of copyright law only or whether recourse to external limitations is unavoidable. Future clarifications from the CJEU on this point are expected.

In the last chapter of this edited volume, Chapter 22, Orit Fischman Afori explores the constitutionalization of copyright law as an alternative path for analysis of the questions of balancing copyright law with the public's interest in access to protected materials. In the contributor's view, a concrete case study for taking this alternative path concerns the role of online intermediaries, such as Internet Service Providers (ISPs) and search engines. The author first critically reflects on the legal basis for imposing obligations upon online intermediaries which are aimed at promoting another party's welfare or even broad social values. Bearing in mind that these intermediaries are private bodies seeking profit, a proposition is presented whereby online intermediaries should be perceived as hybrid private/public bodies. In the view of Fischman Afori, acknowledging this hybrid status is crucial, since it may make it possible to demand compliance with certain core public law principles.

Furthermore, for the author, the powerful alternative path for easing the current copyright crisis functions, *inter alia*, through the remedies granted. In this respect, one of the most outstanding legal principles used within the remedial framework for balancing these conflicting constitutional interests is the principle of proportionality. In the contributor's view, proportionality functions as a universal notion, vesting discretion in the judiciary to craft the final legal solution in a pragmatic way. It is an open standard, similar to reasonableness; however, it is specifically tailored to enable courts to strike a proper balance between competing constitutional values or human rights involved in a certain and particular case. In that regard, the appeal of the measure of proportionality to current copyright law reflects both the emergence of human rights issues into this area of private law and the need for a new powerful, acceptable and universal measure that would facilitate the promotion of new solutions to current challenges in copyright law.

Professor Fischman Afori then examines a few examples of the use of the universal measure of proportionality as a basic prism for evaluating the legitimacy of granting site-blocking orders: the relevant case law of the European Court of Justice (CJEU) and British High Court decisions handed down by Justice Richard Arnold. The author reviews, with a critical eye, this line of decisions as shifting judicial discretion into a procedural-technical mode rather than focusing on policy-oriented reasoning. Finally, the author provides a snapshot outside Europe, along with a short description of the new Israeli legislation, codifying the British High Court's "checklist" of considerations. In her view, all these examples together demonstrate the potential of the new constitutional phase of copyright law, which is facing global challenges to be solved by universal measures. The author concludes that the constitutional remedial standard of proportionality would indeed lead to a more balanced copyright law, one that acknowledges users' rights and the public interest in access to copyright-protected works. Online intermediaries are key players as agents not just for copyright enforcement but also for voicing the vast public interest. As they function as a technological "intermediary," their legal status should also reflect their complicated task.

Overall, pluralist answers have been given by the book's contributors to the complex question of whether pluralism or universalism is the path to follow for the development of international copyright law. Minimalist, moderate and maximalist views have been expressed, depending on the specific topic. This is not a surprise since the pluralism of opinions is an inherent and indispensable quality of academia. There is a general consensus that the universalist ambition of copyright law still exists. All the contributors refer to the need for workable and modernized universal copyright principles. National and regional copyright jurisdictions should evolve within a universal framework in a pluralist way which takes into account national and regional needs. In this sense universalism and pluralism are complementary.

Part I

Regional Copyright Law Harmonization

Chapter 1

EU, BC, WCT: The Compatibility of EU Copyright Law with the International Acquis in the Berne Convention, TRIPS and WCT

Antoon A. Quaedvlieg

European Union (EU) regulation in the field of copyright started in 1991 with the introduction of the Software Directive 91/250. Since then, the EU has given birth to an important body of legislation, accompanied from around 2000 by a regular production of jurisprudence of the Court of Justice regarding the interpretation of those instruments. In this process, the international acquis in the field of copyright has been of great importance. Nevertheless, tensions between the EU and international law may also arise, especially in some cases where it is felt that EU policy objectives were given high priority.

EU legislation formally connects with international copyright law through the EU's adherence to the Trade-Related Aspects of Intellectual Property Rights (TRIPS) and WIPO Copyright Treaty (WCT) treaties. As from January 1, 1996, TRIPS obliged the EU to comply with the provisions of Articles 1-21 and the Appendix of the Berne Convention. (1) The EU also is a member of the WCT, which entered into force on March 6, 2002. Article 1(4) WCT likewise obliges its Contracting Parties to comply with Articles 1-21 of the Berne Convention and its Appendix, this time without making an exception for the moral rights mentioned in Article 6bis.

While the need to keep EU copyright law compatible with the international conventions may put limits to its autonomous creation and interpretation, this is compensated by the considerable advantages of being part of a basic system on which a majority of nations can agree. In this chapter, compatibility of EU copyright law with international law will be understood as a large concept. It means more than just compliance and englobes three more components: (1) complementarity; (2) copyright comity; and (3) commitment.

Complementarity: Thus far, copyright in Europe has only partially been harmonized. Where European legislation shows lacunas, international copyright law fills the gap; the systems are complementary. Also, European copyright law has largely been built on the foundations provided by international copyright law. It, therefore, is only natural to seek guidance there; Directives may even in so many words refer to international law for issues they do not regulate themselves. (2) Apart from concrete rules, international law may also provide systemic and teleological elements against the background of which copyright norms can coherently be interpreted. European copyright law is still defective in that regard. The piecemeal character of the harmonization hampers the application of traditional rules of interpretation. (3) For example, neither the performance right nor the rights of adaptation and arrangement have been harmonized. (4) Furthermore, European law still fails to provide a coherent philosophy (5) laying down principles of European copyright. (6) Only some general rules apply like the objective to establish a high level of protection for authors, the principle of proportionality and the conformity with international law.

Comity and bona fides constitute a second element of compliance with international law. Comity is a term not very familiar in copyright law. It refers to the care and courtesy that is called for in the international community. (7) Apart from that, international public law is ruled by the principle of bona fide (good faith), which is laid down in Article 2(2) of the United Nations Charter. (8) The Vienna Convention on the Law of Treaties of May 23, 1969 (9) declares in the third line of its Preamble that, among others, the principle of good faith is universally recognized.

The principle of comity means that paradoxically, international law obliges the EU to take into account the national copyright traditions of its Member States, especially when these are based on international treaties and shared by a number of states. To our knowledge, that point was first raised by Michel Walter, (10) who based this obligation on an analogy with Article 52(4) of the Charter of Fundamental Rights of the EU. (11) Article 52(4) provides that in so far as fundamental rights recognized in the Charter result from the constitutional traditions common to the Member States, those rights must be interpreted in harmony with those traditions. (12) In the same vein, the legal traditions of the Member States in the copyright domain should be taken into account. This analogy is particularly well-founded in relation to the Conventions. The copyright conventions created an international copyright community. In interpreting copyright law, the existence of that community should not be ignored. The negotiations leading to the treaties, the parliamentary discussions that accompanied their implementation in national law and the subsequent application by the judiciary of those national laws in light of the conventions form of massive body of relevant background material. The Berne (and WCT) countries live in a copyright environment that has been shaped by a common tradition. New European solutions that are at odds with this shared heritage should be met with some caution. That applies even more as the rules of the treaties also apply to the external relations of the EU. (13)

Commitment is the third and last element of compliance. It implies taking responsibility for the further development of copyright. The European institutions bundle highly developed copyright cultures and make them speak with one voice. For that reason, Europe bears a special responsibility for the development of the international copyright system. The European role can take two different shapes. First, Europe gives priority to the development of boldly innovative solutions and considers its international obligations as no more than a loosely binding framework. That, however, would almost certainly damage the solidity of the international framework, as it would plainly justify other countries to take no less freedom in their own, possibly diverging interpretations. If, by contrast, Europe takes the treaties very seriously, that might enhance its own authority as well as that of the conventions. There is a wide spectrum between those two extreme positions, and it will sometimes be necessary to find a compromise between them. Still, it would be foolish to undermine the important basic stability offered by the existing international framework by putting it aside too easily.

This contribution will introduce the three relevant treaties (*see* section 1.1 below), analyze the EU copyright legislation (*see* section 1.2 below) and finally study the way in which the European Court of Justice (ECJ) deals—and sometimes grapples—with the Berne Convention and the WCT (*see* section 1.3 below. *See also* Table 1.1 "Reference of international copyright law instruments in the CJEU's case law"). Neither the neighboring rights (14) nor the issue of the competence of the EU in matters of intellectual property matters (15) will be dealt with in this chapter.

1.1 ADHERENCE OF THE EU TO THE COPYRIGHT TREATIES

Three treaties are central: the Berne Convention, the Trade-Related Aspects of Intellectual Properties (TRIPS) treaty and the WCT.

1.1.1 Berne Convention

The EU as such has not adhered to the Berne Convention. Reasons as to why adherence to the Berne Convention posed a problem are explained in a footnote of Attorney General (AG) la Pergola's Opinion with the *Egeda v.*

Hoasa[1] the Paris Act of the Berne Convention refers, as previous Acts did, to the "*countries* of the Union,"[2] i.e., the States.[3] Therefore, the Berne Convention does not appear to allow membership by international organizations. A proposal by the Commission that only concerned the accession of the Member States[4] to the Berne Convention apparently came too close to an accession of the Union itself and was withdrawn when not approved as a result of the extraordinary transfer of jurisdiction that a decision of this nature would have entailed. From the logical and semantic viewpoints too, the Community cannot be the recipient of an order to confirm respective national legislations.

In 1992, Protocol 28 (on intellectual property), Article 5, paragraph (1) under (b) of the European Economic Area (EEA) Agreement provided for the undertaking of the Member States to adhere to the Berne Convention, Paris Act.[5] In *Egeda v. Hoasa*, the Commission asserted that the provisions of the Convention formed an integral part of Community law since the EEA Agreement came into force. At the same time, the Commission referred to case law that held that primary and secondary Community law had to be interpreted in light of international public law.[6]

The Berne Convention relation of Member States with third countries external to the EU will not be affected by the provisions of the European Treaties when the obligations resulting from the Berne Convention date from before the accession of that EU Member State to the European Community (EC) or the EU. The Court of Justice stated in *Martin Luksan* (2012) that all of the Member States of the EU had already acceded to the Berne Convention, some before January 1, 1958, and others before the date of their accession to the EU:

> Thus, the Berne Convention displays the characteristics of an international agreement for the purposes of Article 351 TFEU, which provides inter alia that the rights and obligations arising from agreements concluded before 1 January 1958 or, for acceding States, before the date

1. Advocate General La Pergola, Opinion delivered on Sep. 9, 1999, in Case C-293/98 Entidad de Gestión de Derechos de los Productores Audiovisuales (Egeda) v. Hostelería Asturiana SA (Hoasa) (2000) ECLI:EU:C:1999:403.
2. Cf. Berne Convention, Preamble and Art. 1.
3. The Opinion refers to Claude Masouyé, *Guide de la Convention de Berne pour la protection des oeuvres littéraires et artistiques (Acte de Paris, 1971)* 8 (1978).
4. The undertaking to adhere to the Berne Convention, Paris Act, was however provided for by Protocol 28 (on intellectual property); Decision of the Council and the Commission of 13 December 1993 on the conclusion of the Agreement on the European Economic Area between the European Communities, their Member States and the Republic of Austria, the Republic of Finland, the Republic of Iceland, the Principality of Liechtenstein, the Kingdom of Norway, the Kingdom of Sweden and the Swiss Confederation, Art. 5, para. (1) under (b), (1994) Official Journal L 1/195.
5. Agreement on the European Economic Area (Dec. 13, 1993) Official Journal L 1/1, 1994.
6. Case C-293/98 Egeda v. Hoasa, AG La Pergola Opinion, para. 12.

of their accession, between one or more States, on the one hand, and one or more third countries, on the other, are not to be affected by the provisions of the (European, AQ) Treaties.[7]

The Martin Luksan decision also made an exception: where an agreement allows but does not require a Member State to adopt a measure contrary to EU law, that State should refrain from adopting such a measure and cannot rely on that agreement to exempt itself from the obligations arisen subsequently from EU law.[8]

1.1.2 Trade-Related Aspects of Intellectual Property

TRIPS was adopted on April 15, 1994, in Marrakesh and signed by 117 states among which the EC. It was approved on behalf of the EC by the Council Decision of December 22, 1994.[9] It entered into force on January 1, 1995, and obliged developed countries to apply the majority of its rules as from January 1, 1996.[10] Article 9(1) TRIPS provides that members must comply with Articles 1 through 21 of the Berne Convention, with the exception however of Article 6bis BC regarding moral rights. The TRIPS Agreement also included a number of new obligations under international law that were added to those resulting from the Berne Convention. The Court of Justice applied Article 9(1) TRIPS as from its 2006 decision in *SGAE v. Rafael Hoteles*. The provisions of the TRIPS Treaty have no direct effect.[11] Still, it is settled case law that EU legislation must, as far as possible, be interpreted in a manner consistent with international law, in particular where its provisions are intended specifically to give effect to an international agreement concluded by the EU.[12]

---

7. Case C-277/10 Martin Luksan v. Petrus van der Let (2012) ECLI:EU:C:2012:65, para. 58. Only Croatia became an EU Member State after the date of this decision (2013); the same however applies to that State. In 1992, it had deposited with WIPO its Notification of succession to the Socialist Federal Republic of Yugoslavia as a Berne Union State.
8. Case C-277/10 Martin Luksan v. Petrus van der Let, paras. 61-64.
9. Council Decision (of 22 December 1994) concerning the conclusion on behalf of the European Community, as regards matters within its competence, of the agreements reached in the Uruguay Round multilateral negotiations (1986-1994) (Dec. 22, 1994) Official Journal L 336, 23/12/1994, pp. 1-2.; *Also see,* for example, Case C-406/10 SAS Institute Inc. v. World Programming Ltd (2012) ECLI:EU:C:2012:259, para. 4.
10. Cf Daniel Gervais, *The TRIPS Agreement, Drafting History and Analysis* 519 (3rd edn, Sweet & Maxwell/Thomson Reuters, 2008).
11. Joined Cases C-403/08 and C-429/08 Football Association Premier League Ltd and Others v. QC Leisure and Others (C-403/08) and Karen Murphy v. Media Protection Services Ltd (C-429/08) (2011) ECLI:EU:C:2011:631, para. 189; Case C-135/10 Società Consortile Fonografici (SCF) v. Marco Del Corso (2012) ECLI:EU:C:2012:140, paras. 45-46.
12. Case C-456/06 Peek & Cloppenburg KG v. Cassina SpA. (2008) ECLI:EU:C:2008:232, para. 31; Joined Cases C-403/08 and C-429/08 Football Association Premier League Ltd., para. 189; Case C-135/10 Società Consortile Fonografici (SCF) v. Marco Del Corso, paras. 51-52, 55-56, 71.

1.1.3 WIPO Copyright Treaty

The EU also adhered to the (WCT, also cited by the Court of Justice of the European Union (CJEU) as "CT"). The WCT was adopted in Geneva on December 20, 1996. It was approved on behalf of the EU by Council Decision 2002/278/EC of March 16, 2000,[13] and entered into force on March 6, 2002. By the same instrument, the EC adhered to the WIPO Performances and Phonograms Treaty (WPPT). Article 1(4) WCT provides that the contracting parties are to comply with Articles 1 to 21 of the Berne Convention, this time without excluding, as TRIPS did, Article 6bis of the Berne Convention from that obligation. Only as late as 2011, however, in its decisions in *Premier League* and *Eva-Maria Painer*,[14] the Court of Justice began to make mention of Article 1(4) WCT besides 9(1) TRIPS.[15]

1.2 THE ROLE OF THE COPYRIGHT TREATIES IN EU LEGISLATION

The European legislation offers rich testimony that Europe is part of a Berne (TRIPS, WCT) shaped world. European Directives to a great extent rely on the copyright terminology and structure created by the Berne Convention and WCT. Directives may even entrust the Berne Convention with the regulation of certain cases they do not provide for themselves. In some cases, EU legislation appears to have anticipated international law. Apart from such examples of complementarity, some important instances can be observed of what can be qualified as copyright "comity."

---

13. 2000/278/EC: Council Decision of 16 March 2000, on the approval, on behalf of the European Community, of the WIPO Copyright Treaty and the WIPO Performances and Phonograms Treaty (Mar. 16, 2000) Official Journal 2000 L 89, 11/4/2000, pp. 6-7; *see, inter alia,* Case C-5/11, Titus Alexander Jochen Donner (2012) ECLI:EU:C:2012:370, para. 3; Case C-128/11 UsedSoft GmbH v. Oracle International Corp. (2012) ECLI: EU:C:2012:407, para. 3; Case C-277/10 Martin Luksan v. Petrus van der Let, para. 4.
14. Joined Cases C-403/08 and C-429/08 Football Association Premier League Ltd, para. 189; Case C-145/10 Eva-Maria Painer v. Standard VerlagsGmbH and Others (2011) ECLI:EU:C:2013:138, paras. 4, 10.
15. As from the 2012 judgment in *Martin Luksan*, a series of decisions followed which exclusively made mention of Art. 1 para. 4, WCT; Case C-277/10 Martin Luksan v. Petrus van der Let, paras. 5, 59; Case C-510/10 DR and TV2 Danmark A/S v. NCB—Nordisk Copyright Bureau (2012) ECLI:EU:C:2012:244 para. 29; Case C-419/13 Art & Allposters International BV v. Stichting Pictoright (2015) ECLI:EU:C:2015:27, paras. 3-4; Case C-301/15 Marc Soulier and Sara Doke v. Premier ministre and Ministre de la Culture et de la Communication (2016) ECLI:EU:C:2016:878, paras. 9, 32, 50 and Case C-138/16 Staatlich genehmigte Gesellschaft der Autoren, Komponisten und Musikverleger registrierte Genossenschaft mbH (AKM) v. Zürs.net Betriebs GmbH (2017) ECLI:EU: C:2017:218, para. 4. In Case C-406/10 SAS Institute v. World Programming Ltd (2012) ECLI:EU:C:2012:259 and in Case C-310/17 Levola Hengelo BV v. Smilde Foods BV (2018) ECLI:EU:C:2018:899, para. 6. However, TRIPS Agreement, Art. 9(1) re-emerged besides WCT, Art. 1(4).

1.2.1 Computer Programs Directive (1991)

Symbolically, the first provision of the first European Copyright Directive—Article 1(1) of the Computer Programs Directive[16] of 1991—started with a reference to the Berne Convention: computer programs were to be protected by copyright:

> as literary works within the meaning of the Berne Convention for the Protection of Literary and Artistic Works.

Article 1, paragraph (3) of the Directive added that a computer program was to be protected if it was original in the sense that it is the author's "own intellectual creation": a criterion clearly inspired by the term of the "own intellectual creation" in Article 2(5) of the Berne Convention, where it functions as a condition for the protection of collections.

Article 1(2) of the Computer Programs Directive stated that the protection would apply to the "expression in any form" of a computer program, essentially copying, though not in identical words, the Berne formula of "whatever may be the mode or form of its expression."[17] Not protected were ideas and principles underlying any element of the computer program. That provision anticipated the later Articles 9(2) TRIPS and 2 WCT.

Apart from that, the structure and terminology for the exploitation rights in the Software Directive showed itself tributary to the Berne Convention. Article 4(a) and (b) provided for the exclusive right to do or to authorize the reproduction (Article 9 of the Berne Convention), translation (Article 8 of the Berne Convention), adaptation, arrangement and any other alteration (Article 12 of the Berne Convention) of a computer program.

The Directive further provided for a right of distribution for computer programs. Article 4 of the Directive included the right of rental of a program in the right of distribution.[18] However, when in 1996, Article 6 WCT introduced a general right of distribution,[19] it separated rental and sale. Article 6 WCT confined the right of distribution to the making available to the public of the original and copies of their works through sale or other transfer of ownership. Rental was separately regulated in Article 7 WCT for the sole categories of computer programs, cinematographic works and works

16. Directive 2009/24/EC of the European Parliament and of the Council of 23 April 2009, on the legal protection of computer programs (Codified version) (Apr. 23, 2009) Official Journal L 111, 5/5/2009, pp. 16-22; Council Directive 91/250/EEC of 14 May 1991, on the legal protection of computer programs (May 14, 1991) Official Journal 122, 17/5/1991, pp. 42-46.
17. Cf the similar wording later in TRIPS Agreement, Art. 10 and WCT, Art. 4.
18. According to Recital 12 in the Preamble of the Directive, public lending remained outside the scope of the Directive.
19. The Berne Convention only mentioned the right of distribution in its Art. 14(1)(i) in the specific context of cinematographic works.

embodied in phonograms.[20] Article 4 of the Copyright Directive 2001/29 subsequently provided the right of distribution to the public "by sale or otherwise." The term "or otherwise" was ambiguous; it could be interpreted both in the large sense of the Computer Programs Directive as well as the more narrow sense of the WCT. The Court of Justice interpreted it in the sense of the WCT or otherwise meant "or other transfer of ownership."[21]

Finally, Recital (19) of the Preamble laid down that the Directive did not affect derogations provided for under national legislation in accordance with the Berne Convention on points not covered by the Directive.

In sum, this Directive showed an approach in which European copyright was to a very high extent integrated into the framework of international law.

1.2.2 Rental and Lending Directive (1992)

The Rental and Lending Directive[22] contains no references to the Berne Convention. That is not surprising, as the Berne Convention does not deal with rental and lending. By contrast, the European Directive may have been inspired by the TRIPS negotiations that started in 1986 and were concluded on December 15, 1993. The entry into force of the rental and lending provisions in TRIPS and the WCT, however, followed after the Directive.[23]

Despite this scarcity of the international context at the moment of its entry into force, Recital (7) of the Preamble of the Directive prescribed that the legislation in the Member States should be:

> approximated in such a way as not to conflict with the international conventions on which the copyright and related rights laws of many Member States are based.[24]

thereby showing great awareness of the degree to which national, regional and international copyright rules are always interwoven. Of particular importance is that the *national laws* are mentioned in many words. That represents an explicit recognition by the European legislator of the phenomenon of copyright comity.

20. *Also see* TRIPS Agreement, Art. 11 ("at least" computer programs and cinematographic works).
21. C-456/06, Peek & Cloppenburg v. Cassina.
22. Directive 2006/115/EC of the European Parliament and of the Council of 12 December 2006, on rental right and lending right and on certain rights related to copyright in the field of intellectual property (codified version) (Dec. 12, 2006) Official Journal L 376, 27/12/2006, pp. 28-35; Council Directive 92/100/EEC of 19 November 1992, on rental right and lending right and on certain rights related to copyright in the field of intellectual property (Nov. 19, 1992) Official Journal L 346, 27/11/1992, pp. 61-66.
23. TRIPS, Art. 11; WCT, Art. 7.
24. As to neighboring rights, *also see* the mention of the Rome Convention in Recital (15).

1.2.3 Cable and Satellite Directive (1993)

The Cable and Satellite Directive[25] contained no references to the Berne Convention.

1.2.4 Term Directive (1993)

Of all the references[26] to the Berne Convention in the Term Directive,[27] none matter more than those to the concept of work. As the concept of work had not yet been harmonized by Community legislation, Article 1(1) Term Directive referred to:

> the rights of an author of a literary or artistic work within the meaning of Article 2 of the Berne Convention.

an obvious example of complementarity. Article 6 of the Term Directive established a harmonized originality standard applicable to photographic works:[28]

> Photographs which are original in the sense that they are the author's own intellectual creation shall be protected in accordance with Article 1 (emphasis added).[29]

Recital (16)[30] of the Term Directive, however, added that a photographic work within the meaning of the Berne Convention had to reflect the author's personality. That element cannot be found in the Berne Convention: the BC nowhere requires that the author's own intellectual creation reflect his personality. Neither is the requirement of personality included in the notion of an "original" work in the Berne Convention. "Original" means no more

25. Council Directive 93/83/EEC of 27 September 1993, on the coordination of certain rules concerning copyright and rights related to copyright applicable to satellite broadcasting and cable retransmission (Sep. 27, 1993) Official Journal L 248, 6/10/1993, pp. 15-21.
26. Cf. Recital 2 (minimum terms of protection Berne and Rome Convention); Recital 5 with reference to Art. 14bis para. 2(b), (c) and (d), Recital 6 referring to the ratio of the Berne term; Recital 13 with regard to collections. An indirect reference to Berne Convention, Art. 14bis(3) is found in Art. 2(2) of the Term Directive.
27. Directive 2006/116/EC of the European Parliament and of the Council of 12 December 2006 on the term protection of copyright and certain related rights (Dec. 12, 2006) Official Journal L 372, 27/12/2006, pp. 12-18 (hereinafter the Term Directive).
28. In Germany, Spain and Italy only photographic works of a higher aesthetic level enjoyed a full copyright (term of) protection. Photographs that did not meet that condition would only enjoy a neighboring rights protection of a more limited duration.
29. Cf. Stef van Gompel & Erlend Lavik, *Quality, Merit, Aesthetics and Purpose: An Inquiry into EU Copyright Law's Eschewal of Other Criteria than Originality* 236 Revue Internationale du Droit d'Auteur 101-295, 121 (2013).
30. Council Directive 93/98/EEC of 29 October 1993 harmonizing the term of protection of copyright and certain related rights, Recital 17 (Oct. 29, 1993) Official Journal L 290, 24/11/1993, pp. 9-13; that text was somewhat shortened in the later version in Recital (16) of Directive 2006/116.

than that the work must constitute an own independent creation. The word "original" only appears in Articles 2(3), 8 and 14bis(1) of the Berne Convention in relation to adaptations of works. Article 2(3) of the Berne Convention uses two meanings of original work in one in the same sentence: translations, adaptations, etc., shall be considered original works in the sense of works independently eligible for protection, without prejudice to the original work. This last work obviously is the creation lying at the basis of the adaptation. In that last sense, the term original is also used in Article 8 of the Berne Convention:

> Authors of literary and artistic works protected by this Convention shall enjoy the exclusive right of making and authorizing the translation of their works throughout the term of protection of their rights in the original works.

If original may, therefore, in the Berne Convention, have a double meaning, it certainly does not have the meaning of reflecting the author's personality.

The introduction of the personality element—inspired by continental notions—created a possibility to *raise* the general standard of originality applied in certain Member States. This was to be of great consequence, for it contained the germs of the later harmonization of the concept of work by the Court of Justice in the *Infopaq* decision of 2009 and later decisions.[31] It will be discussed (*see* below section 1.7) that the rules of copyright comity should arguably have curbed this keenness.

1.2.5 Database Directive (1996)

The Database Directive[32] offers a strong example of complementarity of the rules of the Convention as well as national law with EU law in the way it dealt with the issue of exceptions and limitations to copyright.[33] A complete regulation of the thorny issue of exceptions would have gone far beyond the

31. In Infopaq, the Court referred to Art. 6 and not—or only indirectly—the more neutral Art. 1(1) of the Term Directive. Article 1(1) is however mentioned in the "legal context" of the later judgment in Eva-Maria Painer, although that case specifically concerned the protection of photographic works; Case C-145/10, Eva-Maria Painer.
32. Directive 96/9/EC of the European Parliament and the Council of 11 March 1996, on the legal protection of databases (Mar. 11, 1996) Official Journal L. 77, 27/3/1996, pp. 20-28.
33. Apart from that issue, implicit references to the Berne Convention can be found in the word "collection" in the definition of a database in Art. 1(2)—"database" shall mean a collection of independent works, data or other materials—and in the description of the object of protection in Art. 3: Copyright protection is allowed for databases which [...] constitute the author's own intellectual creation, a wording inspired by Art. 2(5) of the Berne Convention. The list of categories of restricted acts in Art. 5 is—with the exception of the right of display—also inspired by the Berne Convention.

primary goal of assuring that databases enjoyed protection (also)[34] by copyright. For that reason, Article 6(1) and (2)(a-c)[35] contained no more than a minimal regulation of this issue, whereas paragraph (2d) allowed the Member States to provide for limitations:

> where other exceptions to copyright which are traditionally authorized under national law are involved, without prejudice to points (a), (b) and (c).[36]

Article 6(3) completed this reference to national law with the safety valve of the generalized version of the three-step test as provided for, at that time, by Article 13 of the TRIPS Treaty.

The convention was further mentioned in Recital (37), according to which Article 10(1) of the Berne Convention was not to be affected by the Directive. Article 10(1) of the Berne Convention provides that it shall be permissible to make quotations. The European legislator probably most of all wanted to ensure the application of the conditions for the application of the exception, namely that quotations must be compatible with fair practice and that their extent does not exceed that justified by the purpose.[37] Either way, it seems that Article 10(1) of the Berne Convention is given direct effect with regard to databases.

The principle of complementarity, as well as the comity rule, appear in Recital (28) of the Database Directive, providing that the moral rights in databases had to be exercised according to the legislation of the Member States and the Berne Convention.

1.2.6 The Directive on Copyright in the Information Society ("Copyright Directive")

The Copyright Directive 2001/29 harmonized three central exploitation rights: the right of reproduction, the right of communication to the public and the right of distribution. The new right of making available was included in the right of communication to the public. To an important extent, the

34. The Database Directive granted a genuine copyright protection as well as a newly created sui generis database right.
35. *Also see* the Recitals 34-37 of the Directive.
36. Article 6(2d) says nothing about new exceptions in national law, even if based on later European directives such as the Copyright Directive 2001/29. About this: Annemarie Beunen, *Protection for Databases. The European Database Directive and Its effects in the Netherlands, France and the United Kingdom* 99-100, para. 3.4.3.6 (Wolf Legal Publishers, 2007).
37. Cf Jens-L. Gaster, *Der Rechtsschutz von Datenbanken* 104-105, paras. 405-409 (Carl Heymanns, 1999) ("aüsserst restriktiv zu handhaben"). In the same sense: Malte Grützmacher, *Urheber-, Leistungs- und Sui-generis-Schutz von Datenbanken* 281 under (dd) (Baden Baden: Nomos, 1999). In the same sense: Matthias Leistner, *Der Rechtsschutz von Datenbanken im deutschen und europäischen Recht* 126 (C.H. Beck, 2000).

Directive served to implement the new international obligations resulting from the WCT and the WPPT.[38] As Recital (15) puts it, these had significantly updated the international protection for copyright and related rights, "not least with regard to the so-called 'digital agenda'." Apart from Recital (44), stating that the exceptions and limitations provided for in the Directive must be exercised in accordance with international obligations, no other reference to the copyright treaties seems to be made.[39]

In its Article 5, the Copyright Directive introduced a list of exceptions and limitations to copyright which, although extensive, was limitative. Furthermore, in Article 5(5), it subjected the application of the exceptions and limitations to the three-step test, although the three-step test in Article 10 WCT is generally understood only to bind the legislators. However, the Agreed Statement concerning Article 10[40] permitted the contracting parties to devise new exceptions and limitations for the digital environment. The Commission must have feared chaos when all the EU Member States would develop their own initiatives. Supposedly, the answer was found by, on the one hand, designing a closed list of limitations; on the other hand, formulating these in a way sufficiently large as to leave much freedom to the national legislator, subject, however, to an intensified check under the three-step test. As far as it concerned old national exceptions for analog use, Article 5(3)(o) even allowed to keep these as far as they did not affect the free circulation of goods. That is a well-placed gesture of comity.

Apart from the new international obligations resulting from the WCT, only the shy fox of the moral rights shortly appeared again on the edge of the old copyright forest and was sent back in there in the same spirit of complementarity and comity as in the Database Directive: to moral rights national law, the Berne Convention and the World Intellectual Property Organization Treaties apply, but moral rights remain outside the scope of the Copyright Directive.[41]

1.2.7 The Resale Right Directive

The Berne Convention deals with the resale rights in its Article 14ter. According to the Convention, the resale right is optional and subject to the

38. Directive 2001/29, Recital 15; Case C-301/15 Marc Soulier and Sara Doke v. Premier ministre and Ministre de la Culture et de la Communication (2016) ECLI:EU:C:2016:878, para. 32; Case C-135/10 Società Consortile Fonografici (SCF) v. Marco Del Corso (2012) ECLI:EU:C:2012:140, para. 40.
39. *See* however Recital 61, stating that the WPPT obliges to amend the directives 92/100 (on rental, lending and related rights) and 93/98 (satellite & cable).
40. Agreed Statements Concerning the WIPO Copyright Treaty (1996), Art. 10.
41. Directive 2001/29, Recital 19.

rule of reciprocity.[42] The Resale Right Directive[43] made it compulsory for the Member States of the EU. The Commission announced that it would be "essential" for the EU to open negotiations with a view to making Article 14b of the Berne Convention compulsory.[44]

1.2.8 THE ENFORCEMENT DIRECTIVE

Article 2(3)(b) of the Enforcement Directive[45] declares that the Directive shall not affect Member States' international obligations and notably the TRIPS Agreement. Recital (5) in the Preamble with the Enforcement Directive refers to the TRIPS agreement. Recital (6) refers to the Paris, Berne and Rome Conventions, stating that these also contain provisions on the means of enforcing intellectual property rights.

Article 5(a) of the Enforcement Directive almost literally copies the presumption on authorship and ownership in Article 15 paragraph (1) of the Berne Convention.[46] It provides:

> (a) for the author of a literary or artistic work, in the absence of proof to the contrary, to be regarded as such, and consequently to be entitled to institute infringement proceedings, it shall be sufficient for his name to appear on the work in the usual manner.

Surprisingly,[47] Article 5 of the Enforcement Directive did not copy the detailed paragraphs (2-4) of Article 15 of the Berne Convention regarding presumptive right owners such as bodies corporate, publishers, and designated competent authorities. It must, however, be assumed that the principle of complementarity applies.

---

42. Directive 2001/84/EC of the European Parliament and the Council of 27 September 2001, on the resale right for the benefit of the author of an original work of art, Recital 6 (Sep. 27, 2001) Official Journal L 272, 13/10/2001, pp. 32-36.
43. Directive 2001/84/EC of the European Parliament and the Council of 27 September 2001, on the resale right for the benefit of the author of an original work of art (Sep. 27, 2001) Official Journal L 272, 13/10/2001, pp. 32-36. Within the European Union, reciprocity clauses denying nationals of other Member States rights conferred on national authors cannot be relied on: Directive 2001/84, Recital 6.
44. Directive 2001/84, Recital 7.
45. Directive 2004/48/EC of the European Parliament and the Council of 29 April 2004, on the enforcement of intellectual property rights (Apr. 29, 2004) Official Journal L 195, 2/6/2004, pp. 16-25.
46. As confirmed in Recital (19).
47. Thus qualified by Michel Walter & Dominik Goebel, *Enforcement Directive* at European Copyright Law. A Commentary 1232, para. 13.5.5 (Michel M. Walter & Silke von Lewinski eds., Oxford: Oxford University Press, 2010).

1.3 COMPATIBILITY WITH THE CONVENTIONS OF THE EU JURISPRUDENCE

If the courtship between the EU, the Berne Convention and the WCT might be called eventful, this is a thing much owed to the jurisprudence of the ECJ. As was established above, the EU has not adhered to the Berne Convention; however, the Convention is indirectly applicable in the EU via Article 9(1) of the TRIPS Agreement and Article 1(4) of the WCT.[48]

There can be no question that the Court takes the international *acquis* very seriously: it is settled case law of the Court that the provisions of agreements concluded by the Union form an integral part of the Union legal order. The TRIPS Agreement, the WCT and the WPPT are such agreements. As far as the Berne Convention is concerned, one can find very explicit confirmations of the determination of the Court and its provisions in, *inter alia*, the decisions in *Soulier & Doke*[49] and *AKM v. Zürs.net*.[50] Although references are perhaps not always made in a systematic way—they may fail in decisions where one would have expected them—the Court very frequently refers to the international conventions; a list of places in the CJEU's jurisprudence where such references can be found is added at the end of this contribution.[51]

In view of this general disposition to faithfully observe the rules of the Conventions, some examples stand out where the Court followed an interpretation radically different from them, in our view, going as far as jeopardizing basic compliance with the Conventions. That may especially happen where the Court pursues goals of economic policy, of a political nature[52] or of consumer protection.[53] What strikes is that in order to achieve those goals, the Court goes beyond the instrument of exceptions and limitations and may also customize the concept of exploitation rights according to the needs felt in a given case. That challenges the very architecture of international copyright law. Compliance will, therefore, be the issue in sections 1.4 and 1.5 below. Other decisions of the Court, however, provided important building stones for the evolution of international law (*see* below section 1.6). In section 1.7, the tension between furthering harmonization, on the one hand, and respecting copyright comity, on the other hand, will be discussed at the hand of the jurisprudence regarding the concept of

48. Joined Cases C-403/08 and C-429/08 Football Association Premier League Ltd and Others, paras. 10, 189.
49. Case C-138/16 AKM v. Zürs.net, paras. 18-21.
50. Case C-301/15 Marc Soulier, para. 32.
51. Without any pretention of completeness. In some cases, the CJEU merely mentions a Treaty provision listed as "legal context" preceding of the decision.
52. As may have been the case with regard to the "hyperlink"-decision in Case C-466/12 Nils Svensson and Others v. Retriever Sverige AB (2014) ECLI:EU:C:2014:76.
53. Cf. the protection of individuals not pursuing profit in Case C-160/15 GS Media BV v. Sanoma Media Netherlands BV and Others (2016) ECLI:EU:C:2016:644.

work. This overview is merely impressionistic and in no way pretends to be systematic.

1.4 COMMUNICATION TO THE PUBLIC: ARTICLE 11BIS(1) OF THE BERNE CONVENTION; ARTICLE 8 WCT

1.4.1 *SGAE v. Rafael Hoteles*: The Introduction of the Concept of a "New Public"

In some 20 decisions on this matter, the Court framed a formidable, detailed EU doctrine in which it surrounded the concept of communication to the public (including the notion of making available) with a swarm of new rules or notions not found in international law. It is felt that these are hardly helpful in clarifying the notion and sometimes obscure it.[54] To mention only a few of them, there is the redefined notion of "public," which must concern an "indeterminate number of potential listeners"[55] and a "fairly large number of people";[56] the technique of the "individualised assessment";[57] the criterion of the "indispensable role" played by the user and the "deliberate nature" of its "intervention."[58]

We will concentrate on the first decision in this matter only: *SGAE v. Rafael Hoteles,*[59] which is fundamental. *SGAE v. Rafael Hoteles* introduced the "new public" criterion. In paragraph 40, the Court considered:

---

54. Cf. Silke von Lewinski, *Réflexions sur la jurisprudence récente de la Cour de justice de l'Union Européenne en droit d'auteur, en particulier sur le droit de communication au public* at Mélanges en l'honneur du Professeur André Lucas 775-784 (Carine Bernault, Jean-Pierre Clavier, Agnès Lucas-Schloetter, Francois-Xavier Lucas eds., LexisNexis, 2014).
55. Case C-306/05 SGAE v. Rafael Hoteles SA, para. 37; Case C-135/10 Società Consortile Fonografici (SCF) v. Marco Del Corso (2012) ECLI:EU:C:2012:140, para. 85.
56. Case C-306/05 SGAE v. Rafael Hoteles SA, paras. 38, 39; Case C-135/10 Società Consortile Fonografici (SCF) v. Marco Del Corso, para. 86.
57. The concept of "communication to the public" requires an individual assessment in which "account has to be taken of several complementary criteria, which are not autonomous and are interdependent. Since those criteria may, in different situations, be present to widely varying degrees, they must be applied both individually and in their interaction with one another." *See, inter alia,* Case C-135/10 Società Consortile Fonografici (SCF) v. Marco Del Corso, paras. 79,80; Case C-160/15 GS Media BV v. Sanoma Media Netherlands BV and Others, para. 33.33.
58. The user makes an act of communication when it intervenes, "in full knowledge of the consequences of its action," to give access to a protected work to its customers. *See, inter alia,* Case C-306/05 SGAE v. Rafael Hoteles SA, para. 42; Joined Cases C-403/08 and C-429/08 Football Association Premier League Ltd, paras. 194-195; Case C-160/15 GS Media BV v. Sanoma Media Netherlands BV and Others, para. 35; Case C-610/15 The Pirate Bay, para. 26.
59. Case C-306/05 Sociedad General de Autores y Editores de España (SGAE) v. Rafael Hoteles SA (2006) ECLI:EU:C:2006:764.

> It should also be pointed out that a communication made in circumstances such as those in the main proceedings constitutes, according to Article 11bis(1)(ii) of the Berne Convention, a communication made by a broadcasting organisation other than the original one. Thus, such a transmission is made to a public different from the public at which the original act of communication of the work is directed, that is, to a new public.

The Court of Justice, therefore, introduced the criterion of "new public" as an interpretation of the Berne Convention notion of "an organisation other than the original one." According to the fixed case law of the Court, a "new" public is a public that was not already taken into account by the copyright holders when they authorized the initial communication to the public of their work.[60] How far the consequences of this redefinition of the "other organization" criterion as a "new public" criterion stretched became clear in the CJEU *Nils Svensson* decision of February 13, 2014. Here, the ECJ decided that the provision on a website of a clickable link to works freely (and legally) available on another website did not constitute an act of communication to the public, as the public was not "new"; the public targeted by the initial communication (website) consisted of all internet users and exactly the same public was targeted by the website that provided the link.[61]

In our view, the Court has nowhere been so close to a major rupture with the rules of the Convention as in its adoption of the notion of the "new public."

To start with, very strong historical arguments oppose the validity of the Court's interpretation. As one can find confirmed in older Supreme Court case law in various countries[62] and as many authors[63] have argued, after due

60. Case C-306/05 SGAE v. Rafael Hoteles SA, paras. 40, 41; Joined Cases C-403/08 and C-429/08 Football Association Premier League Ltd, para. 197; Case C-466/12 Nils Svensson and Others v. Retriever Sverige AB, paras. 24, 31; Case C-160/15 GS Media BV v. Sanoma Media Netherlands BV and Others, para. 37; Case C-527/15 Stichting Brein v. Jack Frederik Wullems, para. 47; Case C-610/15 The Pirate Bay, para. 44.
61. CJEU Feb. 13, 2014, C-466/12, *Nils Svensson*. The "Cordoba" decision of 7 August 2018, has reduced the impact of *SGAE* and more specifically its application in *Svensson* insofar, that it put beyond doubt that there is communication to the public in case of the posting on one website a photograph which was previously posted on another website. In *Cordoba*, it was considered that the preventive nature of the right of communication to the public had to lead to the conclusion that there was a new pubic. Case C-161/17 Land Nordrhein-Westfalen v. Dirk Renckhoff (2018) ECLI:EU:C:2018:634 ("Cordoba").
62. In Belgium, Switzerland and the Netherlands.
63. This argument and/or other objections were raised by, among others, Ansgar Ohly, *Unmittelbare und mittelbare Verletzung des Rechts der öffentlichen Wiedergabe nach dem "Córdoba"-Urteil des EuGH,* Gewerblicher Rechtsschutz und Urheberrecht (2018); P. Bernt Hugenholtz & Sam C. van Velze, *Communication to a New Public? Three Reasons Why EU Copyright Law Can Do Without a "New Public"* 47(7) International Review of Intellectual Property and Competition Law 797-816 (2016) https://doi.org/10.1007/s403

deliberation, the Brussels Conference of 1948 explicitly rejected the new public criterion with regard to Article 11bis, paragraph (1) part (ii), and replaced it by the criterion of another organization than the original one, an *autre organisme*.[64] Furthermore, the Court's conclusion does not logically follow. A transmission made by a broadcasting organization other than the original one can very well be made to the same public and not only in theory. It very frequently happens in practice and has also occurred in cases decided by the Court.

Second, the breach of the legal criterion in the Berne Convention was fundamental. The right of communication to the public is an exclusive right. The author can exercise that right against everyone, which means that everyone who communicates the work to the public needs his permission. The permission granted to A is not a permission granted to B. That B communicates the work to the same public as the public targeted by A—and therefore, not to a new public—makes no difference. This solution is supported by a simple argument: if granting A the permission to communicate the work to the public (X) would allow all others to do the same, A could never acquire an exclusive license to communicate the work to that public. This would severely reduce the value of the copyright. No one pays for a license; every third party can subsequently use it for free.

The "new public" criterion could even suggest that the permission granted *to* A to broadcast the work to the public (X) in some way constitutes a right for the public (X) to receive that work—from A or even from third parties. However, receiving a work is not subject to any exclusive right at all; apart from the rights it may derive from a subscription with a provider, the public neither has a right to reception nor needs permission for such reception.[65]

What caused the Court to deviate thus radically from the clear text of the Berne Convention? Strangely enough, this has never really been clarified.

19-016-0512-7; Agnès Lucas-Schloetter, *L'harmonisation des droits économiques dans l'Union européenne*, Cahiers de la Propriété Intellectuelle 197-199 (2016); Claes Granmar, *A New Public in the Old World!?* at Liber Amicorum Jan Rosén 357-376 (Gunnar Karnell, Annette Kur, Per Jonas Nordell, Daniel Westman, Johan Axhamn, Stephan Carlsson eds., eddy.se., 2016); Lewinski (n. 54) 782-783; Madeleine de Cock Buning, *Cable Retransmission and Other Secondary Use* at A Century of Dutch Copyright Law 289 (deLex, 2012); S.C. van Velze, *Het "nieuw publiek" criterium hoort niet thuis in het Europese mededelingsrecht* 57-66 (AMI, 2016); Jacqueline M.B. Seignette, *Note with CJEU 8 September 2016, Sanoma v. GS Media*, 47 International Economic Review 315, 321 (2016); Antoon A. Quaedvlieg, *Le droit de communication au public dans la jurisprudence de la CJUE* 55 Propriétés Intellectuelles 125-132 (2015).

64. *Also see:* Annotated Principles of Protection of Authors, Performers, Producers of Phonograms and Broadcasting Organizations in Connection with Distribution by Cable, prepared by ILO, UNESCO and WIPO 131-205 (Copyright, 1984).

65. Cf. Joined Cases C-403/08 and C-429/08 Football Association Premier League Ltd and Others, para. 171.

However, reasons of an economic nature[66] and of consumer protection must almost certainly have prevailed.[67] The key motive may have been the desire to prevent that mere reception would be qualified as communication to the public and to thereby avoid a less fortunate consequence of the Berne criterion of an organization other than the original one: that criterion may apply to even very small cable network installations,[68] the clients of which probably[69] belong to, in the wording of the Court, the direct users considered by the author when he authorized the broadcast of his work.[70]

In *SGAE*, the Court considered:

> The clientele of a hotel forms such a new public. The transmission of the broadcast work to that clientele using television sets is not just a technical means to ensure or improve reception of the original broadcast in the catchment area (42).

First, it strikes that the Court speaks of a technical means to ensure or improve reception of the original broadcast; Recital (27) of the Preamble to the Copyright Directive and Article 8 WCT speak of "physical facilities for enabling or making a communication." It further strikes that the Court seems to reason that there is a new public because there is not just mere reception of the broadcasted work. SGAE probably was inspired by a perfectly honorable motive. The adoption of the alternative criterion of a "new public," however, creates a daunting new problem. The question of what criteria

66. An obvious economic motive was decisive in *BSA*: the Court held that the television broadcasting of the graphic user interface of a computer was not a communication to the public, because the television viewers *could not use the essential element* of the GUI, that is the element enabling interaction between the computer program and the user: Case C-393/09 Bezpečnostní softwarová asociace—Svaz softwarové ochrany v. Ministerstvo kultury (2010) ECLI:EU:C:2010:816, para. 57. *See*, Pierre Sirinelli, *Chronique de Jurisprudence* 227, 235 (Revue Internationale du Droit d'Auteur January 2011); Antoon A. Quaedvlieg, *Het wezenlijk bestanddeel van het werk, note with CJEU 22 December 2010* 21 Business Information Engineering 59, 66 (2011): "een spookschip" (a haunted vessel). Conciliatory, but not endorsing the decision: Valérie-Laure Benabou, *Propriétés Intellectuelles* 206 ff., 212-213 (2011).
67. The technique of teleological interpretation is dominant in the jurisprudence of the Court: Célia Zolynski, *L'élaboration de la jurisprudence de la CJUE* at Mélanges en l'honneur du professeur André Lucas 818 (Carine Bernault, Jean-Pierre Clavier, Agnès Lucas-Schloetter, François-Xavier Lucas eds., LexisNexis, 2014).
68. A similar tendency existed at the time in Germany as well as in France: *see* the contemporary editions of Schricker/Von Ungern Sternberg, *Urheberrecht Kommentar* §20 nr. 35, 477-478 (3rd edn, 2006); André Lucas & Henri-Jacques Lucas, *Traité de la propriété littéraire et artistique* nos 295, 237-239 (3ème éd., 2006). This may have been of influence on the decision. Nevertheless, both authors objected that problems of demarcation remained (Von Ungern Sternberg, §20 nr. 37; Lucas, 238).
69. The owners may coincide with "the owners of reception equipment who, either personally or within their own private or family circles, receive the programme."
70. It is felt that very small cable network installations might be *de minimis* under the Berne Convention. The magic formula of how to exempt larger installations is not easy to find. Putting the Berne criterion aside however creates greater problems.

should be decided when there is a "new" public proved to lead to a legal swamp, of which the later jurisprudence of the Court testifies.

1.5 THE RIGHT OF DISTRIBUTION AND THE EXHAUSTION DOCTRINE: ARTICLE 6 WCT

1.5.1 Decision in *UsedSoft*

Another decision that raises questions about compliance with international law was the *UsedSoft* case in 2012.[71] *UsedSoft* was concerned with the so-called rule of exhaustion. The rule of exhaustion is a general principle of intellectual property developed in systems of national law. German copyright law lent it its name of exhaustion (*Erschöpfung*).[72] As far as copyright is concerned, the exhaustion rule is a corollary of the right of distribution. European law acknowledged the exhaustion rule in the Software Directive and the Copyright Directive 2001/29, both in Article 4(2). Both refer to the first sale (or other transfer of ownership) of a copy as the event triggering the effect of exhaustion.

Article 6 WCT confirmed the distribution right. It was left to the contracting parties to determine the conditions under which the exhaustion of the distribution right would apply after the first sale or other transfer of

71. Case C-128/11 UsedSoft v. Oracle, *Propriétés Intellectuelles*, 333-337 note André Lucas; *Revue Trimestrielle de Droit Commercial* 542ff. (2012); note Frédéric Pollaud-Dullian; *Revue Trimestrielle du Droit Commercial* 790ff. (2012), note Philippe Gaudrat; Benoît Michaux, *Auteurs & Media* 556 (2012); Agnès Lucas-Schloetter, *La revente d'occasion de fichiers numériques contenant des œuvres protégées par le droit d'auteur* at Mélanges en l' honneur du Professeur André Lucas 575, 579 (LexisNexis, 2014); P. Bernt Hugenholtz NJ 118 (2013); F.W. Grosheide AMI nr. 3 76 (2013); M.R.F. Senftleben, AMI 56-60 (2013). Hauke Hansen, *Oliver Wolff-Rojzcyk*, note in Gewerblicher Rechtsschutz und Urheberrecht 908-910 (2012); *also see* Yin Harn Lee, *UsedSoft GmbH v. Oracle International Corp (Case C-128/11): Sales of "Used" Software and the Principle of Exhaustion* 43(7) International Review of Intellectual Property and Competition Law 846-853 (2012); Malte Stieper, *Anmerkung zu EuGH, Urteil vom 3. Juli 2012: C-128/11—UsedSoft* ZUM 668-670 (2012); Martin Senftleben, *Die Fortschreibung des urheberrechtlichen Erschöpfungsgrundsatzes im digitalen Umfeld. Die UsedSoft-Entscheidung des EuGH: Sündenfall oder Befreiungsschlag?* 65(40) NJW 2924-2927 (2012). Christopher Stothers, *When Is Copyright Exhausted by a Software License? UsedSoft v. Oracle,* European Intellectual Property Law Review 787-791 (2012). *UsedSoft* was positively commented by: Alexandra Mendoza-Caminade, *Vers une libéralisation du commerce du logiciel en Europe?* 32 Recueil Dalloz 2142 (2012).
72. *See* the fine thesis of Ulrich Joos, *Die Erschöpfungslehre im Urheberrecht. Eine Untersuchung zu Rechtsinhalt und Auspaltbarkeit des Urheberrechts mit vergleichenden Hinweisen auf Warenzeichenrecht, Patentrecht und Sortenschutz* (Urheberrechtliche Abhandlungen des Max-Planck-Instituts Heft, 1991); with a rich overview of the various doctrines justifying the exhaustion doctrine. Joos warns against putting too much emphasis on the "*Belohnungstheorie*," which essentially is the theory applied by the Court of Justice in *UsedSoft*.

ownership "of the original or a copy of the work." Importantly, however, the Agreed Statement concerning Articles 6 and 7 WCT explicitly provided that the expressions "copies" and "original and copies" referred exclusively to fixed copies that can be put into circulation as tangible objects.

In the case of *UsedSoft*, there was neither a sale nor another transfer of ownership. The customers downloaded a copy of the software directly from Oracle's website. The user was granted a license agreement to use the program. Oracle completed that construction by making this user's right non-assignable, a clause that according to German law has effect against third parties. In this way, Oracle aimed at preventing the development of a market for used software. UsedSoft ignored the legal precautions taken by Oracle and offered for sale "already used" licenses for the Oracle programs. In a decision of considerable complexity, the Court, in essence, reasoned that the transfer by the copyright holder to a customer of a copy of a computer program, accompanied by the conclusion between the same parties of a user license agreement of an unlimited duration, constitutes a "first sale … of a copy of a program" within the meaning of Article 4(2) of Directive 2009/24. In short: selling a right to use for an unlimited period is equivalent to the sale of a copy.[73]

As far as the WCT is concerned, the Court reasoned in paragraph 52 that it followed from Article 6(1) of the Copyright Treaty that the existence of a transfer of ownership changes an "act of communication to the public" into an act of distribution, giving rise to exhaustion.[74] That argument—if valid at all—does not repair the conflict with the Agreed Statement concerning Articles 6 and 7 WCT, which provides that the expressions "copies" and "original and copies" refer exclusively to fixed copies that can be put into circulation as tangible objects.

UsedSoft was essentially inspired by an objective of economic policy and consumer protection. One finds this argument[75] worked out in paragraphs 61-63 of the decision. The Court argued there that it would go beyond what is necessary to safeguard the specific subject matter of the intellectual property concerned if the exhaustion of the distribution right would solely apply to copies of computer programs on a material medium.[76] In essence,[77]

73. Criticized by Philippe Gaudrat in his note with CJEU Jul. 3, 2012, C-128/11, Revue Trimestrielle du Droit Commercial 790, nos. 31, 49 (2012). *Also see* Vincent Varet, *De distorsions le droit (de reproduction) s'est épuisé. À propos de l'arrêt de la CJUE en date du 3 juillet 2012, UsedSoft c./Oracle*, Propriétés Intellectuelles 384-387 (2012), final sentence: "Au fond, on aimerait que la Cour de justice fasse plus de droit et moins d'économie (ou alors en fasse vraiment)."

74. A conclusion which was qualified as "rather surprising" by: Thomas Dreier, *Online and Its Effect on the "Goods" Versus "Services" Distinction* 44 International Review of Intellectual Property and Competition Law 137-140, 138 (2013) https://doi.org/10.1007/s40319-013-0020-y.

75. P.B. Hugenholtz qualified it as the "killer argument" in his note in NJ 2013/118.

76. Paragraphs 61-63, qualified as the "killer argument" by P.B. Hugenholtz, NJ 2013/118.

the *UsedSoft* decision made the preservation of a market for used goods an aim in itself, turning it into a moral imperative of sound competition.[78] Paragraph 52 of the *UsedSoft* decision thus provides a rather striking example of interpreting the WCT in the light of EU law—and the Court's own interpretation of it—than of interpreting EU law in light of international law.

1.6 MAKING AVAILABLE

1.6.1 *Filmspeler* and *The Pirate Bay* (TPB)

If Europe should feel a *commitment* to the development of international copyright, that role will be of particular importance for the clarification of new notions of international law, such as "making available." Article 8 WCT grants authors the exclusive right to authorize any communication to the public of their works:

> including the making available to the public of their works in such a way that members of the public may access these works from a place and at a time individually chosen by them.

Whereas the copyright of making available is, therefore, "included" in the right of communication to the public, the same is not true in the case of the neighboring rights: Articles 10 and 14 WPPT provide the making available right as such, without mentioning the right of communication to the public. The same dissymmetry is repeated in Article 3(1) and Article (2) of the Copyright Directive 2001/29.

If the copyright of making available is "included" in the right of communication to the public, should this mean that "making available" can be limited by the concept of "communication"? This view has found strong support.[79] However, this interpretation could cause the concept of making available in copyright respectively neighboring rights to drift apart. Given

---

77. Reto M. Hilty, Kaya Köklü & Fabian Hafenbrädl, *Software Agreements: Stocktaking and Outlook: Lessons from the UsedSoft v. Oracle Case from a Comparative Law Perspective* 44(3) International Review of Intellectual Property and Competition Law 263-292, 280 (2013) https://doi.org/10.1007/s40319-013-0041-6.
78. Philippe Gaudrat, *Revue Trimestrielle du Droit Commercial* 790 ff., para. 49 (2012).
79. In this sense: P. Bernt Hugenholtz & Sam Van Velze, *Communication to a New Public? Three Reasons Why EU Copyright Law Can Do Without a New Public* 47(7) International Review of Intellectual Property and Competition Law 797, 801, 813 (2016) https://doi.org/10.1007/s40319-016-0512-7; European Copyright Society, *Opinion on the Reference to the CJEU in Case C-466/12 Svensson* 35ff. (2013), https://europeancopyrightsocietydotorg.files.wordpress.com/2015/12/european-copyright-society-opinion-on-svensson-first-signatoriespaginatedv31.pdf (accessed Apr. 29, 2019).

the requirement of the unity and coherence of the EU legal order,[80] that could better be avoided; the same applies to international law.

Contrary to this first approach, the Court of Justice seems inclined to regard the concepts of "communication" and "making available" as one and the same, apparently assuming that if the right of communication to the public now includes the right of making available, it means that the right of communication itself has thereby been enlarged. The Basic Proposal contains fragments that could be read as supporting that position:

> The relevant act is the making available of the work by providing access to it.[81]

It remains that this is not fully satisfactory from a systemic viewpoint: after all, in Article 8 WCT, the notion of "making available" is "included" in the notion of "communication to the public," not the other way round.

The Court also shows a preference for the use of the concept of "making available" rather than "communication to the public." *SGAE* and *Premier League* clearly concerned very traditional situations of communication to the public: hotel transmission and television in a pub. The Court nevertheless subjected them to the new standard of making available. The same approach was followed in the *Filmspeler* case.[82] The multimedia player called "*filmspeler*" was a hardware device on which links ("add-ons") to illegal websites had been pre-installed. The Court of Justice considered that the "*filmspeler*" offered its users direct access to protected works and that its provision had, therefore, to be regarded as an act of communication. It stressed that without the link, purchasers would find it difficult to benefit from the protected works. The "*filmspeler*" certainly facilitated an illegal communication by a third party. However, did the act of selling the *"filmspeler"* constitute an actual act of communication to the public by Mr. Wullems? Providing an online hyperlink to the website on which the work was posted would have made Mr. Wullems part of the chain of communication, but in the *Filmspeler* case, the work or subject matter was given access to by the offline "add-ons." The explanatory memorandum with the Basic Proposal did place "making available" in the context of an immaterial means of communication:

> Communication of a work can involve a series of acts of transmission and temporary storage, such incidental storage being a necessary feature

80. Case C-117/15 Reha Training Gesellschaft für Sport- und Unfallrehabilitation mbH v. Gesellschaft für musikalische Aufführungs- und mechanische Vervielfältigungsrechte eV (GEMA) (2016) ECLI:EU:C:2016:379, para. 28.
81. Basic Proposal for the Substantive Provisions of the Treaty on Certain Questions Concerning the Protection of Literary and Artistic Works to be Considered by the Diplomatic Conference (1996) CRNR/DC/4 WIPO44, para. 10.10. Also *see*, Alexander Tsoutsanis, *Why Copyright and Linking Can Tango* 9(6) Journal of Intellectual Property Law & Practice 495-509, 499, 503, 505 (2014) https://doi.org/10.1093/jiplp/jpu024.
82. Case C-527/15 Stichting Brein v. Jack Frederik Wullems.

of the communication process. If, at any point, the stored work is made available to the public, such making available constitutes a further act of communication which requires authorization.[83]

It is, however, difficult to see how an immaterial communication took place in the case of the sale of copies of the "*filmspeler.*" Perhaps the question should better have been left to national law, including its regulations of indirect copyright infringement.

If in *Filmspeler*, the Court may have pushed far the notion of "communication to the public," it took a memorable step in *TPB* (2017),[84] adapting the old notion to the present-day needs. In TPB, the material act of communication to the public was not performed by the online platform TPB. It was the users of TPB who, as "peers," stored the works on their computers and who uploaded the torrent files that made it possible to find the work. Despite this, the Court held that the operators of the online sharing platform TPB provided their users with access to the works concerned.[85] This time, we do not see any systemic restriction in the notion of "communication." It can very well be argued that the same interpretation has always been within reach, even under Article 11bis, paragraph 1(ii) of the Berne Convention. This provision speaks of an "organization" that communicates the works to the public. The notion of "organization" is not defined by the Convention; it could, however, very well encompass several entities that work together either in or as the formal or informal body that realizes the communication. Thus, if the Court's decision clarified the meaning of the notion of "making available" in Article 8 WCT, it also invited to rethink the text of Article 11bis, paragraph 1(ii).

1.7 THE CONCEPT OF WORK: ARTICLE 2 BERNE CONVENTION

1.7.1 Decisions *Infopaq I*, *BSA*, *Eva-Maria Painer*, *Football Dataco v. Yahoo*

The European Commission had never endeavored to harmonize copyright's philosopher's stone: the work of authorship. In 2004, it still felt that apart from the special cases in which it had already undertaken regulatory activity, the Member States had to stay free to establish the level of originality required for copyright protection. There was no indication that the existing differences created a problem for the functioning of the internal market.[86]

83. CRNR/DC/4 WIPO, 46 para. 10.14.
84. Case C-610/15 Stichting Brein v. Ziggo BV and XS4All Internet BV.
85. Case C-610/15 Stichting Brein v. Ziggo BV and XS4All Internet BV, paras. 36, 37.
86. Commission Staff Working Paper on the review of the EC legal framework in the field of copyright and related rights of 19.7.2004, SEC(2004) 995, 19.7.2004.

The special cases the Commission referred to were the work categories of computer programs,[87] databases and photographs.

One morning in 2009, however, Europe woke up and the general concept of work had been harmonized: that was the morning after the judgment of the Court in *Infopaq I*.[88] The Court ruled that the Copyright Directive 2001/29 was based on the principle that works are protected by copyright only if they are original in the sense that they are their author's "own intellectual creation." Among others, this was considered apparent from the general scheme of the Berne Convention, in particular Article 2(5) and (8), which presupposes that artistic or literary works presupposed are intellectual creations.

The *Infopaq* decision was to be confirmed and elucidated in the later decisions of *BSA*, *Premier League*, *Eva-Maria Painer* and *Football Dataco*. As summarized in the decision in *Football Dataco v. Yahoo*, the Court held that the notion of the author's own intellectual creation referred to the criterion of originality (37, with references); the criterion of originality was satisfied when the author expressed his creative ability in an original manner by making free and creative choices (38, with references).

The consequences of this jurisprudence stretched far, especially in Britain[89] and in countries with a copyright system based on the example of British law. First, these systems used to work with a closed list of works; after *Infopaq,* the open criterion applied to the author's own intellectual creation.[90] Second, the United Kingdom (U.K.) used a low threshold of

---

87. It was estimated that 12 Member States would have to lower their threshold whereas three would have to increase it. Cf. Lionel Bently, at Concise European Copyright Law 217 (Thomas Dreier, Bernt Hugenholtz eds., Kluwer Law International, 2006); Jon Bing, *Copyright Protection of Computer Programs* at Research Handbook on the Future of EU Copyright 408 (Estelle Derclaye ed., Edward Elgar, 2009).
88. Case C-5/08 Infopaq International A/S v. Danske Dagblades Forening; *See* Benoît Michaux, *L'originalité en droit d'auteur, une notion davantage communautaire après l'arrêt Infopaq* 5 Auteurs & Media 473-488 (2009); *also see* the contributions of Tanya Aplin, *Subject Matter* & Ramón Casas Vallés, *The Requirement of Originality* at Research Handbook on the Future of EU Copyright 49, 102 (Estelle Derclaye ed., Cheltenham, Northampton: Edward Elgar, 2009); Estelle Derclaye, *Wonderful or Worrisome? The Impact of the ECJ Ruling on Infopaq on UK Copyright Law* 5 European Intellectual Property Review 247-251 (2010); Eleonora Rosati, *Originality in a Work, or a Work of Originality; The Effects of the Infopaq Decision* 33(12) European Intellectual Property Review 746-755 (2011) https://doi.org/10.4337/9781782548942.00013; Andreas Rahmatian, *Originality in UK Copyright Law: The Old "Skill and Labour" Doctrine under Pressure* 44(1) International Review of Intellectual Property and Competition Law pp. 4-34 (2013); Eleonora Rosati, *Closed National Systems of Copyright-Protectable Works Are No Longer Compatible with EU Law*, Gewerblicher Rechtsschutz und Urheberrecht, Internationaler Teil 1112-1118 (2014).
89. Cf. the elaborate analysis in: Derclaye (n. 88).
90. Eleonora Rosati, *Closed National Systems of Copyright-Protectable Works Are No Longer Compatible with EU Law* 12 Gewerblicher Rechtsschutz und Urheberrecht, Internationaler Teil 1112-1118 (2014).

originality. Apart from the requirement that the work should be original in the sense of "not copied"—which, as we saw, as such probably is closer to the conventional notion of "original" than the continental interpretation of the Court (II)—no other condition applied than the application of some degree of "skill and labour." It was not very clear what this last requirement exactly meant, but it is certain that creativity was not required as an element.[91] After *Infopaq,* however, creativity became the essential element of the notions of "originality" and "intellectual creation." The old skill and labor works were not eligible for protection anymore.

It is no wonder that *Infopaq* led to indignation, if not exasperation. Fairly little of this transpired in the—in continental eyes—almost serene academic qualifications of "harmonization by the back door" and "harmonization by stealth." If publications quote British lawyers who considered *Infopaq* as "a bomb" or as "shocking if not choking," these voices remained anonymous.[92]

There is no doubt that *Infopaq I* and the following decisions were compatible as such with the Berne Convention. However, exactly the same applied to the British copyright system. The British were loyal members of the Berne Convention long before the EC was even founded. Important aspects of that convention were framed under their influence. There were no complaints that the British system hurt the concepts of work and originality in the Berne Convention. That is why it is felt that under the viewpoint of comity and bona fides, the shock therapy applied in order to harmonize the concept of work may be questionable. The shock was the more violent as this jurisprudence could have retroactive effects. That made it very different from the three cases in which the legislator had harmonized the originality criterion for specific categories of works and in which the effects of the new regime had each time, however rudimentary, were accompanied by rules of transitional law.[93] Not a single rule of that kind cushioned the effect of the *Infopaq* decision. Article 10(2) of the Copyright Directive 2001/29 provides that the Directive shall apply without prejudice to any acts concluded and rights acquired before December 22, 2002. As from that date, however, it must be assumed that *Infopaq* retroactively applied. Perhaps some consequences of *Infopaq* may be mitigated by the fact that:

91. *See*, among others, Tatiana-Eleni Synodinou, *The Foundations of the Concept of Work in European Copyright Law* at Codification of European Copyright Law. Challenges and Perspectives 102 (Tatiana-Eleni Synodinou ed., Kluwer Law International, 2012).
92. Mireille van Eechoud, *Along the Road to Uniformity: Diverse Readings of the Court of Justice Judgments on Copyright Work* 3(1) Journal of Intellectual Property, Information Technology and Electronic Commerce Law 60-80 (2012).
93. Software Directive, Art. 1(4); Term Directive, Art. 10(3) and Database Directive, Recital 25, Art. 14.

the respect of acquired rights and legitimate expectations is part of the Community legal order.[94]

Nonetheless, one is not always in an enviable situation when one's legal position depends on a general principle of law only.

It is felt that the respect of international law would paradoxically have commanded respect by the judiciary of the national regimes in the U.K. and systems related to it, which were universally accepted by the members of the Berne Union. This being said, in view of the sluggishness of the European legislator to take action in this crucial matter of the concept of work, one cannot suppress some forbidden sympathy for the boldness of the Court.

The harmonization of the concept of originality also caused considerable uncertainty in Germany.[95] Germany used a high threshold of protection with regard to works of industrial design.[96] The protection of models and designs is regulated in Article 2(7) of the Berne Convention, which leaves the countries of the Union free to determine the extent of application of their copyright laws to works of applied art and models and designs, as well as the conditions under which they shall be protected. Article 17 of the Design Directive 98/71 followed the same policy.[97] It provides that registered designs must be eligible for protection under the law of copyright; however, in wordings fairly close to those of the Berne Convention, it adds that the extent to which, and the conditions under which, such a protection is conferred, including the level of originality required, have to be determined by each Member State.[98] In accordance with this rule, Article 9 of the Copyright Directive provided that the Directive is without prejudice to, *inter alia*, design rights. Despite this, the Court's decision in *Flos v. Semeraro*[99] seemed to suggest that the unified criterion for the level of originality hence had to be applied. That was held by the Dutch Supreme Court in 2013:[100] the Dutch judges argued that as far as the European legislator had wished to

---

94. Term Directive, Recital 25.
95. About the German system *see* Ansgar Ohly, *Where Is the Birthday Train Heading? The Copyright-Design Interface in German Law* at Liber Amicorum Jan Rosén 53 591, 607 (Gunnar Karnell eds., eddy. ab, 2016); Ansgar Ohly, *The Case for Partial Cumulation in Germany* at The Copyright/Design Interface. Past, Present and Future 166ff. (Estelle Derclaye ed., Cambridge University Press, 2018).
96. *See*, among others, Gernot Schulze, *Schleichende Harmonisierung des urheberrechtlichen Werkbegriffs?: Anmerkung zu EuGH "Infopaq/DDF"* Gewerblicher Rechtsschutz und Urheberrecht 1019-1021 (2009).
97. Directive 98/71/EC of 13 October 1998, on the legal protection of designs (Oct. 13, 1998) Official Journal L 289, 28/10/1998, pp. 28-35.
98. Directive 98/71/EC, Art. 17.
99. Case C-168/09, Flos v. Semeraro (2011) ECLI:EU:C:2011:29; cf. Lionel Bently, *The Return of Industrial Copyright?* European Intellectual Property Law Review 654ff. (2012) https://doi.org/10.2139/ssrn.2122379.
100. Supreme Court of the Netherlands (Hoge Raad) Oct. 25, 2013, S&S Import en Export/Esschert Design *("Fire stoves")*, no. 6 (IER 2014), 48-55 note PGFA Geerts; AMI 2014, no. 6 pp. 65-67; ECLI:NL:HR:2013:1036.

leave, in the Design Directive and the Design Regulation, freedom to the Member States as to the standard of originality applicable to designs, this freedom has been limited by the body of case law developed by the Court of Justice as from 2009. However, the German Supreme Court took the opposite position in its judgment in *Geburtstagzug (Birthdaytrain).*[101] Indeed, the wording of *Flos v. Semeraro* is not without ambiguity. On top of that, the decision raises so many questions and contradictions that, in sum, total uncertainty continues to exist.[102]

1.8 CONCLUSION

Four aspects that may be associated with the notion of "compatibility" of EU copyright law with the *acquis* in the international copyright treaties were distinguished in the introduction: simple compliance; complementarity; copyright comity; and commitment to the further evolution of international law.

EU legislation above all provides abundant proof of the huge degree of complementarity of EU and international law, extending to elements such as the presumption of authorship and ownership (Enforcement Directive), the concept of work (Software Directive and the Term Directive), the structure of the exploitation rights (Software Directive, Copyright Directive, Resale right Directive) and the categories of relied on the exceptions and limitations (Software Directive and Database Directive).

An important element of this chapter was to draw attention to the importance of principles common in the copyright traditions of the EU Member States, especially where these have roots in international treaties. This issue was raised by Michel Walter in 2014 and was identified here as an obligation of copyright comity on the basis of the principle of bona fides. Some very clear examples of an explicit recognition of this principle can be found in the present body of European legislation, especially where a subject matter is left to the application of the Berne Convention and national law. That was the case as to the moral rights in the Database and Copyright Directives and the application of old national exceptions for analog use in Article 5(3)(o) of the Copyright Directive. Recital (7) of the Rental and Lending Directive even mentions it as a general principle of the approximation of laws.

---

101. BGH, 13.11. 2013, I ZR-143/12, Gewerblicher Rechtsschutz und Urheberrecht 2014, 175 (*"Geburtstagzug"*).
102. Lionel Bently, *The Return of Industrial Copyright?* European Intellectual Property Law Review 654, 661-662 (2012) https://doi.org/10.2139/ssrn.2122379; Antoon Quaedvlieg, *Het Auteursrecht: een crescendo van rechterlijk activisme* at De invloed van het Europese recht op het Nederlandse privaatrecht 708-739 (M. Wissink eds., Kluwer, 2014).

Whereas there can be no doubt that EU jurisprudence puts compatibility first, it can go as far as jeopardizing basic compliance of EU law with international law, where it is felt that certain policy goals are at stake in terms of fair competition and consumer protection. The introduction of the "new public" criterion in *SGAE* and the application of the exhaustion doctrine to the licensing of digital user's rights in *UsedSoft* were studied as examples. Without denying the importance of the policy goals pursued by the Court, it must, however, be observed that it is willing to realize these in individual cases at the cost of enormous damage to the systemic transparency and solidity of copyright—whereas such decisions might mean relatively little when it comes to the consistent and durable advancement of the policies and the interests underlying them.

Where it concerns commitment to the evolution of international law, a heavier burden rests on the shoulders of the judiciary than on those of the legislator—at least in the past, the Proposal of a Directive on copyright in the Digital Single Market has to all probabilities changed that situation.[103] We restricted ourselves, however, to law already in force. In our view, the Court of Justice realized a historical step by considering that the acts of the platform Pirate Bay formed a direct copyright infringement.

The European jurisprudence would do well to show more awareness of copyright comity. In *Infopaq* and the decisions following it, comity was perhaps not observed enough. The appointment of specialized judges might help.[104]

All in all, the saga of the interactions between the EU institutions and the international copyright instruments yields examples of the force as well as the fragility of the international framework. That the authority of this framework is based not so much on its age but on its eminent legal architecture should inspire more awe.

103. Proposal for a Directive of the European Parliament and of the on copyright in the Digital Single Market, COM/2016/0593 final—2016/0280 (COD).

104. Marcella Favale, Martin Kretschmer & Paul C. Torremans, *Is There an EU Copyright Jurisprudence? An Empirical Analysis of the Working of the European Court of Justice* 79(1) Modern Law Review 31-75 (2016) https://doi.org/10.1111/1468-2230.12166.

Table 1.1 Reference of International Copyright Law Instruments in the CJEU's Case Law

Berne Convention, Paris Act 1971	
1 BC:	DR, TV2 Danmark 2012 (5); Levola 2018 (3).
2 BC:	
paragraph (1)	Infopaq 2009 (4); Painer 2011 (5); SAS Institute 2012 (3); Soulier & Doke 2016 (3); Levola 2018 (4).
paragraph (2)	Levola 2018 (4).
paragraph (5)	Infopaq 2009 (4, 34).
paragraph (6)	Infopaq 2009 (4); Soulier & Doke 2016 (3).
paragraph (8)	Infopaq 2009 (4, 34).
3 BC:	
paragraph (1)	Soulier & Doke 2016 (4).
paragraph (2)	Soulier & Doke 2016 (4).
5 BC:	
paragraph (1)	Soulier & Doke 2016 (5).
paragraph (2)	Soulier & Doke 2016 (5; 32; 50-51); Dirk Renckhoff 2018 (31, indirect).
9(1) BC:	Infopaq 2009, (5, 34); Soulier & Doke 2016 (6; 32); Levola 2018 (5).
10(1) BC:	Painer 2011 (6, 127, 128).
11 BC:	SGAE 2006 (5), Organismos 2010 (5); Premier League 2011 (5, 201), Circul Globus (3, 35).
11bis(1) BC:	SGAE 2006 (6, 40, 41), Organismos 2010 (6); Premier League 2011 (6, 192), DR, TV2 Danmark 2012 (6); *SCF v. Marco del Corso* 2012 (85, indirect); Soulier & Doke 2016 (7, 32); Zürs.net 2017 (5; 18; 21; 25) (indirect); 44 (operative part).
11bis(3) BC:	DR, TV2 Danmark 2012 (6, 28, 30, 48).
11ter BC:	Organismos.
12 BC:	Painer 2011 (7); Art & Allposters 2015 (6; 26-27).
14 BC:	Organismos.
14bis BC:	Martin Luksan 2012 (3, 54, 57, 59-60, 64).
37(1)(c) BC:	Painer 2011 (8, 126).
Trade-Related Aspects of Intellectual Property TRIPS/WTO 1994	
4 TRIPS:	*Promusicae 2008.*
9(1) TRIPS:	SGAE C-306/05 2006; Infopaq 2009 (3); Premier League 2011 (4, 189); Painer 2011 (4); SAS Institute 2012 (4); Levola 2018 (6).
9(2) TRIPS:	SAS Institute 2012 (33); Levola 2018 (6).

10(1) TRIPS:	BSA (3, 33); SAS Institute 2012 (5, 34).
10(2) TRIPS:	*Football Dataco v. Yahoo!* 2012 (3, 31).
14 TRIPS:	*SCF v. Marco del Corso* 2012 (3, neighboring rights).
41(1) TRIPS:	Promusicae 2008 (3, 60).
41(2) TRIPS:	Promusicae 2008 (3, 60).
42 TRIPS:	Promusicae 2008 (4, 60).
47 TRIPS:	Promusicae 2008 (5, 60).
	WIPO Copyright Treaty WCT 1996
1(4) WCT:	Premier League 2011 (10; 189); Painer 2011 (10); Martin Luksan 2012 (5, 59); Art & Allposters 2015 (3-4); Soulier & Doke 2016 (9; 32; 50); Zürs.net 2017 (4); Levola 2018 (7).
2 WCT:	SAS Institute 2012 (6, 33); Levola 2018 (8).
4 WCT:	SAS Institute 2012 (7); UsedSoft 2012 (4).
5 WCT	*Football Dataco v. Yahoo!* 2012 (4, 31).
6 WCT:	Laserdisken 2006 (40-42); Peek & Cloppenburg 2008 (4, 29-32, 34-35); Titus Alexander Jochen Donner 2012 (23-24); UsedSoft 2012 (5, 7, 52, 60); Art & Allposters 2015 (5, 38-40); Dimensione Direct Sales 2015 (3-4, 23-24).
7 WCT:	UsedSoft 2012 (5, 7); *VOB v. Leenrecht* 2016 (3-5, 31-34, 39).
8 WCT:	SGAE 2006 (8, 10, 43); Organismos 2010 (8, 9, 10); *SCF v. Marco del Corso* 2012 (13); UsedSoft 2012 (6, 53).

Chapter 2

The Creeping Unification of Copyright in Europe

P. Bernt Hugenholtz

On April 17, 2019, the European Union (EU) formally adopted the Directive on Copyright in the Digital Single Market (CDSM Directive).[1] The Directive is the twelfth harmonization directive in the field of copyright and neighboring rights in Europe, since the adoption of the Computer Programs Directive in 1991.[2] Now that the approximation of copyright law in Europe is approaching completion, the idea of actual unification of copyright in the EU is gaining ground. Note that harmonization and unification of law, although often confused,[3] are different things. While harmonization compels lawmakers in the Member States to align national law with the norms of a directive, unification creates norms that directly apply to the entire territory of the Union, making national law redundant. Complete unification of copyright would therefore not only lead to "perfect harmonization"—i.e., identical substantive rules across the Union—but would also remove the territorial reach of copyright protection that is inherent to the existing

1. Directive (EU) 2019/790 of the European Parliament and of the Council of 17 April 2019 on copyright and related rights in the Digital Single Market and amending Directives 96/9/EC and 2001/29/EC (17 Apr. 2019) Official Journal L 130, 17/5/2019, pp. 92-125.
2. Council Directive 91/250/EEC of 14 May 1991, on the legal protection of computer programs (14 May 1991) Official Journal L 122/42, 17/5/1991, pp. 42-46.
3. *See,* for example, Communication from the Commission to the European Parliament, the Council, the European Economic and Social Committee and the Committee of the Regions, *Towards a Modern, More European Framework for Copyright* (Dec. 9, 2015) COM (2015) 626 final.

structure of national rights, and which continues to fragment the internal market until this day.

In its 2015 Communication on the modernization of the European copyright framework, the European Commission espoused its "long-term vision" of a unitary copyright "in the form of a single copyright code and a single copyright title," which should eventually replace the national copyright laws of the Member States.[4] According to the Commission:

> The EU should pursue this vision for the very same reason it has given itself common copyright legislation: to build the EU's single market, a thriving European economy and a space where the diverse cultural, intellectual and scientific production of Europe travel across the EU as freely as possible.[5]

Whereas formal unification in the form of an EU Copyright Regulation still seems to be a long way off, the EU legislator and the Court of Justice are gradually removing or reducing the territoriality of copyright in distinct fields, thereby bringing a unified European copyright law slowly but steadily closer. This chapter traces this process of creeping unification of copyright law in the EU. Section 2.1 *below* begins by summarizing the process of harmonization that has led to the current copyright *acquis* and highlights the role of the Court of Justice as the main promotor of approximation. Section 2.2 sets out various ways in which EU law has tackled territoriality in copyright law until today. Section 2.3 describes the increasing role of the EU Charter as a unifying force. Section 2.4 concludes by examining the prospect of formal unification by way of an EU Copyright Regulation.

2.1 HARMONIZATION OF COPYRIGHT

The harmonization of copyright in Europe has its roots in a legendary study conducted by Dr. Dietz in the 1970s for the European Commission.[6] The study, which was completed in 1976, demonstrated that the substantive rules on copyright and related rights of the (then) nine Member States of the European Community (EC) differed considerably from one another and potentially hindered the free movement of cultural goods across the Community. Harmonization of copyright was therefore necessary, Dietz concluded. To this end, Dr. Dietz advised the European Commission to initiate a program of step-by-step harmonization. According to the *Harmonisierungsfahrplan* proposed by Dietz, priority should be given to the most

4. *Ibid.*
5. *Ibid.*
6. Adolf Dietz, *Das Urheberrecht in der Europäischen Gemeinschaft, Studie im Auftrag der Generaldirektion Forschung, Wissenschaft und Bildung der Kommission der Europäische Gemeinschaften* (Baden Baden: Nomos, 1978).

urgent issues: the duration of copyright, private copying, reprography, lending right and the exhaustion of the distribution right. Dr. Dietz's harmonization agenda was eventually carried out by the European lawmaker in the 1990s, albeit not in the order he suggested.

Interestingly, the Dietz study contemplated not only harmonizing but also eventually unifying copyright law in the Community. According to Dietz, immediate unification of copyright was less urgent since, unlike formality-based rights of industrial property such as patents and trademarks, copyright protection arises *ex lege* (automatically) in all countries of the Community. Unification could wait until harmonization was complete, Dietz suggested.[7]

The harmonization of copyright in Europe eventually occurred in three phases: a first, highly productive ten-year period during which the main harmonization directives were issued (1991-2001); a second decade of consolidation and "soft law"; and a third still ongoing period of "harmonization through jurisprudence," during which the Court of Justice has taken over the harmonizing torch from the European legislator.[8]

With the adoption of the new CDSM Directive, copyright harmonization by directive is moving ever closer to completion. A dozen directives on copyright and neighboring rights have approximated the copyright laws of the Member States to a considerable degree.[9] First and foremost, the EU copyright *acquis* encompasses the main exploitation rights conferred by copyright: the rights of reproduction, communication to the public and distribution. Also harmonized are the main remuneration rights, such as the public lending right,[10] the private copying and reprography levies,[11] and the *droit de suite* (artist's resale right).[12] The same goes for the term of copyright,

---

7. *Ibid.*, 305-306.
8. *See*, P. Bernt Hugenholtz, *Copyright in Europe: Twenty Years Ago, Today and What the Future Holds*, 23(2) Fordham Intellectual Property, Media & Entertainment Law Journal 503-524 (2013).
9. *Ibid.*
10. Directive 2006/115/EC of the European Parliament and of the Council of 12 December 2006 on rental right and lending right and on certain rights related to copyright in the field of intellectual property (12 Dec. 2006) Official Journal L 376/28, 27/12/2006, pp. 28-35; replacing Council Directive 92/100/EEC of 19 November 1992, on rental right and lending right and on certain rights related to copyright in the field of intellectual property (19 Nov. 1992) Official Journal L 346/61, 27/11/1992, pp. 61-66.
11. Directive 2001/29/EC of the European Parliament and of the Council of 22 May 2001 on the harmonization of certain aspects of copyright and related rights in the information society, Art. 5(2)(a), (b) (22 May 2001) Official Journal 167/10, 22/6/2001, pp. 10-19 (hereinafter "InfoSoc Directive").
12. Directive 2001/84/EC of the European Parliament and of the Council of 27 September 2001, on the resale right for the benefit of the author of an original work of art (27 Sep. 2001) Official Journal L 272/32, 13/10/2001, pp. 32-36.

which ends 70 years after the death of the creator throughout the Union.[13] Copyright exceptions and limitations are broadly harmonized by the Information Society Directive that lists one mandatory and twenty optional exceptions.[14] The Marrakesh Directive of 2017 offers a mandatory limitation for the benefit of visually impaired persons.[15] The DSM Directive introduces a number of additional mandatory exceptions.[16]

The EU copyright *acquis* also deals with a variety of specific (vertical) issues, ranging from computer software[17] and database protection[18] to the use of orphan works.[19] Governance and supervision of collective rights management have also been harmonized.[20] The rules on copyright enforcement have been extensively approximated by way of the EU Intellectual Property (IP) Enforcement Directive, which applies horizontally to all IP rights protected in the Union.[21] Moreover, the DSM Directive partly harmonizes the law of author's contracts.[22] All in all, only a few areas in copyright law are left untouched by EU legislation.

Mindful of Recital 7 to the Information Society Directive, which states that "differences not adversely affecting the functioning of the internal

---

13. Directive 2011/77/EU of the European Parliament and of the Council of 27 September 2011, amending Directive 2006/116/EC on the term of protection of copyright and certain and related rights (27 Sep. 2011) Official Journal L 265/1, 11/10/2011, pp. 213-217.
14. InfoSoc Directive.
15. Directive (EU) 2017/1564 of the European Parliament and of the Council of 13 September 2017, on certain permitted uses of certain works and other subject matter protected by copyright and related rights for the benefit of persons who are blind, visually impaired or otherwise print-disabled and amending Directive 2001/29/EC on the harmonization of certain aspects of copyright and related rights in the information society, Art. 4 (13 Sep. 2017) Official Journal L 242/6, 20/09/2017, pp. 6-13.
16. Directive (EU) 2019/790 of the European Parliament and of the Council of 17 April 2019 on copyright and related rights in the Digital Single Market and amending Directives 96/9/EC and 2001/29/EC (17 Apr. 2019) Official Journal 130, 17/5/2019, pp. 92-125.
17. Directive 2009/24/EC of the European Parliament and of the Council of 23 April 2009 on the legal protection of computer programs (23 Apr. 2009) Official Journal L 111/16, 5/5/2009/, pp. 16-22; Replacing Council Directive 91/250/EEC of 14 May 1991, on the legal protection of computer programs (14 May 1991) Official Journal L 122/42, 17/5/1991, pp. 42-46.
18. Directive 96/9/EC of the European Parliament and of the Council of 11 March 1996, on the legal protection of databases (11 Mar. 1996) Official Journal L 77/20, 27/3/1996, pp. 20-28.
19. Directive 2012/28/EU of the European Parliament and of the Council of 25 October 2012 on certain permitted uses of orphan works (25 Oct. 2012) Official Journal L 299/5, 27/10/2012, pp. 5-12.
20. Directive 2014/26/EU of the European Parliament and of the Council of 26 February 2014, on collective management of copyright and related rights and multiterritorial licensing of rights in musical works for online use in the internal market (26 Feb. 2014) Official Journal L 84/72, 20/3/2014, pp. 72-98.
21. Directive 2004/48/EC of the European Parliament and of the Council of 29 April 2004 on the enforcement of intellectual property rights (29 Apr. 2004) Official Journal L 195/16, 2/6/2004, pp. 45-86.
22. Directive (EU) 2019/790, Arts. 18-23.

market need not be removed or prevented," some exclusive rights with limited impact on the internal market, such as public performance and adaptation rights, have so far remained unharmonized. The same goes for moral rights (personality rights), which protect non-pecuniary interests of authors and have therefore escaped the attention of European legislators until today. The rules on authorship and copyright ownership, which tend to vary greatly from one country to another, are mostly unharmonized as well.

2.1.1 Judicial Activism by the European Court

This brings me to the important role that the EU Court of Justice has played, and still plays, in completing the European harmonization agenda, by closing various gaps in the copyright *acquis*. Starting with the landmark *Infopaq* case of 2009,[23] the Court has pursued an activist agenda of "harmonization by interpretation"[24] or by "stealth," as some commentators would have it.[25] In *Infopaq*—a case involving the unauthorized reproduction of 11-word fragments of newspaper articles by a news alert service—the Court rather matter-of-factly held that:

> copyright within the meaning of Article 2(a) of Directive 2001/29 is liable to apply only in relation to a subject-matter which is original in the sense that it is its author's own intellectual creation.[26]

From this, the Court derived a harmonized copyright infringement standard:

> In the light of those considerations, the reproduction of an extract of a protected work which, like those at issue in the main proceedings, comprises 11 consecutive words thereof, is such as to constitute reproduction in part within the meaning of Article 2 of Directive 2001/29, if that extract contains an element of the work which, as such, expresses the author's own intellectual creation; it is for the national court to make this determination.[27]

While the Court's holding is roughly in line with the author's right conception of works of authorship that underlies the law of copyright in the continental-European Member States, it came as a surprise since no general

23. Case C-5/08 Infopaq International A/S v. Danske Dagblades Forening (2009) ECLI: EU:C:2009:465.
24. Jonathan Griffiths, *Infopaq, BSA and the "Europeanisation" of United Kingdom Copyright Law*, 16 Media & Arts Law Review (2011), https://ssrn.com/abstract=1777027 (accessed May 5, 2019).
25. Lionel Bently, *Harmonization by Stealth* (paper presented at Fordham IP Conference 2012). *See also* Gernot Schulze, *Schleichende Harmonisierung des urheberrechtlichen Werkbegriffs?*, Gewerblicher Rechtsschutz und Urheberrecht 1019 (2009).
26. Case C-5/08 Infopaq International A/S v. Danske Dagblades Forening, para. 37.
27. *Ibid.*, para. 48.

harmonized standards for works of authorship or copyright infringement formally exist. The directives have only harmonized three distinct categories of works—computer programs,[28] databases[29] and photographs[30]—along the common standard of "the author's own intellectual creation," whereas the directives are completely silent on the standard(s) for assessing copyright infringement. The Court has nevertheless confirmed and expanded its *Infopaq* holding in *BSA* and other cases while consistently repeating that copyright subject matter in the EU requires that a work be "the author's own intellectual creation,"[31] which is the case if "it reflects the author's personality ... by making free and creative choices."[32] In other words, EU law protects original creation; merely investing skill and labor is not sufficient.[33]

Not surprisingly, these decisions by the Court of Justice of the European Union (CJEU) have led to criticism and even condemnation, especially by commentators in the United Kingdom. According to Griffiths, the decisions are "a striking example of judicial activism in the interests of harmonisation."[34] Not deterred by this criticism, the Court has continued to express similar judicial activism in other largely uncharted areas, such as the notion of "public" (communication). According to the Court, communication to the public occurs both in a hotel that merely provides CDs and CD players to its guests;[35] in a public house where customers may view broadcast sports programs on television screens;[36] in a physical rehabilitation center where patients may watch television while undergoing treatment;[37] not however in a dentist's practice where a radio is playing music.[38]

---

28. Directive 2009/24/EC, Art. 1(3).
29. Directive 96/9/EC, Art. 3(1).
30. Directive 2006/116/EC, Art. 6.
31. Case C-393/09 Bezpečnostní softwarová asociace—Svaz softwarové ochrany v. Ministerstvo kultury (2010) ECLI:EU:C:2010:816 (hereinafter "BSA"). *See also* Joined Cases C-403/08 and C-429/08 Football Association Premier League Ltd and Others v. QC Leisure and Others (C-403/08) and Karen Murphy v. Media Protection Services Ltd (C-429/08) (2011) ECLI:EU:C:2011:631.
32. Case C-145/10 Eva-Maria Painer v. Standard Verlags GmbH and Others (2011) ECLI:EU:C:2011:798.
33. Case C-604/10 Football Dataco Ltd and Others v. Yahoo! UK Ltd and Others (2012) ECLI:EU:C:2012:115.
34. Griffiths (n. 24). *See for* a more positive assessment, Raquel Xalabarder, *The Role of the CJEU in Harmonizing EU Copyright Law*, 47 International Review of Intellectual Property and Competition Law 635-639 (2016) https://doi.org/10.1007/s40319-016-0509-2.
35. Case C-162/10 Phonographic Performance (Ireland) Limited v. Ireland and Attorney General (2012) ECLI:EU:C:2012:141.
36. Joined Cases C-403/08 and C-429/08 Football Association Premier League Ltd and Others.
37. Case C-117/15 Reha Training Gesellschaft für Sport- und Unfallrehabilitation mbH v. Gesellschaft für musikalische Aufführungs- und mechanische Vervielfältigungsrechte eV (GEMA) (2016) ECLI:EU:C:2016:379.
38. Case C-135/10 Società Consortile Fonografici (SCF) v. Marco Del Corso (2012) ECLI:EU:C:2012:140.

The European Court of Justice has also developed complicated rules on hyperlinking to copyright-protected works. In *Svensson,* the European Court ruled that a hyperlink is a "communication" that reaches the "public." But if it points to a work lawfully published online, the hyperlink does not reach a "new public," and therefore does not qualify as an act of communication to the public.[39] In *GS Media,* the Court clarified that linking to unlawful content does amount to communication to the public unless the hyperlinking person is an individual acting without knowledge and financial motive.[40] In *Stichting Brein,* the Court extrapolated this line of case law by holding that The Pirate Bay, the notorious platform that facilitates mass-scale "file sharing" of musical works and audiovisual content without the rightholders' permission, is directly liable for communicating these works to the public.[41] The Court's decision in *Stichting Brein* is a prime example of judge-made EU copyright law and stands in marked contrast to earlier decisions by national courts in Europe and the United States that dealt with file-sharing platforms principally in terms of secondary (contributory or vicarious) liability.

The Court's expansive interpretation of the communication right has clearly informed Article 17 of the DSM Directive, which determines that the provider of an "online content-sharing service" (e.g., *YouTube*) "performs an act of communication to the public or an act of making available to the public for the purposes of this Directive when it gives the public access to copyright-protected works or other protected subject matter uploaded by its users." But in remarkable contrast to this new rule, applying pre-DSM Directive law, the Court subsequently held that content-sharing sharing platforms such as YouTube that apply "the appropriate technological measures that can be expected from a reasonably diligent operator" to prevent copyright infringement, do *not* themselves communicate works to the public.[42]

Yet another area where the Court has acted in a harmonizing manner is private copying. While the Information Society Directive, which compels Member States that permit private copying to provide for "fair compensation" to the authors, seemed to have left ample leeway to the Member States,[43] the Court has issued around a dozen judgments on the issue, constructing an elaborate set of rules on private copying levy schemes.[44]

39. Case C-466/12 Nils Svensson and Others v. Retriever Sverige AB (2014) ECLI:EU:C:2014:76.
40. Case C-160/15 GS Media BV v. Sanoma Media Netherlands BV and Others (2016) ECLI:EU:C:2016:644.
41. Case C-610/15 Stichting Brein v. Ziggo BV and XS4All Internet BV (2017) ECLI:EU:C:2017:456.
42. Case C-682/18—YouTube and Cyando (2021) ECLI:EU:C:2021:503.
43. InfoSoc Directive, Art. 5(2)(b).
44. *See, e.g.*, Case C-467/08 Padawan SL v. Sociedad General de Autores y Editores de España (SGAE) (2010) ECLI:EU:C:2010:620; CJEU Jun. 27, 2013, Joined Cases C-457/11 to C-460/11 Verwertungsgesellschaft Wort (VG Wort) v. Kyocera and Others

In *Padawan,* the Court justifies its judicial intervention as follows:

> according to settled caselaw, the need for a uniform application of European Union law and the principle of equality require that the terms of a provision of European Union law which makes no express reference to the law of the Member States for the purpose of determining its meaning and scope must normally be given an independent and uniform interpretation throughout the European Union; that interpretation must take into account the context of the provision and the objective of the relevant legislation.

Consequently, the concept of "fair compensation" in Article 5(2)(b) of the Information Society Directive:

> which does not contain any reference to national laws must be regarded as an autonomous concept of European Union law and interpreted uniformly throughout the European Union.[45]

In *Deckmyn,*[46] another case where the Court was asked to interpret one of the optional limitations of the copyright acquis (in this case, parody), the European Court similarly came up with an "autonomous" interpretation of the limitation at issue. This is especially remarkable, since the Information Society Directive has left the choice of limitations and exceptions to the Member States. As Prof. Xalabarder concludes:

> Member States may choose which limitations to implement in their national laws, but they cannot freely design their scope: the scope of limitations comes "standardized" as designed in the corresponding paragraph of Art. 5.[47]

In *Luksan,* the European Court, once again, ventured into previously unharmonized terrain: here, the law of film production contracts. The Court held that the economic rights to exploit a cinematographic work vest by operation of law, directly, in the author (i.e., principal director) of the film.

(C-457/11) and Canon Deutschland GmbH (C-458/11) and Fujitsu Technology Solutions GmbH (C-459/11) and Hewlett-Packard- GmbH (C-460/11) v. Verwertungsgesellschaft Wort (VG Wort) (2013) ECLI:EU:C:2013:426; Case-C-435/12 ACI Adam BV and Others v. Stichting de Thuiskopie and Stichting Onderhandelingen Thuiskopie vergoeding (2014) ECLI:EU:C:2014:254.; Case-C-463/12 Copydan Båndkopi v. Nokia Danmark A/S (2015) ECLI:EU:C:2015:144; Case-C-166/15 Aleksandrs Ranks and Jurijs Vasiļevičs v. Finanšu un ekonomisko noziegumu izmeklēšanas prokoratūra and Microsoft Corp. (2016) ECLI:EU:C:2016:762.

45. Case C-467/08 Padawan SL v. Sociedad General de Autores y Editores de España (SGAE), paras. 32-33.
46. Case C-201/13 Johan Deckmyn and Vrijheidsfonds VZW v. Helena Vandersteen and Others (2014) ECLI:EU:C:2014:2132.
47. Xalabarder (n. 34) 635-639.

Consequently, national (Austrian) law that allocated these rights to the film producer was deemed incompatible with EU law.[48]

In the *Levola Hengelo* case, which concerned the copyright protection of the taste of a food product, the European Court confirmed that the notion of a work of authorship is fully governed by EU law:

> Accordingly, in view of the need for a uniform application of EU law and the principle of equality, that concept must normally be given an autonomous and uniform interpretation.[49]

The European Court went on to deny copyright protection to the taste of a food product (in the case at hand, a cheese spread) on the ground that the taste of a food product cannot "be pinned down with precision and objectivity."[50]

The *Cofemel* case offers yet another example of the Court's judicial activism. Whereas the EU rules on design protection[51] expressly leave discretion to the Member States in determining the level of originality required for copyright protection of works of applied art, the Court unequivocally applies its previously developed uniform originality standard to (clothing) designs.[52]

As a result of these and other decisions, important areas of copyright law have now been judicially harmonized by the Court. One can only wonder what topics will remain for the EU legislature to tackle in the years to come. According to Prof. Van Eechoud:

> Inevitably … once national courts are taken further down the road to an all-inclusive Community-wide notion of what constitutes a work, there will be no escape from a Community-wide notion of authorship (and initial ownership). And eventually also of moral rights, which has been kept out of the discussion in EU institutions so far with the convenient "excuse" that it has no particular internal market relevance.[53]

The Court's judicial activism is reminiscent of the important role that the Court of Justice played in the years leading up to harmonization. In a series of landmark decisions, the Court measured the exercise of IP rights

48. Case C-277/10 Martin Luksan v. Petrus van der Let (2012) ECLI:EU:C:2012:65.
49. Case C-310/17 Levola Hengelo BV v. Smilde Foods BV (2018) ECLI:EU:C:2018:899, para. 33.
50. *Ibid.*, paras. 42-43.
51. Article 17, Directive 98/71/EC of the European Parliament and of the Council of 13 October 1998, on the legal protection of designs, OJ L 289, 28.10.1998, pp. 28-35; Art. 96(2), Council Regulation (EC) No 6/2002 of 12 December 2001, on Community designs, OJ L 3, 5.1.2002, pp. 1-24.
52. Case C-683/17 Sociedade de Vestuário SA v. G-Star Raw CV (2019) ECLI:EU:C:2019:721, para. 54.
53. Mireille van Eechoud, *Along the Road to Uniformity: Diverse Readings of the Court of Justice Judgments on Copyright Work*, 3 Journal of Intellectual Property, Information Technology and E-Commerce Law 76 (2012).

against the basic freedoms of the internal market—in particular, the free circulation of goods and services.[54] Where the exercise by rightholders was found to be outside the "specific subject matter" of IP, e.g., to impede parallel imports of copyrighted goods between Member States, the Court found it to conflict with these freedoms. These decisions of the Court can be seen as a prelude to the harmonization process and certainly provided an important impetus for the European Commission's original harmonization initiative.[55]

2.2 THE FIGHT AGAINST TERRITORIALITY

Nevertheless, the edifice of European copyright still suffers from one structural weakness: territoriality. Despite three decades of harmonization, copyright in the EU has largely remained national law, with each Member State holding on to its own copyright law. As in the case of other IP rights, the protection conferred on copyright holders by these laws is limited to the borders of each State. Copyright's territoriality reflects the *Schutzland* principle of the Berne Convention, a rule that was confirmed by the European Court of Justice in its *Lagardère* decision.[56]

In all countries where his work is protected by copyright, the rightholder therefore enjoys a bundle of national copyrights. Each national right in this bundle can, in principle, be exercised separately, licensed or transferred in whole or in part. Territorial fragmentation of national copyrights is indeed quite common in actual practice. For example, film distribution and screening rights tend to be granted and exploited per Member State.[57] Territoriality is also at the heart of the collective

54. *See, e.g.,* Case 78/70 Deutsche Grammophon Gesellschaft mbH v. Metro-SB-Großmärkte GmbH & Co. KG (1971) ECLI:EU:C:1971:59.; Case 62/79 SA Compagnie générale pour la diffusion de la télévision, Coditel, and others v. Ciné Vog Films and others (1980) ECLI:EU:C:1980:84 (hereinafter "Coditel I"); Case 58/80 Dansk Supermarked A/S v. A/S Imerco (1981) ECLI:EU:C:1981:17; Case 262/81 Coditel SA, Compagnie générale pour la diffusion de la télévision, and others v. Ciné-Vog Films SA and others (1982) ECLI:EU:C:1982:334 (hereinafter "Coditel II"); Case 158/86 Warner Brothers Inc. and Metronome Video ApS v. Erik Viuff Christiansen (1988) ECLI:EU:C:1988:242; Case 341/87 EMI Electrola GmbH v. Patricia Im- und Export and others (1989) ECLI: EU:C:1989:30.

55. Jean-François Verstrynge, *Copyright in the European Economic Community*, 4 Fordham Intellectual Property, Media and Entertainment Law Journal 6 (1993) https://doi.org/10.54648/leie1992008.

56. Berne Convention for the Protection of Literary and Artistic Works (Sep. 9, 1886), S. Treaty Doc. Nos. 99-27 (hereinafter "Berne Convention"), Art. 5(2); Case C-192/04 Lagardère Active Broadcast v. Société pour la perception de la rémunération équitable (SPRE) and Gesellschaft zur Verwertung von Leistungsschutzrechten mbH (GVL) (2005) ECLI:EU:C:2005:475, para. 46.

57. P. Bernt Hugenholtz & Joost Poort, *Film Financing in the Digital Single Market: Challenges to Territoriality*. International Review of Intellectual Property and Competition Law 51, 167-186 (2020) https://doi.org/10.1007/s40319-019-00900-2.

management and exercise of musical performance rights. Composers and songwriters normally entrust their rights per territory to a locally operating collective management organization with a remit that is traditionally limited to the national borders of its place of establishment.

Another feature of territoriality is that, according to European conflict rules, the law of the country where protection is invoked (the "Schutzland") determines whether there is copyright infringement.[58] In *Hejduk,* a German company was sued before an Austrian court for making photographs available on its website without the permission of the Austrian photographer. The European Court held that the Austrian Court had jurisdiction:

> on the basis of the place where the damage occurred, to hear an action for damages in respect of an infringement of those rights resulting from the placing of protected photographs online on a website accessible in its territorial jurisdiction.[59]

The *Hejduk* ruling implies that making a work available over the Internet has copyright consequences in all jurisdictions where the work can be accessed online. As a result, an online provider wishing to offer a content service throughout the EU is required to obtain licences from all rightholders in all Member States.

The territorial nature of copyright thus poses an immediate obstacle to the integration of the European internal market.[60] Over the years, the European Court and the EU legislator have therefore sought solutions that mitigate the negative effects of territoriality on the internal market. However, these solutions are still incomplete and, in particular with regard to the cross-border exploitation of works online, do not yet provide sufficient solutions. A number of these partial solutions are summarized below.

2.2.1 Exhaustion of the Distribution Right

The Court of Justice has recognized at a very early stage that the territorial exercise of IP rights negatively affects the free movement of goods. In a series of judgments predating the harmonization process, the Court ruled that the distribution right is exhausted once goods protected by rights of IP are introduced on the Community market with the rightholder's consent.[61] This rule of Community exhaustion (or "first sale") was eventually consolidated

58. Regulation (EC) No. 864/2007 of 11 July 2007on the law applicable to non-contractual obligations (Rome II), Art. 8 (11 Jul. 2007) Official Journal L 199, 31/7/2007, pp. 40-49.
59. Case C-441/13 Pez Hejduk v. EnergieAgentur. NRW GmbH (2015) ECLI:EU:C:2015:28.
60. *See* Communication from the Commission to the European Parliament, the Council the European Economic and Social Committee and the Committee for the Regions *A Single Market for Intellectual Property Rights*, Brussels 24 May 2011, COM (2011) 287 final, p. 7.
61. *See, inter alia*, Case 78/70 Deutsche Grammophon Gesellschaft mbH v. Metro-SB-Großmärkte GmbH & Co. KG (1971).

in the Information Society Directive.[62] Consequently, parallel imports of copyrighted goods (such as books and CDs) are permitted between Member States, and markets for copyrighted goods can no longer be divided along national borders.

However, no comparable rule has as yet been developed regarding the provision of copyright-related services. In its *Coditel* judgment of 1980, the European Court of Justice refused to recognize a rule of Community exhaustion in respect of acts of broadcasting and cable transmission.[63] The rightholder in a neighboring Member State (in this case, Belgium) could therefore legitimately oppose the unauthorized retransmission of a feature film broadcast on television in another State (Germany) and retransmitted in Belgium over cable networks, without unduly restricting trade between Member States. The Coditel holding was eventually codified as well in the Information Society Directive. According to Article 3(3) the right of communication to the public cannot be exhausted.[64]

Nevertheless, the European Court of Justice has—controversially—applied the exhaustion rule to computer software "distributed" in intangible form over an Internet server, insofar as this mode of dissemination is deemed economically equivalent to the sale of physical copies of software. According to the Court in *UsedSoft*:

> the right of distribution of a copy of a computer program is exhausted if the copyright holder who has authorised, even free of charge, the downloading of that copy from the Internet onto a data carrier has also conferred, in return for payment of a fee intended to enable him to obtain a remuneration corresponding to the economic value of the copy of the work of which he is the proprietor, a right to use that copy for an unlimited period.[65]

However, in the more recent *Tom Kabinet* decision, the Court did not continue down this road toward "digital exhaustion." For works not categorized as computer programs, the rules of the Information Society Directive imply that "reselling" digital copies online is an act of communication to the public subject to the rightholder's authorization.[66]

---

62. InfoSoc Directive, Art. 4(2).
63. Case 62/79 Coditel, and others v. Ciné Vog Films and others (1980).
64. InfoSoc Directive, Art. 4(2). According to Recital 29, in such cases the "question of exhaustion does not arise."
65. Case C-128/11 UsedSoft GmbH v. Oracle International Corp (2012) ECLI:EU:C:2012:407.
66. Case C-263/18 Nederlands Uitgeversverbond and Groep Algemene Uitgevers v. Tom Kabinet Internet BV and Others (2019) ECLI:EU:C:2019:1111.

2.2.2 The Rise of Country-of-Origin Rules

Another solution to the problem of market fragmentation through territorial rights can be found in the Satellite and Cable Directive of 1993.[67] Under the rules of this Directive, a satellite broadcast is deemed to be a communication to the public solely in the country of origin of the signal, i.e., the country where the "injection" of the program-carrying signal takes place.[68] Consequently, copyright licenses for satellite broadcasting are needed only in the country of origin of the broadcast.[69]

The 2019 EU Online Broadcasting Directive similarly provides for a country-of-origin rule in respect of "ancillary online services" offered by broadcasting organizations, such as online simulcasting and catch-up services.[70] The scope of the new rule is, however, fairly limited, since it applies only to radio programs, television news and current affairs programs and "fully financed own [television] productions of the broadcasting organization."[71] It therefore remains to be seen what positive impact, if any, the new Directive will have on the DSM. The EU Portability Regulation, adopted in 2017, also comprises a country-of-origin rule.[72] This Regulation obliges providers of online audiovisual services offered on a subscription basis (e.g., Netflix) to provide subscribers staying temporarily in another Member State with the same film offering as they enjoy in their home country. In order to make this obligation work, the Regulation stipulates that:

> [t]he provision of an online content service under this Regulation to a subscriber who is temporarily present in another Member State, as well as the access to and the use of that service by the subscriber, shall be deemed to occur solely in the subscriber's Member State of residence.[73]

More generally, country-of-origin rules are on the rise in copyright-related EU legislation. For example, the Orphan Works Directive of 2012 accords "orphan work" status in all Member States to any work or phonogram that is considered an orphan work in a Member State under the

67. Directive 93/83/EEC of 27 September 1993 on the coordination of certain rules concerning copyright and rights related to copyright applicable to satellite broadcasting and cable retransmission (27 Sep. 1993) Official Journal L 248/15, 6/10/1993, pp. 15-21 (hereinafter "Satellite and Cable Directive").
68. Satellite and Cable Directive, Art. 1(2)(b).
69. *See*, for example, Case C-290/21 Staatlich genehmigte Gesellschaft der Autoren, Komponisten und Musikverleger Reg. Gen. mbH (AKM) v. Canal+ Luxembourg Sàrl (2023) ECLI:EU:C:2023:424.
70. Directive 2019/790/EU.
71. Directive (EU) 2019/790, Art. 3(1).
72. Regulation (EU) 2017/1128 of the European Parliament and of the Council of 14 June 2017 on cross-border portability of online content services in the internal market (14 Jun. 2017) Official Journal L 168/1, 30/6/2017, pp. 1-11 (hereinafter "Portability Regulation").
73. Portability Regulation, Art. 4.

rules of the Directive.[74] The "Marrakesh Directive" on the use of works for the benefit of visually impaired persons allows an "authorised entity" established in any Member State to make accessible-format copies of works and to make these available to beneficiaries and other "authorities" anywhere in the Union, subject to the substantive conditions of the Directive.[75] Country-of-origin rules can also be found in the DSM Directive. According to Article 5(3):

> [t]he use of works and other subject matter for the sole purpose of illustration for teaching through secure electronic environments undertaken in compliance with the provisions of national law adopted pursuant to this Article shall be deemed to occur solely in the Member State where the educational establishment is established.[76]

Similarly, the DSM Directive's exception allowing the use of out-of-commerce works:

> shall be deemed to occur solely in the Member State where the cultural heritage institution undertaking that use is established.[77]

2.2.3 Remedies in Competition Law

Less structural, but occasionally effective nonetheless, are the solutions that can be found in EU competition law to prevent territorial market fragmentation through the exercise of national copyright, notably Articles 101 (antitrust) and 102 (abuse of dominance) of the Treaty for the Functioning of the European Union (TFEU)—formerly Articles 81 and 82 of the EC Treaty. Over the years, the European Commission, which is tasked with competition oversight, and the European Court of Justice have produced extensive case law on the issue. For example, in 1982, the European Court ruled that an exclusive territorial license in respect of a film does not per se infringe antitrust law but that such a contract may well amount to a violation "if it has as its object or effect the restriction of film distribution or the distortion of competition on the cinematographic market."[78]

In its *Premier League* decision of 2011, the European Court of Justice held that an exclusive pay television license agreement that obliges the pay television broadcaster not to supply decoding devices to users outside the

74. Directive 2012/28/EU, Art. 4.
75. Directive (EU) 2017/1564 of the European Parliament and of the Council of 13 September 2017 on certain permitted uses of certain works and other subject matter protected by copyright and related rights for the benefit of persons who are blind, visually impaired or otherwise print-disabled and amending Directive 2001/29/EC on the harmonization of certain aspects of copyright and related rights in the information society, Art. 4 (13 Sep. 2017) Official Journal L 242/6, 20/9/2017, pp. 6-13.
76. DSM Directive, Art. 5(3).
77. DSM Directive, Art. 9(2).
78. Case 262/81 Coditel II.

territory covered by that license agreement infringes Article 101 TFEU.[79] The decision is in line with general EU competition law,[80] which distinguishes between active and passive sales to consumers in Member States not covered by a territorial license. Whereas competition law does allow a licensor to oblige a licensee not to actively seek customers outside the licensed territory, a licensee may not be prevented from "passively" selling to such consumers. In other words, an exclusive territorial broadcasting license may never be absolute.[81]

Following the Court's decision in the Premier League, the European Commission started an investigation into anti-competitive licensing practices in the pay television sector. The investigation focused on licensing contracts entered into by a number of major film studios and Sky U.K. Limited (and subsidiaries). This led to commitments by Paramount and Disney to remove or no longer enforce restrictions in their licensing contracts that prevent pay television providers from responding to unsolicited (passive) requests from consumers outside the licensed territory.[82]

More recently, in line with the CJEU's holding in Premier League, the General Court upheld a Commission decision finding that Valve, the operator of the Steam online gaming platform, and several game publishers infringed Article 101 TFEU by geoblocking Steam keys and thus effectively preventing passive sales outside licensed territories.[83]

2.2.4 Multiterritorial Licenses

The EU Collective Rights Management Directive of 2014 explores a completely different solution to the problem of territoriality.[84] In addition to offering detailed rules on good governance and transparency of collective rights management societies, the Directive obliges collecting societies to

---

79. Joined Cases C-403/08 and C-429/08 Football Association Premier League and others.
80. *See, e.g.*, Commission Regulation (EU) No 330/2010 of 20 April 2010 on the application of Art. 101(3) of the Treaty on the Functioning of the European Union to categories of vertical agreements and concerted partnership, Art. 4(b)(i) (20 Apr. 2010) Official Journal L 102, 23/4/2010, pp. 1-7.
81. *See* Giuseppe Mazziotti & Felice Simonelli, *Another Breach in the Wall: Copyright Territoriality in Europe and Its Progressive Erosion on the Ground of Competition Law*, 18(6) info 60-61.
82. Case AT.40023—Cross-border access to pay-TV (Paramount); Case AT.40023—Cross-border access to pay-TV (Disney). The European Commission's decision in Paramount was eventually annulled by the CJEU for lack of proportionality because it did not take into account the adverse effect on the contractual rights of third parties; Case C-132/19 P Groupe Canal + SA.
83. Case T-172/21 Valve Corporation.
84. Directive 2014/26/EU of the European Parliament and of the Council of 26 February 2014 on collective management of copyright and related rights and multi-territorial licensing of rights in musical works for online use in the internal market (26 Feb. 2014) Official Journal L 84/72, 20/3/2014, pp. 72-98.

conclude multiterritorial licenses for online uses of music. Rightholders who have entrusted their rights to a collecting society that is unwilling or unable to do so may withdraw their rights and transfer them to another collecting society that is willing and able to license them on a multi-territory basis. In this way, the EU legislator hopes to break the territorial partitioning of the market through collectively managed music rights and to promote pan-European licensing for the Internet.

2.3 GROWING IMPACT OF THE EU CHARTER AND PRIMARY UNION LAW

Parallel to the step-by-step "deterritorialization" of copyright, a small revolution is occurring in the European case law that bolsters the trend toward a unitary European copyright. The inclusion of IP rights in the EU Charter (Article 17(2) of the Charter) has given copyright entitlements fundamental rights status.[85] The same goes for a variety of copyright exceptions justified by fundamental freedoms, such as freedom of expression (Article 11 of the Charter).

For example, in *Luksan,* the Court of Justice, referring to Article 17 of the Charter, held that a provision in Austrian copyright law providing for the statutory transfer of filmmakers' rights to film producers is contrary to EU law.[86] And in *Deckmyn,* the Court ruled that the parody exception provided for in Article 5(3) of the Information Society Directive is motivated by freedom of expression and is therefore to be liberally interpreted.[87] It is worth noting that far from all Member States have codified a general parody exception. The explicit reference in the judgment to freedom of expression enshrined in the Charter raises the question of whether a parody exception should not also be introduced in every Member State, given that it is the expression of an underlying fundamental right.[88] In his opinion in the *Pelham* case, Advocate-General Szpunar seems to accept this argument. While denying Member States the freedom to introduce exceptions not included in the Information Society Directive's "shopping list," the Advocate-General admits that:

> some ... exceptions reflect the balance struck by the EU legislature between copyright and various fundamental rights, in particular the

85. *See* Christophe Geiger, *"Constitutionalising" Intellectual Property Law? The Influence of Fundamental Rights on Intellectual Property in the European Union*, 37 (4) International Review of Intellectual Property and Competition Law 371 (2006).
86. Case C-277/10 Martin Luksan v. Petrus van der Let.
87. Case C-201/13, Johan Deckmyn and Vrijheidsfonds VZW v. Helena Vandersteen and Others.
88. Note that Art. 17(7) DSM Directive requires EU Member States to introduce a parody exception only in respect of "uploading and making available content generated by users on online content-sharing services."

freedom of expression. Failing to provide for certain exceptions in domestic law could therefore be incompatible with the Charter.[89]

The Court's increasingly frequent references to the fundamental rights enshrined in the EU Charter suggest that there are, in principle, no limits to the European Court's competence to opine in copyright cases. If the *acquis* codified in the directives is simply the expression of general legal principles enshrined in the Charter, there is no reason for the Court to be cautious, even where there is no written secondary law to rely on.

Primary Union law is also occasionally invoked by the European Court of Justice to protect the internal market from fragmentation by territorial copyright. In the *Premier League* case discussed above, the Court ruled that a ban on the resale of Greek decoder cards not only violates antitrust law but also Article 56 TFEU, which guarantees the free movement of services.[90] And in *UsedSoft,* the European Court relied on its long-standing exhaustion case law, that is directly grounded in the free movement of goods, to extend the exhaustion rule to computer software downloaded from the Internet.[91]

In connection with the judicial harmonization by the Court described above, the freedom of the Member States to devise their own solutions within the existing harmonized framework is rapidly diminishing. Driven by fear of state liability for damages resulting from (retrospectively) incorrect transposition,[92] this increasingly leads Member States to (near-)literal transposition of directives. This moves us ever closer to actual unification.

2.4 THE LAST STEP: FORMAL UNIFICATION

As we have seen in the previous sections of this chapter, the unification of copyright is progressively effectuated by way of a variety of legal instruments and doctrines, such as the country-of-origin principle, competition law, application of the EU Charter and other primary Union law. In the meantime, the European Court of Justice is filling in any remaining gaps in the copyright acquis. Nevertheless, a truly unified European copyright has yet to be realized, and geoblocking practices based on territorially exercised

89. Opinion AG Szpunar, Case C-476/17 Pelham and others (2018) ECLI:EU:C:2018:1002, para. 77.
90. Joined Cases C-403/08 and C-429/08 Football Association Premier League and others, paras. 85 et seq.
91. Case C-128/11 UsedSoft GmbH v. Oracle International Corp, paras. 62-63.
92. ECJ Nov. 19, 1991, Case C-6/90 Andrea Francovich and Danila Bonifaci and others v. Italian Republic (1991) ECLI:EU:C:1991:428. For example, following CJEU Apr. 10, 2014, Case C-435/12 ACI Adam BV and Others v. Stichting de Thuiskopie and Stichting Onderhandelingen Thuiskopie vergoeding (2014) ECLI:EU:C:2014:254. The Netherlands was held liable for damages to rightholders for permitting downloading from illegal sources. SEKAM v. The Netherlands, ECLI:NL:RBDHA:2018:10645 (Court of The Hague, 2018).

rights persist across the Union.[93] Also, legislatures in some Member States seemingly cannot suppress their desire to "gold-plate" harmonized standards by introducing more detailed rules at the national level, which inevitably leads to new disparities.[94]

Ideally, unification would be achieved in the form of an EU Copyright Regulation that provides for a unitary copyright title and replaces existing national copyright laws. Significantly, the Lisbon Reform Treaty has introduced a specific competence for the EU legislature to create Union-wide IP rights. Article 118 TFEU expressly instructs the European Parliament and the Council to "adopt measures for the creation of European intellectual property rights to provide uniform protection of intellectual property rights throughout the Union … ."

In 2006, the Institute for Information Law (IViR) carried out a comprehensive evaluation of the copyright acquis at the request of the European Commission. One of the study's main recommendations was to initiate a unification project that might, one day, lead to unified EU copyright law.[95] According to the IViR study, the advantages of unitary EU copyright are undeniable. An EU Copyright Regulation would immediately establish a truly unified legal framework, replacing the multitude of national rules of the present. It would have an instant Union-wide effect, creating an unfragmented single market for copyrights and related rights, both online and offline. It would enhance legal security and transparency for right owners and users alike and greatly reduce transaction costs. Unification could also restore the asymmetry that is inherent in the current acquis, which mandates basic economic rights but merely permits limitations.[96]

In recent years, the idea of unification has become gradually accepted in scholarly[97] and political circles. For example, at the end of 2014, the

---

93. Tatiana Eleni Synodinou, *Geoblocking in EU Copyright Law: Challenges and Perspectives*, 69(2) Gewerblicher Rechtsschutz und Urheberrecht International 136-150 (2020).
94. *See*, for example, Christina Angelopoulos, Arts. 15 & 17 of the Directive on Copyright in the Digital Single Market Comparative National Implementation Report, CIPIL, Cambridge 2023.
95. Institute for Information Law, *The Recasting of Copyright & Related Rights for the Knowledge Economy* (DG Internal Market, 2006); Mireille van Eechoud, P. Bernt Hugenholtz, Lucie Guibault, Stef van Gompel & Natalie Helberger, *Harmonizing European Copyright Law. The Challenges of Better Lawmaking* (Kluwer, 2009).
96. *Ibid.*, 316-317.
97. *See, inter alia,* Reto Hilty, *Copyright in the Internal Market*, 35 International Review of Intellectual Property and Competition Law 760 (2004); Estelle Derclaye & Trevor Cook, *An EU Copyright Code: What and How, If Ever?*, Intellectual Property Quarterly 259 (2011); Frank Gotzen, *The European Legislator's Strategy in the Field of Copyright Harmonization at Codification of European Copyright Law* 43-54 (Tatiana-E. Synodinou ed., Kluwer 2012); Reto Hilty, *Reflections on a European Copyright Codification* at Codification of European Copyright Law 355 (Tatiana-E. Synodinou ed., Kluwer 2012); Tatiana Synodinou, *The Desirability of Unification of European Copyright Law*, at The Routledge Handbook of European Copyright Law (Eleonora Rosati ed., 2021); Mireille

European Copyright Society, a group of leading European copyright professors, sent a public letter to the European Commission urging it to initiate a unification project.[98] A year later, the European Commission committed itself to the idea of unitary copyright in an official Communication to the Council and the European Parliament.[99] In doing so, the Commission acknowledged that the road to a European Copyright Regulation is still long and complex. Evidently, as the European Commission observes in its Communication:

> Towards a modern, more European framework for copyright, the introduction of a unitary copyright system would have to be accompanied by the establishment of EU copyright courts operating at various levels, similar to the courts already designated under the EU trademark and design right systems. But these difficulties should not lead to the abandonment of this vision as a long-term objective.

Earlier, the Wittem Group had already demonstrated with its European Copyright Code[100] that there is sufficient support in academic circles for European unification and that remaining differences between the copyright laws of the Member States are by no means unbridgeable.

All in all, a transition from the current, highly harmonized—and increasingly "deterritorialized"—system to a truly unitary copyright system would be evolutionary rather than revolutionary. The real question is not whether we will ever get there but when. As Dr. Dietz predicted in 1976, such a transition will become easier, indeed almost natural, after the harmonization of substantive copyright law has been completed. In any case, any remaining doctrinal resistance against unification based on diverging national legal traditions[101]—objections that have, in the past, marred both harmonization and unification efforts—is becoming obsolete now that

---

van Eechoud, *Territoriality and the Quest for a Unitary Copyright Title*, International Review of Intellectual Property and Competition Law 55, 66-88 (2024) https://doi.org/10.1007/s40319-023-01412-w.

98. European Copyright Society, *Letter to Commissioner Oettinger on Unification of Copyright Law*, https://europeancopyrightsociety.org/wp-content/uploads/2015/12/ecs_letter_to_oettinger_fin-1.pdf (accessed on Mar. 24, 2025).

99. Communication from the Commission to the European Parliament, the Council, the European Economic and Social Committee and the Committee of the Regions, *Towards a Modern, More European Framework for Copyright* (Dec. 9, 2015) COM (2015) 626 final.

100. Wittem Group, *European Copyright Code*, https://www.ivir.nl/copyrightcode/european-copyright-code/ (accessed May 5, 2019). *See* P. Bernt Hugenholtz, *The European Copyright Code. The Wittem Project* at Codification of European Copyright Law 339-354 (Tatiana E. Synodinou ed., Kluwer 2012); Eleonora Rosati, *The Wittem Group and the European Copyright Code,* Journal of Intellectual Property Law & Practice 862 (2010).

101. *See* Andreas Rahmatian, *European Copyright Inside or Outside the European Union: Pluralism of Copyright Laws and the "Herderian Paradox,"* International Review of Intellectual Property and Competition Law 912-940 (2008) https://doi.org/10.1007/s40319-016-0531-4.

substantive copyright law in the Member States has been all but approximated.

The main remaining obstacles to unification are political and economical. Several major stakeholders, such as collective rights management organizations and film production companies, will not be keen on abandoning their business models based on territorial exclusivity. And some Member States will be reluctant to fully relinquish their remaining autonomy in the field of copyright, even if advanced harmonization has not left much room for national discretion or digression. Moreover, whether the EU wishes to invest any political capital at all in a copyright unification project seems rather unlikely in the aftermath of Brexit. However, Brexit may present an unexpected opportunity. Absent the United Kingdom, only a few smaller Member States (Ireland, Cyprus and Malta) will represent the British "copyright" tradition inside the EU. This will, most likely, make a unified European copyright law that is systematically based on "author's rights" principles much easier to accomplish.

So, how do we get there from here? Commentators and the European Commission have in the past advocated a variety of interim steps,[102] such as recodification of the entire acquis in a single EU Copyright Directive,[103] the introduction of an optional EU copyright title that would co-exist with national copyrights,[104] codification of EU copyright standards in a Commission Recommendation, et cetera. As this chapter has demonstrated, unification is already creeping into the system of EU copyright law at various levels and in different ways. We have, in my opinion, reached a stage where interim steps are no longer needed.[105] The time to start formal unification is now.

102. *See* Gotzen (n. 97) 49-54; Rote Hilty (n. 97) 360-363.
103. Communication from the Commission to the European Parliament, the Council the European Economic and Social Committee and the Committee for the Regions *A Single Market for Intellectual Property Rights*, Brussels 24 May 2011, COM (2011) 287 final, p. 11.
104. *Ibid.*
105. To be sure, the transition from a structure of national copyrights to a uniform unitary title will require a range of transitional rules regarding the ownership of existing works; *see* Mireille van Eechoud, *Territoriality and the Quest for a Unitary Copyright Title*, International Review of Intellectual Property and Competition Law 55, 66-88, p. 84 (2024) https://doi.org/10.1007/s40319-023-01412-w.

Chapter 3

Globalization of Collective Rights Management and the Role of National CMOs

*Rudolf Leška**

Sate sanguine divom,
Tros Anchisiade, facilis descensus Averno;
noctes atque dies patet atri ianua Ditis;
sed revocare gradum superasque evadere ad auras,
hoc opus, hic labor est. …
Vergil[1]

Collective management organizations (CMOs) are private entities acting for the public good for the benefit of users, consumers and rightholders alike by providing access to a large amount of cultural goods, reducing transactional costs and ensuring appropriate distribution among authors and other rightholders. In the dynamics of abruptly changing copyright policies in Europe and elsewhere, it is possible to note an ongoing deterioration of these

* The original contribution was made possible by the institutional support of long-term research projects at the University of Finance and Administration as part of the junior project "Transformations of Individual and Collective Copyright Management."

1. Aen. 6.125-129:

O goddess-born of great Anchises' line,
The gates of hell are open night and day;
Smooth the descent, and easy is the way:
But to return, and view the cheerful skies,
In this the task and mighty labor lies.
(Dryden trans.).

traditional features of collective rights management (CRM) for the declared sake of competition, global market and free flow of cultural goods on the Internet.

After summing up the outstanding legal issues of today's CRM, I will argue that the current European Union (EU) policy in this field and the means chosen for the establishment of the Digital Single Market (DSM) in Europe are ill-founded, should not serve as inspiration for other countries and must be revisited as they lead to a fossilization of the oligopoly of major publishers and global platforms and, ultimately, to a lesser cultural diversity. Instead of creating a supranational borderless market with large corporate-like CMOs, we must look for other solutions when delivering multiterritorial licenses to users—solutions based on established licensing standards and the territorial nature of copyright.

3.1 TRADITIONAL FEATURES OF COLLECTIVE MANAGEMENT AND LICENSING

Attributes of CRM are well-researched in the literature.[2] They usually include (or at least included until very recently)—without hierarchical order—a territorial monopoly for the management of certain rights (either established by law or by practice), an obligation to act for the common good of all rightholders (e.g., with no preference of one repertoire over another), an obligatory extent of representation (disallowing "cherry-picking" by rightholders),[3] the obligation to represent a rightholder when approached, the obligation to license the repertoire if requested by a user under an *ex ante* published tariff (obligation to contract), nonprofit nature, policing and enforcement of copyright and the execution of a social, cultural and educational mission. Accommodating the two seemingly conflicting principles of nondiscrimination and solidarity[4] between rightholders (national and foreign, large and small) as well as between "sister" organizations, CRM

2. For a comprehensive overview of collective management cf. Daniel Gervais ed., *Collective Management of Copyright and Related Rights* (3rd edn, Kluwer, 2016).
3. It should be noted that obligatory representation of the full repertoire has not been introduced only to ease the CMOs their operations and make the administration less costly (representation only for certain rights or certain repertoire makes licensing and distribution more complex and more expensive) but also to protect the author or the artist. If a critical number of authors and artists is represented by a CMO by being fully bound to the representation agreement, the user cannot push them to direct license for unreasonably low remuneration.
4. The principle of solidarity within the organization can be documented on distribution rules (favoring works of cultural value assessed within the local cultural context) and on deductions for social, cultural and educational purposes which are to a certain extent applied also to proceeds which are otherwise due to foreign rightholders. This is of special importance in the case of small CMOs in countries which are net importers of cultural goods the remuneration for which is sent abroad.

has served its purpose of achieving collaborative harmony in the international exchange of cultural goods.

As such, CMOs continue to play a vital and irreplaceable role within the creative ecosystem and, needless to say, in national cultural policies—mainly in continental Europe.

3.2 THE NEED FOR MULTITERRITORIAL LICENSING

Development of Internet services, data compression and better availability of the Internet for wide audiences created a demand for online reception of art[5] and *eo ipso* for the licensing of such online uses. Obviously, traditional licensing schemes based on the principle of territorial clearance of rights were not ready to quickly adapt to this demand, even though the problem was not entirely new.

In the sphere of mechanical rights, the desire of major record companies to obtain a pan-European license for the production and sale of compact discs in the 1990s led to several global deals. In 1996, four such agreements were in place, namely between STEMRA (Netherlands) and Polygram, SACEM/SDRM (France) and Sony, GEMA (Germany) and Warner/BMG and lastly, a deal covering continental Europe between SACEM/SDRM, MCPS (U.K.) and GEMA on the one side and EMI on the other.[6] These agreements were nevertheless still based on the traditional reciprocal representation of CMOs. Although record companies were able to acquire licenses for (nearly) any part of the global repertoire under these arrangements (based on the CMOs' own representation agreements with rightholders and reciprocal agreements with the CMOs' sisters' organizations), the proceeds from such deals were distributed to rightholders through the individual national CMOs. The system was therefore still firmly based on the territoriality principle. Later, MCPS and Polygram took a step further. Under their 1997 deal,[7] which came into effect on July 1, 1997, Polygram group purchased from MCPS a European-wide mechanical license. MCPS contracted directly with music publishers, to the dismay of European continental CMOs, thus avoiding their involvement and, of course, their commission.[8] It is obvious that the major music publishers saw this as advantageous as they saved on the commission which would be otherwise charged by two CMOs.

5. I prefer to use the word art instead of the—now modern—content, a term which obscures the true nature of the protected subject matter in policy discussions.
6. Nils Bortloff, *Collective Management of Rights in Musical, Literary and Dramatic Works in Europe,* 6 German American Law Journal 67, 75 (1997).
7. The system was reportedly opened for any record company, not only for Polygram, which was the first to make such request. Jeff Clark-Meds, *Polygram Deal Angers EU,* Billboard Magazine 6, 101 (1996).
8. *Ibid.*, 101. According to this news report, MCPS's unilateral move led to several terminations of reciprocal agreements by continental CMOs.

In the area of the right of public performance, the need for a multiterritorial license was substantiated not only by business reasons but also by the legal necessity to deal with overspills from one territory to another during the act of communication to the public.

Historically, the issue of cross-border use by a single act of communication—whether licensed or not—first appeared with the operation of luxurious trans-European expresses and ocean-faring steamers[9] and later with the discovery of radio transmission.[10] Even in cases where radio transmission is directed to a particular territory, inadvertent overspill to neighboring countries is unavoidable, especially in a region as fragmented as Europe. This problem was not unknown to the policymakers and copyright lawyers of the time, but it became accepted by rightholders as a natural phenomenon which is de facto not substantially harming their material interests, and the doctrine largely supported the emission theory.[11] Even under the opposite theory of reception advocated by the World Intellectual Property Organization Director General Árpád Bogsch,[12] inadvertent occasional overspill of terrestrial broadcasts was considered a *de minimis* exception from copyright.[13] Interestingly, the issue was never really settled. Contractual solutions found their way into standard broadcasting license deals if concluded individually with the rightholders, without involving CMOs when licensing such overspills.[14]

9. Two cases, even though they involve patent rather than copyright infringement, are reported from the USA, where the courts refused to extend patent protection to the vessels on the high seas, even if registered under the U.S. flag. Cf., Ocean Science & Engineering, INC. v. The United States, 595 F.2d 572 (Ct. Cl. 1979) and Decca Ltd v. The United States, 544 F.2d 1070 (1976).
10. In cases from 1950s and 1960s involving Hertzian transmission by a U.S. based radio station to Canada, the Canadian courts considered the transborder broadcast to be infringing, as it was directed to Canada. In the case CAPAC v. International Good Music, Inc., S.C.R. [1963] (Can.) 80% of the audience was Canadian. Cf. *also,* an Ontario case of Jenner v. Sun Oil Co, 2 D.L.R. 526 [1952]. A U.S. case tried in the 9th District had a similar result: the court held that the infringement occurred exclusively in the country of reception (Canada), even if the signal was broadcast from the USA; Allarcom Pay Television, Ltd. v. General Instrument Corp., 69 F.3d 381 (9th Cir. 1995).
11. Meaning that the rights' clearance needs to take only in the country in which the communication originates.
12. Sam Ricketson, *The Berne Convention for the Protection of Literary and Artistic Works: 1886-1986* 442-452 (Kluwer, 1987); *See also* Iris C. Geik, *Direct Broadcast Satellites and the Determination of Authors' Rights under the Berne Convention: Lucy in the Sky Without Rights?,* 15 Suffolk Transnational Law Journal 563 (1992); Andreas P. Reindl, *Choosing Law in Cyberspace: Copyright Conflicts on Global Networks,* 19 Michigan Journal of International Law 799 (1998).
13. Ricketson (n. 12) 445.
14. To our knowledge, none of the CMOs has been ever authorized to license such overspill on behalf of a sister organization abroad. Likewise, the broadcasters did not usually seek a license clearance with foreign CMOs to get clearance for their broadcast available in neighboring or foreign regions.

The emergence of commercial satellite technology[15] posed yet another new challenge for the traditional territorial licensing models. After legal battles fought elsewhere,[16] the European Communities (ECs) decided to provide a legislative answer. In the 1993 Directive on the coordination of certain rules concerning copyright and rights related to copyright applicable to satellite broadcasting and cable retransmission[17] (the "SatCab Directive"), the European legislator revolutionized the approach to one-to-many communication in situations where the communication is emitted by a broadcasting organization to different territories using satellite technology.[18] It is well known that the Directive introduced a legal fiction under which satellite

15. Meaning both communications satellites and younger direct-to-home satellites.
16. For example, the Austrian Supreme Court found in two cases in favor of rightholders, claiming that the satellite broadcast was infringing their copyright in countries of reception; OGH, 4 Ob 19/91, International Review of Intellectual Property and Competition Law (IIC) 1992, 703; OGH, 4 Ob 44/92, International Review of Intellectual Property and Competition Law (IIC) 1993, 665; Austria was not a European Economic Community (EEC) Member State at that time.
17. Council Directive 93/83/EEC of 27 September 1993 on the coordination of certain rules concerning copyright and rights related to copyright applicable to satellite broadcasting and cable retransmission (Sep. 27, 1993) Official Journal L 248, 10/06/1993, pp. 15-21 (hereinafter "the SatCab Directive").
18. In its rather unclear judgment, the Court of Justice extended the application of the SatCab Directive also to rebroadcasting by providers of satellite packages. Cf., Joined Cases C-431/09 and C-432/09 Airfield, Canal Digitaal v. Sabam and Airfield v. Agicoa Belgium BVBA (2011) ECLI:EU:C:2011:648. The Court of Justice had an opportunity to revisit this judgment in case C-290/21, Staatlich genehmigte Gesellschaft der Autoren, Komponisten und Musikverleger Reg. Gen. mbH (AKM) v. Canal + Luxembourg Sàrl (2023) ECLI:EU:C:2023:424. Instead of correcting some of the obvious flaws of the Airfield ruling (such as the simple fact that *rebroadcasting*—be it by satellite or other means—is under the copyright law treated differently than *broadcasting*), the court reiterated the Airfield findings and extended the emission theory enacted by the SatCab directive for broadcasting also to rebroadcasting if such rebroadcasting happens by means of the satellite technology. This creates a very strange situation. Before this judgment, it was common practice in the EU that CMOs in the Member States licensed rebroadcasting (by wire or wireless) on the national basis. The Court of Justice seems to suggest that in case of rebroadcasting by satellite, the operator has to clear individual programs in all of the countries where the signal originates. Therefore, while the cable operator might conveniently clear the rights in the whole bundle in the country of operation, the satellite operator would need to clear individual programs in several countries where they operate although the catch-up service (quite common these days) would be cleared in the country of reception. The outcome is a total fragmentation of the internal market instead of a digital single market the Commissioned (and perhaps the court) dreamt of. It should be noted though that the court was deciding under the law as it stand before the new SatCab2 directive [Directive (EU) 2019/789 of the European Parliament and of the Council of 17 April 2019 laying down rules on the exercise of copyright and related rights applicable to certain online transmissions of broadcasting organisations and retransmissions of television and radio programmes, and amending Council Directive 93/83/EEC (Apr. 17, 2019) Official Journal L 130, 17/05/2019, pp. 82-91; transposition in the Member States was due on Jun. 7, 2021] and it is uncertain how much of it could be applicable under the new directive and its direct injection theory.

broadcasting is generally deemed to take place in the Member State where the program-carrying signals are uplinked.[19] This legal fiction applies both in the process of rights clearance as well as in the assessment of the infringement of one's exclusive rights.[20]

As mentioned, with the development of the global information infrastructure, the need for global licensing arrangements has become more pressing than ever, even though copyright-related problems eventually turned out to be not as prohibitive for the development of technology as prophesized.[21] Unsurprisingly, the market has developed its own solutions to the problem of cross-border online licensing.

As early as 2000, the most important performing rights organizations associated with the International Confederation of Societies of Authors and Composers (CISAC) agreed on a multiterritorial licensing framework dubbed the Santiago Agreement, an ambitious undertaking intended to solve the problem of a global license with the use of established practices and the system or reciprocal representation agreements (RRAs) between collecting societies. Under this system, a user was granted multiterritorial worldwide license to use music from the repertoire of the represented CMOs for a webcasting or on-demand service (streaming, downloading), including music synchronized with audiovisual material (videos), upon the condition that the user registers at the CMO in the place of the user's residence. A year later, the music mechanicals collecting societies agreed in Barcelona to extend this system also to the licensing of mechanical rights (the Barcelona Agreement).[22]

Unfortunately, the Prodi Commission (with Competition Commissioner Mario Monti, also the author of the "Monti Report")[23] decided to disrupt this system of multiterritorial licensing, which the EC considered a violation of competition rules, and the operations under both agreements ceased at the

19. *See*, SatCab Directive, Art. 1(2)(b)-(d).
20. This has been confirmed by the AKM judgment (n. 18).
21. Prof. Trimble shows that in practice, the internet continues to work notwithstanding the theoretical possibility of the application of a bundle of rights; Cf., Markéta Trimble, *The Multiplicity of Copyright Laws on the Internet,* 25 Fordham Intellectual Property Media & Entertainment Law Journal 339, 341-343 (2015).
22. Notably, this system was not an entirely new invention and CISAC members had experience with application of a similar model under the Sydney Agreement of 1987 which was intended for licensing overspills of satellite broadcasting even before the adoption of the SatCab Directive (one CMO could have granted license for the entire footprint of the satellite after consulting with CMOs from the territories concerned).
23. Mario Monti, *A New Strategy for the Single Market at the Service of Europe's Economy and Society,* Report to the President of the European Commission José Manuel Barroso, http://ec.europa.eu/archives/commission_2010-2014/president/news/press-releases/pdf/20100510_1_en.pdf (accessed Mar. 24, 2025). More on Monti report *see supra.*

end of 2004.[24] The Barroso Commission, appointed in November 2004, continued with the same policy. It was mainly this pressure of the EU Competition Authority (the Commission) that ensured that the achieved solutions were neither prolonged nor developed further, and it is the Commission's own political responsibility that the development of seamless licensing of digital uses within the EU was halted in 2004.

The International Federation of the Phonographic Industry (IFPI) decided to notify the Commission of its Simulcasting Agreement[25] for licensing certain simulcasts of phonograms and in 2000 applied for a negative clearance or for an exemption from the cartel rules of Article 81(3)[26] of the Treaty establishing the EC;[27] this was granted only after several amendments and upon the condition that the CMOs will allow the users to seek license at any of the CMOs which should compete in the area of administrative cost pricing (while the price charged for the license was calculated as a bundle of the CMOs' tariffs). The IFPI applied the same principles of what I would term joint licensing to its reciprocal agreements concerning webcasting, phonograms for background music on websites and new media (on-demand offerings of audio and audiovisual programs). Unfortunately, IFPI agreements do not involve CMOs administering rights in the performances of performing artists (as opposed to phonogram producers) and have so far had only limited, if any, practical impact.

Steps taken by the Commission in its search for the alleged anticompetitive nature of the RRAs (*see* the CISAC decision referred to below) substantially influenced also other actors in the field who started applying more caution when developing cross-border licensing schemes, effectively freezing the entire sector. It turned out that the main barrier to the pan-European licensing was the European Commission and not the Member States' copyright laws.

3.3 LARGE CMOs Go Global (New Business Models)

Some CMOs navigating through the uncharted stormy waters of European CRM did not follow the IFPI solution and—partly in line with the

24. Cases COMP/38.126 (Santiago Agreement) and COMP/38.377 (Barcelona Agreement). The agreements are reprinted in Volume 16, Paolo Spada ed., *Gestione collettiva dell'offerta e della domanda di prodotti culturali* (Quaderni di AIDA Giuffrè, 2006).
25. Commission Decision of 8 October 2002 relating to a proceeding under Art. 81 of the EC Treaty and Art. 53 of the EEA Agreement (Case No COMP/C2/38.014—IFPI "Simulcasting") (Text with EEA relevance) (notified under document number C(2002) 3639) (Oct. 8, 2002) Official Journal L 107, 30/4/2003, pp. 58-84.
26. Consolidated version of the Treaty on the Functioning of the European Union, Art. 101(3), Official Journal C 326, 26/10/2012, pp. 47-390.
27. Case No COMP/C2/38.014—IFPI "Simulcasting."

Commission's idea[28]—developed supranational licensing hubs and joint ventures which are no longer based on traditional RRAs but rather on direct licensing.

This was primarily enabled by the Commission's opinion that exclusivity clauses in representation agreements between CMOs and rightholders represent prohibited restraint of trade. Such clauses included a duty of a CMO to not accept for membership any person or entity which is already affiliated with another CMO or has the nationality of a foreign country where a sibling CMO operates.[29] The Commission considered among anticompetitive practices, i.a., clauses prohibiting a represented author from entrusting the CMO with only certain rights or certain works.[30] Although the General Court did not share the Commission's concern and partly annulled its decision, while also mentioning that the Commission failed to prove that the parallel conduct of CMOs was the result of concertation rather than a rational means of ensuring the effectiveness of licensing arrangements, the seven-year legal battle did little to aid the development of online licensing in Europe.

This forced the European CMOs to allow individual rightholders (mostly publishers) to withdraw parts of their repertoire from collective management entirely or with respect to certain rights.[31]

It is not only the big players who are trying to cherry-pick represented rights. In Czechia, there have been already several instances in which a composing artist prohibited others from performing their songs after the split of a band to monopolize live performances for themselves. This was done by withdrawing the right of live public performance from collective administration.[32] Obviously, allowing such actions contradicts the underlying public

---

28. The Commission applauded the CELAS undertaking in the CISAC decision as an example worth following.
29. This was subject to Commission's investigation already in 1981 when the German neighboring rights CMO was found guilty for constraint of trade by not accepting membership application of foreign performers (Commission Decision of 29 October 1981 relating to a proceeding under Art. 86 of the EEC Treaty (IV/29.839—GVL) (Oct. 29, 1981) Official Journal L 370, 28.12.1981, pp. 49-59); Opinion of the Commission was confirmed by the then European Court of Justice in Case C-7/82, GVL v. Commission (1983) ECLI:EU:C:1983:52.
30. This led to the investigation of 24 collecting societies and a decision of the Commission in case No COMP/C2/38.698—CISAC in which the Commission found certain clauses of the RAAs anticompetitive. Although the Commission's decision was annulled in part by the General Court; Case T-442/08, CISAC v. Commission ECLI:EU:T:2013:188.
31. As documented above, the situation was not entirely new with respect to the mechanical rights deal made with MCPS by Polygram Group in 1997. The difference lies in the fact that some European continental CMOs considered it to be in breach of their respective RAAs which were terminated.
32. The first documented case was the rock band "Citron," some of whose members split and formed a second band "Limetal." Certain songs were coauthored by Radim Pařízek who withdrew his songs from collective administration at the Czech CMO Ochranný svaz autorský pro práva k dílům hudebním (OSA), but only for live public performance of his

policy in collective management of the bulk repertoire with the ultimate task of making the works available. In the past, a CMO would probably not allow such partial withdrawal unless the author terminated his or her representation in its entirety, thus losing all the benefits related to the representation. It seems, however, that in the current state of competition policy in the Union, such withdrawal must be respected.

This new rightholder's "benefit" has been utilized mainly by major music publishers who have in certain instances withdrawn their popular repertoire from national CMOs in order to monetize directly their "digital rights," including mechanical rights (i.e., digital reproduction right), and public performance rights (i.e., making available right).

Some CMOs have seen this not as a threat to their position but rather as an opportunity, leading to the formation of supranational licensing hubs. One of the first was Central European Licensing and Administration Services (CELAS) and Pan-European Central Online Licensing (PAECOL). CELAS, jointly owned by GEMA and PRS for Music,[33] was formed in 2007 for cross-border digital licenses as an exclusive supplier of digital rights to the repertoire of EMI Music Publishing. The German company PAECOL, a fully owned subsidiary of the German CMO GEMA, managed digital mechanical licensing of Sony/ATV's Anglo-American catalog.[34] Following Sony's acquisition of EMI Music Publishing in 2012, a new joint venture owned by GEMA, PRS for Music and Sony/ATV Music Publishing named SOLAR[35] was established to license the Sony/ATV Music Publishing and EMI Music Publishing catalogs.[36] The London-based SOLAR replaced the previous schemes CELAS and PAECOL. In 2018, SOLAR fully authorized the licensing hub ICE to license its repertoire.[37]

---

songs. This was done on purpose to prevent the other members from performing those songs at concerts of their new band; Cf. a press report, Darek Štalmach, *Limetal není Citron. Nehrajte mou hudbu, trvá na svém Pařízek*, iDNES.cz https://www.idnes.cz/ostrava/zpravy/rozpad-kapely-citron-ma-dohru-byvali-clenove-nemohou-hrat-jeho-pisne.A160111_2217623_ostrava-zpravy_woj (accessed Mar. 24, 2025); Since then, other similar cases related to a similar "solution" of conflicts between former band members were reported in Czechia.

33. Sebastian Felix Schwemer, *Emerging Models for Cross-Border Online Licensing,* at User Generated Law: Re-constructing Intellectual Property Knowledge in the Knowledge Society 82 (Thomas Riis ed., Edward Elgar Publishing, 2016).
34. Sony/ATV, PRS for Music and GEMA launch joint venture, https://www.prsformusic.com/press/2014/sony-atv-prs-for-music-and-gema-launch-joint-venture (accessed Mar. 24, 2025).
35. Run by SOLAR Music Rights Management Ltd. London, cf. www.celas.eu (accessed Mar. 24, 2025).
36. Schwemer (n. 33) 82. The deal was extended in October 2018; https://www.iceservices.com/sony-atv-and-solar-extend-their-pan-european-digital-licence-administration-agreement/ (accessed Mar. 24, 2025).
37. Sony/ATV and SOLAR extend their pan-European digital licence administration agreement, https://www.iceservices.com/sony-atv-and-solar-extend-their-pan-european-digital-licence-administration-agreement/ (accessed Mar. 24, 2025).

Warner Chappell collaborated with BUMA/STEMRA (Netherlands), PRS for Music (U.K.), SABAM (Belgium), SACEM (France), SGAE (Spain) and STIM (Sweden) on the Pan European Digital Licensing (PEDL) System. All of these CMOs have a non-exclusive right to grant pan-European licenses to digital and mobile service providers for the Anglo-American Warner Chappell repertoire.[38]

Warner Chappell is also using MINT Digital Services[39] when licensing the use on iTunes. MINT is presented as a joint venture of SESAC (U.S.A.)[40] and SUISA (Switzerland) but it actually consists of three companies. SESAC Digital Licensing AG, Vaduz, Liechtenstein,[41] and SUISA Digital Licensing AG, Triesen, Liechtenstein,[42] are providing licenses. SUISA Digital Licensing AG is at its website informally named as "Mint SUISA Digital Licensing." The last one is MINT Digital Services AG registered in Zürich, Switzerland.[43] While the shareholders are neither publicly disclosed, according to the MINT's template agreement, this society might be owned by SESAC Holdings, Inc.[44] and SUISA.[45] SUISA provides administration services to SESAC Digital Licensing AG and SUISA Digital Licensing AG. Currently, MINT provides mechanical and performance licenses to around 70 DSPs for many CMOs, among which the identifiable are SESAC, SUISA, SOZA, ACUM, AKKA/LAA, Autodia, EAU, GCA, LATGA, Armauthor, AlbAutor, several IMEs, and publishers (Warner Chappell mentioned above).

Universal Music Publishing and SACEM launched another pan-European joint venture with the acronym DEAL (Direct European Administration and Licensing) which does not exist anymore.

38. Schwemer (n. 33) 155; *See also* Warner/Chappell Music Launches Its Pan-European Digital Licensing (P.E.D.L.) Initiative, https://investors.wmg.com/news-releases/news-release-details/warnerchappell-music-launches-its-pan-european-digital-licensing (accessed Mar. 24, 2025).
39. *Cf.* www.mintservices.com (accessed Mar. 24, 2023).
40. The actual collective management organization is named SESAC Performing Rights, LLC. It is part of a complex structure of corporations.
41. Registration No. FL-0002.550.490-1. Formerly registered in Eschen, Liechtenstein. According to its statute owned at least originally by SESAC Holdings UK Ltd. which in turn is owned by SESAC Holdco I LLC, New York (according to the financial statement published in the commercial register on Mar. 3, 2025). The latter company is registered in Delaware under the file 5265288.
42. Registration No. FL-0002.551.444-2.
43. Registration No. CHE-173.015.914.
44. SESAC Holdings, Inc., registered in New York, owned by private equity funds. *Cf.* Leading Music Rights Organization SESAC to be Acquired by Blackstone, https://www.blackstone.com/news/press/leading-music-rights-organization-sesac-to-be-acquired-by-blackstone/ (accessed Mar. 23, 2025).
45. SESAC Digital Licensing, AG Publisher Affiliation Agreement for Online Licensing Representation in Territories Outside the United States. Article II, Letter J. Available at https://www.sesacdigital.li/dl/SESAC_Standardnutzungsvertrag_EN_2022-01-31.pdf.

The Pan European Licensing Initiative of Latin American Repertoire is a SGAE affiliated licensing hub for Sony/ATV Latin repertoire and Independent Music Publishers' European Licensing (IMPEL), founded in 2010 as an organization affiliated with MCPS, was a counterpart to the major players' initiatives but in 2018 transformed to a collecting organization in its own right (as IMPEL Collective Management Limited based in London). It serves independent publishers alongside a digital rights agency, MERLIN,[46] which licenses global digital music services.

As far as the Anglo-American repertoire of BMG is concerned, GEMA is authorized by the publisher to provide pan-European licenses.

Another licensing platform was founded in 2013 as ARMONIA, a French-based Economic Interest Grouping of CMOs[47] which licensed on-demand and webcasting rights in music for more than 33 territories. It terminated in 2022 and was removed from the commercial register in 2023.

A joint venture between PRS for Music (U.K.), STIM (Sweden) and GEMA (Germany) called ICE is the largest licensing hub in terms of repertoire and together with MINT one of only two that survived until today. It was launched in 2010 and originally focused on database integration.[48] ICE is a non-entity grouping of three corporations (International Copyright Enterprise Services Ltd.,[49] ICE International Copyright Enterprise Germany GmbH,[50] and ICE Operations AB based in Stockholm),[51] which offers data administration and online processing services to CMOs (PRS for Music, GEMA, STIM, POLARIS Nordic, SABAM, BUMRA/STEMRA) and publishers (SONY/ATV, ARESA, SOLAR MUSIC, WARNER/CHAPPELL) and multiterritorial online licensing of the repertoire of its three owners. One of its notable achievements is negotiating a global deal with Facebook.[52]

Similar development has been observed in the licensing of nonmusical repertoire, though on a much smaller scale—one example is the online licensing service OnLineArt, a Brussels-based cooperative (OnLineArt

---

46. Music and Entertainment Rights Licensing Independent Network Ltd, Dublin.
47. Once included were AKM (Austria), SPAUTORES (Portugal), SUISA (Switzerland), SABAM (Belgium), ARTISJUS (Hungary), SACEM (France), SACEM (Luxembourg), SIAE (Italy) and SGAE (Spain).
48. About, https://www.iceservices.com/company/about/ (accessed Mar. 24, 2025).
49. Based in London, Registration No. 08983089. Owned by STIM, PRS for Music and GEMA in equal shares. Cf. 2023 Annual Report of International Copyright Enterprise Services Ltd.
50. Based in Berlin, registered with the Charlottenburg District Court (Amtsgericht Charlottenburg) under the number RB 162426, owned by ICE Operations AB which is by itself a member this grouping.
51. Corporate registration number 556723-5907. Owned by STIM, PRS for Music and GEMA in equal shares according to the information from the last general meeting's minutes of October 2, 2023, available in the Swedish commercial register.
52. Dani Deahl, *Facebook Signs Music Licensing Deal with European Rights Company ICE*, The Verge, https://www.theverge.com/2018/2/21/17036088/facebook-music-licensing-royalties-copyright-ice (accessed Mar. 24, 2025).

S.C.R.L.) associating 17 CMOs which administer the rights of visual artists around the world, providing a one-stop-shop for digital on-demand licenses to the repertoire of its members.[53]

Impacts of these developments on the cultural policy and the EU's quest for a pan-European license and later announced DSM are analyzed below.

3.4 SHIFTS IN THE EU AGENDA CONCERNING CRM

Facilis Descensus Averno

Although the agenda of the EU in the field of CRM has a long history, it has not achieved any consistency and remains rather confusing.

Since the 1990s, the Commission has undertaken certain consultations on harmonization with the professional public and the Member States.[54]

Later, in its 2004 resolution on collective management, the European Parliament took a rather traditional stand.[55] It stressed the indispensable character of CRM in the sphere of copyright and called for a "rapid, fair and professional acquisition of rights" (paragraph 6). The Parliament expressly pointed out the territorial character of copyright and seems to be of the opinion that this by itself is not an obstacle to the development of global distribution mechanisms. Furthermore, the Parliament explicitly mentions that collective management is an "important factor in stimulating cultural creativity and influencing the growth of cultural and linguistic diversity" (paragraph 22).

The resolution was shortly followed by a Commission Communication on the same topic[56] with a different view of the problem of cross-border licensing and its solutions. The Commission has asked itself the question:

> whether it should be left for the market to develop Community-wide licensing further, while respecting the basic rules of intellectual property protection, including its territorial nature, or whether the Community

53. *See*, https://onlineart.info/ (at the time of access Mar. 24, 2025, under website reconstruction).
54. For their overview, cf. para. 3.3. of the Communication from the Commission to the Council, the European Parliament and the European Economic and Social Committee: The Management of Copyright and Related Rights in the Internal Market of 16 April 2004, COM/2004/0261 final, https://eur-lex.europa.eu/LexUriServ/LexUriServ.do?uri=CELEX:52004DC0261:EN:HTML (accessed Mar. 24, 2025) (hereinafter "the 2004 Communication").
55. European Parliament resolution on a Community framework for collective management societies in the field of copyright and neighboring rights of 15 January 2004 (Jan. 15, 2004), 2002/2274(INI), http://www.europarl.europa.eu/sides/getDoc.do?type=TA&language=EN&reference=P5-TA-2004-0036 (accessed Mar. 24, 2025).
56. The 2004 Communication.

> legislator should seek to facilitate greater Community-wide licensing. (paragraph 1.2.4).

Unfortunately, it has answered this question by preferring the latter: regulatory action rather than market solutions, pointing toward a complex regulation of CRM on the EU level.

The 2004 Communication was followed by the 2005 Recommendation on collective cross-border management of copyright for music services (the "2005 Recommendation"),[57] which foreshadowed Directive 2014/26/EU (hereinafter the "CRM Directive").[58] It can also be read as a public announcement of the justification for the Commission's involvement and disruption of the CISAC-developed "Santiago" and "Barcelona" models for a one-stop-shop with multiterritorial licenses. However, the Commission has not recommended even the IFPI/Simulcasting model with a preference for direct licensing and competition between CMOs.[59]

The European Parliament replied to the 2005 Recommendation with its own observations in the 2007 Resolution.[60] Again, the Parliament position remained conservative, stressing possible solutions within the framework of reciprocal agreements (paragraphs N, O) and "the existing network of national CRMs" (paragraph J). Among the focal points of this 2007 Resolution remained the conviction that "music is not a commodity" (paragraph H); "national CRMs should continue to play an important role in providing support for the promotion of new and minority rightholders, cultural diversity, creativity and local repertoires" (paragraph I). Importantly, the Parliament was concerned:

> about the potentially negative effects of some provisions of the Recommendation on local repertoires and on cultural diversity given the potential risk of favouring a concentration of rights in the bigger CRMs, and whereas the impact of any initiative for the introduction of competition between rights managers in attracting the most profitable rightholders must be examined and weighed against the adverse effects

---

57. Commission Recommendation on collective cross-border management of copyright and related rights for legitimate online music services of 18 May 2005 (2005/737/EC) (May 18, 2005) Official Journal L 276, 21/10/2005, pp. 54-57, https://eur-lex.europa.eu/legal-content/EN/ALL/?uri=CELEX%3A32005H0737 (accessed Mar. 24, 2025).
58. Directive 2014/26/EU of the European Parliament and of the Council of 26 February 2014 on collective management of copyright and related rights and multiterritorial licensing of rights in musical works for online use in the internal market (Feb. 26, 2014) Official Journal L 84, 20/03/2014, pp. 72-98.
59. Critically: Josef Drexl, *Competition in the Field of Collective Management: Preferring "Creative Competition" to Allocative Efficiency in European Copyright Law,* at Copyright Law: A Handbook of Contemporary Research 256 (Paul Torremans ed., Edward Elgar Publishing, 2007); Drexl correctly argues that the Commission's focus on "output, price and quality" omits to take into account the very purpose of copyright law: the promotion of creativity and cultural diversity, *ibid.*
60. 2002/2274(INI).

of such an approach on smaller rightholders, small and medium-sized CRMs and cultural diversity.

The back-and-forth between the Parliament and the Commission continued in 2008, first with the Commission's Communication on Creative Content Online.[61] The Communication touched upon many issues, including "multi-territory licensing for creative content." In this regard, the Communication identified transactional costs as allegedly detrimental to the exploitation of European works outside of their national markets and declared its willingness to remedy the situation of multiterritory licensing by, *inter alia*, promoting competition on the market for rights management (in relationships between CMOs and rightholders).

The European Parliament essentially reiterated its view in the 2008 Resolution,[62] which is sharply critical of the Commission's CISAC investigation and the resulting chilling effect on the stakeholders' attempts to solve the lack of EU-wide licensing based on available business models.

The Commission introduced its plan to reform the CRM framework in the 2010 Communication "A Digital Agenda for Europe,"[63] following the Europe 2020 Strategy[64] in which the Commission pledged to work on modernization of the framework for copyright. The Digital Agenda for Europe identified a revision of CRM as one of the key actions for the achievement of simplified copyright clearance—a fact which was elaborated in the 2011 intellectual property strategy "A Single Market for Intellectual Property Rights."[65] In this ambitious strategy, the Commission explicitly mentions a sort of "super CMO," namely the creation of European rights brokers able to license and manage the world's musical repertoire on a

61. Communication from the Commission to the European Parliament, the Council, the European Economic and Social Committee and the Committee of the Regions on creative content online in the Single Market of 3 January 2008 {SEC(2007) 1710} (Jan. 3, 2008) COM/2007/0836 final, https://eur-lex.europa.eu/LexUriServ/LexUriServ.do?uri=COM:2007:0836:FIN:EN:HTML (accessed Mar. 24, 2025).
62. European Parliament resolution of 25 September 2008 on collective cross-border management of copyright and related rights for legitimate online music services (2010/C 8 E/19).
63. Communication from the Commission to the European Parliament, the Council, the European Economic and Social Committee and the Committee of the Regions of 19 May 2010 A Digital Agenda for Europe (May 19, 2010) COM(2010) 245 final, https://eur-lex.europa.eu/legal-content/EN/ALL/?uri=celex:52010DC0245 (accessed Mar. 24, 2025).
64. Communication from the Commission: EUROPE 2020, A strategy for smart, sustainable and inclusive growth of 3 March 2010 (Mar. 3, 2010) COM(2010) 2020 final, https://eur-lex.europa.eu/LexUriServ/LexUriServ.do?uri=COM:2010:2020:FIN:EN:PDF (accessed Mar. 24, 2025).
65. Communication from the Commission to the European Parliament, the Council, the European Economic and Social Committee and the Committee of the Regions A Single Market for Intellectual Property Rights: Boosting creativity and innovation to provide economic growth, high quality jobs and first class products and services in Europe of 24 May 2011 (May 24, 2011) COM/2011/0287 final, https://eur-lex.europa.eu/legal-content/EN/TXT/?uri=celex:52011DC0287 (accessed Mar. 24, 2025).

multiterritorial level and a European rights management regime, perhaps combined with the European Copyright Code.

In the following Communication on content in the DSM,[66] the Union announced the structured stakeholder dialogue "Licensing Europe" (touching mostly on subjects other than collective management, such as portability) at a time when a CRM Directive bill was already pending.[67]

After the Commission's attempt to apply the Services Directive[68] to CRM (arguing that statutory monopoly of CRM contravenes EU law) was squashed by the Court of Justice in its OSA judgment,[69] the CRM agenda was moved to the CRM Directive, which was being negotiated at the time. The CRM Directive, however, does not deal with the question of legal monopoly of a CMO in a Member State (prohibiting the users from getting licenses for their offline use from abroad); this principle has remained valid so far, even though most Member States no longer have any such provisions in their laws.

Regrettably, the CRM Directive as a result of the above-mentioned developments mostly followed the Commission's view without taking into account much from the resolutions of the European Parliament. Although the Directive anticipated the announcement of the DSM policy by the Juncker Commission on May 6, 2015,[70] it aims to serve the same goals—removing supposed barriers to cross-border digital use of cultural goods (music in this case).

In the CRM Directive, the Commission proposed what it claimed to be its own regulatory solution to the problem of pan-European licensing. It should be noted, however, that the CRM Directive does not deal with pan-European licensing of protected subject matter other than music, such as phonograms and artistic performances or general nonmusical repertoire, which is usually licensed individually by rightholders for on-demand uses. Yet this is not entirely true. For example, simulcasting and webcasting rights

---

66. Communication from the Commission on content in the Digital Single Market of 18 December 2012 (Dec. 18, 2012) COM/2012/0789 final, https://eur-lex.europa.eu/legal-content/EN/TXT/?qid=1404312217584&uri=CELEX:52012DC0789 (accessed Mar. 24, 2025).
67. For the CRM Directive's legislative procedure, *see* Proposal for a Directive of the European Parliament and of the Council on collective management of copyright and related rights and multiterritorial licensing of rights in musical works for online uses in the internal market, 2012/0180/COD, https://eur-lex.europa.eu/procedure/EN/2012_180 (accessed Mar. 24, 2025).
68. Directive 2006/123/EC of the European Parliament and of the Council of 12 December 2006 on services in the internal market (Dec. 12, 2006) Official Journal L 376, 27/12/2006 pp. 36-68.
69. Case C-351/12, OSA—Ochranný svaz autorský pro práva k dílům hudebním o.s. v. Léčebné lázně Mariánské Lázně a.s. (2014) ECLI:EU:C:2014:110.
70. European Commission—Press release, A Digital Single Market for Europe: Commission sets out 16 initiatives to make it happen, http://europa.eu/rapid/press-release_IP-15-4919_en.htm (accessed Mar. 24, 2025).

concerning sound recordings and artistic performances remain in most, if not all, Member States collectively administered, and their cross-border licensing remains limited,[71] in part due to competition concerns. They were not addressed by the CRM Directive either.

One of the constant arguments of the Commission against territorially-based licensing schemes in favor of a universal pan-European digital license is the naive idea that the monitoring of illegal use in the online environment can take place from a distance.[72] This could not be farther from the truth. In fact, piracy in the online environment is very often locally focused. The biggest Czech illegal services are targeting their offer at Czech consumers, in the Czech language and with a major share of local repertoire. One of the biggest cyberlockers, Hellspy.cz/Hellshare.cz (now terminated), even used to geoblock access from other countries to prevent monitoring from abroad (a measure introduced after the Megaupload investigation by U.S. authorities).[73] The Central and Eastern European markets are of little interest to the major publishers or big licensing hubs as their share in the EU revenue is insignificant. Yet the operation of pirate services has substantial harmful effects on the local market. To our knowledge, none of the music publishers who withdrew their repertoire from collective management has taken any legal action in Central Europe. Therefore, local CMOs have fought lengthy legal battles with the operators of such services on their own, helping publishers whose rights they might not even administer—and paying for the court and legal costs from management fees deducted from remuneration due to those who have not withdrawn their repertoire. The unrepresented

71. As mentioned above, a multilateral contractual system of clearance of phonogram webcasting and simulcasting rights (and to limited extent on-demand rights as far as they concern the broadcasting organization's ancillary online service) has been developed by IFPI, but it does not allow for the licensing of artistic performances which are in many Member States administered by CMOs different from the phonogram producers' collecting organizations. The latter are usually affiliated with IFPI while the former are associated in the Societies' Council for the Collective Management of Performers' Rights (SCAPR) which has not yet introduced a system similar to IFPI. This is in part due to the significant conceptual differences in the treatment of performers' exclusive rights and rights to remuneration from broadcasting of their performances between EU Member States (in some Member States, the broadcaster obtains a statutory license for the use of performances by broadcasting, including simulcasts, in some the broadcaster needs to obtain a contractual license to use performances from a performers' organization, in others from a phonogram producers' organization if the phonogram producer is allowed under the law of such Member States to get the performers' rights assigned).
72. Case No. COMP/C2/38.014—IFPI "Simulcasting."
73. Tomáš Stibor, *Služby Hellspy a Hellshare v. zahraničí končí*, Objevit.cz, https://www.objevit.cz/sluzby-hellspy-a-hellshare-v-zahranici-konci-t7970 (accessed Mar. 24, 2025), concerning geoblocking of the service by its operator who stated they would limit the availability of the service to Czechia, Slovakia and Poland. Since the transposition of the DSM Directive in the Czech law in January 2023 and after a lengthy dispute with OSA, Hellspy and Hellshare terminated their services.

publishers are then freeriding on the enforcement service, which the local CMO does for them at the expense of local authors.

As with any other activity, policing of the online environment in individual Member States requires presence, good contacts and knowledge of the local situation, the local market, consumer preferences and the language, without all of which, it is rather difficult to enforce rights online. The fact that since the CRM Directive has been in effect,[74] no foreign CMO has taken any legal action against online piracy in the region is the best evidence that the system does not work the way the Commission dreamed of.

The Commission claimed that the solution lies in the rightholders' freedom of choice (freedom to choose one or more CMOs and freedom to choose the extent of represented rights and repertoire) as well as in the newly introduced European licensing passport system under which only those CMOs which possess the necessary capacities (personal, financial, technological) are authorized to grant multiterritorial licenses to users. This drew a dividing line between CMOs, which are now categorized into two groups: with and without the passport. CMOs which do not comply with the criteria or which simply decide not to pursue the passport application may ask another CMO for an online mandate of the former's repertoire. It is no surprise that these services can be offered only by major European CMOs which have enough resources for such an undertaking.

As the classics have taught us, the road to hell is paved with good intentions. It became clear long ago that the Commission tenaciously insists on rather dubious means by which it wishes to achieve the commendable goal of smooth cross-border licensing (a goal which was actually accomplished already in 2004 by the CMOs themselves). Instead of letting the private parties find commercially viable solutions within the realm of private law, the Commission opted for a regulatory solution using public law instruments with disregard to the impact of the regulation on cultural diversity.

3.5 CULTURAL DIVERSITY AND NATIONAL CULTURAL POLICY

Hoc Opus, Hic Labor Est

Although it was easy for the EU administration to undermine the established and essentially working system of CRM, it will be much more difficult to find a user-friendly operational alternative to the RRAs—deregulation might prove to be a bigger challenge than regulation. The most important thing is

74. While major publishers are not represented for certain online uses in the Central European region.

to license,[75] and if rightholders and CMOs have the opportunity to license, they can be guaranteed to take it. It would be wrong to assume that publishers and authors of whom CMOs are composed (and who usually run or oversee CMOs' operations) do not wish to license uses of their works or in other words gain profit.

The current CRM Directive is to certain degree an experiment with an inadequate prior assessment of the economic, social and cultural impacts on users, creators and the creative industries.[76]

It is already clear that the stated goals of the CRM Directive were not reached and likely will not be reached any time soon if the Commission continues to rely on regulation instead of agreements between the concerned parties. It goes without saying that regulatory intrusions in the private sphere should be limited to the most obvious and necessary cases which need a remedy of market failure—which was not demonstrated by the Commission in this case.

As Schwemer rightly noted:

> [i]nstead of the previous system of mono-territorial licensing, an emerging system of mono-repertoire licensing has been created.[77]

With the quest for transparency, the licensing hubs seem to go exactly in the opposite direction. While it was easy for users to understand where to license, which repertoire and for what tariff, the licensing hubs do not operate transparently at all, providing only limited information available on their website. The user thus cannot assess in advance the repertoire represented, nor the price. It can be supposed that the transaction costs of an average online music service have risen rather than dropped. On top of that, the user is no longer certain that he or she will get the license. Unlike CMOs, individual publishers and new licensing hubs do not have the obligation to grant a license. Mandatory membership proved to be the best public policy

---

75. Daniel Gervais made an important point concerning illegal use on the internet "The solution—at this point, the only solution—is to *license* massive Internet uses in a way that respects all of those involved in the creation, performance, publication, production and use of copyright content"; *See,* Daniel Gervais, *Collective Management of Copyright: Theory and Practice in the Digital Age,* at Collective Management of Copyright and Related Rights 30 (Daniel Gervais ed., 3rd ed., Kluwer, 2016) (emphasis in the original).
76. The Commission published a study in 2005 following up on consultations with stakeholders: Study on a Community initiative on the cross-border Collective Management of Copyright. Commission Staff Working Document, Jul. 7, 2005. The study argues that the best solution to cross-border licensing would be the freedom of rightholders to choose CMOs on their own and related measures. The concerns and objections expressed by stakeholders, however, remained largely unanswered. Besides that, the Monti Report (n. 23) highlighted the challenges for the (digital) single market, including the claimed lack of copyright transparency and licensing, but without analyzing these issues any further (cf. Monti Report (n. 23) 45).
77. Sebastian Felix Schwemer, *The Licensing of Online Music Streaming Services in Europe,* at Handbook on the Economics of Copyright: A Guide for Students and Teachers 155-156 (Richard Watt ed., Edward Elgar Publishing, 2014).

in ensuring access to a license for anyone—one-stop-shop licensing in Europe now seems more remote than ever before.[78]

Effective collection and distribution by itself should be a matter of course, but this must not be the end of the CMOs' mission, as the Commission believes—a position surely welcomed by successful publishers and best-selling authors and performers.[79] The vast majority of the creative ecosystem and CMO membership (in nominal terms rather than in terms of market share) is formed by less successful authors and artists or small publishers and independent labels, often outside the mainstream. Their interests are not addressed by the CRM Directive. These creators and interpreters form the necessary base from which popular authors and artists can recruit. In other words, there would be no Mozart without plenty of Salieris and the policymaker's mission is not to cater to the Mozarts but to protect the Salieris to keep the ecosystem alive.[80] In terms of cultural policy, this should include social, cultural and educational services (provided by governments, Non-Governmental Organizations or—traditionally—the CMOs), preference for culturally important (even if not popular) works in the distribution scheme, promotion of non-mainstream repertoire among users and the public, scholarships and support programs for creators and publishers, collective policing (which small rightholders cannot afford), industry-wide bargaining, etc. No economic competition—regardless of how efficient—can resolve these issues. It is not purely accidental that EU Member States have accumulated the richest and most diverse cultural heritage in the world. The EU publishes the most books, outperforming markets in the USA and China,[81] and produces the most films.[82] Naturally, most of this production will never be global hits and in these terms, the American creative production is much more economically efficient (fewer works more widely distributed). If the EU representatives openly announced

78. I have summarized problems related to the licensing hubs as follows: (1) questionable legality (CMOs are only allowed to outsource certain technical activites under the CRM Directive), (2) limited transparency, (3) no control by rightholders, (4) no contribution to cultural and social missions of the CMOs, (5) no obligation to licence, (6) data shared with selected rightholders, (7) profit making nature, (8) conflict of Interest and preference of repertoire, (9) HQ outside of the EU, (10) complicated policying.

79. Schroff and Street call this policy "rewarding those who are already commercially successful"; Simone Schroff & John Street, *The Politics of the Digital Single Market: Culture vs. Competition vs. Copyright,* 21 Information, Communication & Society 1305 (2018) https://doi.org/10.1080/1369118x.2017.1309445.

80. Music fans shall excuse my metaphor influenced by the Forman made Amadeus film. Salieri was actually a successful composer of his time with and his legacy is lasting.

81. *International Publishers Association's Annual Report 2015-2016*, https://internationalpublishers.org/annual-report-2015-2016/ (accessed Mar. 24, 2025).

82. Feature films (data used for the year 2015); Total number of national feature films produced, UNESCO Institute for Statistics, http://data.uis.unesco.org/Index.aspx?DataSetCode=CUL_DS (accessed Mar. 24, 2025). With around 1,600 films produced in 2015, Europe is comparable only to India in terms of sheer numbers, outperforming the U.S. production more than twice.

that their policy was to create fewer works but distribute them more efficiently, it would be completely acceptable, as these politicians would then have to gain public votes in support of such policy. The problem is mainly that while all of the policy papers repeatedly mention cultural diversity, in fact they do not actually consider this aspect of cultural policy very much.

Thus, the true winners, for now, are the big publishers and big international users operating online platforms. Google, Apple or Spotify might have saved on transactional costs and major publishers indeed might have obtained better deals. But it would be very unrealistic to believe that the situation today is easier for a local emerging music service which has to negotiate its licenses directly with major publishers on commercial terms instead of a government-overseen tariff. Giving the big publishers the right to withdraw their popular repertoire from administration while leaving there the less popular repertoire harms other CMO members (small publishers and less successful authors) as it deprives the CMOs of significant proceeds (as use shifts more and more to the Internet, this issue will steadily become more pressing) and simultaneously makes the administration costs higher (less popular repertoire used in pieces is more costly to administer—report, process and distribute).

If the current policy and regulatory framework do not change, it seems inevitable that the "competition" will lead to: (1) a fossilizing oligopoly of major publishers and global platforms, (2) the rise of new barriers to enter the market for local and small services seeking to operate on the Internet (which will have to negotiate pricing individually with publishers instead of relying on the published tariffs),[83] (3) worse access to works and uncertainty for users (certain repertoire might be provided exclusively to users[84] or might not be licensed at all), (4) restriction of the cultural autonomy of Member States,[85] (5) increased administration costs for small CMOs and lower income for small publishers and local authors, (6) less money for the cultural ecosystem in small Member States (as the globally less successful are mostly

83. A local musical service from a country such as Czechia or Slovakia which has no ambitions for pan-European operation, e.g., due to language or user preference barriers, cannot rely anymore on one license granted by OSA and SOZA. It must individually negotiate licenses with major publishers and obtain the license for the local repertoire from their local CMO.

84. Unlike publishers, CMOs are only allowed to grant non-exclusive licenses.

85. CRM is an important instrument of cultural policy. The Commission, having limited powers in the sphere of culture, circumvented its lack of competence by relying on competition law. The true nature of CRM lies not in trade but in cultural policy. The importance of CRM for cultural policy can be documented also on the Czechoslovak experience. In a country established as a union of the Slovak and Czech nations, both maintained a certain cultural autonomy and after World War II, a Slovak CMO (named SOZA) operated separately from the Czech CMO (OSA). After the federalization of Czechoslovakia in 1968, both federal republics sought high autonomy in the realm of cultural policy and both understood CRM as a crucial instrument for achieving this objective.

local creators of non-English repertoire, often in small countries where there are no big CMOs with the ability to obtain cross-border licenses), (7) increased distribution of global Anglo-American and English language repertoire, (8) less diverse and fewer works created and licensed, (9) freeriding of the unrepresented rightholders on local offline and online enforcement activities, and (10) the formation of a few dominant European "super collecting societies" instead of a patchwork of national CMOs.

3.6 CLOSING REMARKS

The Union legislature should expressly allow the Member States to regulate CRM on their own, based on their social and legal traditions and cultural policy. But as any horizontal deregulation in the Union (loosening regulation already established on the Union level) is very unlikely, the action must be taken by the Union. At the very least, CMOs must be explicitly allowed to require obligatory membership of rightholders for their full repertoire in the whole scope of collectively administered rights.

But even if the Union legislature remains inactive, CMOs must remain faithful to their mission of fostering creativity, creative production and distribution of works and performances. This can be done even under the new framework by different means. For example, various hardship funds and educational, cultural or social services and scholarships could be made available only to those authors and interprets who have been members for a certain period of time and who have not withdrawn any part of their repertoire or rights; in other words, those who are showing solidarity with the other members.

For collective management of rights, universalism would lead to less diversity which should not be the desirable outcome for any copyright policymaker. It is self-evident that the current competition-based CRM policy must be revisited if the Union and its Member States truly wish to preserve and develop the exceptional diversity and richness of European culture while ensuring cultural productivity and broad access to creative goods. The initiative must be entrusted to stakeholders who should advance their contractual relationships, including better and broader RRAs, allowing better and technically improved cooperation between CMOs. In other words, rather than destroying and achieving the same result through regulation, let us support the development of contractual market solutions.

Chapter 4

U.S. (Non)Compliance with Its International Copyright Obligations under Berne, TRIPS and the 1996 WIPO Copyright Treaties

Jane C. Ginsburg[*]

The United States (U.S.) adhered to the Berne Convention in 1988 (effective 1989). Declaring U.S. copyright law already in substantial compliance with its new obligations,[1] Congress made "minimalist"[2] amendments to conform U.S. law to treaty norms, particularly with respect to formalities[3] but left some significant lacunae. Notably, it did not enact protections for authors' "moral" rights of attribution and integrity, and, notwithstanding the Convention's express command, Congress did not restore copyright protection to foreign Berne Convention works that had fallen prematurely into the public domain in the U.S. Subsequent legislation in 1990 introduced moral rights protection to a very limited class of "works of visual art,"[4] and in 1994, as part of U.S. implementation of its adherence to the World Trade Organization

* Thanks for research assistance to Andrew McWhorter, Columbia Law School class of 2019, and to Makena Binker Cosen, Columbia Law School class of 2025.

1. *See, e.g.,* 100th Congress, S. Rep. Nos. 100-352, at 9-10 (1988); Jane C. Ginsburg & John M. Kernochan, *One Hundred and Two Years Later: The U.S. Joins the Berne Convention,* 13 Columbia-Volunteer Lawyers for the Arts Journal of Law & the Arts 1 (1988).
2. Final Report of the Ad Hoc Working Group on U.S. Adherence to the Berne Convention 53 (1986), reprinted in 10 Columbia-Volunteer Lawyers for the Arts Journal of Law & the Arts 513, 622 (1986).
3. *See, e.g.,* Ginsburg & Kernochan (n. 1), 9-17.
4. *See* Visual Artists Rights Act, 17 USC §106A (2012).

Agreement on Trade-Related Aspects of Intellectual Property Rights (TRIPS),[5] Congress restored the copyrights in qualifying foreign works.[6] The U.S. ratified the 1996 World Intellectual Property Organization (WIPO) Copyright Treaties in 1998; a package of legislation that year implemented the WIPO Treaties' new international obligations to protect technological measures protecting works of authorship, and to protect copyright management information (CMI), but did not otherwise amend the law to conform to treaty norms.[7]

As this summary indicates, the U.S. has not always enthusiastically embraced its international obligations.[8] Today, combining crabbed interpretation of the scope of conventional norms with the overoptimistic assessment of the conformity of U.S. copyright law with those obligations, the U.S. remains out of step with the treaties with respect to its coverage of moral rights, and Berne's prohibition on formalities. It is also unclear whether the U.S. has fully implemented the WIPO Treaties' "making available right."

Before addressing these three shortcomings, I will briefly set out the Berne treaty structure, of which one U.S. appellate court has revealed distressing ignorance.

4.1 THE BASIC STRUCTURE OF THE BERNE CONVENTION

The Berne Convention rests on two pillars, national treatment (nondiscrimination against foreign authors), and substantive minima. Substantive minima require Member States to grant specific protections to foreign Berne Union authors; these protections may already exist in domestic law, but if they do not, the country of origin must nonetheless afford them to foreign Berne Union authors, though it need not accord those protections to its own authors.[9] When domestic law fails to afford treaty-level protection, it does not suffice to grant the foreign work national treatment; the Member State must provide the coverage the treaty mandates, even though it surpasses what

5. Agreement on Trade-Related Aspects of Intellectual Property Rights (Apr. 15, 1994), 1869 UNTS 299.
6. *See* 17 USC §104A (2012); Uruguay Round Agreements Act, Pub. L. 103-465, 108 Stat. 4809 (1994). This legislation survived constitutional challenge, *see* Golan v. Holder, 565 U.S. 302 (2012).
7. Digital Millennium Copyright Act, Pub. L. 105-304, 112 Stat. 2860 (1998); Jane C. Ginsburg, *Copyright Legislation for the "Digital Millennium,"* 23 Columbia-Volunteer Lawyers for the Arts Journal of Law & the Arts 137 (1999).
8. Indeed, the Berne Convention Implementation Act of 1988, Pub. L. No. 100-568, 102 Stat. 2853, states that the "provisions of the Berne Convention … shall not be enforceable in any action brought pursuant to the provisions of the Berne Convention itself."
9. *See* Berne Convention for the Protection of Literary and Artistic Works (Sep. 9, 1886), S. Treaty Doc. No. 99-27, Art. 5(1), (3).

local authors will enjoy. It is precisely the role of substantive minima to fill the gap between Member States' domestic norms and the protections the treaty requires.

In *Fahmy v. Jay-Z,*[10] the Ninth Circuit misapprehended this basic feature of the Berne Convention. The case concerned the assertion of moral rights by the heir of an Egyptian composer against the composition's sampling in a U.S. sound recording. The composer had granted rights to an Egyptian record producer, who in turn licensed its incorporation by the U.S. producer, but the heir contended that the U.S. recording was a derivative work and therefore subject to the composer's right to prevent distortion or mutilation of the underlying work.[11] The court, accurately, stated that:

> No provision of the Act recognizes a moral right to prevent distortions or mutilations of copyrighted music.[12]

Turning to international obligations, the court continued:

> The [Berne] Convention guarantees only that holders of foreign copyrights are afforded "the same protection" as holders of domestic copyrights, a policy known as the "principle of national treatment." … In other words, parties to the Convention, such as the US, are not required to grant foreign copyright holders rights which are not granted to its domestic copyright holders. Since our federal law does not accord protection of moral rights to American copyright holders as to non-visual art, neither does it recognize Fahmy's claim to moral rights.[13]

This is simply incorrect; if the right at issue comes within Berne's substantive minima, as is the case with moral rights,[14] parties to the Berne Convention indeed are required to grant foreign copyright holders those rights. While the court's manifest error made no difference to the outcome of the case,[15] it is very regrettable that any U.S. court, and particularly one whose docket frequently includes copyright cases,[16] could so misconstrue the Berne Convention. That said, the court's error was effectively harmless because Congress has made clear that parties in an infringement action may not directly invoke Berne Convention protections.[17] Thus, while Berne

10. Fahmy v. Jay-Z, 891 F.3d 823 (9th Cir. 2018).
11. The court indicated that that the heir's claim over derivative works sought to exercise economic, not moral, rights in any event, *see ibid.,* 830-831.
12. *Ibid.*, 831.
13. *Ibid.*
14. *See* Berne Convention Art. 6bis.
15. For example, because Berne does not prohibit waivers of moral rights, and the Egyptian contract could have been interpreted to forego moral rights claims.
16. The Ninth Circuit covers both the Central District of California (Hollywood) and the Northern District of California (Silicon Valley).
17. *See* Berne Convention Implementation Act of 1988, Pub. L. No. 100-568, 102 Stat. 2853:

mandates the protection of moral rights, if the requisite protection does not exist in U.S. law, the claim will fail.

4.2 U.S. SHORTCOMINGS RESPECTING SUBSTANTIVE MINIMA

4.2.1 Moral Rights

Berne Convention Article 6bis provides:

> Independently of the author's economic rights, and even after the transfer of the said rights, the author shall have the right to claim authorship of the work and to object to any distortion, mutilation or other modification of, or other derogatory action in relation to, the said work, which would be prejudicial to his honor or reputation.

In addition, the quotation right set out in Article 10 requires the Member States to permit the:

> mak[ing of] quotations from a work which has already been lawfully made available to the public, provided that their making is compatible with fair practice, and their extent does not exceed that justified by the purpose … .

but further mandates:

> mention shall be made of the source, and of the name of the author if it appears thereon.[18]

When the U.S. joined the Berne Convention, it declined to amend Title 17 to provide specific protection for moral rights. Instead, it contended that existing U.S. law provided protection for these rights, including:

> various provisions of the Copyright Act and the Lanham Act, various state statutes, and common law principles such as libel, defamation, misrepresentation and unfair competition, which have been applied by

---

Sec. 3 Construction of the Berne Convention.

(a) Relationship with Domestic Law—The provisions of the Berne Convention—
   (1) shall be given effect under title 17, as amended by this Act, and any other relevant provision of Federal or State law, including the common law; and
   (2) shall not be enforceable in any action brought pursuant to the provisions of the Berne Convention itself.

(b) Certain Rights Not Affected—The provisions of the Berne Convention, the adherence of the United States thereto, and satisfaction of United States obligations thereunder, do not expand or reduce any right of an author of a work, whether claimed under Federal, State, or the common law—
   (1) to claim authorship of the work; or
   (2) to object to any distortion, mutilation, or other modification of, or other derogatory action in relation to, the work, that would prejudice the author's honor or reputation.

18. Berne Convention, Art. 10(1)(3).

courts to redress authors' invocation of the right to claim authorship or the right to object to distortion.[19]

The Berne Convention Implementation Act specifically declared that:

> [t]he Amendments made by this Act, together with law existing on the date of enactment of this Act, satisfy the obligations of the United States in adhering to the Berne Convention and no further rights or interests shall be recognized or created for that purpose.[20]

Although the U.S. had relatively weak moral rights at the time, at least two factors supported its conclusion that various state and federal laws, taken together, sufficed to satisfy the Berne requirement. First, other common law countries—most notably, the United Kingdom (U.K.)—relied on common law, rather than specific guarantees of moral rights, to meet Berne Article 6bis obligations. (Since then, the U.K. and other Commonwealth countries have enacted explicit guarantees of moral rights.)[21] Second, Dr. Arpad Bogsch, then WIPO's Director General, had asserted that the U.S. could join Berne without changing its law in respect of Berne Article 6bis.[22]

Since the U.S.' adherence to the Berne Convention, three significant legal developments underscore the parsimonious coverage of moral rights in the U.S. First, the U.S. passed the Visual Artists Rights Act (VARA), codified at 17 USC., section 106A. While this law expressly provides rights of attribution and integrity to "works of visual art," its narrow definition of that term, and its many exclusions, make the law inapplicable to most copyright-protected works, and to many uses of the works that it does cover. Most importantly, a VARA violation pertains only to the physical original (or a series of 200 or fewer signed and numbered copies) or a painting, drawing, sculpture or of certain photograph; alterations or non-attribution of mass market reproductions fall outside the law's scope.[23]

---

19. S. Rep. No. 100-352, at 9-10 (1988). The principal provisions of the Copyright Act that the United States relied on in support of Berne adherence were §106(2) (right to create derivative works) and §115(a)(2).
20. Berne Convention Implementation Act of 1988, Pub. L. 100-568, §2(3), 102 Stat. 2853.
21. *See, e.g.*, Copyright, Designs and Patents Act 1988, c. 48 (U.K.); Copyright Amendment (Moral Rights) Act 2000 (Cth) (Austl.).
22. S. Rep. No. 100-352, at 10.
23. The Copyright Office notes that VARA excludes subject matter like musical works or sound recordings because the music industry protects authors' attribution and integrity through contracts that are unavailable for visual artists. United States Copyright Office, Authors, Attribution, And Integrity: Examining Moral Rights in the United States, a Report of the Register of Copyrights 63 (2019) (hereinafter *Copyright Office Moral Rights Report*). Courts have promptly dismissed VARA claims over works that are not works of visual art. *See, e.g.,* Hijrahannah v. Def Jam Recordings, No. 14 C 0872, 2014 WL 3586055, at *2 (N.D. Ill. Jul. 21, 2014) (dismissing VARA claims concerning the use of his sheet music by other artists); Kettenburg v. Univ. of Louisville, No. CIVA 3:06CV79, 2005 WL 4444092, at *2 (W.D. Ky. Jun. 16, 2005) (dismissing VARA claim regarding proper attribution for plaintiff's creative writing class assignment).

Second, in 1998 the U.S. adopted 17 USC. Section 1202 concerning the protection of CMI, as part of the Digital Millennium Copyright Act's (DMCA's) implementation of new international obligations introduced in the 1996 WIPO treaties. Article 12 of the WIPO Copyright Treaty (WCT) provides:

> (1) Contracting Parties shall provide adequate and effective legal remedies against any person knowingly performing any of the following acts knowing, or with respect to civil remedies having reasonable grounds to know, that it will induce, enable, facilitate or conceal an infringement of *any right covered by this Treaty or the Berne Convention*:
> (i) to remove or alter any electronic rights management information without authority;
> (ii) to distribute, import for distribution, broadcast or communicate to the public, without authority, works or copies of works knowing that electronic rights management information has been removed or altered without authority.
>
> (2) As used in this Article, "rights management information" means information which identifies the work, the author of the work, the owner of any right in the work, or information about the terms and conditions of use of the work, and any numbers or codes that represent such information, when any of these items of information is attached to a copy of a work or appears in connection with the communication of a work to the public.[24]

The violation consists in the knowing removal or alteration of CMI having reasonable grounds to know that the removal or alteration will facilitate:

> any right covered by this Treaty or the Berne Convention.[25]

Authorship attribution and integrity rights are Berne Convention rights under Article 6bis and, as to attribution rights, indirectly under Article 10(3).[26] As a result, under the international norm, author-identifying information is protected rights management information, and its knowing removal would violate a right covered by the Berne Convention. Because Berne specifies the independence of moral and economic rights, the removal of the author-identifying information by third parties, including the holder of the economic rights, as well as the dissemination of an altered version of the work whose CMI does not disclose the changes, could violate and facilitate

24. WIPO Copyright Treaty (Dec. 20, 1996) TRT/WCT/001, Art. 12 (emphasis added).
25. *Ibid.*, Art. 12(1) (emphasis added).
26. Berne Convention, Art. 10(3).

the violation of the author's 6bis rights.[27] The U.S. implementation of WCT Article 12 departs from the international text in one important way. §1202 states:

> (a) False Copyright Management Information—No person shall knowingly and with the intent to induce, enable, facilitate, or conceal infringement—
> (1) provide copyright management information that is false, or
> (2) distribute or import for distribution copyright management information that is false.
>
> (b) Removal or Alteration of Copyright Management Information—No person shall, without the authority of the copyright owner or the law—
> (1) intentionally remove or alter any copyright management information,
> (2) distribute or import for distribution copyright management information knowing that the copyright management information has been removed or altered without authority of the copyright owner or the law, or
> (3) distribute, import for distribution, or publicly perform works, copies of works, or phonorecords, knowing that copyright management information has been removed or altered without authority of the copyright owner or the law, knowing, or, with respect to civil remedies under section 1203, having reasonable grounds to know, that it will induce, enable, facilitate, or conceal *an infringement of any right under this title.*[28]

Apart from the extremely limited coverage of VARA, authorship attribution is not a "right under this title."[29] Removal of authorship information does not violate §1202 unless it facilitates infringement of an economic right. If the creator no longer owns, or never did own, exclusive economic rights under copyright, the creator would have no claim. While an authorized exploiter who deleted authorship-identifying information would violate Article 12 of the WCT, that text is not self-enforcing in the U.S. The

27. At least when the author has not transferred moral rights (and to the extent that the country where the work is exploited permits transfers of moral rights).
28. H.R. 2281, 105th Cong. §1202 (1997) (emphasis added).
29. The Copyright Office advises against amending §1202 to require that authors be cited, pointing to the potential burden and complexity of such a proposal. While industry examples of voluntary provision of metadata for sound recordings and photographs are positive, mandatory implementation may not be advisable, considering concerns about burdens on the creative industries, impact on anonymous works, allocation of responsibility for implementing such systems, and enforcement challenges. *Copyright Office Moral Rights Report* 90-92.

possibility that authorized exploiters would remove or alter author-identifying information is not negligible,[30] but an authorized exploiter is not a copyright infringer, so, unless the author can demonstrate that the absence or alteration of author-identifying information would facilitate infringement by unauthorized downstream users, she would have no §1202 claim. A 2019 Copyright Office Study acknowledged "that the dual intent standard raises a high bar and excludes a large amount of misconduct that should at least raise the potential of civil liability."[31]

Third, the Supreme Court in *Dastar Corp. v. Twentieth Century Fox Film Corp.*,[32] held that the term "origin of goods" in section 43(a) of the Lanham Federal Trademarks Act refers to the source of the physical product and not to the person who created the underlying content. Before *Dastar*, authors could invoke the Lanham Act as a partial source of attribution and integrity rights, since courts had construed it to afford a remedy for false attribution of authorship. The Supreme Court's decision has now undermined much of the law under section 43(a) on which the U.S.' claimed right of attribution rested at the time of Berne adherence.[33]

---

30. Platforms originally stripped works of CMI online to make their file sizes compatible with the narrow bandwidth of dial-up connections and then, to speed up website loading times. Despite advances in broadband technology capable of supporting larger file sizes, the practice persists. A 2015 study found that, while some metadata formats remain on certain social media platforms, others were consistently stripped out. With the development of new technologies for CMI attachment, corresponding methods for its alteration or deletion also arise. *See Social Media Sites Photo Metadata Test Results*, Embedded Metadata Manifesto, http://www.embeddedmetadata.org/social-media-test-results.php (showing that, while Exif metadata was retained on Pinterest and Tumblr, IIM and XMP metadata was stripped off on Tumblr, and Exif, IIM, and XMP metadata were stripped off on Twitter and Flickr) at 86.
31. Preliminary drafts of international treaties and U.S. proposals to amend copyright law to safeguard CMI associated with a work included a knowledge requirement to avoid inadvertent violations but lacked the intent element for causing or facilitating infringement. However, concerns arose during negotiations about the broad scope of these provisions, which could hinder legitimate activities and correction of inaccurate information. *Ibid.*, 95-95.

    While it is not necessary to prove actual infringement to sustain a 1202 claim, some courts treat the absence of infringement as an indicium of lack of intent. *See* Doe v. Github, Inc., No. 22-cv-06823-JST, 2023 U.S. Dist. LEXIS 86983, at *30 (N.D. Cal. May 11, 2023); Stevens v. CoreLogic, 899 F.3d 666 (9th Cir. 2018); Steele v. Bongiovi, 784 F. Supp. 2d 94, 98 (D. Mass. 2011).

    The Copyright Office proposed to add a section to 1202A, specifying that the intentional removal or alteration of CMI would be actionable only if done with the intent to *conceal* the author's attribution information. This measure aims to ease the dual intent standard, to enable authors who have transferred their rights to retain standing, and to protect those innocently altering or removing CMI. *Copyright Office Moral Rights Report* 98-99.
32. 539 U.S. 23 (2003).
33. Ba sed on a review of lower court decisions interpreting *Dastar*, the Copyright Office believes that there are still some claims that may be made under the Lanham Act for violating attribution or integrity rights. *See Copyright Office Moral Rights Report* 54-58. While the Copyright Office does not advise amending the Lanham Act, it holds that any

Finally, regarding the Berne Convention quotation right's requirement of author attribution, Article 10 does not afford Member States an option to provide quotation rights;[34] it directs their allowance, subject to a variety of conditions, including mandatory mention of the source and of the name of the author, if it appears on the work. Article 10(1)'s other conditions (fair practice; proportionality) resemble two of the U.S. fair use exception's factors (amount and substantiality of the portion taken; effect on the value of or potential market for the work),[35] but neither the text of 17 USC. Section 107 nor its judicial interpretation has mandated mention of the name of the author of the copied work. The U.S. could come closer to compliance with international norms under the Berne Article 10 quotation right were its courts to include authorship attribution as a consideration under the first fair use factor: nature and purpose of the use. The "nature of the use" would take into account whether the defendant credited the source and the author.[36] Incorporation of attribution into the fair use factors would not, however, make attribution mandatory, as required by Berne Article 10; it would simply require courts to consider the presence or absence of authorship credit as part of the fair use balance.

Authorship attribution has occasionally figured in court's analyses;[37] however, to contend that it has weighed significantly in the balance would overstate. But nothing in the statute or prior case law precludes the development of a more vigorous attribution consideration as part of the

legislation should be drafted narrowly to protect only against consumer confusion, without extending copyright protection or granting authors further control over permissible uses of underlying works. *Ibid.*, 58-59.

For critiques of *Dastar*'s evisceration of the attribution right, *see, e.g.*, Jane C. Ginsburg, *The Right to Claim Authorship in US Trademarks and Copyright Law,* 41 Houston Law Review 263 (2004); Greg Lastowka, *The Trademark Function of Authorship,* 85 Boston University. Law Review 1171 (2005) https://doi.org/10.2139/ssrn.656138; Justin Hughes, *American Moral Rights and Fixing the Dastar "Gap"* 2007 Utah Law Review 659 (2007) https://doi.org/10.2139/ssrn.618783.

34. Berne Convention, Art. 10(1).
35. *See* 17 USC §107(3)(4) (2012).
36. Courts might also take into account a defendant's failure to include authorship attribution as part of the analysis of the "effect of the use upon the … value of the work" under the fourth fair use factor, *see*, Jane C. Ginsburg, *Essay: Fair Use Factor Four Revisited: Valuing the "Value of the Copyrighted Work,"* 67 Journal of the Copyright Society of the U.S.A. 19 (2020), http://ssrn.com/abstract=3537703.
37. The leading case is Weissmann v. Freeman, in which the defendant's failure to credit his erstwhile co-author contributed to the court's holding the use unfair; Weissmann v. Freeman 868 F.2d 1313, 1324 (2d Cir. 1989); *See also*, Marcus v. Rowley, 695 F.2d 1171, 1176 (9th Cir. 1983). When defendants did credit the source of the copied material, some courts have found authorship attribution a point in favor of fair use. *See, e.g.*, Lathan v. City of Whittier Alaska, No. 3:10-cv-00070-TMB, 2011 U.S. Dist. LEXIS 159477, at *34 (D. Alaska Aug. 4, 2011); Williamson v. Pearson Educ., Inc., No. 00 CIV. 8240(AGS), 2001 WL 1262964, at *5 (S.D.N.Y. Oct. 19, 2001); Rubin v. Brooks/Cole Pub. Co., 836 F. Supp. 909, 918 (D. Mass. 1993); Maxtone-Graham v. Burtchaell, 803 F.2d 1253, 1256 (2d Cir. 1986).

evaluation of the first factor. That technique would conform to the *Charming Betsy*[38] doctrine—the general principle that domestic statutes should be interpreted in light of the U.S.' international obligations.[39]

Courts may come to consider attribution as part of the fair use analysis with the rise of AI-generated images "in the style of" living artists. Emulating a given artist's style has not traditionally been considered copyright infringement.[40] Assuming, *arguendo*, that the fair use status of the inputs were to turn on the infringement analysis of the outputs (a highly contested proposition), feeding an artist's corpus into an AI system and then asking the system to create a new work in the style of the targeted artist (assuming the work imitates, rather than cuts and pastes from preexisting works) would not infringe. However, by making it possible to generate outputs in the style of a given artist, the AI system may, some artists fear, supersede the demand for the real artist's works.[41] Market-substitutional copying generally does not qualify as a fair use, but in this instance the substitution results from

38. Murray v. Schooner *Charming Betsy* 6 US64, 2 L.Ed.208 (1804).

39. *See, e.g.,* Restatement (Third) of the Foreign Relations Law of the United States §114 (1987); *see generally* Ralph G. Steinhardt, *The Role of International Law as a Canon of Domestic Statutory Construction,* 43 Vanderbilt Law Review 1103 (1990); For an in-depth exploration of the role of the Charming Betsy canon in U.S. implementation of Berne minimum moral rights, *see* Graeme Austin, *The Berne Convention as a Canon of Construction: Moral Rights after Dastar,* 61 New York University Annual Survey of American Law 111, 144-150 (2005). The *Charming Betsy* doctrine is not inconsistent with ss. 2 and 3 of the 1988 Berne Convention Implementation Act; Berne Convention Implementation Act §2, 17 USC §101, 102 Stat. 2853(1988). Section 2 is compatible with *Charming Betsy* because it confines the applicable law to U.S. law, which Congress declares in conformity with the Berne Convention. U.S. courts therefore should interpret U.S. law to ensure the accuracy of that declaration; *Ibid.,* s. 3 directs courts not to rely on the Berne Convention to expand rights to claim authorship, but given the declaration that the U.S. already conforms to Berne attribution norms, an interpretation of U.S. law that is consistent with Berne would not expand U.S. attribution rights; *Ibid.,* 3.

40. *See, e.g.,* Hayuk v. Starbucks 157 F Supp 3d 285 (S.D.N.Y. Dist Ct, 2016); McDonald v. West 138 F Supp 3d 448 (S.D.N.Y. Dist Ct, 2015); Dean v. Cameron 53 F Supp 3d 641 (S.D.N.Y Dist Ct, 2014); Kroencke v. GMC 270 F Supp 2d 441 (S.D.N.Y. Dist Ct, 2003) at 444: "Nothing in the Copyright Act of 1976 (which refers to the infringed 'work' in the singular) or in the precedents of this Circuit supports the view that a plaintiff's entire *oeuvre*, or even an aggregated portion of it, may be used as the point of comparison where the works included therein bear little or no relation to one another beyond 'style')"; Judith Ripka Designs, Ltd v. Preville 935 F Supp 237 (S.D.N.Y. Dist Ct, 1996), at 248: "The copyright laws do not protect styles, but only particular original designs" (citing Peter Pan Fabrics, Inc. v. Martin Weiner Corp 274 F 2d 487 (2nd Cir, 1960) at 489).

41. *See, e.g.,* Jose Antonio Lanz, "Greg Rutkowski Was Removed From Stable Diffusion, But AI Artists Brought Him Back," *Decrypt* (Jul. 29, 2023); Richard Currie, "Musicians Threaten to make Oasis 'Live Forever' with AI," *The Register* (Apr. 21, 2023); Sarah Andersen, "The Alt-Right Manipulated My Comic. Then A.I. Claimed It," *The New York Times* (Dec. 31, 2022); Andy Baio, "Invasive Diffusion: How One Unwilling Illustrator Found Herself Turned Into an AI Model," *Waxy* (Nov. 1, 2022); Andrew Deck, "AI-generated Art Sparks Furious Backlash from Japan's Anime Community," *Rest of World* (Oct. 27, 2022).

emulating style, rather than incorporating portions of the inputted works into the outputs. The outputs, even if hewing to the "style" side of the "style/expression" divide, may nonetheless compete with the artist's future prospects: why pay an artist to create a work when one can request an image-generation program to create a similar substitute for free (or for the usage or subscription cost of the service)? But this substitution effect may not be cognizable under factor four of section 107, which inquires into the effect on the market for or value of the copyrighted work (i.e., the works copied into the system), not the market for or value of the artist's present and future oeuvre in general.

Under the Berne Convention[42] Article 9(2), and WCT[43] Article 10, the "three-step test" authorizes Member States to create exceptions and limitations to the reproduction right; the third step requires that the exception or limitation "not unreasonably prejudice the legitimate interests of the author." An AI output that competes with an artist's oeuvre in general or with her future work may not supplant the market for any particular copied work, but that output may indeed "unreasonably prejudice the legitimate interests of the author" in making a living and continuing her creative activities. To put the U.S. in compliance with its international obligation to conform national copyright exceptions to the three-step test, U.S. courts could look beyond section 107's lack of an explicit direction to address an exception's impact on the legitimate interests of the author. U.S. courts could incorporate an inquiry into that impact as an additional fair use consideration. Even under a solely work-based interpretation of section 107(4), one may observe that the wholesale copying of an artist's works into training data in order to enable stylistically similar outputs jeopardizes not only the artist's future employment or commissions but also devalues the actual works copied because the image-generation program can produce outputs that compete with already-created works as well.

4.2.2 Prohibition of Formalities

Berne Convention, Article 5(2) provides:

> The enjoyment and the exercise of these rights [the rights which their respective laws do now or may hereafter grant to their nationals, as well as the rights specially granted by this Convention] shall not be subject to any formality.

42. Berne Convention (Jul. 24, 1971), 828 UNTS 221, (entered into force Nov. 19, 1984, accession by Singapore Sep. 21, 1998) https://www.wipo.int/wipolex/en/text/283693 [Berne Convention].
43. WIPO Copyright Treaty (Dec. 20, 1996), 36 ILM 65 (1997) (entered into force Mar. 6, 2002, accession by Singapore Jan. 17, 2005) https://www.wipo.int/wipolex/en/text/295157 [WCT].

From the outset of the mid-nineteenth-century movement for international copyright, authors advocated the abolition or restriction of formalities. Proper compliance with multiple national formalities was cumbersome, costly, and often unsuccessful, hence authors' demand as early as the first international Congress aimed at securing authors' rights, held in Brussels in 1858, that authors be protected in all countries so long as they satisfied whatever formalities their home countries imposed. The 1886 and 1896 versions of the Berne Convention adopted this approach.[44]

In practice, however, it turned out to be difficult to prove to foreign authorities that the author had complied with the country of origin's formalities.[45] As a result, the 1908 Berlin revision prohibited the imposition of formalities on foreign authors altogether, although Member States remained free to require that domestic authors affix notice, register claims, and/or deposit copies with local authorities.[46] And, to ensure that an author's failure to carry out domestic formalities—with a consequent loss of protection in the country of origin—would not affect the availability of international protection, the Berlin revisers specified that:

> apart from the provisions of this Convention, the extent of protection, as well as the means of redress afforded to the author to protect his rights, shall be governed exclusively by the laws of the country where protection is claimed.[47]

The effect of this language was to confer copyright throughout the Berne Union, automatically and upon creation, on every Convention-covered work created by an author who was a national of a Berne Union Member State, or first published within a Member State. The no-formalities rule thus fundamentally undergirds the Berne Convention system of universal international authors' rights.

But what are "formalities" in the Berne sense? Article 5(2) declares that:

> the enjoyment and the exercise of these rights shall not be subject to any formality.[48]

Although earlier texts refer to "conditions and formalities," it has long been understood that the term "any formality" encompasses both "formal and material conditions" on the existence or enforcement of rights.[49] "These rights" are:

---

44. Sam Ricketson & Jane C. Ginsburg, *International Copyright and Neighbouring Rights: The Berne Convention and Beyond* §§6.85-6.87, 6.104-6.105 (3rd ed., Oxford University Press, 2022).
45. *Ibid.*, §§6.88-6.89.
46. *Ibid.*, §§3.12, 6.89.
47. Berne Convention, Art. 5(2) (Art. 4(2) in the Berlin revision).
48. *Ibid.*
49. *See generally* Ricketson & Ginsburg (n. 44), §§6.104-6.106.

> the rights which the[] respective laws [of the countries of the Union] do now or may hereafter grant to their nationals, as well as the rights specially granted by this Convention.[50]

Thus, a foreign author is entitled to national treatment in Berne Member States (but without having to comply with any formalities the state may impose on its own authors), as well as to any additional Convention-guaranteed rights, even if these are not afforded to local authors.

The "enjoyment" of local or Berne minimum rights extends to:

> everything which must be complied with in order to ensure that the rights of the author with regard to his work may come into existence. These would include such requirements as registration, the deposit or filing of copies, the payment of fees, or the making of declarations,[51]

such as the notice of copyright which the U.S. before Berne adherence had required published works to bear; nonaffixation of the notice would result in the work's falling into the public domain.[52]

In addition to the initial attachment of protection (since 1908 automatic upon creation for authors from other Berne Member States), the concept of "enjoyment" of copyright would include the persistence of protection for the minimum Berne term of copyright; obligations to register and renew copyrights, such as existed in the 1909 U.S. Copyright Act,[53] thus would fall under the prohibition.[54] In the 1976 Act, the U.S. abandoned its two-term structure of copyright, in favor of the Berne life + 50 standard.[55] As a result, for works created as of the Act's effective date of January 1, 1978, there was no more renewal term, and accordingly no more renewal registration. As to works published before 1978, transitional rules required renewal of works

50. Berne Convention, Art. 5(1).
51. Ricketson & Ginsburg (n. 44), §6.105 (quoting the German delegate Dr. Meyer at the 1884 Diplomatic Conference).
52. Howard B. Abrams, *The Law of Copyright* §8:10, 1 (2018); William Gable, *Restoration of Copyrights: Dueling Trolls and Other Oddities under Section 104A of the Copyright Act,* 29 Columbia Journal of Law & the Arts 181, 196 (2005).
53. Copyright Act of 1909, Chapter 320 §§1, 24, 35 Stat. 1075 (1909) (repealed 1976).
54. Stef F. von Gompel, *Formalities in Copyright Law* 195 (Kluwer Law International, 2011); The scope of rights (including any limitations or exceptions) also comes within the "enjoyment" of Berne and national rights. In addition to Art. 5(1)'s command that "Authors shall enjoy" rights under national law and under Berne minima, Berne Arts. 11, 11bis, 11ter, 12 and 14bis all provide that "authors shall enjoy" the specific minimum rights to public performance, adaptation and cinematographic works. A Member State may neither condition the initial attachment of copyright on compliance with formalities nor subsequently deny coverage of particular rights to authors who fail to meet declaratory obligations. Thus, for example, a Member State may not subject the translation right (a minimum right under Art. 8) to registering the work or filing a notice of reservation of rights.
55. Copyright Act of 1976, Pub.L. 94-553, §302, 90 Stat. 2541 (1976).

then in their first term of copyright,[56] but in 1992, Congress provided for automatic renewal of works published before 1978 that were then in their first term of copyright.[57]

Berne precludes not only formalities that condition the existence of copyright but also those that freight its "exercise."[58] Without the second prohibition, an author might be *vested* with copyright, but unable to enforce her rights unless she complies with a variety of prerequisites to suit or to availability of remedies.[59] Copyright-specific conditions on access to judicial process or to injunctive relief (including seizure and destruction of infringing Articles) or to actual damages, therefore, contravene Berne norms. When it joined the Berne Convention, effective 1989, the U.S. limited its requirement that works be registered as a prerequisite to initiating an infringement action to "United States works."[60] Congress recognized that subjecting foreign Berne Convention works to a pre-suit registration requirement violated Berne minimum protections, but preserved the requirement for domestic works, as Berne permits.[61]

4.2.2.1 Which "Conditions" on the Existence or Enforcement of Rights Does Article 5(2) Permit?

4.2.2.1.1 Permissible Conditions

By contrast, general litigation obligations, such as payment of filing fees, or general procedural or evidentiary requirements, while they may affect the enforcement of a copyright claim, are not "formalities" in the Berne sense so long as they apply to all actions, whatever the subject matter.[62] Moreover,

56. *Ibid.,* §304.
57. Copyright Renewal Act of 1992, Pub.L. 102-307, 106 Stat. 264 (1992).
58. Berne Convention, Art. 5(2).
59. von Gompel (n. 54), 200.
60. 17 USC §411(a) (2012); a "United States work" is defined in s. 101.
61. Berne Convention, Art. 5(3). *See* Final Report of the ad Hoc Working Group on U.S. Adherence to the Berne Convention 53 (1986) *reprinted in* 10 Columbia-Volunteer Lawyers for the Arts Journal of Law & the Arts 513, 565 (1986). The Supreme Court unanimously ruled that a copyright infringement lawsuit can only proceed once the copyright is registered with the U.S. Copyright Office. Fourth Est. Pub. Benefit Corp. v. Wall-Street.com, LLC, 139 S. Ct. 881, 887, 203 L. Ed. 2d 147 (2019).
62. Arguably, 17 USC § 512(c)'s system of notice and takedown could be considered a "formality" because notice is a prerequisite to relief. Nonetheless, the argument is unpersuasive because the information that §512(c)(3) requires is not a condition precedent to seeking relief akin to the §411 pre-suit registration obligation, but corresponds to what one would have to prove in court. The requirements that, in a civil action, the author prove that she is the author, that she created the work, that she published it on a particular date, and that the work is original, are not "formalities," but are the facts in issue. Berne Convention, Art. 5(2) does not dispense the author from proving those facts in the proceeding that will determine if she is entitled to relief. It means that the author need not register a document attesting to those facts before she can even initiate a procedure to seek

Berne specifically permits certain mandatory declaratory obligations. For example, under Berne Article 3, a work will not be protected in the Union unless its author's nationality or its place of first publication meets the condition of being a Berne Member State. Article 2(2) allows Member States to make fixation in material form a condition of protection. U.S. Copyright law's fixation requirement[63] thus does not run afoul of Berne. Once a work does qualify for protection under the Convention, however, Member States may not impose declaratory or other conditions precedent to the enjoyment or exercise of domestic and conventional rights. With this possible exception: with respect to works still under copyright in their countries of origin, but in the public domain in a newly-acceding Member State (or still under copyright in the new Member State, but in the public domain in other Member States), Article 18(1) requires Member States to restore the copyrights in these works, but Article 18(3) allows Member States to determine "the conditions of application of [the restoration] principle."

A Member State may not decline to restore copyrights in qualifying foreign works in the local public domain: Article 18(3) makes clear that the restoration principle must be applied. But that provision grants Member States considerable latitude to determine how to restore copyright in formerly public domain foreign works. "Conditions" on the implementation of restoration might well include declaratory obligations. For example, section 104A of the U.S. copyright law reinstates copyright automatically,[64] but protects "reliance parties" who had exploited the work in good faith before its restoration, by requiring restored copyright owners to file a "Notice of Intent to Enforce Restored Copyright" in the Copyright Office or by service on the reliance party.[65] In other words, before she may enforce her copyright against a reliance party, the author or copyright owner of a formerly public domain work must comply with a detailed declaratory obligation[66] in order to put reliance parties on notice of the restored owner's claims. By virtue of Article 18(3), this declaratory obligation, albeit a significant limitation on the enforcement of copyright, seems fully compatible with Berne norms.

---

relief (at which she will have to prove the facts). Transposed to §512(c)(3), the facts in the notice are the facts that must be pleaded to obtain the temporary restraining order-like remedy of a takedown. They are the procedure, they are not a screen barring the author from access to the process.

63. 17 USC §201(a) (2012).
64. *See* 17 USC §104A(a)(1)(A) (2012).
65. *Ibid.*, §104A(c).
66. The details are set out in *Ibid.*, §104A(e).

4.2.2.1.2 Incentives Versus Obligations: Rewarding the Effectuation of Declaratory Measures by Offering Litigation or Remedial Enhancements

If Berne prohibits the imposition of sanctions for noncompliance with declaratory obligations, another approach might be to substitute carrots for sticks. Under U.S. copyright law, authors who comply with registration or other requirements enjoy evidentiary advantages and qualify for additional remedies. Authors, domestic or foreign, who do not register their works with the copyright office within the prescribed deadlines are not entitled to those benefits. Are these "carrots" Berne-compatible?

4.2.2.1.2.1 Evidentiary Advantages

Evidentiary advantages might provide meaningful incentives to authors or rightholders to register their works and record transfers of rights, thus facilitating title searching. For example, to encourage compliance with declaratory measures, the U.S. accords presumptive probative value to the publicly-recorded information if the registration is made within five years of first publication.[67] Presumptions of originality arising from timely registration may significantly enhance the author's ability to enforce her rights, particularly if courts would otherwise impose a high burden of proof of the original character of the author's expression.[68] While the copyright-specificity of this "carrot" might call its Berne compatibility into question, leading authorities have suggested that measures to "facilitate proof of authorship" are not prohibited formalities.[69]

With respect to recordation, the U.S. Copyright Act states that recordation provides constructive notice of the recorded information;[70] it also designates the copyright owner as the first grantee to record the transfer of title in the event of conflicting transfers.[71] To the extent that recordation

67. *See, e.g.,* 17 USC §410(c) (2012) (certificate of registration serves as prima facie proof of information there recorded, if registration is effected within five years of publication), §412 (statutory damages and attorney's fees available only if work registered before infringement occurred, "unless … registration is made within three months after the first publication of the work").
68. *See, e.g.,* Cour d'appel [CA] [regional court of appeals] Paris, 1re chambre civile, Sep. 8, 2015, 143/2015, *reversing* Tribunal de grande instance [TGI] [ordinary court of original jurisdiction] Paris, Mar. 27, 2014, 12/05634 (reversing trial court's ruling that plaintiff heir of French author Albert Camus had failed to prove the expressive originality of Albert Camus' unpublished letters).
69. *See* Jörg Reinbothe & Silke von Lewinski, *The WIPO Treaties on Copyright: A Commentary on the WCT, the WPPT and the BTAP* 89, §7.3.39 (2nd ed., Oxford University Press, 2015); Copyright 142, 154, §§73-76 (1993) (permissibility of laws giving registration information the effect of a rebuttable presumption of the correctness of the information).
70. 12 USC §205(c) (2012).
71. *Ibid.,* §205(d).

perfects or evidences title to property in general,[72] rather than solely to copyright, its lack of copyright-specificity indicates that it is not a forbidden formality in the Berne sense.

4.2.2.1.2.2 Remedial Advantages

Berne's prohibition on formalities requires that copyright remedies, such as injunctive relief and actual damages, remain available to foreign authors who have not locally registered their works or undertaken other locally-imposed declaratory measures. Although the Berne Convention itself specifies no remedies other than border seizures of infringing copies,[73] Berne anticipates that Member States will supply the "means of redress."[74] These are determined by local law,[75] but, over and above the national treatment rule, they remain subject to the general no-formalities proviso.[76] By the same token, the TRIPS Accord requires Member States to include injunctive relief within the available panoply of remedies;[77] TRIPS' incorporation of the Berne no-formalities rule means that Member States may not condition remedies on compliance with formalities.

If Berne and TRIPS preclude conditioning express or implicit conventional minimum remedies on fulfillment of formalities, might the Member States create incentives for compliance with declaratory measures by subjecting additional remedies to a compliance obligation? In other words, might there be a category of Berne+ remedies for which imposition of formalities would be permissible? When the U.S. joined the Berne Convention in 1989, it retained the provision in the Copyright Act that limited availability of statutory damages and attorney's fees to works which had been registered before the infringement occurred.[78] This provision was thought to afford meaningful incentives to registration that are:

72. *See, e.g.,* Massachusetts General Laws Annotated, Chapter 183, §4 (West) (requiring recordation of a notice of lease or assignment in order for a conveyance of an estate to be valid); Tex. Prop. Code Ann. §13.002 (West) (recordation provides notice of the instrument to all persons); Cal. Civ. Code §1213 (West) (a recorded conveyance of real property serves as constructive notice of the conveyance to subsequent purchasers).
73. Berne Convention, Art. 16.
74. *Ibid.,* Art. 5(2).
75. *Ibid.*
76. It has been suggested that Berne does not in fact require Member States to include injunctive relief within their remedial arsenals, and that Member States might therefore condition that remedy on compliance with declaratory measures, leaving undeclaring authors with some form of equitable remuneration in lieu of injunctions. *See* Christopher Sprigman, *Reform(aliz)ing Copyright,* 57 Stanford Law Review 485, 555-560 (2004) https://doi.org/10.4324/9781315092621-8. For detailed rebuttal of this contention, *see* Jane C. Ginsburg, *"With Untired Spirits and Formal Constancy": Berne Compatibility of Formal Declaratory Measures to Enhance Title-Searching,* 28 Berkley Technology Law Journal 1583, 1593-1597 (2013) https://doi.org/10.2139/ssrn.2262924.
77. TRIPS, Art. 41(1).
78. Pub. L. 94-553, tit. I, §101, 90 Stat. 2583 (1976) (codified as amended at 17 USC §412 (2012)).

compatible with Berne since it deals with certain specific remedies rather than the ability to obtain redress at all.[79]

In general, the argument holds that remedies that exceed the protections mandated by international instruments are not subject to the Berne minima no-formalities rule. So long as the Member State requires its own authors to comply with any declaratory obligations with respect to these remedies, then imposing the same obligations on foreign authors remains consistent with the rule of national treatment, and that is all Berne demands. It is true that Berne does not enumerate the remedies of statutory damages and attorney's fees whose availability would be subject to compliance with Member State formalities, but neither does it enumerate the basic remedies of actual damages or injunctive relief. The only treaty-mandated remedy is seizure of infringing copies.[80] If treaty specification were to sort remedies into treaty-required and treaty+, then all remedies other than seizure would be Berne+, and, under the argument that Berne+ remedies may be conditioned on compliance with formalities, almost all copyright enforcement could be so freighted—a result manifestly inconsistent with the text and purpose of Article 5(2).

While Berne does not distinguish between "basic" and "enhanced" enforcement tools, TRIPS effectively does because it includes the additional measures of statutory damages and attorneys' fees among its specified remedies, but it does not require Member States to provide them.[81] It might follow that conditioning the availability (to local and foreign authors alike) of these remedies on some act of public filing is TRIPS-compatible.[82]

The non-mandatory character of these remedies, however, does not necessarily mean that a Member State that chooses to include them may also condition them on compliance with formalities. Structurally, one may contend that all of the TRIPS provisions pertaining to copyright, whether substantive or remedial, are subject to the overarching no-formalities rule by virtue of TRIPS' incorporation of Berne's norms.[83] As a result, even optional remedies may not be made subject to compliance with formalities. Member States' freedom to determine the "means of redress," including by devising

79. Final Report of the ad hoc Working Group on U.S. Adherence to the Berne Convention 53 (1986) *reprinted in* 10 Columbia-Volunteer Lawyers for the Arts Journal of Law & the Arts 513, 565 (1986).

80. *See* Berne Conv. Art. 16.

81. TRIPS, Art. 45(2).

82. If TRIPS permitted the imposition of formalities that Berne does not, TRIPS would be in conflict with itself, since it directs Member States to "comply with articles 1 through 21 of the Berne Convention (1971)," TRIPS Art. 9(2). That conflict would also implicate Barne Conv. Art. 20, which permits Member States "to enter into special agreements among themselves, in so far as such agreements grant to authors more extensive rights than those granted by the Convention, or contain other provisions not contrary to this Convention."

83. TRIPS, Arts. 2(2), 9(1).

remedies additional to the basic forms of monetary and injunctive relief, does not release them from the general Berne prohibition on formalities or entitle them to selective adherence to the no-formalities rule. Article 5(2) makes it clear that Berne minima, including the no-formalities rule, continue to bolster the designation of the laws of the country of protection to govern the scope of protection and remedies because Article 5(2) prefaces that delegation by specifying "apart from the provisions of this Convention." "Apart from" should be understood as "in addition to," not "excluding the provisions of this Convention." The latter reading would eviscerate the Berne minima, reducing the Convention to one based solely on national treatment. The no-formalities rule underpins the "enjoyment and exercise" of "the rights which [member States'] respective laws do now or may hereafter grant to their nationals, as well as the rights specially granted by this Convention." Thus, member States may define the "means of redress," but because those means form part of the "exercise" of national rights, those means must conform to the prohibition on formalities. Suppose, for example, that a Member State provided an expedited judicial or administrative process for copyright infringement claims, but only if the rightholder had registered the work before the alleged infringement occurred. This procedural advantage, albeit innovative and perhaps unique to that Member State, is nonetheless a "means of redress." Article 5(2) does not distinguish between traditional or basic remedies and additional, unusual, or new remedies: *all* remedies come within "the means of redress." Under this reading, there is no such thing as a Berne+ remedy, and therefore no basis to impose formalities on the availability of some remedies but not others.

4.2.3 Making Available Right

WCT Article 8 provides:

> authors of literary and artistic works shall enjoy the exclusive right of authorizing any communication to the public of their works, by wire or wireless means, including the making available to the public of their works in such a way that members of the public may access these works from a place and at a time individually chosen by them.

The WCT "making available" right applies to the offering to the public of on-demand access to a work in the form of a stream or a download. The text of WCT Article 8 ("making available to the public of their works in such a way that members of the public may access these works from a place and at a time individually chosen by them") encompasses all forms of on-demand access, whether or not the access results in a retention copy. Thus, it does not matter whether the member of the public obtains access to the work via a real-time "stream" or via the delivery to her computer or another device of a digital copy that she subsequently "opens" in order to see or hear the work.

Article 8 is designed to be "technology neutral" in order to avoid obsolescence. Even in 1996, it was understood that the line between exploitations involving the creation of copies, and exploitations involving real-time (more or less) listening and/or viewing without retaining a copy was becoming increasingly indistinct. The WIPO "Internet Treaties" acknowledged and anticipated the overlapping nature of "performance" and "copy" in digital communications, and, seeking a technologically neutral solution, therefore aimed to cover both.

Compliance with the WCT moreover requires a Member State to cover not only actual transmissions of streams and downloads but also the offering to communicate the work on demand as a stream or a download.[84] The act that triggers the making available right is the offer to communicate the work to the public on an on-demand basis; while actual individualized communications to members of the public are of course covered as well, the innovation of the WIPO Treaties was to enable authors to license, or to seek redress from, persons or entities who hold works out to the public as available for access by streaming or downloading.

The "umbrella solution" adopted at the 1996 Diplomatic Conference that yielded the WCT[85] allows Member States to implement Article 8 making available right through a variety of means, including, for example, an all-embracing "making available" right, or a combination of a public performance right covering streams and a digital distribution right covering downloads. Whatever the means chosen, however, the Member State must ensure that its law covers the offering to the public of on-demand access to a work both as a stream and as a download.[86]

The U.S. Copyright Act does not include a right titled "making available," or "communication to the public." At the time of ratification, U.S. authorities did not anticipate the difficulties that have subsequently ensued. As the 2013 study by the U.S. Department of Commerce ("Green Paper")[87] explains:

> When the U.S. implemented the WIPO Internet Treaties in the DMCA, it did not include an explicit "making available" right, as both Congress and the Administration concluded that the relevant acts were encompassed within the existing scope of exclusive rights.[88] In addition to the

84. *See, e.g.,* Ricketson & Ginsburg (n. 44), §12.59; WIPO Guide to the Copyright and Related Rights Treaties Administered by WIPO (2003) at CT-86.
85. *See* Mihaly Ficsor, *The Law of Copyright and the Internet: The 1996 WIPO Treaties, Their Interpretation and Implementation* 204-210 (Oxford University Press, 2002).
86. *See, e.g.,* Communication to the Public by Telecommunication: Scope of s. 2.4(1.1) of the *Copyright Act*—Making Available, CB-CDA 2017-085 (Copyright Board of Canada, Aug. 25, 2017).
87. U.S. Department of Commerce Internet Policy Task Force, Copyright Policy, Creativity and Innovation in the Digital Economy 14-16 (2013) ["Green Paper"].
88. H.R. Rep. No. 105-551, pt. 1, at 9 (1998); *WIPO Copyright Treaties Implementation Act and On-Line Copyright Liability Limitations Act: Hearing on H.R. 2281 and H.R. 2180*

existing reproduction and public performance rights, the distribution right, adopted in the 1976 Copyright Act, applied to digital transmissions as well as the distribution of physical copies.[89] And the legislative history indicates that this right was intended to incorporate the prior law's "publication" right,[90] which included the mere offering of copies to the public.[91]

Section 106(3) covers the right:

> to distribute copies or phonorecords of the copyrighted work to the public by sale or other transfer of ownership, or by rental, lease, or lending.

And section 106(4)(5) and (6) cover the rights to perform and display the work publicly, including by transmission:

> by means of any device or process, whether the members of the public capable of receiving the performance or display receive it in the same place or in separate places and at the same time or at different times.

U.S. compliance with its WCT obligations, therefore, turns on whether the U.S. Copyright Act, as interpreted by the courts, confers the exclusive right to offer on-demand to the public work for streaming and downloading. Coverage of only the actual delivery of a stream or download does not suffice, nor does coverage of only offers of streams but not of downloads (or vice versa).

Before the Subcomm. on Courts and Intellectual Property of the H. Comm. on the Judiciary, 105th Cong. 34 (1997) (Statement of Bruce Lehman, Assistant Secretary of Commerce for Intellectual Property).

89. Notably the legislative history from 1965 made reference to the potential for the "transmission of works by … linked computers, and other new media of communication" that "may be expected to displace the demand for authors' works by other users from whom copyright owners derive compensation." Supplementary Register's Report on the General Revision of the U.S. Copyright Law 14 (1965).
90. The right to "distribute" first emerged in the "Preliminary Draft for Revised US Copyright Law" in late 1962, and was substituted for "publish" to avoid the confusion that had developed surrounding the term "publication" and courts' attempts to avoid the harsh effects of "publication" without proper notice (forfeiture of federal copyright protection); *See generally* Peter Menell, *In Search of Copyright's Lost Ark: Interpreting the Right to Distribute in the Internet Age,* 59 Journal of the Copyright Society of the U.S.A. 1 (2011) https://doi.org/10.2139/ssrn.1679514; Benjamin Kaplan, *Publication in Copyright Law: The Question of Phonograph Records,* 103 University of Pennsylvania Law Review 469, 488-489 (1955) https://doi.org/10.2307/3310086.
91. *See* Menell (n. 90), 57; *see also* 2 Melville B. Nimmer & David Nimmer, *Nimmer on Copyright* §8.11[B][4][d] (2023) (henceforth Nimmer & Nimmer). At the time, the right to "publish" was understood to encompass the offering of copyright works to the public, and there was no requirement to prove actual distribution of copies; *See* David O. Carson, *Making the "Making Available Right" Available: 22nd Annual Horace S Manges Lecture, February 3, 2009,* 33 Columbia Journal of Law & the Arts 135, 160-161 (2010); Restatement (Third) of the Foreign Relations Law of the United Stated §114 (1986).

The U.S. implementation of the making available right reveals the potential shortcomings of relying on multiple exclusive rights collectively to cover the full range of acts comprised within the making available right: some features of the right may end up left out. U.S. case law has assigned the offering and communication of digital streams to the public performance right and downloads to the reproduction and distribution rights.[92] Although case law and statutory authority clearly establish that the U.S. distribution right embraces delivery of digital copies,[93] decisions interpreting the scope of the distribution right differ regarding the essential question of coverage of offers to download. A number of courts have concluded that the distribution right incorporates the concept of "making available" reflected in the WIPO Treaties.[94] Some other courts have disagreed.[95] Indeed, so confident was one district court that the mere offer of downloads could not violate the distribution right, that the court declined to follow the rule of statutory interpretation (the *Charming Betsy* doctrine) that calls upon courts to interpret statutes consistently with U.S. international obligations.[96] That court held instead that the *Charming Betsy* doctrine applies only when a statute is ambiguous, and that the scope of the distribution right, as interpreted in the 8th Circuit, unambiguously foreclosed its application to offers to distribute.[97] All of these cases, however, have focused solely on the scope of the distribution right and predate subsequent academic scholarship reviewing previously unanalyzed legislative history.[98] For the moment, only federal district courts have ruled on the question, but their rulings have ranged from assimilating making available to "publication" (whose statutory definition encompasses offers to distribute) to requiring actual downloads. The latter group of decisions thus would leave a gap in U.S. coverage of the full range of the making available right.

---

92. *See, e.g.,* United States v. Am. Soc'y of Composers, Authors & Publishers, 627 F.3d 64, 69 (2d Cir. 2010).
93. *See, e.g.,* Capitol Records, LLC v. ReDigi Inc., 934 F. Supp. 2d 640, 651 (S.D.N.Y. 2013) ("ReDigi"); Arista Records LLC v. Usenet.com, Inc., 633 F. Supp. 2d 124, 147 (S.D.N.Y. 2009) ("Usenet.com"); London-Sire Records, Inc. v. Doe 1, 542 F. Supp. 2d 153, 173 (D. Mass. 2008).
94. A&M Records v. Napster, Inc., 239 F.3d 1004, 1014 (9th Cir. 2001) ("Napster"); Universal City Studios Prods. LLLP v. Bigwood, 441 F. Supp. 2d 185, 191 (D. Me. 2006); Motown Records Co. v. DiPietro, No. 04-CV-2246, 2007 WL 576284 (E.D. Pa. Feb. 16, 2007); UMG Recordings, Inc. v. Alburger, Civil No. 07-3705, 2009 WL 3152153, at *3 (E.D. Pa. Sep. 29, 2009).
95. These cases have not, however, required direct evidence of the dissemination of copies, but have allowed proof based on circumstantial evidence or inference. *See* Capitol Records, Inc. v. Thomas, 579 F.Supp.2d 1210, 1225 (D. Minn. 2008); London-Sire Records, Inc., 542 F.Supp.2d at 169; Atl. Recording Corp. v. Howell, 554 F. Supp. 2d 976, 981-984 (D. Ariz. 2008).
96. *See* Murray v. Schooner Charming Betsy, 6 U.S. (2 Cranch) 64, 118 (1804).
97. *See* Capitol Records v. Thomas, 579 F. Supp. 2d 1210 (D. Minn., 2008).
98. Menell (n. 90); Nimmer & Nimmer (n. 91), §8.11[B][4][d] (2023).

In a thorough study of the making available right, however, the U.S. Copyright Office concluded that, despite the inconsistent case law, "Section 106(3) is properly construed to cover offers to distribute copyrighted works via download."[99] The Copyright Office examined related provisions of the copyright act and the legislative history of the 1976 Act distribution right and applied the *Charming Betsy* doctrine in support of that conclusion. The Report specifies that the "offer" contemplated by the making available right:

> permits a finding of infringement only where a party has a copy of a work and makes one or more copies available for members of the public to obtain. Accordingly, while a person who uploads a copyrighted work to a share folder for downloading by the public has made an offer sufficient to implicate Section 106(3), one who simply makes a statement purporting to "offer" copies that she does not in fact possess has not done so.[100]

The coverage of "making available" by the public performance and display rights also poses interpretive difficulties. While the legislative history indicates that Congress anticipated and sought to extend the public performance right to pay-per-view transmissions,[101] the definition of a public performance arguably implies completed rather than incipient transactions. The text of the definition states:

> whether the members of the public capable of receiving the performance or display receive it in the same place or in separate places and at the same time or at different times.[102]

Reading the statute literally to require that members of the public have received the performance or display for the performance or display to have occurred, however, leads to absurd results. In a copyright variant of the tree falling unseen in the forest, even traditional broadcasting might not be a public performance: if no one turns on the radio, then no members of the public receive the performance. It would be more consistent with Congress' intent to read "receive it" as a conditional "could receive it" rather than a declaratory phrase.

The Copyright Office Report concluded that the public performance and display rights' coverage of transmissions was not only limited to transmissions actually effected but also to offers to transmit—including to stream—performances of copyrighted works.

While acknowledging the lack of direct judicial authority, the Office concludes that reading the statutory provisions in light of the purposes

99. United States Copyright Office, *The Making Available Right in the United States, a Report of the Register of Copyrights* 26 (2016) (hereinafter *Copyright Office Making Available Report*).
100. *Ibid.*, 29; Accordingly: Copyright Board of Canada (n. 86), para. 163.
101. H.R. Rep. 94-1476, 64-65 (1976), *reprinted in* 1976 USCC.A.N. 5659, 5678.
102. 17 USC §101 (2012) (emphasis supplied).

articulated by Congress indicates that the public performance right encompasses offers to stream. To begin with, excluding such offers would require reading the text in a manner that is inconsistent with Congress's clear intention to make a performance's accessibility, not its actual receipt, the determining factor under the Transmit Clause. As one commenter observed, if the phrase "transmit ... to the public" is to be read literally:

> it would follow there is no transmission to "the public" if the service does not in fact communicate the performance of the work to a substantial number of people.
>
> Indeed:
>
> [t]he Act ... suggests that "the public" consists of a large group of people outside of a family and friends.
>
> But, as shown:
>
> what matters, in determining whether the audience for a transmission is "the public," is capacity by "members of the public" to receive the transmission, not actual receipt.[103]

The Office also concluded that the Supreme Court had clarified that services offering members of the public individualized delivery of on-demand content came within the scope of the public performance right, regardless of the technical means by which the offered content was communicated.[104]

Finally, certain kinds of hyperlinks, particularly framing and inline linking, might also be considered to make works available to viewers of websites on which content residing on third-party servers seems to appear to be integrated into the website. U.S. case law has divided over whether this form of presentation of third-party copyrighted works constitutes public display by the linker. The Court of Appeals for the Ninth Circuit in a 2007 decision, *Perfect 10 v. Amazon*,[105] announced a rule insulating linkers from liability, and many U.S. courts since then have followed it.[106] Under the Ninth Circuit's "server rule":

> the owner of a computer that does not store and serve ... electronic information to a user is not displaying [or distributing] that information,

103. *Copyright Office Making Available Report* (n. 99), 39-40 (citations omitted).
104. *See* ABC v. Aereo, 134 S.Ct. 2498 (2014).
105. Perfect 10 v. Amazon, 508 F.3d 1146 (9th Cir. 2007).
106. Notwithstanding criticism from other courts (*see infra*), the Ninth Circuit has reaffirmed its adherence to the "server test." *See* Hunley v. Instagram, LLC, 73 F.4th 1060 (9th Cir. 2023). For a defense of the "server test," *see* Michael P. Goodyear, *Embedding Permission Culture: A New Approach to the Server Test Quandary*, 75 Oklahoma Law Review 263 (2023) https://doi.org/10.2139/ssrn.4042401.

> even if such owner in-line links to or frames the electronic information.[107]

Therefore, a defendant who provides a hyperlink of any kind (through simple linking, deep linking, framing, or inline linking) cannot incur direct copyright liability unless that defendant also "store[s] and serve[s]" the copyrighted material to which the link points.[108]

While a number of district courts and the Seventh Circuit[109] have endorsed the Ninth Circuit's "server test," other courts have questioned or declined to apply the test. For example, a district court held that "when defendants caused the embedded Tweets to appear on their websites, their actions violated plaintiff's exclusive display right; the fact that the image was hosted on a server owned and operated by an unrelated third party (Twitter) does not shield them from this result."[110] Indeed, courts have criticized the server test's apparent incompatibility with the language and legislative history of the Copyright Act. As a district court observed:

> The Copyright Act defines "display" as "to show a copy of" a work, 17 U.S.C. § 101, and not "to make and then show a copy of the copyrighted work." … The Ninth Circuit's [server test] approach, under which no display is possible unless the alleged infringer has also stored a copy of the work on the infringer's computer, would seem to make the display right merely a subset of the reproduction right … The Copyright Act makes clear, however, that to "show a copy" is to display it.[111]

In effect, under the server rule, authors' initial making available of their works online results in a kind of digital exhaustion of public display rights, in contrast to U.S. courts' refusal to recognize an equivalent outcome when redissemination of a digital file occurs through distribution of copies.[112]

The server rule adopted in *Perfect 10 v. Amazon* may put the U.S. at risk of falling short of its obligation to protect copyright owners' "making available" right under the WCT and the WIPO Performances and Phonogram Treaty (WPPT). Some commentators have contended that the server rule "eviscerates" the making available right by allowing other websites to inline

---

107. Perfect 10 v. Google, 416 F. Supp. 2d 828, 843-845 (C.D. Cal. 2006), aff'd. sub nom Perfect 10 v. Amazon, 508 F.3d 1146 (9th Cir. 2007).
108. For extensive criticism of the "server rule," *see* Jane C. Ginsburg & Luke Ali Budiardjo, *Liability for Providing Hyperlinks to Copyright-Infringing Content: International and Comparative Law Perspectives*, 41 Columbia Journal of Law & the Arts 153, 179-192 (2018).
109. *See* Flava Works, Inc. v. Gunter, 689 F.3d 754 (7th Cir. 2012).
110. Goldman v. Breitbart News Network, LLC, 302 F.Supp.3d 585, 586 (S.D.N.Y. 2018).
111. McGucken v. Newsweek LLC, No. 19 CIV. 9617 (KPF), 2022 WL 836786, at *6 (S.D.N.Y. Mar. 21, 2022). For a further critique of the "server test," *see* Jane C. Ginsburg & Luke Ali Budiardjo, *Embedding Content or Interring Copyright: Does the Internet Need the "Server Rule"?*, 42 Columbia Journal of Law & the Arts 417 (2019).
112. *See, e.g.*, Capitol Records, LLC v. ReDigi Inc., 910 F.3d 649 (2d Cir. 2018).

or frame their copyrighted content without permission, thus divesting the copyright holders of the ability to control how their works are disseminated online.[113]

The Copyright Office's Report noted many of these arguments, but simply concluded that there remained doubt about whether:

> a court might deem certain forms of inline linking or framing distinguishable from the technology in Perfect 10 for purposes of the server test.[114]

and that:

> [c]onclusive resolution of these issues will require further guidance from courts.[115]

Courts, however, have yet to provide consistent guidance; as a result, assertions that the U.S. has properly implemented the WIPO Treaties "making available" right may be overoptimistic, if not disingenuous.

---

113. Letter from Nancy E. Wolff, Counsel, PACA, Digital Media Licensing Association, Inc. to Maria A. Pallante, Register of Copyrights, U.S. Copyright Office (Sep. 15, 2014), 4 (responding on behalf of visual arts trade associations to the U.S. Copyright Office's Jul. 15, 2014 Notice of Inquiry). *See also Copyright Office Making Available Report* (n. 99), 49 (noting these arguments). *See* generally Jane C. Ginsburg & Luke Ali Budiardjo, *Liability for Providing Hyperlinks to Copyright-Infringing Content: International and Comparative Law Perspectives*, 41 Columbia Journal of Law & the Arts 153, 179-87 (2018).
114. The Ninth Circuit in *Hunley, supra* (n. 106), however, declined to confine the application of the server test to internet searches.
115. *Copyright Office Making Available Report* (n. 99), 50-51. Since the Report, the Ninth Circuit in VHT, Inc. v. Zillow Grp., Inc., 918 F.3d 723, 736 (9th Cir. 2019), in dicta, indicated that it would not interpret the Copyright Act to include a "making available" right that covered "an exclusive right to 'make available for display', a position neither supported by the statute nor embraced by this court. See Perfect 10, Inc. v. Amazon.com, Inc., 508 F.3d 1146, 1160 (9th Cir. 2007)."

Chapter 5

Is the U.S. Fair Use Doctrine Compatible with Berne and TRIPS Obligations?

Pamela Samuelson & Kathryn Hashimoto[*]

The flexible, multipurpose United States (U.S.) fair use limitation on copyright's exclusive rights is for many international authors' rights professionals a somewhat alien concept.[1] Although the U.S., like the European Union (EU), has adopted many specific exceptions to copyright's exclusive rights,[2] the most robust and widely used limit on U.S. copyrights is fair use.[3] This doctrine, which was codified in the Copyright Act of 1976 (1976 Act), directs courts to consider four factors in making fair use determinations: (1)

---

* We are grateful for input from Colleen Chien, Rochelle Cooper Dreyfuss, Daniel Gervais, Bernt Hugenholtz, Justin Hughes, Amy Kapczynski, Jerome Reichman, and Martin Senftleben. This chapter was first prepared for a presentation at the University of Cyprus Law School's "Universalism or Pluralism in International Copyright Law" conference on May 31-Jun. 1, 2018. We thank Tatiana Synodinou for the invitation to prepare this work.

1. *See, e.g.*, P. Bernt Hugenholtz & Martin R.F. Senftleben, *Fair Use in Europe: In Search of Flexibilities* (November 2011), Institute for Information Law, University of Amsterdam, https://www.ivir.nl/publicaties/download/Fair%20Use%20Report%20PUB.pdf.
2. *See* 17 U.S.C. §§108-122. *See generally* Ruth L. Okediji, *Reframing International Copyright Limitations and Exceptions as Development Policy,* at Copyright Law in an Age of Limitations and Exceptions 429 (Ruth L. Okediji ed., Cambridge Univ. Press, 2017) (setting forth various exceptions and limitations in U.S. copyright law).
3. 17 U.S.C. §107. Between 1978 and 2009, U.S. courts decided approximately 330 copyright cases in which fair use defenses were raised. One of us read all of them in the order in which they were written and analyzed them in Pamela Samuelson, *Unbundling Fair Uses*, 77 Fordham Law Review 2537 (2009).

the purpose of the challenged use; (2) the nature of the copyrighted work; (3) the amount taken; and (4) actual or potential harms to markets for the work.[4]

The thesis of this chapter is that the U.S. fair use limitation is compatible with the "three-step test" set forth in Article 9(2) of the Berne Convention for the Protection of Literary and Artistic Works[5] and in Article 13 of the Agreement on Trade-Related Aspects of Intellectual Property Rights (TRIPS).[6] These provisions regulate the permissible scope of limitations and exceptions (L&Es) in national copyright laws.[7] Under these treaties, L&Es are supposed to be for "certain special cases" and they must neither interfere with "a normal exploitation" of protected works nor "unreasonably prejudice the legitimate interests" of authors and other rightholders.[8] The generality of the U.S. fair use provision and its seeming indeterminacy have caused some commentators to assert that the U.S. fair use doctrine does not satisfy the three-step test under these treaties.[9] It is certainly true that fair use has privileged some uses that would have been

4. 17 U.S.C. §107.
5. Berne Convention for the Protection of Literary and Artistic Works, Art. 9(2) (Sep. 9, 1886), S. Treaty Doc. No. 99-27 [hereinafter Berne Convention].
6. Agreement on Trade-Related Aspects of Intellectual Property Rights, Annex IC, Art. 13 (Apr. 15, 1994), 1869 U.N.T.S. 299 [hereinafter TRIPS].
7. The three-step test has also been incorporated in other WIPO-administered treaties as well as in EU Directives. *See, e.g.*, WIPO Copyright Treaty (20 Dec. 1996) TRT/WCT/001 [hereinafter "WCT"]; Directive 2001/29/EC of the European Parliament and of the Council of 22 May 2001 on the harmonization of certain aspects of copyright and related rights in the information society, Art. 5(5), OJ L 167, 22.6.2001 [hereinafter "InfoSoc Directive"].
8. Berne Convention, Art. 9(2); TRIPS, Art. 13.
9. *See, e.g.*, Mihaly J. Ficsor, *The Law of Copyright and the Internet: The 1996 WIPO Copyright Treaties, Their Interpretation and Implementation* 284, §5.5 (Oxford Univ. Press, 2002); Herman Cohen Jehoram, *Restrictions on Copyright and Their Abuse*, 27 European Intellectual Property Law Review 359, 362 (2005); Andre Lucas, *For a Reasonable Interpretation of the Three-Step Test*, 32 European Intellectual Property Law Review 277, 278-279 (2010); Sam Ricketson, *The Berne Convention for the Protection of Literary and Artistic Works: 1886-1986* 482 (Kluwer, 1987). *See also* Ruth Okediji, *Toward an International Fair Use Doctrine*, 39 Columbia Journal of Transnational Law 75, 117 (2000), https://doi.org/10.2307/1123488 (recommending development of an international fair use doctrine, but expressing concern that fair use was inconsistent with the three-step test). Okediji's views have evolved on this issue, as have those of Ficsor and Ricketson. *See* Mihaly J. Ficsor, *Conflict of the Canadian Legislation and Case Law on Fair Dealing for Educational Purposes with the International Norms, In Particular with the Three-Step Test* 14 (September 2022), http://www.copyrightseesaw.net/en/papers [hereinafter Ficsor, Conflict] (U.S. fair use is consistent with three-step test); P. Bernt Hugenholtz & Ruth L. Okediji, *Final Report: Conceiving an International Instrument on Limitations and Exceptions to Copyright* 3 (March 2008), https://www.opensocietyfoundations.org/sites/default/files/copyright_20080506.pdf; Sam Ricketson, *WIPO Study on Limitations and Exceptions of Copyright and Related Rights in the Digital Environment* 67-69 (April 2003), WIPO Standing Comm. on Copyright and Related Rights (SCCR 9/7), http://www.wipo.int/edocs/mdocs/copyright/en/sccr_9/sccr_9_7.pdf [hereinafter Ricketson, WIPO Study] (some fair uses are consistent with the test).

infringements or required compensation in other nations, but that alone does not support the view that the fair use doctrine violates international norms.[10]

In expressing our agreement with the views of several previous commentators that U.S. fair use is compatible with the three-step test,[11] this chapter makes two main points. First, the U.S. fair use doctrine was accepted as consistent with the three-step test when the U.S. joined the Berne Convention in 1989. Its statutory embodiment recites several specific criteria that provide guidance to its interpretation, and the fair use case law has evolved to refine the types of special cases to which it applies, in accord with the first step of the test. Because fair use cases carefully assess harms that challenged uses would cause to markets for protected works and other legitimate interests, the fair use doctrine satisfies the second and third steps of the test. Second, the U.S. fair use doctrine has remained consistent with the three-step test since the U.S. joined the World Trade Organization (WTO) in 1994. Several developments since then reinforce our conclusion that the U.S. fair use doctrine satisfies the TRIPS three-step test, notwithstanding certain criticisms.[12]

---

10. *See, e.g.*, Jane C. Ginsburg, *Fair Use for Free, or Permitted-but-Paid?*, 29 Berkeley Technology Law Journal 1383, 1414-1431 (2014) (discussing licensing regimes for educational uses of copyrighted works in the EU). In France, digitization of in-copyright books was held unlawful. *See, e.g.*, Matthew Saltmarsh, *Google Loses in French Copyright Case*, N.Y. Times (Dec. 18, 2009), https://www.nytimes.com/2009/12/19/technology/companies/19google.html. Fair use decisions upholding educational uses and book digitization are discussed *infra* notes 152-157, 169-175 and accompanying text.
11. *See, e.g.*, Justin Hughes, *Fair Use and Its Politics—At Home and Abroad,* at Copyright Law in an Age of Limitations and Exceptions 234, 246-254 (Ruth L. Okediji ed., Cambridge Univ. Press, 2017); Tyler Newby, Note, *What's Fair Here Is Not Fair Everywhere: Does the American Fair Use Doctrine Violate International Copyright Law?*, 51 Stanford Law Review 1633 (1999), https://doi.org/10.2307/1229532; Martin R.F. Senftleben, *The International Three-Step Test—A Model Provision for EC Fair Use Legislation*, 1 Journal of Intellectual Property, Information Technology and Electronic Commerce Law 67 (2010); William Patry, *Fair Use, the Three-Step Test, and the Counter-Reformation*, Patry Copyright Blog (Apr. 2, 2008), https://williampatry.blogspot.com/2008/04/fair-use-three-step-test-and-european.html [hereinafter "Patry Blog"]; Richard J. Peltz, *Global Warming Trend? The Creeping Indulgence of Fair Use in International Copyright Law*, 17 Texas Intellectual Property Law Journal 267, 273 (2009); Eric Schwartz, *An Overview of the International Treatment of Exceptions*, 2 Program on Information Justice and Intellectual Property 20 (2014). *See also* Daniel J. Gervais, *(Re)structuring Copyright: A Comprehensive Path to International Copyright Reform* 66 (Edward Elgar, 2018) (recognizing that fair use may seem semantically incompatible with the three-step test, but may be normatively compatible); Pamela Samuelson, *Possible Futures of Fair Use*, 90 Washington Law Review 815, 850-853 (2015). Professors Aplin and Bently have argued that those fair uses that fall within a broad understanding of "quotations" are not subject to the three-step test. *See* Tanya Aplin & Lionel Bently, *Displacing the Dominance of the Three-Step Test: The Role of Global Mandatory Fair Use,* at The Cambridge Handbook of Copyright Limitations and Exceptions 37 (Shyamkrishna Balganesh et al. eds, Cambridge Univ. Press, 2021).
12. *See infra* ss. 5.2.3 and 5.2.4.

5.1 THE U.S. FAIR USE DOCTRINE IS CONSISTENT WITH THE BERNE THREE-STEP TEST

To situate our argument that the U.S. fair use doctrine complies with the Berne three-step test, this chapter briefly revisits the origins of that test. It then explains why the U.S. fair use doctrine was compatible with it when the U.S. joined the Berne Convention in 1989.

5.1.1 Origins of the Three-Step Test in the Berne Convention

What is now known as the "three-step test" became part of the Berne Convention as a result of the 1967 revision session held in Stockholm, Sweden.[13] An important goal for the organizers of the Stockholm meeting was to attain formal recognition of an authorial right to control reproductions of protected works in the Berne Convention. Many nations had already adopted such a right in their domestic laws. However, the treaty had not previously made that right an international standard.

Because many nations had already enacted various L&Es to their domestic reproduction rights,[14] delegates to the Stockholm meeting perceived the need to formulate a provision offering guidance on the range of permissible exceptions to the new standard exclusive right.[15] After vigorous debate about the possible contours of such a provision, the delegates ultimately settled on a framework for assessing the acceptability of L&Es.[16]

The new Article 9(1) of Berne thus provided that "[a]uthors of literary and artistic works protected by this Convention shall have the exclusive right of authorizing the reproduction of these works, in any manner or form." It was complemented by the new Article 9(2):

> It shall be a matter for legislation in the countries of the Union to permit the reproduction of such works in certain special cases, provided that such reproduction does not conflict with a normal exploitation of the work and does not unreasonably prejudice the legitimate interests of the author.

Article 9(2)'s first step focuses on exceptions for "certain special cases," that is, exceptions identifying types of uses exempted, generally recognizing,

13. For a masterful history of the three-step test, *see* Martin Senftleben, *Copyright, Limitations and the Three-Step Test: An Analysis of the Three-Step Test in International and EC Copyright Law* (Kluwer Law Int'l, 2004). Concerning the origins of the test, *see ibid.,* at 43-82.
14. Among the L&Es typically found in national laws were those permitting quotations, reproductions of public speeches, news articles, reports of current events, private uses, photocopying by libraries, print-disabled access to texts, and public safety purposes. Ricketson, WIPO Study (n. 9) at 20.
15. Senftleben (n. 13) at 48-51.
16. *Ibid.*

if implicitly, the public policy purposes the L&Es were intended to serve.[17] The second step considers whether the exception would "conflict with a normal exploitation of the work" in typical or expected markets for the works.[18] The third step considers whether the exception would otherwise "unreasonably prejudice the legitimate interests of the author," which suggests some degree of prejudice might be acceptable if counterbalancing interests were present.[19]

Although the precise meaning of each step was not firmly agreed upon at that time, Article 9(2) aimed to accommodate a wide variety of specific copyright L&Es already adopted in national copyright laws,[20] as well as the United Kingdom's (U.K.'s) more open-ended and multipurpose fair dealing provision,[21] which historically allowed unauthorized uses of copyrighted works for a variety of purposes: research or private study; criticism or review; and reporting on current events.[22] The U.K. would not have proposed or strongly supported Article 9(2) if Berne Union colleagues perceived this multipurpose provision to be unacceptable.[23]

5.1.2 The U.S. Fair Use Doctrine Is Consistent with Berne Article 9(2)

When the U.S. formally joined the Berne Convention in 1989, it asserted that its fair use doctrine was Berne-compliant.[24] Berne Union members, international copyright experts, and World Intellectual Property Organization

17. *Ibid.,* at 133-152.
18. *Ibid.,* at 168-194.
19. *Ibid.,* at 210-221.
20. *See, e.g.,* Ricketson, WIPO Study (n. 9) at 20-26.
21. For a discussion of the compatibility of fair dealing with the Berne three-step test, *see, e.g.,* Christophe Geiger, Daniel Gervais & Martin Senftleben, *The Three-Step Test Revisited: How to Use the Test's Flexibility in National Copyright Law*, 29 American University International Law Review 581, 612-616 (2014), https://doi.org/10.2139/ssrn.2356619. Owing in large part to the influence of British copyright law on its former colonies, many countries have fair dealing provisions in their national laws. *See, e.g.,* Jonathan Band & Jonathan Gerafi, *The Fair Use/Fair Dealing Handbook* 1 (March 2015), http://infojustice.org/wp-content/uploads/2015/03/fair-use-handbook-march-2015.pdf.
22. The U.K. fair dealing provision is in the Copyright, Designs and Patents Act 1988, §§29-32, and now includes additional purposes such as illustration for instruction; caricature, parody, or pastiche; and quotation.
23. *See, e.g.,* Senftleben (n. 13) at 50, 163.
24. *See generally* U.S. Adherence to the Berne Convention: Hearings Before the Subcommittee on Patents, Copyrights & Trademarks of the Committee on the Judiciary (1986) 99th Cong. 427-522 (discussing compatibility issues for U.S. copyright law with Berne requirements, although not mentioning fair use specifically). Practically speaking, whether the U.S. fair use defense is consistent with the three-step test would most likely be tested today under the auspices of a TRIPS-based challenge. However, since the Berne

(WIPO) officials accepted this assertion.[25] Notably, no one suggested that the U.S. needed to change its fair use provision,[26] even though the U.S. was required to make several significant changes to the 1976 Act to bring its law into conformity with other Berne requirements.[27]

Although Berne Union members were mostly civil law countries whose statutory L&Es were more specific than the U.S. fair use provision, this common law doctrine traced its roots back more than a century and a half before the U.S. accession to Berne.[28] Between these origins and the mid-twentieth century, the fair use case law had evolved into readily recognized categories of cases.[29] The fair use limitation and its conventional use-cases were so well-accepted that Congress codified it in the revised copyright statute.[30] Under the 1976 Act, a large number of additional judicial

---

test served as the model for the three-step test adopted in TRIPS and elsewhere, it is important to explore the interplay between the fair use doctrine and the language of Berne 9(2).

25. *See, e.g.,* Patry Blog (n. 11) (identifying numerous European copyright professionals, including the Director General of WIPO, who appeared before Congress about Berne implementation and voiced no objections to the U.S. fair use doctrine). The interpretation of the three-step test, under Berne and other international treaties, is governed by the Vienna Convention, particularly Arts 31 and 32. *See* Vienna Convention on the Law of Treaties (May 23, 1969) 1155 U.N.T.S. 331. Article 31(1) mandates that "[a] treaty shall be interpreted in good faith in accordance with the ordinary meaning to be given to the terms of the treaty in their context and in the light of its object and purpose"; Art. 31(3) recognizes any subsequent agreements or practice as additional considerations.
26. Senftleben (n. 13) at 167.
27. Congress changed rules that had previously been conditions of copyright protection (e.g., putting notices of copyright on published copies of protected works) and of exercising one's rights under U.S. copyright law (e.g., requiring registration as a precondition of bringing infringement lawsuits). The U.S. also "restored" copyrights of foreign nationals that U.S. law had considered in the public domain for failure to comply with U.S. formalities, added architectural works to the subject matters of U.S. copyright law, and extended moral rights of attribution and integrity to authors of visual art works. For a discussion of the need for these changes, *see, e.g.,* Jane C. Ginsburg & John M. Kernochan, *One Hundred and Two Years Later: The U.S. Joins the Berne Convention,* 13 Columbia-VLA Journal of Law & the Arts 1 (1988). Even with these changes, U.S. copyright law is arguably noncompliant with Berne due to its incomplete implementation of Berne moral rights norms.
28. Justice Story's decision in Folsom v. Marsh, 9 F. Cas. 342 (C.C.D. Mass. 1841) is often said to have originated the fair use doctrine. Professor Sag traces it back to 1710 in the English case law on the right of fair abridgement. *See* Matthew Sag, *The Pre-history of Fair Use*, 76 Brooklyn Law Review 1371, 1373 (2011).
29. *See* Alan Latman, Fair Use of Copyrighted Works, Study No. 14 of Copyright Law Revision, Studies Prepared for the Subcommittee on Patents, Trademarks, and Copyrights (Comm. Print, 1960). *See also* William F. Patry, *The Fair Use Privilege in Copyright Law* (2nd ed., BNA Books, 1995) (describing 17 categories of fair use cases).
30. H.R. Rep. No. 94-1476, at 65 (1976).

decisions have interpreted fair use and put more meaningful flesh on the bones of the doctrine so that its contours could reasonably be understood.[31]

The codified §107 begins by clarifying that notwithstanding the exclusive rights set forth in §106, "the fair use of a copyrighted work … is not an infringement of copyright."[32] It then identifies six favored purposes, namely, "criticism, comment, news reporting, teaching …, scholarship, or research."[33] It next sets forth four factors to be considered when making a fair use determination: "(1) the purpose and character of the use, including whether such use is of a commercial nature or is for nonprofit educational purposes; (2) the nature of the copyrighted work; (3) the amount and substantiality of the portion used in relation to the copyrighted work as a whole; and (4) the effect of the use upon the potential market for or value of the copyrighted work."[34]

By enumerating specific purposes in the fair use provision's preamble, fair use, like the U.K. fair dealing provision, articulates several types of special cases to which it applies.[35] U.S. fair use is notably more specific than the U.K. fair dealing provision by its articulation of other factors besides purposes that should be taken into account when making a judgment about whether a challenged use is fair. Consideration must also be given to how much was taken and what effect the use has had or will have on the work's market.[36] While the U.S. fair use doctrine is not limited to the statutorily favored uses, the extensive fair use case law shows that the cases fall into numerous predictable patterns.[37]

In *Unbundling Fair Uses*, one of us identified several meaningful "clusters" of fair use cases.[38] One cluster has privileged uses that promote

31. *See, e.g.*, Harper & Row Publishers, Inc. v. Nation Enters., 471 U.S. 539 (1985) (news article quoting from "heart" of unpublished book held unfair); Sony Corp. Am. v. Universal City Studios, Inc., 464 U.S. 417 (1984) (time-shift copying of broadcast television programs held fair).
32. 17 U.S.C. §107.
33. *Ibid.*
34. *Ibid.* Other factors may also be considered. *See, e.g.*, Harper & Row, 471 U.S. at 549 (characterizing list of factors as "nonexclusive"). For example, public interest considerations have sometimes played a part in the analysis. *See, e.g.*, Sony, 464 U.S. at 454.
35. 17 U.S.C. §107.
36. *Ibid.* Similar factors have been considered in some U.K. fair dealing cases, although the statute does not require it. *See, e.g.*, Hubbard v. Vosper, 2 Q.B. 84, 94 [1972] (Eng.); Lionel Bently & Brad Sherman, *Intellectual Property Law* 224-226 (4th ed., Oxford Univ. Press, 2014) (listing common factors and cases considering them).
37. *See, e.g.*, Michael J. Madison, *A Pattern-Oriented Approach to Fair Use*, 45 William & Mary Law Review 1525 (2004), https://doi.org/10.31228/osf.io/c2kdh.
38. *See* Samuelson (n. 3) at 2541-2542. The term "cluster" denotes cases involving similar fact patterns. *See also* Barton Beebe, *An Empirical Study of U.S. Copyright Fair Use Opinions, 1978-2005*, 156 University of Pennsylvania Law Review 549 (2008); Madison (n. 37); Neil Weinstock Netanel, *Making Sense of Fair Use*, 15 Lewis & Clark Law Review 715 (2011); Matthew Sag, *Predicting Fair Use*, 73 Ohio State Law Journal 47 (2012), https://doi.org/10.2139/ssrn.1769130.

freedom of expression, freedom of speech, and news reporting activities.[39] A second cluster, often involving fair quotations, has enabled ongoing authorship.[40] A third cluster has fostered learning-related uses, such as for teaching, scholarship, and research.[41] A fourth has provided some breathing room for private uses of copyrighted works.[42] A fifth has allowed uses for investigative or adjudicative purposes.[43] Other fair use case clusters have supported fair competition, ongoing innovation, and access to information.[44]

The fair use cases within each cluster have similar fact patterns, which enables prediction of reasonably likely outcomes.[45] Some fact patterns within a cluster tend to cut in favor of fair use, while others disfavor fair use in particular cases.[46] In general, a use is likely to be fair when the putative fair user took from a copyrighted work no more than was reasonable in light of his/her purposes and when that use did not supplant demand for the original.[47]

The compatibility of the U.S. fair use doctrine with the Berne three-step test is also supported by the frequency with which functions served by the U.S. fair use doctrine are achieved elsewhere through specific L&Es.[48] The right of fair quotation, for instance, is dealt with in the U.S. through fair use,[49] although under Berne and in other national or regional laws by specific exceptions.[50] Parodies and satires are frequently found to be fair uses in U.S. courts,[51] while specific exceptions permit them elsewhere.[52] Fair use privileges some news reporting uses,[53] but specific exceptions do this in other countries.[54] Uses of copyrighted works in the course of legal

39. Samuelson (n. 3) at 2546-2553.
40. *Ibid.,* at 2568-2580.
41. *Ibid.,* at 2580-2587.
42. *Ibid.,* at 2588-2592.
43. *Ibid.,* at 2592-2597.
44. *Ibid.,* at 2602-2615.
45. Because there are relatively few learning-related and private use cases and those decided have produced mixed results, these clusters are the least predictable of the fair use decisions. *Ibid.,* at 2582, 2588.
46. Transformative uses are, for instance, more likely than non-transformative (i.e., consumptive) uses to be fair. *See, e.g.,* Campbell v. Acuff-Rose Music, Inc., 510 U.S. 569, 579 (1994).
47. *See, e.g.,* Bill Graham Archives v. Dorling Kindersley, Ltd., 448 F.3d 605, 613 (2d Cir. 2006).
48. *See generally* Lionel Bently (general ed.), *International Copyright Law & Practice* §8[2] (Matthew Bender 1988 & Supp. 2018) (discussing national exceptions).
49. *See, e.g.,* New Era Publ'ns Int'l v. Carol Publ'g Grp., 904 F.2d 152 (2d Cir. 1990).
50. *See, e.g.,* Berne Convention, Art. 10(1); InfoSoc Directive, Art. 5(3)(d).
51. *See, e.g.,* Campbell v. Acuff-Rose Music Corp., 510 U.S. 569 (1994).
52. *See, e.g.,* InfoSoc Directive, Art. 5(3)(k); Nigerian Copyright Act (2004) Cap. C28, Second Schedule.
53. *See, e.g.,* Nunez v. Caribbean Int'l News, 235 F.3d 18 (1st Cir. 2000).
54. *See, e.g.,* InfoSoc Directive, Art. 5(3)(c).

proceedings is usually fair use in the U.S.,[55] but handled through specific exceptions outside the U.S.[56] Reverse-engineering of computer programs for purposes such as extracting information necessary to achieving interoperability has been addressed through fair use in the U.S.,[57] but it is lawful in the EU through a specific exception.[58] Text-mining has been held to be fair use in U.S. courts;[59] Japan adopted a text- and data-mining (TDM) exception in 2009, which it broadened by amendment in 2018, while the U.K. added a narrower exception in 2014, Singapore enacted a TDM provision in 2021, and the EU created two TDM exceptions as part of its 2019 Directive on Copyright in the Digital Single Market.[60] These six examples do not exhaust the list, but they illustrate the point: Fair use does, in practice, pertain to "certain special cases."

The second step of the Berne test considers whether a challenged L&E conflicts with the normal exploitation of the copyrighted work. This step closely aligns with fair use's fourth factor, which considers "the effect of the use upon the potential market for or value of the copyrighted work."[61] Uses have often been adjudged unfair because of proven harms to the market or perceptions that such harms were reasonably likely.[62] Because market harm is often the most important factor in fair use cases,[63] fair use complies with the conflict-with-normal-exploitation part of the three-step test.

Moreover, uses that would unreasonably prejudice the legitimate interests of their authors are unlikely to be fair. The unpublished nature of a work, for instance, has weighed against fair use when it thwarted the author's

55. *See, e.g.,* Bond v. Blum, 317 F.3d 385 (4th Cir. 2003).
56. *See, e.g.,* InfoSoc Directive, Art. 5(3)(e).
57. *See, e.g.,* Sega Enters. Ltd. v. Accolade, Inc., 977 F.2d 1510 (9th Cir. 1992).
58. *See, e.g.,* Directive 2009/24/EC of the European Parliament and of the Council of 23 April 2009 on the legal protection of computer programs, Art. 6, OJ L 111, 5.5.2009, pp. 16-22 [hereinafter "Software Directive"].
59. *See, e.g.,* Authors Guild, Inc. v. HathiTrust, 755 F.3d 87 (2d Cir. 2014).
60. *See* Copyright Act, Art. 47-7 (2009), *amended and superseded*, Act No. 30 of May 25, 2018, Art. 30-4(ii) (Japan); Copyright, Designs and Patents Act 1988, Art. 29A (U.K.); Copyright Act 2021 (2020 Rev. Ed., Act No. 22 pf 2021), s. 244 (Sing.); Directive (EU) 2019/790 of the European Parliament of the Council of 17 April 2019 on copyright and related rights in the Digital Single Market and amending Directives 96/9/EC and 2001/29/EC, OJ L130/92, 6.6.2019 [hereinafter "CDSM"]. A new Ukrainian copyright law, which includes a TDM provision, entered into force in January 2023. *See* Tian Lu, *New Ukrainian Law on Copyright and Related Rights*, IPKat (Jan. 24, 2023), https://ipkitten.blogspot.com/2023/01/guest-post-new-law-on-copyright-and.html.
61. 17 U.S.C. §107.
62. *See, e.g.,* Fox News Network, LLC v. TVEyes, Inc., 883 F.3d 169 (2d. Cir. 2018) (news monitoring services' use of Fox news was unfair because of harm to licensing market); Princeton Univ. Press v. Michigan Document Servs., Inc., 99 F.3d 1381, 1385-1391 (6th Cir. 1996) (photocopied coursepacks of in-copyright works and excerpts held unfair because of harm to licensing market).
63. *See, e.g.,* Harper & Row, 471 U.S. at 566.

right to control the first publication of the work.[64] Uses of unlawfully acquired copies of works or uses that invade the author's privacy will also cut against fair use.[65] Fair use is also less likely when the "heart" of the work is taken.[66] U.S. courts have sometimes opined that some putative fair uses should be permitted, subject to compensation.[67] The U.S. fair use defense can satisfy the Berne third step.[68]

The three-step test resembles the U.S. fair use provision in both form and function.[69] Like fair use, the three-step test itself utilizes abstractly worded criteria for assessing the acceptability of certain types of uses of protected works.[70] Common law adjudication is simply the way in which the U.S. evolves its fair use law. This explains why Justin Hughes has characterized fair use as a mechanism for creating new copyright L&Es.[71] Since the Supreme Court's decision in *Campbell v. Acuff-Rose Music, Inc.*, for example, parodies have often been held fair uses.[72] The U.S. Court of Appeals for the Ninth Circuit in *Sega Enterprises, Ltd. v. Accolade, Inc.*,[73] established that reverse-engineering computer program code for interoperability purposes is fair use.[74] Under Professor Hughes' conception, fair use is not itself an L&E within the meaning of the Berne three-step test and hence does not run afoul of it.[75]

The affinity between fair use and the three-step test helps to explain why many commentators have concluded that the U.S. fair use doctrine is

64. 471 U.S. at 552-553.
65. 471 U.S. at 563 (use of purloined copy undercut fair use argument); Monge v. Maya Magazines, Inc., 688 F.3d 1164, 1169, 1177-1178 (9th Cir. 2012) (privacy invasion disfavored fair use defense).
66. *See, e.g.*, Harper & Row, 471 U.S. at 565. *But see* Campbell, 510 U.S. at 588 (taking the heart of a work may be necessary in order to parody it).
67. *See, e.g.*, Campbell, 510 U.S. at 578 n. 10.
68. *But see* Jane C. Ginsburg, *Letter from the US: Exclusive Rights, Exceptions, and Uncertain Compliance with International Norms: Part II (Fair Use)*, Revue Internationale du Droit d'Auteur (2014) (manuscript at 23), https://scholarship.law.columbia.edu/cgi/viewcontent.cgi?article=2898&context=faculty_scholarship.
69. *See, e.g.*, Peltz (n. 11) at 273.
70. *See, e.g.*, Daniel J. Gervais, *Towards a New Core International Copyright Norm: The Reverse Three-Step Test*, 9 Marquette Intellectual Property Law Review 1, 28 (2005); Martin Senftleben, *Bridging the Differences Between Copyright's Legal Traditions—The Emerging EC Fair Use Doctrine*, 57 Journal of the Copyright Society of the U.S.A. 521, 546-550 (2009).
71. Hughes (n. 11) at 236; *See also* Senftleben (n. 13) 162-168 (positing that each favorable fair use decision allows a new, specific case of fair use in accordance with the first step as enunciated by the WTO panel).
72. Campbell, 510 U.S. at 579-582; for an example of a parody fair use case post-Campbell, *see, e.g.*, Liebowitz v. Paramount Pictures Corp., 137 F.3d 109 (2d Cir. 1998).
73. 977 F.2d 1510 (9th Cir. 1992).
74. 977 F.2d at 1514.
75. Hughes (n. 11) at 250-254.

compatible with the three-step test.[76] Some have even conceptualized the three-step test as an open L&E for the digital age.[77]

5.2 FAIR USE IS CONSISTENT WITH THE TRIPS THREE-STEP TEST

As a founding member of the WTO, the U.S. committed itself to comply with the intellectual property norms set forth in TRIPS.[78] Indeed, TRIPS negotiations were already underway when the U.S. joined Berne in 1989. The U.S. has consistently asserted that its fair use doctrine is TRIPS- as well as Berne-compatible.[79]

The close relationship between TRIPS and Berne arises from the TRIPS requirement that WTO members comply with Articles 1-21 of Berne, which obviously includes Article 9(2).[80] Yet, Article 13 of TRIPS separately provides its own three-step test.[81] After comparing the Berne and TRIPS tests, this Part explains why the U.S. fair use doctrine is TRIPS-compatible, notwithstanding recent criticisms.

5.2.1 Comparing the TRIPS Three-Step Test with the Berne Test

The TRIPS three-step test is similar to its Berne counterpart in key respects; yet, it is notably different in other respects. For one thing, Berne's Article 9(2) pertained only to exceptions to the reproduction right, whereas Article 13 extends its test to all L&Es that affect exclusive rights.[82]

Second, the wording and tone of the Berne provision is different from Article 13. The former is stated permissively: "It shall be a matter for legislation in the countries of the Union to permit. … "[83] This displays Berne's deference to its member nations as independent actors having considerable latitude to pursue their national interests in copyright legislation

76. *See, e.g.,* Australian Law Reform Commission, Copyright and the Digital Economy: Final Report 116-122, https://www.alrc.gov.au/publication/copyright-and-the-digital-economy-alrc-report-122/ (citing several academic experts in concluding that fair use complies with the three-step test).
77. *See, e.g.,* Hugenholtz & Senftleben (n. 1) at 17; Senftleben (n. 70) at 542-543.
78. *See generally* J.H. Reichman, *Universal Minimum Standards of Intellectual Property Protection under the TRIPS Component of the WTO Agreement*, 29 International Lawyer 345 (1995).
79. *See, e.g.,* Carlos M. Correa, *Trade Related Aspects of Intellectual Property Rights: A Commentary on the TRIPS Agreement* 146-148 (Oxford Univ. Press, 2007).
80. TRIPS, Art. 9(1). Expressly excluded are moral rights obligations under Art. 6*bis* and derivative provisions.
81. TRIPS, Art. 13.
82. Berne Convention, Art. 9(2); TRIPS, Art. 13. TRIPS also sets forth a similar three-step test for exceptions to other IP rights. TRIPS, Arts. 17, 30.
83. Berne Convention, Art. 9(2).

within Berne's broad framework.[84] The TRIPS provision has a more restrictive tone, for it states that "[m]embers shall confine" their L&Es to those that comply with the three-step test.[85] This wording signals the drafters' intent to constrain national freedom to adopt L&Es.

Third, Article 13's third step considers whether an L&E would unreasonably prejudice the legitimate interests of "rightholder[s]," instead of those of "authors," as in Berne.[86] This shifts the TRIPS test's focus to L&Es that impact the commercial interests of firms from WTO Member States who engage in international trade in copyrighted works.[87]

Fourth, unlike the Berne Convention, TRIPS is seemingly agnostic about whether national legislatures or other law-making bodies, such as courts or administrative agencies, are responsible for adopting L&Es subject to the three-step test.[88]

Fifth and most importantly, TRIPS provides a strong enforcement mechanism that Berne lacked.[89] Under it, one WTO Member State can challenge another's L&Es as violating Article 13's three-step test and have that dispute adjudicated.[90] If, after considering the evidence, a WTO panel agrees with the complainant, the violator is expected to change its laws in conformity with the panel's ruling. Failure to comply may be followed by negotiations for compensation or, finally, by authorization to impose trade sanctions against the violator.[91] A case in point is the EU's successful challenge to the U.S. Fairness in Music Licensing Act (FMLA),[92] to which we will shortly turn.

---

84. *See, e.g.,* Christophe Geiger, *The Role of the Three-Step Test in the Adaptation of Copyright Law to the Information Society* 3, UNESCO e-Copyright Bulletin (January-March 2007), http://unesdoc.unesco.org/images/0015/001578/157848e.pdf; Ruth L. Okediji, *The International Copyright System: Limitations, Exceptions and Public Interest Considerations for Developing Countries* 5 (Int'l Centre for Trade & Sustainable Development, Issue Paper No. 15, 2006).
85. TRIPS, Art. 13.
86. *Ibid.*; Berne Convention, Art. 9(2).
87. *See generally* Susan K. Sell, *Private Power, Public Law: The Globalization of Intellectual Property Rights* (Cambridge Univ. Press, 2003).
88. Under Berne Convention Art. 9(2), deciding what L&Es to create is "a matter for legislation"; TRIPS Art. 1(1) is more eclectic about how the L&Es should be created. *See* Hughes (n. 11) at 252.
89. TRIPS, Art. 64.
90. *See generally* Rochelle Cooper Dreyfuss & Andreas F. Lowenfeld, *Two Achievements of the Uruguay Round: Putting TRIPS and Dispute Settlement Together*, 37 Virginia Journal of International Law 275 (1997).
91. TRIPS, Art. 64. *See also* World Trade Organization, Understanding the WTO: Settling Disputes, https://www.wto.org/english/thewto_e/whatis_e/tif_e/disp1_e.htm (last visited Dec. 31, 2023).
92. Pub. L. No. 105-298, 112 Stat. 2830 (1998) (codified at 17 U.S.C. §110(5)). *See* WTO Report of the Panel WT/DS160/R of 15 June 2000 on United States—Section 110(5) of the U.S. Copyright Act [hereinafter "§110(5) Panel Report"].

5.2.2 Why Some Have Questioned the Compatibility of Fair Use with TRIPS' Three-Step Test

Critics of the U.S. fair use provision have leveled five types of TRIPS violation charges against it. First and most commonly, some say that the U.S. fair use provision is too general to satisfy the "certain special cases" criterion.[93] Second, some regard fair use as too indeterminate to satisfy the three-step test, for such claims are adjudicated on a case-by-case basis and outcomes are fact-intensive.[94] Third, some charge that certain fair use decisions of the past decade have gone too far.[95] Fourth, fair use is said to be non-compliant because it lacks an explicit factor to detect unreasonable prejudices to the legitimate interests of rightholders.[96] Fifth, courts do not require attribution of source and authorship in fair use cases, as TRIPS arguably requires.[97]

The first two charges find some support in the WTO panel decision that ruled against the FMLA's expansion of §110(5)'s exception to the U.S. public performance right, which allowed many businesses, including restaurants and retail establishments, to play recorded music without paying royalties to copyright owners.[98] Shortly after enactment of the FMLA, the EU initiated a WTO dispute against the U.S. charging that the §110(5) exception was incompatible with the TRIPS three-step test.[99]

The WTO panel agreed with the EU that the amended provision did not satisfy the "certain special cases" step of the test. It construed the term "certain" as requiring the exception to be clearly defined in national legislation, thereby creating "a sufficient degree of legal certainty."[100] It interpreted the term "special" to mean that the exception must be "limited in its field of application or exceptional in scope," as well as "narrow in a

93. *See* sources cited (n. 9). Some leading commentators are skeptical that a facial TRIPS challenge to the U.S. fair use doctrine could succeed, although an "as applied" challenge to particular fair use decisions might be plausible. *See, e.g.,* Gervais (n. 11) at 66; Hughes (n. 11) at 254-255. Professor Hughes thinks it would be "politically disastrous" for a WTO member to make a "frontal challenge" to the U.S. fair use doctrine. Hughes (n. 11) at 246.
94. *See, e.g.,* Okediji (n. 9) at 114-123.
95. Ginsburg (n. 68) at 22-23.
96. *Ibid.,* at 23.
97. Jane C. Ginsburg, *The Most Moral of Rights: The Right to be Recognized as the Author of One's Work*, 8 George Mason Journal of International Commercial Law 44, 49-52 (2016).
98. §110(5) Panel Report (n. 92). It should be noted that the panel's ruling lacks precedential effect on future disputes interpreting the three-step test. *See, e.g.,* Geiger, Gervais & Senftleben (n. 21) at 600-601.
99. §110(5) Panel Report (n. 92) at 1-7. The exception pertained to businesses with a certain square footage using a certain number of speakers. 17 U.S.C. §110(5)(B). The FMLA expanded the footage and speaker limits.
100. §110(5) Panel Report (n. 92) ¶6.108.

quantitative as well as qualitative sense."[101] The panel took note of the large percentage of businesses that §110(5)(B) would exempt and ignored the U.S.'s policy-based arguments supporting the exception.[102] The panel also decided that §110(5)(B) failed the second and third steps of the test because of the effects on rightholders' markets.[103] Under that panel's interpretation of Article 13, a failure to satisfy any step of the test would be fatal to a respondent's defense of the exception.[104]

The panel's ruling was understandable given the high proportion of establishments that the amended §110(5) exempted from copyright liability.[105] Public performances of music have a long history as an important source of revenue for copyright owners.[106]

Even so, some commentators on the §110(5) panel's interpretation of the three-step test have criticized it for taking too restrictive an approach to the first step of the test,[107] for its unwillingness to consider policy rationales for challenged L&Es,[108] and for being insufficiently deferential to national policy interests.[109] Commentators recommend that WTO panels, when ruling on future Article 13 challenges, consider the larger objectives and principles that TRIPS as a whole was intended to serve, including those set forth in Articles 7 and 8.[110]

Article 7 states that the treaty's objectives are "to promote technological innovation" as well as "the transfer and dissemination of technology, to the mutual advantage of producers and users of technological knowledge," and this should be done "in a manner conducive to social and economic welfare, and to a balance of rights and obligations."[111] Article 8 recognizes the rights of WTO members to adopt laws "necessary to protect public health and nutrition and to promote the public interest in sectors of vital importance to

---

101. *Ibid.*, ¶6.109.
102. *Ibid.*, ¶6.133.
103. *Ibid.*, ¶¶6.211, 6.266.
104. *Ibid.*, ¶6.160. Another WTO panel, which reported on a dispute over a Canadian patent L&E affecting pharmaceutical products, similarly ruled that the three steps of Art. 30's similar test are cumulative and failure to satisfy any one is fatal. *See* WTO Report of the Panel WT/DS114/R of 17 Mar. 2000 on Canada—Patent Protection of Pharmaceutical Products, ¶7.20.
105. §110(5) Panel Report (n. 92) ¶¶6.125-6.127. *See also* Helen A. Christakos, Note, *WTO Panel Report on Section 110(5) of the US Copyright Act*, 17 Berkeley Technology Law Journal 595, 604 (2002) (noting the §110(5) panel's reliance on a Congressional Research Service study).
106. §110(5) Panel Report (n. 92) ¶2.17.
107. *See, e.g.*, Christakos (n. 105) at 604.
108. *See, e.g.*, Annette Kur, *Of Oceans, Islands, and Inland Water—How Much Room for Exceptions and Limitations under the Three-Step Test?*, 8 Richmond Journal of Global Law and Business 287, 326 (2009), https://doi.org/10.2139/ssrn.1317707.
109. *See, e.g.*, Molly Land, *Rebalancing TRIPS*, 33 Michigan Journal of International Law 433, 465 (2012).
110. *See, e.g.*, Geiger, Gervais & Senftleben (n. 21) at 597-599.
111. TRIPS, Art. 7.

their socio-economic and technological development," as long as those laws otherwise comport with the agreement.[112] TRIPS is not just a trade agreement aimed at benefiting rightholders; it was intended to be an instrument through which Member States could craft their intellectual property rules to foster development, thereby furthering social as well as economic goals.[113]

5.2.3 Why Fair Use Is Consistent with the TRIPS' Three-Step Test

As a primary instigator and active promoter of the TRIPS Agreement, the U.S. sought to establish international copyright norms that were comparable to its national rules and continued to assert, as it had when joining the Berne Convention, that its fair use doctrine was compatible with its obligations under the TRIPS Agreement.[114] Just as no one suggested that the U.S. needed to amend or repeal its fair use provision in order to join the Berne Convention, no one suggested that such an amendment or repeal was necessary for the U.S. to comply with Article 13 of the TRIPS Agreement. Nor in the years since TRIPS came into effect has any WTO Member State charged the U.S. with noncompliance with TRIPS because of its open-ended fair use doctrine.[115]

A facial challenge to the U.S. fair use limitation seems highly unlikely now, especially given the numerous empirical studies in the past decade or so that verify that the U.S. fair use case law falls into predictable patterns.[116] Especially influential has been the U.S. Supreme Court's *Campbell* decision,[117] which affirmed that a rap parody version of a popular song could qualify as fair use.[118] The Court recognized that fair use provides "breathing space" for second-generation creators to build on the works of previous creators.[119] Indeed, fair use, along with the idea/expression distinction, plays a key role in keeping U.S. copyright law compatible with constitutional free

112. TRIPS, Art. 8.
113. *See, e.g.*, Land (n. 109) at 463-469; Geiger, Gervais & Senftleben (n. 21) at 597-599.
114. During a review session of the TRIPS Council in 1996, the U.S. stated that "[t]he fair use doctrine of US copyright law embodies essentially the same goals as Article 13 of TRIPS, and is applied and interpreted in a way entirely congruent with the standards set forth in that Article." *See* Council for Trade-Related Aspects of Intellectual Property Rights, Review of Legislation on Copyright and Related Rights: United States 4 (Oct. 30, 1996) WTO Doc. IP/Q/USA/1.
115. Some nations may have decided not to challenge the consistency of fair use with the three-step test, despite its seeming vulnerability under the §110(5) panel decision; yet it seems significant that no nation has regarded the fair use doctrine and its principles of openness and flexibility so abhorrent as to challenge it.
116. *See, e.g.*, Beebe (n. 38) at 609-610; Madison (n. 37) at 1645-1665.
117. Campbell v. Acuff-Rose Music, Inc., 510 U.S. 569 (1994).
118. *See, e.g.*, Samuelson (n. 11) at 817-825 (discussing post-Campbell cases).
119. Campbell, 510 U.S. at 579.

speech and free expression norms.[120] The robust application of the fair use doctrine in American copyright jurisprudence was in clear view at the time the U.S. and other nations acceded to TRIPS and has become even clearer since then.

Several additional developments since 1994 reinforce our conclusion about the consistency of the U.S. fair use doctrine with the TRIPS three-step test. First, fair use is spreading in the international community. Numerous other countries, including Sri Lanka, the Philippines, Singapore, South Korea, and Taiwan, have adopted fair use or fair use-like provisions in their national copyright laws.[121] In 2007, Israel replaced its fair dealing provision with a more open-ended fair use rule modeled on the U.S. provision.[122] In 2012, Canada amended its fair dealing provision to make it more expansive and flexible, similar to the U.S. fair use doctrine.[123] Interest in more open-ended flexible fair use-like exceptions has been growing in other countries as well.[124] Australia has considered replacing its "narrow purpose-based exceptions" with "a principles-based, fair use exception, similar to the well-established system operating in the U.S. and other countries."[125] The European Commission even solicited comments about whether the EU should consider adopting a fair use-like provision.[126] Fair use would not be expanding globally if the adoption of such an exception would put these nations out of compliance with their TRIPS obligations.

Second, an Agreed Statement to the 1996 WIPO Copyright Treaty (WCT) concerning L&Es expressed a receptive attitude toward copyright L&Es:

---

120. *See, e.g.,* Eldred v. Ashcroft, 537 U.S. 186, 219-220 (2003).
121. *See, e.g.,* Hughes (n. 11) at 257-261.
122. *See, e.g.,* Orit Fischman Afori, *An Open Standard "Fair Use" Doctrine: A Welcome Israeli Initiative*, 30 European Intellectual Property Law Review 85, 85 (2008).
123. *See*, e.g., Michael Geist, *Fairness Found: How Canada Quietly Shifted From Fair Dealing to Fair Use,* at The Copyright Pentalogy: How the Supreme Court of Canada Shook the Foundations of Canadian Copyright Law 157 (Michael Geist ed., Univ. of Ottawa Press, 2013).
124. *See*, e.g., Niva Elkin-Koren & Neil Weinstock Netanel, *Transplanting Fair Use Across the Globe: A Case Study Testing the Credibility of U.S. Opposition*, 72 Hastings Law Journal 1121, 1125-1126 (2021). *See also* Peter K. Yu, *The Quest for a User-Friendly Copyright Regime in Hong Kong,* 32 American University International Law Review 283, 339 (2016); Jerome H. Reichman, *The Limits of "Limitations and Exceptions" in Copyright Law*, at Copyright Law in an Age of Limitations and Exceptions 292, 301-304 (Ruth L. Okediji ed., Cambridge Univ. Press, 2017) (discussing efforts to liberalize copyright exceptions in Brazil, South Africa, and other nations).
125. Australian Government Productivity Commission, Intellectual Property Arrangements 9, https://www.pc.gov.au/inquiries/completed/intellectual-property/report/intellectual-property.pdf.
126. *See, e.g.,* Martin Senftleben, *The Perfect Match: Civil Law Judges and Open-Ended Fair Use Provisions*, 33 American University International Law Review 231, 232 (2017).

> It is understood that … Contracting Parties [can] carry forward and appropriately extend into the digital environment limitations and exceptions in their national laws which have been considered acceptable under the Berne Convention. Similarly, these provisions should be understood to permit Contracting Parties to devise new exceptions and limitations that are appropriate in the digital network environment.
>
> It is also understood that [the WCT] neither reduces nor extends the scope of applicability of the limitations and exceptions permitted by the Berne Convention.[127]

Notwithstanding the WCT's restatement of the three-step test,[128] the Agreed Statement reflects a consensus that existing Berne-compatible L&Es satisfied that test and that suitable new exceptions would as well. It is thus fair to infer that the Agreed Statement serves as a kind of savings clause for L&Es already in existence, including U.S.-style fair use provisions, and signals an openness to new copyright L&Es, such as those for TDM, crafted for the digital age.

Third, there is growing recognition that in an era of rapid technological change, flexible open-ended L&Es, such as fair use, can play a useful role in balancing the legitimate interests of rightholders, subsequent creators (such as fan fiction authors), and the public (such as in making backup copies of music) in regulating various uses of copyrighted works that do not have market-destructive effects.[129] These days, legislatures simply cannot anticipate new uses of works in digital form and decide which ones should be permitted through crafting of a specific exception.[130] Applying fair use or a similar flexible doctrine can enable courts to weigh various factors in order to reach principled decisions.[131]

Fourth, some European courts and commentators have been warming to open-ended limits on copyright's exclusive rights.[132] Some European cases

---

127. WCT, Agreed Statement to Art. 10.
128. WCT, Art. 10.
129. *See, e.g.,* Christophe Geiger, Jonathan Griffiths & Reto M. Hilty, *Towards a Balanced Interpretation of the "Three-Step Test" in Copyright Law,* 12 European Intellectual Property Law Review 489 (2008); Hugenholtz & Senftleben (n. 1) at 2; Hughes (n. 11) at 238-239; Samuelson (n. 3) at 2602-2615.
130. *See, e.g.,* Samuelson (n. 3) at 2602.
131. *See, e.g.,* Ian Hargreaves, *Digital Opportunity: A Review of Intellectual Property and Growth* 41-52 (May 2011) (recommending greater flexibility in U.K. and EU copyright law to accommodate future technologies); P. Bernt Hugenholtz, *Fair Use in Europe,* Communications of the ACM 26 (May 2013). The European Parliament's Committee on Legal Affairs in 2015 drafted an initial report on copyright reform calling for adoption of a fair use-style copyright exception, although this was subsequently modified in the final report. *See* Jeremy Malcolm, *European Parliamentarians to Vote Tomorrow: Fix Our Broken Copyright Law!*, Electronic Frontier Foundation (Jun. 15, 2015), https://www.eff.org/deeplinks/2015/06/european-parliamentarians-vote-tomorrow-fix-our-broken-copyright-law.
132. *See, e.g.,* Hugenholtz & Senftleben (n. 1) at 4.

have endorsed the concept of a public interest exception,[133] while others have relied upon fundamental human rights, including freedom of expression,[134] as limits on copyrights. These limits are less precise than the U.S. fair use doctrine and hence seemingly more vulnerable to challenges for noncompliance with the three-step test.[135]

Fifth, a group of leading European copyright scholars has criticized the WTO §110(5) panel decision as unduly "restrictive" and "inflexible" in its analysis of the three-step test.[136] These scholars recommend that WTO panels engage in a more comprehensive balancing approach rather than insisting that a challenged L&E must satisfy each step of the test cumulatively.[137] In considering the "certain special cases" step, it should not be necessary for L&Es to be narrow (quantitatively as well as qualitatively) and clearly defined.[138] In considering the second step, a rightholder's expectation of income may be relevant to whether there is a conflict with a normal exploitation, but not dispositive, as due regard should be paid to the purposes of the L&E.[139]

Their "Declaration for a Balanced Interpretation of the Three-Step Test in Copyright Law,"[140] offers "an appropriately balanced interpretation of the Three-Step Test under which existing exceptions and limitations within domestic law are not unduly restricted and the introduction of appropriately balanced exceptions and limitations is not precluded."[141] Such a balanced interpretation recognizes and is in harmony with so-called open-ended provisions such as fair use and fair dealing.

---

133. *See, e.g.,* Peltz (n. 11) at 277-278.
134. *Ibid.,* at 278-280. In a Belgian case involving the parodic use of a comic book cover image, the CJEU articulated a broad approach to copyright L&Es, relying not on the three-step test but instead focusing on purpose and proportionality, particularly in light of fundamental rights such as freedom of expression. Case C-201/13 Deckmyn v. Vandersteen, 3.9.2014, ECLI:EU:C:2014:2132; *see also* Martin Senftleben, *Copyright, Creators and Society's Need for Autonomous Art—The Blessing and Curse of Monetary Incentives,* at What If We Could Reimagine Copyright? 25, 46-47 (Rebecca Giblin & Kimberlee Weatherall eds., ANU Press, 2017) (noting the CJEU's characterization of strong free speech interests as user rights).
135. Canada's Supreme Court has articulated six factors to consider in fair dealing cases and indicated other factors may apply in appropriate cases. *See* CCH Canadian Ltd. v. Law Soc'y of Canada, 4.3.2004, 1 S.C.R. 339, 2004 S.C.C. 13, ¶¶53, 60 (Can.).
136. *See* Geiger, Griffiths & Hilty (n. 129) at 490.
137. *Ibid.* The §110(5) panel's decision was not appealed; hence, the WTO Appellate Body has not had the opportunity to consider the proper interpretation of the three-step test.
138. *Ibid.*
139. *Ibid.*
140. *See* Christophe Geiger, Reto Hilty, Jonathan Griffiths & Urma Suthersanen, *Declaration: A Balanced Interpretation of the Three-Step Test in Copyright Law*, 1 Journal of Intellectual Property, Information Technology, and E-Commerce Law 119 (2010) (also known as "The Munich Declaration" or "The Max Planck Declaration").
141. *Ibid.,* at 120.

Sixth, under the Obama Administration, the U.S. proposed a general fair use-friendly provision as part of the intellectual property chapter of the Trans-Pacific Partnership (TPP):

> Each party shall endeavor to achieve an appropriate balance in its copyright and related rights system, among other things by means of limitations or exceptions ..., including those for the digital environment, giving due consideration to legitimate purposes such as, but not limited to: criticism; comment; news reporting; teaching, scholarship, research, and other similar purposes; and facilitating access to published works for persons who are blind, visually impaired or otherwise print-disabled.[142]

This provision met with favor among the TPP partners and appeared in the final text of the TPP.[143] Although the Trump Administration subsequently withdrew from the TPP, the willingness of TPP partners to agree to this text signals further international acceptance of fair use-like L&Es.

Seventh, there has been growing acceptance in the international arena of conceptualizing fair use and other L&Es as providing users with "rights" as a matter of copyright law.[144] Among the scholars who have embraced this conception are Tanya Aplin and Lionel Bently of the U.K., Pascale Chapdelaine, Carys Craig, Abraham Drassinower, Michael Geist, and David Vaver of Canada, Niva Elkin-Koren of Israel, and Rochelle Cooper Dreyfuss of the U.S.[145] These scholars understand the rights of users and the larger public interest as legitimate counterweights to the interests of copyright holders in exercising their exclusive rights. Indeed, the Canadian Supreme Court has issued a series of decisions articulating the user rights concept in interpreting Canada's fair dealing provision.[146] This case law has endorsed a broad, liberal approach to fair dealing activities for research, private study,

---

142. Trans-Pacific Partnership Agreement, Art. 18.66, https://ustr.gov/sites/default/files/TPP-Final-Text-Intellectual-Property.pdf. Art. 18.65 restated the three-step test, to which Art. 18.66 was subject.
143. *Ibid.*
144. *See, e.g.*, Carys J. Craig, *Globalizing User Rights–Talk: On Copyright Limits and Rhetorical Risks,* 33 American University International Law Review 1, 33-37 (2017).
145. *See, e.g.*, Aplin & Bently (n. 11) at 37-43 (as to Berne's fair quotation right); Pascale Chapdelaine, *Copyright User Rights: Contracts and the Erosion of Property* (Oxford Univ. Press, 2015); Abraham Drassinower, *Taking User Rights Seriously,* at In the Public Interest: The Future of Canadian Copyright Law 462, 474 (Michael Geist ed., Irwin Law, 2005); Rochelle Cooper Dreyfuss, *TRIPS-Round II: Should Users Strike Back?,* 71 University of Chicago Law Review 21 (2004), https://doi.org/10.4324/9781315085463-10; Niva Elkin-Koren, *Copyright in a Digital Ecosystem: A User Rights Approach,* at Copyright Law in an Age of Limitations and Exceptions 132 (Ruth L. Okediji ed., Cambridge Univ. Press, 2017); David Vaver, *Copyright Defenses as User Rights,* 60 Journal of the Copyright Society of the U.S.A. 661 (2013). *See also* Reichman (n. 124) at 302 (describing Brazil's copyright reforms, which refer expressly to "users' rights").
146. *See, e.g.*, CCH Canadian Ltd. v. Law Soc'y of Canada, 4.3.2004, 1 S.C.R. 339, 2004 S.C.C. 13 (Can.).

and other purposes.[147] Some U.S. decisions have similarly suggested that fair use "is better viewed as a right granted by the Copyright Act" than just as a defense to infringement.[148] The U.S. Court of Appeals for the Ninth Circuit agreed.[149]

If courts and legislatures have recognized certain L&Es as conferring rights on users of copyrighted works, this should be pertinent in the analysis of the third step of the three-step test: If users have "rights" to engage in certain activities, then exercising those rights should be unlikely to cause unreasonable prejudice to rightholders' legitimate interests.[150]

5.2.4 Has U.S. Fair Use Become Noncompliant Because of Recent Decisions?

Notwithstanding the strong arguments thus far proffered for the compatibility of the U.S. fair use doctrine with the Berne and TRIPS three-step tests, two American critics have asserted that certain recent court decisions have taken such an expansive view of fair use as to put the U.S. out of compliance with its treaty obligations.[151] We respectfully disagree.

Among the decisions so criticized are the U.S. Court of Appeals for the Second Circuit's rulings in *Authors Guild, Inc. v. HathiTrust* and *Authors Guild, Inc. v. Google Inc.*[152] The Guild sued Google and the digital repository

147. A group of five Canadian copyright cases, including CCH, endorsing the user rights doctrine, is referred to as the "Copyright Pentalogy." *See generally The Copyright Pentalogy* (n. 123). Mihaly Ficsor, a former WIPO official, has criticized these cases and the user rights doctrine as being in violation of the three-step test. *See* Ficsor, Conflict (n. 9).

148. Bateman v. Mnemonics, Inc., 79 F.3d 1532, 1542 n. 22 (11th Cir. 1996) (computer software). *See also* SunTrust Bank v. Houghton Mifflin Co., 268 F.3d 1257, 1260 n. 3 (11th Cir. 2001) (literary work).

149. Lenz v. Universal Music Corp., 815 F.3d 1145, 1152-1153 (9th Cir. 2016) (copyright owner must consider whether use of a short segment of recorded music in a user-generated video was a fair use). The 1976 Act explicitly characterizes fair use as a "right" in 17 U.S.C. §108(f)(4).

150. But *see* Lionel Bently & Tanya Aplin, *Whatever Became of Global, Mandatory, Fair Use? A Case Study in Dysfunctional Pluralism,* at Is Intellectual Property Pluralism Functional? 8, 22-27 (Susy Frankel ed., Edward Elgar, 2019) (because the fair quotation right under Berne Convention Art. 10(1) is a global mandatory rule, it should not be subjected to the three-step test).

151. *See, e.g.,* The Scope of Fair Use: Hearing Before the Subcommittee on Courts, Intellectual Property, and the Internet of the House Committee on the Judiciary (2014) 113th Cong. 14-22 (statement of June M. Besek, Executive Director, Kernochan Center for Law, Media and the Arts) [hereinafter Besek Statement]; Ginsburg (n. 68).

152. Authors Guild, Inc. v. Google Inc., 804 F.3d 202 (2d Cir. 2015) (making digital copies of books for search and providing snippets a fair use); Authors Guild, Inc. v. HathiTrust, 755 F.3d 87 (2d Cir. 2014) (creation of a repository of digital content from research libraries is a fair use). An appeals court in China seemed to embrace open norms in combining U.S. fair use factors and the three-step test to consider whether "exceptional

HathiTrust for infringing copyrights when digitizing in-copyright books from research library collections. The Second Circuit ruled that this digitization was fair use because these defendants created full-text searchable databases to enable TDM.[153] The court concluded that Google's book digitization project and HathiTrust's use of the digitized copies resulted in no harm to book markets because users could not view more than a few "snippets" of text in response to search queries yielding results from in-copyright books.[154]

In considering the compatibility of these rulings with the three-step test, we note that the Court of Justice of the European Union (CJEU) has upheld library digitization of in-copyright books.[155] Many nations have broad library/archival privileges.[156] Some WTO members have either adopted or proposed specific copyright exceptions to allow text-mining and to enable better access to books for print-disabled people.[157] The *Authors Guild v. Google* and *Authors Guild v. HathiTrust* decisions thus seem unlikely cases to test the consistency of U.S. fair use with the three-step test.

These critics also challenged the U.S. Court of Appeals for the Second Circuit's ruling in *Cariou v. Prince* as violating TRIPS.[158] This lawsuit challenged Richard Prince's appropriation of 30 of Patrick Cariou's photographs of Jamaican Rastafarians for a series of paintings that sold for considerable sums.[159] Prince transformed images in the photographs by cutting them up, magnifying and rearranging many elements, and painting over some parts.[160] The Second Circuit held that Prince's use of 25 photographs was fair use as a matter of law and remanded the case for consideration of fair use defenses as to the other 5.[161] Given the many

---

circumstances" justified Google Books' scanning and making snippets as a "free use" beyond the law's enumerated exceptions; it ultimately ruled that Google had not carried its burden of persuasion. *See* Yong Wan, *Similar Facts, Different Outcomes: A Comparative Study of the Google Books Project Case in China and the United States,* 63 Journal of the Copyright Society of the U.S.A. 573 (2016).

153. *See* Besek Statement (n. 151) at 6-7; Ginsburg (n. 68) at 9-12, 17-18. They contend that the wholesale copying of millions of copyrighted works for a different purpose than the original could not be "transformative." Besek Statement (n. 151) at 5-11.
154. Google, 804 F.3d at 207-208; HathiTrust, 755 F.3d at 97, 99-100.
155. *See* Case C-117/13, Technische Universitat Darmstadt v. Eugen Ulmer KG, 11.9.2014, ECLI:EU:C:2014:2196. It should be noted that making the work available in digital format on dedicated terminals is subject to a duty to pay adequate remuneration. *Ibid.*, ¶48.
156. *See, e.g.,* Canadian Copyright Act, R.S.C. 1985, c. 42 (as amended), §30.1.
157. WIPO maintains a list of countries that have signed onto or otherwise acceded to the Marrakesh Treaty to Facilitate Access to Published Works for Persons Who Are Blind, Visually Impaired, or Otherwise Print Disabled. *See* Contracting Parties, Marrakesh VIP Treaty, https://www.wipo.int/wipolex/en/treaties/ShowResults?start_year=ANY&end_year=ANY&search_what=C&code=ALL&treaty_id=843.
158. Ginsburg (n. 68) at 19-22 (criticizing Cariou v. Prince, 714 F.3d 694 (2d Cir. 2013)).
159. Cariou, 714 F.3d at 699, 709.
160. 714 F.3d at 699-700.
161. 714 F.3d at 712.

parody/satire/burlesque exceptions in other national copyright laws,[162] the *Cariou* decision also seems an unlikely vehicle with which to challenge the U.S. fair use doctrine as noncompliant with its TRIPS obligations.[163]

A more recent case involving appropriation artist Andy Warhol, *Andy Warhol Foundation for the Visual Arts, Inc. v. Goldsmith*,[164] was decided by the U.S. Supreme Court in 2023 and may appease these critics who have decried fair use decisions such as *Cariou.* On commission from *Vanity Fair* magazine in 1984, Warhol created a series of drawings and silkscreen portraits of the musical artist Prince, based on a photo that the magazine had licensed from professional photographer Lynn Goldsmith for one-time use as a source image.[165] The district court, relying on *Cariou*, found Warhol's use of the Goldsmith photo for his Prince Series was a transformative fair use,[166] but the Second Circuit reversed and found the Prince Series was not fair use as a matter of law.[167] The Supreme Court affirmed the Second Circuit's ruling that the first fair use factor favored Goldsmith, though the Court focused solely on the Andy Warhol Foundation's 2016 commercial license to *Condé Nast* (parent company to *Vanity Fair*) to publish one of Warhol's prints as part of a special commemorative issue following the death of Prince.[168]

These critics also objected to the successful fair use defense in *Cambridge University Press v. Becker.*[169] This lawsuit, which began in 2008, challenged the policy of Georgia State University allowing professors to post book chapters for their students on electronic course reserves for nonprofit educational purposes.[170] Twice the district court, in an extensive, detailed opinion, determined that most of the challenged uses were fair use, which the plaintiff publishers appealed; twice the U.S. Court of Appeals for the Eleventh Circuit remanded the case with instructions for the district court to

---

162. *See, e.g.,* Copyright, Designs, and Patents Act 1988, §30A, added by Copyright and Rights in Performances (Quotation and Parody) Regulations 2014/2356 (U.K.). It is, moreover, highly unlikely that any major copyright industry group would lobby their government to initiate a WTO dispute challenging the Cariou decision.
163. Cariou did not have a viable moral rights claim in the U.S. His photographs did not qualify for moral rights protection under U.S. law because they were reproduced in a book. 17 U.S.C. §§101 (definition of "work of visual art"), 106A. In any event, TRIPS does not oblige WTO nations to protect moral rights. TRIPS, Art. 9(1).
164. 598 U.S. 508 (2023).
165. 598 U.S. at 515. The case arose in 2016 when Goldsmith contacted the Andy Warhol Foundation (AWF) with infringement claims following publication of Warhol's "Orange Prince" on the cover of a special magazine edition commemorating Prince. *Ibid.*
166. Andy Warhol Foundation for the Visual Arts, Inc. v. Goldsmith, 11 F.4th 26, 38 (2d Cir. 2021).
167. 11 F.4th at 32.
168. 598 U.S. at 526.
169. Ginsburg (n. 68) at 5-9 (discussing Cambridge Univ. Press v. Becker, 863 F. Supp. 2d 1190 (N.D. Ga. 2012), *rev'd sub nom.*, Cambridge Univ. Press v. Patton, 769 F.3d 1232 (11th Cir. 2014)).
170. Becker, 863 F. Supp. 2d at 1201-02.

correct aspects of its fair use analysis.[171] Ultimately, the district court found that the use of 37 of 48 works was fair use.[172] The publishers chose not to appeal from this ruling.[173]

There have been thus far no Article 13 disputes over specific judicial decisions interpreting L&Es. However, some commentators accept that overbroad interpretations of L&Es could be successfully challenged.[174] The *Becker* court's careful fact-finding about each challenged use may make it less vulnerable to a TRIPS challenge than if the court had issued a more categorical ruling (e.g., stating that posting book chapters online is per se fair use).[175]

Another recent Supreme Court case, *Google LLC v. Oracle America, Inc.*, was a landmark decision concerning computer software, in which the Court ruled that Google's use of 37 packages of the Java application program interface (API) to develop its Android platform was a fair use,[176] a decision that further vexed commentators who think that fair use and the transformativeness doctrine have been overbroadly applied.[177] As part of its fair use analysis, the Court treated as significant the nature-of-the-work factor and determined that the Java API declarations were further from the core of copyright, and it also weighed the public benefit in its evaluation of market effects to hold in favor of Google.[178] A similar decision in 2012[179] by the CJEU that a computer program's functionality cannot be protected by

---

171. In the initial bench trial, the district court found fair use with respect to 43 of 48 works. Cambridge Univ. Press v. Becker, 863 F. Supp. 2d 1190 (N.D. Ga. 2012), *rev'd sub nom.*, Cambridge Univ. Press v. Patton, 769 F.3d 1232 (11th Cir. 2014). On remand, the district court revised its analysis in accordance with the Eleventh Circuit's direction, yet nonetheless found that 44 of 48 works were fair uses. Cambridge Univ. Press v. Becker, 371 F. Supp. 3d 1218 (N.D. Ga. 2016), *vacated and remanded sub nom.*, Cambridge Univ. Press v. Albert, 906 F.3d 1290 (11th Cir. 2018).
172. Cambridge Univ. Press v. Becker, 446 F. Supp. 3d 1145 (2020).
173. Had the case continued, it is interesting to speculate whether Cambridge University Press might have approached U.K. officials to consider bringing a TRIPS complaint against the U.S. on the ground that the Becker decision was inconsistent with Art. 13, as a broad fair use ruling on educational use copying might be challengeable. *See* Gervais (n. 11) at 90-91. Whether the U.K. government would have been receptive to such a request, however, is questionable.
174. *See, e.g., ibid.*, at 66.
175. The Delhi High Court upheld a photocopy shop's fair dealing defense for copying book chapters (and sometimes whole books) for nonprofit educational uses. As dismayed as the publishers may be about that decision, the U.K. has not initiated a TRIPS violation complaint. Cambridge Professor Lionel Bently does not believe it constitutes a TRIPS violation. *See* Gopika Lekshmi, *Rapporteur, Copyright and Coursepacks: A Collision of Competing Values* (November 2016), https://www.law.ox.ac.uk/sites/default/files/migrated/copyright_and_coursepacks_final_report.pdf.
176. 593 U.S. 1 (2021).
177. *See, e.g.*, Jane C. Ginsburg, *Letter from the US, Part I: The Fair Use Pendulum Oscillates*, Revue Internationale du Droit d'Auteur (October 2021) (manuscript at 3, 18-25), https://ssrn.com/abstract=3964178.
178. Google, 593 U.S. at 26-29, 39-40.

copyright, based on interpretations of the EU's Software Directive and InfoSoc Directive, suggests compatibility of U.S. fair use with specific exceptions in EU law that, again, make a challenge of non-compliance with TRIPS unlikely.

A consideration weighing against TRIPS challenges to digital fair use cases is that copyright policymakers and courts, both domestically and internationally, have had to evolve this law to respond to the challenges of digital networked environments. As Professors Geiger, Gervais, and Senftleben have pointed out, delegates who participated in the negotiation of the WCT sought to maintain a balance between authorial rights and the public interest.[180] As stated in the WIPO Basic Proposal:

> When a high level of protection is proposed, there is reason to balance such protection against other important values in society. Among these values are the interests of education, scientific research, the need of the general public for information to be available in libraries and the interests of persons with a handicap that prevents them from using ordinary sources of information.[181]

The preamble to the WCT mirrors this priority by explicitly naming education, research, and access to information as part of a larger social good that needs to be balanced against the rights of authors and other rightholders.[182] Advanced technological developments have enabled many new uses of works, including mass digitization, digital lending, and online courses. It is difficult to imagine all of the new uses in the digital age that technology and the Internet can enable, and it is even harder to conceive what progress in the future would look like if digital improvements were stymied by overly strong copyrights. The fair use doctrine has functioned as a flexible balancing mechanism within copyright law to address new technologies such as these, which were not or could not have been contemplated by legislators at the time.[183]

It is understandable that some commentators disagree with some digital fair use decisions on the grounds that such uses should be licensed.[184] However, courts have been quite careful thus far in applying fair use to challenged technological uses. They have allowed search engines to facilitate

179. Case C-406/10, SAS Institute Inc. v. World Programming Ltd., 2.5.2012, ECLI:EU:C:2012:259; *see also supra* text accompanying (nn. 57-58).

180. Geiger, Gervais & Senftleben (n. 21) at 589-591.

181. Diplomatic Conference on Certain Copyright and Neighboring Rights Questions, Basic Proposal for the Substantive Provisions of the Treaty on Certain Questions Concerning the Protection of Literary and Artistic Works to be Considered by the Diplomatic Conference, Art. 12 n. 12.09 (Aug. 30, 1996) WIPO Doc. CRNR/DC/4 [hereinafter WIPO Basic Proposal].

182. WCT, Preamble.

183. *See, e.g.,* H.R. Rep. No. 94-1476, at 66 (1976).

184. *See, e.g.,* Ginsburg (n. 10).

access to online information, but ruled against certain news monitoring uses as excessive.[185] Even if a few court rulings interpret fair use in an overly broad way, that does not mean that the fair use doctrine itself violates the TRIPS three-step test.

5.2.5 The Attribution Challenge to Fair Use

Professor Jane Ginsburg has leveled an additional charge against fair use as noncompliant with TRIPS because U.S. fair quotation decisions do not routinely require source or author attribution.[186] This argument relies on the TRIPS Article 9(1) requirement that WTO members comply with Berne Articles 1-21,[187] which obviously includes Article 10. Berne Article 10(1) requires the adoption of an exception allowing authors to make fair quotations from other authors' published works,[188] while Article 10(3) states that "mention shall be made of the source, and of the name of the author if it appears thereon" when the fair quotation right is exercised.[189] Because U.S. courts do not require attribution in all quotation-type fair use cases, Professor Ginsburg argues, the U.S. is noncompliant with Berne and TRIPS norms.[190]

There are two main reasons why we find the attribution attack on fair use unpersuasive. First, TRIPS expressly excludes Berne-based moral rights obligations from consideration in WTO disputes.[191] It would be inconsistent with that intent to allow attribution moral rights to be litigated at the WTO through the backdoor mechanism that Ginsburg proposes.[192] Second, by shifting attention to the "legitimate interests of the *rightholder*" in Article 13,

185. *See, e.g.*, Authors Guild, Inc. v. Google Inc., 804 F.3d 202 (2d Cir. 2015) (digitizing books to index contents and enable snippets held fair use); Fox News Network, LLC v. TVEyes, Inc., 883 F.3d 169 (2d Cir. 2018) (watch-related functions of news monitoring service held unfair).
186. *See* Ginsburg (n. 97) at 49-52. Professor Ginsburg appears to have walked back from this stance in subsequent articles. *See, e.g.*, Jane C. Ginsburg, *Fifty Years of U.S. Copyright: Toward a Law of Authors' Rights?*, 50 American Intellectual Property Law Association Quarterly Journal (March 2023), https://ssrn.com/abstract=4230363 (describing 1976 Act compared to preceding statutes as more author-centric and consonant with international standards and Berne).
187. TRIPS, Art. 9(1). This does not apply to Art. 6*bis* and related rights. *Ibid.*
188. Berne Convention, Art. 10(1).
189. *Ibid.*, Art. 10(3).
190. *See* Ginsburg (n. 97) at 52. *But see* Bently & Aplin (n. 150) at 4 (unclear if Art. 10(3) is a condition of the fair quotation right or an ancillary obligation). In a separate article, these authors state that U.S. fair use cases may need to pay more attention to attribution, although they do not say failure to do so violates treaty obligations. *See* Aplin & Bently (n. 11) at 55.
191. TRIPS, Art. 9(1).
192. Article 9(1) of TRIPS excludes not only Art. 6*bis* but also "rights derived therefrom." Article 10(3)'s source/author attribution requirement would seem to be one of the rights derived from Art. 6*bis*.

instead of those of the "*author*" as Berne does, the TRIPS test is focused on the economic effects of L&Es on firms operating in the global market,[193] not on the interests of authors.

Although Professor Ginsburg is correct that U.S. courts do not always require attribution as a condition of exercising fair use, attribution is sometimes taken into account, even if not required.[194] Authors often have good reasons to cite sources and identify authors, whether out of professional courtesy, to validate arguments, or to avoid charges of plagiarism. Uses may, moreover, be easily justified as fair even though no attribution is provided or required. Some intellectual creations are, for instance, so well-known (e.g., Mickey Mouse or Harry Potter) as to be self-attributing. In cases such as *Campbell*, parodists did not need to identify the author of the parodied song. Anyone who knew the Orbison song would have realized the work that was being mocked.

Another consideration is that in enacting legislation to implement the Berne Convention, the U.S. Congress declared that the treaty was not self-executing; its implementation would be solely dependent on domestic legislation.[195] Congress has granted attribution rights only to a narrow class of works of visual art,[196] and even these rights are subject to fair uses.[197]

The utilitarian U.S. copyright law system has never embraced and is ill-suited for moral rights-infused copyright rules.[198] The U.S. position has been that attribution rights are more satisfactorily serviced through contracts, industry practices, and "pro-attribution norms."[199]

Finally, Professor Ginsburg identified no case(s) that would be suitable vehicles for a TRIPS challenge. It is highly unlikely that any WTO Member State would be so upset about the lack of a source/attribution requirement in fair use cases as to bring a TRIPS challenge on this basis.

---

193. *See, e.g.,* Neil W. Netanel, *The Next Round: The Impact of the WIPO Copyright Treaty on TRIPS Dispute Settlement,* 37 Virginia Journal of International Law 441, 453 n. 44 (1997); WIPO Basic Proposal (n. 181) Art. 1, n. 1.05.
194. *See, e.g.,* Nunez v. Caribbean Int'l News Corp., 235 F.3d 18 (1st Cir. 2000) (newspaper's attribution of authorship weighed in favor of fair use). *See also* Greg Lastowka, *Digital Attribution: Copyright and the Right to Credit*, 87 Boston University Law Review 41, 84-89 (2007) (discussing cases considering attribution in fair use cases).
195. Berne Convention Implementation Act of 1988 §2(1), Pub. L. No. 100-568, 102 Stat. 2853, 2853.
196. *See* Pub. L. No. 101-650, title VI, 104 Stat. 5089 (codified at §106A and in scattered sections of 17 U.S.C.). Another attribution-like right can be found in §1202 of the Digital Millennium Copyright Act, which provides protection against intentional removal or alteration of copyright management information. 17 U.S.C. §1202.
197. 17 U.S.C. §107 (referring to §§106, 106A).
198. *See, e.g.,* Rebecca Tushnet, *Naming Rights: Attribution and Law,* 2007 Utah Law Review 789, 789 (2007).
199. *See, e.g., ibid.* at 791. *See also* Catherine Fisk, *Credit Where It's Due: The Law and Norms of Attribution,* 95 The Georgetown Law Journal 49 (2006), https://doi.org/10.1257/rct.2422-1.0 (describing communities of norms and attribution as a feature of employment law).

5.3 CONCLUSION

The U.S. has steadfastly maintained that its copyright law, including its fair use doctrine, complies with its international treaty obligations. This chapter has offered reasons for concluding that the U.S. fair use doctrine does satisfy Berne and TRIPS three-step tests for permissible L&Es, the doubts of some commentators notwithstanding. Indeed, there has been growing recognition that open-ended L&Es such as fair use allow copyright law to be adapted to a wide range of new uses of protected works made possible by the extraordinary technological advancements in the digital age.

Chapter 6

The Compatibility of Canada's Copyright Law with International Copyright Conventions

Ysolde Gendreau

The international copyright scene today is no longer dominated by the Berne Convention. Yet, even though its practical contemporary relevance comes mostly from its incorporation in the Trade-Related Aspects of Intellectual Property Rights (TRIPS) agreement, the Berne Convention remains the golden standard when one examines a country's compliance with an international copyright text. Of course, it has stopped growing since the Paris Act of 1971; but its rules continue to address the fundamentals of copyright law to an extent such that it is still possible to debate their interpretation today and bring additional light to the understanding of copyright law. The consequence of its relative decline of influence, however, has led to the creation of new international instruments of which the 1996 World Intellectual Property Organization (WIPO) treaties are the prime examples. One therefore hopes that a look at the compatibility of Canada's copyright law with the Berne Convention and, in particular, the WIPO Copyright Treaty will help to appreciate how a state can today implement its international obligations in ways that do—or do not—take into consideration the minimum standards that have evolved since 1886.

Before addressing some contemporary issues of its compatibility with such international standards, Canadian copyright law must be understood as the by-product of its colonial history.[1] The dividing line here is 1921 when the basis of today's law was enacted.[2] Up till then, Canadian copyright law was a mix of the various copyright statutes in force in England whose application extended to its colonies with legislation adopted by the federal Parliament of Canada since 1867, the year of the birth of Canada as we know it today.[3] Canada's participation in the Berne Convention was effected then through England which, as an imperial power, would also sign the Convention in the name of its colonies.

The revision of the Convention in Berlin in 1908 created the impetus for England to undertake a sweeping review of its copyright statutes. Indeed, English copyright law at the time was spread among a great variety of statutes that could each address specific copyright issues. It would prove more coherent and modern to have just one statute in which to articulate copyright policies.[4] The Copyright Act of 1911, also known as the Imperial Copyright Act, thus became the new rallying point for copyright law in England.[5] It was also known as the Imperial Copyright Act because of the new imperial copyright policy that England wanted to further: if all the British colonies were to adopt it, then copyright law would become unified throughout the Empire. The sun would never set on the British copyright empire!

The colonialist agenda, however, met some resistance. Not all dominions within the Empire were ready to accept it without protest. The British Parliament thus devised two possibilities for its colonies: either they could accept the Imperial Act as such and merely declare that it applies within their territories or they could choose to enact their own legislation on the basis of the Imperial Act. Australia, for instance, chose the first path and voted its Copyright Act 1912 very soon after the Imperial Act.[6] Canada, however, preferred to create its own version. Work on it lasted many years and was moreover interrupted when the energy of the government was naturally diverted toward Canadian participation in the war effort. It is thus only 10 years after the Imperial Copyright Act that the Canadian Parliament finally enacted its Copyright Act in accordance with its undertaking to adopt its own

1. *See* Pierre-Emmanuel Moyse, *Canadian Colonial Copyright: The Colony Strikes Back,* at An Emerging Intellectual Property Paradigm: Perspectives from Canada (Ysolde Gendreau ed., Edward Elgar 2008) 107; Myra J. Tawfik, *History in the Balance: Copyright and Access to Knowledge,* at From "Radical Extremism" to "Balanced Copyright": Canadian Copyright and the Digital Agenda 69 (Michael Geist ed., Irwin Law 2010).
2. *Copyright Act*, 1921, S.C. 1921, c. 24.
3. *British North America Act, 1867*, 30 & 31 Vict., c. 3.
4. *See* Uma Suthersanen, *The First Global Copyright Act,* at A Shifting Empire: 100 Years of the Copyright Act 1911, 1 (Uma Suthersanen & Ysolde Gendreau eds., Edward Elgar 2013).
5. *An Act to amend and consolidate the Law relating to Copyright*, 1 & 2 Geo. V, c. 46.
6. *See* Sam Ricketson, *The Imperial Copyright Act 1911 in Australia* at A Shifting Empire: 100 Years of the Copyright Act 1911, 52 (Uma Suthersanen & Ysolde Gendreau eds., Edward Elgar 2013).

version of the 1911 Act.[7] Its actual implementation was further delayed till 1924.

Canada's self-affirmation during what was supposed to be a process of British copyright imperialism can be seen as one of the manifestations of greater ambition for national sovereignty,[8] an ambition that was growing around the Empire. On the international stage, the result of this movement was the Statute of Westminster in 1931 that gave full international autonomy to some British dominions.[9] This meant that these British dominions, i.e., countries like Canada, for example, could sign international instruments in their own right. Decisions on Canada's international obligations have since then been made in Canada.

It is in light of this history that one can divide the evolution of the compatibility of Canada's copyright law with the Berne Convention into three stages. The first one corresponds to the age of the eager and dutiful beginner. Then comes the time of the pragmatic or realistic international partner who, in the end, develops into a passive/aggressive individualist.

6.1 THE DUTIFUL/EAGER BEGINNER

The 1921 Copyright Act is based on a British statute that was designed to implement the 1908 Berlin Act of the Berne Convention. Since then, there has been the Berne Additional Protocol of 1914, which allowed Canada to restrict protection in respect of United States (U.S.) works, but most importantly the 1928 Rome Act of the Convention. That version of the Berne Convention is most famous for its inclusion of the obligation to protect two moral rights prerogatives, the right of paternity and the right of integrity, in its Article 6*bis*. Since the Canadian copyright legislation closely follows that of its English parent, one can readily imagine that the adoption of moral rights provisions in Canadian copyright law could not be taken for granted.[10] The traditional hostility of copyright countries toward moral rights is well known and can still be traced in many statutes around the copyright world.[11]

7. On this issue, *see* in general Ysolde Gendreau, *No Copyright Law is an Island,* at A Shifting Empire: 100 Years of the Copyright Act 1911, 226 (Uma Suthersanen & Ysolde Gendreau eds., Edward Elgar 2013).
8. *See* Sara Bannerman, *The Struggle for Canadian Copyright: Imperialism to Internationalism, 1842-1971* (UBC Press 2013).
9. Statute of Westminster, 1931, 22 Geo. V, c. 4.
10. Elizabeth Adeney, *Moral Rights in Canada: An Historical and Comparative View,* at An Emerging Intellectual Property Paradigm: Perspectives from Canada 163 (Ysolde Gendreau ed., Edward Elgar 2008).
11. *See* Sam Ricketson, *The Berne Convention for the Protection of Literary and Artistic Works*: *1886-1986* 455-476 (Kluwer and Centre for Commercial Law Studies 1987); Gillian Davies & Kevin Garnett, *Moral Rights* (2nd edn, Sweet & Maxwell 2016); Elizabeth Adeney, *The Moral Rights of Authors and Performers: An International and Comparative Analysis* (Oxford University Press 2006).

Canada's seriousness about its international duties translated itself in a paraphrase of Article 6*bis* for the implementation of its obligation to ensure the protection of the minimum moral rights of the Convention.[12] It has meant that this 1931 amendment of the Copyright Act made Canada the first copyright country to introduce moral rights. The use of this drafting technique has also meant that compliance with the Convention could not be challenged. Yet, if their legislative status had to be acknowledged, the fate of Canadian moral rights in the courts reveals quite a different picture.

Over the years, few cases concerning moral rights have been brought before the Canadian courts. Up until 1971, none had proved successful for the authors.[13] Courts and commentators were quick to identify reasons for its lack of appeal: they were ensconced in legal fuzziness. No term of protection was associated with them. No remedies were specified. Some terminological differences existed between the English and French versions. The requirement of evidence of prejudice to the author's honor or reputation was unavoidable. Perhaps more importantly, from a Canadian theoretical perspective, the very beginning of the provision was creating difficulties: "[i]ndependently of the author's copyright" was raising the possibility that these rights were not truly part of copyright. Because the division of powers in the Canadian federation allocates exclusive jurisdiction over copyright to the federal Parliament, a right that is not part of copyright falls out of its ambit and thus becomes the proper subject matter of the provincial legislative assemblies. Altogether, these considerations proved to be too much for Canadian authors and rendered the provision rather meaningless. It has been famously described by an eminent lawyer and commentator as "conceived in vagueness, poorly drafted, sententious in utterance, and useless in practical application."[14] A very obvious response to this situation was that, on several occasions, authors preferred to avail themselves of other "safer" copyright provisions or legal concepts that could act as substitute remedies to redress their situation.[15]

12. "Independently of the author's copyright, and even after assignment, either wholly or partially, of the said copyright, the author has the right to claim authorship of the work, as well as the right to restrain any distortion, mutilation, or other modification of the work that would be prejudicial to his honour or reputation." *Copyright Amendment Act 1931*, S.C. 1931, c. 8, s. 5. *See* Emile Colas, *Le droit moral de l'artiste sur son œuvre*, 59 Canadian Bar Review 521 (1981); David Vaver, *Author's Moral Rights in Canada,* 14 International Review of Intellectual Property and Competition Law 329 (1983) https://doi.org/10.60082/2817-5069.1834; Ysolde Gendreau, *Moral Rights* at Copyright and Confidential Information Law in Canada 161 (Gordon F. Henderson ed., Carswell, 1984).
13. *See*, for example, Gnass v. Cité d'Alma (Jun. 30, 1977), Doc. No. 200-09-0000232-745 (Quebec Court of Appeal) (unpublished); John Maryon Int'l Ltd. v. N.B. Telephone Co., (1982) 141 D.L.R. (3d) 193 (New Brunswick Court of Appeal).
14. Harold G. Fox, *Some Points of Interest in the Law of Copyright,* 6 University of Toronto Law Journal 100, 126 (1945) https://doi.org/10.2307/824283.
15. *See*, for example, Netupsky v. Dominion Bridge Co., [1972] S.C.R. 368; Gnass v. Montréal (Ville), [1974] C.S. 414; Le Nordet v. 82558 Canada Ltée, [1978] C.S. 904;

Relegated to the oubliettes of Canadian copyright practice, the Berne paraphrase came back with a vengeance in 1971 in the case of *Snow v. The Eaton Centre Ltd*, the one case that made moral rights a top copyright preoccupation in the country.[16] Red ribbons had been placed around the necks of a flight of geese sculpted by Snow and hanging from the ceiling of the main shopping center in Toronto in order to contribute to the festive look of the place for the end-of-the-year holiday season. The author succeeded in obtaining an injunction to have the ribbons removed. It took no less to have a good part of the Canadian copyright community request that moral rights should become a priority in the ongoing revision of the Copyright Act. Indeed, since the 1950s, the Canadian government had been dragging its feet from study to report to the white paper on copyright revision.[17] The task had become so daunting that it resigned itself to a layered approach that started with the more pressing issues. By the 1980s, these included everyone's favorite item on the agenda of copyright reform in those days: computer programs. Moral rights were included in the legislative program and thus became part of Phase I of the Canadian revision process in 1988.[18]

Around the end of the 1980s, something was afoot about moral rights in the copyright countries. In addition to Canada, the United Kingdom (U.K.)[19] and even the U.S.,[20] a few years later, introduced new provisions about moral rights that share common features. Australia followed suit in 2000.[21] If one takes the Canadian text as an example, one sees a definite intention to restrict the application of moral rights to specific situations. The rights are qualified by a terminology that is meant to ensure that only the

---

Patsalas v. National Ballet of Canada, (1986) 13 C.P.R. (3d) 522 (Ontario High Court). Before moral rights were introduced in the Act, authors were already using this method: LeSueur v. Morang & Co. (1911), 45 S.C.R. 95; Joubert v. Géracimo (1916), 26 B.R. 97. On moral rights in Canada before 1931, *see* Elizabeth Adeney, *Moral Rights: A Brief Excursion into Canadian History,* 15 Intellectual Property Journal 205 (2001).

16. (1983) 70 C.P.R. (2d) 105 (Ontario High Court). *See* David Vaver, *Snow v. The Eaton Centre: Wreaths on Sculpture Prove Accolade for Artists' Moral Rights,* 8 Canadian Business Law Journal 81 (1983-1984).
17. Royal Commission on Patents, Copyright, Trade Marks and Industrial Design, *Report on Copyright* (Queen's Printer 1957); Economic Council of Canada, *Report on Intellectual and Industrial Property* (Information Canada 1971); Government of Canada, *From Gutenberg to Telidon: A White Paper on Copyright* (Consumer and Corporate Affairs Canada 1984); Canada, House of Commons, Standing Committee on Communications and Culture, *Report of the Sub-Committee on the Revision of Copyright: A Charter of Rights for Creators* (Supply & Services Canada 1988).
18. An Act to Amend the Copyright Act and to Amend other Acts in Consequence Thereof, S.C. 1986-87-88, c. 15. *See* David Vaver, *The Canadian Copyright Act Amendments of 1988* 4 Intellectual Property Journal 121 (1988-1989).
19. Copyright, Designs and Patents Act 1988, c. 48, ss.77-89.
20. Visual Artists Rights Act of 1990, Pub. L. No. 101-650, 104 Stat. 5128, introducing 17 U.S. Code §106A.
21. Copyright Amendment (Moral Rights) Act 2000, introducing ss. 189-195 AZO into the Copyright Act 1968 (Cth).

more grievous cases can give rise to an action: the right of paternity may only be invoked "where reasonable in the circumstances"[22] and the demonstration of prejudice to the "author's honor or reputation" is specifically required in cases of violation of the right of integrity.[23] The difficulties that had been identified with the previous text were addressed: a term of protection was stated,[24] remedies were spelled out,[25] and no general positioning in reference to the copyright in the work was made. The text is also upfront about the thorny issue of assignment: a concession to the "purity" of moral rights was made in that the rights are declared to be unassignable; but, in the typical copyright fashion, waivers "in whole or in part" can be made.[26] Overall, the provisions are much more detailed than the previous paraphrase of the Berne Convention and exude an air of reluctance about the whole exercise.

The compliance of the new provisions with the Berne Convention does not seem to have been seriously questioned. To be sure, a country cannot be faulted for filling in where the Convention has been silent. The great irony of the situation is that, since the new regime, moral rights provisions that were supposed to provide a tighter control on the authors' willingness to enforce them have produced in 30 years more positive outcomes for authors than the looser prior text in 57 years.[27] Given this result, it would seem ill-advised to challenge the compliance of today's Canadian text with the Berne Convention.

This somewhat "happy end" to the story of moral rights in Canada should not make one forget that the initial text was already considered compliant and that the parliamentarians of 1931 were very concerned about the need to respect their new international obligations. Indeed, it was even said at the time that, if it were to realize that it could not meet these obligations because they went against Canadian interests, then Canada should simply withdraw from the Convention.[28] The debates at that time did

---

22. Copyright Act, R.S.C. 1985, c. C-24, s. 14.1 (1) (hereinafter Copyright Act).
23. Copyright Act, s. 28.2 (1).
24. Copyright Act, s. 14.2.
25. Copyright Act, s. 34 (2).
26. Copyright Act, s. 14.1 (2).
27. For example Ateliers Tango Argentin v. Festival d'Espagne et d'Amérique latine, [1997] R.J.Q. 3030 (Quebec Superior Court); Boudreau v. Lin, (1997) 75 C.P.R. (3rd) (Ontario Court, General Division); Vaillancourt v. Carbone 14, [1999] R.J.Q. 490, (Quebec Superior Court); Paris v. Ecomusée de Hull inc., [2003] J.Q. no. 18065; Dolmage v. Erskine, (2003) 23 C.P.R. (4th) 495; Enrietti—Zoppo v. Colla, [2007] O.J. No. 5183 (Ontario Small Claims Ct); Ghanotakis v. Expertises didactiques Lyons inc., 2004 CanLII 35492; Jacobs v. Canada (Attorney General), 2009 FC 628; Aînouche v. Actualités Côte-des-Neiges inc., 2010 QCCQ 11302; Coulombe v. Parc maritime du St-Laurent de l'Île d'Orléans, 2010 QCCQ 8917; Suttie v. Canada (Attorney General), 2011 FC 119; Isle-Principia (U.S.A.) inc. v. Guimond, 2013 QCCS 3730; Vallée v. Fédération québécoise des municipalités, 2013 QCCQ 14130; Chung v. Brandy Melville Canada Ltd, 2016 QCCQ 2735; Saad v. Le Journal de Montréal, 2017 QCCQ 122.
28. Bannerman (n. 8) p. 123.

not make it necessary to go that far, but they did highlight the spirit in which Canada wanted to act as a new international citizen. This spirit may partly explain its evolution over the next decades when it developed into a more assertive international citizen.

6.2 THE PRAGMATIC/REALISTIC PARTNER

The Berne Convention was to be updated on two other occasions after the Rome Conference: in Brussels in 1948 and in Paris in 1971. Because adhesion to the new versions of the Convention is not automatic and the Convention specifically regulates the relationships among states that are bound by different levels of its text,[29] Canada, like other Member States, had to decide each time whether it wanted to adhere to the new texts. Contrary to many other countries, Canada remained at the Rome level of the Berne Convention till adhesion to the Paris text became a normal consequence of membership in the TRIPS Agreement within the World Trade Organization (WTO) Agreement of 1994.[30] These decisions gave the country more leeway in the pursuit of its own interests. Nowhere is this more obvious than in its relationship with its neighbor, the U.S.

North American geography and history have made the Canada-United States relationship very special. Around the same time as Canada was undergoing its Phase I amendments of the Copyright Act, a Canada-United States Free Trade Agreement was being negotiated.[31] Even if this precursor of the North American Free Trade Agreement (NAFTA) and of the TRIPS Agreement did not contain an intellectual property chapter, one copyright issue made its way into the text: the retransmission right.[32] U.S. copyright owners were very dissatisfied with the fact that their television programs were being relayed by cable in Canada without any compensation. On the other hand, the Canadian cable companies felt all the more justified in their position that a 1954 court decision had clearly stated that the text of the Canadian Copyright Act could not be interpreted so as to impose the payment of royalties for retransmissions by cable.[33] Without any internal willingness to change the situation, only an international negotiation process could create the necessary pressure to see otherwise.

To introduce a retransmission right while one is bound only by the Rome Act of the Berne Convention means not having to worry about its

29. Berne Convention, Art. 32. *See* Ricketson (n. 11) pp. 813-825.
30. This is not to say that the issue was not discussed in the meantime. *See* David Vaver, *Copyright in Foreign Works: Canada's International Obligations,* 66 Canadian Bar Review 76 (1987).
31. Free Trade Agreement between the Government of Canada and the Government of the United States of America, T.S. No. 41355.
32. Article 2006.
33. Canadian Admiral Corporation Ltd. v. Rediffusion, Inc., [1954] Ex. C.R. 382.

Article 11*bis*(1)(ii) which states that "[a]uthors of literary and artistic works shall enjoy the exclusive right of authorizing: … any communication to the public by wire or by rebroadcasting of the broadcast of the work, when this communication is made by an organization other than the original one". Not only was Canada not bound by this text but, at the time, the U.S. also was not a member of the Convention itself. Since the impetus behind the amendment came from the U.S. and since that country had crafted its own retransmission regime without any constraint from the Convention, it only made sense that the retransmission right that the Canadian Parliament would adopt would be modeled after the U.S. system, where concern about double payment, if remuneration were to exist for the retransmission of local or network signals, was manifest.[34]

The drafting technique that the Canadian Parliament chose was to set up the operating provision of cable retransmission as an exception to copyright. Set in Part III of the Act, entitled "Infringement of copyright and moral rights and exceptions to infringement," it could thus identify the retransmissions of distant signals as an activity that requires the payment of royalties. All the other conditions apply to the retransmissions of both local and distant signals, including one that the signal be "retransmitted simultaneously and without alteration, except as otherwise required or permitted by or under the laws of Canada."[35]

It is therefore fundamental to the working of the retransmission right in Canada that its justification depends on the existence or absence of a new public that the retransmission achieves. To require the payment of royalties only when a work reaches a new audience, because the original signal is too far to be picked up by that audience or because it is retransmitted on a later occasion, stems from a different policy consideration in the framing of the law than one which is based on an authorization, as in the case of the Berne Convention, when the "communication is made by an organization other than the original one."[36]

Even if, at the time when Canada implemented the retransmission right, neither it nor the U.S. was bound by the Paris—or even Brussels—text of the Berne Convention, it may seem surprising that no attention seems to have been paid to the Berne rule as a policy guide. The Canada-United States Free Trade Agreement was but two years prior to the entry of the U.S. into the Berne Union.[37] It is difficult to imagine that the U.S. was not aware at that time of the contents of the Convention and of the role it would play in the negotiations of the TRIPS Agreement that had started in Punta del Este a year

34. Melville B. Nimmer & David Nimmer, *Nimmer on Copyright* (vol. 2, LexisNexis 2014), § 8.18[E] and especially 8.18 [E][4][a].
35. Copyright Act, s. 31(2)(c).
36. Berne Convention, Art. 11*bis*(1)(ii).
37. The agreement was reached in 1987 and the United States became a member of the Berne Convention in 1989.

earlier in 1986. Probably as befits a trade agreement, economic expediency has held greater sway than eventual treaty compliance by either one of the parties. Indeed, the issue could also have been in the mind of the Canadian negotiators who cannot not have been aware of the differences between the Rome text and the Paris text of the Convention: adhesion to the 1971 text of the Berne Convention only came in 1998. After all, it is precisely because new rules that were added during the Brussels and Paris revision conferences did not suit the Canadian Parliament that Canada stayed bound to the Rome text of the Convention for so long.

The jump from the Rome text to the Paris text of the Berne Convention did have an impact on the drafting of the Copyright Act: not only were modifications made in 1994 in the wake of the TRIPS Agreement,[38] which imposed an update of national laws in light of the last text of the Convention, but the Paris text of the Convention also worked its way into Phase II of the revision of the Canadian Copyright Act in 1997.[39] For instance, since the Rome text of the Convention did not authorize countries to entertain an ephemeral recording exception, the Supreme Court had declared in 1991 that it could not interpret the then-current Act in such a way as to create a situation that would be analogous to one where such an exception existed in the law.[40] The exception thus became part of the debates during the revision process and, just as the Paris text of the Berne Convention allowed it, the decision was made to create such an exception.[41] If the rules of the Paris text of the Berne Convention could be used to legitimate the existence of an exception, why would they not also be relevant when another important regime in the communications world, such as that of the retransmission right, is at stake? The lack of effectiveness of the Berne Convention could explain such behavior when the Convention was the only reference; but its incorporation in the TRIPS Agreement, for the very reason of the existence of the dispute resolution mechanisms of the WTO, should have made the country more interested in aligning itself with its requirements. On the contrary, it looks more like the then-present text of the Canadian Copyright Act was perceived as already compliant with the Convention and that further action based on the new international norms needed only be with respect to "new" issues rather than on the basis of some self-assessment of the existing law.

One is left with the result that the present retransmission regime in Canada, which works in synch with that of its neighbor, does not comply with the Berne Convention today unless one wants to read into the "organization other than the original one" of Article 11*bis*(1)(ii) a euphemism for an "organization that reaches a new public *because* the organization

38. World Trade Organization Agreement Implementation Act, S.C. 1994, c. 47.
39. Act to amend the Copyright Act, S.C. 1997, c. 24.
40. Bishop v. Stevens, [1990] 2 S.C.R. 467.
41. Copyright Act, ss. 30.8 and 30.9.

is other than the original one." What is interesting in this situation is that no one seems to care. That, in itself, says much about the prevailing attitude toward enforcement of the Berne Convention, even in an era of WTO mechanisms. It would not be the only example of such a climate.

One advantage of this willful blindness toward that provision of the Berne Convention is that, in Canada, it has kept the notion of a "new public" out of the interpretation of "communication." Only in the statutory cable retransmission provisions is there an indirect reference to a "new public" through the distinction between local and distant signals.[42] As much cannot be said about the discussions in the European Union about the interpretations of the European Court of Justice of the definition of "communication" where the idea of a "new public" is central to several cases on Internet transmissions.[43] These cases attract much attention and, as seen from the outside, it seems difficult to make the debate evolve beyond that new theoretical framework. A drawback of the disappearance of Article 11*bis*(1)(ii) in a debate on cable retransmission could be that its policy considerations are not perceived as key elements in the discussions on Internet transmissions.[44] Over the years, a widely recognized legal environment in which secondary transmissions are subject to the copyright owner's consent whenever they are made by an "organization other than the original one," rather than when they reach a new public, could steer the Internet discussions in a direction that has not yet been fully explored.

Such consequences on the interpretation of copyright law digress from the observation that, with the advent of intellectual property rules in trade agreements, actual compliance with the Berne Convention has surprisingly started to be of less import than one would have expected. They nevertheless tend to indicate that attitude toward international law can have an impact on what may seem like purely national legal developments. If strict business considerations now prevail over the need to abide by international agreements, then one may assume that the political attitude toward international

---

42. *See* the text accompanying (n. 35).
43. Among many, *see* Case C-306/05 Sociedad General de Autores y Editores de España (SGAE) v. Rafael Hoteles SA (2006) ECR I 11519; Case C-403/08 Football Association Premier League v. QC Leisure (2011) ECR I 09083; Case C-351/12 OSA v. Lébčebné ECLI:EU:C:2014:110 (2014); Cases C-431/09 and C-432/09 Airfield, Canal Digitaal v. Sabam and Airfield v. Agicoa Belgium BVBA (2011) ECR I 9363; Case C-466/12 Svensson v. Retriever Sverige AB (2014) ECLI:EU:C:2014:76; Case C-348/13 BestWater International GmbH v. Mebes (2014) ECLI:EU:C:2014:2315; Case C-160/15 GS Media BV v. Sanoma Media Netherlands BV (2016) ECLI:EU:C:2016:644.
44. Much has been (and is still being) written on this issue. For some examples, *see* Fabienne Brison & Sari Depreeuw, *The Right of Communication to the Public in the European Union*, at Research Handbook on Copyright Law 96 (Paul Torremans ed., 2nd edn, Edward Elgar 2017); Gaetano Dimita, *The WIPO Right of Making Available*, at Research Handbook on Copyright Law 135, 142-160 (Paul Torremans ed., 2nd edn, Edward Elgar 2017); João Pedro Quintais, *Copyright in the Age of Online Access: Alternative Compensation Systems in EU Law* 164-182 (Wolters Kluwer 2017).

compliance has markedly changed since the 1930s concern with punctilious respect of supranational norms. It is also safe to venture that when the waters of non-compliance are tested and do not bring about any rebuke, it becomes easier, on the next occasion, to display greater boldness.

6.3 THE PASSIVE/AGGRESSIVE INDIVIDUALIST

Phase II of the revision process of the Canadian Copyright Act took place in 1997, i.e., just one year after the WIPO copyright treaties of 1996. In order not to disturb the compromises reached during its negotiations among the various stakeholders, it was decided not to include digital considerations and the new international rules in it: a new revision process would be undertaken shortly thereafter. Fifteen years later, the Copyright Modernization Act, in 2012, has brought Canadian copyright law into the digital times.[45] If, from an international perspective, the avowed aim was to translate the WIPO treaties into Canadian law, the rules of the Berne Convention nevertheless continue to hover in the background. Recent judicial developments, moreover, have provided a rare opportunity to examine how the courts are to look at international copyright norms when an interpretation of the Canadian Copyright Act is sought.

One rule above all dominates the discussions about legislative compliance with international norms: the three-step test. Originating in Article 9(2) of the Berne Convention, where it was introduced in the Paris text of 1971 along with the recognition of the reproduction right, its extension to all types of uses of works was achieved in the WIPO treaties. The WIPO Copyright Treaty moreover specifically requires that the test apply to exceptions to all rights provided in the Berne Convention, i.e., beyond the reproduction right:

> Contracting Parties shall, when applying the Berne Convention, confine any limitations of or exceptions to rights provided for therein to certain special cases that do not conflict with a normal exploitation of the work and do not unreasonably prejudice the legitimate interests of the author.[46]

Because Canada had not been bound by the Paris text of the Convention before 1998, the identification of new exceptions during Phase II of the revision in 1997 was subject to the three-step test only with regard to exceptions to the right of reproduction. The 2012 amendments thus mark the beginning of the relevance of the three-step test for *all* exceptions in the Act, both old and new, since one of the purposes of these amendments was to implement the WIPO Copyright Treaty.

45. Copyright Modernization Act, S.C. 2012, c. 20.
46. WIPO Copyright Treaty, Art. 10(2).

Not enough time has elapsed since the introduction of the retransmission right in 1988 to witness a different take on the attitude toward compliance with the Berne Convention—via the WIPO treaties—in 2012. Just as in that previous example, the new relevance of the Convention does not seem to have led to a re-examination of the existing exceptions to copyright rights in light of the international standard. No exception was abrogated because of it. If reference could be made to the three-step test, it was in relation to the new exceptions that were being created. Here, examples abound.

The most notable Canadian exception must be the one for user-generated content (UGC), more commonly known as the UGC exception or the YouTube exception.[47] Designed to allow any Internet user to post videos that can incorporate existing works so they can be shared among friends and any interested persons, the UGC exception relies on several conditions that are meant to ensure that the activity remains as non-commercial as possible and that the Internet intermediaries be exempt from liability for the use of potentially infringing content:

> ***29.21*** (1) It is not an infringement of copyright for an individual to use an existing work or other subject-matter or copy of one, which has been published or otherwise made available to the public, in the creation of a new work or other subject-matter in which copyright subsists and for the individual—or, with the individual's authorization, a member of their household—to use the new work or other subject-matter or to authorize an intermediary to disseminate it, if
>
> (a) the use of, or the authorization to disseminate, the new work or other subject-matter is done solely for non-commercial purposes;
>
> (b) the source—and, if given in the source, the name of the author, performer, maker or broadcaster—of the existing work or other subject-matter or copy of it are mentioned, if it is reasonable in the circumstances to do so;
>
> (c) the individual had reasonable grounds to believe that the existing work or other subject-matter or copy of it, as the case may be, was not infringing copyright; and

47. Copyright Act, s. 29.21. *See* Teresa Scassa, *Acknowledging Copyright's Illegitimate Offspring: User-Generated Content and Canadian Copyright Law,* at The Copyright Pentalogy: How the Supreme Court of Canada Shook the Foundations of Canadian Copyright Law 431 (Michael Geist ed., University of Ottawa Press 2013); Joost Bloom, *Private International Law Aspects of User-Generated Content,* 26 Intellectual Property Journal 205 (2014); Fraser Turnbull, *The Morality of Mash-Ups: Moral Rights and Canada's Non-Commercial User-Generated Content Exception,* 26 Intellectual Property Journal 217 (2014); Marian Hebb, *UGC and Fan Fiction: Rethinking Section 29.21,* 26 Intellectual Property Journal 237 (2014).

(d) the use of, or the authorization to disseminate, the new work or other subject-matter does not have a substantial adverse effect, financial or otherwise, on the exploitation or potential exploitation of the existing work or other subject-matter—or copy of it—or on an existing or potential market for it, including that the new work or other subject-matter is not a substitute for the existing one.

(2) The following definitions apply in subsection (1).

intermediary means a person or entity who regularly provides space or means for works or other subject-matter to be enjoyed by the public.

use means to do anything that by this Act the owner of the copyright has the sole right to do, other than the right to authorize anything.

It is still too early to know what results the interpretation of that provision will yield. One can already see that there are many potential sources of abuse by users: whose "non-commercial purposes" are relevant in the analysis? How much effort is required to identify the sources and eventually the names of the authors of the used work? How alert must one be to the potentially infringing character of the used work? What is a "substantial adverse effect, financial or otherwise"? The answers to these questions would help to assess the exception in light of the three-step test that has become the reference for the validation of exceptions. Can the potentially very broad scope of the exception be countered by a strict application of the conditions to which it is subject? On paper, these conditions seem reasonable and warranted; in reality, how can a copyright owner prove that they were not respected? Is compliance with the three-step test a matter of textual conformity only or is it a test of the reality on the ground?

The UGC exception is not the only new exception that can be challenged by the three-step test. It partakes of a series of exceptions that were introduced in response to a social and judicial climate in the country that is very favorable to them. Since the beginning of the century, cases brought before the Supreme Court of Canada gave it the opportunity to enunciate a copyright philosophy that puts greater emphasis on the user of works than on their originators. The movement started with a decision on a conflict between an author and the buyer of copies of his works who decided to transfer the inks of posters and notecards onto other surfaces and thus sell them at a higher price. The Court set the issue in this broader framework:

> The *Copyright Act* is usually presented as a balance between promoting the public interest in the encouragement and dissemination of works of the arts and intellect and obtaining a just reward for the creator (or, more accurately, to prevent someone other than the creator from appropriating whatever benefits may be generated) …

The proper balance among these and other public policy objectives lies not only in recognizing the creator's rights but in giving due weight to their limited nature. In crassly economic terms it would be as inefficient to overcompensate artists and authors for the right of reproduction as it would be self-defeating to undercompensate them.[48]

This line of reasoning was taken up in the next copyright case that it heard, a case about photocopies of legal texts of all sorts that were made in the library of the Law Society of Upper Canada.[49] The Court there seized the opportunity to state that exceptions in the Copyright Act are actually "users' rights" that thus respond to the rights of copyright owners.[50] Since that 2004 decision, this conception of exceptions has stayed in the collective imagination of the Canadian copyright community. By sheer coincidence, the Supreme Court rendered five copyright decisions during the summer of 2012, two of which perpetuate that understanding of the role of exceptions in Canadian copyright law,[51] the same year that the Act was updated.

The 2012 amendments thus provided the opportunity to create many exceptions that were not directly mandated by the WIPO Copyright treaties, but that nevertheless remain subject to the three-step test. Given the surrounding ambiance, it comes as no surprise that the new exceptions can be regarded as embodying the legal analysis of exceptions by the Supreme Court. If the UGC exception can be seen as one of its manifestations that has caught the public's attention abroad, other exceptions have attracted just as much—if not more—attention at home. In particular, the arrival of a seemingly inexhaustible array of exceptions in the education sector has caused much debate, all the more so that they seemed to be the direct extension of the conclusions of one of the year's Supreme Court decisions.[52] The importance of exceptions in the Act has reached a point where, in a paper version, 47 pages out of the 201 pages that represent the entire statute are devoted to its various exceptions (thus 23.3%), the vast majority being free exceptions, in addition to the 10 pages that represent the private copying regime for musical works, performers, and record producers.

The problem with some of these exceptions does not come merely from the compatibility of their text with the three-step test, but also from their relationships among themselves. In the case of exceptions in the field of education, new exceptions were introduced to reflect the current digital

48. Théberge v. Galerie d'art du Petit Champlain inc., 2002 SCC 34, paras. 30-31. Compare this result with the one in Case C-419/13, Art & Allposters International BV EU:C:2015:27.

49. CCH Canadian Ltd. v. Law Society of Upper Canada, 2004 SCC 13.

50. *Ibid.*, para. 48.

51. SOCAN v. Bell Canada, 2012 SCC 36; Alberta (Education) v. Access Copyright, 2012 SCC 37.

52. Alberta (Education) (n. 51).

environment in which educational institutions operate today.[53] Some groundwork had already been done during the Phase II amendments in 1997 when exceptions were already part of the agenda of that reform.[54] What makes the 2012 intervention in this context more remarkable is that, in addition to a digital update of the specific exceptions that govern educational institutions, the purpose of "education" was added to the list of fair dealing purposes that coexist along specific exceptions in the Act.[55] Given the broad reading of the fair dealing purposes that the Supreme Court mandated in its 2004 decision, one is left with the impression that were a specific educational exception not be found applicable to a particular situation, fair dealing for education can then come to the rescue and validate the identified use.[56] Similarly, the UGC exception can be regarded as one of a group of new exceptions that target private uses: reproduction for private purposes,[57] fixation of signals and recording programs for later listening or viewing (time-shifting),[58] and backup copies[59] are all activities that could qualify as private copying in addition to the private copying regime for musical works that continues to exist as an independent part of the Act.[60] Does this fragmentation of a notional private copying exception have a bearing on their compliance with the three-step test? Is it easier to comply with the three-step test when the situations are separated from each other rather than when there is just one all-encompassing exception? Moreover, because these new exceptions rely on conditions that are similar to those that exist for the UGC exception,[61] the same queries about the evaluation of these conditions apply to them as well.

Space does not permit one to mention all exceptions where there may be a conflict with the three-step test. However, the educational and private copying examples can be regarded as illustrations that the matter can quickly become more complex than the usual assessment of one or the other of these exceptions on its own. Indeed, they also raise the possibility that an examination of the compliance of exceptions could pertain to exceptions as a group rather than as individual ones. Any given exception that applies to the education sector could pass the test as a single exception, but the

---

53. Specific exceptions for education are to be found in ss. 29.3-30.4, 30.3, 30.4 of the Copyright Act.
54. *Supra* (n. 39).
55. Copyright Act, s. 29.
56. Some of the post-2012 education cases do focus on the interpretation of the exception of fair dealing for education: Copibec v. Université Laval, 2017 QCCA 199 (the parties reached a settlement agreement after the Court of Appeal of Quebec authorized the class action proceedings led by the collective management society); York University v. Access Copyright, 2021 SCC 32. *See* also Access Copyright v. British Columbia Ministry of Education, 2017 FCA 16.
57. Copyright Act, s. 29.22.
58. Copyright Act, s. 29.23.
59. Copyright Act, s. 29.24.
60. Copyright Act, Part VIII, ss. 79-88.
61. *See* the text accompanying, (n. 47).

appraisal of the situation could lead to a different result if the analysis were conducted on the basis of several exceptions as a whole. One question remains unanswered with respect to the educational exceptions in Canada: even if there continue to be uses in the educational context that involve the payment of royalties,[62] what proportion do they represent in the overall use of works in the educational section? This question can be avoided when the test is handled one exception at a time, but it becomes legitimate when the entire scheme is judged as a whole.

Whatever approach one takes, the fact remains that, more than 10 years later, the compatibility of the Canadian exceptions with the three-step test has not been judged sufficiently serious to warrant international input. The trade agreements that Canada has signed since then make no mention of them;[63] a request for a WTO panel has not happened. One can venture some reasons for this lack of interest. The Canadian market is small and the country is not a superpower, hence its sphere of copyright influence is practically non-existent.[64] Yet, the international community was quick to react when another intellectual property right was at stake: both the European Union and the U.S. brought Canada to WTO panels shortly after some exceptions were introduced in the Patent Act.[65] One can imagine that this experience would have made the Canadian government particularly careful when treading on other intellectual property exceptions and one may thus tend to judge that the government's assessment of the situation made it confident that its copyright exceptions would not be challenged. Another, more cynical, explanation for the indifference toward Canadian copyright law is that, more than 20 years after it was rendered, the decision in the WTO panel decision on section 110(5) of the U.S. Copyright Act[66] has not brought about its modification. Whereas the possibility of resorting to the WTO dispute settlement mechanisms had been considered one of the goals of the inclusion of intellectual

62. Copyright Act, ss. 30.02 and 30.03.
63. ACTA (Anti-Counterfeiting Trade Agreement, 2011); CETA (Canada–European Union Comprehensive Economic and Trade Agreement, 2016); CPTPP (Comprehensive and Progressive Trans-Pacific Partnership, 2018); CUSMA (Canada–United States–Mexico Agreement, 2018).
64. One notable exception is the UGC exception that was considered in Hong Kong; concern over its compliance with the TRIPS Agreement led to its rejection. *See* Peter K. Yu, *Can the Canadian UGC Exception Be Transplanted Abroad?,* 26 Intellectual Property Journal 177 (2014).
65. Canada—Term of Patent Protection—AB-2000-7—Report of the Appellate Body, WT/DS170/AB/R, Sep. 18, 2000; Canada—Patent Protection of Pharmaceutical Products—Complaint by the Communities and their Member States—Report of the Panel, WT/DS114/R, Mar. 17, 2000. The Patent Act was quickly amended as a result of these two decisions: An Act to amend the Patent Act, S.C. 2001, c. 10 (assented to on Jun. 14, 2001).
66. United States—Section 110(5) of the U.S. Copyright Act—Report of the Panel, WT/DS160/R, Jun. 15, 2000.

property in the negotiation of the WTO Agreement, the hopes and expectations that this new enforcement environment had raised may have been dashed when it became apparent that its application was not universal … . It is difficult to believe in the efficiency of the WTO dispute settlement process, at least when it applies to copyright matters when the major player in the field can pay a mutually agreed compensation in lieu of modifying its rules for future application. As the next-door neighbor who had to defend itself in the WTO patent cases, the Canadian government can be acutely aware of this evolution in the understanding of the WTO process as it applies to copyright.

The lack of interest in an examination of Canadian copyright law exceptions through the lens of the three-step test echoes the Canadian Supreme Court's view on the relationship between the Copyright Act and the international copyright agreements. In *SOCAN v. Entertainment Software Association*,[67] a case that focused on the making available right, the Court was invited to pronounce itself on the desirability to consider the WIPO Copyright Treaty for the interpretation of that right as it has been implemented in Canada. Two interpretations were submitted to the Court: (1) the making available right only refers to the act of offering works online, so that it would coexist independently with the public communication right when the public actually decides to access the work; two occasions for the payment of royalties would thus be created; and (2) the Act merely confirms that the public communication right is engaged the moment the work is made available to the public; only one opportunity for the negotiations of royalties would exist. According to the Court, both interpretations would reflect a proper implementation of the Treaty.

The Court favored the second one for various reasons. First, it declared that international conventions are important to understand the context of a law and that there is always a presumption of conformity. Then, it said that, even if treaties can be relevant, the role of the courts is to interpret the will of the legislator even if it means that this will go against the obligation to implement the treaties; this duty of interpretation flows from the principle of the separation of powers. "International law cannot be used to support an interpretation that is not permitted by the words of the statute."[68]

Earlier decisions by the Court have found that Internet transmissions, whether by streaming or by downloading, constitute single protected activities and must therefore generate only one royalty payment. There cannot be a payment for the making available of the work followed by a

67. 2022 SCC 30. This is the second time that the parties have been before the Supreme Court since their first dispute which gave rise to one of the five Supreme Court decisions in 2012. *See* SOCAN v. Entertainment Software Association, 2012 SCC 34.

68. The Court here refers to one of its earlier decisions, Kazemi Estate v. Islamic Republic of Iran, 2014 SCC 62, at para. 60.

payment for its communication (streaming) or its downloading (reproduction). Even if the act of making a work available can be seen as a physically different activity from its transmission, it does not mean that it constitutes a "separately compensable activity."[69] Anything that may lead to two distinct payment bases for one transmission activity cannot be supported by the statute and violates the principle of technological neutrality.

However, the Court's understanding of technological neutrality may be regarded as somewhat idiosyncratic. In its 2012 ESA decision, the majority of the Court had analyzed streaming as a form of communication to the public and had compared downloading to "simply a technological taxi that delivers a durable copy of the same work to the end user."[70] It was able to make this distinction because of a technical interpretation of the structure of the provision that defines the economic rights provided by the Act: streaming must be ultimately characterized as a form of public performance because it is evanescent, whereas downloading cannot come within this conceptualization because a copy of the work ends up in the memory of the device where it is downloaded. Ten years later, the Court offers a more legally informed analysis and states that transmission by downloading involves the right to authorize the reproduction of the work (the equivalent here of the act of making a work available in the streaming context) and the reproduction right for the actual downloading of the work. One can think of two major difficulties with this characterization. First, the Court seems to have no difficulty with the consequence that two rights are involved in the downloading context while it insists that there must be only one right of communication for the sake of technological neutrality when streaming is at stake.[71] Second, it does not find it strange that no right of communication is involved when the work travels from its initial site to the user's device when such communication is identified to characterize what happens between point A and point B in the streaming context. What prevents it, apart from its dogmatic stance on the technical qualification of the right of communication, from seeing a communication right followed by a reproduction right in the downloading context? Just as its preference for the combination of the right to authorize a reproduction with the right of reproduction relies on two rights, it would still result in two rights. The Court seems to find support for its analysis in a statement from the U.S. Copyright Office which equates streaming with the public performance right and downloading with the distribution right.[72] Yet, it fails to see that the reliance on the U.S. distribution

69. 2022 SCC 30, para. 59.
70. 2012 SCC 34, para. 5.
71. "The making available of a stream and a stream are both protected as a single communication to the public, while the making available of a download is protected as an authorization to reproduce, and the download is protected as a reproduction." SOCAN v. ESA, 2022 SCC 30, para. 75.
72. SOCAN v. ESA, 2022 SCC 30, para. 109.

right does not involve a second right in the transaction as it is suggesting for the Canadian downloading context.[73]

Since the ESA case only concerns the communication right because it started in a dispute between users and the performing rights organization (SOCAN), the Court's comments on the reproduction right can be seen as mere obiter dicta, though they are very detailed and would thus have good persuasive force. They are not the only problematic elements in the Court's reasoning: a look at the French-language version of the provisions and at the parallel rules governing the making available of performers' performances and sound recordings[74] offers additional arguments for challenging its interpretation of the implementation of the WIPO Copyright Treaty. Although it claims to fully respect Canada's international obligations, its very own undermining of its cherished notion of technological neutrality, which is woven throughout its reasoning, makes one doubt that it wants to make sure that Canada is aligned with international copyright law. After all, it does not shy away from stating that "[t]here is no 'international copyright' law."[75] Nor is it very much concerned by the existence of international treaties:

> while a treaty can be highly relevant to statutory interpretation, it cannot overwhelm *clear* legislative intent. The court's task is to interpret what the legislature (federally and provincially) has enacted and not subordinate this to what the federal executive has agreed to internationally.[76]

A close reading of the decision allows one to challenge that the legislative intent behind the implementation of the making available right was so clear that the Court's interpretation of the text at stake was obvious. This attitude toward international agreements is in sharp contrast with the one that prevailed in the Court's 1990 decision where the status of Canada within the Berne Convention played a major role in the interpretation of the law.[77]

Over nearly a century since it started to be an independent member of the Berne Convention, Canada has evolved from a dutiful member of the Union to an increasingly bolder individualist with no consequences to speak of. This apparent nonchalance toward what remains the historically central international instrument in the field may be the consequence of never having committed formally to its developments beyond its first participation in the Union in its own right. The current attitude would therefore be in line with its previous attitude. Another explanation, which is linked to the first one, is that Canada was brought into the Paris Act of the Berne Convention at a time

73. The Court would not be able to refer to the Canadian distribution right because it expressly applies to the distribution of tangible objects that incorporate protected works. Copyright Act, s. 3 (1) (j).
74. Copyright Act, ss. 15 (1.1)(d) and 18 (1.1)(a).
75. SOCAN v. ESA, 2022 SCC 30, para. 78.
76. *Ibid.*, para. 48 (emphasis added).
77. Bishop v. Stevens, (n. 40).

when the Convention had already become less relevant as a standard maker. A corollary of this argument is that, as new rules were added to the Convention, the country did not develop over the years the practice of conceiving its copyright law in light of the Berne standards and its offspring in the WIPO treaties. Depending on one's perspective, one may say that Canada is either paying lip service to the Berne Convention and the WIPO treaties or is openly defiant. Whichever conclusion is true, it is safe to say that Canada's contribution to international copyright law is that of a country that will look first to its own interests before participating unreservedly in the elaboration of international copyright norms.

Chapter 7

Evolutions of Copyright Law in Africa: Compatibility with International Norms and Directions

Marisella Ouma

Copyright in Africa has developed over the years to keep up with international laws and developments at a local, national and regional level. The Berne Convention has undoubtedly been the most influential legal document in drafting the national laws within the continent. This chapter shall examine the evolution of copyright within the different legal systems in Africa, the main factors that influence the development of copyright such as the ever-changing technologies, as well as the needs of the copyright industries, and the legislative framework in the increasingly globalized economy, as well as the diversity of laws.

The issue of harmonization or approximation of copyright laws has been discussed at regional level through the various economic blocs as well as the two main continental organizations that deal with intellectual property. However, no specific instrument addresses the issue. Despite the lack of a regional instrument, the copyright laws within the continent have the minimum requirements as provided under the Berne Convention and this may provide a basis for harmonization of the laws.

In the absence of a regional framework and taking into account the fact that Africa has 55 countries, which have developed their national laws independent of each other, the chapter will draw examples from some of the countries based mainly on the legal systems and the geographical area to provide a representative overview.

7.1 BACKGROUND

Africa is a large continent covering 30.37 million square kilometers with 55 countries and an estimated population of 1.4 billion as of September 2023. The official languages include English, Arabic, French, Kiswahili, Portuguese and Spanish.[1] The countries are culturally diverse and at different levels of economic development with the strongest economies being Nigeria, South Africa Egypt and Algeria. The copyright industries that have grown exponentially in the last 20 years include the film and music industry, book publishing, animation, computer games, software and the visual arts. The Nigerian entertainment industry, for instance, is estimated to employ over one million people and generates over USD 7 billion for the economy.[2]

Mali, Senegal, Nigeria, the Democratic Republic of Congo and South Africa also have vibrant music industries. Other industries that continue to grow within the copyright sector include animation, which has taken root in Ghana and Kenya, and book publishing, especially in South Africa, Nigeria and Kenya.

Most countries have copyright laws that have been enacted over the years to address new developments at national, regional and international levels. There is currently no specific continental system of copyright protection at the continental level but most countries have included the minimum provisions of the Berne Convention even in cases where they are not party to the Berne Convention.[3]

At the regional level, not much has been done to formulate intellectual property policies and laws, in particular as far as copyright and related rights are concerned. There are two regional intellectual property organizations namely the African Regional Intellectual Property Organization (ARIPO) and the *Organisation Africaine de la Propriété Intellectuelle* (OAPI) The Africa Union established the Pan African Intellectual Property Organization (PAIPO), ostensibly to administer intellectual property at a continental level but the Statute has yet to come into force. The African Continental Free Trade Area (AfCFTA) adopted the Protocol on Intellectual Property in 2023 which seeks to, among other things, establish an intellectual property office within the AfCFTA Secretariat.

1. English is used as the official language in at least 23 countries, Arabic in 8 countries, French in 29 countries, Swahili 2 countries, Portuguese in 6 countries and Spanish in 1 country. There are more than 1,500 local languages spoken in the different countries in Africa some of which are also recognized as either official or national languages.
2. *See* The Business of Entertainment Harnessing Growth Opportunities in Entertainment, Media, Arts and Lifestyle, PWS, https://www.pwc.com/ng/en/assets/pdf/the-business-of-entertainment-final.pdf (accessed May 5, 2018).
3. Uganda is a good example of a country that has a modern copyright law, which included the provisions of the Berne Convention though it is not a party to the Convention.

ARIPO only recently included copyright and related rights in its mandate.[4] OAPI has included provisions of copyright and related rights in the Bangui Agreement, according to which the organization has been established, and it also provides legislative texts on intellectual property. The two organizations have recently signed a Memorandum of Understanding where they have agreed to work on intellectual property together for the mutual benefit of their members.

There are eight sub-regional economic communities in Africa which are recognized by the African Union.[5] These are the Arab Maghreb Union (AMU/UMA), The Economic Community of West African States (ECOWAS), the East African Community (EAC), the Intergovernmental Authority on Development (IGAD), the Southern African Development Community (SADC), Common Market for Eastern and Southern Africa (COMESA), the Economic Community of Central African States (ECCAS), and the Community of Sahel-Saharan States (CENSAD). Some of the above organizations have made efforts to include copyright within their legal and administrative framework for the benefit of their respective Member States.

With the adoption of the AfCFTA Protocol on intellectual Property Rights,[6] there is room for further consideration of copyright issues in the annex on intellectual property as they are part and parcel to trade in goods and services within the continent. The regional economic blocs play a crucial role in the harmonization of copyright law in Africa.

4. Lusaka Agreement, Art. III provides for the objectives of the Organization which shall be discussed further in s. 5.4.1.1.
5. The Regional Economic Communities (RECs) of the African Union, au.int (accessed Mar. 25, 2025).
6. This is one of the Protocols to the Agreement establishing the Africa Continental Free Trade Area negotiated under what is known as Phase II of the negotiations. The protocol on Intellectual Property rights was adopted in 2023 by the State Parties. The Protocol covers the general rules on intellectual property and the specific provisions will be negotiated by State Parties under the annexes to the Protocol.

Figure 7.1 Map of Africa

Source: https://www.nationsonline.org/maps/africa-political-map.jpg.

7.2 HISTORY AND DEVELOPMENT OF COPYRIGHT LAW IN AFRICA

7.2.1 Evolution of Copyright in Different Legal Systems

Copyright in Africa developed along three different legal systems. This was greatly influenced by the colonial era and the countries that colonized them. These systems were namely (1) The Civil Law System; (2) The Common Law System; (3) and the Roman-Dutch Law/Common Law System.

7.2.1.1 The Civil Law System

The civil law system was introduced mainly in the French, Portuguese and Spanish colonies.[7] The civil law (*droit d'auteur*) seems to emphasize the author and the rights that accrue to him there-from. Copyright, in this case, is seen to be an extension of the author's personal and resonates with the natural rights theory of copyright law. The system protects the economic interests of the author as well as the author's moral rights. In this case, the moral rights are inalienable and cannot be transferred to third parties even when the economic rights are transferred to third parties.

The law clearly distinguishes between copyright and neighboring (related) rights. This is one of the distinguishing features between copyright under the civil law system and copyright under the common law system.[8]

7.2.1.2 The Common Law System

The origins of the English Copyright Act of 1911[9] can be traced back to the 1710 Statute of Anne. It codified and rationalized the protection of copyright by abolishing the common law copyright and the different subject-specific statutes that existed in England prior to 1911. The common law approach to copyright lays emphasis on the need to protect the investment and labor, which in turn will encourage production of new works.[10] The economic rights take the center stage in copyright protection. Unlike the civil law system, there is no clear distinction between copyright and neighboring (related rights).

7. Equatorial Guinea was the only country in Africa that was colonized by Spain. Although Tanzania was initially colonized by Germany, after the World War, the British took over and their legal system was largely influenced by common law.
8. Lionel Bently & Brad Sherman, *Intellectual Property Law* 32 (4th edn, Oxford University Press, 2014).
9. An Act to amend and consolidate the Law relating to Copyright, Geo.6 5, c. 46 (1911) (hereinafter "Imperial Act, 1911").
10. Bently & Sherman (n. 8).

This is the system that has shaped the development of copyright and related rights in countries that were former British Colonies as will be discussed in section 7.2.2.1 below.

7.2.1.3 The Roman-Dutch Law

The history of copyright law in South Africa predates most of the other copyright laws as it can be traced back to 1803, in the form of Roman-Dutch "common law." This was part of the Copyright Act of the Batavian Republic of which the Cape was a province.[11] By 1910, this law was applicable in all states, except the Orange Free State which had its own Roman-Dutch copyright common law.[12] In 1916, the Copyright Act of South Africa declared the Imperial Act 1911 applicable in South Africa and in effect repealed all the previous copyright laws.

The Roman-Dutch Law influenced the legal systems of several other countries, as well, such as Eswatini, Lesotho, Zimbabwe and Namibia.

7.2.2 Evolution of Copyright Law in African Countries

7.2.2.1 Colonial Era

As discussed in section 7.2.1 above, European countries implemented the copyright laws from their respective countries in the colonies. The colonial powers did not take into consideration existing traditional legal systems and their national laws became part and parcel of the legal regimes within thc colonies. In the French colonies, the French copyright law was transplanted, and enacted for the benefit of the French citizens and not the indigenous population. Likewise, in the British colonies, the laws applied were the laws of the United Kingdom (U.K.) and were not applicable to the indigenous people within the colonies.[13]

---

11. Owen H. Dean, *Handbook on South African Copyright Law* 1-3 (Juta and Company, 1987).
12. For Further Reading on History of Roman Dutch Law, *see* Robert W. Lee, *The History of the Roman Dutch Law,* 10 Journal of the Society of Comparative Legislation, n. 2 (1910), 261-268 https://www.jstor.org/stable/752590 (accessed Jun. 7, 2018) https://doi.org/10.2307/1324386.
13. They developed a three-tier system for the application of the laws including copyright laws. The first tier was the English law as applied in the U.K. and included copyright. The second tier was laws enacted within the colonies as applicable to the inhabitants and the third tier was customary/traditional law. For Further reading *see* Sandra Fullerton Joireman, *Inherited Legal Systems and Effective Rule of Law: Africa and the Colonial Legacy,* 39(4) Journal of Modern African Studies (2001) https://doi.org/10.1017/s0022278x01003755, https://pdfs.semanticscholar.org/635c/b82fbc80ca14a599428c1d06643b2293bdd9.pdf (accessed Sep. 23, 2018).

In the British colonies, the 1911 Act was enacted through various Orders-In-Council except for the self-governing territories. It came into force in various colonies and protectorates. In Ghana, the 1911 U.K. Copyright Act was enacted through the Ghana Copyright Ordinance of 1914 and the Copyright Regulations of 1918. In South Africa, the Imperial Act 1911 was declared the operative law while in Nigeria, the Order-in-Council No. 912 of 1912 extended the application of the British Copyright Act to both protectorates; Northern and Southern Nigeria.[14]

In South Africa, the 1916 Copyright Act of South Africa declared the Imperial Act 1911 applicable in South Africa and repealed the previous Copyright law.[15]

The East Africa Order in Council of 1897 made English common law applicable to Kenya, which was then a British Protectorate. This was later replaced with the Imperial Act 1911.

The situation in Morocco is not different as its legal regime was influenced by the French legal system, during the colonial period. In 1912, a law protecting literary works, among other things, was established. This was followed by the Copyright Law in 1916 and other laws enacted in 1926 and 1927. The laws took cognizance of the rights of the author to his or her work.

Egypt has been a civil law country since 1883 when the French codes replaced Islamic law. This also applies to copyright law. In Mozambique, the law on copyright and related rights was enacted in 1966.[16] This was much later than in most countries and not much attention was given to copyright issues at the legislative level.

The laws in the colonial era mainly focused on literary, musical, artistic and dramatic works and it was an offense to distribute, sell, hire or exhibit copyright infringing works within the territories. However, in some cases, for instance, in Ghana, the exceptions and limitations were granted under "fair dealing." There were no express provisions for civil remedies.[17]

7.2.2.2 Post Independence

After independence, most African countries retained the copyright laws that they had during the colonial period. This was a transitional period and not much emphasis was placed on copyright. With time and the development of the copyright industries, several countries amended their laws or enacted new laws to take into account the developments in relation to the international

14. Order-in-Council No. 912 of 1912.
15. Copyright Law in South Africa can be traced back to the Batavian Republic, as far back as 1803.
16. Decree No. 49.980 of Apr. 27, 1966, which became applicable in Mozambique.
17. Poku Adusei, Kwame Anyimadu-Antwi & Naana Halm, *Ghana,* at Access to Knowledge in Africa: The Role of Copyright 60 (Chris Armstrong, Jeremy De Beer, Dick Kawooya, Achal Prabhala & Tobias Schonewetter eds., UCT Press, 2010).

landscape as well as the technological advances at a national, regional and global level.

There were developments at the International Level such as the Rome Convention for the Protection of Performers, Producers of Phonograms and Broadcasting Organizations of 1961[18] and other copyright-related instruments, the World Trade Organization (WTO) Trade-Related Aspects of Intellectual Property (TRIPS) Agreement,[19] the WIPO Copyright Treaty (WCT),[20] the WIPO Performances and Phonograms Treaty (WPPT),[21] the Beijing Treaty for the Protection of Audiovisual Performances,[22] and the Marrakesh Treaty for the Visually Impaired.[23]

As they amended their laws, several countries took into account the provisions of the Berne Convention, which each country had to comply with under the TRIPS Agreement once it became a member of the WTO. There are several factors that were taken into consideration in the development of new laws or amendment of existing laws; (1) Need to have national laws that reflect the copyright situation in each country and which take into account the needs of the local authors and rights holders; (2) Growth of different copyright industries within and beyond the national boundaries; (3) Requirement to comply with international laws on copyright and related rights. This was particularly urgent as failure to comply with the provisions of the Berne Convention as contained in the TRIPS Agreement would attract sanctions; (4) The ever-changing technologies especially in the digital environment present challenges and opportunities which need to be addressed by copyright law.

So far, the laws that have been revised and enacted most recently are the Copyright Act of Malawi of 2016,[24] the Copyright Act of Lesotho of 2015 and the Liberia Copyright Act 2016. Kenya, Nigeria and South Africa are in the process of reviewing their laws. Eswatini still applies the 1912 Copyright Act but they are in the process of amending the law to take into account these developments.

7.2.3 Advent of Digital Technologies

The national laws in most African Countries as stated above are in compliance with the Berne Convention. The advent of digital technologies

18. International Convention for the Protection of Performers, Producers of Phonograms and Broadcasting Organizations (Oct. 26, 1961) TRT/ROME/001.
19. Agreement on Trade-Related Aspects of Intellectual Property Rights (Apr. 15, 1994), 1869 UNTS 2.
20. WIPO Copyright Treaty (Dec. 20, 1996) TRT/WCT/001.
21. WIPO Performances and Phonograms Treaty (Dec. 20, 1996) TRT/WPPT/001.
22. Beijing Treaty on Audiovisual Performances (Jun. 24, 2012) TRT/BEIJING/001.
23. Marrakesh Treaty to Facilitate Access to Published Works for Persons Who Are Blind, Visually Impaired, or Otherwise Print Disabled (Jun. 27, 2013) TRT/MARRAKESH/001.
24. Act No. 26/2016 (hereinafter Malawi Copyright Act).

and, specifically, the Internet has brought about challenges and opportunities in copyright and related rights. It was not until recently that much attention was given to the provisions of the law in light of the new technologies.[25] The creation and use of copyright works in the digital environment have grown exponentially, especially in the last 20 years.

The basic principles of copyright law are still applicable in the digital environment and works are protected as such. The main areas that most countries are currently focusing on are the protection and administration of copyright in the digital networks including issues of access, collective management and dissemination of the works. Legislation is being amended to make specific provisions in relation to address some of these issues that have been brought about by digital technologies. In Malawi, the 2016 Act includes the right of making available as part of the right of communication to the public.[26] It also makes it illegal to circumvent technological protection measures or remove electronic right management information.[27] The law is, however, silent on the liability of Internet service providers for copyright infringement. Similar provisions are to be found in the national copyright laws of Nigeria, Uganda and Senegal.

The inclusion of the right of making available is even more important in the administration and management of rights within the digital environment. In Kenya, for instance, the current Act does not make a specific provision for the right of making available and this is presumed to be part of the right of communication to the public. This has presented some challenges.[28]

Infringement over the Internet has increased over the years and other than the technological protection measures, Internet service providers or intermediaries stand the risk of being liable for infringement as a result of acts committed by users. The copyright laws are generally silent on the issue of liability of the Internet service provider but in several jurisdictions like

25. For long time, the effect of the digital environment was seen to be remote there was limited internet access and as well as access to the relevant digital technologies. However this has since changed with the average internet penetration in Africa being about 43%. (As of January 2024, Morocco, Lybia and Seychelles have the highest penetration rates of 90.7%, 88.4% and 86.7%, respectively. The lowest penetration rates are found in South Sudan, Burundi and The Central African Republic Statista: Share of internet users in Africa as of January 2024, by country www.statista.com (accessed Mar. 25, 2025).
26. Section 29 provides for the right of communication to the public and this right under s. 2 is defined to cover the right of communication to the public.
27. Malawi Copyright Act, s. 85.
28. The Copyright (Amendment) Bill of 2017 makes proposals for the inclusion of the right of making available. Prior to the repeal of s. 30A of the Act, there was a provision for the right of making available in relation to the rights of performers. The section was declared unconstitutional by the Court as there was no proof of public participation when the law was amended to include the said provision.

South Africa, Ghana, Malawi, Zambia and Zimbabwe, the provisions are included in the Electronic Transactions Laws.[29]

7.3 COMPATIBILITY WITH INTERNATIONAL LAWS

It has become clear that several countries developed their copyright laws based on the laws that had been transplanted into the countries during the colonial era. The main treaties considered are the Berne Convention, the TRIPS Agreement, the WCT, the WPPT, the Beijing Treaty for the Protection of Audiovisual Performances and the Marrakesh Treaty.

7.3.1 The Berne Convention

The accession to the Berne Convention was done at different stages. The Order in Council issued under the 1888 Act of the U.K. extended the application of the Berne Convention to all British Dominions. Most African countries were not part of the negotiations for the Convention and only acceded to it post-independence. It is notable that Tunisia is the only African Country to have ratified the Berne Convention.[30]

Angola, Eretria, Ethiopia, South Sudan and Sierra Leone have yet to accede to the Berne Convention but they have included the minimum provisions of the Convention in their national laws. It is notable that Sierra Leone, Ethiopia and Angola are members of the WTO and thus are bound by the provisions of the Berne Convention through the TRIPS agreement.[31]

Table 7.1 Parties to the Berne Convention

Contracting Party	*Signature*	*Instrument*	*Date*	*Date in Force*
Algeria	-	Accession	January 19, 1998	April 19, 1998
Benin	-	Declaration of Continued Application	January 3, 1961	August 1, 1960
Botswana	-	Accession	January 15, 1998	April 16, 1998

29. The Copyright (Amendment Act) of Kenya, seeks to include the provisions in relation to the liability of Internet Service Providers in the Act.
30. Tunisia signed the Berne Convention on Sep. 9, 1886, ratified it on Sep. 5, 1887, and it came into force on Dec. 5, 1887.
31. TRIPS Agreement, Art. 9 provides that Members shall comply with Arts. 1 to 21 of the Berne Convention and the Berne Appendix. However, the signatory states are not obliged to provide for moral rights as provided for under Art. 6bis of the Berne Convention.

Burkina Faso	-	Accession	April 26, 1963	August 18, 1963
Burundi	-	Accession	January 12, 2016	April 12, 2016
Cape Verde	-	Accession	April 7, 1997	July 7, 1997
Cameroon	-	Declaration of Continued Application	September 21, 1964	January 1, 1960
Central African Republic	-	Accession	May 31, 1977	September 3, 1977
Chad	-	Accession	August 4, 1971	November 15, 1971
Comoros	-	Accession	January 17, 2005	April 17, 2005
Congo	-	Declaration of Continued Application	May 8, 1962	August 15, 1960
Cote d' Ivoire	-	Accession	July 8, 1961	January 1, 1962
Democratic Republic of the Congo	-	Declaration of Continued Application	October 8, 1963	June 30, 1960
Djibouti	-	Accession	February 13, 2002	May 13, 2002
Egypt	-	Accession	March 2, 1977	June 7, 1977
Equatorial Guinea	-	Accession	March 26, 1997	June 26, 1997
Eswatini	-	Accession	September 14, 1998	December 15, 1998
Gabon	-	Accession	December 19, 1961	March 26, 1962
Gambia	-	Accession	December 7, 1992	March 7, 1993
Ghana	-	Accession	July 11, 1991	October 11, 1991
Guinea	-	Accession	August 13, 1980	November 20, 1980
Guinea-Bissau	-	Accession	April 18, 1991	July 22, 1991
Kenya	-	Accession	March 11, 1993	June 11, 1993

Contracting Party	*Signature*	*Instrument*	*Date*	*Date in Force*
Lesotho	-	Accession	June 27, 1989	September 28, 1989
Liberia	-	Accession	December 8, 1988	March 8, 1989
Libya	-	Accession	June 28, 1976	September 28, 1976
Madagascar	-	Declaration of Continued Application	February 11, 1966	January 1, 1966
Malawi	-	Accession	July 12, 1991	October 12, 1991
Mali	-	Declaration of Continued Application	March 19, 1962	March 19, 1962
Mauritania	-	Accession	October 16, 1972	February 6, 1973
Mauritius	-	Accession	February 9,1989	May 10, 1989
Morocco	-	Accession	June 16, 1917	June 16, 1917
Mozambique	-	Accession	August 22, 2013	November 22, 2013
Namibia	-	Declaration of Continued Application	September 21, 1993	March 21, 1990
Niger	-	Declaration of Continued Application	May 2, 1962	August 3, 1960
Nigeria	-	Accession	June 10, 1993	September 14, 1993
Rwanda	-	Accession	November 3, 1983	March 1, 1984
Sao Tome and Principe	-	Accession	March 14, 2016	June 14, 2016
Senegal	-	Accession	June 30, 1962	August 25, 1962
South Africa	-	Declaration of Continued Application	October 3, 1928	October 3, 1928
Sudan	-	Accession	September 28, 2000	December 28, 2000
Togo	-	Accession	January 28, 1975	April 30, 1975
Tunisia	September 9, 1886	Ratification	September 5, 1887	December 5, 1887

Uganda	-	Accession	January 28, 2022	April 28, 2022
United Republic of Tanzania	-	Accession	April 26, 1994	July 25, 1994
Zambia	-	Accession	September 13, 1991	January 2, 1992
Zimbabwe	-	Declaration/ Notification of Succession	September 18, 1981	April 18, 1981

Source: *WIPO Administered Treaties, Contracting Parties to the Berne Convention,* http://www.wipo.int/treaties/en/ShowResults.jsp?treaty_id=15 (accessed September 4, 2022).

From Table 7.1, it is clear that different countries acceded to the Berne Convention after independence, but there was no urgency to do so before the TRIPS Agreement came into force.

In Ghana, the Copyright Act 85 of 1961 and the Copyright (Fee) Regulation of 1969 (Legislative Instrument 174) were promulgated. More copyrightable works were included under copyright such as cinematographic works, films, sound recordings and broadcasts.

The 1969 law was repealed and replaced by the Copyright Law 1985 [Provisional National Defence Council Law (PNDCL 110)]. Under this law, protection was extended to foreign works in compliance with the provisions of the Berne Convention. The law also made provisions to allow for flexibility specifically to take into account works such as music where the authors were not able to reduce it to sheet music. The distinctive provision of this Act was the provision of moral rights, namely integrity and attribution, which were granted in perpetuity. In 1991, Ghana acceded to the Berne Convention.

The Act was in operation until 2005 when the Copyright Act 690 of 2005 was passed. One of the main reasons for the promulgation of the 2005 Act was to ensure compliance with the Berne Convention as well as provide for the protection of copyright in the digital environment in line with the WPPT and the WCT.

Senegal passed its Copyright Law in 1973. Prior to that, the applicable law was the French Law on copyright. Since Senegal had acceded to the Berne Convention in 1961, the provisions of the Copyright Law 1973 were in line with the provisions of the Berne Convention. More recently, the Copyright Law No. 2008-09,[32] repealed the 1973 Copyright Act, while being tailored to meet the requirements of the TRIPS, WPPT and the WCT to which it is party.

32. The Law No. No. 2008-09 of Jan. 25, 2008 on Copyright and Related Rights.

In 1965, South Africa repealed the 1916 Act, which was subsequently repealed by Act No. 98 of 1978. The Act had several Amendments between 1992 and the most recent is the proposed Copyright Amendment Bill No. 2 of 2018.

7.3.2 Analysis of the Berne Convention Provisions in National Laws

The Berne Convention is the basis for national laws in most African countries.

7.3.2.1 Basic Principles of the Berne Convention

The three basic principles of the Berne Convention are namely: (1) National Treatment; (2) Automatic Protection; and (3) Independence of Protection are enshrined in the national laws. The laws provide for territorial protection of copyright and related rights but this is extended to authors in countries who are Members of the Berne Convention.

For instance, under the South African Copyright Act, copyright subsists automatically in works that are eligible for copyright protection, where the author or one of the joint authors qualifies either by virtue of domicile, citizenship or residence.[33] A similar provision is found in the Copyright Act of Kenya[34] and the Copyright Act of Malawi among others.

There is no provision for registration of copyright in most of the laws although quite a number of countries provide for voluntary registration/or notification of copyright systems. The registration or notification may not be included expressly in the law but may be inferred from existing provision. The Copyright Act of Kenya provides as one of the duties of the Copyright Office, the maintenance of a database and the provision of voluntary registration under the Copyright Regulations.[35] The Ghana Copyright Act provides that the Copyright Administrator shall maintain a register of copyright works and the main purpose of the registration is to maintain a record of the works, publicize the rights of copyright owners and give evidence of ownership and authentication of intellectual property.[36] This may be construed as a formality for copyright protection but the law expressly

33. *See* the South African Copyright Act, ss. 3(1) and 4.
34. The Copyright Act (Cap. 130 of the Laws of Kenya), s. 23.
35. Section 5(f) provides that Kenya Copyright Board shall "maintain an effective data bank on authors and their works." The Regulations go further to empower the Copyright Office to open and maintain a register of works and prescribes the mode and form of registration in Regulations 8 to 12. The Regulations however clearly state the registration of copyright is not a prerequisite to the enjoyment of copyright and related rights.
36. Ghana Copyright Act No. 690 of 2005, s. 5(1)-(3).

states that enjoyment of copyright shall not be independent of the registration.[37] Other countries that have put in place voluntary registration systems are Malawi, Botswana, Nigeria, and Uganda.

More countries are contemplating the introduction of the voluntary registration system mainly to create repositories of the works, which the authors may use as prima facie evidence of ownership and facilitate enforcement of their rights. The laws expressly state that there shall be no formalities for the subsistence of copyright.

7.3.2.2 Subject Matter and Eligibility for Protection

The subject matter of copyright protection as provided for in the Berne Convention is replicated in the national laws. On the issue of fixation, a country like Zimbabwe is flexible as fixation is not a requirement for copyright protection.[38] Originality remains a requirement for eligibility of copyright protection.[39] The issue of originality has been subject to several court cases and the courts have developed jurisprudence on same.[40]

With the advent of computer programs, the subject matter has been expanded to include computer programs. In some countries, computer programs are protected as literary works as they are defined as such, while in other countries, computer programs are recognized independently as subject matter for protection under copyright.

Countries that adopted the common law system and were part of the English Colonies like Kenya, Nigeria, Ghana, and as well as Zimbabwe (which has its roots in the Roman-Dutch system, however) provide for the protection of sound recordings, broadcasts and performers under the copyright regime without a clear distinction. They are included in the works eligible for copyright protection. This is not in conformity with the provisions of Article 2 of the Berne Convention. However, it is important to note that although they are included as works eligible for copyright protection, the laws make separate provisions in relation to the related rights.

In countries such as Senegal, Niger, and Burkina Faso, which were influenced by the civil law system, the national law clearly makes a distinction between copyright and related rights as stated in section 7.2.1.1. The works listed as eligible for copyright protection are in line with the

37. Ghana Copyright Act No. 690 of 2005, s. 5(4).
38. Zimbabwe Copyright and Neighbouring Rights Act Chapter 26.05, s. 10; Under the Act, the only requirement for copyright protection is originality. The rationale for this was to cater for those rights holders who were not able to reduce the works into a fixed format especially in relation to written music so as not de disenfranchise them in terms of their creative works. The Malawi Copyright Act of 2016, s. 26(2) is more precise on the issue of fixation.
39. Zimbabwe Copyright Law Chapter 26.03, s. 10.
40. Faulu Kenya Deposit Taking Micro Finance Ltd v. Safaricom Ltd eKLR [2012]; In this case, the court held that concepts are not protected by copyright.

Berne Convention and these are: (1) Literary works including computer programs and any works expressed in any discernible language; (2) dramatic works; (3) choreographic works; (4) circus acts; (5) musical works with or without words; (6) audiovisual works and visual arts.[41]

Courts have developed jurisprudence on this matter. In the case South African case of *Waylite Diary v. National Bank Ltd*,[42] the court held that appointment pages in a printed diary were not entitled to copyright protection as they did not fall within the subject matter of protection. It was not an artistic work as there was no originality; it was commonplace.

7.3.2.3 Rights Granted

Both economic and moral rights are granted under the national laws. These rights are similar at the national level and this may be attributed to several factors the most pronounced one being the influence of the laws that they inherited post-independence, which in most cases were compliant with the Berne Convention. The moral rights granted under the laws are not transferrable even when the economic rights are transferred. The rights are inalienable and this is an area of convergence for all the countries regardless of the system of law in their respective countries.

For example, section 20(1) of the South African Copyright Act provides:

> Notwithstanding the transfer of the copyright in a literary, musical or artistic work in a cinematograph film or in a computer program, the author shall have the right to claim authorship of the work, subject to the provisions of this Act, and to object to any distortion, mutilation or other modification of the work where such action is or would be prejudicial to the honor and reputation of the author.

This is the standard provision that is found in most of the laws. However, the South African Law goes further to provide that the author who authorizes the use of his work or a work associated with a computer program may not prevent or object to modifications that are absolutely necessary on technical grounds or for the purpose of connected exploitation of the work.[43]

7.3.2.4 Limitations to Copyright Protection

Article 2bis of the Berne Convention leaves it to the Member States to make provisions in relation to limitations to copyright in the case of certain speeches, certain uses of lectures and addresses, and the right to make the

41. Law No. 2008-09 of Jan. 25, 2008 on Copyright and Neighbouring Rights in Senegal, Art. 6 (hereinafter "Senegal Copyright Act, 2008").
42. Waylite Diary v. First National Bank Ltd (1) SA 645 (A) (1995).
43. Peter Ramsden, *A Guide to Intellectual Property Law* 37(Juta and Co. Ltd., 2011).

collection of such works. Several countries exclude the above works from protection under copyright.

7.3.2.5 Term of Protection and Public Domain

The Berne Convention provides for the minimum term of protection in relation to the different works. In national law, the term of protection is the life of the author plus 50 years or in the case of cinematographic works or works of anonymous or pseudonymous works, the term would be 50 years from the date of publication. Several countries like Ghana have extended the term to the life of the author plus 70 years or 70 years from the date of publication as the case may be.

The application of these different terms of protection will be subject to the application of the principle of national treatment. Thus, where a country like Kenya only offers 50 years of protection post the life of the author, the author from Ghana, Senegal or Mozambique will only enjoy protection in Kenya, Botswana, Namibia, and South Africa for the life of the author plus 50 years, but will continue to enjoy the rights for another 20 years in Ghana and other countries with the 70-year term.

The lapse of the copyright term is one of the ways in which the works fall into the public domain.

7.3.2.6 Limitations and Exceptions to Copyright

The exceptions and limitations to exclusive rights go beyond the right of reproduction as provided for under Article 9 of the Berne Convention. These have been extended under the TRIPS Agreement to include other exclusive rights granted under the national laws. However, the exceptions and limitations are subject to the three-step test.[44]

Uganda, in its Copyright Act of 2006 attempts to provide for the exceptions and limitations not only subject to the three-step test but also within the doctrines of fair use and fair dealing. This contrasts with the other exceptions and limitations in other national laws within the continent, which usually provide for fair dealing and do not include the three-step test in the laws. A closer analysis of section 15 of the Copyright Act of 2006 reveals that different approaches are used for different exceptions and limitations.

On the one hand, although in section 15(1) of the Act fair use is named in its wording, what is actually indicated are the exceptions in line with fair dealing and this includes use of works for purposes of private use, teaching, purposes of news and reporting current affairs, for judicial proceedings. On the other hand, section 15(1)(b) alludes to fair practice in relation to quotation from a published work. The exception to the right of reproduction is subject to the three-step test in relation to literary and artistic works or

44. TRIPS, Art. 13.

scientific work by a public library, noncommercial documentation center, or scientific or educational institution.

The test is further applicable when determining whether or not the use falls within the ambit of fair use.[45] The issue as to whether an action falls within the fair use principle is thus left to the Court for determination on a case-by-case basis. In the United States (U.S.), fair use is subject to an established criterion for determination.[46] The jurisprudence on this has yet to be developed in Uganda. This is one of the divergent issues on the domestication of the Berne Convention within the continent.

The Copyright Act of Senegal takes a more pragmatic approach where the exceptions and limitations are clearly classified and listed. First, exceptions that are specific to the right of communication to the public are listed.[47] The second part provides for exceptions in relation to the right of reproduction. The third part covers exceptions that are common to the right of communication to the public and the right of reproduction, such as for the purposes of illustration for teaching, parody, analysis and quotation, for information purposes, and the use of graphic or three-dimensional works located in a public place.[48]

This third part is where the general and specific exceptions to all the exclusive rights granted under the Copyright Act are constituted. This is the case with the Copyright Act of South Africa, too. Some of the general exceptions are for purposes of fair dealing, judicial proceedings, quotations, by way of illustration, reproduction by a broadcaster by means of its own facilities for their broadcasts, information, and reproduction for use of news reporting.[49]

The above discourse illustrates the dynamics in drafting laws, which although anchored in the Berne Convention have divergent ways of domesticating the same. They are still influenced by the laws based on the legal system, whether civil law, common law or Roman-Dutch systems of law. The concept of fair use as provided for in the Copyright Act of Uganda was influenced by the doctrine of fair use under the U.S. Copyright Law. The fair use doctrine as stated earlier, relies on judicial interpretation based on

45. Copyright and Neighbouring Rights Act 2006 (Uganda), s. 15(2).
46. The fair use principle in the U.S. prescribes four factors to be used in the determination by the Court on what amounts to fair use namely: (1) purpose and character of the use; (2) nature of the copyrighted work; (3) substantiality of the portion of the work used and; (4) effect of the use on the potential market or value of the work; https://www.uleth.ca/lib/copyright/content/fair_dealing_week/fair_dealing_vs_fair_use.asp (accessed Oct. 5, 2018).
47. Senegal Copyright Act 2008, Arts. 38-39 provide exceptions if the communication to the public is for private use and use in religious services.
48. Senegal Copyright Act 2008, Arts. 42-46.
49. Ramsden (n. 43).

four established principles, while fair dealing is left to the courts to decide where there are no specific guidelines as to what constitutes fair in dealing.[50]

The AfCFTA Protocol on Intellectual Property Rights, The Protocol has extensive provisions on exceptions and limitations, including areas that are still under negotiation at the international level.[51] It also provides for exceptions that support the preservation of cultural heritage as well as for the reproduction of a reasonable portion of any published works upon request for purposes of research or private study. It is important to note that the Berne Convention provides for the three-step test in relation to the right of reproduction.[52] In this respect, provisions under the Protocol are deemed to be "Berne Plus." Thus, in drafting the annex, it is important to apply the three-step test for the exceptions and limitations to be adopted at the national level in light of the provisions of the AfCFTA Protocol on Intellectual Property.

The Berne Convention provides the minimum standards for protection of copyright law and since most of the countries have adopted the three basic principles of copyright as provided for under the Berne Convention, it is trite to state that the same facilitates the universality of copyright within the pluralistic system that exists in the Continent.

7.3.2.7 The Appendix to the Berne Convention

The Special Provision Regarding Developing Countries, known as the Appendix to the Berne Convention was adopted in 1971 primarily to facilitate access to printed works by developing countries so as to promote development. The principle behind it was that strict copyright protection was an impediment to accessing the requisite knowledge required by the developing countries from the developed countries.

However, the provisions were found to be cumbersome and lengthy and did not serve the purpose for which the Appendix was intended. Consequently, very few countries included the provisions in their laws. Nigeria and Malawi have incorporated the Appendix in their national laws but they have hardly been utilized.

50. Ben Sihanya, *Intellectual Property and Innovation Law in Kenya and Africa: Transferring Technology for Sustainable Development* 232 (Sihanya Mentoring & Innovative Lawyering, 2016); *See also* Giuseppina D'Agostino, *Healing Fair Dealing? A Comparative Copyright Analysis of Canada's Fair Dealing to UK Fair Dealing and U.S Fair Use,* 53 McGill Law Journal 309-363 (208) https://doi.org/10.2139/ssrn.1014404.
51. Examples are exceptions and limitations for educational and research purposes, and libraries and archives which are on the agenda of the World Intellectual Property Organization (WIPO) Standing Committee on Copyright and Related Rights (SCCR).
52. Article 9(2) of the Berne Convention *"It shall be a matter of legislation of the countries of the Union to permit the reproduction of such works in certain special cases, provided that such reproduction does not conflict with a normal exploitation of the work and does not unreasonably prejudice the legitimate interests of the author."*

7.3.3 The TRIPS Agreement

The TRIPS Agreement has consolidated the universality of the Berne Convention as countries, which had not ratified or acceded to the Berne Convention were forced to adhere to its minimum requirements. A country like Uganda, which has yet to accede to the Berne Convention has provisions that are compatible with the Berne Convention due to their membership to the WTO.

The TRIPS Agreement extends the application of the three-step test to all other exclusive rights. The national laws save for the Copyright Act of Uganda do not specifically make reference to the three-step test but they provide for exceptions and limitations, which are presumed to be within the three-step test.

For the countries that are not members of the WTO but are State Parties to the Agreement, the provisions of the Protocol will be applicable, and to that extent make them compliant with the TRIPS Agreement.

7.3.4 WIPO Copyright Treaties

The treaties were mainly adopted to address the developments in the digital environment.[53] The ratification or accession has been slow and only 13 of the 55 countries have ratified or acceded to the two treaties.[54]

7.3.5 Marrakesh Treaty for the Visually Impaired

The Marrakesh Treaty for the Visually Impaired is another treaty that has brought about universality in the national laws within the continent. The Treaty requires Member States to make provisions for the limitations and exceptions that allow for access to printed works by visually impaired persons. Prior to the adoption of the Marrakesh Treaty, several countries did not have the exceptions and limitations for the visually impaired. These provisions have recently been included in the laws. The Copyright Act of Malawi 2016 has specific provisions on exceptions and limitations for the visually impaired. The Act provides for exceptions for reproduction of works

53. The Beijing Treaty for the Protection of Audiovisual Performances is left out as it has yet to come into force and there are only seven Countries from Africa that have recently acceded to or ratified the Treaty.

54. For the WCT, Algeria, Botswana, Burkina Faso, Burundi, Gabon, Ghana, Guinea, Mali, Namibia, Nigeria, Senegal and Togo are party; WIPO Administered Treaties, http://www.wipo.int/treaties/en/ip/wct/ (accessed Oct. 9, 2018); While in the case of the WPPT, the Contracting States are Algeria, Botswana, Burkina Faso, Gabon, Ghana, Guinea, Madagascar, Mali, Namibia, Nigeria, Senegal and Togo; WIPO Administered Treaties, http://www.wipo.int/treaties/en/ip/wppt/ (accessed Oct. 9, 2018).

for use by persons with disabilities.[55] These provisions are replicated in the proposed amendments to the Copyright Laws in Kenya, South Africa, and Nigeria.[56]

The Marrakesh Treaty also obliges the Member States to facilitate access to the visually impaired even in cases where technological protection measures have been applied. It also ensures that the published works are readily available commercially in accessible format copies.

7.4 REGIONAL PROTECTION OF COPYRIGHT

The development of copyright has over the years been a matter for the different countries to deal with at the national level. It was not until recently that matters of copyright were considered at the regional level. However, other than the Annex to the Banjul Agreement under the OAPI, there are no copyright protocols or regional instruments that harmonize the laws either at the continental level or within the regional economic blocs. Copyright has, as stated earlier, developed within the context of national laws. The following paragraphs shall give a brief overview of the current status.

7.4.1 Intellectual Property Organizations

The main organizations that are mandated to administer intellectual property rights on behalf of their members are the ARIPO and the Organization of African Intellectual Property (OAPI). The PAIPO was recently established under the African Union.

7.4.1.1 African Regional Intellectual Property Organization

The African Intellectual Property Organization was established under the Lusaka Agreement. One of its objectives is:

> to promote the harmonization and development of intellectual property laws and matters related thereto, appropriate to the needs of its members and the region as a whole.

In 2002, ARIPO expanded its mandate to include copyright and related rights, with the aim of promoting the provision of effective protection and management of copyright and related rights among the Member States. Article III was amended to include a specific objective on copyright and related rights:

---

55. Copyright Act of Malawi of 2016, s. 49.
56. Eleven Countries namely Botswana, Burkina Faso, Ghana, Kenya, Lesotho, Liberia, Malawi, Nigeria, Tunisia and Uganda have acceded to or ratified the Treaty.

> to promote, in its members, the development of copyright and related rights and ensure that copyright and related rights contribute to the economic, social and cultural development of members and of the region as a whole.[57]

ARIPO has since embarked on a number of initiatives to help the Member States align their laws to the existing international norms as well as developments in copyright at national, regional and international levels.

There are 19 Member States that are party to the Lusaka Agreement and these include Botswana, Cape Verde, The Gambia, Ghana, Kenya, Kingdom of Eswatini, Kingdom of Lesotho, Liberia, Malawi, Mauritius, Mozambique, Namibia, Rwanda, São Tomé and Príncipe, Seychelles, Sierra Leone, Somalia, Sudan, Swaziland, Tanzania, Uganda, Zambia and Zimbabwe. Several countries are granted observer status. The following countries are recognized as potential members and include Angola, Algeria, Burundi, Egypt, Eritrea, Ethiopia, Libya, Nigeria, South Africa and Tunisia.[58]

There are several ARIPO activities geared toward the promotion and development of copyright and related rights. The first one is to ensure that the Member States update their copyright laws to ensure that they take cognizance of developments at the national, regional and international levels. To this end, ARIPO has developed a model law on copyright and related rights as well as guidelines for ratification of the International Copyright Conventions.[59] In 2021, the Member States adopted the Kampala Protocol on Voluntary Registration of Copyright and Related Rights.[60] The purpose of the Protocol was to guide the Member States in the process of voluntary registration and notification of copyright and related rights. There is no other specific regional law on copyright and related rights under ARIPO and the

57. Agreement on the Creation of the ARIPO adopted by the Diplomatic Conference for the adoption of an Agreement on the Creation of an Industrial Property Organization for English-Speaking Africa at Lusaka (Zambia) on Dec. 9, 1976, and amended by the Administrative Council of ARIPO on Dec. 10, 1982, Dec. 12, 1986 and Nov. 27, 1996, and as amended by the Council of Ministers on Aug. 13, 2004 (Dec. 9, 1976), Art. III(i) (hereinafter "the Lusaka Agreement").
58. The Lusaka Agreement, Art. VI mandates the Organization to cooperate with non-Member States.
59. The ARIPO Guidelines for the Domestication of the Marrakesh Treaty were published in 2016; *See* https://www.aripo.org/storage/copyright-publication/1687439173_ARIPO%20Guidelines%20for%20the%20Domestication%20of%20the%20%20Marrakesh%20Treaty.pdf (accessed Mar. 25, 2025). ARIPO has published the Model Copyright Law and guidelines for ratification of the Berne Convention, WCT, WPPT and the Beijing Treaty.
60. The Protocol was adopted by the Member States in Kampala, Uganda on Aug. 28, 2021. The voluntary registration system does not create an obligation for registration of copyright and related rights for the Member States. It is deemed to be an administrative tool as it is more of a notification system.

Member States are encouraged to provide for at least the minimum standards within the Berne Convention.[61]

7.4.1.2 *Organisation Africaine De La Propriété Intellectuelle*

The OAPI was established under the Bangui Agreement in 1977 to administer intellectual property rights on behalf of the French-speaking countries in Africa.

The objectives of OAPI include among others: (1) contribute to the promotion and protection of literary and artistic property as an expression of cultural and social values; (2) encourage creating associations of authors at the national level; (3) and centralize, coordinate and disseminate information on copyright and related rights among the Member States. These are all geared toward the promotion of economic development through the effective protection of intellectual property and related rights.

Just like ARIPO, OAPI initially only dealt with industrial property but the Bangui Agreement was revised to include copyright and related rights as part of its mandate.[62] However, unlike ARIPO, which does not have a specific regime on copyright and related rights, Annex VII of the Bangui Agreement makes provisions for the protection of copyright and related rights.[63] The provisions in relation to copyright and related rights are in line with the minimum provisions of the Berne Convention in relation to the subject matter of protection, rights protected, limitations on economic rights, flexibilities, ownership of rights and assignment and licensing.[64]

The administration of the rights is left to the Member States of the Organization to deal with at the national level. The Annex under part five has clear provisions on measures, remedies and sanctions concerning unauthorized commercial use of copyright and related rights and of its infringements.[65] The OAPI Member States each have their own national laws in relation to copyright and related rights.

61. This is in contrast to the European Union which has Directives and regulations on copyright and related rights that are binding on the Member States.
62. The Agreement Revising the Bangui Agreement of Mar. 2, 1977, on the Creation of an African Intellectual Property Organization (Mar. 2, 1977), annex VII, TRT/OA002/002 has provisions for copyright and related rights (hereinafter the Bangui Agreement).
63. Bangui Agreement, annex VII, Art. 1 provides for common rules on protection of copyright and related rights as well as the promotion of the cultural heritage among the OAPI Member States.
64. Part two of the Annex covers the rights of performers, producers of sound recordings and broadcasting organizations. Part three covers the common provisions such as remuneration for private copying, and public domain, while part four provides for the collective administration of copyright and related rights. It is interesting to note that the users under Art. 51 are expected to pay the national collective management organizations for the use of works that have fallen in public domain.
65. Bangui Agreement, annex VII, Art. 61.

OAPI currently has 17 Member States namely, Benin, Burkina Faso, Cameroun, Central Africa Republic, Comoros, Congo, Côte d'Ivoire, Gabon, Guinea, Guinea Bissau, Equatorial Guinea, Mali, Niger, Mauritania, Niger, Senegal, Chad and Togo.

7.4.2 Regional Economic Communities

There are several regional economic communities (RECs) in Africa as mentioned in section 7.1 which provides the background to this chapter.[66] To determine whether there is harmonization or divergence of copyright within the continent, we shall look at the ECOWAS, the EAC, the SADC, and the COMESA.

7.4.2.1 Economic Community of West African States

The ECOWAS was established in 1975. It currently has 15 Member States. Unfortunately, not much has been done to address issues of intellectual property and in particular copyright under ECOWAS. The closest reference to copyright is Article 41 that permits Member States to introduce or continue to execute restrictions and prohibitions that have an impact on the protection of national artistic and cultural property.[67] This goes against the provisions of the Berne Convention where the rightholder is granted the right to control the exclusive rights such as the right to import and communicate the works to the public. The provision may end up stifling cross-border trade in copyright goods. It does not serve to harmonize the copyright regime at the regional level.

7.4.2.2 East African Community

The EAC is a regional intergovernmental organization of six Partner States: the Republics of Burundi, Kenya, Rwanda, South Sudan, the United Republic of Tanzania, and the Republic of Uganda, with its headquarters in

66. These are the Arab Maghreb Union (AMU/UMA), the Economic Community of West African States (ECOWAS), the East African Community (EAC), the Intergovernmental Authority on Development (IGAD), the Southern African Development Community (SADC), Common Market for Eastern and Southern Africa (COMESA), the Economic Community of Central African States (ECCAS), Community of Sahel-Saharan States (CENSAD).
67. Henry Kibet Mutai, *Intellectual Property Rights Promotion and Protection Under the Tripartite FreeTrade Area: Prospects for an Intellectual Property Protocol*, https://www.tralac.org/publications/article/10133-intellectual-property-rights-promotion-and-protection-under-the-tripartite-free-trade-area-tfta-proposals-for-an-intellectual-property-protocol.html (accessed Apr. 20, 2019).

Arusha, Tanzania. It was established under the EAC Treaty of 1999, which came into force in 2000.[68]

Although there are currently no specific provisions within the EAC statutes and regulations the EAC is currently working on an Intellectual Property Policy of which the overall objective is to create a dynamic, vibrant and balanced system in the EAC Partner States with the ultimate aim of establishing an Intellectual Property System for the ASEAN Economic Community (AEC) to stimulate and drive innovation and creativity. The EAC has had numerous opportunities to address Intellectual Property and specifically copyright but it has always been relegated as the EAC strives to achieve the more tangible aspects of the EAC of the four EAC Pillars such as trade, education and agriculture, to name a few.[69] States to come up with the mode of cooperation. In September 2018, the EAC held a consultative forum on the proposed EAC Intellectual Property Policy, but it seems to have been geared toward industrial property as addressed from a science and technology perspective. It is important to note that the objectives of the Partner States in relation to copyright are mainly to promote and protect creativity and innovation and enhance the protection of intellectual property. The onus is on the Partner States to ensure that this is achieved as there is no set policy or regulatory framework to guide the process until the policy is adopted.

The Partner States are left to provide for copyright protection and as discussed in section 7.3.2.1 above, although they are in conformity with the Berne Convention, the laws are not harmonized as they developed independently.

7.4.2.3 Southern African Development Community

The SADC has a membership of 16 countries which include the following: Angola, Botswana, Comoros, Democratic Republic of Congo, Lesotho, Madagascar, Malawi, Mauritius, Mozambique, Namibia, Seychelles, South Africa, Eswatini, United Republic of Tanzania, Zambia and Zimbabwe.

7.4.2.4 Common Market for Eastern and Southern Africa

The COMESA is a REC that was established in 1994.[70] It currently has 21 Member States. COMESA has a copyright policy and one of the objectives is to ensure comprehensive protection of copyright and related rights

68. https://www.eala.org/documents/view/the-treaty-for-the-establishment-of-the-east-africa-community-1999-2006 (accessed March 2025).
69. The four main pillars in the EAC are the Customs Union, The Common Market, the Monetary Union and the Political Federation.
70. The Treaty Establishing the COMESA was signed on Nov. 5, 1993 in Kampala, Uganda and was ratified a year later in Lilongwe, Malawi on Dec. 8, 1994.

including enforcement. To achieve its objectives, it has signed a memorandum of understanding with the ARIPO to cooperate on matters of intellectual property. There is no specific instrument of copyright and related rights. Member States are left to address copyright matters at the national level.

7.5 PROTECTION OF IP AT THE CONTINENTAL LEVEL

7.5.1 Pan African Intellectual Property Organization

The PAIPO was established under the African Union (PAIPO) in January 2016 when the Statute was adopted. Under Article 3 of the Statute of the PAIPO, the mandate is as follows:

> PAIPO shall be responsible for intellectual property and other emerging issues related to the intellectual property system as a tool for economic, cultural, social and technological development of the continent as well as set intellectual property standards that reflect the needs of the African Union, its Member States and RECs, ARIPO and OAPI.

PAIPO was established to promote of harmonization of intellectual property systems of the Member States with particular regard to protection, exploitation, commercialization and enforcement.[71] However, this has not happened as only six countries have signed the Statute, only one ratification and one deposit. This could be attributed to various factors such as the bias toward science and technology as well as other continental dynamics in intellectual property rights administration.[72]

7.5.2 African Continental Free Trade Area

On March 21, 2018, in Kigali, Rwanda, 44 African Countries affixed their signatures to the Agreement establishing the AfCFTA. The Agreement came into force on May 30, 2019.

The ever-changing digital technologies continuously create the need for updating copyright laws within the region. As stated earlier, at the continental level, there was no instrument on copyright and related rights and intellectual property rights as a whole.[73] The State Parties to the Africa Continental Free Trade Agreement adopted the AfCFTA Protocol on Intellectual Property Rights 2023. This is the first instrument at the continental level on the

71. Statute of the Pan African Intellectual Property Organization (Jan. 30, 2016), obj. 4 para. 1.
72. As of September 2023, signatories to the Statute were Sierra Leone, Ghana, Comoros, Chad, Guinea and Tunisa.
73. *See* s. 7.1 above.

protection of intellectual property, albeit within the context of trade in the AfCFTA.

The Protocol recognizes the importance of intellectual property in trade and seeks to avoid discrimination in protecting intellectual property among the State Parties, especially those that are not members of the WTO. It also seeks to promote innovation and creativity and recognizes the role of the regional intellectual property organization and the need to address the fragmentation of intellectual property instruments within the continent.

The AfCFTA Protocol on Intellectual Property requires State Parties to provide for balanced copyright frameworks to ensure protection, access to and use of works for education, research, scientific inquiry and preservation of cultural materials for the advancement of welfare and sustainable development. The frameworks should take into consideration the rapid technological advances, and mandate fair and adequate remuneration for facilitating cross-border flows of authors and performers for educational and cultural materials. The Protocol established the AfCFTA Intellectual Property Office which shall, *inter alia,* co-ordinate interactions and activities of the intellectual property stakeholders, work with existing regional intellectual property institutions and promote and protect intellectual property across the continent.

The Protocol covers the general rules on intellectual property and the specific provisions will be negotiated by State Parties under the annexes to the Protocol.[74] All other provisions shall be negotiated under the Annex to the Protocol on Copyright and Related Rights.

7.6 UNIVERSALISM OR PLURALISM

Since Copyright was first introduced in Africa, many copyright laws have been enacted over the years, influenced mainly by the Berne Convention. The African countries have developed their copyright laws independently within the continent and at different times. It is noteworthy that although the copyright legislation has been adopted by jurisdictions of three distinct legal systems in Africa, the individual copyright laws share similar provisions, which may be attributed to the Berne Convention as well as the TRIPS Agreement.

Digital technologies have brought about several challenges, which were not envisaged. Although several countries are yet to ratify the WCT and the WPPT, some of the provisions have been included in the national laws.

On matters of copyright and related rights, there is no uniform continental regime and neither are there regional regimes, except for Annex VII of the Banjul Agreement to which the OAPI Member States are parties. National legislation conforms to the minimum standard of protection as set

74. Article 11 of the AfCFTA Protocol on Intellectual Property Rights.

out in the Berne Convention. The facilitation of merging of the universal copyright law by the African Union, through the African Continental Free Trade Area Agreement, the Regional Intellectual Property Organizations and the Regional Economic Blocs is work in progress.

Universalism has primarily to do with the approximation of the national laws to comply with the international copyright treaties, and in particular with the Berne Convention. Recent developments indicate the move toward harmonization of laws within the African continent. The provisions of the AfCFTA Protocol on Intellectual Property to a certain extent are working toward approximation of the laws at the continental level.

Part II

Pluralism or Universalism in International Copyright Lawmaking

Chapter 8

Berne Convention: The Epicenter of Universalism or the Contrary?

Dionysia Kallinikou

Universalism[1] originates from the philosophical and theological concept that some norms have a universal application. We also find universalism in anthropology, metaphysics, social and natural sciences, political theories and international law.[2] Theories and doctrines of universalism are valid for everyone. What is right and fair should be applicable everywhere. However, there is no agreement about what values or principles are universal because diversity is reflected in different factors, such as regions, ideologies, culture, legal traditions and economy.

Human rights and rule of law are comprised of universal principles and values. The principle of universal protection of authors, as well as the balance of rights, derives from Article 27 of the Universal Declaration of Human Rights:[3]

> (1) Everyone has the right to participate freely in cultural life of the community, to enjoy the arts and to share in scientific advancement and

1. For the term universalism and the below analysis, *see*: Wikipedia, http://en.wikipedia.org/wiki/Universalism (accessed November 2023); James D. Ingram, *Universalism/Universalization*, Wiley Online Library, http://doi.org/10.1002/9781118474396.wbept1017 (November 2023).
2. Emmanuelle Jouannet, *Universalism and Imperialism: The True-False Paradox of International Law?,* 18 The European Journal of International Law 379, 381 (2007) https://doi.org/10.1093/ejil/chm029; Gustavo Gozzi, *The Particularistic Universalism of International Law in the Nineteenth Century*, 52 Harvard International Law Journal 73, 75-78 (2010).
3. Universal Declaration of Human Rights (Dec. 10, 1948) A/RES/217(III).

its benefits. (2) Everyone has the right to have the moral and material interests resulting from any scientific, literary or artistic creation of which he is the author.

The Marrakesh Treaty to facilitate access to published works for persons who are blind, visually impaired or otherwise print-disabled (2013) is in line with the above-mentioned principles and includes human rights aspects. Intellectual property is also protected by Article 17(2) of the Charter of Fundamental Rights of the European Union (EU).[4]

The protection of authors, creators and artists is a matter of justice and fairness. The recognition and protection of their rights which aims at the protection of creation and creativity is a reward of the spiritual toil and an incentive for their contribution to the development of economy, culture and cultural heritage.

8.1 THE ORIGIN, THE NATIONAL TREATMENT AND THE MINIMUM PROTECTION

The origin of international copyright protection is based on the bilateral copyright agreements[5] between countries and the French Decree of March 28, 1852,[6] as a result of the protection of all foreign works without the condition of reciprocity, regardless of the place of publication or the nationality of the author.

The principle of universal copyright legislation was declared at the International Congress on Literary and Artistic Property that took place in Brussels, in September 1858.[7]

4. Charter of Fundamental Rights of the European Union, Official Journal C 326, 26/10/2012, pp. 391-407, Doc. 12012P/TXT.
5. Volume I, Sam Ricketson & Jane C. Ginsburg, *International Copyright and Neighbouring Rights: The Berne Convention and Beyond* 1.29 (Oxford University Press, 2005). *See also:* Brander Matthews, *The Evolution of Copyright,* 5 Political Science Quarterly 583, 601 (1890) http://www.compilerpress.ca/Competitiveness/Anno/Anno%20Matthews%20The%20Evolution%20of%20Copyright.htm (accessed Mar. 17,2025); Harry G. Henn, *Quest for International Copyright Protection,* 39 Cornell Law Review 43, 45 (1953), https://scholarship.law.cornell.edu/cgi/viewcontent.cgi?article=1620&context=clr (accessed Mar. 17, 2025).
6. Ricketson & Ginsburg (n. 5), 2.05; Sam Ricketson, *The Birth of the Berne Union,* 11 Columbia-Volunteer Lawyers for the Arts Journal of Law & the Arts 9 (1986-1987), https://heinonline.org/HOL/LandingPage?handle=hein.journals/cjla11&div=3&id=&page= (accessed Mar. 17, 2025).
7. Ricketson & Ginsburg (n. 5); Samuel Ricketson, *The Birth of the Berne Union,* 11 Columbia-Volunteer Lawyers for the Arts Journal of Law & the Arts 9 (1986-1987), https://heinonline.org/HOL/LandingPage?handle=hein.journals/cjla11&div=3&id=&page= (accessed Mar. 17, 2025).

The initiative for negotiations and meetings that led to the Berne Convention of 1886 belongs to the Association Litteraire et Artistique Internationale and to its President Victor Hugo.

The Berne Convention for the Protection of Literary and Artistic Works, signed in Berne, on September 9, 1886,[8] by 10 states, is the oldest and most fundamental international convention on copyright. Nowadays, almost all countries have signed the 1971 Paris Act of the Berne Convention.[9]

Article 1 of the Berne Convention, which has remained almost unchanged since the original text of 1886, provides that "The countries to which this Convention applies constitute a Union for the protection of the rights of authors in their literary and artistic works."

The first paragraph of the Preamble of the Berne Convention points out that the desire of the Union countries is the protection of authors' rights in an effective and uniform manner, as possible.

Even if uniformity has not been fully achieved,[10] the above provisions have a universal value because they emphasize the protection of authors at an international level.

According to the Guide of the Berne Convention, the goal of the protection is to produce "as far as possible the same regime for all who enjoy such protection."[11]

It comes out from the Records of Berne Convention that the terms "universal" and "uniform" in copyright law[12] are sometimes equally used, although they do not have the same meaning. "Uniform" copyright law provides that the protection is the same and does not vary between countries. "Universal" copyright law is based on an idealistic approach providing that the protection of authors is a general and permanent principle valid everywhere.

During the Diplomatic Conferences (between 1884 and 1886) concerning the Act of 1886, the first idea was to favor a "universal codification" of copyright law. This opinion was based on the concept of natural law[13] according to which authors' rights should be protected universally in all countries.

---

8. Berne Convention for the Protection of Literary and Artistic Works (Sep. 9, 1886), S. Treaty Doc. No. 99-27, www.wipo.int/edocs/.../en/berne/trt_berne_001en.pdf (accessed November 2023) ("Hereinafter Berne Convention").
9. Total number of contracting parties of the Paris Act: 176, www.wipo.int/treaties/en/ip/berne (accessed November 2023).
10. Mihaly Ficsor, *Guide to the Copyright and Related Rights Treaties Administered by WIPO-WIPO and Glossary of Copyright and Related Rights by WIPO* 20 (WIPO, 2003).
11. *Guide to the Berne Convention for the Protection of Literary and Artistic Works (Paris Act, 1971)* 7 (WIPO, 1978).
12. For the notion of a universal copyright law *see also* Ricketson & Ginsburg (n. 5), 2.02-2.05.
13. Ricketson & Ginsburg (n. 5), 2.02; Ricketson (n. 6), 4.

The German Delegation[14] at the first Conference in Berne (1884) proposed to abandon national treatment in favor of a "uniform regulation" within the framework of an International Convention concerning the protection of copyright.

International codification was desired by some delegations, but finally, national treatment was supported. The idea of a uniform international law was rejected because it was difficult to amend all national laws at once. A realistic view was supported and the final draft of the Act excluded the idea of a uniform international law on copyright.[15]

The Berne Convention adopted two important principles that remain unchanged: the national treatment and the minimum rights *jure conventionis.*[16]

According to Article 5(1):

> Authors shall enjoy, in respect of works for which they are protected under this Convention, in countries of the Union other than the country of origin, the rights which their respective laws do now or may hereafter grant to their nationals, as well as the rights specially granted by this Convention.

This provision treats foreigners in the same way as nationals. It means that creative works which have a country of origin,[17] a Union country, benefit in all other countries of the Union from the same protection, as each country grants to works of its own nationals.[18] Protection of the country of origin is governed by domestic law according to Article 5(3) of the Berne Convention. The national treatment may be refused for works of applied arts, for the resale right, for the comparison of terms and for works eligible for protection according to the criterion of first publication.

The principle of national treatment does not mean that the treatment is identical to all Union countries because the scope of protection varies from one country to another.

---

14. 1886-Berne Convention Centenary-1986, *The Berne Convention for the Protection of Literary and Artistic Works from 1886 to 1986* 90 (WIPO, 1986); *See also* Ricketson & Ginsburg (n. 5), 2.24; Silke Von Lewinski, *International Copyright Law and Policy* 2.44-2.45 (Oxford University Press, 2008).
15. Ricketson (n. 6), 4; Jane Ginsburg, *International Copyright: From a "Bundle" of National Copyright Laws to a Supranational Code?* 4-6, http//papers. ssrn.com/abstract =222508 (accessed November 2023).
16. Stephen M. Stewart, *International Copyright and Neighbouring Rights* 5.04 (London-Butterworths, 1983).
17. *See,* Berne Convention, Art. 5(4) for protection in the country of origin.
18. WIPO summary of the Berne Convention for the Protection of Literary and Artistic Works (1886), www.wipo.int/treaties/en/ip/berne/summary_berne.html (accessed Aug. 25, 2018); At the Congress of the Société des Gens de Lettres in 1878 the principle of national treatment was formulated, as follows:

    > In countries outside the country of origin, every literary, scientific and artistic work shall be treated according to the same laws as works of national origin.

National treatment has the advantage that courts in countries where copyright was infringed can issue judgments according to their own national law.

The first paragraph of the Preamble of Berne Convention indicating the purpose to give protection of authors' rights in a manner "as effective ... as possible" takes into consideration that the social, cultural and economic conditions are not the same in all Union countries and the balance of interest is divergent in the various copyright systems and doctrines.

In order to guarantee a minimum level of harmonization, Article 5(1) includes in the assimilation "the rights specially granted by this Convention," in other words, the minimum rights prescribed in the Berne Convention.

The minimum protection mainly relates to the protected works, the rights and the duration. Berne Convention provides for economic and moral rights and permits certain exceptions and limitations to economic rights. The Appendix to the Paris Act permits developing countries to implement non-voluntary licenses for translation and reproduction in certain cases.

President Numa Droz,[19] in the Second Conference in Berne (1885), in his closing speech, made the following address:

> Today's date is a milestone in the history of international law ... Of course, like any convention between Sovereign States, our work does have the character of a compromise. It was no in our power, neither could it be our intention, to effect the disappearance of the legislative peculiarities of all Contracting States, which after all are due to differences of doctrine, practice and procedure and tied up with the institutions of each country and its legal culture ... all are enabled to enter the Union and at the same time retain those features of their statute and caselaw to which they are attached, provided they are also consent to assure authors of effective protection on the points settled by the Convention.

Berne Convention is a multilateral international Convention for the protection of authors, as it concerns their literary and artistic works, open[20] to all countries establishing a Union to the totality of the contracting parties.

Minimum standards and substantive Berne provisions are extended beyond the Berne Union by the Trade-Related Aspects of Intellectual Property Rights (TRIPS) Agreement[21] and the WIPO Copyright Treaty (WCT).[22]

Except for the provisions of the Berne Convention on moral rights, all the substantive provisions of the Berne Convention are incorporated in the

19. 1886-Berne Convention Centenary-1986 (n. 14), 128.
20. Stewart (n. 16), 5.06.
21. Agreement on Trade-Related Aspects of Intellectual Property Rights (Apr. 15, 1994), 1869 UNTS 299 (hereinafter "TRIPS Agreement").
22. WIPO Copyright Treaty (Dec. 20, 1996) TRT/WCT/001 (hereinafter "WCT").

TRIPS Agreement and they become therefore obligations of the World Trade Organization member countries under the TRIPS Agreement.[23] TRIPS Agreement imposed further substantive provisions concerning computer programs, compilations of data, rental rights and enforcement.

Substantive provisions of the Berne Convention are also applied in the context of the WCT.[24] This Treaty imposes further obligations concerning computer programs, compilations of databases, right of distribution, right of rental, right of making available to the public, as well as obligations concerning technological measures and rights management information.

Berne Convention represents the classical international copyright system of harmonization and lies at the core of all international treaties on copyright.

National treatment and minimum rights is the basic method applied by the Berne Convention to achieve international protection tolerating national differences and divergences of laws, doctrines and judgments.

Berne Convention is characterized as the "most important instrument for transplanting copyright law worldwide."[25]

Berne Convention does not represent uniformity but addresses universal permanent principles, values and standards, such as the effective protection of authors' rights in their literary and artistic works, the recognition of moral and economic rights, the balance of rights by introducing limitations and exceptions not only to the extent of the economic rights but also to the term of protection.

8.2 BERNE PROVISIONS AND NATIONAL NORMS

The transplantation of international copyright[26] by the method of national treatment and minimum rights permits national preservation of laws, doctrines and norms.

National legislation and case law have differences between the countries of the Union, but national divergences are tolerated by the Berne Convention.[27]

23. TRIPS Agreement, Art. 9(1).
24. WCT, Art. 1(4); Regarding the so-called compliance clause *see* Jörg Reinbothe & Silke Von Lewinski, *The WIPO Treaties 1996* 35-36 (Butterworths- LexisNexis, 2002).
25. Paul Edward Geller, *Legal Transplants in International Copyright: Some Problems of Method*, 13 UCLA Pacific Basin Law Journal 199, 200 (1994) https://doi.org/10.5070/p8131022070.
26. *See Ibid.,* 199 et seq.
27. Jane Ginsburg, *Berne Without Borders: Geographic Indiscretion and Digital Communications, Stephen Stewart Memorial Lecture, Intellectual Property Institute,* Columbia Law School, Pub Law Research Paper No. 01-30, 7 (2001), http://papers.ssrn.com/paper.taf?abstract_id=292010 (accessed November 2023).

8.2.1 Moral and Economic Rights

Moral rights are recognized by Article 6bis of the Berne Convention, as it concerns the right of paternity and the right of integrity. Moral rights safeguard the personal connection between the author and his work and their protection is an issue of fundamental importance in the context of the digital technology in which there is a danger of modification, distortion and mutilation of protected works.

Many countries of the Union and in particular France[28] provide a wider protection of moral rights. Greek Copyright Law recognizes, apart from the right of paternity and the right to integrity, the right of divulgation, the right of access to work and the right of rescission.[29] It is also provided in this law that, after the expiry of the duration of copyright protection, the State, represented by the Minister of Culture, may exercise the rights relating to the acknowledgment of the author's paternity and the rights relating to the protection of the integrity of the work.[30]

Economic rights are recognized, under the Berne Convention, as exclusive rights, subject to certain limitations and exceptions, which are: the right of translation, the right of reproduction, the right of adaptation, arrangement and other alteration, the right of public performance and of communication to the public of a performance, the right of public recitation and of communication to the public of a recitation, the right of broadcasting and as it concerns cinematographic works the right of adaptation, reproduction, distribution, public performance and communication to the public.

The economic rights are differently implemented in the countries of the Union and new questions have arisen as a result of the digital technology. The reproduction and dissemination of works became rapid and easy. Authors have the possibility to create new forms of works, to distribute them rapidly but there is a big difficulty in controlling distribution and exploitation. The framework of exclusive rights was maintained, and the existing rights were interpreted broadly, but the control in the digital world remained difficult.

The reproduction right has been defined and adapted to the digital environment by the Information Society Directive (InfoSoc Directive)[31] and national legislations, but the principle recognized by Article 9 of the Berne

28. Code de la Propriété Intellectuelle, L. 121-1 to L. 121, *codes.droit.org/CodV3/propriete_intellectuelle.pdf* (November 2023).
29. Law 2121/1993 (Greek Copyright Act), Art. 4, www.wipo.int/wipolex/en/details.jsp?id=1790 (accessed November 2023).
30. Greek Copyright Act, Art. 29(2).
31. Directive 2001/29/EC of the European Parliament and of the Council of 22 May 2001 on the harmonization of certain aspects of copyright and related rights in the information society Official Journal L 167, 22/06/2001 pp. 10-19.

Convention remains intact and is fully applied in the digital environment according to the agreed statement of WCT.[32]

The right of communication to the public, including the right of making available, is provided in the framework of WCT and the InfoSoc Directive. National legislations adopted definitions and provisions similar to the international treaties and the *acquis communautaire* or have adapted the right to the digital environment. The notion of the "new public" emerged in a lot of discussion after the *Svensson*[33] judgment of the European Court of Justice (ECJ) and different interpretations.[34]

8.2.2 Protected Works

Subject matter of protection under Article 2(1) of the Berne Convention "literary and artistic works" including "every production in the literary, scientific and artistic domain" whatever may be the mode or form of its expression. The provision contains a non-exhaustive list of these works and many national legislations or case law protect other forms of works not included in the list.

Although it is not expressly mentioned, a work to be protected should be original. The notion of "original work" is found in Article 2(3) of the Berne Convention as it concerns the "translations, adaptations, arrangements and other alterations of a literary or artistic work," as well as in Article 14bis(1) concerning the "cinematographic" works.

Originality is not interpreted in a uniform way in the Union countries and there are many differences between national legislations, doctrines and case law. Legal systems are not the same and the differentiation between civil law and common law tradition still exists.

The British approach to originality is that of "skill, labor or judgment in producing the work" or similar criteria, such as effort and time.

The civil law approach has a subjective character and the predominant criterion is "the mark of the author's personality." This concept is generally accepted in the French system of *droit d' auteur* and in other continental tradition countries, where the character of personal creation and individuality prevails. The personal element is of basic importance also in Greek theory and jurisprudence. A work is original when it is the result of a personal contribution, when it expresses the author's personality, when it represents some individuality and when it is statistically unique.

32. Agreed statement concerning the WIPO Copyright Treaty (Dec. 20, 1996) Concerning Art. 1(4).
33. Case C-466/12 Nils Svensson and others v. Retriever Sverige AB (Feb. 13, 2014).
34. *See* indicatively: Stavroula Karapapa, *The Requirement for a "New Public" in the EU Copyright Law*, 1 European Law Review 63-81 (2017);Eleonora Rosati, *When Does a Communication to the Public under EU Copyright Law Need to Be a "New Public,"* https://papers.ssrn.com (accessed November 2023).

The United States Supreme Court in *Feist Publications v. Rural Telephone Service Co*[35] denied the "sweat of the brow" approach and held that originality is a constitutional requirement and "Rural's white pages lack the requisite originality." This decision should be interpreted as making clear that copyright protection rewards originality, not effort. The Supreme Court stated that Rural's selection is:

> selection of a sort, but it lacks the modicum of creativity necessary to transform mere selection into copyrightable expression. Rural expended sufficient effort to make the white pages directory useful, but insufficient creativity to make it original.

The EU Copyright Directives use the concept of "author's own intellectual creation" as it concerns the originality of three types of works: computer programs, databases and photographs. The ECJ in the *Infopaq*[36] case ruled that:

> the reproduction of an extract of a protected work which ... comprises 11 consecutive words thereof, is such as to constitute reproduction in part within the meaning of Article 2 of Directive 2001/29, if that extract contains an element of the work which, as such, expresses the author's own intellectual creation; it is for the national court to make this determination.

The adoption of the originality standard, as the "author's own intellectual creation" in the *Infopaq* case, was developed in posterior judgments of the ECJ and in particular, *BSA v. Ministry of Culture*,[37] *FAPL*,[38] *Painer v. Standard*,[39] *Football Dataco*[40] and *SAS Institute*.[41]

The criterion of originality, as "the author's own intellectual creation," is also used by Article 14 of Directive on Copyright in the Digital Single Market (CDSM Directive) (EU) 2019/790, as it concerns works of visual art in the public domain. According to the above Article 14 "when the term of

35. Feist Publications Inc v. Rural Telephone Service Co Inc, No. 89-1909, 499 U.S.340 (Supreme Court of the United States, 1991).
36. Case C-5/08 Infopaq International v. Danske Dagblades Forening (2009) ECLI:EU:C:2009:465, paras. 48-51. *See also* Tatiana-Eleni Synodinou, *The Foundations of the Concept of Work in European Copyright Law, Codification of European Copyright Law-Challenges and Perspectives* 97 (Walters Kluwer, 2012).
37. Case C-393/09 BSA v. Ministerstvo Kultury (2010) ECLI:EU:C:2010:816, para. 51.
38. Joined Cases C-403/08 and C-429/08 Football Association Premier League Ltd and Others v. QC Leisure and Others (C-403/08) and Karen Murphy v. Media Protection Services Ltd (C-429/08) (2011) ECLI:EU:C:2011:631, para. 155.
39. Case C-145/10 Eva Maria Painer v. Standard VerlagsGmbH, Axel Springer AG and others (2011) ECLI:EU:C:2011:798, para. 87.
40. Case C-604/10 Football Dataco Ltd, Football Association Premier League Ltd and others v. Yahoo UK Ltd, Stan James (Abington) Ltd and others (2012) ECLI:EU:C:2012:115, paras. 37-39.
41. Case C-406/10 SAS Institute Inc v. World Programming Ltd (2012) ECLI:EU:C:2012:259, para. 45.

protection of a work of visual art has expired, any material resulting from an act of reproduction of that work is not subject to copyright or related rights, unless the material resulting from that act of reproduction is original in the sense that is the author's own intellectual creation."

The question is if the criterion of "author's own intellectual creation" may be considered the minimum common standard in EU for the originality concept about all works. The interpretation depends on the evaluation of national courts, taking into consideration the differences in Members States' copyright protection.

The element of "intellectual creation" is implicitly required in the Berne Convention as basic element of protected works. The notion of "intellectual creations" is found in Article 2(5) of the Berne Convention, as it concerns the "collections of literary or artistic works."

The principle of works "created by humans" is generally accepted in the copyright field, but this concept is under discussion because of the famous "monkey selfie picture," the robots and artificial intelligence (AI).

Animal-made works of art[42] may be considered abstract creations, but, according to the classical tradition principles, they cannot be protected by copyright. The U.S. Copyright Office[43] expressly declared the human authorship requirement. The District Judge William Orrick decided, in January 2016, that copyright does not protect animals' works and "Naruto" is not an author within the meaning of the Copyright Act.[44]

AI works[45] is a new issue that raises numerous questions The main problem is, if the output generated by Generative AI programs may be protected by copyright and if the training process infringes copyright in intellectual works used for this training. The U.S. Copyright Office excludes from protection and registration non-human content.[46] Human authorship is required for "work" to be protected by copyright. The training of the AI

42. Animal-made art challenges human monopoly on creativity, https://www.wired.com/2012/02/animal-art/ (accessed Mar. 17, 2025).
43. *Copyrightable Authorship-US Copyright Office*, https://www.copyright.gov/.../ch300-copyrightable-auth (accessed Mar. 17, 2025).
44. Naruto v. David John Slater, No. 3:2015cv04324—Document 45 (N.D. Cal. 2016); Naruto v. David John Slater, No. 16-15469 (9th Cir. 2018); *See also* Andres Guadamuz, *The Monkey Selfie: Copyright Lessons for Originality in Photographs and Internet Jurisdiction*, 5 Internet Policy Review (2016) https://doi.org/10.14763/2016.1.398, https://papers.ssrn.com/sol3/papers.cfm?abstract_id=2752461 (accessed Mar. 17, 2025).
45. Andres Guadamuz, *Artificial Intelligence and Copyright* 14-19 (WIPO Magazine, 2017); Kalin Hristov, *Artificial Intelligence and the Copyright Dilemma,* 57 IDEA-The Journal of the Franklin Pierce Center for Intellectual Property 431,440 (2017), https://ipmall.law.unh.edu/sites/default/files/hosted_resources/IDEA/hristov_formatted.pdf (accessed Mar. 17, 2025); Paul Lambert, *Computer Generated Works and Copyright: Selfies, Traps, Robots, AI and Machine Learning,* 39 European Intellectual Property Review 12, 13 (2017) https://doi.org/10.31228/osf.io/np2jd, https://osf.io/np2jd (accessed Mar. 17, 2025).
46. Compedium of the United States Copyright Office, 2021, s. 312.2.

system by preexisting works protected by copyright, without the authorization of the author, is an infringement, unless existing exceptions or limitations are applied, such as text and data mining[47] or fair use. The criteria of protection by a sui generis right is also proposed similarly to the database maker's right.[48]

Is the Mars Rover's selfie in the public domain or the owner of copyright is National Aeronautics and Space Administration?[49] In copyright law, the author has a central role[50] and it is difficult to accept "the death of the author"[51] or *un droit d'auteur sans auteur*.[52]

8.2.3 Authorship

Article 1 of the Berne Convention speaks about the protection of the rights of authors in their literary and artistic works. Berne provisions do not contain the definition of the notion of author[53] for the obvious reason that some national laws recognize only natural persons as authors, whereas some others recognize legal entities as copyright owners. Berne Convention is open to all legal and philosophical systems regarding the authorship and entrusts the determination to the countries of the Union.

The author is the human creator and the originator of the work.[54] The U.S. Constitution (Article 1, section 8, Clause 8) recognizes to Congress the power to:

> promote the progress of science and useful arts, by securing for limited times to authors … the exclusive right to their … writings.

---

47. *See* Arts. 3 and 4 of Directive (EU) 2019/790 of 17 April 2017 on copyright and related rights in the Digital Single Market and amending Directives 96/9/EC and 2001/29/EC.
48. Tatiana Synodinou, at Copyright and the Challenges of AI, (Begoña González Otero & João Pedro Quintais, Kluwer Copyright blog, Sep. 25, 2018) https://copyrightblog.kluweriplaw.com/2018/09/25/singularity-copyright-challenges-artificial-intelligence/ (accessed November 2023); *AI Intelligence-Criteria for Protection*, https://europeancopyrightsocietydotorg.files.wordpress.com/2018/06/synodinou-ai-and-ownership.pdf (accessed November 2023).
49. Daniel Schönberger, *Deep Copyright: Up-And Downstream Questions Related to Artificial Intelligence (AI) and Machine Learning (ML)* at Droit d'auteur 4.0/Copyright 4.0.
50. Lionel Bently, *Copyright and the Death of the Author in Literature and Law*, 57 The Modern Law Review 973, 974 (1994) https://doi.org/10.1111/j.1468-2230.1994.tb01989.x.
51. Roland Barthes, *Image, Music and Text,* available at: 25, 236 (1986) TS Act 2000, Arts. 142-148 (1977) cited by Bently (n. 50).
52. Alain Strowel, *Liberté, Propriété, Originalité: Retour aux sources du droit d'auteur, Profiles de la Création* 141 (Bruxelles-Publications des Facultés Universitaires Saint-Louis, 1997).
53. Guide to the Berne Convention (n. 11), 11.
54. *See* Adolf Dietz, *The Concept of Author under the Berne Convention*, 155 Revue Internationale du Droit d' Auteur 3, 4-43 (1993).

Authors and creators are at the center of the copyright system[55] but in the digital world, where computer systems perform human tasks and users become authors, it is more difficult to define this notion.

Civil law tradition countries, such as France, Germany and Greece, follow the anthropocentric principle of authorship. This is the "principle of truth" phrased in the Greek copyright system by George Koumantos:[56]

> no other but the real author and his work can be considered to have acquired primary copyright in any manner.

Legal entities cannot be considered authors with the exception of specific cases, such as anonymous or pseudonymous works, collective works in France or in case of assignment and transfer of economic rights.

On the contrary, in common law tradition countries, the author or creator is usually the first owner of copyright, but the ownership depends on the circumstances under which the work was created and a legal entity may be considered the owner of copyright. Under the United Kingdom (U.K.) copyright system, in a sound recording, the first owner of copyright is the record producer.[57] Under the U.S. Copyright Act, if a work is made for hire, then the employer is considered to be the author even if the employee has created the work unless written agreement to the contrary.[58] The employer may be a legal entity or an individual.

The EU Software Directive[59] and Database Directive[60] leave to national legislation the determination of the author as a natural person or a legal entity.

Regarding cinematographic works, Article 14bis2(a) of the Berne Convention provides that "ownership" of copyright is a matter for legislation in the country where protection is claimed. This provision does not use the term "author" but speaks about ownership and leaves the countries of the Union free to adopt the system they want, recognizing authors as initial rightholders or producers as owners or both authors and producers. Under the U.K. Copyright system, the joint authors and first owners of copyright in a

---

55. *See* the analysis of Jane Ginsburg, *The Author's Place in the Future of Copyright*, Working Paper No. 512 (Mar. 5, 2015), http:web.law.columbia.edu/law-economic-studies/working papers (accessed November 2023).
56. George Koumantos, *Copyright* 164 (8th edn, Ant. Sakkoulas, 2002).
57. U.K. Copyright, Designs and Patents Act 1988, s. 9(2)(aa).
58. U.S. Copyright Act 1976, §201(b).
59. Directive 2009/24/EC of the European Parliament and of the Council of 23 April 2009 on the legal protection of computer programs, Art. 2(1) (Apr. 23, 2009) Official Journal L 111, 5/5/2009, pp. 16-22.
60. Directive 96/9/EC of the European Parliament and of the Council of 11 March 1996 on the legal protection of databases, Art. 4(1) (Mar. 11, 1996) Official Journal L 77, 27/3/1996, pp. 20-28.

film are the principal directors and the film producer.[61] The Rental Directive,[62] the Satellite Directive[63] and the Term Directive[64] explicitly provide that the principal director shall be considered the author or one of the authors of cinematographic or audiovisual works.

8.2.4 Limitations and Exceptions

Copyright has been evolved into a system of exclusive rights but the need to recognize some limitations and exceptions in specific cases has been acknowledged in the Diplomatic Conference of 1884. President Numa Droz, in his speech to the delegates, declared that "… limitations on absolute protection are dictated … by the public interest … ."[65]

Berne Convention allows national laws to provide certain limitations and exceptions on economic rights. These limitations concern: (1) the three-step test (Article 9(2)); (2) quotations and use of works by way of illustration in publications, broadcasts, sound or visual recordings for teaching purposes (Article 10); (3) reproduction of certain articles or broadcast works and use of works seen or heard in the course of reporting current events (Article 10bis) and ephemeral recordings for broadcasting purpose (Article 11bis(3)). These limitations are optional except for the provision concerning the quotations.[66]

Article 2bis of the Berne Convention gives national legislation the possibility to limit the protection of certain oral works, such as political speeches and speeches delivered in the course of legal proceedings, as well as lectures, addresses and other works of the same nature delivered in public. Authors enjoy the exclusive right of making a collection of such works.

Legislation in the Union countries may exclude from copyright protection the official texts of a legislative, administrative and legal nature and the official translations of those texts (Article 2(4) of the Berne Convention).

---

61. U.K. Copyright, Designs and Patents Act 1988, s. 9(2)(ab).
62. Directive 2006/115/EC of the European Parliament and of the Council of 12 December 2006 on rental right and lending right and on certain rights related to copyright in the field of intellectual property, Art. 2(2) (Dec. 12, 2006) Official Journal L 376, 27/12/2006, pp. 28-35.
63. Council Directive 93/83/EEC of 27 September 1993 on the coordination of certain rules concerning copyright and rights related to copyright applicable to satellite broadcasting and cable retransmission, Art. 2(5) (Sep. 27, 1993) Official Journal L 248, 6/10/1993, pp. 15-21.
64. Directive 2006/116/EC of the European Parliament and of the Council of 12 December 2006 on the term of protection of copyright and certain related rights, Art. 2(1) (Dec. 12, 2006) Official Journal L 372, 27/12/2006, pp. 12-18.
65. Ricketson & Ginsburg (n. 5), 13.01.
66. Herman Cohen Jehoram, *Restrictions on Copyright and Their Abuse*, 27(10) European Intellectual Property Review 359, 360 (2005).

News of the day or miscellaneous facts having the character of mere items of press information are excluded from protection (Article 2(8) of the Berne Convention). This provision implies that news and facts themselves are not copyrightable but, on the contrary, the articles of a journalist are protected by copyright. The recently proposed EU press publishers' right may harm journalists and photographers and would benefit publishers and big institutions by creating "broad rights of ownership in news and other information."

Term protection may be also considered a limitation in time (Article 7 of the Berne Convention).

Another kind of limitation is compulsory or legal licenses replacing the exclusive rights with a right of equitable remuneration. Article 11bis of the Berne Convention allows national legislation to determine the conditions for compulsory licenses concerning broadcasting and other rights.

National law, whether in common or in civil law countries, has been framed in order to ensure the balance between the interests of the creator and the need of the public to have access to creative works. Exceptions and limitations enable the users to reproduce and communicate to the public the work without infringing the exclusive rights of the author and are explained by respect for fundamental freedoms (freedom of expression and of the press, right of information), by the public interest (education, libraries, museums and archives) or by the impossibility of the rightholders to exercise their exclusive rights (reproduction for private use).

The members of the Berne Union have in their national laws used the limitations to copyright. However, there have been different approaches. Some countries have adopted very few limitations and others have used them all. Courts, in general, have been faithful to the restrictive philosophy of the Berne Convention. There are two main systems of limitations:[67]

- The "open system" of limitations is that of the "fair use" applied by the American copyright system or the "fair dealing" applied in common law countries. Fair use[68] is a doctrine codified in the U.S. Copyright Act 1976 (§107) allowing certain limitations to copyright and taking into consideration four criteria, such as the purpose and the character of the use, the nature of the copyrighted work, the amount of the work used and the effect of the use on the potential market or value of the copyrighted work.

67. Anne Lepage, *Overview of Exceptions and Limitations to Copyright in the Digital Environment*, 3 e-Copyright Bulletin 5-7 (2003).

68. Marshall Leaffer, *Understanding Copyright Law* 427 et seq. (3rd edn, Matthew Bender, 1999).

- The "closed system" of limitations is that of the civil law tradition countries, where the law expressly provides a specific list of limitations and exceptions. This is the system adopted in France, Germany, Greece and other countries of civil law tradition.

In the framework of the balance of interests, Article 5 of the InfoSoc provides an exhaustive list of limitations. Only one of the exceptions is mandatory, the exception of temporary acts of reproduction which are incidental to certain other acts. All other exceptions are optional. The ECJ, generally, holds the principle of strict interpretation of limitations and exceptions in several cases, such as in *Infopaq* and other judgments.[69]

The Directive (EU) 2019/790 on Copyright in the Digital Single Market introduces new mandatory exceptions on text and data mining (Articles 3-4), on the use of works and other subject matter in digital and cross-border teaching activities (Article 5) and on the preservation of cultural heritage (Article 6).[70]

The three-step test instituted by Article 9(2) of the Berne Convention, as a limitation to the right of reproduction, provides, also, a framework for the balance of interests:

> It shall be a matter for legislation in the countries of the Union to permit the reproduction of such works in certain special cases, provided that such reproduction does not conflict with a normal exploitation of the work and does not unreasonably prejudice the legitimate interests of the author.

The three-step test has since become part of almost all international treaties and EU Directives. According to Article 5(5) of the InfoSoc Directive, all exceptions are subject to the three-step test, as it is imperative for the legislator to define the scope of the limitations, as well as for the judge. The three-step test has been incorporated into certain national laws of Member States through a specific provision (i.e., Article 28C of Greek Copyright Law). At a Community level, it has caused an extensive scientific discussion and many questions, while a more open and dynamic

69. Case C-435/12, ACI Adam BV and others v. Stichting de Thuiskopie, Stichting Onderhandelingen Thuiskopie vergoeding (2014) ECLI:EU:C:2014:254, paras. 22-23.
70. *See* Jonathan Griffiths, Tatiana Synodinou & Raquel Xalabader, *Comment of the European Copyright Society Addressing Selected Aspects of the Implementantion of Articles 3 to 7 of Directive (EU) 2019/790 on Copyright in the Digital Market*, 72(1) GRUR International (December 2022), https://doi.org/10.1093/grurint/ikac137, https://www.researchgate.net/publication/366296049_Comment_of_the_European_Copyright_Society_Addressing_Selected_Aspects_of_the_Implementation_of_Articles_3_to_7_of_Directive_EU_2019790_on_Copyright_in_the_Digital_Single_Market (accessed Mar. 17, 2025).

interpretation is sought, aiming at the broadening of the scope of limitations and exceptions.[71]

8.3 FUTURE PERSPECTIVES

In the twentieth century, globalization[72] knocked the area of copyright through the Special 301 Report, prepared annually by the Office of the United States Trade Representative identifying countries which do not provide "adequate and effective" protection of intellectual property rights, as well as through the TRIPS Agreement and the rules for enforcement, subject to a dispute settlement mechanism and through the conversion of the intellectual work in a commercial product.

In the twenty-first century, when the Internet has offered the ability of easy access to the public for knowledge and information, copyright is called to protect creators in the digital world. The spread approach is that Internet democratized the knowledge and access to information. The cultural dimension of new technologies is a challenge for copyright regulation. Creators and rightholders search for new business models, as well as for technical and legislative solutions to protect copyright from unauthorized uses.

The WCT and the incorporation of the Berne Convention to its provisions updated the international protection of authors in the digital environment, but problems did not disappear.

The complex structure and technology of the Internet have an important influence on what can be done legally and what political options are at hand. The use of new technologies' market, as the manner for expanding the horizon of the global commercial exploitation, based on its interconnection and interoperability with other markets, in close co-operation with the banking system, allows the multiplication of the global commercial turnover. This expansion may result in free and easy access for the users to the creative works. The income, which is made by the intermediate sectors of the new technologies, based on the transmission and distribution of the creative works to their end-users, could allow economically these industries to offer knowledge and information for free to the society of users. The figures of these enterprises' balance sheets prove their economic growth.

The new technologies' market has not been faced in its totality, including the sectors of software business and enterprises providing "Over The Top" services and applications. Social media offer a new ecosystem of

71. *Declaration on a Balanced Interpretation of the Three-Step Test in Copyright Law*, https://www.ip.mpg.de/fileadmin/ipmpg/content/forschung_aktuell/01_balanced/declaration_three_step_test_final_english1.pdf (accessed Mar. 17,2025).
72. Samuel K. Murumba, *Globalizing Intellectual Property: Linkage and Challenge of a Justice Constituency*, 19 University of Pennsylvania Journal of International Law 435, 438-440 (2014).

connectivity and a new political power. "Over The Top" services play an important role in communication, providing content over the Internet and bypassing traditional distribution. These are the sectors that seem to gain the upper hand, economically and technologically in the market.

Apart from solitary entities and individuals, it is noticed that copyright experts and legislators have mainly focused on manufacturers of technical devices used for private copying, uploading and downloading of creative works, on intermediaries providing Internet services and recently on online content sharing service providers.

In a digital environment, the main questions which are raised would focus on the economic and moral dimensions of copyright for the creators and other rightholders, as well as on the legal and technical manner of licensing and enforcement and on the determination of the liable entities and individuals for payment of appropriate licensing or of fair remuneration fees.

In the intellectual property market, the creator/the rightholder is on the one side and the public is on the other side. The aim is that an artistic work should be used by the public. Nowadays, the digital market business factors (hardware, software, Internet Service Providers (ISPs) and platform enterprises), in combination with the Internet, act as intermediaries. It is evident that the Berne Convention plays a balancing role. However, the increasing involvement of new technologies in the intermediaries and the vast technical development have triggered the balance between creators/rightholders and the public.

The failure to provide appropriate fees to creators/rightholders for the use of their works—that has a direct negative impact on their livelihoods—known as the "Value of market research for creators" proves that creators receive almost nothing in the digital era, but their artistic works, used as "market vehicles" to sell hardware, software, ISPs and platforms' content and services, enable the intermediaries huge economic growth. The sought "transformation" of the artistic work to "commercial good" used for so-called information and education purposes deprives the creators/rightholders of their appropriate intellectual property rights. The public is invited to use the artistic works "free of charge."

However, it is evident that the public pays the cost of advertising, as well as the cost of direct licensing by platforms of content and services to the intermediaries. In the meantime, the intermediaries collect massively these paid amounts, together with the continuously increasing stock market value of their shares, and consequently, their business grows rapidly, resulting in market oligopolies.

Under these circumstances, the concept of "public interest" could be considerably modified, when it is going to be used for an attempt to limit, through intellectual property laws, the creators' property and moral rights or for an attempt to limit, through anti-trust laws, the economic, business and political power of the intermediaries' oligopolies, in the digital market, which is technically mastering all fields of economy, including the intellectual property market.

The "Value Gap" is partly solved by Article 17 of Directive (EU) 2019/790 (CDSM Directive) increasing the liability of online platforms for user-generated content under specific conditions. Protection for authors and performers is also provided by the CDSM Directive, as it concerns the exploitation of works and performances. In particular, Article 18 stipulates the principle of appropriate and proportionate remuneration in exploitation contracts, Article 19 sets out the transparency obligation, Article 20 provides the contract adjustment mechanism, Article 22 lays down the right of revocation and Article 21 provides that disputes concerning the transparency obligation and the contract adjustment mechanism may be submitted to a voluntary alternative dispute resolution procedure. These provisions are very important because they protect authors and performers usually in the weaker contractual position, when they grant a license or transfer their rights for the purpose of exploitation.[73]

"Net neutrality" and "open Internet" regulations could be preserved, despite the opposite order (December 14, 2017) of the U.S. Federal Communication Commission, but not to the detriment of the creators and other rightholders.

The adjustment of digital rights and further harmonization of the duration of the copyright may respond to the challenge of the digital age.

Blockchain[74] technology promises new approach for rights' management and licensing arrangements that benefit copyright holders without intermediaries.

The twenty-first century is the age of AI. We all know that AI systems have advantages and threats but they play a central role in the digital transformation of the single market. Despite the economic, social and political impact of this technology, new difficulties are opened up for copyright. Authors and creators support human-created works. Copyright should only protect human creativity. This principle is very important but algorithms and AI machines overturn the existing principles. AI regulation and ethics are under study and discussion.

AI Act[75] is the first text of AI law in the world to establish rules for different risk levels.: unacceptable risk, high risk, generative AI, limited risk. Generative AI, such as Chat GPT, has to comply with transparency obligations regarding copyright works or other material used as training data.

73. Recital 72 of (EU) Directive 2019/790.

74. EU Blockchain Observatory and Forum, https://www.eublockchainforum.eu (accessed November 2023).

75. Regulation (EU) 2024/1689 of the European Parliament and of the Council of 13 June 2024 laying down harmonised rules on artificial intelligence and amending Regulations (EC) No 300/2008, (EU) No 167/2013, (EU) No 168/2013, (EU) 2018/858, (EU) 2018/1139 and (EU) 2019/2144 and Directives 2014/90/EU, (EU) 2016/797 and (EU) 2020/1828 (Artificial Intelligence Act).

Providers of foundation models used in AI systems have also the obligation to "draw up and make publicly available a sufficiently detailed summary of the content used for training the general-purpose AI model."[76]

The rule should be that any use of works protected by copyright for AI activities requires the authorization of the creator or of other rightholder or remuneration in accordance with the EU legislation and the provisions of international treaties.

Amending the Berne Convention may be a possibility, but it is an unlikely situation. The authors have no reason for this demand.[77] Despite the digital problems and dilemmas, the Berne Convention rules belong to the tradition and have secured the international protection of authors, in a balanced manner, for a long time.

Berne Convention provides authors with a high level of protection at the international level by traditional principles that were maintained through the centuries. The flexibility of Berne provisions enabled the countries of the Union to preserve their national standards, their culture, their economy and their ideology. However, it is very difficult to achieve consensus for resolving the different problems.

National treatment and the provisions guaranteeing minimum rights are basic principles of international law in the field of intellectual property and are associated with the principle of cultural diversity and respect for all cultures, as these principles are confirmed in the United Nations Educational, Scientific and Cultural Organization (UNESCO) Convention on the protection and promotion of the diversity of cultural expressions (2005), as well as in the UNESCO Convention for the safeguarding of intangible cultural heritage (2003).

Berne Convention addresses universal principles and values without interference with national legal cultures and doctrines. Cultural diversity is very important in the framework of the digital environment and should be preserved.

Berne Convention is the reference point to control the compatibility of national provisions to international norms and represents a worldwide international harmonized system of authors' protection.

For all these reasons, the Berne Convention should remain "a uniting force" for the protection of creators and works of literature, art and science.[78]

---

76. Article 53(1)(d) and Recital 107 of the AI Act.
    See also the comments of Joao Pedro Quintais, *Generative AI, Copyright and AI Act*, IVIR, May 9, 2023, Kluwer Copyright Blog, https://copyrightblog.kluweriplaw.com/2023/05/09/generative-ai-copyright-and-the-ai-act/ (accessed Mar. 17, 2025).
77. Georges Koumantos, *The Future of the Berne Convention*, 11 Columbia-Volunteer Lawyers for the Arts Journal of Law and Arts 225, 236 (1986).
78. Eugen Ulmer, *One Hundred Years of the Berne Convention*, 17 International Review of Intellectual Property and Competition Law 707, 715 (1986) https://doi.org/10.4324/9781315092621-10.

Chapter 9

Universality or Diversity? The WIPO Role and Strategy in International Copyright Lawmaking

Jørgen Blomqvist[*]

Historically, copyright first came about at the national level in the form of codification of established practices regarding the issuance of privileges, and the early copyright laws showed quite some diversity. This was also the case in 1886 when the adoption of the Berne Convention[1] instituted international copyright protection. The very structure of the early Acts of the Convention bears witness to this, not least in the balance between national treatment and minimum rights.

National treatment, that is, the obligation for contracting parties to grant for works from other contracting parties at least the same protection as they grant for their own works, was the predominant obligation under the Berne Convention. Minimum rights were, compared to the latest 1971 Paris Act, scarce. The Berne Convention granted a quite limited right of translation in Article 5, and the presence of limitations and exceptions regarding reproduction of press articles[2] and use of works in publications for educational and scientific purposes, as well as chrestomathies,[3] seemed to presuppose the existence of a right of "publication" of works, that is, reproduction and

* All views and opinions expressed in this article are those of the author and do not represent any views or opinions of WIPO, its Member States or its International Bureau.

1. Berne Convention for the Protection of Literary and Artistic Works (Sep. 9, 1886), S. Treaty Doc. No. 99-27.
2. Berne Convention, Art. 7.
3. *Ibid.*, Art. 8.

(possibly) dissemination to the public. No underlying rights, however, were explicitly spelled out in the Convention. Neither was the right of public performance of dramatic, dramatico-musical and musical works,[4] because it was only referred to as a right to which Article 2 applied, that is, a right subject to national treatment; it was not formulated as a minimum right.

If one compares this starting point of the international norm-setting in the field of copyright and related rights with a more recent example, the Beijing Treaty,[5] there is a clearly visible difference. Not only does the Beijing Treaty contain a fully-fledged catalog of moral and economic rights,[6] but its Article 4 also limits the application of national treatment to the minimum rights and rights of equitable remuneration which are granted by the Treaty. Accordingly, the balance between national treatment and minimum rights has tipped over to a point where the former will have only very limited practical significance, if any.

This example illustrates how, over the years of international norm-setting in the field of copyright and related rights, there has been a tendency toward moving from a general framework allowing a very high degree of freedom regarding the contents of the national substantive rules toward a much more thorough international harmonization. The purpose of this chapter is to examine the role which has been played in this respect by the World Intellectual Property Organization (WIPO). WIPO is the United Nations (UN) specialized agency for intellectual property rights (IPRs). Apart from WIPO in a narrow sense, the examination in principle could also encompass WIPO's predecessor organization, the Bureaux Internationaux Réunis pour la Protection de la Propriété Intellectuelle (BIRPI), which was composed of the two distinct Bureaus for the Berne and Paris Conventions, respectively. From a formal point of view, the Berne Bureau and BIRPI were not intergovernmental organizations as WIPO is today. They were part of the Swiss Federal Government, which served as the secretariat for the Berne Union, established by the original Berne Act and subsequent Acts of the Convention. In order to complete the picture, we could also go slightly further and include the United Nations Educational, Scientific and Cultural Organization (UNESCO) and International Labour Organization which together with WIPO perform a number of administrative functions regarding the Rome Convention.[7] Henceforth, however, in order to maintain a contemporary rather than historical focus, BIRPI and the other organizations will not be separately examined.

4. *Ibid.*, Art. 9.
5. Beijing Treaty on Audiovisual Performances (Jun. 24, 2012), 3376 UNTS I-56432, (hereinafter Beijing Treaty).
6. Beijing Treaty, Arts. 5-11, 13-17.
7. Rome Convention for the Protection of Performers, Producers of Phonograms and Broadcasting Organizations (Oct. 26, 1961) 496 UNTS I-7247.

When we look closer into the role of WIPO, we need to realize that the organization that we often refer to rather loosely, in reality, is several quite distinct things. As such, WIPO is an intergovernmental organization, that is, basically an association the members of which are national governments. The Member States exert their power over the organization through its various Governing Bodies, such as the WIPO Assembly.[8] The organization has a secretariat, the International Bureau, headed by a Director General. Already here it becomes clear that it is not quite straightforward to talk about a strategy and a role in international copyright rulemaking. The various Member States will most commonly not hold identical views and positions on many such matters, and the rulemaking is, therefore, a result of sometimes difficult political compromises, whether expressed in the form of normative acts, soft law, or policy guidelines for the work of the International Bureau.

In addition to this, the organization can be said to have a double role, both legislative and executive. First, it is the forum of, and its International Bureau is serving in a secretarial capacity, the Member States' governments when enacting new international instruments, or enacting new versions of existing such instruments. Second, at the request of individual Member States, it is providing advice to governments and legislators on new legislation and updating of existing legislation. In the past, such advice has typically been given under several different forms, such as the elaboration of model laws, whether as an executive activity of the International Bureau or a collective endeavor encompassing the Member States' governments in a committee of experts; the provision of draft copyright laws, adapted to the legal tradition and economic realities of the individual countries; the provision of comments and suggestions regarding existing legislation; and the provision of comments and suggestions regarding draft new legislation elaborated by the government requesting the advice.

In the following, we shall first examine the importance of the legislative activities of and within the organization in section 9.1 below, and then we shall take a closer look at the advisory activities in section 9.2 below. In section 9.3 below we shall look briefly at the present state of play before concluding in section 9.4 below. It is necessary, however, to further limit the scope of our examination, because, in terms of size, a full description of how these different fields have evolved over the Centuries in which the organization has existed in different incarnations would be more fitting for a thesis than for a chapter such as the present. We shall therefore focus on the developments during the last 40-50 years, that is, more or less since the adoption of the 1971 Paris Act of the Berne Convention and the subsequent

8. The structure of the organization is quite complex. For further details, *see* Carolyn Deere Birkbeck, *The World Intellectual Property Organization: A Reference Guide* 67-105 (Edward Elgar Publishing, 2016).

adoption of the Phonograms Convention[9] in 1971 and the Satellite Convention[10] in 1974. Even within this timespan, there is a good reason to concentrate on understanding the last 25 years, where important developments have taken place.

9.1 NORM SETTING AT WIPO

At the point in time when our examination starts, the situation was under change. The preceding revision of the Berne Convention had been tumultuous. It had been prepared in the, at the time, traditional way through cooperation between the International Bureau and the host government of the upcoming diplomatic conference, in this case Sweden, and as part of the preparation, a number of meetings of governmental experts had taken place. A number of developing countries had expressed concerns that increasing levels of minimum rights would not be acceptable to them, and it had only been possible under great difficulties to reach an agreement at the 1967 Stockholm Revision Conference. Even that agreement, however, proved unacceptable for some countries and only the 1971 Paris Revision Conference succeeded in reaching a lasting agreement.[11] It was clear, though, that any future revision of the Convention would be very difficult, if possible at all, due to the increasing political disagreements. In the words of former WIPO Director General Arpad Bogsch:

> WIPO and the Berne Union try to keep pace with those changes [in technology and in the socio-economic environment] and seek solutions to the new problems as they emerge. Since the 1971 (Paris) conference of revision of the Berne Convention, such solutions are sought in ways other than a new revision of the Berne Convention. The high number of the countries party to that Convention (76 at the date of the centenary in 1986), the greater differences in wealth among the member countries and the enormous cultural variety among them make it difficult if not unlikely, at least on major issues, to obtain the unanimity that is required for any revision of the Berne Convention (Berne (Paris) Convention, Article 27(3)).[12]

9. Convention for the Protection of Producers of Phonograms Against Unauthorized Duplication of Their Phonograms (Oct. 29, 1971) UNTS I-12430.
10. Brussels Convention Relating to the Distribution of Programme-Carrying Signals Transmitted by Satellite (May 21, 1974) UNTS I-17949.
11. *See,* for example, Sam Ricketson & Jane C. Ginsburg, *International Copyright and Neighbouring Rights: The Berne Convention and Beyond* 117ff. (3rd edn, Oxford University Press, 2022).
12. Arpad Bogsch, *The First Hundred Years of the Berne Convention for the Protection of Literary and Artistic Works,* 22(9) WIPO Copyright 291, 327 (1986). As of the end of the year 2024, the number of Member States of the Berne Union is 181.

However, certain pressing problems in the field of related rights, notably due to the limited scope and membership of the Rome Convention, had found their solutions through the adoption of the Phonograms and Satellite Conventions.

Obviously, when the Member States of an intergovernmental organization disagree on fundamental issues, it cannot pursue a role or strategy aiming at universalism. The differences in opinion reflect that the Member States, or groups among them, either already have or intend to pass national legislation at different levels of protection because they have differing national views of opinion and strategies as to what would be the optimal solution for their countries. This does not rule out, however, that the picture may reveal several nuances when examined in closer detail. Disagreements do not necessarily cover all issues, and the ongoing technological development made close international cooperation useful, not least in terms of gathering information, analyzing the issues and discussing possible solutions to the various problems that were emerging.

We enter here what Sam Ricketson termed the "period of guided development."[13] It lasted from the 1970s until the beginning of the 1990s, and during that time, various committees of WIPO and UNESCO met and discussed a number of topical questions, namely: reprography, computer use and storage of works, protection of computer programs, videocassettes, cable television, expressions of folklore, rental of phonograms, private copying, direct broadcast satellites, employed authors, publishing contracts and piracy.[14] Those discussions did not result in binding norms, except for those that later crystallized into the Trade-Related Aspects of Intellectual Property Rights (TRIPS) Agreement,[15] the WIPO Copyright Treaty (WCT) and the WIPO Performances and Phonograms Treaty (WPPT).[16] Some of the meetings passed resolutions or recommendations, notably regarding reprography[17] and the storage and use of protected works in computer memories,[18] but frequently the meeting reports were the only formal outcome of the discussions. And even such resolutions did not do much in terms of unification. As Arpad Bogsch later commented on the resolution regarding

13. Ricketson & Ginsburg (n. 11), 126ff.
14. Bogsch (n. 12), 326ff.
15. Agreement on Trade-Related Aspects of Intellectual Property Rights (Apr. 15, 1994), 1869 UNTS 299, (hereinafter "TRIPS").
16. WIPO Copyright Treaty (Dec. 20, 1996) 2186 UNTS I-38542, Arts. 4, 5, 6, 7, 14 (hereinafter "WCT"); WIPO Performers and Phonograms Treaty (Dec. 20, 1996) 2186 UNTS I-38543, Arts. 8, 12, 9, 13, 23 (hereinafter "WPPT").
17. *Sub-Committee of the Executive Committee of the International Union for the Protection of Literary and Artistic Works on Reprographic Reproduction sitting together with Sub-Committee of the Intergovernmental Copyright Committee on Reprographic Reproduction* 11(8) WIPO Copyright 159, 175 (1975).
18. *Second Committee of Governmental Experts on Copyright Problems Arising from the Use of Computers for Access to or the Creation of Works* 18(9) WIPO Copyright 239, 254ff. (1982).

reprography: "The resolution is far from recommending in any precise manner what national laws could or should provide for."[19] Thus, it is rather obvious from the context that universality in the sense of aiming at identical provision at the national level was way beyond the achievable at that time, and it was certainly not a part of the organization's role or strategy.

Less would have to do, but what WIPO actually accomplished deserves no denigration. The organization still played a significant role in its endeavors toward a certain degree of uniformity, namely a common approach to the issues and a common analysis of the problems, caused by the emerging technologies. The various discussions of topical issues were based on elaborate and detailed documents, prepared either by the International Bureau of WIPO or by external experts, and thereby the International Bureau played a significant role in guiding the discussions and showing possible solutions.[20] One may also mention a number of examples, whether in the form of definitions or rules, which originated during that period and which are generally accepted, included in later international instruments, or at least clearly prevailing trends, in national legislation around the Globe.

Reprographic reproduction in schools, libraries or private enterprises cannot be made without limitations or licensing; either the extent must be limited by national law or a suitable compensation system must be implemented (or both); computer programs are protected under copyright law, and to the extent they are original they must be seen as creative expressions; private reproduction of computer programs is not permitted in general, but only to the extent necessary for purposes of lawful use, compatibility, safety and back-up; the right of reproduction applies to reproduction in digital media, such as computer memories or external digital memories, such as DVDs or USB keys; the rules concerning broadcasting apply regardless whether the broadcast is terrestrial or via satellite.

In the field of cable television, agreement was even reached on a set of annotated principles drafted in the style of legislative texts.[21] They were surely influential too, even though perhaps a bit too wordy for most national drafting styles.

However, we can also see areas where, despite thorough discussion, no clear consensus emerged, such as the question of whether rights owners should receive compensation for the reproduction of their works or recordings made on blank media sold to the general public, such as cassette tapes, blank CDs or DVDs, or computer memory sticks. Here, views remain at odds

19. Bogsch (n. 12), 328.
20. *Ibid.*, 327.
21. Subcommittees of the Executive Committee of the Berne Union, of the Intergovernmental Committee of the Universal Copyright Convention and of the Intergovernmental Committee of the Rome Convention on Television by Cable, *Annotated Principles of Protection of Authors, Performers, Producers of Phonograms and Broadcasting Organizations in Connection with Distribution of Programs by Cable* 20(4) WIPO Copyright 131, 146ff. (1984).

as they also do in relation to the anchoring of such systems in the international treaty system, including notably its rules on national treatment.[22] Another issue where no agreement was reached was that of the applicable law in case of direct satellite broadcasting covering more than one national territory.[23] In this case, even geopolitical tensions contributed to the disagreements. The solution suggested and argued for by the International Bureau (and even in daily parlance named after the then Director General, the "Bogsch theory") implied that the applicable law should be the law of all countries where the satellite signal could be received. Due to inevitable overspill, this would give rights owners in Eastern European countries influence on the clearance of rights for broadcasting originating from the neighboring Western European countries, something that the latter could not accept.[24]

As the above description shows, there was not much room for any ambitious strategy or role for the organization to play in terms of international harmonization, let alone unification, of national legislation during much of the period of "guided development." Things changed a little, however, toward the end of that period. At the time when General Agreement on Tariffs and Trade (GATT) negotiations were underway which would eventually lead to the establishment of the World Trade Organization (WTO) and the adoption of the TRIPS Agreement, WIPO undertook an exercise which revealed a shift in focus away from norm-setting at the treaty level toward exerting a more targeted influence on national legislation. First, in 1988 a Committee of Experts summarized and synthesized a large number of "principles" describing the protection of various categories of works,[25] and in the following two years, a Committee of Experts discussed a Model Law on copyright and related rights. The work was based on elaborate documents containing an annotated draft model law,[26] and the documentation for the last of the committee meetings in 1990,[27] prepared by the International Bureau, summarized the previous discussions and listed a number of "Issues in Respect of Which Further Advice is Sought." It is interesting to note that the

22. *See,* for example, regarding the TRIPS Agreement, Daniel Gervais, *The TRIPS Agreement, Drafting History and Analysis* 210f. (5th ed., Sweet & Maxwell, Thompson Reuters, 2021).
23. Bogsch (n. 12), 332.
24. Jørgen Blomqvist, *Primer on International Copyright and Related Rights* 51 (Edward Elgar Publishing, 2014).
25. *Committee of Governmental Experts on the Evaluation and Synthesis of Principles on Various Categories of Works*, (Geneva. Jun. 27 to Jul. 1, 1988), 24(10), (11) and (12) WIPO Copyright, 364ff., 445ff. and 506ff. (1988).
26. *Committee of Experts on Model Provisions for Legislation in the Field of Copyright, First Session* at WIPO Meetings 25(5) WIPO Copyright 146ff. (1989); *Committee of Experts on Model Provisions for Legislation in the Field of Copyright, Second Session* at WIPO Meetings 25(12) WIPO Copyright 362ff. (1989).
27. *Committee of Experts on Model Provisions for Legislation in the Field of Copyright. Third Session* at WIPO Meetings 26(9) WIPO Copyright 241ff. (1990).

ambition was to "inspire and influence governments and legislators to improve their intellectual property laws and opt for solutions that will increase the degree of similarity among legislations whenever the special interests of a country do not require different solutions."[28] Thus, universality was the ideal aim, but the reality of diversity, based on differing interests, had to be factored in. In addition, the form of the planned outcome of the exercise shows that the intention was to obtain as much harmonization as politically possible, but in the form of an overall harmonization rather than an outright uniformity of national legislation. In the words of the 1988-1989 Program and Budget of WIPO:

> The norms (standards) will take the form of guidelines or model provisions for national or regional legislations and, in respect of questions for which the conclusion of a multilateral treaty has serious chances of being successful, the norms (standards) will take the form of draft treaties. Guidelines are indications of how to achieve certain objectives, and "model" provisions are mere examples ("models"). Either may or may not be followed by legislators. Neither creates obligations for anyone ...
>
> [...]
>
> In the field of literary and artistic works, uniform solutions, in the form of guidelines or model provisions for legislations, will be proposed.[29]

The understanding of the term "model provisions" was further elaborated in the document prepared for the last of the meetings:

> The word "model" has various meanings. One of the meanings is, indeed, that a model is a standard of excellence, something ideally good. But the other and more frequently used meaning is that a model is a guide or an example, for the preparation and creation of something (something—in our case, of national laws—that itself serves certain purposes and, thus, should correspond to those purposes). In the Program of WIPO, the word "model" is used in the latter meaning [...].[30]

Even so, no Model Law was adopted by the meetings, and views differed on a number of issues when the last session was concluded. The immediate outcome was, therefore, the working documents, containing legislative provisions with numerous alternative solutions and square brackets; the meeting reports, reflecting the different views on the various issues;

28. *Ibid.*, 242.
29. Program and Budget of WIPO for the 1988-1989 biennium, WIPO Document AB/XVIII/2, Annex A, item PRG.04, here quoted from 26(9) WIPO Copyright, 242 (1990).
30. *Committee of Experts on Model Provisions for Legislation in the Field of Copyright* (n. 27), 244 (emphasis in source text).

and an understanding that afterward the Model Law would be published by the International Bureau under its own responsibility.[31] Thus, even if ambitions had been higher and aimed at some level of harmonization, or even unification in limited areas, the practical reality was that the political will to accept compromise in respect of many issues simply was not there. In the end, no Model Law was ever published. It did not make sense to publish such a document, because the next major copyright issue that would occupy WIPO was the preparation of the "Possible Protocol to the Berne Convention" which eventually became the WCT. When entering into a phase of political negotiations with the aim of reaching an agreement on a new international instrument, it would be uncomfortable for all parties if the International Bureau were to publish such a document which might influence, or even freeze, the different positions.

The work was not in vain, however, as it gave a useful base for the work of the International Bureau advising governments of developing countries, and soon governments of countries in transition from planned economy toward market economy as well, on how to establish national legislation that is compatible with the international instruments. This will be discussed in section 9.2 below.

Compared to the previous revisions of the Berne Convention—and the preparation of the Rome Convention as well—the preparation of the WCT and the WPPT changed, as it was no longer spearheaded by a prospective host government with the assistance of the International Bureau. Now, the work took place in two Committees of Experts, which eventually for all practical purposes worked as a single committee dealing with both instruments, under the chairmanship of the same government representative throughout, namely Mr. Jukka Liedes of Finland. At the outset, the work was based on elaborate memoranda prepared by the International Bureau and then discussed in the Committees, but as discussions increasingly moved from the technical to the political level, the procedure changed. Progress was slow until the adoption of the TRIPS Agreement in April 1994, but later the same month it was decided that the working papers from the International Bureau for the next committee meetings should be considered informal working papers only. They should be circulated for comments by governments for subsequent inclusion in the papers before being discussed by the Committees. The following sessions of the Committees went even further by deciding that all discussions were to be based solely on government proposals and, apart from compiling and organizing the presentation of those proposals, the International Bureau was only requested to prepare a limited number of memoranda on few and carefully defined issues.[32] This development illustrates how the strategy in this work was quite narrowly aiming at

31. *Ibid.*, 243f.
32. *World Intellectual Property Organization 1992-2007* 48 (WIPO Publication No. 1011E, Geneva, 2007).

adopting international instruments going as far in terms of harmonization as governments could actually agree on. During the negotiations, nobody ever mentioned the possibility of going away from the established system of the Berne and Rome Conventions—which had also been adopted in the TRIPS Agreement—that harmonization took the form of minimum requirements regarding the substantive rights, that is, "reined in diversity" rather than "universality."

It is interesting to notice, however, that the actual outcome of the Treaties and the subsequent national legislation in some areas actually has been close to universality, for example, as regards the protection against unlawful deletion or tampering with rights management information,[33] where the provisions in the implementing national statutes are practically identical. The implementation of the protection against circumvention of technological protection measures, however, presents much more important national differences.[34]

If we now turn our attention to more recent times, there has been a significant development in the Organization's policies since the turn of the century. Most prominent in this respect is the WIPO Development Agenda, which was adopted by the WIPO General Assembly at its session in September-October 2007.[35] Looking at Cluster B of this Agenda, which contains the principles relating to norm-setting, flexibilities, public policy and public domain, there is a conspicuous lack of references to unification of national legislation. On the contrary, a good deal of the principles rather point toward a policy of leaving the highest possible level of flexibility for national legislators, not least in developing and least-developed countries. For example, WIPO's norm-setting activities shall "take into account different levels of development";[36] and the Organization's activities, including norm-setting "should take into account the flexibilities in international intellectual property (IP) agreements, especially those which are of interest to developing countries and Least Developed Countries (LDCs)";[37] WIPO should "initiate discussions on how, within WIPO's mandate, to further facilitate access to knowledge and technology for developing countries and LDCs to foster creativity and innovation and to strengthen such existing activities within WIPO";[38] and, in supporting the UN development goals, including the Millennium Declaration, address in its working documents for norm-setting activities issues such as, among others, "safeguarding national implementation of intellectual property rules," "potential flexibilities, exceptions and limitations for Member States" and "the possibility of additional

33. WCT, Art. 12; WPPT, Art. 19.
34. Guilda Rostama, *Scoping Study on the Impact of the Digital Environment on Copyright Legislation Adopted Between 2006 and 2016*, WIPO Document SCCR/35/4, 36ff.
35. General Report adopted by the Assemblies para. 334, WIPO document A/43/16.
36. *Ibid.*, Annex A, item 15 and Annex B, item 10.
37. *Ibid.*, Annex A, item 17 and Annex B, item 12.
38. *Ibid.*, Annex A, item 19 and Annex B, item 14.

special provisions for developing countries and LDCs."[39] All the items quoted seem to point toward lesser constraints for national legislators, rather than toward any tendency toward universality. Even more clearly, they point toward a political acceptance of and a strategic move toward a stronger emphasis on different levels of obligations for developing and least-developed countries on the one side and developed countries on the other. Thus, even if it has been argued that the Berne Appendix and its additional flexibilities for developing countries have not been particularly successful,[40] it represents a general strategy, which may not have been predominant for a while, but now it has been formally revived.

The international treaties adopted since then, the Marrakesh[41] and Beijing Treaties, however, do not contain provisions allowing different levels of protection for different categories of Contracting Parties, and such provisions have not appeared in the discussions regarding the protection of broadcasting organizations, either. It is, however, interesting to note that the Marrakesh Treaty seems to display a certain ambition of universality. Each of the main operative provisions of the Treaty starts out with a rather succinct and obligatory rule, which is followed by a more elaborated provision indicating how Contracting Parties may implement the obligatory rule. This way of drafting very much resembles a model law, and that falls well in line with the overall purpose of the Treaty which is not only to propagate limitations and exceptions for the benefit of persons with reading impairments but in particular also to facilitate the international circulation of special format copies, made for the use of the beneficiaries. Obviously, for such international cooperation, nearly identical or at least quite similar provisions in all relevant national legislation are a major enabling and facilitating factor.

The quite opposite tendency can be observed in relation to the Beijing Treaty. Here the main underlying problem was that national protection of performing artists, as regards audiovisual fixations of their performances, had developed without the guidance of international treaties. It varied from no legal protection at all, via a high level of contractual rights based on a rather slim layer of copyright (as in the U.S.A.), to medium and high levels of protection based on related, or neighboring, rights. The main purpose of the Beijing Treaty was to bring this area from disparate national systems, which covered only national beneficiaries, to an international system where performers would enjoy protection in other countries party to the Treaty where the audiovisual fixations of their performances are used. Here, the existing differences in protection level for all practical purposes made any ambition of unification illusory. Making the different systems work together

39. *Ibid.*, Annex A, item 22.
40. Blomqvist (n. 24), 191.
41. Marrakesh Treaty to Facilitate Access to Published Works for Persons Who Are Blind, Visually Impaired or Otherwise Print Disabled (Jun. 27, 2013) UNTS I-54134.

was in itself an ambitious endeavor. Let us just mention Article 11 of the Treaty, on the right of broadcasting and communication to the public. One may argue that it is one of the most important rights, granted in the Treaty because it is the legal basis for ongoing payment of royalties to the performers. Nevertheless, the provision was aptly termed an *à la carte* provision when it was negotiated at the Diplomatic Conference in 2000, because in reality, it enables Contracting Parties to pick and choose their level of protection, including no protection at all, while other countries would then be entitled not to grant national treatment, but only material reciprocity. The *raison d'être* of the provision is the fact that without it, performers could not claim any rights whatsoever in other countries, as it follows from the provision on national treatment in Article 4 of the Treaty.

The discussions on the protection of broadcasting organizations, which has been on the agenda of the SCCR since the Committee first took up its work in 1998, also seem to be leaving a very high degree of flexibility for national legislators. This is evidenced by a focus on the protection of the emitted signal, which leaves out any rights in acts, committed after the fixation of the signal. Also the level of protection in relation to other emission techniques than terrestrial, satellite and non-interactive cable emissions is highly controversial. Obviously, the lower the level of minimum rights in an international treaty, the more flexibility there will be for implementing national legislation, and the more possibility there will be for diversity, rather than uniformity. Furthermore, there are significant national diversities in the existing legislation, for example, in the way that not all countries protect broadcasting organizations under copyright or related rights, but rather under telecommunication law. Thus, as the negotiations stand, there is little reason to expect that a future treaty will be a unifying exercise.[42]

Let us finally take note of the fact that no explicit strategy or policy regarding universality or diversity is formulated in WIPO's Program of Work and Budget for the 2024-2025 biennium[43] as regards the normative activities of the Organization. This document, obviously, primarily shows the activities and priorities of the International Bureau, but presumably, they are written and adopted on the background of the overall strategy and policy of the organization as such. For copyright, its aim is "[f]acilitating discussions in the SCCR on substantive agenda items and copyright-related emerging issues, including exceptions and limitations as per the SCCR agenda."[44] Among the expected results of the work of the Copyright Sector in the biennium, we find: "[d]evelopment of balanced and effective international normative frameworks for IP"; and "[d]evelopment of balanced and effective

42. Third Revised Draft Text for the WIPO Broadcasting Organizations treaty, WIPO document SCCR/44/3.
43. Program of Work and Budget for 2024-2025, WIPO 2023.
44. *Ibid.,* 31.

IP, innovation and creative ecosystems in Member States."[45] These results clearly appear to remain true to the policies formulated in the Development Agenda, and they seem to reflect a very high degree of political common sense. At a very basic level, it is probably justified to generalize by saying that national governments accept to submit themselves to international norms only to the extent they consider it advantageous for their national interests. That is what governments are there for. Among those interests is to ensure protection abroad of its nationals at the highest possible level. Equally important, however, is to maintain the highest possible national sovereignty and flexibility, not least in the act of balancing the opposing interests of rights owners, users, the general public and special interest groups, which is at the heart of any national copyright policy and, accordingly, legislation. For many countries that mainly import works and other protected subject matter from abroad, the balance of payments regarding use of foreign rights versus income from own works used abroad inevitably also plays a role. WIPO, both the organization as such and its International Bureau, is guided by the Member States and therefore cannot but take a realistic stance. Unless there is a special reason for unified national provisions, a reason which is perceived as advantageous by all countries in question, it is not a realistic strategy.

9.2 WIPO'S LEGISLATIVE ASSISTANCE

We will now turn toward the other main function of WIPO that has influence on national legislation, the legislative assistance to developing countries. Such assistance is given only at the request of the country in question, in accordance with the general principles followed by the UN and its specialized agencies, and it is tailored advice, taking into account specific country needs and situations.[46] The advice is confidential as far as WIPO's International Bureau is concerned, whereas the receiving governments are free to publicize it if they so choose.[47,48]

The legislative assistance offered by WIPO is demand-driven, not only in terms of given only when asked for but also in terms of its form and extent,

45. *Ibid.,* 34.
46. https://www.wipo.int/ip-development/en/policy_legislative_assistance/ (accessed Jan. 25, 2024).
47. The author of this chapter has worked on providing such advice while employed by WIPO. For this reason, several observations in the following are kept in general terms, in order not to reveal any content of advice given to specific countries, and, in general, it has not been possible to provide documentation in the form of references to specific national legislation. In so far, the following represents but a generalizing and non-exhaustive personal account.
48. Arpad Bogsch, *The First Twenty Five Years of the World Intellectual Property Organization from 1967 to 1992* 52 (WIPO Publication No. 881(E), Geneva, 1992).

and in practice, it normally depends on the prevailing situation in the country in question. In some very few countries, there is no copyright statute at all and in others, there is a statute, but it is outdated and perhaps reflects the situation in the country before, or shortly after, its independence. In such cases, it is not unusual that the Government will choose to start from scratch and request a draft statute, which is compatible with the applicable international treaty framework. In the past, the Model Law on Copyright for Developing Countries adopted by the Committee of Governmental Experts convened by the Tunisian Government in Tunis from February 23 to March 2, 1976, (the Tunis Model Law) was prepared as a general basis on which the advice could be based. It was supplemented with comments by the Secretariat of UNESCO and the International Bureau of WIPO and subsequently published.[49] With no more than 18 sections in the statute, it was short and concise, but it still provided for flexibilities. By means of square brackets, a number of options were kept open, in particular relating to the main differences between the common law and the civil law traditions, such as the requirement of fixation as a precondition for protection, the ownership of works created in employment relationships and the rules regarding ownership or legitimation to exploit rights in audiovisual ("cinematographic") works. Also, the *droit de suite* (artists' resale right), which is optional under Article 14ter of the Berne Convention, is included in square brackets. In addition, two annexes provide optional provisions for those developing countries that may choose to implement and make notifications regarding the Appendix to the Berne Convention and thereby introduce certain nonvoluntary licenses for translation, broadcasting and reproduction of protected works for educational purposes.

While short and concise, some may also consider the Model Law somewhat over-ambitious because the drafters had been tempted to include provisions about the *domaine public payant,* that is, an obligation to pay a fee for use of public domain works, the proceeds of which are to be used for certain purposes to the benefit of authors. Then, as now, that might be more an issue for political discussion than a "must-have" in the national legislation of developing countries. The commentary rightly states that such a legal system "is already known to certain legislations," but it does not spell out explicitly that it is not obligatory under any of the international conventions.[50]

In addition, and after several years of preparation, the Intergovernmental Committee of the Rome Convention adopted a commented Model Law Concerning the Protection of Performers, Producers of Phonograms and Broadcasting Organizations in 1974.[51]

---

49. Tunis Model Law on Copyright, reprinted in 12(6) WIPO Copyright 165 (1976).
50. *Ibid.*, 179.
51. Model Law Concerning the Protection of Performers, Producers of Phonograms and Broadcasting Organizations (WIPO Publication 811(E)), 10(6) WIPO Copyright 163 (1974).

With the passing of time, those Model Laws became outdated, and, as described above in relation to WIPO's norm-setting activities, attempts were made to prepare new versions during the early 1990s. The outcome of that activity was an elaborate draft as well as quite meticulous records of the differing views in the many fields where governments did not agree. As also mentioned above, the International Bureau did not publish any new model law. Instead, the advice to developing countries, and later also countries in transition from a planned economy toward a market economy, was based on increasingly diversified draft laws, adapted to the legal traditions, drafting traditions and, indeed, level of development of the recipient countries. It also became increasingly common that countries while requesting a draft law also specified particular wishes, such as limitations and exceptions covering distance education, persons with disabilities or provisions covering decompilation of computer programs. At the same time, the International Bureau became increasingly aware that the term "model law" by some observers was understood as an indication of supremacy—that it was promoted as an ideal model that preferably should be followed—where the underlying intention was an example for further discussion on how a national law could be drafted.

Even so, nobody in his or her right mind would restart the drafting from scratch every time a new request for assistance was made, and the specialized staff of the International Bureau obviously also used a stock of boilerplate texts. It is free for anyone to try to identify the main tenor of such texts by comparing national legislation from different developing countries and transition countries, adopted during different eras. Even without having done so, but based on observations done while working with much different national legislation over a span of years, it is probably safe to state that WIPO has had quite a significant influence on national legislation. The two Model Laws were a unifying factor at their time, and many of their elements can be identified in national legislation adopted from the late 1970s and well into the 1980s.

Starting in the first half of the 1990s and lasting throughout the Decade, much new national legislation in developing and transition countries began to implement the specific additional provisions, which had been included in the TRIPS Agreement. This was at least to some extent a consequence of the fact that the International Bureau of WIPO after the adoption of the Agreement broadened its technical, including legislative, assistance to requesting countries. Where it earlier mainly dealt with the instruments adopted under WIPO's auspices, it now also included the TRIPS Agreement, as mandated in Article 4 of the 1995 Agreement Between the WIPO and the WTO.[52] If one takes the time it would take to look through a large number

52. Agreement between the World Intellectual Property Organization and the World Trade Organization (Dec. 22, 1995), https://www.wto.org/english/tratop_e/trips_e/wtowip_e.htm (accessed Jan. 25, 2024).

of statutes of developing, least-developed and transition countries, adopted during those years, one would notice a certain level of uniformity. It was inevitable for the staff of the International Bureau to use boilerplate texts, not least during the hectic years when many developing countries sought advice in preparation for the entry into force of the TRIPS substantive provisions for developing countries in 2005. The uniformity one would find doing such an exercise, however, would not be complete, and for several reasons. Drafting styles are different. Even within the common law and civil law traditions, respectively, there are several different "dialects." Some national legislators have decided to modify the provisions in order to adapt them to the specific conditions in their countries. Differences in the wordings that one will find in, for example, WIPO's very comprehensive database of national legislation, WIPO lex,[53] may also simply be due to the several translations to and from the national language, which many texts have undergone during their preparation and after their adoption.

A further layer was added to much national legislation following the adoption of the WCT and WPPT in 1996, but in reality, it can be observed also in laws adopted before the adoption of the treaties. During the preparation of the Treaties, it became clear that a number of provisions dealing with issues raised by digital technology and the Internet would be unavoidable and it was therefore also an integrated part of the advice, given by the International Bureau. Since the adoption of those Treaties, obviously, provisions dealing with such issues have been an indispensable part of any modern legislation, just as, in later years, provisions dealing with audiovisual performances as protected under the Beijing Treaty and exceptions and limitations for the benefit of persons with reading impairments as mandated by the Marrakesh Treaty became increasingly commonplace. Now, after the entry into force of those Treaties, it is an integrated element in the legal advice provided by the International Bureau.

What has been a common element during these years where the international legal framework developed is the fact that the legislative advice is demand-driven. This relates to whether such advice has been given at all in the first place, but to the overall direction and extent of the advice as well. If to take a hypothetic example, a country would ask for a draft Bill that is as simple and straightforward as possible, it would be difficult for the International Bureau to take into account a number of limitations and exceptions, which usually are implemented through lengthy and detailed provisions. However, if a country emphasizes its intention to benefit as much as possible from the flexibilities available, a draft Bill would typically be longer and more complex.

Even so, the International Bureau is, of course, working in a rational way and there is no reason to draft new wordings from scratch when variations in the substantive contents of the provisions do not necessitate it.

53. WIPO Lex, https://www.wipo.int/wipolex/en/index.html (accessed Jan. 25, 2024).

This simple fact of everyday life at the office obviously implies a certain trend toward universality, regardless of whether it is a part of a strategy or not. In practice, these texts find their way more or less unchanged into the adopted legislation of some countries, but in others, they are re-drafted as part of the legislative process, for example, in order to conform with the national legislative drafting style. It is a clear tendency, however, that the demands of the receiving countries are increasingly specific and boilerplate texts are no longer sufficient to meet the requirements. In certain cases, the advice has taken the form of ongoing interaction between the International Bureau and a drafting committee in the receiving country, resulting in a national report from that committee to the national government, or direct ongoing exchanges of views and suggestions between the Bureau and the relevant government officials.

To find an explanation for these developments, and to look for a formulated strategy of the organization as well, we may again take a look at the WIPO Development Agenda. It does not point toward a policy of universality. On the contrary, in Cluster A which deals with technical assistance and capacity building, item 13 stresses that the organization's legislative assistance "shall be, *inter alia,* development-oriented and demand-driven, taking into account the priorities and the special needs of developing countries, especially LDCs, as well as the different levels of development of Member States and activities should include time frames for completion."[54] In item 1, almost the same wording is found as a general programmatic declaration for WIPO's technical assistance, however, supplemented with the following statement, which also seems relevant as regards the legislative assistance: "In this regard, design, delivery mechanisms and evaluation processes of technical assistance programs should be country specific."[55] Of course, these wordings do not seem to prevent the International Bureau from using a variety of "*prêt-à-porter*" solutions, rather than bespoke or tailor-made texts, where appropriate, but it certainly does not encourage widespread use of "one size fits all" solutions. As a political statement, it clearly points more toward diversity than universality.

A similar tendency is mirrored in item 14, which deals with the technical assistance offered by WIPO under the agreement between WIPO and WTO.[56] According to this item, "WIPO shall make available advice to developing countries and LDCs, on the implementation and operation of the rights and obligations and the understanding and use of flexibilities contained in the TRIPS Agreement."[57] Again, the emphasis on flexibilities, which

54. WIPO Development Agenda, WIPO document A/43/16, 154.
55. *Ibid.,* 153.
56. Agreement between the World Intellectual Property Organization and the World Trade Organization (Dec. 22, 1995), https://www.wto.org/english/tratop_e/trips_e/wtowip_e.htm (accessed Jan. 25, 2024).
57. WIPO Development Agenda, WIPO document A/43/16, 154.

mirrors views that were strongly advocated by developing countries during the drafting of the Development Agenda, shows the political desire of developing countries to retain the greatest possible freedom to arrange their respective national legislation as they see fit.

The 2024-2025 Program and Budget of WIPO are in accordance with this emphasis. It describes the main line of action for the Copyright Development activities as follows: "Assisting national copyright offices and other competent public institutions in copyright related strategic planning and policymaking, as well as in their implementation of these strategies and policies, with the aim of supporting Member States in making more effective use of the copyright ecosystem to achieve their goals for sustainable development."[58] Read together with the general principles of Member State-driven assistance, which controls WIPO as well as the UN as a whole, this wording does not indicate anything like a mandate to work toward unification of national legislation, unless the recipients specifically would request it.

9.3 STATE OF PLAY

For a global overview of the implementation of certain aspects of the international instruments, there is reason to note the study by Dr. Guilda Rostama, prepared for the WIPO Standing Committee on Copyright and Related Rights.[59] This study covers all WIPO Member States and examines a number of specific themes in their national legislation, adopted between 2006 and 2016, namely: (1) the digital environment and the copyright value chain; (2) the limitations and exceptions in the digital environment; (3) the impact of digital technology on the protected subject-matter and on the management of copyright; and (4) new digital players and copyright. Thus, the study does not intend to give a complete picture of the state of national legislation in the field, nor of the outcome of the legislative advice, offered by the International Bureau. Obviously, a number of countries have amended their legislation and implemented international treaties without seeking the assistance of WIPO. The study is of a descriptive nature and does not conclude on its findings. To this author, however, it seems safe to conclude that even when looking at this quite well-defined area, where the International Bureau of WIPO has been very active for almost three decades, quite

58. WIPO Program of Work & Budget 2024/25, 32, available at https://www.wipo.int/about-wipo/en/budget/ (accessed Jan. 25, 2024).
59. Scoping Study on the Impact of the Digital Environment on Copyright Legislation Adopted Between 2006 and 2016, prepared by Guilda Rostama, WIPO document SCCR/35/4. The author of this chapter contributed to the preparation of the study by commenting on a draft version.

some uniformity has materialized, but certainly it has not ruled out significant diversity at the national level either.

The diversity seems even more distinct when we look at some of the more specific studies which have been prepared under the auspices of WIPO. We may note, for example, that "[o]f the 188 countries of the world that are members of the WIPO, the laws of only forty-five countries contain provisions that specifically permit museums to make certain uses of works in their collection without the prior authorization of the rights holder."[60]

Or, we may take note of Kenneth Crew's remarks in the executive summary of his study on exceptions for libraries and archives:

> Copyright statutes also reflect the tension that can exist among a country's competing objectives. The details of the library exceptions reveal much about the relationship of copyright law to library services. They also can manifest a compromise among cultural, historical, and economic objectives, typically by permitting libraries to make socially beneficial uses of copyrighted works, while setting limits and conditions aimed at protecting the interests of copyright owners, publishers, and other rightsholders.[61]

An even more specific indication of the diversity in national legislation on limitations and exceptions in the field of copyright and related rights is available in the WIPO document summarizing responses from Member States to a questionnaire on limitations and exceptions in national legislation.[62] This document reports on the replies from 61 Member States to a comprehensive questionnaire, containing 103 questions. They range from general issues relating to limitations and exceptions to specific questions regarding legislative provisions in five specific areas: educational activities; libraries and archives; persons with disabilities; religious, social and cultural exceptions; and questions regarding digital technology.

By way of examples, more or less randomly picked from the document, we may notice that on the more general level, a clear majority (44) of the responding countries (61) have opted for a "closed" system of limitations and exceptions specifically provided for in the legislation. Still, 3 countries have an open system such as the United States (U.S.) system of "fair use" while 12 countries have a mixed system and 1 country is categorized as "other."[63] More diverse is the implementation of the three-step test in national

60. Study on Copyright Limitations and Exceptions for Museums, prepared by Jean-François Canat and Lucie Guibault, in collaboration with Elisabeth Logeais, WIPO Document No. SCCR/30/2, 53.
61. Kenneth D. Crews, JD, PhD, *Study on Copyright Limitations and Exceptions for Libraries and Archives: Updated and Revised* 7 (WIPO Document No. SCCR/30/3).
62. Updated Report on the Questionnaire on Limitations and Exceptions, prepared by the Secretariat of the WIPO Standing Committee on Copyright and Related Rights, WIPO Document No. SCCR/21/7.
63. *Ibid.*, 8.

legislation. This has been done in 28 countries, while 23 have not and 8 have done so partially.[64] A prevalent majority (56) of responding countries (60) have limitations and exceptions permitting the use of works for private or personal purposes, but when it comes to including a remuneration system for such uses, responses diverge with 32 countries having such systems while 28 do not (including the 4 that do not have a private use exception).[65] A core provision among the limitations and exceptions is that dealing with quotation. It is found in the national legislation of 50 responding countries while missing in that of 11 responding countries. At first sight, this may seem surprising as some even claim that Article 10 of the Berne Convention dealing with this is obligatory,[66] but the absence of a specific provision does not necessarily imply that there is no "right of quotation" as it well might be embedded in broader provisions, such as those permitting "fair use" or "fair dealing." Still, it illustrates that the different legislative traditions, not just common law versus civil law, but also the different "dialects" within these traditions, tend to maintain diversity, rather than promote universality. Nevertheless, there are certainly also examples of provisions that have won general acceptance, such as targeted limitations and exceptions allowing reproduction for educational purposes which is reported from 51 responding countries while 4 do not have them and 3 countries report them as being covered by general exceptions,[67] but even here, the text of the report shows a number of variations at national level. No statistical exercises shall be attempted here, everybody interested can by skimming through the report make up his or her own mind. This writer certainly saw more diversity than universality.

The very existence and impressive volume of these and more[68] WIPO studies bear witness to the fact that despite many years of both norm-setting and technical assistance in the legislative field, a significant diversity exists among national legislation. This is not surprising; it is quite in line with the explicit political strategy of individual solutions and a high level of flexibility when implementing international norms at the national level. Obviously, the increased focus on limitations and exceptions in the work of WIPO may eventually lead to a higher degree of uniformity in this specific and yet important field, but as it is reflected in the WIPO Secretariat's summary of

---

64. *Ibid.*
65. *Ibid.,* 10.
66. *See,* e.g., Blomqvist (n. 24), 159ff.
67. Updated Report on the Questionnaire on Limitations and Exceptions, prepared by the Secretariat of the WIPO Standing Committee on Copyright and Related Rights, WIPO Document No. SCCR/21/7, 20.
68. For an overview, *see* http://www.wipo.int/copyright/en/limitations/ (accessed Jan. 26, 2024).

the regional consultations and the international conference on the subject, held in 2019, developments in this regard take time.[69]

9.4 CONCLUSION

When concluding on the role and strategy of WIPO in the international unification of copyright legislation, it does not make sense to try to compare the present situation with a hypothetical one, where WIPO would not have existed. The organization plays such a central role in international copyright and related rights that had it not existed, somebody would have invented it anyway. It is also indisputable that the organization has played, and still plays, a crucial role in the international harmonization of national legislation, even if the norm-setting activities presently are moving slowly. History shows that windows for international norm-setting sometimes open, enable the adoption of some instruments, and then close again. Thus, windows for copyright and related rights treaties were open in the years 1967-1974, 1994-1996 and 2012-2013, and they will certainly open again, possibly with subsequent diplomatic conferences on the rights of broadcasting organizations and on the protection of traditional cultural expressions in the coming years. The international norms bring about a certain level of harmonization and the latest addition, the Marrakesh Treaty on limitations and exceptions for persons with reading impairments, may in principle be interpreted as a step toward unification. It has a very particular structure containing both short, general mandatory rules laying out the principles and longer, more specific optional provisions, which almost resemble a model law that may well be followed closely in the national legislation of many countries. But in the language of bureaucracy, "in principle" is one of the most common negations, and the said structure assures countries party to the Treaty the liberty to divert from the detailed solution provided.

This should not be a surprise. Countries have different ideals, and they sometimes conflict. As a legal institution, copyright and related rights are closely connected to both economy and culture, and the basic conditions for both vary enormously between countries. Levels of affluence and development are vastly different, and it is difficult to imagine how it should be possible to reach an agreement on universally applicable norms at such a level of detail that they would be useful as national legislation. Those of us who are shorter, taller, broader or otherwise differ from the average human dimensions have a profound skepticism toward the concept of "one size fits all." In practice, more often than not it ends up fitting nobody really well. National governments are there to find the best solutions for their own

69. Report on Regional Seminars and International Conference on Limitations and Exceptions, WIPO document SCCR/40/2, 7-19.

country, and they are, for good reasons, just as reluctant as regards uniform solutions for all countries.

In conclusion, WIPO does in practice play a role in obtaining uniformity in national legislation, which cannot be neglected. It follows from the function of the international norms in certain cases where relatively detailed international provisions have been called for, and it follows from natural and rational practices in the process of providing technical assistance to developing, least developed and transition countries. The basic principle of only granting a certain level of minimum rights, however, as well as the politically determined role and strategy of the organization do not aim at universality as an ideal objective. On the contrary, the role and strategy of WIPO are probably best described as being to ensure an up-to-date well-functioning system of international copyright and related rights protection while at the same time safeguarding the highest possible level of autonomy for national legislation.

Chapter 10

Toward a New Berne Convention

Daniel Gervais

The Berne Convention was last substantially revised at a difficult diplomatic conference in Stockholm in 1967. These difficulties were caused in large part by the post-colonial emergence of dozens of new developing countries. Four years later, in Paris, developing countries negotiated the addition of an appendix to the Stockholm text to provide them with a way—a very complicated way—to issue compulsory licenses for the translation and reproduction of books. Was that the last revision of the treaty? As of March 2025, the Berne Union had 181 Member States. The conventional wisdom is that the Convention can never be revised because unanimity is required to revise the substantive part of the Convention, and it is simply impossible to get the near-universal current membership of the Berne Union to agree on anything. Though this view is certainly reasonable and indeed probably correct, there are two reasons why it is possible to begin work on a new Berne Convention. The first reason is rather technical: the rule of unanimity could be translated as a search for consensus. Consensus has been the rule at the General Agreement on Tariffs and Trade (GATT)[1]/World Trade Organization (WTO) since 1948 and, most of the time it actually works, and the WTO had 166 members as of March 2025, a number not that far from the Berne Union membership.[2] Moreover, the unanimity rule requires that all

1. The General Agreement on Tariffs and Trade (Oct. 30, 1947), 64 UNTS 814.
2. WTO rules permit even a single Member State to block agreement. *See* Marrakesh Agreement Establishing the World Trade Organization (Apr. 15, 1994), 33 I.L.M. 1226, 1232. Yet it seems to function, presumably because actors show a systemic interest in making it work. *See also* Joost Pauwelyn, *The Transformation of World Trade,* 104 Michigan Law Review 1 (2005) 26-29.

members present at a revision conference—that is, not that all members of the Union—agree, which, in this author's opinion, could be done on a motion by the chair to which no one objects.[3] That is often how many decisions are made in international bodies. The history of the Convention shows that revisions are possible. After all, they have happened several times, including the last time in Paris in 1971. It is also true, however, as Professor Ricketson noted, that:

> [a]greement became more difficult at each conference, but substantive progress was nonetheless made.[4]

He then concluded that it was:

> "not inconceivable that if there were sufficient goodwill and determination among Berne members, consensus could be reached on some basic changes or modifications to the existing text as part of a full revision of that text" but that "it may be accepted that revision of the Berne text presently remains highly unlikely."[5]

I agree. Yet, as academics, aren't we allowed to dream?

The second argument is that work on a new Berne Convention would open a much-needed discussion on the future of copyright. Since the adoption of the Trade-Related Aspects of Intellectual Property Rights (TRIPS) Agreement in 1994, the World Intellectual Property Organization (WIPO) has proceeded to adopt several new treaties based on the foundations of the Berne Convention, namely the Beijing Treaty on Audiovisual Performances (adopted in 2012; 47 parties as of April 2024); the Marrakesh Treaty to Facilitate Access to Published Works for Persons Who are Blind, Visually Impaired or Otherwise Print Disabled (2013, 94 parties as of April 2024); the WIPO Copyright Treaty (WCT, 1996, 116 parties as of April 2024); and the WIPO Performances and Phonograms Treaty (WPPT, 1996, 112 parties as of April 2024). As of this writing, WIPO was working on a new treaty to protect broadcasts (with a narrow focus on signal piracy in the latest discussions) and possibly considering another instrument on limitations and exceptions. What is emerging is a tapestry of standards with diverse membership. It may be time to weave a new agreement on what copyright should be about, as generative Artificial Intelligence (AI) shakes the

3. Article 27(3) of the Paris Act refers to "unanimity of the votes cast." Previous Acts required unanimous consent of countries "composing" the Union. *See also* Hans Ballreich & Hans Peter Kunz-Hallstein, *Revision of the Paris Convention: The Principle of Unanimity,* 9 International Review of Intellectual Property and Competition Law 21, 22 (1978). Of course, in the Paris Convention the unanimous consent rule is customary law and not enshrined in the text of the treaty itself.
4. Sam Ricketson, *The International Framework for the Protection of Authors: Bendable Boundaries and Immovable Obstacles,* 41 Columbia-Volunteer Lawyers for the Arts Journal of Law & the Arts 341, 349 (2018).
5. *Ibid.*, 353.

foundations of the house built on what were thought to be solid foundations laid in Berne in September 1886.

The argument that the Berne Convention can never be revised because of perennial North-South conflicts or divergent views among interest groups also seems unconvincing to me. It implies that the only way forward is to adopt a plurality of discrete instruments, each with a new right or exemption, followed by a long path to ratify them (or not), or even to adopt countermeasures, that is, different and possibly incompatible norms in other contexts, such as regional or bilateral trade agreements. A more comprehensive solution seems to me to be a better way forward. A broader approach may be both normatively balanced and politically more palatable because it is comprehensive. It may have a better chance of being adopted and, more importantly, of becoming a unified norm. In a "package," hopefully, everyone can find something they like and thus be willing to compromise and accept something they do not like. Otherwise, we are stuck with a pure power game, and both normativity and evidence-based policy-making will be the victims.

It is the perceived impossibility of achieving unanimity that led to the elaboration in the 1980s and 1990s (when there were fewer than 100 members of the Berne Union) not of a new Act of the Convention, but rather of a possible Protocol to the Convention, an optional additional treaty that would not require an amendment of the Convention.[6] That decision was made at the very top. The former WIPO Director-General Arpad Bogsch put it very clearly:

> WIPO and the Berne Union try to keep pace with those changes and seek solutions to the new problems as they emerge. Since the 1971 (Paris) conference of revision of the Berne Convention, such solutions are sought in ways other than a new revision of the Berne Convention. The high number of the countries party to that Convention …, the greater differences in wealth among the member countries and the enormous cultural variety among them make it difficult if not unlikely, at least on major issues, to obtain the unanimity that is required for any revision of the Berne Convention.[7]

---

6. As a former U.S. Register of Copyright Ralph Oman noted, "the perceived political impossibility of amending the Berne Convention through a formal revision conference—a procedure that requires unanimity—prompted a search for an administrative alternative to a formal revision conference." Ralph Oman, *Berne Revision: The Continuing Drama,* 4 Fordham Intellectual Property Media & Entertainment Law Journal 139, n. 14.5 (1993). As Oman also noted, the U.S. was also hoping to use the protocol to bridge the gap between copyright and related rights by bringing sound recordings fully into the copyright picture as works. That effort failed and a separate instrument, the WPPT was signed concurrently with the WCT. *See Ibid.*, 148.
7. Arpad Bogsch, *The First Hundred Years of the Berne Convention for the Protection of Literary and Artistic Works at WIPO Publication, Copyright* 291, 327 (1986); *see also,*

This possible protocol in turn laid the foundation for the WCT adopted on December 20, 1996.[8] The WIPO official most directly responsible for the WCT diplomatic conference and its preparation was Dr. Mihály Ficsor, Assistant Director-General. As he stated a few months after the adoption of the WCT:

> [The idea of a protocol instead of a new Act] was attractive for those who were interested in an appropriate level of copyright protection. The other reason was that, while for a revision of the Berne Convention unanimity is needed (see Article 27(3)) (which now with the more than 120 member countries of the Berne Union would be obviously difficult to achieve), a special agreement, by definition, may be concluded by any group of member countries of the Union (among themselves and also with countries outside the Union).[9]

In the same vein, Reinbothe and von Lewinksi explained the choice of a protocol by combining the political difficulties encountered in 1967 and the unanimity requirement:

> Whereas it was revised regularly until 1971, the last two Revision Conferences of 1967 in Stockholm and 1971 in Paris showed that the increasingly active role played by developing countries changed the political climate and made it extremely difficult to reach the necessary compromises. This experience might have discouraged the WIPO International Bureau from initiating, within the regular rhythm of 20 years, a new revision of the Berne Convention, all the more since this would have required unanimity. One had to expect even an aggravation of the North-South conflict, in addition to the arising of new conflicts of interests, such as between different groups of industrialized countries. At the same time, an adaptation of the Berne Convention to new technical and economic developments seemed necessary.[10]

One advantage of the approach proposed in this chapter is that new instruments such as the WCT must comply with Article 20 of the Convention and thus may only contain "provisions not inconsistent with" the Convention. In contrast, a new treaty would not be a "special agreement" and could therefore rewrite the rules more freely. More importantly, even if it is not adopted as a new treaty, the work of experts in rewriting copyright rights,

---

Sam Ricketson, *The Berne Convention for the Protection of Literary and Artistic Works: 1886-1986* 16.37 (Geneva: WIPO, 1987).

8. WIPO Copyright Treaty (Dec. 20, 1996) TRT/WCT/001 [hereinafter "WCT"].
9. Mihály Ficsor, *The Spring 1997 Horace S. Manges Lecture: Copyright for the Digital Era—The WIPO "Internet" Treaties* 21 Columbia-Volunteer Lawyers for the Arts Journal of Law & the Arts 197, 223 (1997).
10. Jorg Reinbothe & Silke von Lewinski, *The WIPO Treaties 1996: Ready to Come into Force*, 24(4) European Intellectual Property Review 199 (2002).

exceptions and limitations would in itself be valuable material for interpreting existing norms and facilitating their forward-looking implementation by WIPO Member States.

In my 2019 book (revised edition) *Restructuring Copyright*, I proposed the text of a new treaty as a starting point for a global conversation on copyright reform.[11] It is also worth noting that the idea explored in this chapter of a possible new Act of the Convention made a noted appearance in a report published by a European Union *Comité des Sages* in January 2011.[12] The Committee's charge was to find ways to bring Europe's cultural heritage online. Its detailed report suggested refreshing or "adapting the Berne Convention on this point in order to make it fit for the digital age," which "should be taken up in the context of WIPO and promoted by the European Commission."[13] Indeed, this became one of the key recommendations of the report.[14]

Working toward a new Act of the Berne Convention could greatly improve the current dynamics of intellectual property (IP) negotiations. This dynamic has two main characteristics. First, it is not a dialogue, but rather a "ships passing in the night" approach. By this I mean that we have, on the one hand, "pro-IP" lobbies pushing for TRIPS-Plus norms and national measures to increase the level of protection, and, on the other hand, so-called anti-IP or anti-protection lobbies, mostly pushing for separate agreements on limitations and exceptions (L&Es). Second, a smarter copyright policy is not or no longer a binary and simplistic debate about balancing rights and exceptions.[15] Now, it is a complex interplay between rightholders' rights versus users' rights, a complex matter where one considers that many people are both rightholders and users (e.g., reusers or authors of derivative works).[16] User rights can (like some part of authors' rights) be grounded in other bodies of law, such as human rights, and the interface between IP and human rights is fuzzily delineated and, not surprisingly, the object of significant debates among scholars.[17] These rights-based discourses often

11. Daniel Gervais, *Restructuring Copyright* (Edward Elgar, revised edition, 2019).
12. European Union & Comité des Sages, *The New Renaissance, Report of the "Comité des Sages" Reflection group on bringing Europe's Cultural Heritage,* online bib-01/2011 5 (Jan. 10, 2011) https://op.europa.eu/en/publication-detail/-/publication/79a38a23-e7d9-4452-b9b0-1f84502e68c5 (accessed Apr. 24, 2024).
13. *Ibid.*, 5, 19.
14. *Ibid.*, 20-21.
15. Silke von Lewinski, *International Copyright over the Last 50 Years: A Foreign Perspective,* 50 Journal of Copyright Society U.S.A. 581, 597 (2003).
16. The now famous statement made in a Supreme Court of Canada decision, citing David Vaver, comes to mind: "Both owner rights and user rights should therefore be given the fair and balanced reading that befits remedial legislation." CCH Canadian Ltd. v. Law Society of Upper Canada 48 SCC 13 (2004); 1 SCR 339 [2004].
17. *See* Ruth L. Okediji, *Does Intellectual Property Need Human Rights?*, 51 New York University Journal of International Law & Politics 1 (2018); Laurence R. Helfer, *Human Rights and Intellectual Property: Conflict or Coexistence?*, 5 Minnesota Intellectual

turn into the shoals on which reform efforts get stranded and, eventually, sink.

Some copyright rights are mostly non-controversial. For example, the right of an author to have her name on her work, unless it is unreasonable under the circumstances—the right of attribution—is not usually a major source of opposition. Perhaps you would reply that I am unaware of Foucault's (and Barthes') pronouncement of the death of the author. His name was on his books, and I suspect his heirs are cashing the publishers' checks. Not only did poststructuralism fail to signal the end of the norm of attribution but there is also a new countervailing discourse of attribution as a consumer or user right: knowing what you're reading, listening to, or watching comes from (intellectually). In the right of attribution, we may have an example of something stakeholders on both "sides" could agree on. Admittedly, it is not a particularly decisive starting point, but it is a starting point, nonetheless.

The list of low-hanging fruit goes beyond a reasonable right of attribution. Some exceptions also seem beyond serious debate, at least in principle, such as exceptions for print-disabled users.

What other areas can we find common ground on? For example, could we agree that copyright should not pick and choose between business models? Not a very controversial suggestion, except for legacy industries that benefit from legally distorted business models, and they will be seen for what they are. They could get transitional measures. But today many copyright laws are unduly selective, and I propose that this must end.

Let us try to go one step further. From a pragmatic point of view, would it not be much more efficient to structure copyright in such a way that it corresponds to its primary objective, leaving it to authors, other rights holders, distributors and users to define the authorized uses, rather than trying to make each use artificially correspond to one or more legal fragments such as reproduction, public performance, communication, distribution, adaptation and so on? In other words, is it efficient or even useful to ask a copyright holder who wants to authorize the online distribution of his work whether this requires, say, one or six reproductions, one or four communications to the public, making available, perhaps a form of digital distribution, etc.?

Consider the simple example of a digital camera taking a picture of a three-dimensional object that is itself protected by copyright (say, a sculpture). Suppose that the image file can then be processed and used to create a three-dimensional copy of the sculpture using a 3D printer. According to traditional copyright hermeneutics, we would first look at the computer file

Property Review 47 (2003) https://doi.org/10.2139/ssrn.459120; Daniel Gervais, *How Intellectual Property and Human Rights Can Live Together: An Updated Perspective at Intellectual Property and Human Rights* (Paul Torremans ed., 3rd edn., Kluwer, 2015).

created by the camera. This file is not an image; it is computer code that "describes" how a computer can create an image. So, we would ask whether this computer code, which is treated by the law as a literary work, is a reproduction of the object, an adaptation, or something else. Then we would consider whether the transmission of the file from one computer to another can be a public performance or a communication to a public (which in turn means deciding what is a public), whether a public display occurs at some point, etc. in countries with a discrete display right in their copyright law, such as the United States (U.S.), and the list goes on. Remember that each right fragment in the copyright "bundle" (reproduction, public performance, communication, distribution, adaptation/derivation, display) may be owned by a different party, or may even be further subdivided by language, medium, etc. This implies that a license may be required for the use of each such fragment, in each territory of use.

This kind of classic copyright reasoning strikes me as jumping through too many unnecessary hoops. If hundreds of millions of end users are unable to understand this high degree of complexity (which often requires obtaining two or more licenses for the same use) and to figure out who owns what and where they become licensees who enter into (non-negotiable) contracts with content owners and distributors, and a less than optimal form of private ordering may then shape the actual use of copyright, with very few normative springs to help us jump through the hoops. Indeed, this change in the role of private ordering may have been underestimated. In the pre-digital realm, many and perhaps most of the problems arising from the fragmentation of the bundle or copyright (among uses, users, media, and territories) could be remedied by private ordering because a limited number of professional entities were involved. When the licensee is a typical consumer, the picture is different, because copyright is not used to shape financial flows in professional distribution channels, but rather to restrict personal uses that were previously exempted or at least tolerated under first sale or private use or some form of fair use. Moreover, in the context of mass use, licenses are typically adhesion contracts, including contracts that allow the drafter to change the terms of the contract by notifying the other party or by simply posting a new version of the "contract" on a website. What if, instead, copyright had fair rules that could not be deviated from in consumer contracts? Another point to keep in mind is that, normatively, copyright policy has traditionally been resistant to the accumulation of rights fragments around a single use. Beyond private ordering, solutions to avoid the difficulties posed by fragmentation are sometimes included in the legislation, such as defaulting to a "dominant" right fragment. For example, since broadcasting can (and should) be considered a single economic activity, the "dominant fragment," namely communication to the public, can be used as the main vector for setting tariffs and implementing licensing agreements. This explains why several national laws contain an exception for so-called ephemeral recordings—even though they are far from ephemeral and can be kept for months for the use of the reproduced fragment in the context of broadcasting. These ephemeral recordings are often technically indispensable, but of secondary importance when the main economic operation (in this case, reaching a public through broadcasting) is the focus of the analysis. The need to provide for such exceptions is just one sign of a lack of alignment between the structure of copyright fragments and the underlying policy objective of copyright.

In the camera and 3D-printing example described above, the better questions to ask are whether there should be a right for commercially relevant uses of the files containing the image-making and 3D-printing instructions, and then whether there is a reasonable, normatively grounded way to monetize the value of those files. A better answer might look more like an open-access subscription model—leaving aside for the moment the extremely skewed financial flows generated by some of the players operating under that kind of model. A better option is needed, because otherwise, the likely result will be years of litigation, frustrated users, and possibly stunted technological development, and, lest we forget too quickly what happened in the music realm, less revenue for copyright holders and, ultimately, the redirection of financial flows, often to the detriment of authors and users. A lose-lose all around; once again.

Copyright needs to be rebalanced, and I propose two interrelated mobilizing principles for doing so. First, I argue that some fragmentation is useful to tailor permissions to use protected works in particular markets, but this fragmentation should not be according to technological acts tied to old technologies like printing or live broadcasting. My suggestion is that fragmentation should be done by contract, that is, the underlying economic right should be a simpler right that is divisible by contract—subject to special, unwaivable rules for consumer contracts. This allows the system to respond to any technological change. Second, copyright must focus on uses that significantly restrict the market or the possibilities for exploiting the product, rather than on a right to authorize prohibiting technical operations performed on the work or a copy thereof. The approach I propose is therefore to emphasize the effect of the use rather than its technical nature.[18] It is not unauthorized "reproduction" (even the making of ten thousand copies) of a book that may harm the author or publisher, but the distribution to the public of these copies. For example, I can make 10,000,000 copies of a song on my computer in seconds. That causes no harm to anyone. It is the dissemination of copies that is relevant.[19]

---

18. Shira Perlmutter, *Convergence and the Future of Copyright,* 24 Columbia-Volunteer Lawyers for the Arts Journal of Law & the Arts 163, 172-173 (2001).
19. Two American authors have in fact proposed that copyright be replaced by a right of distribution to the public. Their analysis of the problem is interesting, but it must be noted that distribution is not the only way to enter a market; Ernest Miller & Joan Feigenbaum,

This explains why I have limited sympathy for past efforts to reform copyright along the lines of adding "technical form of use" fragments. For example, the creation of a right of "transmission" or "making available" on the Internet, which may have solved certain problems specific to the Internet, did not solve either the conceptual or the pragmatic issues examined here.[20] For one thing, its interaction with pre-existing fragments of law is unlikely to produce the desired results. For example, while I do not believe that the U.S. Congress actually intended to expropriate songwriters when it added the digital performance right for labels, empirically that is exactly what has happened. The passage of the Music Modernization Act in 2018 provided a limited fix.

The proposed approach is to have a simpler right, with appropriate limitations built into the scope of the copyright itself.[21] The idea of putting limits on the scope of the right is, of course, something that is already well known. For example, a performance or communication must be in or to a public for these fragments of the right to apply.

To stay within the boundaries of the major international instruments, I suggest that we use the flexibility provided by the three-step test. The test allows states to provide for limitations and exceptions to copyright rights:

- in certain special cases;
- that do not conflict with the normal commercial exploitation of the work; and
- do not unreasonably prejudice the legitimate interests of the author [in TRIPS: rightholder].

The test lived in a relatively obscure part of the international copyright landscape until 1994 when, with the adoption of the WTO TRIPS Agreement, it became the cornerstone of almost all limitations and exceptions to all IP rights in international law.[22] It is now used as the model for exceptions to all copyright rights in TRIPS (Article 13); Article 10(1) and (2) of the WCT

Taking the Copy Out of Copyright at Digital Rights Management Workshop 233-244 (2001), https://link.springer.com/chapter/10.1007/3-540-47870-1_15 (accessed Apr. 24, 2024).

20. Mark Lemley, *Dealing with Overlapping Copyrights on the Internet,* 22 University of Dayton Law Review 547, 582-583 (2002) https://doi.org/10.31235/osf.io/8ezns.
21. Nicolas Suzor, *Free-Riding, Cooperation, and "Peaceful Revolutions" at Copyright,* 28(1) Harvard Journal of Law & Technology 137, 192 (2014).
22. Agreement on TRIPS (Apr. 15, 1994), 1869 UNTS 299, contains a list of material excluded for copyright ability, namely "ideas, procedures, methods of operation or mathematical concepts as such"; *see also ibid.*, Art. 13, which extended the three-step test of the Berne Convention to cover any copyright right (including, e.g., public performance).

(December 20, 1996); Article 16(2) of the WPPT;[23] Article 13(2) of the Beijing Treaty;[24] and Article 11 of the Marrakesh Treaty.[25]

Most purpose-specific exceptions and limitations pass the first step of the test if they have reasonable limitations (consistent with their purpose). It could be argued, for example, that an exception limited to a class of users is limited in scope unless that class is defined in an unreasonably broad manner. The second step is normative in nature: an exception is not allowed if it covers a form of exploitation that has, or is likely to acquire, significant economic importance. In other words, if the exception is used to limit an economically significant market or, a fortiori, to compete with the copyright holder, the exception is prohibited.[26] The WTO panel in the U.S. section 110(5) case used this type of approach.[27] Applying the third step requires a definition of the "unreasonable" prejudice.[28] The presence of the word "unreasonable" indicates that some level or degree of prejudice is justified. For example, while a country may completely exempt the making of a small number of private copies, it may be required to impose a compensation scheme, such as a levy, when the level of prejudice becomes unjustified, unless licensing solutions emerge organically. The inclusion of a reasonableness/justifiability criterion allows legislators to strike a balance between the rights of authors and other copyright holders and the needs and interests of users. In other words, there should be a public interest justification for limiting copyright. Of course, while the public interest may coincide with the interests of users, they are not synonymous. It is also in the public interest that there be a balanced protection for authors and other rights holders. Any exemption without compensation must therefore be measured against any demonstrable loss of income to authors and other rights holders. An exception that significantly reduces existing sales or licensing revenues or, under the second step, prevents the rightholder from attempting to sell or

23. WIPO Performances and Phonograms Treaty (Dec. 20, 1996) TRT/WPPT/001.
24. Beijing Treaty on Audiovisual Performances (Jun. 24, 2012), http://www.wipo.int/wipolex/en/details.jsp?id=12213.
25. In TRIPS, it is also the test for exceptions to industrial design protection (Art. 26(2)) and patent rights (Art. 30). There is, however, a crucial difference in the case of patent rights, which may impact how the rule is interpreted when applied to copyright. The last (third) step of the test in Art. 30 requires that exceptions do not unreasonably prejudice the legitimate interests of the patent owner, taking account of the legitimate interests of third parties.
26. An example of the scope of an exception based on non-commercially significant use can be found in HR 3261, 108th Cong. (2003) s. 4(b), also known as the Database and Collections of Misappropriation Act.
27. U.S. Copyright Act, s. 110(5), para. 6. 180 (Jun. 15, 2000) WTO Document WT/DS160/R.
28. It is worth noting that "not unreasonable prejudice" is not quite the same as "reasonable prejudice"; "Not unreasonable" connotes a slightly stricter threshold (*see ibid.*, para. 6.225).

license is almost certainly inconsistent with the second and probably also the third step of the test.

The three-step test allows national legislators to rescope copyright with an inherent teleological limitation that can then serve as a normative anchor for a rescoped copyright. The idea is to re-scope the right not just by adhering to the three-step test, but by actually using it. Nothing in the text of Berne or TRIPS requires that limitations on the right be a separate step from the definition of the right itself. Conversely, if an exception or limitation to copyright is seen as an area not protected by copyright, the three-step test can be said to preserve the area covered by copyright. It thus provides the contours of "unfair" use.[29]

The three-step test has suffered two major blows that need to be addressed. First, there are at least 11 different versions of the test at the international level. Two WTO dispute settlement panels have had some difficulties in interpreting it, partly as a result of working on two different versions in parallel. Second, some countries have denatured the test by changing its locus and placing it in their domestic law where it is performing a wholly different function than what the Berne drafters intended. The purpose of the test was to impose an obligation *on states* to limit and in some cases compensate for certain exceptions (e.g., by moving certain exceptions into the category of compulsory licenses). The appropriate place for the test is thus not in national law, but rather as a guide for policymakers. The test examines exceptions and limitations systemically. If they are incorporated into national law and applied by a court, they will be evaluated on a case-by-case basis based on the effect of the exception and limitation in the particular facts of the dispute. This is partly a problem because national and international decisions can influence the interpretation of the norm at the other level.

Bearing that in mind, it seems reasonable to suggest that copyright owners would be satisfied with a strong economic right that applies in cases where a use is demonstrably prejudicial to their commercial interests or, in the language of the test, where such use conflicts with normal exploitation. Other uses, such as private use or use for research, would in almost all cases fall outside the scope of a new effects-based right. Such a standard, incorporating notions of normality and reasonableness, would be more flexible and dynamic, allowing copyright to evolve through judicial interpretation as new technological uses are invented. It would be "naturally" dynamic because normalcy is not set in stone: What constituted normal commercial use 15 or 20 years ago has changed dramatically and irreversibly, and more changes will come.

29. Ruth Okediji, *Towards an International Fair Use Standard*, 39 Columbia-Volunteer Lawyers for the Arts Journal of Transnational Law 79 (2000) https://doi.org/10.2307/1123488.

My proposal, in short, is that the economic component of copyright should be a right to authorize or prohibit uses that demonstrably interfere with actual or foreseeable commercial exploitation. This right would, of course, be subject to limitations and exceptions, but in line with the mobilizing principles articulated above, the goal is to build intrinsic limits into the scope of the right itself and to make it independent of the technical nature of the use made. Because it is market- and effect-based, and not a reflection of the technical operations performed on copies of works, it is, as I said earlier, technologically neutral. In sum, I propose that copyright be structured teleologically rather than technologically. To be consistent with international norms, the law should be interpreted by defining "use" to encompass current technological uses (reproduction, performance, communication), but using the three-step test to take into account commercial exploitation.[30] This also reduces the work that must be done by L&Es and simplifies the analysis.

Structuring the right in this way would in many cases imply a temporal component. The proposed approach would protect strong exclusive rights used during initial preparations for actual commercial exploitation against unauthorized uses affecting commercial exploitation that are not covered by an exception or limitation.[31] After this initial phase, the right would weaken to allow certain uses, some of which could be subject to a right to remuneration in appropriate cases. This does not seem to me to be fundamentally inconsistent with the "permitted but paid" notion suggested by Professor Jane Ginsburg.[32]

The approach I propose can be justified normatively because it produces a desirable result, and pragmatically because efforts to stop or control Internet use have not been particularly successful, either technically or commercially. The proposed approach structurally realigns copyright with the reality of online uses.

This brings me back to moral rights and even a step beyond to the humanity of copyright. As noted above, attribution is a well-established and accepted principle. The moral right can serve not only authors but also users who might want to know who wrote or created a work. I also suggest that there should be a right to prevent first publication. This has long existed at common law, even in the absence of a statutory moral right. These are examples of things that most stakeholders could agree on, as long as

30. *See, e.g.,* the Swiss (Federal) Copyright Act, Art. 10:2. In order to comply with international norms, the right should be interpreted by defining "use" to encompass current technical uses (reproduction, performance, communication), using the three-step test to factor in commercial exploitation.
31. "Specific" in this context does not refer to how the exception or limitation is formulated. Fair use would be included, for example, even though it is not "specific." Its specificity comes in its case-by-case application by courts.
32. Jane C. Ginsburg, *Fair Use for Free or Permitted-But-Paid*, 29 Berkeley Technology Law Journal 1383 (2014).

appropriate limits are put in place. In the case of generative AI, there needs to be a discussion at the international level about the need for a human author to be the cause of the originality required (as implied by the Berne Convention) for a work to be protected by copyright.[33] Professor Ricketson opined that the "need for authors to be 'human' is a longstanding assumption in national copyright laws."[34] He is correct.[35] And it must remain so.

A right of integrity should also be recognized, although it should not unduly limit the possibilities offered by digital technology to transform and re-use works, consistent with freedom of expression concerns. It is suggested that the scope of the right of integrity should be limited to cases where the harm to honor and reputation is both significant and demonstrable. This would align the infringement test with a more objective standard. The use of the work of an author who strongly believes in choice in an anti-abortion campaign comes to mind as a violation of the restructured right I propose.

Structural reform must include a reform of remedies. Remedies affect the scope of the right. The approach I propose is not to require countries to eliminate statutory or pre-established damages, because it is true that in many cases actual damages are difficult to prove. However, the range of statutory damages assessed in cases other than those of commercial-scale piracy should be in line with the nature of the use by individuals, that is, in most cases in the range of a few hundred dollars or euros per view (and not necessarily per work). The amount could be increased at the discretion of the court in cases of continued or repeated unauthorized use by the user.[36]

Where does this leave the need for new L&Es? The 1967 Stockholm experience of trying to include a list in the Convention of the same kind as that found in Article 5 of the Information Society (InfoSoc) directive,[37] failed, opening the door to the three-step test. A new Act of the Convention should take account of the Marrakech Treaty and use existing inventories of national laws, as was done in 2014 for libraries and archives.[38] I suspect that,

33. Daniel Gervais, *The Human Cause*, at Research Handbook On Intellectual Property And Artificial Intelligence (Ryan Abbott ed., Edward Edgar, 2022), pp. 21-38.
34. Sam Ricketson, *People or Machines: The Berne Convention and the Changing Concept of Authorship,* 16 Columbia-Volunteer Lawyers for the Arts Journal of Law & Arts (1991-1992) 1, 8.
35. An analysis of multiple national laws led another scholar to a similar conclusion. *See* Andres Guadamuz, *Artificial Intelligence and Copyright*, WIPO Magazine (October 2017) ("Most jurisdictions, including Spain and Germany, state that only works created by a human can be protected by copyright."), https://www.wipo.int/wipo_magazine/en/2017/05/article_0003.html.
36. The amount could be increased at the court's discretion in cases of repeat or continued bad faith use.
37. Directive 2001/29/EC of the European Parliament and of the Council of 22 May 2001 on the harmonisation of certain aspects of copyright and related rights in the information society (May 22, 2010) Official Journal L 167, 22/06/2001, pp. 10-19.
38. WIPO published a study of existing *exceptions and limitations revealing a variegated worldwide picture. See Kenneth Crews, Copyright Limitations and Exceptions for*

if such a process were used, there would not be a large number of exceptions and limitations that could be made mandatory.

Finally, let me return to the question raised by the theme chosen for this book, namely, whether what I am proposing is universalistic in nature, as the theme chosen for this book suggests.

The two major "universalisms" that have dominated copyright history for over a century and continue to do so, although the duopoly is weakening as pluralism grows, will find something here. The U.S., with its rhetorical insistence on capitalism as the engine of growth, should welcome a model that reflects the commercial concerns of those who create, distribute, and use content. Europe, with its post-nation-state universalism that places a premium on Culture (which I have written here with a capital C to maximize the semiotic space and anthropological role the term can capture), should welcome an approach that seeks to give creators who want to hone their skills and master their craft a chance to do so, while giving users access to more culture and information than ever before.

Europe and the U.S. typically agree on strong copyright protection in trade agreements and elsewhere but for different reasons. U.S. negotiators see copyright as an incentive for private capital to invest in the production and distribution of successful commercial products by U.S. companies. The worldwide success of American music, movies, television, software and books supports this view. Europeans see copyright as a tool to support the cultural economy and an indispensable facet of European humanist universalism. I am not arguing that these views are wrong, but that they do not work as they should to justify the current, confused regime. More fundamentally, the simplistic implementation of the idea of a "strong copyright" regime based on the current model of a multiplicity of fragmented and disparate rights, exceptions and limitations in different instruments is ill-suited to this century.

A new Berne Convention therefore looks to me like a universalist approach, one that not only brings the two major copyright families but also the rest of the world, into its wake. However, there is not necessarily an irresolvable tension between universalism and pluralism in this proposal, for at least two reasons. The first is that, despite TRIPS, Berne, the WCT and WPPT, and Marrakech, there is no such thing as an international copyright. Copyright is a territorial right—which in almost all cases means national. Second, and relatedly, as I have argued elsewhere, each country must be allowed, and indeed normatively required, to calibrate its IP regime to its own needs and circumstances, bearing in mind that those needs and circumstances will change over time. Thus, universal norms provide a framework within which calibrated pluralist copyright regimes are developed; pluralist regimes, but within universalist boundaries.

Libraries: Typology Analysis (2019) WIPO document SCCR/38/4, https://www.wipo.int/meetings/en/doc_details.jsp?doc_id=432051 (accessed Apr. 24, 2024).

Chapter 11

Pluralism and Universalism in International Copyright Law: The Role of an International Acquis

Graeme B. Dinwoodie

Contemporary scholarship has explored in some depth the role of pluralism and universalism in law in a number of areas.[1] But the contest between these animating philosophies is not new in international copyright law. In the 1880s, at its founding, the international copyright system was faced with what might be seen as a binary choice between universalism and pluralism, between a single global code and a range of distinct national rules.[2] But a literal reading of the constituent terms of that dichotomy oversimplifies the

1. *See* generally Paul Schiff Berman, *Global Legal Pluralism as a Normative Project,* 8 UC Irvine Law Review 149 (2018); Paul Schiff Berman, *Can Global Legal Pluralism Be Both "Global" and "Pluralist"?*, 29 Duke Journal of Comparative & International Law 381 (2019) https://doi.org/10.2139/ssrn.3385847.
2. *See* Jane C. Ginsburg, *International Copyright: From a "Bundle" of National Copyright Laws to a Supranational Code?*, 47 Journal of the Copyright Society of the U.S.A. 265, 268-269 (2000) https://doi.org/10.2139/ssrn.222508 (noting that the intergovernmental meeting in 1883 to form the Berne Union revealed a "universalist" group that "favored a codified and uniform law of international copyright" and another that "preferred as little unification and as much national independence as possible"); 1 Sam Ricketson & Jane Ginsburg, *International Copyright and Neighbouring Rights: The Berne Convention and Beyond* §§ 2.02-2.04, 42-44 (2nd ed., 2005) (describing the choice as one between "universalism" and "pragmatism"); cf. Jane C. Ginsburg, *From Hypatia to Victor Hugo to Larry and Sergey: "All The World's Knowledge" and Universal Authors' Rights*, 1 Journal of the British Academy 71 (2013) https://doi.org/10.5871/bacad/9780197265666.003.0004 (discussing universalism in relative terms).

impulses that were at play in the formulation of the Berne Convention[3] and it fails to capture the complexity of the design choices facing the system that we now have.

Despite that, the philosophies of universalism and pluralism remain useful lenses through which to think about how to conceive of the international copyright system going forward. International copyright law arguably requires re-conceptualization to take account of social, political and technological changes that have occurred since 1886. That system might appropriately reflect a different balance of universalism and pluralism than embodied in the original Berne Convention. Some of that rebalancing also underlies arguments advanced by scholars and policymakers in the European Union (EU) that the process of harmonization of national rights should give way to discussion of a unitary EU copyright title with regional effect throughout the Union.[4] And, a universalist vision might embrace or prioritize an evolving mix of features, including ones that reflect in different ways uniformity, international regulation—which might constrain national choice but not require uniformity—and global (or at least transborder) reach.[5]

11.1 THE BERNE MODEL

Countries participating in the discussions that led to the Berne Convention possessed a common desire to achieve cross-border or international protection for the works of their own nationals. There are a series of mechanisms for achieving that goal. Most directly, nation-states could unilaterally accord the same protection to foreign nationals as was granted to domestic authors. Some countries, such as France, had already adopted this strategy from the

3. *See* Berne Convention for the Protection of Literary and Artistic Works (Sep. 9, 1886), S. Treaty Doc. No. 99-27 (hereinafter Berne Convention).
4. *See* P. Bernt Hugenholtz, *Is Harmonization a Good Thing? The Case of the Copyright Acquis,* at The Europeanization of Intellectual Property Law: Towards a European Legal Methodology 57, 71-73 (Pila & Ohly eds., Oxford University Press, 2013); European Parliament Resolution of 9 July 2015 on the Implementation of Directive 2001/29/EC of the European Parliament and of the Council of 22 May 2001 on the Harmonisation of Certain Aspects of Copyright and Related Rights in The Information Society, 28 (Jul. 9, 2015) (2014/2256(INI)) (calling "on the Commission to study the impact of a single European Copyright Title on jobs and innovation, on the interests of authors, performers and other rightholders, and on the promotion of consumers' access to regional cultural diversity").
5. This spatial dimension is arguably the sense in which Jane Ginsburg has argued that "the no-formalities rule [in Article 5(2) of the Berne Convention] thus fundamentally undergirds the Berne Convention system of universal international authors' rights." *See* Jane C. Ginsburg, *"With Untired Spirits and Formal Constancy": Berne Compatibility of Formal Declaratory Measures to Enhance Copyright Title-Searching,* 28 Berkeley Technology Law Journal 1583, 1589 (2013) https://doi.org/10.2139/ssrn.2262924.

mid-nineteenth century.[6] Indeed, for countries that considered copyright to be a natural right it is hard, as a matter of principle, to deny the correctness of that approach.[7] Natural rights have a universalist character,[8] something that needs to be borne in mind as human rights instruments come to play a more important role in defining international copyright norms.[9]

For other countries, particularly those that grounded copyright in more instrumentalist justifications, whether to offer protection to foreign authors was a more open intellectual choice. To what extent would such an extension of protection further the objectives underlying the grant of copyright? Resolution of this question was informed not only by calculations about the climate of creativity that one wished to encourage and the relative value of domestic and foreign production but also by considerations of domestic political economy; foreign authors do not vote, and in the late nineteenth century, patterns of immigration had yet not complicated such nationalistic assessments. Thus, it was not until 1891 that the United States (U.S.) enacted the Chace Act to extend protection to foreign authors.[10] And even when this occurred the U.S. Congress still included inward-looking devices such as the Manufacturing Clause designed to protect domestic industries from some of the consequences of granting rights to foreign authors, namely, drying up the ready supply of good foreign works to copy for free.[11]

National treatment was chosen in 1886 as the means by which to guarantee protection to foreign authors, rather than the more complex reciprocity model that tended to emphasize a more suspicious "trust but verify" approach to international relations.[12] But of course, the Berne Convention was not just about mechanisms for ensuring the local protection of foreign authors, or the protection of domestic authors abroad as the local governmental actors might think of that question. In order to facilitate and enhance trade in an economy that was increasingly cross-border, authors and publishers needed some certainty not only about the *existence* of protection but also about the *nature or content* of the copyright law that would regulate the exploitation of their work. Indeed, some agreement on substantive norms beyond the cross-border protection of authors was required to make the

6. *See* Decree of Mar. 28, 1852 (Fr.); Ricketson & Ginsburg (n. 2), §1.24 at 22.
7. *See* Ricketson & Ginsburg (n. 2), §2.02 at 42.
8. *See* Universal Declaration of Human Rights (Dec. 10, 1948) A/RES/217(III), Art. 27.
9. *See generally* Laurence R. Helfer & Graeme W. Austin, *Human Rights and Intellectual Property Mapping: the Global Interface* (Cambridge University Press, 2011); *see also* United Nations General Assembly, *Human Rights Council: Report of The Special Rapporteur in the Field of Cultural Rights* (Dec. 24, 2014) A/HRC/28/57.
10. *See* Act of Mar. 3, 1891, c. 565, §3, 26 Stat. 1101.
11. *See* 26 Stat. 1106 (1891); *see generally* Marshall Leaffer, *International Copyright from an American Perspective,* 43 Arkansas Law Review 373 (1990). The Manufacturing Clause expired on Jul. 1, 1986. *See ibid.,* 398 n. 131.
12. *See* Berne Convention, Art. 5(1).

political economy of national treatment acceptable to those with an instrumentalist bent.

Thus, the conceptual model embedded in Berne in 1986 was one of national treatment combined with some relatively low-level substantive guarantees of protection.[13] Article 5(1) provides that:

> [a]uthors shall enjoy … the rights which their respective laws do now or may hereafter grant to their nationals, as well as the rights specially granted by this Convention.[14]

This is a model that endorses, even within an international system, the principle of territoriality and the legislative autonomy of Member States to tailor their national copyright law to their own policy dictates within mild constraints.[15] Within the concepts or themes explored in this chapter, this might be seen as a largely pluralist model, consistent with the premise of territoriality.

The foundational choice that confronted negotiating countries in 1886 is often presented as one between that pluralist, territorial model and a more comprehensive universal copyright law, establishing uniform standards to be applied in all adherent countries. This alternative approach was advocated by several countries in the lead up to Berne, most notably, Germany.[16] We have tended to label this latter approach as "universalist" but its distinguishing feature, which set it apart from the model ultimately adopted, was its desire for substantive uniformity and thus a limit on plural approaches to copyright.

This quest for universal uniformity proved too ambitious. Agreement on a comprehensive code would have required substantial compromise on the part of most nations and thus was beyond the negotiating parties. As a practical matter, the acceptability of a single supranational code depends in large part upon the closeness of that code to a country's existing law. And to the extent that any agreement reached would have been built around the standards prevailing in the dominant copyright-respecting nations, this might have impeded growth in the membership of the union established by the

13. *See* Graeme B. Dinwoodie, *A New Copyright Order: Why National Courts Should Create Global Norms,* 149 University of Pennsylvania Law Review 469, 490 (2000) https://doi.org/10.2307/3312732.
14. *Ibid.*
15. Indeed, the obligation of Art. 5(1) applied only to "in respect of works for which [authors] are protected under this Convention, in countries of the Union other than the country of origin." *See* Berne Convention, Art. 5(1). As Art. 5(3) of the Berne Convention lays out even more explicitly, "protection in the country of origin is governed by domestic law." *See also ibid.,* Art. 5(4) (providing complex definition of "country of origin"). Thus, Member States are accorded even greater latitude as regards domestic works. For example, the United States imposes on U.S. works the formality of registration prior to an action for infringement, which Art. 5(2) of the Convention bars being required of foreign works. *See* 17 USC §411(a); Berne Convention, Art. 5(2).
16. *See* Ricketson & Ginsburg (n. 2), §2.24 at 62.

Berne Convention.[17] Thus, the choice made in 1886 was animated both by pluralism and universalism. The drafters opted to pursue a conceptual structure more likely to result in an international copyright system that was universal in reach and ambition, while more pluralist in content.

This refinement of the relationship between pluralism and universalism reflects an understanding of international copyright law that accommodates within an international system or regime a role for plural laws or norms. One might cast that as marking a difference between a focus on international copyright *law*, and an international copyright *system* or international copyright *regime*. The latter phrase—an international copyright *system*—perhaps best captures the diverse components that regulate the exploitation of creative works of authors on an international level.

11.2 POST-BERNE DEVELOPMENTS

It is of course also true that—viewed in terms of applicable norms or rules—the international system has since 1886 reflected an evolving balance of norms grounded in national, regional and international instruments. But the choice is not, I would suggest, between a plural approach to copyright law and a universal approach to copyright law. Rather, the evolution has sought to accommodate a pluralist approach to copyright law within a system that is universal in reach and which may aspire for increasingly persuasive reasons to install more uniform norms.[18]

The content of our international copyright system these days is filled far more extensively than in 1886 by norms that derive from regional or international sources than from national ones.[19] Yet, the basic structure of an international system reflecting space for the pluralist value of national autonomy persists. The Agreement on Trade-Related Aspects of Intellectual Property Rights (TRIPS) did not on its face alter that structure.[20] It was very

17. *See* Ginsburg (n. 2), 269 ("the underlying rationale was that a flexible international treaty would permit more countries to accede to the Union, thus increasing membership"). Similar arguments about the dominant model of ever-developing acts of the Convention now underlie complaints by developing countries about the nature of the international provisions. *See* Ruth L. Okediji, *The Limits of International Copyright Exceptions for Developing Countries,* 21 Vanderbilt Journal of Entertainment & Technology Law Journal 689 (2019) https://doi.org/10.2139/ssrn.3383726.
18. *See* Dinwoodie (n. 13), 478-481.
19. *See* Ginsburg (n. 2).
20. *See* TRIPS (Apr. 15, 1994), 1869 UNTS 299; *see generally* Graeme B. Dinwoodie & Rochelle C. Dreyfuss, *A Neofederal Vision of TRIPS: The Resilience of International Intellectual Property Regime* Chs. 1-2 (Oxford University Press, 2012); *But see* Ruth Okediji, *Toward an International Fair Use Doctrine*, 39 Columbia Journal of Transnational Law 75, 104-105 (2000).

much built on the Berne model and afforded Member States substantial latitude to tailor their copyright laws to their own policy preferences.[21]

But the creation of a binding dispute settlement procedure and a standing quasi-judicial institution to interpret TRIPS may have been seen by that institution—the World Trade Organization (WTO) Dispute Settlement Body (DSB)—as an invitation to develop "autonomous" international copyright law.[22] Examples of judicial activism in this field are not hard to find. The Court of Justice of the European Union (CJEU) has sought to develop "autonomous" principles of EU copyright law, and thus elide national autonomy unless the directive being interpreted has explicitly reserved a question to national law.[23] Indeed, that Court has done so on occasion even when directives intentionally (and sometimes explicitly) have left matters to national law.[24] The resulting harmonization creep that has

21. *See* Dinwoodie & Dreyfuss (n. 20), 41-42.
22. *See* Dinwoodie (n. 13), 501-502; *see ibid.,* 502-517 (arguing that the WTO should resist the urge to adopt an activist interpretive philosophy).
23. *See* Eleonora Rosati, *Copyright and the Court of Justice of the European Union* 42-43 (Oxford University Press, 2019) (tracing the history of this approach and listing the multiple occasions on which the Court has deployed it to develop a European concept that has an "independent and uniform interpretation throughout the European Union"); *see,* e.g., Case C-201/13 Deckmyn v. Vandersteen (2014) EU:C:2014:2132 (parody as autonomous concept in defining meaning of defense to copyright infringement even though that was a defense which was optional for Member States to provide). The Court might instead have eradicated some differences that the directive left open by invocation of EU-level rules external to copyright law, such as the free expression guarantee of Art. 11 of the Charter of Fundamental Rights (as regards the parody in Deckmyn) or through fundamental notions of free movement (in Case C-128/11 Usedsoft GmbH v. Oracle International Corp. (2012) EU:C:2012:407, where the Court also used this principle of interpretation). *See* P. Bernt Hugenholtz, *The Creeping Unification of Copyright in Europe,* at Pluralism and Universalism in International Copyright Law (Tatiana Synodinou ed., Kluwer, 2019) pp. 77-95, at 72, 87, 92; Case C 476/17, Pelham GmbH v. Ralf Hütter (2018) EU:C:2018:1002, para. 77 (Advocate General Szpunar).
24. Sometimes this has been clear from the limited scope of the harmonization instrument. Thus, the Court has arguably extended the "authors' own intellectual creation" test of originality to all works of authorship notwithstanding its legislative adoption with respect to only three specific types of work, namely, software, databases and photographs. *See* Case C-5/08 Infopaq International A/S v. Danske Dagblades Forening (2009) EU:C:2009:465; Case C-393/09 Bezpečnostní softwarová asociace v. Ministerstvo kultury (2010) EU:C:2010:816. But sometimes the Court has acted in the face of explicit textual authority of Member States to follow diverse approaches. *See* Case C-168/09 Flos SpA v. Semeraro Casa e Famiglia SpA (2011), EU:C:2011:29, para. 34. The virulence of this approach is such that Member States have been unduly keen to fall in line with what is seen as the oncoming Europeanization. *See, e.g.,* Enterprise and Regulatory Reform Act 2013, §74(2); *see generally* Lionel Bently, *The Return of Industrial Copyright* 34 European Intellectual Property Review 654 (2012). The end point of this dynamic in the context of copyright protection for designs appears to be Case C-683/17 Cofemel-Sociedade de Vestuário SA v. G-Star Raw CV (2019), EU:C:2019:363, in which the Advocate-General has proposed that Member States do not have the freedom to choose the level of originality necessary for the protection of works of applied art, industrial

shriveled national autonomy in European copyright policy has not been replicated in the WTO (in any of the intellectual property disputes in which reports have been issued). There might be textual reasons for this restraint,[25] but the more powerful explanation might be the weaker institutional legitimacy of the WTO as against that of the EU.[26] Recent attacks on the Organization by the U.S., and efforts to cobble the Appellate Body, are unlikely to embolden it.[27]

Likewise, the World Intellectual Property Organization (WIPO) Internet treaties (the WIPO Copyright Treaty (WCT) and the WIPO Performances and Phonograms Treaty (WPPT)) did not alter the basic conceptual structure of Berne, even if they suggest important evolutions in the process of international copyright lawmaking.[28] Nor have multiple bilateral or plurilateral TRIPS-plus agreements altered that structure. Those agreements have both reshaped the political dynamics at play in taking advantage of the latitude afforded the WTO Member States[29] and stacked the deck toward the

---

designs and works of design. This is despite Art. 17 of the Design Directive, which states that: "A design protected by a design right registered in or in respect of a Member State in accordance with this Directive shall also be eligible for protection under the law of copyright of that State as from the date on which the design was created or fixed in any form. The extent to which, and the conditions under which, such a protection is conferred, including the level of originality required, shall be determined by each Member State." *See* Directive 98/71/EC of the European Parliament and of the Council of 13 October 1998 on the legal protection of designs (Oct. 13, 1998) Official Journal 1998 L 289, 28/10/1998, pp. 28-35.

25. *See* Understanding on Rules and Procedures Governing the Settlement of Disputes, Marrakesh Agreement Establishing the World Trade Organization, Annex 2, Art. 3(2).
26. The mode of implementation of international treaty obligations and EU directives also varies in ways that encourage the CJEU to approach interpretation in this fashion. Many EU Member States have taken simply to adopt the language of the directive, thus facilitating the Court effectively treating the Directive as a Regulation. This may reflect the fact that directives—while not regulations—do typically have a level of detail not found in international treaties, which require greater interpolation and allow greater divergence in what states do to comply. It might also be because Member States thus avoid the specter of Francovich damages. *See* P. Bernt Hugenholtz, *The Creeping Unification of Copyright in Europe,* at Pluralism and Universalism in International Copyright Law (Tatiana Synodinou ed., Kluwer, 2019) pp. 77-95, at 92.
27. *See* Statements by the United States at the Meeting of the WTO Dispute Settlement Body, Geneva 12, https://geneva.usmission.gov/wp-content/uploads/sites/290/Feb25.DSB_.Stmt_.as-deliv.fin_.public.pdf (accessed Jun. 5, 2016).
28. *See* WIPO Copyright Treaty (Dec. 20, 1996) TRT/WCT/001; WIPO Performances and Phonograms Treaty (Dec. 20, 1996) TRT/WPPT/001; Graeme B. Dinwoodie, *The WIPO Copyright Treaty: A Transition to the Future of International Copyright Lawmaking?,* 57 Case Western Reserve Law Review 751 (2007) https://doi.org/10.1093/oso/9780195128857.005.0009 (discussing how the WIPO Copyright Treaty did suggest changes to the nature of the international copyright system); *see generally* Pamela Samuelson, *The US Digital Agenda at WIPO,* 37 Virginia Journal of International Law 369 (1997).
29. *See* Henning Grosse Ruse-Khan et al., *Principles for Intellectual Property Provisions in Bilateral and Regional Agreements,* 44 International Review of Industrial Property 878

adoption of particular national models that may over time become the international norm.[30]

To be sure, these developments over the last 20 years each in their own way have contributed to the reshaping of contemporary international copyright law in important respects. Most importantly for current purposes, they have all shifted the balance of applicable norms within a system of increasingly universal reach in the direction of those norms with an international or regional pedigree. And thus the space for plural national policy choices has shrunk. But this has occurred within a system that nominally at least is conceptually structured as it was in 1886.

There is much to be said for national autonomy and the maintenance of a pluralist approach to copyright.[31] The number and range of countries now participating in the international copyright system makes the values of individual national tailoring even more vital than they were in 1886. This is a paradox of the development of global systems. As the geographic reach of the system expands, often stimulating a simplistic impulse to universalize and homogenize, the more we may actually need to attend to the diversity of the participants and endorse the value of national autonomy.

By the same token, as the post-1994 trade system, advances in digital communication technologies, and varied other social forces, effect deeper integration in the creation and consumption of creative works—and intensify the inter-dependence of markets that was part-motivation for Berne in 1886—the demand for convergence of national norms regulating authorial works is surely well-founded.[32] In some circumstances, pluralism might be dysfunctional.[33] Indeed, the acceleration in social and commercial assimilation might argue not only for a shift toward more extensive global norms but also toward procedural and institutional mechanisms that foreswear the very deliberate internationalization that characterized copyright lawmaking in the

(2013); *see, e.g.,* United States-Australia Free Trade Agreement (May 18, 2004) 43 I.L.M. 1248, Art. 17(4); Comprehensive and Progressive Agreement for Trans-Pacific Partnership (Mar. 8, 2018) (hereinafter "CPTPP"), https://international.gc.ca/trade-commerce/trade-agreements-accords-commerciaux/agr-acc/cptpp-ptpgp/text-texte/index.aspx?lang=eng (accessed Jun. 5, 2019); *see generally* Peter K. Yu, *Currents and Crosscurrents in the International Intellectual Property Regime,* 38 Loyola of Los Angeles Law Review 323, 392-400 (2004); Peter K. Yu, *The RCEP and Trans-Pacific Intellectual Property Norms,* 50 Vanderbilt Journal of Transnational Law 673, 675 (2017).

30. Cf. Matthias Leistner, *Intermediary Liability in a Global World,* at Pluralism and Universalism in International Copyright Law 11 n. 54 (Tatiana Synodinou ed., Kluwer, 2019) (arguing that U.S. free trade agreements helped the DMCA become the model for notice & takedown but recognizing other influences as well).
31. *See* Graeme W. Austin, *Valuing "Domestic Self-Determination" in International Intellectual Property Jurisprudence* 77 Chicago-Kent Law Review 1155 (2002).
32. *See* Dinwoodie (n. 13), 478-481.
33. Lionel A.F. Bently & Tanya Aplin, *Whatever Became of Global Mandatory Fair Use? A Case Study in Dysfunctional Pluralism,* at Is Intellectual Property Pluralism Functional? (Susy Frankel ed., Edward Elgar, 2019) (arguing that the marginalization of Art. 10(1) of the Berne Convention highlights the dangers of pluralism in copyright).

twentieth century.[34] Thus, we also need mechanisms that will more quickly and more extensively create or recognize global norms for the treatment of copyright works.[35]

At first blush, there might appear to be some tension between these propositions. National autonomy is even more crucial than was formerly the case given the expanded scope of the international system, but so too is the development of global norms. This was one of the many tensions that Rochelle Dreyfuss and I took into account when, in tackling what we saw as the challenges of TRIPS, we broached the concept of an "international *acquis*" in our book "A Neo-Federalist Vision of TRIPS: The Resilience of the International Intellectual Property Regime."[36]

In that book, we devoted substantial time to debunking the suggestion that TRIPS constituted a supranational code imposing a single substantive set of norms on the diverse membership of TRIPS. Yet, the fact that we spoke of an "international" *acquis* has brought up the question of whether this portends an augmentation of international or universal norms and thus a further shift in the balance between national and international authorities. That is to say, how might an "international copyright *acquis*" shape the development of international copyright law; would it contribute inexorably to the development of a universalist approach in international copyright law? In the next Part of this chapter, I respond to that question, taking account of the nature of the international copyright system discussed above.

11.3 THE INTERNATIONAL *ACQUIS*

By "international *acquis,*" we meant consciously to borrow (but also to adapt for our own purposes) the term as used by various other institutions and scholars. For the EU, the term describes the body of existing legal principles and commitments to which new members of the EU must ascribe.[37] "Acquis" has been used by the Appellate Body of the WTO to explain why panel reports should be relevant in adjudicating future disputes.[38] And it has been understood by scholars as a device to fill gaps and create predictability in a cross-border arena.[39] In international copyright law, the WTO panel in the

34. *See* Dinwoodie (n. 28) (noting the lack of nationally-tested models prior to negotiation of international rules in the WIPO Copyright Treaty).
35. *See* Dinwoodie (n. 13) (arguing for enhanced role of national courts).
36. *See* Dinwoodie & Dreyfuss (n. 20), Chapter 7.
37. *See* R. Michael Gadbaw, *Systemic Regulation of Global Trade and Finance: A Tale of Two Systems,* 13 Journal of International Economic Law 551, 567 (2010) https://doi.org/10.1093/jiel/jgq031.
38. Appellate Body Report, Japan—Taxes on Alcoholic Beverages, WT/DS8/AB/R, WT/DS10/AB/R, WT/DS11/AB/R 14 (Oct. 4, 1996).
39. *See* Petros C. Mavroidis, *No Outsourcing of Law? WTO Law as Practiced by WTO Courts,* 102 American Journal of International Law 421, 465 (2008) https://doi.org/10.2

United States—Section 110(5) case, which was the first TRIPS panel to refer to an *"acquis"* (in that case, the Berne *acquis*), appeared to add another dimension to the concept, regarding the *acquis* as a body of principles reflected in a treaty regime even if not always expressed.[40]

The over-arching goal of articulating an international copyright *acquis* was to create a legal framework to structure future lawmaking, at both the national and international levels. At the international level, this would be important in reducing the problem of fragmentation about which international law scholars have written generally in the last 12 years.[41] That phenomenon is clearly present in international copyright law, as norms are generated by the WTO, WIPO, and human rights bodies, to name only three prominent expositors.[42] Adjudicating international law claims becomes harder in that climate, as the panel in *United States—Section 110(5)* acknowledged when confronted with the challenge of reconciling the Berne Convention, the TRIPS Agreement, and the WCT.[43] The Vienna Convention on the Law of Treaties only gets you so far.[44]

Fleshing out an *acquis* rather than relying simply on the bare bones of international treaties would also help guide and render more efficient international negotiations. It would codify the values of Member State autonomy and the rights of users that are largely implicit in older treaties.[45] It would also harness the different expertise of the diverse array of institutions promulgating copyright-relevant norms. And it would ameliorate the problems of capacity that can bedevil developing countries new to copyright law and help address challenges presented by a weak domestic political economy.[46] Too often the international norms are stated to be those set out in the TRIPS Agreement or the Berne Convention, but these are necessarily incomplete as templates for national adoption. And that incompleteness will tend to have a systemic character, given that the current model is grounded in the minimum rights of authors. While we did not see the

---

307/20456639; Michael Wabwile, *Re-Examining States' External Obligations to Implement Economic and Social Rights of Children,* 22 Canadian Journal of Law & Jurisprudence 407, 433 (2009) https://doi.org/10.1017/s0841820900004756 (noting gap-filling role).

40. *See* Panel Report, United States—Section 110(5) of the U.S. Copyright Act (Jun. 15, 2000) WT/DS/160/R §6.42 (hereinafter United States—Section 110(5) Panel Report).
41. *See, e.g.,* United Nations International Law Commission, *Fragmentation of International Law: Difficulties Arising from the Diversification and Expansion of International Law: Report of the Study Group on the Fragmentation of International Law, Finalized by Martti Koskenniemi*, §242 (Apr. 13, 2006) UN Doc. A/CN.4/L.682.
42. *See* Dinwoodie & Dreyfuss (n. 20), 147-156.
43. *See* United States—Section 110(5) Panel Report (n. 40), §6.70.
44. *See* Vienna Convention on the Law of Treaties (May 23, 1969) 1155 UNTS 331.
45. *See* Dinwoodie & Dreyfuss (n. 20), 192-193.
46. *See ibid.,* 178-180.

acquis as a model law, it might serve some of the same functions as a well-balanced model law might do.[47]

We only briefly sketched the substantive content of the international *acquis* in "A Neo-federalist Vision," urging other scholars to take on the task.[48] But one important point for present purposes is that we drew the content of the *acquis* from national as well as international intellectual property law along with associated jurisprudence and scholarship, including sources such as human rights law that one might not regard as part of copyright law.[49] And this is at one with the premise noted above, namely, that the international copyright system is more than simply the content of international copyright instruments or laws. The *international system* of 1886 clearly contemplated the role of *national laws* in providing content to international norms; and indeed, the interpretative methodology adopted by WTO panels in applying the Vienna Convention on the Law of Treaties in TRIPS cases does so too.[50]

For example, in determining the meaning of permissible exceptions under the minor exceptions doctrine referenced in the documents of the Berne conferences, the panel in *United States—Section 110(5)* was alert to the wide range of exceptions and limitations that existed appropriately under diverse national laws.[51] From those national examples, the panel extrapolated a number of universal principles that validated a plural range of national laws. For example, the panel rejected the argument that the minor exceptions doctrine should be restricted to noncommercial uses, relying in part upon the wide variation in exemptions found in national laws.[52]

An ambitious articulation of universal principles that draws upon plural sources is especially important at this time.[53] Public international law is not the only way that copyright law is effectively universalized, or global

47. The so-called Tunis Model Law of Copyright for Developing Countries prepared by WIPO in 1976 is far out of date. *See* Jorgen Blomqvist, *Universality or Diversity? The WIPO Role and Strategy in International Copyright Lawmaking,* at Pluralism and Universalism in International Copyright Law (Tatiana Synodinou ed., Kluwer, 2019). Various non-governmental organizations have asked WIPO to update that law.
48. The principles according to which we sought to develop the international copyright *acquis* and the copyright specific content that we ourselves identified can be found in Chapter 7 of the book. *See* Dinwoodie & Dreyfuss (n. 20).
49. *See* Dinwoodie & Dreyfuss (n. 20), 177.
50. *See* Panel Report, Canada—Patent Protection of Pharmaceutical Products (Mar. 17, 2000) WT/DS114/R §7.69 (relying on national laws permitting the use of patented products for scientific experimentation to justify the regulatory review exception).
51. *See* United States—Section 110(5) Panel Report (n. 40), §6.55.
52. *See ibid.,* §6.58.
53. This effort to meld the universal and the plural is also seen in the work of Lionel Bently & Tanya Aplin, although arguably along different dimensions. They argue that "'fair practice' in Art. 10(1) of the Berne Convention has an autonomous and pluralistic meaning that embraces notions of moral and economic harm, distributive justice concerns, freedom of expression principles, and, in limited circumstances, custom." *See* Bently & Aplin (n. 33). This approach has some echoes of the suggested approach to Art.

copyright solutions imposed. If Berne created a structure that might be called "International Copyright Law 1.0," we may now be seeing an international system that we can label "International Copyright Law 2.0," not because of any particular international instrument but because of the accumulated effect of a number of developments. Thus, we suggested in "Neo-Federalist Vision" that we were in what might (borrowing the language of the American constitutional scholar Bruce Ackerman) be called an "international constitutional moment," when the time is ripe for a new paradigm.[54] The strength of that claim has only grown in the last eight years.

Numerous forces have challenged the theoretical paradigm of Berne 1886, namely, that "the international system did not articulate positive copyright law" but instead "established parameters within which national political processes created the substantive balance appropriate to the circumstances of each different domestic order."[55] The institutional, political, technological, and social forces of the twenty-first century belie the simplicity or balance of that model. Indeed, it might even sound naive.

A number of challenges require a more elaborated international system and one which makes explicit that which formerly was instantiated by autonomous national political processes, institutions and norms.[56] These include developments in private international law, where a sizeable body of national case law involving transborder copyright disputes has grown over the last 20 years.[57] A number of countries have liberalized rules of jurisdiction, abrogating rules of exclusive jurisdiction and allowing adjudication of foreign copyright infringement claims.[58] Under the so-called

---

10*bis* of the Paris Convention. *See* George H.C. Bodenhausen, *A Guide to the Application of the Paris Convention for the Protection of Industrial Property* 144 (WIPO Geneva, 1968).

54. Bruce J. Ackerman, *Reconstructing American Law* (Harvard University Press, 1984); Others have adopted this device in international law. *See, e.g.,* Anne-Marie Slaughter & William Burke-White, *An International Constitutional Moment,* 43 Harvard International Law Journal 1, 2 (2002).
55. *See* Dinwoodie (n. 28), 755.
56. Of course, the imperfect nature of national political processes might cause one to seek refuge in the international system. *See* Ruth L. Okediji, *The Regulation of Creativity under the Internet Treaties,* 77 Fordham Law Review 2379, 2404-2408 (2009) https://doi.org/10.2139/ssrn.1433848 (discussing the institutional capacity of developing countries to exercise effective design choices at the national level).
57. *See generally,* James J. Fawcett & Paul Torremans, *Intellectual Property and Private International Law* (2nd ed., Oxford University Press, 2011).
58. *See, e.g.,* Boosey & Hawkes Music Publishers, Ltd. v. Walt Disney Co., 145 F.3d 481, 484 (2d Cir. 1998) (reversing district court's dismissal of claims under foreign copyright laws on forum non conveniens grounds); Pearce v. Ove Arup P'ship, [1999] 1 All E.R. 769, 784-804 (C.A.) (hearing claim for infringement of Dutch copyright); Lucasfilm Ltd v. Ainsworth [2011] UKSC 39 (accepting jurisdiction over U.S. copyright claim). Other decisions have offered a broad range of options for where to bring suit without formally enhancing the *scope* of jurisdiction beyond that forum. *See, e.g.,* Case C-441/13 Pez Hejduk v. Energieagentur.nrw GmbH, EU:C:2015:28 at [33].

predicate act theory, U.S. courts have extended jurisdiction over domestic infringement to encompass monetary claims for follow-on infringement abroad, without always considering whether the foreign acts amounted to infringement under foreign laws.[59] And liberal approaches to choice of law (and related broad interpretations of infringing acts, such as "public performance") have facilitated ready localization of cross-border disputes in a single country.[60] These different mechanisms, especially when considered in tandem with the enhanced importance of cross-border business models and geographic dispersal of assets, have effectively allowed national courts to adjudicate global copyright disputes.[61]

A universal system that paid greater respect for pluralism within its confines would match the liberalization of jurisdiction and choice of law in copyright over the last 20 years with a structured international system of jurisdiction and recognition of judgments that allowed an ongoing contest of plural approaches.[62] In the last decade, two soft law projects (one based in the U.S. and one in Europe) have grappled with the need for such a system and the special challenges that might be presented by copyright law (and by intellectual property law in general).[63] These projects brought together a

---

59. *See* Los Angeles News Serv. v. Reuters T.V. Int'l Limited, 149 F.3d 987 (9th Cir. 1998), later proceeding, 340 F.3d 926 (9th Cir. 2003); Tire Eng'g & Distribution, LLC v. Shandong Linglong Rubber Co., 682 F. 3d 292, 307 (4th Cir. 2012); *Remarks by Graeme Dinwoodie*, 30 Brooklyn Journal of International Law 885, 889-890 (2005); *see also* Graeme B. Dinwoodie, *The Architecture of the International Intellectual Property System*, 77 Chicago-Kent Law Review 993, 1007 n. 75 (2002).
60. *See* NFL v. Primetime 24 Joint Venture, 211 F.3d 10, 13 (2d Cir. 2000) (finding that performance occurs at the place of initiation of the signal in the United States as well as at places of receipt); Twentieth Century Fox Film Corp. v. iCrave TV, 53 U.S.P.Q.2d 1831 (W.D. Pa. 2000); Spanski Enters., Inc. v. Telewizja Polska, S.A., 883 F.3d 904 (D.C. Cir. 2018).
61. The extent to which this is true varies with the mechanism in question. Insofar as the ability to hear foreign copyright infringement claims opens the door to courts applying multiple different copyright laws to a transborder dispute, it might reduce the temptation to localize an entire dispute in the forum and thus may enhance respect for different laws. That is not necessarily true of the predicate act theory, and even less so of expansive localization. And even where a court might in theory have open to it the possibility of applying multiple different copyright laws to a transborder dispute, it would not be a huge surprise if in practice courts treated those laws as essentially the same and thus apply a single law (very often the forum). In this regard, it is notable that the Court of Justice of the European Union has taken a far more relaxed view toward the consolidation of copyright claims under different national laws in a single proceeding than it has in the patent context. Case C-145/10 Painer v. Standard Verlags et al. EU:C:2011:798 at [81]-[82]. Cf. C-539/03 Roche Nederland BV v. Primus, EU:C:2006:458; *see also* Council Regulation (EC) No. 44/2001 of 22 December 2000 on Jurisdiction and the Recognition and Enforcement of Judgments in Civil and Commercial Matters, Art. 6(1) (Dec. 22, 2000) Official Journal L 12/1, 16/01/2001.
62. *See* Dinwoodie (n. 59).
63. *See* American Law Institute, *Intellectual Property: Principles Governing Jurisdiction, Choice of Law and Judgments in Transnational Disputes* (2008); European Max-Planck

wide range of experts and have already been cited in national courts.[64] Yet, the U.S. and China, most notably, are presently vetoing the inclusion of copyright or other forms of intellectual property within the pending negotiation of a Draft Hague Convention on Jurisdiction and Recognition of Judgments.[65] Indeed, despite that effort at exclusion, Article 11 of the draft provides that in intellectual property cases:

> a judgment ruling on an infringement shall be [recognised and] enforced only to the extent that it rules on a monetary remedy in relation to harm suffered in the State of origin.[66]

This is precisely the wrong approach at a time when national courts have indicated the need to rethink the enforcement of injunctive relief in intellectual property cases.[67]

As multinational intermediaries assume ever more relevance in the enforcement of copyright law, and thus serve as the regulators of access to and use of copyright works, the preservation of territorial pluralism is at the whim of private corporate efficiency calculations.[68] Corporations may for understandable reasons seek to apply a common set of standards to conduct occurring on their platform or using their services.[69] And the balance of different public interests that the national systems injected into the international copyright system is also absent from such lawmaking because in this context there is no transparent discussion of the appropriate balance between

---

Group on Conflict of Laws in Intellectual Property (CLIP), *Conflict of Laws in Intellectual Property: The CLIP Principles and Commentary* (Oxford University Press, 2013). Further work in this space is being pursued by the International Law Association Committee on Intellectual Property and Private International Law.

64. *See, e.g.,* Lucasfilm Ltd v. Ainsworth, UKSC 39 (2011) at [93]-[94].
65. *See* Hague Conference on Private International Law, Special Commission on the Recognition and Enforcement of Foreign Judgments (May 24-29, 2018), 2018 Draft Convention, Working Document No. 262 REV, Art. 2(m), https://assets.hcch.net/docs/23b6dac3-7900-49f3-9a94-aa0ffbe0d0dd.pdf. (accessed Jun. 7, 2019).
66. *See ibid.,* Art. 11. The bracketed language is in the original, suggesting that it is a matter of continuing debate.
67. *See* Pro Swing Inc. v. Elta Golf Inc. SCC 52 (2006) (Canada) (indicating that it may be time to reconsider the historical reluctance to enforce foreign injunctive orders in trademark cases). National courts on both sides of the Atlantic have struggled with questions of trans-border enforcement in the copyright context. *See* SAS Institute Inc. v. World Programming Ltd. EWHC 3452 (2018) (Comm) (U.K.) (enforcement of non-copyright U.S. cause of action that impinged on EU copyright policy as embodied in decision of the Court of Justice); SARL Louis Feraud Int'l v. Viewfinder, Inc. 489 F.3d 474 (2d Cir. 2007) (potential conflict between French copyright law and free speech guarantees of the U.S. Constitution).
68. For a discussion of the role of platforms in the context of speech regulation, *see* Kate Klonick, *The New Governors: The People, Rules, and Processes Governing Online Speech,* 131 Harvard Law Review 1598, 1602 (2018).
69. It is not clear whether automation in detection and enforcement will impose even more rigid uniformity or whether, with enhanced efficiency, it will make national differentiation more practical.

plural and uniform, between national and global, or between author and user.[70]

Although international law allows room for preserving those balances by regulating intermediary behavior, national legislative efforts to structure and confine that private ordering have been weak. Conditioning immunity for intermediaries on the use of filtering obligations may represent the next challenge of this type (following upon the application of technological protection measures by rightholders and the ubiquity of notice and takedown practices).[71] In the recently adopted Directive on Copyright in the Digital Single Market,[72] the EU has effectively required a certain subset of intermediaries, namely, online content-sharing service providers (OCSSP),[73] *inter alia,* to make, in accordance with high industry standards of professional diligence, "best efforts to ensure the unavailability of specific works … for which the rightholders have provided the service providers with the relevant and necessary information."[74] In short, they will be required to engage in the filtering of content.

Recognizing that the incentive structure built into Article 17—which effectively imposes this obligation—will make the OCSSP (and the filtering software of the OCSSP) the arbiter of access to materials making use of the copyrighted works, the EU legislator has sought to regulate the decision-making activities of the OCSSP. Thus, Article 17(7) decrees that:

> the cooperation between [OCSSPs] and rightholders shall not result in the prevention of the availability of works … uploaded by users, which

70. *See* Graeme B. Dinwoodie, *Private Ordering and the Creation of International Copyright Norms: The Role of Public Structuring,* 160 Journal of Institutional and Theoretical Economics 161, 189 (2004) https://doi.org/10.1628/0932456047738613 84.
71. *See ibid.* (discussing the application of technological protection measures by rightholders and notice & takedown practices); *see also* Jerome H. Reichman, Graeme B. Dinwoodie & Pamela Samuelson, *A Reverse Notice & Takedown Regime to Enable Public Interest Uses of Technically Protected Copyrighted Works,* 22 Berkeley Technology Law Journal 981, 985 (2007) https://doi.org/10.4337/9781848449442.00013.
72. Directive (EU) 2019/790 of the European Parliament and of the Council of 17 April 2019 on copyright and related rights in the Digital Single Market and amending Directives 96/9/EC and 2001/29/EC (Apr. 17, 2019), Official Journal 130, 17.5.2019, pp. 92-125.
73. Article 2(6) defines "online content-sharing service provider" as "a provider of an information society service of which the main or one of the main purposes is to store and give the public access to a large amount of copyright-protected works or other protected subject matter uploaded by its users, which it organises and promotes for profit-making purposes." It also excludes specifically "Providers of services, such as not-for-profit online encyclopaedias, not-for-profit educational and scientific repositories, open source software-developing and- sharing platforms, [access providers], online marketplaces, business-to-business cloud services and cloud services that allow users to upload content for their own use."
74. *See ibid.,* Art. 17(4)(b).

do not infringe copyright and related rights, including where such works or other subject matter are covered by an exception or limitation.[75]

In this, EU legislators have simply mimicked the provision in the Information Society Directive (InfoSoc Directive) to ensure that technological protection measures did not silently impose unbalanced norms (again reflecting an unarticulated balance between local and global) on the European public.[76] That provision, Article 6(4), arguably had the makings of a vehicle to monitor private technological overrides of legislated balance. But the relatively toothless mechanisms that were enacted nationally meant that that provision was never really made effective.[77]

Article 17(9) does go further, but reeks of aspiration rather than any real vision. It requires that the service provider shall put in place "an effective and expeditious complaint and redress mechanism" for users who object to the filtering of their content, and requires both that complaints be processed without undue delay, and that rightholders justify the reasons for their requests to block access. This seems unambitious. In the other direction, the Article requires that "decisions to disable access to or remove uploaded content shall be subject to human review."[78] This seems unrealistic.

11.4 CONTINUING CHALLENGES

I do not mean to be entirely pessimistic or critical. As these challenges to the long-standing conceptual model of international copyright law accumulate, there have been efforts to respond to the realities of plural national approaches in an increasingly interdependent climate. Thus, as the global political economy has pressed hard for the formal international copyright model of minimum standards when national political economies are threadbare, scholars and activists have sought to shine a light on the balance embedded in international copyright law.

75. Indeed, the Directive explicitly provides that "Member States shall ensure that users in each Member State are able to rely on any of the following existing exceptions or limitations when uploading and making available content generated by users on online content-sharing services: (a) quotation, criticism, review; (b) use for the purpose of caricature, parody or pastiche."

76. Directive 2001/29/EC of the European Parliament and of the Council of 22 May 2001on the harmonization of certain aspects of copyright and related rights in the information society, Art. 6 (May 22, 2001) Official Journal L 167, 22/06/2001 pp. 10-19.

77. For one proposal, *see* Reichman, Dinwoodie & Samuelson (n. 71). Again, here, the penalty that Member States might impose upon intermediaries for violating these obligations is not clear.

78. Article 17(9) also requires, more specifically, that "Member States shall also ensure that out-of-court redress mechanisms are available for the settlement of disputes" and "that users have access to a court or another relevant judicial authority to assert the use of an exception or limitation to copyright and related rights."

Ten years ago, Bernt Hugenholtz and Ruth Okediji spearheaded a project that drew out in accessible form existing provisions of the international agreements that mandated exceptions.[79] Tanya Aplin and Lionel Bently have recently authored a couple of articles advancing an argument for a broad reading of the mandatory quotation right in Article 10(1) of the Berne Convention that would, they argue, serve to require WTO Member States to validate a sizeable range of fair uses.[80] Current understandings of Article 10(1) may be unlikely to sustain the strong form of Aplin & Bently's argument.[81] However, as shown by the receptiveness of some courts in their treatment both of soft law such as the "ALI Principles Governing Jurisdiction, Choice Of Law, and Judgments in Transnational Disputes,"[82] and of scholarly criticism of the interpretation of the three-step test in diverse fora,[83] these arguments may yet help to shape the debate in a space with scant dispositive authoritative interpretations.

In the meantime, the Marrakesh Treaty to Facilitate Access to Published Works for Persons Who Are Blind, Visually Impaired, or Otherwise Print Disabled, mandated exceptions to ensure access to special format copies of books, including audiobooks and digital files for the blind and visually impaired.[84] And recent bilateral agreements, such as the EU—Canada

---

79. P. Bernt Hugenholtz & Ruth L. Okediji, *Conceiving an International Instrument on Limitations and Exceptions to Copyright* (2008), www.ivir.nl/publicaties/hugenholtz/finalreport2008.pdf.
80. Bently & Aplin (n. 33); Tanya Aplin & Lionel A.F. Bently, *Displacing the Dominance of the Three-Step Test: The Role of Global, Mandatory Fair Use,* at Comparative Aspects of Limitations and Exceptions in Copyright Law (Ng-Loy Wee Loon, Haochen Sun & Shyam Balganesh eds., Cambridge University Press, 2019); *see also* Berne Convention, Art. 10(1).
81. *See* Case C-476/17 Pelham GmbH v. Ralf Hütter (2018) EU:C:2018:1002 [63]-[70] (Advocate General Szpunar) (discussing the nature of the quotation exception).
82. *See* above (n. 51).
83. *See* Case C-161/17 Land Nordrhein-Westfalen v. Dirk Renckhoff (2018) EU:C:2018:279 (Advocate General Campos Sánchez-Bordona) at [122] n. 82 (refusing to apply the three-step test in Art. 5(5) of the InfoSoc Directive cumulatively, relying on the Max Planck declaration on the three-step test). Of course, the Court of Justice did not follow the advice of the Advocate-General in *Renckhoff. See* Case C-161/17, Land Nordrhein-Westfalen v. Dirk Renckhoff (2018) EU:C:2018:634.
84. *See* Marrakesh Treaty to Facilitate Access to Published Works for Persons Who Are Blind, Visually Impaired or Otherwise Print Disabled (Jun. 27, 2013) UNTS I-54134. The treaty came into force on Sep. 30, 2016. *See generally* Laurence R. Helfer, Molly K. Land, Ruth L. Okediji & Jerome H. Reichman, *The World Blind Union Guide to the Marrakesh Treaty: Facilitating Access to Books for Print-Disabled Individuals* 44 (Oxford University Press, 2017). *See* Marrakesh Treaty, Art. 4(1)(a). Article 4(1)(b) of the Treaty also authorizes (but does not require) other exceptions. The exceptions enacted by a Member State under Art. 4(1) must formally comply with the three-step test. But if Member States adopt the form of exceptions suggested by Art. 4(2) of the Treaty, they will presumptively be compliant with the three-step test. *See* Helfer (n. 84), at 44. For EU implementation, *see* Directive 2017/1564/EU of the European Parliament and of the Council of 13 September 2017 on certain permitted uses of certain works and other subject matter

Comprehensive Economic and Trade Agreement, contain mandatory safe harbors for intermediaries.[85] Together, these efforts represent one front in the reformulation of international copyright law; trying to breathe into the exceptional provisions of the international instruments the same energy that advocates of authors' rights have injected into those guarantees.[86]

Likewise, we suggested in "Neo-Federalist Vision" that the *acquis*, should articulate principles that reflect the increased interdependence of nation-states, and exploit the potential for pooling of resources.[87] Here too, public international law recently has made some progress. Even with international mandatory exceptions, which require that national laws permit particular uses, the principle of territoriality can interfere with the effectiveness of those exceptions. But that too can be attenuated. Thus, the Marrakesh Treaty (building to some extent on the treatment of patent compulsory licenses under the Doha declaration)[88] also requires Member States to allow for the cross-border exchange of special format copies of books, including audiobooks and digital files, and other print material between those countries that are parties to the treaty (and who comply with the standard three-step test for exceptions in international copyright law).[89]

At the regional level, the three exceptions in the Digital Single Market Directive, while open to criticism on other grounds, reflect in different ways a conceptual evolution to take account of the new international copyright climate.[90] Thus, the exceptions are mandatory, reflecting a shift toward uniformity. And the uses they validate are added to the defenses that Article

protected by copyright and related rights for the benefit of persons who are blind, visually impaired or otherwise print-disabled and amending Directive 2001/29/EC on the harmonisation of certain aspects of copyright and related rights in the information society (Sep. 13, 2017) Official Journal L 242, 20/09/2017, pp. 6-13; Regulation (EU) 2017/1563 of the European Parliament and of the Council of 13 September 2017 on the cross-border exchange between the Union and third countries of accessible format copies of certain works and other subject matter protected by copyright and related rights for the benefit of persons who are blind, visually impaired or otherwise print-disabled (Sep. 13, 2017) Official Journal L 242, 20/09/2017, pp. 1-5.

85. *See* Comprehensive Economic and Trade Agreement Between Canada of the One Part, and the European Union and its Member States, of the Other Part, Art. 20(11), Official Journal L 11, 14/1/2017, pp. 23-1079.

86. This was an important feature of the international acquis that was sketched in *A Neo-Federalist Vision*. *See* Dinwoodie & Dreyfuss (n. 20), 182-189, 198-201.

87. *See Ibid.,* 193-194.

88. *See* TRIPS, Art. 31*bis*.

89. *See* Marrakesh Treaty, Arts. 5-6. The U.S. Senate ratified the treaty in 2018, and the implementation legislation (the Marrakesh Treaty Implementation Act) was signed into law by the President on October 10, 2018. That legislation amended s. 121 of the Copyright Act, which had already established limitations and exceptions allowing certain authorized entities to provide published works in accessible formats to those who have print disabilities. It also inserted a new section (s. 121A) allowing authorized entities to both export and import works in accessible formats between the United States and other countries who have signed the Marrakesh Treaty.

90. *See* Arts. 3-6.

6(4) of the InfoSoc Directive says should not be technologically negated. Moreover, they cannot be contracted around.[91] Finally, in addition to the three mandatory exceptions being portable across borders in Europe—because they are mandatory—the benefit of the provision mandating extended collective licensing to allow cultural heritage institutions in their country to copy and provide access to out-of-commerce works permanently in the collection of the institution must be available to such institutions in other Member States.[92] This parallels the policy impulse behind the Portability Regulation.[93] Ordinarily, rules of exhaustion (unregulated by international law and even under EU law) would prevent a work lawfully made in one EU Member State by virtue of an exception or limitation in the source country from automatically being lawful in the country of import. A copy made by virtue of a national exception is not placed on the market "with the consent of the copyright owner," even if such differences interfere with the free movement of goods.[94]

---

91. *See* Directive on Copyright in the Digital Single Market (n. 72), Art. 7. These are not the first exceptions that are immune to private re-ordering. *See* Directive 2009/24/EC of the European Parliament and the Council of 23 April 2009 on the Legal Protection of Computer Programs, Art. 8, Official Journal L. 111, 5/5/2009, pp. 16-22.
92. *See* Directive 2019/790/EU, Art. 9(1) ("Member States shall ensure that licences granted in accordance with Article 8 may allow the use of out-of-commerce works or other subject matter by cultural heritage institutions in any Member State").
93. *See* Regulation (EU) 2017/1128 of the European Parliament and of the Council of 14 June 2017 on cross-border portability of online content services in the internal market (Jun. 14, 2017), Official Journal L 16, 30/06/2017, pp. 1-11.
94. *See* Lionel Bently, Brad Sherman, Dev Gangjee & Phillip Johnson, *Intellectual Property Law* 15 (Oxford University Press, 2018) (suggesting that "where intellectual property rights subsist in country A, but are subject to a compulsory licence (i.e., any person may exploit the intellectual property right on payment of a fee), the rights are not exhausted when goods are manufactured under such a licence. Here, the intellectual property right owner will be able to use national laws to prevent imports into country B"). The language of the first sale provision is more ambiguous in the United States. Section 109(a) makes the exhaustion turn on the copy in question being "lawfully made." *See* 17 USC §109(a). Although the United States Supreme Court has endorsed the concept of international exhaustion, meaning that copyright will be exhausted as regards goods lawfully placed on a foreign market, *see* Kirtsaeng v. John Wiley & Sons, Inc., 568 U.S. 519 (2013), the goods in that case were lawfully put on the market because the copyright owner had itself consented to the foreign sale. It is not settled whether goods lawfully placed on a foreign market because of an exception in that country should be regarded as "lawfully made." *See Geophysical* Service, Inc. v. TGS-NOPEC Geophysical Co. 850 F.3d 785 (5th Cir. 2017) (remanding to district court to "decide whose law governs the determination whether the copies imported by TGS were lawfully made under § 109"). However, it would be a radical attenuation of prevailing understandings of territoriality is the U.S. courts found that the law of the place of foreign manufacture applied, as this would effectively extend the exceptions of other countries into the United States. A middle ground might be achieved through case sensitive application of conflicts principles, including the extent of connection with a foreign law and compliance of the foreign country with international standards. Cf. Daniel J. Gervais, *The TRIPS Agreement: Drafting History and Analysis* §§2.99, 222 (4th ed., Sweet & Maxwell, 2012). Insofar as

11.5 CONCLUSION

All these last examples surely shift the balance of national and international norms in the international copyright system in favor of the latter. That can be characterized as a move toward universality and away from pluralism. But it occurs within a broader system that seeks to formulate universal principles that still validate a plural range of national *laws*. A fleshed-out *acquis* would serve various useful functions in the current international copyright climate. But the development of an *acquis* does not predetermine any precise reconfiguration of the international copyright system or suggest any preference for universality over pluralism.

---

this is treated as a matter of exhaustion, rather than the creation of new exceptions, it would arguably be immune from challenge as non-compliant with the three-step test. Cf. TRIPS, Art. 6(1).

Chapter 12

Revision of the Berne Convention: Utopia or Realistic Dream?

Michel M. Walter[*]

12.1 INTRODUCTION

In the first edition of this book on "Pluralism and Universalism in International Copyright Law," the status of the international copyright acquis under the last version of the Berne Convention of 1967/1971 was briefly described in conjunction with the substantive provisions added by the Trade-Related Aspects of Intellectual Property Rights (TRIPS) Agreement and the WIPO Copyright Treaty (WCT).[1] In this context, some gaps of protection were identified,[2] and the question asked whether a more holistic approach as regards the circumscription of the exclusive rights granted to authors would appear to be worth discussing. Furthermore, the problems

1. Also, *see* Dionysia Kallinikou, *Berne Convention: The Epicenter of Universalism or the Contrary?,* at Tatiana Eleni Synodinou, Universalism or Pluralism in International Copyright Law 299 (1st edn, Kluwer Law International, 2019).
2. *See* Michel Walter, *The Author's Exclusive Rights According to the Berne Plus-Plus Copyright Framework, Their Adaptation to New Technical and Societal Challenges and the Limits of Such Adaptation,* at Tatiana Eleni Synodinou, Universalism or Pluralism in International Copyright Law 375, 379 (1st edn, Kluwer Law International, 2019).

caused by the lack of consistent liability regimes[3] and—in particular in the digital sector—effective enforcement mechanisms were alluded to. Moreover, the question was raised whether the traditional exclusive rights granted to the author should be supplemented with claims to an equitable remuneration or a (mandatory) management by Collective Management Organizations (authors' societies). With this latter aspect, exclusive rights can be maintained and at the same time made more user-friendly in some fields, in particular of (mass) exploitation of protected works, if necessary supplemented by a regime of extended licenses.

In the following, we will attempt to explore these topics in greater depth and summarize some of them in the form of proposals for a possible revision of the Berne Convention, however difficult such a revision may be. Of course, it is not possible to discuss all the problems that arise, and the author is also aware of the fact that there are numerous legal and political obstacles to such a general reform. One of these problems—apart from the political and economic drifting apart of the members of the international community of states—is the sometimes widely divergent legal traditions of the Union countries, which often is described as the copyright vs *droit d'auteur* dichotomy. However, this does not preclude "thinking out loud" about the possibilities of a more comprehensive further development and reform of the Berne, even if this may seem somewhat utopian at first glance.

A further obstacle to a (more comprehensive) revision of the Berne Convention itself is seen in the principle of unanimity, which is enshrined in Article 27 of the Berne Convention. Although the Convention is to be revised on an ongoing basis in a view to the introduction of amendments designed to improve the system of the Union (paragraph 1), and for this purpose, conferences shall be held successively in one of the countries of the Union among the delegates of the said countries (paragraph 2), any revision of the Convention, including the annex, requires unanimity among the votes cast (paragraph 3). This makes the success of revision conferences difficult because it is to be assumed that, against the background of a diversified world order and in view of the different economic, political and social ideas in North and South as well as in East and West, unanimous decisions can hardly be reached. This is why, back in the 1970s, the idea of an Additional Protocol to the Berne Convention, which had initially been considered, eventually was dropped, and the TRIPS Agreement and the WCT were adopted in the guise of special agreements within the meaning of Article 20.[4]

Although the principle of unanimity enshrined in the Berne Convention guarantees continuity, it is also an almost insurmountable obstacle to the

3. Cf. Francis Gurry, *Copyright in the Digital Environment: Restoring the Balance, 24th Annual Horace S Manges Lecture, April 6, 2011,* 41 Columbia-Volunteer Lawyers for the Arts Journal of Law & Arts 459 (2011).
4. *See* Jørgen Blomquist, *Primer on International Copyright* 22.

further development of the Convention. However, as will be shown below,[5] though this requirement indeed is an obstacle, it is probably less insurmountable than is generally assumed.

Another fundamental question is to be answered at the outset, namely whether the general approach of the Berne Convention should be maintained or whether alternative solutions would better fulfill the basic purpose of the Convention:

(a) The current system is based on two pillars: On the one hand, the principle of national treatment and, on the other, the anchoring of a minimum standard of protection. While the principle of national treatment neutralizes the "xenophobic" attitude of national copyright law, at least for works covered by the Convention and replaces it with the principle of equal treatment, the minimum rights granted by the Convention provide for an autonomous minimum standard of protection and thus for a framework of copyright protection that all countries of the Union are to guarantee. The latter seems indispensable in an increasingly smaller, interconnected world and guarantees a more or less universal minimum level of protection while at the same time leaving room to maneuver for national and regional developments and fields of experimentation by limiting "harmonization" to the essentials.

    On the other hand, the principle of national treatment, which is limited to works covered by the Convention, at the same time constitutes unequal treatment of authors of works who are not nationals of a Union country[6] and thus also serves as an incentive for and an indirect influence on countries not yet belonging to the Berne Convention to join the Union. This indirect "pressure" was not completely ineffective; however, its effects also should not be overestimated. This in turn was the reason why a different track was taken with the TRIPS Agreement in order to achieve recognition of the Berne system—with the exception of moral rights (Article 9(2) of the TRIPS Agreement)—within the framework of an agreement devoted to trade policy[7] besides further developing in substance with some regard (TRIPS-Plus elements).[8]

(b) However, it could be argued that such discrimination against "foreign works" is to be regarded as a violation of copyright seen under the perspective of human rights, which should no longer be maintained. From this point of view, since its reform in 1992, the

5. *See* s. 12.4 below.
6. More precisely: works which do not originate from a Union country and whose authors neither are nationals of nor have their habitual residence in a country of the Union.
7. *See* e.g., Silke von Lewinsky, *International Copyright Law and Policy*, 3.01 (2008).
8. *See* Jørgen Blomquist, *Primer on International Copyright* 23.

Swiss Copyright Act has granted equal protection to domestic and foreign authors irrespective of the author's nationality or place of habitual residence or the work's origin;[9] this also applies, in principle, to the Copyright Ordinance of Hong Kong.[10] The character of copyright protection as a human right, on the one hand, follows from the Universal Declaration of Human Rights,[11] according to which "everyone has the right to the protection of the moral and material interests resulting from any scientific, literary or artistic production of which he is the author." (Article 27(2) of the Declaration).[12] It is to be admitted, of course, that the Universal Declaration of Human Rights—as a Resolution of the United Nations (UN) General Assembly—is not legally binding. This objection, however, does not apply to the provision of the International Covenant on Economic, Social and Cultural Rights (ICESCR),[13] Article 15(1)(b) of which is worded identically in essence. According to this provision, the Contracting States must recognize the right of everyone "to benefit from the protection of the moral and material interests resulting from any scientific, literary or artistic production of which he is the author." The UN Social Covenant has so far been ratified by no fewer than 173 states; it is legally binding and is supplemented by an additional Protocol dating from 2008, which also provides for individual complaints to the UN Human Rights Committee;[14] it has so far been ratified by 31 states after all. In this context, the European Court of Justice (ECJ) in its recent judgment in the *Kwantum/Vitra* case[15] likewise assumed that the equal treatment of foreign authors is laid out in the restricted acts as provided for in Union law as well as in the international copyright treaties, unless Union law, which has exclusive jurisdiction, expressly derogates from this principle.

9. With regard to claims to an equitable remuneration in the field of "secondary exploitation of industrial sound recordings"; however, the principle of reciprocity applies with regard to neighboring rights (Art. 35(4) of the Swiss Copyright Act).
10. This Ordinance also grants unconditional protection to foreign works but reserves the right to take retaliatory measures in the event of a lack of reciprocity (Arts 177 et seq. Copyright Ordinance idF 2022).
11. Resolution of the General Assembly of the United Nations (Declaration on Human rights) of 10 December 1948 no 217A.
12. Also, *see* Kallinikou (n. 1) 299.
13. Adopted by the UN General Assembly on Dec. 16, 1966.
14. Apart from investigation procedures and state complaints.
15. ECJ Oct. 24, 2024, case C-227/23 *Kwantum/Vitra* MR-Int 80 (2024) = jusIT 220 (Thomas Rainer Schmitt) (2025) = ZUM 104 (2024) (Marc Huckschlag) = GRUR 1800 (2024) (Benjamin Raue).

Whereas this assumption may be criticized from several perspectives, it is in line with a possible rethinking of national and Union copyright in this regard.[16]

In addition to the fundamental recognition of copyright protection as a human right, further arguments can be put forth in favor of an unconditional equal treatment of foreign works, as there are the questionability of linking to the place of first publication as an essential point of attachment, the limited effect on the behavior of third countries, and the inherent "clan liability" of creators as well as a harmonization with the system of the Paris Convention.

(c) However, the fact that the international copyright system has been in place for decades, as well as the fact that the copyright concepts of the various states in detail differ greatly, despite the minimum protection established in the Berne Convention due to the continuing dualism of universalism and pluralism, speaks against such approach for the time being. Irrespective of the above considerations, it shall be assumed, therefore, that the *status quo* is to be maintained in principle, at least for the time being. On the other hand, the possibilities of a sensible further development of the existing protection system shall be explored. In the first place, structural issues will be discussed, and then one or the other further topic shall be addressed where a need for action may exist. The focus will also be on the fact that the international copyright acquis has become highly complex due to the historically evolved regulations, which is why also a reintegration of the existing copyright-related international treaties in one revised Berne Convention shall be envisaged.

12.2 POTENTIAL FOR A STRUCTURAL REVISION

12.2.1 The Points of Attachment Set Out in the Convention

(a) The relationship to a Union country, which works must have in order to enjoy the protection of the Berne Convention, is set out in Article 3 of the Berne and may be understood as the Union's autonomous rule on the treatment of aliens.[17] Primarily, protection under the Berne extends to nationals of a Union country,[18] whereas the place of first publication is irrelevant so far. Second, the Berne

16. For details *see* Michel Walter, *Der internationale Schutz des Urheberrechts in der Europäischen Union nach dem Urteil des EuGH in der Rechtssache "Kwantum/Vitra": Am Beispiel von Werken der angewandten Kunst',* MR International 75 (2024).
17. *See* Jørgen Blomquist, *Primer on International Copyright* 31ff.
18. With regard of anonymous and pseudonymous works *see also* the presumption rule set out in Art. 15(4) of the Berne.

also applies to works first published in a country of the Union; with this regard, the concept of "publication" is defined relatively narrowly in the third paragraph of this provision and extends only to publications in physical form in sufficient quantity, whereas the mere communication to the public is not to be regarded as publication in a country of the Union. Furthermore, nationals of third countries enjoy the protection of the Convention if they have their habitual residence in a Union country. In contrast, Article 4 is based on the producer's headquarters or habitual residence with regard to cinematographic works (lit a), while for works of architecture and works of visual arts incorporated in a building or other structure, the country where such works have been erected or incorporated in (lit a) is recognized as an additional point of attachment for the protection under the Convention.[19]

(b) The points of attachment set out in the Convention still make sense in principle. As far as the author's nationality is concerned, this criterion takes account of the basic idea of providing an incentive for third countries to ratify the Convention or accede to it in the interests of their own nationals, even if this "pressure" may not always have been effective. The attaching to the country of first publication in the first line serves to protect publishers (producers) having their headquarters or residence in a Union country but is also in the interests of authors from third countries, who would otherwise hardly find contractors to market their works in a Union country. In view of the narrow definition of the term "publication," a close link with this country is ensured.

Although an extension of this protection to works that have been "published" electronically seems worth considering, no agreement could be reached in this regard during the negotiations that led to the conclusion of the WCT in 1996.[20] In my opinion, a prerequisite for the inclusion of electronic publications would in any case be a certain permanence of accessibility, as may be the case for e-books, which are also included in traditional libraries or permanently established online journals. With respect to the fact that a clear localization is required in order to serve as a criterion for attachment, such an extension would probably have to be based on the headquarters or habitual residence of such "online-publishers," as is the case for cinematographic works as well.

19. As to the points of attachment also *see* Thomas Dreier, at Thomas Dreier & P Bernt Hugenholtz, Concise European Copyright Law 22 (2nd edn, 2016); Silke von Lewinsky, *International Copyright Law and Policy* 5.08 (2008); Sam Ricketson & Jane Ginsburg, *International Copyright and Neighbouring Rights—The Berne Convention and Beyond* I 6.01 (2005).

20. *See e.g.*, Mihály Ficsor, *The Law of Copyright and the Internet—The 1996 WIPO Treaties, Their Interpretation and Implementation* 2.43 to 2.45 (2002).

However, it still seems questionable whether an agreement could be reached in this respect.

(c) Nationals of third countries who have their habitual residence in a Union country are to be treated on a par with nationals of such country since the Stockholm revision of the Convention. It follows from the wording of the provision that they are completely assimilated to nationals and, therefore, entitled to enjoy national treatment as well as the minimum rights granted under the Convention;[21] a revised version of the Convention could make this even more clear.

12.2.2 The Country of Origin-Exception

According to Article 5(3) of the Berne Convention, it is a matter of national legislature of the country of origin of a work to autonomously organize protection on its "home" territory. However, if the author is not a national of the country of origin, he or she enjoys national treatment but cannot claim the minimum rights of the Convention. This "country of origin exception" is based on the idea that international treaties should—with respect to international comity—not conflict with the regulatory sovereignty of Union countries for their domestic territory and should, in principle, only regulate the legal status of "foreign works."

This basic assumption can be called into question.[22] After all, the Berne Convention as a "Union" is also based on common values. In my opinion, it is difficult to see why the countries of the Union should not be expected to grant the minimum protection of the Convention to works of their own origin to the same extent as is mandatory for "foreign works." Moreover, the country of origin-exception is only to be explained historically and runs counter to the principle of equal treatment; it even turns against the own nationals in cases where their works are first published in a third country. The strengthening of this equal treatment principle is an important pillar of the Berne and should, therefore, work "in both directions" and thus also consolidate the position of the Berne as a "Union." Giving up this exception would also help to harmonize the legal framework and smoothen the application of the Convention. Last but not least, the description of the country of origin in Article 5(4) of the Berne remains problematic and is not convincing in all perspectives, in particular as regards the rule of the shorter term of protection in the case of simultaneous publications in several Union

21. *See* Silke v. Lewinski, *International Copyright and Policy* 5.14f. (2008); Sam Ricketson & Jane Ginsburg, *International Copyright and Neighbouring Rights—The Berne Convention and Beyond* I no 6.05 (2nd edn, 2006).
22. As to a more positive evaluation *see* Sam Ricketson, *The International Framework for the Protection of Authors: Bending Boundaries and Immovable Obstacles*, Columbia-Volunteer Lawyers for the Arts Journal of Law & Arts 341 (346) (2018).

countries (Article 5(a) of the Berne Convention). The application of this principle appears rather arbitrary in the present context.

Of course, it should not be overlooked that the abolition of the country of origin-exception could also meet with skepticism. In this context, one could think of certain formality requirements that continue to exist in some Union countries, for instance, in the United States of America, albeit in a reduced form. According to the United States (U.S.) Copyright Act, a work's registration is a prerequisite for claiming certain rights such as statutory damages or reimbursement of costs, which is permitted—irrespective of Berne's formality ban—only under the country of origin-exception.

12.2.3 The Conflict of Laws Rules of the Berne Convention

Since its Berlin version (1908), Article 4(2) of the Berne Convention incidentally also includes a provision on applicable law, when Article 5(2) of the 1967/71 version provides that[23] "the extent of protection, as well as the means of redress afforded to the author to protect his rights, shall be governed exclusively by the laws of the country *where* protection is claimed." This provision originally indeed was to be understood as the application of the *lex fori*, but it was soon recognized in doctrine that it was to be interpreted in the sense of the application of the law of the "country of protection" in which the act of use or infringement takes place.[24] The European Union (EU) Rome II Regulation, therefore, tried to improve this wording in circumscribing this principle with regard to the law "applicable to a non-contractual obligation arising from an infringement of an intellectual property right" in such a way that this "shall be the law of the country *for which* protection is claimed." This circumscription, however, is misleading as well and has given rise to misinterpretations.[25] In a revised version, this wording could be further clarified to the effect that the existence, scope, and duration of protection, as well as the means of redress afforded to the author to protect his rights, shall be governed exclusively by the laws of the country "where the exploitation or infringement takes place or produces effects that are not only marginal (country of protection)."

12.2.4 National Treatment Principle and Material Reciprocity

(a) The principle of national treatment is one of the two pillars on which the Berne Convention is built, and there is no need to amend

23. "Apart from the provisions of this Convention" (minimal protection).
24. *See e.g.*, Michel Walter, at U Loewenheim, Handbuch des Urheberrechts § 64 no 2 (3rd edn, 2021).
25. *Ibid.*, § 64 46.

it in this respect. However, it appears worthwhile considering whether all of the exceptions of this fundamental principle, as provided for under the current rules of the Convention, shall be upheld in a revised Convention. These exceptions apply to certain works of applied art (Article 2(7) of the Convention), to the special issue of the term of protection (comparison of the terms of protection under Article 7(8) of the Convention), and to the resale right (Article 14ter of the Convention). In this context, it is to be recalled that the respective country of comparison differs from case to case. Whereas in regard to the application of the special rule for works of applied art and with respect to the comparison of the terms of protection, the comparison must be made with the country of origin; material reciprocity, as provided for the resale right, is based on the law of the country to which the author is a national.

(b) Whereas the current version of the Berne Convention includes works of applied art among the objects of protection, since this category of works is expressly[26] listed in Article 2, it follows from the aforementioned provision of Article 2(7) that the countries of the Union are free to protect works of applied art only as designs and, moreover, are free to provide a term of protection reduced to 25 years from production only,[27] according to Article 7(8) of the Berne. The maintaining of the complicated material reciprocity provision of Article 2(7), for its part, seems questionable and makes the application of the Berne disproportionately complicated.[28] According to this reciprocity rule, Union countries may only grant design protection and refuse copyright protection if this is the case in the country of origin of the work, provided that such protection exists at all in the country of protection. Since in such case the protection in any case can be shortened to the term granted for designs in the country of origin on account of the comparison of terms of protection, the application of material reciprocity appears to be dispensable.

(c) However, it seems advisable to retain the comparison of terms of protection rule according to Article 7(8) of the Convention, which is only optional under the Berne.[29] This is because this rule is a basic measure firmly anchored in the legal tradition of the Union countries, though it makes the computation of the terms of

26. By way of example.
27. Article 12 of the TRIPS Agreement did not modify this rule for works of applied art (and photographs).
28. *See* with this regard e.g., ECJ Oct. 24, 2024, case C-227/23 *Kwantum/Vitra* (n. 15) and Walter (n. 16).
29. Its application is mandatory under Art. 7(1) of the EU Term-Directive.

protection considerably more difficult. On the other hand, it seems worth considering to compare the terms granted in the country of protection with the author's home country instead of the country of origin. This would eliminate the difficulties in determining the country of origin and would at least provide the theoretical possibility of influencing the legislation of the author's respective home country, which is not the case for a comparison with the country of origin if not corresponding with the country of which the author is a national. In addition, synchronization with the reciprocity rule for the resale right would be established, and the—questionable—circumscription of the country of origin could be completely dropped in this context.

(d) As far as the application of material reciprocity with regard to the resale right is concerned, it will have to be retained for the time being as well, since a certain degree of influence on the legislation of those countries that do not yet have provided for a resale right cannot be ruled out in this respect. However, the description of the principle of reciprocity could be clarified in the sense of reciprocity "in principle" in order to facilitate the application of this provision, also with a view to the international art trade.

12.2.5 Disputes Concerning the Interpretation of the Convention

(a) A major shortcoming of the current Berne system is that the Convention neither provides a (judicial) interpretative body nor a dispute settlement mechanism. It is true that Article 33(1) of the Convention sets out that disputes between Union countries concerning the interpretation or application of the Convention may be brought before the International Court of Justice by application in conformity with the Statute of the Court. This means that the International Court of Justice has jurisdiction in principle.[30] However, this jurisdiction of the International Court of Justice has so far proved to be toothless because each country can declare that it does not consider itself bound when depositing its instrument of ratification or accession, and a number of Union countries have made use of this option. In such cases, the International Court of Justice has jurisdiction under its Statute only in the case of a general submission subject to reciprocity or by submission in an individual case.[31]

30. Article 36(1) of the Statute of the International Court of Justice.
31. Article 36(1) and (2) of the Statute of the International Court of Justice.

In addition, it is only a matter of settling disputes between Union countries, in which other considerations, especially political ones, often play a greater role than the need to clarify contentious copyright issues regarding the interpretation of the Berne Convention. Moreover, the decisions of the International Court of Justice only have a direct effect on the states involved, although an indirect effect on other states can be assumed. Finally, we must not lose sight of the fact that the International Court of Justice, according to its Statute, which forms an integral part of the UN Charter, is a court specializing in international law issues, which has hardly any experience with copyright issues.

(b) The establishment of a permanent and specialized court at the international level—e.g., within the framework of World Intellectual Property Organization (WIPO)—would, therefore, represent a significant improvement of the international system. The clarification of legal issues of international copyright by national courts often proves difficult in practice due to a lack of familiarity with the complicated international legal framework and, above all, does not lead to uniform case law. Even highly qualified supranational courts as the ECJ are occasionally overstrained with complex international copyright issues. As an example, the interpretation of minimum rights anchored in the WCT in the sense of maximum protection in construing national or regional law (in this case, EU law)[32] may be mentioned.[33]

Such a regulation would (also) have to give courts—at least the national supreme courts—the possibility to refer to such an international special court. With this regard, the preliminary ruling procedure, as provided for in Article 267 of the Treaty for the Functioning of the European Union (TFEU), could serve as a model. A modification of the current provision of Article 33 would, therefore, represent a significant progress for a uniform interpretation and, if necessary, cautious further development of the Berne system.

---

32. That can go beyond due to the minimum protection principle of Art. 19 of the Berne Convention.
33. *See* ECJ Apr. 17, 2008, case C-456/06 *Peek & Cloppenburg/Cassina/Le Corbusier* [2008] ECR I-2731 = [2008] MR 198 (Michel Walter) = [2008] GRUR Int 593 (Marcus v. Welser). *See* Michel Walter, *The Author's Exclusive Rights According to the Berne Plus-Plus Copyright Framework, Their Adaptation to New Technical and Societal Challenges and the Limits of Such Adaptation*, at Tatiana Eleni Synodinou, Universalism or Pluralism in International Copyright Law 376 (1st edn, Kluwer Law International, 2019).

12.3 ON A REDRAFTING OF THE BERNE MINIMUM RIGHTS

12.3.1 Fine-Tuning the Moral Rights of Authors

(a) The moral rights set out in Article 6bis of the Berne, in addition to the exploitation rights, play a central role in the Berne system of copyright protection, in which the right to claim authorship and the prohibition of alterations are, in principle laid down unconditionally, whereas their waivability or alienability is discussed controversially. The importance of moral rights may even become more important in a world of digital mass use, which is why their cautious strengthening appears to be of eminent importance and could continue to play a role precisely where management and control with the help of exploitation rights could fail in an increasingly technologized environment.[34] As regards the circumscription of moral rights laid down in the Berne, their scope could be clarified to some extent, even if a cautious approach would have to be taken with regard to the different status that these rights enjoy from a comparative law perspective.[35] Even if the right to "claim authorship of the work" is also to be understood as embracing the right to determine whether and with which designation (true name of the author, pseudonym or anonyme) a work is to be credited when it is used, a clarification would appear to be appropriate and also be acceptable for those countries that approach personal rights with a certain degree of skepticism.

With regard to the prohibition of alterations, the provision is limited to such modifications that could be detrimental to the author's "honour or reputation," which is a rather cautious description and is ultimately limited to clearly significant alterations. In this respect, it would seem worth considering extending this description to some extent, for example, to the effect that in any case such changes shall be prohibited which interfere with "legitimate interests of the author" instead of aiming at the author's "honour or reputation." Moreover, at least the inalienability of moral rights should be anchored in a revised version of the Berne.

(b) According to the second paragraph of Article 6bis, the post mortem moral rights of the author must not necessarily have to be exercised

34. *See* Mira Sundara Rajan, *Moral Rights: The Future of Copyright Law?,* 14(4) Journal of Intellectual Property Law & Practice 257 (2019) https://doi.org/10.1093/jiplp/jpz008.

35. Also, *see* Alain Strowel, *The Moral Interests of Authors as Universal Signs of the Law of Autonomy: And Their Plural Recognition Within or Outside Copyright Law*, at Tatiana Eleni Synodinou, Universalism or Pluralism in International Copyright Law 393, 404 (1st edn, Kluwer Law International, 2019).

by the legal successors (heirs) of the author. Rather, they "shall be exercisable by the persons or institutions authorized by the legislation of the country where protection is claimed." In this context, the wording "*at least* until the expiry of the property rights" leaves room for national concepts that recognize everlasting moral rights. In view of the divergent national regulations, this will also have to be upheld, but individual protection could at least be defined for the duration of the protection of property rights, which also corresponds to the legal tradition of most Union countries.

However, the second sentence of this provision, according to which countries whose legislation at the time of ratification (of this version) of the Convention or accession to it does not contain provisions for the protection of moral rights granted under paragraph 1 after the author's death may provide that some of these rights shall not be maintained after the death of the author, could be deleted as a historical relic.

12.3.2 More Open Circumscription of the Exploitation Rights

(a) According to the existing system of the Berne Convention, the exploitation rights reserved to the author are understood as exclusive rights and circumscribed in detail with a view to different fields of exploitation and by categories of works. This corresponds to the concept of the national legislature but differs significantly from them in terms of systematization, a fact which does not make their application easier. This is due, on the one hand, to the historical development and the merely gradual developing of the minimum rights, but on the other hand, also to the cumbersome revision work, which has come to a complete standstill as regards the Berne as such since the seventies of the last century for the reasons already mentioned.

For example, the establishment of an exclusive distribution right that is conceived separate from the reproduction right has not yet been recognized in the latest version of the Berne Convention apart from film copyright. This gap was only filled in with the WCT (Article 6 of the WCT). Also, the rights of communication to the public are fragmented and systematically incoherent, partly differentiated by type of work and yet incompletely regulated. For example, despite repeated attempts with the TRIPS Agreement and the WCT, there is still no general display right for works of visual arts, although this is generally granted in national laws, and hardly any resistance is to be expected in the event of an amendment. The systematic complexity is particularly evident in the wording of Article 8 of the WCT as regards the making available right extending to the specific use of copyright subject matter on the Internet (by way of an umbrella clause).

(b) As far as the rights of exploitation of works in tangible form are concerned, a revised version of the Berne could retain the right of reproduction, as described in Article 9(1) of the Convention in its last version,[36] and add the distribution and rental rights, as defined in Articles 6 and 7 of the WCT in a modified form. Apart from a rewording and a clearer systematization, such a revision could also extend the rental right to all types of works and would no longer be limited to computer programs, cinematographic works and works recorded on sound carriers. This restriction does not appear to be appropriate and is probably primarily due to the lobbying power of the software and the film and recording industries. In this case, it would further be discussed how to deal with the right of exhibiting (works of visual arts) and whether the principle of exhaustion should continue to be reserved for the Union countries.[37]

(c) With regard to the various forms of communication to the public, a somewhat modified and more comprehensive[38] and at the same time simplified wording could be envisaged following the model of Article 3 of the EU Information Society Directive. Of course, the restriction by the criterion of a distance element[39] would have to be dropped.[40] Since a differentiation according to different categories of works does not appear to be necessary and the current provisions of the Berne Convention are also incomplete in this respect, the definition of the different types of communication to the public could be considerably simplified and at the same time made more flexible. In any case, works of visual arts and choreographic works should be included.[41] At the same time, the possibility of restricting the traditional broadcasting right by means of Hertzian waves to a mere claim to an equitable remuneration in national legislature (Article $11^{bis}(2)$ of the Convention) could be eliminated, since the acquisition of the relevant licenses is ensured by means of collecting societies that are subject to the obligation to contract.

36. If necessary, supplemented by clarifications, such as those contained in Art. 2 of the Information Society Directive.
37. *See* Walter (n. 2), 378.
38. As to such holostic approach *see* already Walter (n. 2), 375, 381.
39. In Union law this only is to be deduced from Recital 23: "This Directive should harmonise further the author's right of communication to the public. This right should be understood in a broad sense covering all communication to the public not present at the place where the communication originates."
40. Article 8 WCT is limited to transmissions over a distance because communication to the public gathered on one place is already dealt with in other articles of the Berne Convention, the application of which is expressly reserved.
41. *See* Walter (n. 2), 377.

(d) In view of the difficulties in classifying and including new types of use that enter the stage in regard of new technical developments and emerging business models, a widening of the catalogue of types of use reserved to the author by means of a more open complementary provision appears to be worthy of discussion as well. Some national laws, such as the German Copyright Act, realize this goal by generally reserving to the author the right to exploit the works created by him in tangible and intangible form and simply specifying the exploitation rights (restricted acts) conveyed to him by way of example only.[42] *Daniel Gervais* is also in favor of such open wording, but at the same time proposes to restrict it by reserving to the author only those uses—to summarize briefly—"that demonstrably interfere with actual or predictable commercial exploitation."[43]

This approach can serve as a starting point for further considerations,[44] but in my opinion, the exclusively commercial approach appears to be too strict since it presupposes the existence of markets that are not always given. To give an example: The use of works to train Artificial Intelligence (AI) constitutes a relevant use that is not restricted to acts of reproduction in the course of using copyright works for training purposes; however—due to the novelty of this use—there is (as yet) no market for such use or is exempted by (in my view premature) intervention by the legislator through the exception provided for text and data mining under the Single Market Directive in the EU.[45] A complementary general circumscription of the uses to be reserved to the author would also favor a more functional concept instead of a mere technical one.

12.3.3 Exclusive Rights and Claims to an Equitable Remuneration

(a) The system of the Berne Convention, in principle, is based on exclusive rights with respect to the uses reserved to the author. In some cases, however, it allows their substitution by mere claims to equitable remuneration, as is the case, for example, for the broadcasting (without wire) under Article $11^{bis}(2)$ of the Berne

42. *"The author shall enjoy* the *exclusive right ...; this right shall include in particular ... ".*
43. *See* Daniel Gervais, *Toward a New Berne Convention in Tatiana Eleni Synodinou, Universalism or Pluralism in International Copyright Law* 339 (349) (1st edn, Kluwer Law International, 2019); Daniel Gervais, *(Re)Structuring Copyright: A Comprehensive Path to International Copyright Reform* 207, 213 and 304 (2017).
44. As to other suggestions *see* Gervais, *(Re)Structuring Copyright* (n. 43) 207.
45. *See* Michel Walter, *On the "Taming" of Artificial Intelligence under EU Copyright Law on the Assumption That the TDM-Exception Applies to the Training of Generative AI Models,* Gedenkbundel Antoon Quaedvlieg 312 (2025).

Convention.[46] As regards works of music with or without text, Article 13(1) of the Berne allows to install a system of compulsory licenses. These exceptions to the basically exclusive nature of exploitation rights conveyed on authors are primarily to be explained historically and should therefore be scrutinized for a revised Berne Convention. Against the background of the establishment of collective management organizations for most of the relevant uses, both exceptions no longer seem appropriate. This also applies to the background of the second of the abovementioned exceptions in favor of compulsory licenses in the area of musical works, namely the prevention of a monopoly position of producers of phonograms because collecting societies are subject to an obligation to contract. Both exemptions could therefore be canceled in a revised version of the Berne Convention.

(b) However, the system of the Berne lacks a basis and minimum standards for autonomous claims to appropriate remuneration for certain uses outside the scope of exclusive rights. This is except for the resale right pursuant to Article 14ter, which is, however, not a mandatory minimum right and shall not be dealt with here in detail.[47] Such claims are becoming increasingly important in a world of (digital) mass use, especially for certain uses that are relevant for the society as a whole and worthy to be facilitated and supported, such as by libraries, archives, museums and other "cultural heritage" institutions or such of scientific research and teaching or other educational institutions. Such claims to an equitable remuneration take account of the fact that in certain areas, the exercise of exclusive rights may be undesirable from a socio-political point of view. Moreover, the costs for the establishment of licensing systems may also be too high and their handling too time-consuming (transfer costs so-called), while a complete exemption through exceptions and limitations would mean promoting common interests at the expense of authors only. Such remuneration systems are already established in the national and regional legislature of the European Union countries, for example, the so-called library levy. This is the case in particular in Union law, where in principle even an exclusive right is provided for the

46. In such case a downgrading to mere remuneration claims is limited in its effects to the respective country of the Union. *See* Walter (n. 2), 387.

47. *See* with this regard in detail Samuel Ricketson, *Proposed International Treaty on droit de suite/Resale Royalty Right for Visual Artists*, WIPO Study SG15-0565 (2015); Samuel Ricketson, *WIPO Toolkit on Artist's Resale Right, Standing Committee on Copyright and Related Rights* (43rd Session Geneva, Mar. 13 to 17, 2023).

public lending of copyright material, but with the possibility for Member States to downgrading it to a mere remuneration claim.[48]

(c) The main field of application, however, is the realm of exceptions and limitations to which the *Three-Step Test* is to be applied. Examples include the "fair compensation" provided, e.g., in Union law for private copying or the "textbook remuneration" enshrined in numerous national legal systems. In this respect, one could consider providing for an extension clause in connection with this test[49] or taking this consideration into account as part of the third step. Although this may meet with criticism in those countries that traditionally only recognize either an exclusive right on the one hand or fair use on the other, it would seem sensible if a graduated balance could be found in this respect through the further development of international law. In this way, the Berne Convention could again assume the role of an engine for the further development of copyright law and legal harmonization. This seems to be the order of the day, especially in times of an increasing drifting apart of social systems and a galloping further development of technical possibilities, business models, and the resulting increase in access to copyrighted material.

Future areas of application for such autonomous or supplementary remuneration claims could also be the sensitive area of the use of AI.[50] This is not only in relation to the use of protected works as training material but above all in connection with the commercialization of AI facilities and/or the use of the output "generated" with the help of such systems.[51]

12.3.4 Exclusive Rights and Collective Management Organizations

Not covered by the current system of the Berne Convention is the collective management of rights, which a revised convention should also be concerned with, at least in principle. On the one hand, collective management is of growing importance in a globalized and increasingly digitalized world; on the other hand, the management of exclusive rights by collecting societies also forms an intermediate stage between individually licensed exclusive

48. Jointly with the rental right set out in the Rental and Lending Rights Directive 1992.
49. On this alternative the text proposed below is based on.
50. *See* Martin Senftleben, *Generative AI and Author Remuneration*, 54 International Review of Intellectual Property and Competition Law 1535 (2023) https://doi.org/10.1007/s40319-023-01399-4; Christophe Geiger and Vincenzo Iaia, "The forgotten creator: Towards a statutory remuneration right for machine learning of generative AI," *Computer law and security review (CLSR)* 2024, Article 105925; Walter (n. 45).
51. In this context, a distinction is to be made between AI-generated works that were generated more or less autonomously and those in which AI was only used as a tool.

rights and the granting of mere remuneration claims. This is with respect to the fact that collecting societies are subject to a contracting obligation. The provision of such mandatory collective administration by the national legislature in specific cases should, therefore, also be addressed in international copyright law.[52]

12.3.5 Provision of a Complete System of Exceptions or Limitations?

(a) The actual version of the Berne Convention does not provide for a closed system of exceptions or limitations. Only a few exceptions are provided for explicitly (on an optional basis), such as the right to quote (Article 10(1) of the Convention), reporting on current events (Article $10^{bis}(2)$ of the Berne) or the use for educational or teaching purposes (Article 10(2)) and ephemeral reproductions by broadcasting organizations (Article 11bis(3) of the Berne Convention). Apart from this, the General Report of the main Committee of the Brussels Conference refers to a general recognition that the national legislature in the field of communication to the public is free to provide for further exceptions of lesser importance (*petites reserves* so-called).[53] Above all, however, a general clause in the form of the *Three-Step Test* so-called was established in the Stockholm/Paris version of the Berne Convention for the first time that initially was limited to the reproduction right (Article 9(2) of the Convention). Already, the TRIPS Agreement extended this legal instrument to all exclusive rights (Article 13 of the TRIPS Agreement), which was adopted by the WCT as well (Article 10 of the WCT).[54]

(b) Of course, the Marrakesh Agreement of 2013 must be mentioned in this context; however, it only deals with a specific use in a small segment in order to facilitate access to works that had already been made accessible to the public for persons who are blind, visually impaired, or otherwise print disabled. Generally, however, the question is to be answered as to whether a revised version of the Berne should provide for a complete system of mandatory or facultative exceptions or limitations, as is the case, e.g., in Union law (more or less successful).[55] However, such efforts would be difficult to realize with respect to the different traditions of the

52. *See* Walter (n. 2), 389.
53. Cf with this regard the General Report of the Brussels Conference, Documents de la Conférence de Bruxelles 100.
54. *See* Walter (n. 2), 387.
55. *See* in the first place Art. 5 of the Information Society Directive.

national copyright systems. Furthermore, it does not seem advisable to separate one side of the coin of the copyright protection system from the other, since the required "fair balance" cannot be struck in separate treaties.[56] Moreover, it could also appear questionable whether strict universalism in this area is at all preferable to a pluralistic approach.[57] We should, therefore, be cautious about the suggestion made to agree upon a separate Copyright Limitations Treaty based on the model of the Marrakesh Treaty.[58] Without going into this in more detail in the given context, it may be noted that a special agreement on the subject of exceptions and limitations would only make the international contractual situation even more confusing.

(c) As far as the—incomplete—list of exceptions and limitations contained in the Berne is concerned, one could think of structuring this list[59] and complement it with some regards. In the proposed text for a revised version of the Berne at the end of this article, such task has not yet been carried out.

12.3.6 Copyright Contract Law and Direct Remuneration Claims

(a) Copyright contract law, dealing with the transfer or the licensing of the rights conveyed by the author to third parties, has not been dealt with so far in the international copyright treaties. Detailed regulation often proves difficult, even under national law. Also, the European legislator only addressed this filed of law at a late stage and only in a few provisions of the Digital Single Market (DSM) Directive of 2019.[60] A regulation of copyright contract law issues within the framework of a revised Berne Convention, therefore, appears difficult to realize, even if this seems desirable.[61] However, consideration could be given to at least establishing the general

56. *See* Rachel Xalabarder, *Towards an International Common Core of Exceptions and Limitations*? at Tatiana Eleni Synodinou, Universalism or Pluralism in International Copyright Law 407, 441 (1st edn, Kluwer Law International, 2019).
57. Cf Jørgen Blomquist, *Universality or Diversity? The WIPO Role and Strategy in International Copyright Lawmaking,* at Tatiana Eleni Synodinou, Universalism or Pluralism in International Copyright Law 317, 334 (1st edn, Kluwer Law International, 2019).
58. *See* Martin Senftleben, *A Copyright Limitations Treaty Based on the Marrakesh Model: Nightmare or Dream Come True?,* SSRN Electronic Journal January 2017 https://doi.org/10.2139/ssrn.3064823.
59. Also with this regard *see* Daniel Gervais, *(Re)Structuring Copyright: A Comprehensive Path to International Copyright Reform* 216 (2017).
60. Articles 18 bis 23 of the DMS Directive.
61. Cf Agnès Lucas-Schloetter, *Copyright Contract Law in Tatiana Eleni Synodinou*, Universalism or Pluralism in International Copyright Law 597 (1st edn, Kluwer Law International, 2019).

principle in an appropriate way that, in the event of a contractual disposal of authors' rights, creators are nevertheless entitled to receive a fair share of the exploitation proceeds (claim to an equitable remuneration).

(b) Apart from this, it seems worth considering, at least in principle, to stipulate at international level that the national legislature could vest authors in their capacity as the original holders of their copyrights with a—collectively enforceable—right to remuneration directly against end users in appropriate cases. This is irrespective of the fact that the exclusive right as such may have been transferred to third parties (producers) through the granting or transfer of rights. Thus, in appropriate cases the right of control could remain with the right holder (producer) and could be exercised individually, whereas an appropriate economic share could be guaranteed to authors in a direct way and without burdening the contractual relationship. This is also based on the experience that linking a fair remuneration to the proceeds from the work's exploitation realized by the author's direct contractual partner often proves to be cumbersome and unpromising, especially in the case of exploitation chains.

12.3.7 Liability Systems and Enforcement

(a) As already alluded to above, the international copyright treaties do not provide for a coherent liability system, which is a basic prerequisite for the enforcement of copyright claims. Setting up such systems is therefore left to regional and national legislature, which does not seem satisfactory. Nonetheless, in view of the very different concepts and traditions in this area, international solutions are unlikely to be found. Even in the narrower regional area of the EU, it has only recently become clear how difficult it is to reach agreement on at least the basic principles of liability for "large" online content-sharing service providers (platforms), as now provided for in Article 17 of the DSM Directive.[62] However, it seems worth considering at least clarifying in international copyright law that the Union countries must ensure the enforcement of copyright claims through efficient liability regimes and that any "save harbor" regulation must not lead to the enforcement of legitimated claims becoming inefficient, if not impossible. This is the dilemma that the digital millennium has just faced (and still faces to some extent):

62. *See* Matthias Leistner, *Intermediary Liability in a Global World*, at Tatiana Eleni Synodinou, Universalism or Pluralism in International Copyright Law 471 (1st edn, Kluwer Law International, 2019); Walter (n. 2), 375, 385 commenting on the then Art.13 of the Digital Single Market Directive RL.

Far-reaching "safe harbor" regimes deprive powerful intermediaries, to whose liability traditional copyright law is linked, of liability or make it dependent on the fulfillment of overly strict conditions, while the individual user as the ultimately liable infringer cannot be addressed or can only be pursued with insurmountable difficulties. This is apart from the consideration that the enforcement of claims against a large number of end-users is not desirable from a socio-cultural perspective either.

(b) With regard to the enforcement of copyrights, the available "measures, procedures and remedies" as set out in the TRIPS Agreement could be adopted. Some of them could be rendered mandatory and supplemented to some extent. In order to avoid overloading the Convention, the reference system as provided for in the TRIPS Agreement and the WCT with regard to the substantive provisions of the Berne Convention (Articles 1 to 21) could be used and supplemented by specific "plus elements."

12.4 ON THE FEASIBILITY OF A COMPLETE REVISION

Of course, the difficulties related to a general revision should not be underestimated, but nevertheless appears to be a goal worth striving for. As mentioned above, the unanimity principle enshrined in the Berne Convention appears to be a major obstacle to a comprehensive revision of the Berne Convention. However, this does not mean that all states participating in a revision conference would have to agree to a revised treaty instrument. The aforementioned provision of Article 27(3) of the Berne Convention expressly states that only the votes cast count, which is why abstentions that in international practice can occur time and again (even in a coordinated form) do not count as votes against.[63] Moreover, only the states actually represented at a revision conference are decisive, and they also have the option of ultimately not ratifying or acceding to a renegotiated agreement regardless of their approval of the revised treaty text at the revision conference. Although this is not a desirable goal, it considerably weakens the effectiveness of the unanimity principle.

In addition, the principle of unanimity is not set in stone. Although it was the rule in earlier times, it only makes sense in cases involving a manageable number of contracting states with a comparable legal and cultural background,[64] which was the case in the earlier years of the Berne

63. With this respect also *see* Sam Ricketson, *The International Framework for the Protection of Authors: Bending Boundaries and Immovable Obstacles*, 341 Columbia-Volunteer Lawyers for the Arts Journal of Law & Arts 341, 352 (2018).

64. Cf Hanspeter Neuhold, *Die Wiener Vertragsrechtskonvention 1969*, 15/1 Archiv des Völkerrechts 1, 17 (1971).

but has long since ceased to be the case with currently 181 Union countries. Already when the Vienna Convention on the Law of Treaties was concluded in 1969,[65] the International Law Commission (ILC) deduced the principle of a two-thirds majority from state practice, which also formed the basis for the conclusion of this convention and was laid down in the text of the Convention for future treaties.

According to the Vienna Convention, the adoption of the text of a treaty at an international conference takes place by the vote of two-thirds of the States present and voting, unless by the same majority they shall decide to apply a different rule (Article 9(2) of the Vienna Convention). This rule limits the required majority to two-thirds of the states participating in a conference that are present and also take part in the vote. Pursuant to this rule, also lower (or higher) quorums can be decided by a two-thirds majority. Under the rules of the Vienna Convention on the Law of Treaties, a possible revision conference could therefore replace the unanimity principle with a two-thirds majority in line with recent state practice.

12.5 CONCLUSION

In conclusion, an attempt will be made to summarize some of the above considerations in a draft revised version of the substantial provisions of the Berne Convention in its Articles 1 to 21, although not all issues can be addressed. For the sake of clarity, the existing sequence of Articles will be retained, however not throughout the draft. At the same time, the text will be reorganized in some cases. The Plus elements as laid down in the TRIPS Agreement and the WCT are taken into account in their substantive part but not in relation to the protection of technical measures and the enforcement provisions of the TRIPS Agreement. The liability issues mentioned are addressed only in principle, whereas a more author-friendly structure of film copyright is not dealt with at all in the draft. The actual regulations on exceptions and limitations have also been adopted uncritically for the time being and have not yet been supplemented.

Overall, this is an initial attempt only for further discussion that needs to be further developed and supplemented (“*work in progress*”):

Article 1

The countries to which this Convention applies constitute a Union for the protection of the rights of authors in their literary and artistic works *that constitute human intellectual creations.*[66]

65. Vienna Convention on the Law of Treaties of May 23, 1969.

66. This ample circumscription of an originality requirement is common to all copyright legislations and already set out in Art. 2(5) as regards the protection of collections and in Art. 14bis(1) with respect to cinematographic works. It appears to make sense to generally

Article 2

(1) The expression "literary and artistic works" shall include every production in the literary, scientific and artistic domain, whatever may be the mode or form of its expression, such as books, pamphlets and other writings; lectures, addresses, sermons and other works of the same nature; dramatic or dramatico-musical works; *computer programs, whatever may be the mode or form of their expression*;[67] choreographic works and entertainments in dumb show; musical compositions with or without words; *works of visual arts such as* drawing, painting, architecture, sculpture, engraving and lithography, *including performance art*; photographic works to which are assimilated works expressed by a process analogous to photography; works of applied art; illustrations, maps, plans, sketches and three-dimensional works relative to geography, topography, architecture or science.

(2) It shall, however, be a matter for legislation in the countries of the Union to prescribe that works in general or any specified categories of works shall not be protected unless they have been fixed in some material form.

(3) *Without prejudice to the copyright in the original work and to Article 12,* translations, adaptations, arrangements of music and other alterations of a literary or artistic work shall be protected as original works, provided that they *constitute an intellectual creation.*

(4) It shall be a matter for legislation in the countries of the Union to determine the protection to be granted to official texts of a legislative, administrative and legal nature, *including official preparatory material,* and to official translations of such texts.

(5) Collections of literary or artistic works such as encyclopaedias and anthologies *or other material* which, by reason of the selection and arrangement of their contents, constitute intellectual creations shall be protected as such, without prejudice to the copyright in each of the works forming part of such collections. *This also applies to compilations of data or other material, whether in machine readable or other form.*[68]

(6) The works mentioned in this article shall enjoy protection in all countries of the Union, *according to the provisions of Articles 3 and*

---

refer to such clarification, even if not interpreted in the same way in all Union countries (*see* Kallinikou (n. 1), 299 (306).

67. *See* Art. 10(1) of the TRIPS Agreement and Art. 4 of the WCT.
68. *See* Art. 10(2) of the TRIPS Agreement and Art. 5 of the WCT.

4. This protection shall operate for the benefit of the author and his successors in title.

(7) Subject to the provisions of Article 7(4) of this Convention, it shall be a matter for legislation in the countries of the Union to determine the extent of the application of their laws to works of applied art and industrial designs and models, as well as the conditions under which such works, designs and models shall be protected. ... *deleted* ...[69]

(8) *The protection granted under this Convention extends to expressions and not to ideas, procedures, methods of operation or mathematical concepts as such.*[70]

(9) The protection of this Convention shall not apply to news of the day or to miscellaneous facts having the character of mere items of press information *which do not constitute human intellectual creations.*[71]

Article 3

(1) The protection of this Convention shall apply to:
  (a) authors who are nationals of one of the countries of the Union, for their works, whether published or not;
  (b) authors who are not nationals of one of the countries of the Union, for their works first published in one of those countries, or simultaneously in a country outside the Union and in a country of the Union;

(2) Authors who are not nationals of one of the countries of the Union but who have their habitual residence in one of them shall, for the purposes of this Convention, be assimilated to nationals of that country *in the sense of the preceding paragraph 1(a).*[72]

(3) The expression "published works" means works published with the consent of their authors, whatever may be the means of manufacture of the copies, provided that the availability of such copies has been such as to satisfy the reasonable requirements of the public, having regard to the nature of the work. The performance of a dramatic, dramatico-musical, cinematographic or musical work, the public

69. "Works protected in the country of origin solely as designs and models shall be entitled in another country of the Union only to such special protection as is granted in that country to designs and models; however, if no such special protection is granted in that country, such works shall be protected as artistic works."

70. *See* Art. 2 of the WCT.

71. For sake of clarity, this reference to the precondition of an intellectual creation should be added in order to establish equal treatment journalistic works. Alternatively, this paragraph may be deleted.

72. This is to make even more clear that this provision is to be understood in the sense of complete assimilation rather than in the sense of national treatment excluding the minimum rights granted in the Convention. In doctrine, the provision unanimously is understood in this sense.

recitation of a literary work, the communication by wire or the broadcasting of literary or artistic works, the exhibition of a work of art and the construction of a work of architecture shall not constitute publication.

(4) A work shall be considered as having been published simultaneously in several countries if it has been published in two or more countries within thirty days of its first publication.

[*(5) Authors of works made available to the public in such a way that members of the public may access them from a place and at a time individually chosen by them are deemed published in a country of the Union if the publisher of such work (e.g., e-book publisher or online-publisher) has his headquarters or habitual residence in one of the countries of the Union, provided that the making available is carried out in a permanent form.*][73]

Article 4

The protection of this Convention shall apply, even if the conditions of Article 3 are not fulfilled, to:

(a) authors of cinematographic works the maker of which has his headquarters or habitual residence in one of the countries of the Union;

(b) authors of works of architecture, erected in a country of the Union or of other artistic works incorporated in a building or other structure located in a country of the Union.

Article 5

(1) Authors shall enjoy, in respect of works for which they are protected under this Convention, in *all* countries of the Union ~~other than the country of origin~~, the rights which their respective laws do now or may hereafter grant to their nationals, as well as the rights specially granted by this Convention.

(2) The enjoyment and the exercise of these rights shall not be subject to any formality; such enjoyment and such exercise shall be independent of the existence of protection in the country of origin of the work. Consequently, apart from the provisions of this Convention, the *existence, scope, and duration of protection*, as well as the means of redress afforded to the author to protect his rights, shall be governed exclusively by the laws of the country

73. Also, *see* the Report of the Country of Origin Study Group of the ALAI [2012] 232 Revue Internationale du Droit d'Auteur 2; cf Jørgen Blomquist, *Primer on International Copyright* 34.

where the exploitation or infringement takes place or produces its effects that are not only marginal (country of protection).

Paragraphs (3)[74] *and (4)*[75] *deleted*

Article 6[76]

... deleted ...[77]

Article 6bis

(1) Independently of the author's economic rights, and even after the transfer *or licencing* of the said rights, the author shall have the *inalienable and non-waivable* right to claim authorship of the work, *including the right to determine whether to be credited or not and under which name,* and to object to any distortion, mutilation or other modification of, or other derogatory action in relation to, the said work, which would be prejudicial to his *legitimate interests.*

(1a) The right according to paragraph (1) extends to the right to prevent the use of one's name on any work the author did not create, or on any work of the author that has been adapted or modified, including a modification carried out by means of artificial intelligence.

(2) The rights granted to the author in accordance with the preceding paragraph shall, after his death, be maintained, at least until the

---

74. "(3) Protection in the country of origin is governed by domestic law. However, when the author is not a national of the country of origin of the work for which he is protected under this Convention, he shall enjoy in that country the same rights as national authors."
75. "(4) The country of origin shall be considered to be ... ."
76. "(1)Where any country outside the Union fails to protect in an adequate manner the works of authors who are nationals of one of the countries of the Union, the latter country may restrict the protection given to the works of authors who are, at the date of the first publication thereof, nationals of the other country and are not habitually resident in one of the countries of the Union. If the country of first publication avails itself of this right, the other countries of the Union shall not be required to grant to works thus subjected to special treatment a wider protection than that granted to them in the country of first publication.
(2) No restrictions introduced by virtue of the preceding paragraph shall affect the rights which an author may have acquired in respect of a work published in a country of the Union before such restrictions were put into force.
(3) The countries of the Union which restrict the grant of copyright in accordance with this Article shall give notice thereof to the Director General of the World Intellectual Property Organization (hereinafter designated as 'the Director General') by a written declaration specifying the countries in regard to which protection is restricted, and the restrictions to which rights of authors who are nationals of those countries are subjected. The Director General shall immediately communicate this declaration to all the countries of the Union."
77. This rule of retaliation should be deleted in the endeavour to extend (unconditional) national treatment if one of the points of attachment is complied with. In practice, this rule is no more applied (*see* Jørgen Blomquist, *Primer on International Copyright* 37f.; Silke v. Lewinski, *International Copyright and Policy* no 5.50 (2008)).

expiry of the economic rights. *After the expiry of these rights, it shall be a matter of the legislation of the countries of the Union to determine whether and for what period moral rights shall continue to exist and by which persons or institutions they may be exercised. … deleted … .*[78]

(3) The means of redress for safeguarding the rights granted by this Article shall be governed by the legislation of the country *of protection.*

Article 7bis

In case of a transfer or licencing of the rights granted to authors under the Convention, the author shall have the right to claim fair compensation; it shall be a matter for legislation in the countries of the Union to determine whether this claim is directed against the transferee or licencee in the chain of exploitation, against the user, or against both of them.

Article 7

(1) The term of protection granted by this Convention shall be the life of the author and fifty years after his death.

(2) However, in the case of cinematographic works, the countries of the Union may provide that the term of protection shall expire fifty years after the work has been made *accessible*[79] to the public with the consent of the author, or, failing such an event within fifty years from the making of such a work, fifty years after the making.

(3) In the case of anonymous or pseudonymous works, the term of protection granted by this Convention shall expire fifty years after the work has been ~~*lawfully*~~ made *accessible* to the public *with the consent of the author, or, failing such authorized making accessible within this period fifty years after the making.* However, when the pseudonym adopted by the author leaves no doubt as to his identity, the term of protection shall be that provided in paragraph (1). If the author of anonymous or pseudonymous work discloses his identity during the above-mentioned period, the term of protection applicable shall be that provided in paragraph (1). The countries of the Union shall not be required to protect anonymous or pseudonymous

---

78. "However, those countries whose legislation, at the moment of their ratification of or accession to this Act, does not provide for the protection after the death of the author of all the rights set out in the preceding paragraph may provide that some of these rights may, after his death, cease to be maintained."

79. Since the right of "making available" is specific to the exclusive right under Art. 8 WCT the term of making a work accessible to the public appears more appropriate.

works in respect of which it is reasonable to presume that their author has been dead for fifty years.

(4) It shall be a matter for legislation in the countries of the Union to determine the term of protection of ~~*photographic works and that of*~~ works of applied art[80] in so far as they are protected as artistic works; however, this term shall last at least until the end of a period of twenty-five years from the making of such a work.

(5) The term of protection subsequent to the death of the author and the terms provided by paragraphs (2), (3) and (4), shall run from the date of death or of the event referred to in those paragraphs, but such terms shall always be deemed to begin on the 1st of January of the year following the death or such event.

(6) The countries of the Union may grant a term of protection in excess of those provided by the preceding paragraphs.

(7) … *deleted* …[81]

(7) The provisions of the preceding *paragraphs* shall also apply in the case of a work of joint authorship, provided that the terms measured from the death of the author shall be calculated from the death of the last surviving author. (ex-Article 7bis)

(8) In any case, the term shall be governed by the legislation of the country *of protection*; however, *it shall be a matter for* the legislation of that country to provide, that the term shall not exceed the term fixed in the *country of which the author is a national.*

(9) *Whenever a country of the Union grants a term of protection exceeding the minimal terms as set out in the previous paragraphs it shall be a matter for such legislation to dedicate the proceeds from the exploitation during such periods to social, cultural or educational purposes managed by the persons or institutions authorized by national legislation.*[82]

Article 8

Without prejudice to Article 11 authors of literary and artistic works protected by this Convention shall enjoy the exclusive right of making and of authorizing the translation, adaptation, arrangement of music and

---

80. *See* Art. 9 WCT.

81. “Those countries of the Union bound by the Rome Act of this Convention, which grant, in their national legislation in force at the time of signature of the present Act, shorter terms of protection than those provided for in the preceding paragraphs, shall have the right to maintain such terms when ratifying or acceding to the present Act.”

82. This is to make clear that in case of granting longer terms than the minimum term provided in the Berne Convention (para. 6) the national legislature is free to shape such regime in the form of a *domaine public payant* so-called.

other alterations *or modifications* of a literary or artistic work, provided that they *constitute human intellectual creations.*[83]

Article 9

(1) Authors of literary and artistic works shall enjoy the exclusive right of authorizing or prohibiting the exploitation of their works in tangible form through

(a) the direct or indirect, temporary or permanent reproduction of these works, in any manner or form, in whole or in part,

(b) the distributing to the public of the original or of copies of their works by means of sale or other transfer of ownership,[84] *as well as*

(c) the commercial rental, except for computer programs, where the program itself is not the essential object of the rental,[85] *and except for the rental of cinematographic works for the purpose of communication to the public.*

(2) Any sound or visual recording shall be considered as a reproduction for the purposes of this Convention *as is the case with regard to any reproduction in digital form on whatever physical device.*

Article 10 (replacing ex-Articles 11 to 11ter)

(1) Authors of literary and artistic works shall enjoy the exclusive right of authorizing or prohibiting any communication to the public of their works, by wire or wireless means, including broadcasting via satellite and including the making available to the public of their works in such a way that members of the public may access them from a place and at a time individually chosen by them.

(2) In the absence of any contrary stipulation, permission granted in accordance with paragraph (1) of this Article shall not imply permission to record, by means of instruments recording sounds or images, or to otherwise reproducing the work communicated to the public in the sense of the preceding paragraph.

Article 10bis

Without prejudice to Articles 9 and 10, authors of literary and artistic works shall enjoy the exclusive right to authorize or prohibit any other use made of their works in material or immaterial form, provided that such use is not merely insignificant.

---

83. Whereas originality is a general prerequisite for copyright protection (Art. 1 of the proposal), a further clarification as regards adaptations appears to make sense.
84. Article 6 of the WCT.
85. Article7(2)(i) of the WCT.

Article 10ter

It shall be a matter for legislation in the countries of the Union to provide for a collective management through collecting societies of the rights granted to authors under this Convention on a facultative or mandatory basis in certain cases, including the establishing of a regime of extended licences.

Article 11 (ex-Article 14)

(1) Authors of literary or artistic works shall have the exclusive right of authorizing *or prohibiting*:

 (i) the cinematographic adaptation and reproduction of these works *in the sense of Article 9*, and the distribution of the works thus adapted or reproduced *as well as their commercial rental according to Article 9*;

 (ii) the communication to the public of the works thus adapted or reproduced *in the sense of Article 13*.

(2) The adaptation into any other artistic form of a cinematographic production derived from literary or artistic works shall, without prejudice to the authorization of the author of the cinematographic production, remain subject to the authorization of the authors of the original works.

(3) ... *deleted* ... [86]

Article12 (ex-Article 14bis)

(1) Without prejudice to the copyright in any work which may have been adapted or reproduced *(Article 8)*, a cinematographic work *that constitutes a human intellectual creation* shall be protected as an original work. The owner of copyright in a cinematographic work shall enjoy the same rights as the author of an original work, including the rights referred to in the preceding Article.

(2) (a) Ownership of copyright in a cinematographic work shall be a matter for legislation in the country *of protection*.

 (b) However, in the countries of the Union which, by legislation include among the owners of copyright in a cinematographic work authors who have brought contributions to the making of the work, such authors, if they have undertaken to bring such contributions, may not, in the absence of any contrary or special stipulation, object to the reproduction, distribution, *rental, and* communication to the public in the sense of Article13, or to the

86. "The provisions of Article 13 (1) shall not apply."

subtitling or dubbing of texts, of the work, *provided that authors receive a fair compensation.*[87]

(c) The question whether or not the form of the undertaking referred to above should, for the application of the preceding subparagraph (b), be in a written agreement or a written act of the same effect shall be a matter for the legislation of the country where the maker of the cinematographic work has his headquarters or habitual residence. However, it shall be a matter for the legislation of the country of the Union where protection is claimed to provide that the said undertaking shall be in a written agreement or a written act of the same effect. The countries whose legislation so provides shall notify the Director General by means of a written declaration, which will be immediately communicated by him to all the other countries of the Union.

(d) By "contrary or special stipulation" is meant any restrictive condition which is relevant to the aforesaid undertaking.

(3) Unless the national legislation provides to the contrary, the provisions of paragraph (2) (b) above shall not be applicable to authors of scenarios, dialogues and musical works created for the making of the cinematographic work, nor to the principal director thereof. However, those countries of the Union whose legislation does not contain rules providing for the application of the said paragraph (2) (b) to such director shall notify the Director General by means of a written declaration, which will be immediately communicated by him to all the other countries of the Union.

Article 13 (ex-Article 14ter)

(1) The author, or after his death the persons or institutions authorized by national legislation, *may*, with respect to original works of art and original manuscripts of writers and composers, enjoy the *unwaivable and* inalienable right to *a fair* interest in any sale of the work subsequent to the first transfer by the author of the work.

(2) The protection provided by the preceding paragraph may be claimed in a country of the Union only if *the* legislation in the country to which the author belongs *so provides in a sufficient and effective manner*, and to the extent *provided* by the country where this *interest* is claimed.[88]

87. Apart from this minor modification, this provision on film copyright has not yet been revised.

88. Apart from these minor modifications the provision concerning the *droit de suite* has not yet been revised.

(3) The procedure for collection and the amounts shall be matters for determination by national legislation.

Article 14

(1) *Authors of literary and artistic works shall enjoy the unwaivable and inalienable right to an equitable remuneration for the public lending of the original or copies of their works.*

(2) *It shall be a matter for legislation in the countries of the Union to grant an exclusive right of public lending in lieu of the claim to an equitable remuneration according to the preceding paragraph.*

Article 15

(1) In order that the author of a literary or artistic work protected by this Convention shall, in the absence of proof to the contrary, be regarded as such, and consequently be entitled to institute infringement proceedings in the countries of the Union, it shall be sufficient for his name to appear on the work in the usual manner. This paragraph shall be applicable even if this name is a pseudonym, where the pseudonym adopted by the author leaves no doubt as to his identity.

(2) The person or body corporate whose name appears on a cinematographic work in the usual manner shall, in the absence of proof to the contrary, be presumed to be the maker of the said work.

(3) In the case of anonymous and pseudonymous works, other than those referred to in paragraph (1) above, the publisher whose name appears on the work shall, in the absence of proof to the contrary, be deemed to represent the author, and in this capacity shall be entitled to protect and enforce the author's rights. The provisions of this paragraph shall cease to apply when the author reveals his identity and establishes his claim to authorship of the work.

(4) (a) In the case of unpublished works where the identity of the author is unknown, but where there is every ground to presume that he is a national of a country of the Union, it shall be a matter for legislation in that country to designate the competent authority who shall represent the author and shall be entitled to protect and enforce his rights in the countries of the Union.

(b) Countries of the Union which make such designation under the terms of this provision shall notify the Director General by means of a written declaration giving full information concerning the authority thus designated. The Director General shall at once communicate this declaration to all other countries of the Union.

Article 15bis (ex-Article 2bis)

(1) It shall be a matter for legislation in the countries of the Union to exclude, wholly or in part, from the protection provided by the preceding Article political speeches and speeches delivered in the course of legal proceedings.
(2) It shall also be a matter for legislation in the countries of the Union to determine the conditions under which lectures, addresses and other works of the same nature which are delivered in public may be reproduced by the press, broadcast, communicated to the public by wire and made the subject of public communication as envisaged in Article 11bis (1) of this Convention, when such use is justified by the informatory purpose.
(3) Nevertheless, the author shall enjoy the exclusive right of making a collection of his works mentioned in the preceding paragraphs.

Article 15ter (ex-Article 10)

(1) It shall be permissible to make quotations from a work which has already been lawfully made available to the public, provided that their making is compatible with fair practice, and their extent does not exceed that justified by the purpose, including quotations from newspaper articles and periodicals in the form of press summaries.
(2) It shall be a matter for legislation in the countries of the Union, and for special agreements existing or to be concluded between them, to permit the utilization, to the extent justified by the purpose, of literary or artistic works by way of illustration in publications, broadcasts or sound or visual recordings for teaching, provided such utilization is compatible with fair practice.
(3) Where use is made of works in accordance with the preceding paragraphs of this Article, mention shall be made of the source, and of the name of the author, if it appears thereon.

Article 15^{quater} (ex-Article 10bis)

(1) It shall be a matter for legislation in the countries of the Union to permit the reproduction by the press, the broadcasting or the communication to the public by wire, of articles published in newspapers or periodicals on current economic, political or religious topics, and of broadcast works of the same character, in cases in which the reproduction, broadcasting or such communication thereof is not expressly reserved. Nevertheless, the source must always be clearly indicated; the legal consequences of a breach of this obligation shall be determined by the legislation of the country where protection is claimed.

(2) It shall also be a matter for legislation in the countries of the Union to determine the conditions under which, for the purpose of reporting current events by means of photography, cinematography, broadcasting or communication to the public by wire, literary or artistic works seen or heard in the course of the event may, to the extent justified by the informatory purpose, be reproduced and made available to the public.

Article 15^{quinquies} (ex-Article 11)

It shall be a matter for legislation in the countries of the Union to determine the regulations for ephemeral recordings made by a broadcasting organization by means of its own facilities and used for its own broadcasts. The preservation of these recordings in official archives may, on the ground of their exceptional documentary character, be authorized by such legislation.

Article 15^{sexies} (ex-Article 9(2) amended)

(1) Countries of the Union may, in their national legislation, provide for limitations of or exceptions to the rights granted to authors of literary and artistic works under this Convention in certain special cases that do not conflict with a normal exploitation of the work and do not unreasonably prejudice the legitimate interests of the author.[89]

(2) *Limitations of or exceptions in the sense of the preceding paragraph may in particular be provided for to the extent necessary to respond to serious diseases in times of a pandemic, including vaccination, treatment and containment.*[90]

(3) *Where the use is made according to such limitations of or exceptions to the rights granted to authors of literary and artistic works under this Convention is not merely insignificant, the countries of the Unions shall provide for an unwaivable and inalienable claim to an equitable remuneration to compensate them adequately for such use. It shall be a matter of national legislation to dedicate the proceeds from such remuneration in whole or in part to social, cultural or educational purposes managed by the persons or institutions authorized by national legislation.*

89. Three-Step Test so-called as set out in Arts. 13 of the TRIPS Agreement and 10(1) of the WCT.

90. *See* Sean M. Flyn, *Copyright and COVID*, at Jens Schovsbo, Intellectual Property Rights in Crisis 140 (2024).

Article 16

(1) Infringing copies of a work shall be liable to seizure in any country of the Union where the work enjoys legal protection.
(2) The provisions of the preceding paragraph shall also apply to reproductions coming from a country where the work is not protected, or has ceased to be protected.
(3) The seizure shall take place in accordance with the legislation of each country.

Article 17

The provisions of this Convention cannot in any way affect the right of the Government of each country of the Union to permit, to control, or to prohibit by legislation or regulation, the circulation, presentation, or exhibition of any work or production in regard to which the competent authority may find it necessary to exercise that right *in the legitimate public interest.*

Article 18

(1) This Convention shall apply to all works which, at the moment of its coming into force, have not yet fallen into the public domain in the country of *protection* through the expiry of the term of protection.
(2) If, however, through the expiry of the term of protection which was previously granted, a work has fallen into the public domain of the country where protection is claimed, that work shall not be protected anew.
(3) The application of this principle shall be subject to any provisions contained in special conventions to that effect existing or to be concluded between countries of the Union. In the absence of such provisions, the respective countries shall determine, each in so far as it is concerned, the conditions of application of this principle.
(4) The preceding provisions shall also apply in the case of new accessions to the Union and to cases in which protection is extended by the application of Article 7 or by the abandonment of reservations.

Article 19

The provisions of this Convention shall not preclude the making of a claim to the benefit of any greater protection which may be granted by legislation in a country of the Union.

Article 20

The Governments of the countries of the Union reserve the right to enter into special agreements among themselves, in so far as such agreements grant to authors more extensive rights than those granted by the Convention, or contain other provisions not contrary to this Convention. The provisions of existing agreements which satisfy these conditions shall remain applicable.

Article 21

(1) *It shall be a matter for legislation in the countries of the Union to establish fair liability regimes ensuring the effectiveness of the rights and claims granted to authors of literary and artistic works in particular in cases of mass use. If certain intermediaries are exempted from liability (safe-harbor provisions), equivalent liability rules must be provided for.*

(2) *Without prejudice to Article 17 Union countries shall provide for the measures, procedures and remedies necessary to ensure the enforcement of the rights covered by this Convention. Those measures, procedures and remedies shall be fair and equitable and shall not be unnecessarily complicated or costly, or entail unreasonable time-limits or unwarranted delays.*[91] *Union countries shall in any case comply with Articles 41 through 50 as well as Articles 51 through 60 and 61 (enforcement of intellectual property rights) of the TRIPS-Agreement with the following modification and amendments:*

...

(3) *The Union countries shall comply with Articles 11 and 12 of the WIPO Copyright Treaty concerning technological measures and copyright information.*

Article 21bis

(1) Special provisions regarding developing countries are included in the Appendix.

(2) Subject to the provisions of Article 28(1)(b), the Appendix forms an integral part of this Act.

91. *See* Art. 3 of the EU Enforcement Directive.

Part III
International Copyright Law *Acquis*

Chapter 13

The Moral Interests of Authors as Universal Expressions of the Law of Autonomy: And Their Plural Recognition Within or Outside Copyright Law

Alain Strowel

Moral rights, as we know and call them in Continental Europe since the second half of the nineteenth century, are a way to recognize some fundamental claims of the creative persons with regard to the product of their mind and their intimate relationship with it. Those rights thus aim at preserving a special relationship with the creations of a human person rather than at protecting a thing. If copyright is a form of (intellectual) property, its branch comprising moral rights is not (and should not be seen as linked to proprietary interest). This is clear for the right of attribution (referred to as the "right to claim authorship" in Article 6bis of the Berne Convention (BC)):[1] it symbolizes and incorporates the unbreakable bond between an author and a work. The second core moral right is the right of disclosure: it turns around the person of the author and her right to deploy her personality. This right secures "*dignitary* interests" (according to the words of Paul Goldstein) that "are deeply rooted in norms of privacy that are older, wider,

1. Berne Convention for the Protection of Literary and Artistic Works (Sep. 9, 1886), S. Treaty Doc. No. 99-27, Art. 6bis (hereinafter "Berne Convention or BC").

and more deeply entrenched than in the specific doctrine of moral rights."[2] The third core moral right, the right of integrity or to respect the work of authorship, looks more focused on the (intangible) thing, but it is also directly related to the person of the author and how s/he is to be considered within the human community: indeed, in its formulation under Article 6 bis BC, it allows the human author "to object to any distortion, mutilation or other modification of, or other derogatory action in relation to, the said work, *which would be prejudicial to his honor or reputation.*" Its exercise is thus conditioned by the existence of a negative impact on the honor or reputation of a person.

Those rights, as explained below (*see* section 13.3), are part of what can be called the "law of autonomy," i.e., all the legal norms that primarily aim at fostering the autonomous deployment of (human) personalities. Moral rights "embody the legal protection of authors' dignitary interests in connection with their creative works."[3] For instance, the right of attribution can be traced back to the fundamental right of dignity. In the European Union (EU), this right is enshrined in Article 1 of the Charter of Fundamental Rights. This right is foundational and operates as the basis from which other fundamental rights (such as the right to life, liberty and privacy) derive. It implies the right to be recognized and treated with respect as a human person. Similarly, the right of disclosure and the right of integrity rely on the fundamental right of privacy that includes the right to one's reputation (Article 7 EU Charter). In Continental Europe, where updated versions of the fundamental rights have been incorporated in rather recent texts of "constitutional nature" (such as the 1950 European Convention of Human Rights or the EU Charter legally binding since December 1, 2009), the moral rights within the author's rights can thus be viewed as fundamental rights (that said, the economic rights are also part of a fundamental right, the right to property, *see* Article 17 EU Charter). This does not mean that those rights are sacred or discretionary, they have limitations as other fundamental rights.

In other parts of the world, the personal and non-economic interests of authors can be protected under other legal doctrines or principles or can be recognized by social norms. Privacy, as the root of the right of disclosure, can typically be a social norm embedded in the varying interpersonal relations within human communities and cultures. Thus, there are other ways to recognize and give effect to the basic claims and the shared interests underlying moral rights. My view is that the claims that have translated into moral rights as we know them in the author's rights countries (in Continental Europe and beyond) are *universal*, or at least widely shared among humans, but that the interests those rights protect can also be promoted by other legal concepts (within or outside copyright law) or even by social norms (thus

2. Paul Goldstein, *Moral Rights on the Internet* 298 (Fabienne Brison, Severine Dusollier, Marie-Christine Janssens & Hendrick Vanhees eds., ALAI—Larcier, 2015).
3. *Ibid.*, 296.

outside or beyond the law). In this sense, there is also a *plural recognition* of the personality interests, whether by law or other norms.

The pluralist view is illustrated in the first part of the chapter that briefly focuses on the claim of attribution (*see* section 13.1 below) and its varying expressions.

The second section (section 13.2) addresses a broader legal pluralism issue. It is a reminder of the usual tensions between moral rights as they are known in the author's right systems and in the Anglo-American copyright traditions and the need to go beyond those oppositions (and other ones) between the civil law and the common law approaches.

The title of the chapter underlines the plural recognition of the moral interests of authors. There is, however, still an element encapsulated in the title that requires some explanation in this introduction: "The Moral Interests of Authors as Universal Expressions of the *Law of Autonomy*," What does the "law of autonomy" mean? This is discussed in a third section (section 13.3), where I first distinguish two dimensions of copyright laws and rules. First, they are part of what I call "the law of growth" or what others would call the "law of wealth": like many other property institutions that focus on the allocation of market resources, they favor the appearance of new markets and their expansion by promoting innovation and creativity (and, according to some observers, they ensure the "wealth of nations" to use the title of the well-known book of Adam Smith). Katharina Pistor has recently coined the term "code of capital" to designate the economic laws which create wealth (as well as inequality).[4] I prefer the more neutral term of "law of growth" that is also more correlated to the recent focus on growth in our capitalist societies since at least World War II (and economic growth aims at ensuring more wealth). Copyright rules are just one example among many other (economic) laws that are supposed to foster the markets and thus economic growth. Second, copyright laws have also been considered to form part of another dimension of modern law that can be designated as "the law of autonomy," aiming to protect and promote the development of individuals. There are many legal embodiments of this law of autonomy (in particular in the way the law has treated the personality interests, the body (including women) and death-related issues). Moral rights do belong to this second dimension of modern law, and this sheds a new light and has some consequences, as further explained in section 13.3 of the present chapter. More could and should be done to strengthen the non-pecuniary or moral

4. Katharina Pistor, *The Code of Capital* (Princeton University Press, 2020). This author "argues that the law selectively 'codes' certain assets, endowing them with the capacity to protect and produce private wealth. With the right legal coding, any object, claim, or idea can be turned into capital—and lawyers are the keepers of the code" (presentation of the book on https://press.princeton.edu/books/hardcover/9780691178974/the-code-of-capital?srsltid=AfmBOorZy8XBGmMFXAIRmY-ZdCGvlvoSeWfeUskKykzr7hDZmikdW55z, accessed Oct. 28, 2024).

(but the term is not well-chosen) dimension of copyright law,[5] which aims to empower the individual and enhance his/her autonomy.

In the fourth and last section 13.4, I make some simple proposals, and I envisage a few ways in which moral rights can possibly be redesigned in the EU harmonization or unification context so as to make them better in line with the promotion of the authors' autonomy.

I then conclude in section 13.5 with some brief remarks on the role of moral rights in the context of the massive production of content made possible by generative Artificial Intelligence (genAI) and the spreading of the so-called digital replicas (in particular of creators).

13.1 THE MORAL INTEREST OF ATTRIBUTION: A UNIVERSAL CLAIM AND ITS PLURAL RECOGNITIONS

The same claims, such as the claim to be recognized as a creator, might have taken other forms in past times and in other cultures where individual rights were not so prominent and where other systems of legal or social norms rule(d).

Let us take a minute to consider the moral right of attribution, the right for the author to be credited for her work, recognized in Article 6bis of the BC. As stressed by the Copyright Principles Project and P. Samuelson in particular:

> attribution is a norm in many cultures and legal systems and is reflected in a variety of ways, including through well-established norms against plagiarism.[6]

The rules against plagiarism, often compared to theft or robbery, are the corollary of a complex social norm of attribution.[7] It is true that one is, to a certain extent, permitted to copy the works of someone else if s/he attributes them to their real author. To assess the prevalence of the claim to be recognized as an author over time, one should thus enquire how the pervasive

5. What the moral dimension of an intellectual property right is depends on the perspective adopted. I associate the moral dimension of copyright with the emphasis and focus on the person of the creator, but others might link the moral dimension of copyright with some features that favor the public interest (or the interest of the public), such as the idea/expression dichotomy or some exceptions in favor of the community (*see* Steven Ang, *The Moral Dimension of Intellectual Property Rights* 130ff., 180 (Edward Elgar, 2013) on the personhood vein and the moral rights).
6. Pamela Samuelson & Members of the Copyright Principles Project (CPP), *The Copyright Principles Project: Directions for Reform,* 25 Berkeley Technology Law Journal 3 (2010) Available at: https://repository.law.umich.edu/articles/1381.
7. Stuart P. Green, *Plagiarism, Norms, and the Limits of Theft Law: Some Observations on the Use of Criminal Sanctions in Enforcing Intellectual Property Rights* 55(1) Hastings Law Journal 171 (2002) https://doi.org/10.2139/ssrn.315562.

social norms against plagiarism, relying in particular on reputational stigma, have allowed the protection of this interest in earlier times.[8] Indeed, anti-plagiarism norms were known in Europe before the consecration of the Romantic view of the "author" and of moral rights through the nineteenth-century case law, and thus well before their consolidation by legislation in the twentieth century, such as the 1957 Copyright Act in France or the 1965 Law in Germany.[9]

Those norms have probably not achieved the same results as moral rights have, but one should not overestimate the effects of our modern moral rights either. In certain contexts, they struggle to be recognized (although they exist in law books). For instance, what about the effectiveness of the moral rights of attribution and integrity in the field of video games? As many video games integrate several elements that derive from previous works, it is quite difficult to identify the many authors of a single production, and this reduces the effect that moral rights, and in particular the right to claim authorship, can have.[10] That moral rights do affect the practice in most fields of art and creation is a belief and also a daydream, shared by lawyers advocating the *droit d'auteur* approach. One should be realistic about the influence of those rights in practice.

However, it is well possible that in certain cultures and legal-political systems, such as China, the preservation of the personality interests of the individual creators—and, more generally, of the individuals—is not well assured. Comparative studies in culture, anthropology or political science could probably help to support this view. Individuals might thus face higher barriers to ascertain their personality interests in certain cultures and legal-political systems, but it is also doubtful that aspirations to be credited for the intellectual work done are completely absent.

Today, the universal claim to be credited for one's work can be enforced differently because standardized forms of copyright licenses have flourished, and it is easier to make a claim through the choice of a type of license. Indeed, the "widespread use of Creative Commons licenses that require reusers of CC-licensed works to acknowledge the authorship of the reused work" shows that the claim of attribution is widely shared.[11] Thus, the interest that underlies the right that was once called the "right of paternity"—

---

8. *Ibid.,* 177ff.
9. Volume I, Stig Strömholm, *Le droit moral de l'auteur en droit allemand, français et scandinave avec un aperçu de l'évolution internationale* (PA Norstedt & Söners Förlag, 1967) (for the history of the notion); Mira T. Sundara Rajan, *Moral Rights. Principles, Practice and New Technology* (Oxford University Press, 2011).
10. *See*, Volume 2, J. Stein, *Authorship and Moral Rights in Video Games* (Press Start, 2015).
11. Samuelson & Members of the CPP (n. 6) 66; *See also,* Mira T. Sundara Rajan, *The Attribution Right: Authorship and Beyond* at Moral Rights in the 21st Century 245ff. (Fabienne Brison, Severine Dusollier, M-C. Janssens & Hendrick Vanhees eds., ALAI—Larcier, 2015).

and the outdated name is the sign of an old-fashioned social order—can nowadays live and be reinforced by standard contractual terms.

The interest behind the right of attribution can also be enforced through tort law, a field of law that relies heavily on simple moral norms. The principles of tort law can indeed protect against misappropriation of a work or against some harm to the reputation.[12] Tort law is not standardized in the same way as property law, as there is no fixed list of torts (no *numerus clausus* as for property rights), and courts can thus innovate to protect the reputation (of an author).[13] A formal recognition of the right of attribution in copyright law is thus not a precondition for enhancing the attribution interest. Many other rights, in particular, personality rights, have had a "real life" before being formally recognized in the law.[14] This is the case with the image right that can be enforced through tort law actions (such as through extra-contractual liability principles) in countries where it is not officially enshrined in legislation. The possibility to launch an action, even though a right has not (yet) been incorporated into the statutes, is evidence that remedies exist.

In countries where the collective management of copyright is well developed, such as in the Nordic countries, the possibility and the practice of collective management organizations (CMOs) to fight for the moral interests of their members is also a strong factor leading to the effective recognition of moral rights.

Today, new technologies are seen as facilitating the infringement of some moral rights, at least with regard to the integrity of digital content and files. But at the same time, moral interests can be better served by new technologies and services. For instance, as noticed by M. T. Sundara Rajan, services such as Apple's iTunes make it possible to find and maintain the accurate attribution of recorded music.[15]

Social norms regarding plagiarism, standard contractual terms (of the Creative Commons licenses), tort law principles, CMO activism, or new digital technologies can thus partly make up for the absence of a formal right

12. Arguably, the U.S. caselaw of the nineteenth century "came close to developing a tort of moral rights invasion", *see,* Patrick R. Goold, *The Lost Tort of Moral Rights Invasion,* 51(4) Akron Law Review, Art. 4 (2017), https://ideaexchange.uakron.edu/akronlawreview/vol51/iss4/4/?utm_source=ideaexchange.uakron.edu%2Fakronlawreview%2Fvol51%2Fiss4%2F4&utm_medium=PDF&utm_campaign=PDFCoverPages (accessed Oct. 28, 2024).
13. Henry E. Smith, *Modularity and Morality in the Law of Torts,* 4(2) Journal of Tort Law, Art. 5 (2011) https://doi.org/10.2202/1932-9148.1112.
14. *See*, Francois Jongen & Alain Strowel (with E. Cruysmans), *Droit de l'information et de la communication* 383ff., 445ff. (Larcier, 2017).
15. Sundara Rajan (n. 11) 249; iTunes works with Gracenote's music recognition technology and has allowed to identify some recordings (the Hatto's) as hoaxes, *see* the story reported by Mark Singer, *Fantasia for Piano: Joyce Hatto's Incredible Career,* The New Yorker, https://www.newyorker.com/magazine/2007/09/17/fantasia-for-piano (accessed Oct. 28, 2024).

of attribution. That said, the formal recognition of the right of attribution can help to fulfill the personality interests, at least if the right is not fully waivable by law or does not need to be ascertained to exist. More could thus be done in a country such as the United States (U.S.) where, except for the authors of works of visual art,[16] the "U.S. Copyright law has not yet provided general protection to authors as to their attribution interests," although those interests are sometimes protected in the U.S. by contracts, union rules (that replace the role of CMOs in other countries), state laws, fair use rulings (when paying attention to whether the author has been credited), and laws protecting against misrepresentations and deception.[17]

13.2 UNIVERSAL PROTECTION OF MORAL INTERESTS BEYOND THE TWO COPYRIGHT TRADITIONS

It is usual to oppose the model of Continental European systems with numerous and broad moral rights and the Anglo-American systems with less developed moral rights. The main differences can probably be summarized as follows:

Moral Rights in Continental European Systems	*Moral Rights in Anglo-American Systems*
For all authors and works	Only for some authors or works
Various rights beyond attribution and integrity	When recognized, rights limited to attribution and integrity
Robust rights	When recognized, fragile rights
Unwaivable	Waivable
Unconditional	Conditional

Of course, such high-level comparison is rather rough—and one has to go beyond and highlight convergences beyond this contrasting presentation.[18] Also, a strict comparison does not properly take into account the variations and nuances between the national laws within the civil law tradition. The French, German, Italian, Dutch, Belgian, Nordic, and Central

16. *See,* the Visual Artists Rights Act of 1990, 17 USC §106A (2006).
17. Samuelson & Members of the CPP (n. 6) 1243.
18. Alain Strowel, *Droit d'auteur et copyright, Divergences et convergences* (Bruxelles, Bruylant et Paris, L.G.D.J. 1993); Alain Strowel, *Droit d'auteur et copyright. Convergences des droits, régulation différente des contrats* at Mélanges en l'honneur du Prof. André Lucas 699-717 (LexisNexis, 2014).

European countries, etc., versions of moral rights vary quite substantially.[19] Neither does such a comparison take into consideration the diversity shown by the national systems of the common law countries, such as the United Kingdom (U.K.), the U.S., Canada, Australia or other Commonwealth-influenced countries. Some of those systems offer real protection for the moral interests within or outside copyright law. The differences among the civil law countries, on the one hand, and among the common law countries, on the other hand, suggest that there is no universal model for the protection of the moral interests of the authors, not even two main models that could simply be opposed.

However, some features of the moral rights that exist throughout the world can be linked to fundamental differences between the two traditions of author's right and copyright:

Author's Right Systems	*Copyright Systems*
Focus on author	Focus on market and public
Personalist justification	Utilitarian justification
Natural law theory	Positivist view
More protective approach	Incentive-based approach
Early focus on works of art	Early focus on useful works
No formalities	Formalities
Flexible and synthetic rights	More limited rights
List of narrowly interpreted exceptions	Broad fair use type of exception
(Initial) owner = creator	Works made for hire and other ways to have a "corporate copyright"
Statutory regulation of contracts	Wide freedom of contracts

Again, this second table oversimplifies the many divergences and convergences between the two main traditions and the fact that several countries have a hybrid model (for instance, relying on the theory of the unity of arts, France allows copyright to be used for protecting utilitarian articles, contrary than the U.K.; the U.K. has a narrowly formulated fair dealing provision that differs from the broad U.S. fair use exception, etc.). Traditionally, moral rights have been associated with the author's right model as they are a better fit with a legal model that focuses on the author and her personality and recognizes fundamental rights of (creative) persons.

Analyzed through the prism of comparative law, the absence of a "universal" model for moral rights also points to a drafting issue and the

19. For a recent review of the legal situation in various countries, *see* the issue of Sundara Rajan (n. 9) 257-258.

divergences in formulating the law in different legal systems. The difficulty is thus not so much to reach an agreement on the issue of protecting moral interests, but to find a way of drafting rules which could fit with the different legal traditions. There are many differences between the way rules are drafted in civil law countries and the way they are drafted in common law countries. Although I see the drawbacks of using a conceptual way of designing those rights in civil law countries, I believe moral rights should be formulated in broad terms and have a broad coverage. It is the way that was chosen for Article 6bis of the BC, but more could be done for the limitations to those rights (*see* section 13.4 below).

13.3 COPYRIGHT TORN BETWEEN THE "LAW OF GROWTH" AND THE "LAW OF AUTONOMY"

In a less conventional way, I propose here to think about moral rights through the prism of two other "ideal types" in the sense of Max Weber, thus two constructions of abstract models (or two idea-constructs) that help put the chaos of complex realities in order.[20] In particular, I draw on the view described by Antoine Bailleux, who pleads and distinguishes the "law of growth," comprising rules favoring the functioning and the expansion of the market, from the "law of autonomy," which includes all the rules that aim to protect the development of individuals and their human capabilities in particular.[21] Many rules of economic law that have been adopted, in particular since World War II, aim at encouraging and improving market transactions and thus contribute to economic growth. Intellectual property (IP) rules, which are supposed to incentivize investments in innovation, are part of this ideal type of law that favors economic growth over other objectives. A publication of the World Intellectual Property Organization (WIPO) that highlights the link with economic growth is aptly entitled: "Intellectual Property. A Power Tool for Economic Growth."[22] This WIPO self-advocacy paper, based on the premise that "IP is good," shows that IP is a "power tool" for economic expansion and thus also for development. According to this positive (and probably a bit one-sided) view, IP is thus an ingredient for an economic "plus" or "surplus," it is definitely not about a "zero sum game." Potential economic gains guaranteed by IP exclusivity provide a powerful incentive to innovate and develop new products or services in the interest of society as a whole.

20. *See* the entry "ideal type" on Wikipedia.
21. Antoine Bailleux, *Le droit en transition. La science juridique saisie par la critique du modèle croissanciel*, https://dial.uclouvain.be/pr/boreal/object/boreal:188564 (accessed Oct. 28, 2024).
22. Kamil Idris, *Intellectual Property. A Power Tool for Economic Growth* (WIPO Publications, 2003).

Copyright law is, less obviously than patent law, a strong means to incentivize the production of new works as its effect on the creative process is controversial (after all, how many artists and persons engage in creation because of copyright?). But copyright is at least an insurance for publishers and distributors to recoup their costs, and thus, it promotes the dissemination and, in the end, the "consumption" of works. Copyright mainly provides for rights (i.e., the reproduction and distribution rights) to control the making and marketing of products embedding works and their limits, such as exhaustion; it also confers rights (i.e., the communication to the public right) that support various services relying on protected content (e.g., the broadcasting or streaming of audiovisual content). In that sense, copyright law, like other branches of property law, is a way to control resources[23] for maximizing their use, and it is thus part of the "law of growth."

But modern law is also influenced by the superior objective of enhancing the autonomy of persons and their capabilities, that is, their real opportunities to do and be what they have reason to value.[24] Within copyright, the rules on ownership of rights *vis-à-vis* the patrons or employers or the contractual rules that protect the individual authors *vis-à-vis* their publishers and distributors could be designed to enhance the autonomy of the creative people and thus to implement what I call here the "law of autonomy." By securing the right of the author to be recognized as such, by ensuring that works cannot be marketed without the consent of the creator and by allowing the creator to control the fate of his work and to ensure its integrity, the moral rights are also clearly part of this legal dimension.[25] Of course, more could be done to enhance the creative capabilities of people through (copyright) law by recognizing, for instance, the collaborative and collective aspect of some creations, and thus the right to reuse the elements of creations that belong to the human communities.

Copyright mainly belongs to the "right of growth," and it only contains some ancillary components that are part of the "law of autonomy." Interestingly, from a fundamental rights perspective, copyright is viewed as property in the case law of the Court of Justice of the EU (which relies on Article 17(2) of the Charter on Fundamental Rights of the EU).[26] The fact

---

23. Julie E. Cohen, *Property as Institutions for Resources: Lessons from and for IP*, 94(1) Texas Law Review 1-57 (2015) https://doi.org/10.2139/ssrn.2478051 (available also on ssrn).
24. *See* the entry "capability approach" authored by Ingrid Robeyns, *The Capability Approach* (Stanford Encyclopedia of Philosophy, 2016), https://plato.stanford.edu/entries/capability-approach/ (accessed Oct. 28, 2024).
25. In that sense, as put by Sundara Rajan (n. 9, at 257) the moral rights "offer a fascinating counterpoint to the powerful economic considerations that dominate modern copyright discourse."
26. Alain Strowel, *Article 17: La propriété intellectuelle* at Charte des droits fondamentaux de l'Union européenne. Commentaire article par article, 453-485 (Fabrice Picod, Cecilia Rizcallah & Sebastien Van Drooghenbroeck eds., Larcier, 2023, 3rd ed).

that protection is viewed from a property perspective also allows legal persons to invoke the fundamental right protection of copyright. In this sense, classifying it as property breaks the link between copyright and the natural person. However, the Court of Justice does not view the property protection of copyright under Article 17(2) as absolute.[27] The recognition as property has therefore not led to a systematic "propertization" of copyright leading to its continuous extension (in the sense of *in dubio pro proprietate*). The European framework, whether the EU Charter or the European Convention on Human Rights (first protocol), nevertheless contributes to erase the link (appearing in particular in the Universal Declaration of Human Rights (UDHR)) between copyright and the person of the creator.[28]

On the contrary, away from the property approach, some constitutional courts have invoked the right to deploy a personality as a basis for copyright.[29] This brings copyright closer to the "law of autonomy." Also, Article 27(2) of the UDHR stresses the role of the person of the creator:

> Everyone has the right to the protection of the moral and material interests resulting from any scientific, literary or artistic production of which he is the author.

Article 27(2) of the UDHR offers a "universal declaration" and thus a global recognition of the importance of the "moral interests" of the author. Those universal interests can be implemented in a plurality of ways, including outside copyright law (*see* section 13.1 above).

The two legal dimensions of copyright, as a law of growth and a law of autonomy, are mirrored in the two strands that pervade the case law on copyright: most decisions focus on the protection of a thing (property rule), while some, including those on moral rights, tend to protect more against taking (rule of conduct). This is because copyright not only confers rights on a market product but also permits to initiate action against wrongful appropriation. Cases for breach of the right of attribution are based on some form of misappropriation of the dignitary interests of the author to be linked to her work. The same misappropriation approach could serve as the basis for many actions involving the violation of the integrity of a work. Integrity is a virtue and thus points towards a moral notion or value; the right of integrity

27. *Ibid.*
28. With the risk that this right is no more than "a property right in its superb autarcy": the expression is from Gérard Farjat, *Pour un droit économique* 68ff. (Presses Universitaires de France, 2004) and taken up by Fabrice Siiriainen, *Le droit à la culture et l'accès aux œuvres de l'esprit. Réflexions sur la "fonction" du droit d'auteur dans le cadre de sa "fondamentalisation*" at Droit économique et droits de l'homme 448 (Laurence Boy, Jean-Baptiste Racine & Fabrice Siiriainen eds., Larcier, 2009).
29. The German constitutional court has anchored and construed the moral or personal dimension of copyright on the basis of Arts. 1(1) and 2(1) of the German Basic Law (Grundgesetz). Interestingly copyright also finds a common constitutional basis in the provisions on the freedom to create.

objectivizes the value of integrity with regard to the production of the mind of a person.

Other notions and building blocks of copyright tend to point toward moral values. For instance, originality, as a condition for protection, is defined under EU copyright law as the requirement that the creation be "the author's own intellectual creation."[30] This means in particular that the copyright-protected work should not have been copied and should result from an act of creative freedom. The requirement of free (and creative) choices[31] is at the heart of copyright as interpreted by the Court of Justice of the EU: there is no protection when there is no freedom to create.[32]

The same morality of copyright can be deduced from the requirements for copyright infringement to be established. Indeed, to prove copyright infringement, the evidence of substantial similarities between the protected work and the allegedly infringing content is not sufficient; some copying or taking must also be demonstrated or could be presumed (and therefore the possibility for the alleged infringer to have access to the work is a precondition for copyright infringement). The "taking" condition adds an element of morality to the copyright balancing act. This also implies that copyright law embeds moral values better than patent law does: someone who has never copied an invention made by a third party can nevertheless be prohibited from using, making, selling, promoting, etc., her own invention just because someone else (more quickly) filed for patent protection.

The risk, however, exists that the control against "taking" becomes a right to solely control a "thing" through copyright. This risk of a focus on property exists for the control of copies (through the reproduction or distribution right), for the control of derivative works (through the adaptation right) and even for the control by some moral rights. Although moral rights are less about controlling a thing and more about preserving a relation

30. The wording is applied to the originality of photographs (Art. 7 of the Directive 93/98/EEC) of databases (Art. 3(1) of Directive 96/9/EC) and of computer programs (Art. 1(3) of Directive 2009/24/EEC) and has been considered by the CJEU as the standard for originality of other types of works. *See,* Council Directive 93/98/EEC of 29 October 1993 harmonizing the term of protection of copyright and certain and related rights, Art. 7 (Oct. 29, 1993) Official Journal L 290, 24/11/1993, pp. 9-13; Directive 96/9/EC of the European Parliament and of the Council of 11 March 1996 on the legal protection of databases, Art. 3(1) (Mar. 11, 1996) Official Journal L 77, 27/3/1996, pp. 20-28; Directive 2009/24/EC of the European Parliament and of the Council of 23 April 2009 on the legal protection of computer programs, Art. 1(3) (Apr. 23, 2009) Official Journal L 111, 5/5/2009, pp. 16-22; Case C-5/08, Infopaq International A/S v. Danske Dagblades Forening (2009) ECLI:EU:C:2009:465.

31. The reference to "free and creative choices" is mentioned first in Case C-145/10 Eva Maria Painer v. Standard VerlagsGmbH, Axel Springer AG and others (2011) ECLI: EU:C:2011:798, para. 89ff.

32. *See,* Julien Cabay & Alain Strowel, *La nouveauté: un indice d'originalité à l'épreuve d'Internet* at 20 ans de nouveau droit d'auteur 17-68 (Julien Cabay, Véronique Delforge, Virginie Fossoul et Maxime Lambrecht eds., Anthemis, 2015).

between the author and her creation, there is a risk of focusing on some "thing" to preserve "as such" and without consideration for the person and her evolving nature, from youth to maturity, and even as a deceased one for the postmortem duration of copyright.

The two strands—control of a thing versus control against taking—can thus resurface within moral rights. The protection against taking from someone is clearly the focus of the right of attribution or right to be credited; the same with the *droit de divulgation* (right of disclosure) that preserves against any taking and making public a work that the author has not yet authorized for public disclosure. The integrity right, when it is subject to the proof of some prejudice to the author, is also a right that relies on the taking justification; when the integrity is preserved independently from the existence of any prejudice for the author's reputation, there is a stronger risk that the exercise of the rights aims to protect a thing as such. The same could be true of the withdrawal right that exists as a moral right in certain national laws.

13.4 TOWARD AN EU FRAMEWORK FOR MORAL RIGHTS IN LINE WITH THE LAW OF AUTONOMY

While there is a good case in favor of further harmonization of economic rights within the EU (thus beyond the *acquis communautaire*), it is less clear, if one takes into account the "realpolitik" of copyright, that harmonization of moral rights is a reasonable objective that should actively be pursued in Europe (there is no *acquis communautaire* on this particular issue). At an EU level, the topic of moral rights has been advocated by some academics, but a study commissioned by the European Commission at the end of the 1990s concluded, after consulting interested parties, that harmonization of moral rights should not be put on the agenda of the Commission.[33] However, around 30 years later, more convergence on the economic rights and

33. The outcome of this consultation and the responses sent to representative organizations was summarized as follows:

> The analysis of the answers to the questionnaire sent to some representative organisations … indicates that most interested parties are very cautious about any initiative which would be taken in order to harmonise the level of protection of moral rights in Europe. This attitude seems motivated by the fear that a compromise on the moral right issue, if reached at Community level, would jeopardise the high level of protection already enjoyed in some countries. Indeed, the harmonisation process could end up for instance with the adoption of waivable moral rights. Different rights holders organisations have pointed out that energy should preferably be devoted to other, more important problems.

(*see*, Marjut Salokannel, Alain Strowel & Estelle Derclaye, *Study Contract Concerning Moral Rights in the Context of the Exploitation of Works Through Digital Technology Final Report* (1999) Nr ETD/99/B5-3000/E°28). Among others, the following groups responded: Pyramide, European Federation of Journalists, European Federation of Newspaper Publishers, European Federation of Publishers, International Association of

dimensions of copyright has taken place through the case law of the Court of Justice of the EU. It has thus become more difficult to pursue the harmonization and/or to envisage a unification with an EU copyright title without any strong reference to moral rights.

Article 6bis of the BC constitutes the foundation for any European harmonization or unification in this field. This international standard could eventually be literally incorporated into an EU instrument, making it directly applicable and thus more effective. This incorporation into EU law would also allow the Court of Justice of the European Union (CJEU) to interpret and apply it in a way that could ensure more convergence between the Member States.

One little step further would be to add a provision on the characteristics of the attribution and integrity rights as defined in Article 6bis, for instance, making it clear that those two rights cannot be assigned but only waived, and only in special circumstances and in part. In order to find a reasonable compromise on this, a distinction could be made between the issue of inalienability and the extent to which those rights are waivable. The rights should be considered inalienable, but limited waivers should be valid. A clear and informed consent to the waivers would be required, and some safeguards could be added, although the consent should not necessarily be in writing. The exercise of moral rights by the legal successors of the creator would also require a special provision. This could be named a "Berne plus" solution.

A slightly more ambitious harmonization could be considered; many European (continental) countries already provide more and stronger rights than those of Article 6bis. One improvement would be to add the disclosure or divulgation right while defining the legal characteristics of the moral rights (in particular, their inalienability and partial waivability). This would constitute a "Berne plus-plus" proposal.

Beyond the recognition of the rights and their features, the statutory provisions on moral rights should define their limitations. Two kinds of limitations can be thought of. One would be to include some specific misuse provision in the case of moral rights. A second possible limitation which could be incorporated into law would be a codification of the balance of interests involved in moral rights infringement cases. In practice, in many cases involving a possible infringement of moral rights, the courts have conducted various balances of interests. This has been well demonstrated for the right of integrity by our regretted Dutch colleague, Antoon Quaedvlieg,

Audiovisual Writers and Directors (AIDAA)/Société des auteurs et compositeurs dramatiques (SACD), International Federation of the Phonographic Industry (IFPI), Federation Internationale des Aucteurs (FIA), Federation Internationale des Musiciens (FIM), European Writers' Congress, European Visual Artists, European Grouping of Societies of Authors and Composers (GESAC), Swedish Association of Journalists, Finnish Association of Journalists, Directors' and Producers' Society DPRS.

in his inaugural lecture at the Nijmegen (now Radboud) University.[34] For instance, the right of integrity has been relativized by the courts when the originality of the work is modest, when the work has a utilitarian function (as for works of applied arts), or when its intended use belongs to a purely industrial context. Why would it not be possible to codify some criteria of those balancing acts into the law in order to avoid a pure ad hoc balancing by the judges, something that is sometimes feared (in particular in some Anglo-American countries)?

A long time ago, Adolf Dietz proposed to introduce a provision that would include the parameters to be used for determining whether moral rights have been infringed.[35] Such a drafting solution could be acceptable, including maybe in the U.S. which has for a long time lived with another open provision based on noninfringement criteria, the fair use provision (Article 107 Copyright Act). Of course, we still have to decide which criteria have to be introduced into the statutory list. The nature and intensity of the modifications in case of the infringement of the integrity right could be included. The existence of an employment relationship could be another factor. How prejudicial the infringing act is to the honor or the reputation of the author could be another.

The proposal for harmonization should also allow a Member State to respect the EU standard without necessarily embedding all the protection aspects within copyright law (*see* section 13.1 above), although in this case, some guarantees ought to be thought of in order to ensure an equivalent protection outside copyright law.

In sum, there are advantages resulting from a possible harmonization, if not unification, of moral rights throughout Europe:

- nonwaivable moral rights could help to avoid that works are completely tailored to the standardized formats and requirements commonly applied to entertainment products;
- such rights recognized at EU level could increase the bargaining power of authors and performers when dealing with producers;
- in some cases (by reinforcing the position of creators), moral rights can contribute to the preservation of an authentic and lively marketplace for original, provocative and stimulating ideas, and the freedom of expression can thus benefit from those rights;
- new provisions on moral rights could bring the creator's perspective to the center of the copyright system, an objective that should be promoted;

34. Antoon Quaedvlieg, *Auteur en aantasting, werk en waardigheid* (Nijmegen, 2002).
35. Adolf Dietz, *Legal Principles of Moral Rights (Civil Law), General Report* at Le droit moral de l'auteur: The Moral Right of the Author 54ff. (ALAI, Antwerp Congress, Sep. 19-24, 1993).

- strengthening the moral interests of the authors could help to improve the "bad reputation" associated by a large public with IP and copyright that appear in the hands of big media companies;
- the EU legislation could become a model for third countries, helping to shape a better legal environment for creators of those countries, etc.

Other reasons for considering such a harmonization exist and it thus makes sense to think a little bit more about what should be included in a reasonable proposal for protecting the moral interests of the authors.

13.5 CONCLUDING REMARKS: DIGNITARY INTERESTS IN THE AGE OF GENERATIVE ARTIFICIAL INTELLIGENCE (GENAI) AND DIGITAL REPLICAS

Like other doctrines and rules of copyright, the validity and value of moral rights have continuously been put into question by new types of works and new processes and technologies. For example, the fact that movies are the result of many contributors has in practice prevented some coauthors on films from exercising their rights and has prompted some legislators to downsize the moral rights in the case of audiovisual productions. Similarly, moral rights do not fit well with the technical and utilitarian nature of computer programs, and there are some hesitations in certain countries as to whether software developers enjoy the same moral rights as other authors. Today, content can be mass-produced by GenAI, and the generated outputs relying on the training of machines with tons of data and myriads of protected works have prompted the latest great controversy and battleground over the rights of creators. Can a just and reasonable remuneration system be put in place and work, whether based on contracts around the exclusive rights of creators or on some compensation schemes defined by the law?

The displacement of human creators and the risks that they lose some streams of revenue is not the sole issue raised by the GenAI deployment in the creative sectors. As GenAI tools can be used to produce "digital replicas," in other words, to imitate the style and other distinctive features directly linked to the persons of authors and artists, including their voice and likeness, there is also a huge burgeoning debate on the dignitary or personal interests of creators.[36] Even in the U.S., some laws against digital replicas (and deepfakes) that clone voices, faces or body movements have been considered (or adopted in certain states such as New York and Louisiana). AI tools to generate those replicas can be used in many domains, including to

36. *See* Report of the U.S. Register of copyrights, Copyright and Artificial Intelligence. Part 1: Digital Replicas, Jul. 2024, 2-6, https://www.copyright.gov/ai/Copyright-and-Artificial-Intelligence-Part-1-Digital-Replicas-Report.pdf.

clone the works, the likeness or the performances of creators. The laws against the use of unauthorized digital replicas are not based on copyright (or on a related right): in the U.S., as underlined in a report on digital replicas by the Copyright Office, "copyright does not […] protect an individual's identity in itself, even when incorporated into a work of authorship."[37] In contrast, the author's rights approach makes it possible, thanks to the institution of moral rights, to protect an individual's identity in consideration of a work of authorship. Whether moral rights as such are the best instrument against digital replicas remains debatable, but at least the fundamental rights behind those rights (*see* the introduction above) that are part of the law of autonomy (as explained under section 13.3 above) could help to address some issues linked to the spread of digital replicas (other initiatives to reduce disinformation online are a good complement against deepfakes).[38] In any case, the moral rights of authors in relation to their copyrighted works are not as relevant to limit the abusive use of digital replicas as the moral rights of performers (as their performance in relation to which they enjoy similar moral rights usually involves some vocal or facial aspects). In the U.S., the (draft) laws against digital replicas aim to address issues of privacy, unfair competition, consumer protection and fraud. Some researchers in the U.S. claim that to address this issue, one should turn to trademark law instead of copyright and that moral rights are not the best solution.[39] The U.S. Copyright Office has admitted that the copying of an individual's identity is a topic of interest for artists, and in 2019 already, it prepared a report on the moral rights of attribution and integrity that recommended the adoption by the Congress of another legal solution: a federal right of publicity.[40] Adopting a right of publicity might allow to address the issue of digital replicas; it might even permit to protect an artistic style where a particular style is closely identified with an individual performer[41] (although an artistic style cannot be protected under copyright whether in the U.S. or elsewhere).

If one adopts the lenses of a European lawyer, the justification of a possible right of publicity to address the attribution and integrity issues linked to digital replicas is based on the fundamental rights to dignity and

---

37. *Ibid.*, 17.
38. *See* Alain Strowel & Jean De Meyere, *The Digital Services Act: Transparency as an Efficient Tool to Curb the Spread of Disinformation on Online Platforms?,* 14(1) Journal of Intellectual Property, Information Technology and Electronic Commerce Law 66-83 (2023) https://doi.org/10.4018/978-1-59140-932-8.ch013.
39. Derek E. Bambauer & Robert Woods, *AI, Artists, and Anti-Moral Rights (April 10, 2024)*, University of Florida Levin College of Law Research Paper No. 24-19, Available at SSRN: https://papers.ssrn.com/sol3/papers.cfm?abstract_id=4790497.
40. U.S. Copyright Office, Authors, Attribution, and Integrity: Examining Moral Rights in the United States 6 (2019), https://www.copyright.gov/policy/moralrights/full-report.pdf.
41. Report of the U.S. Register of copyrights, Copyright and Artificial Intelligence. Part 1: Digital Replicas, July 2024, 56.

privacy of creators[42] (already mentioned in the introductory part as the source of moral rights). This shows again that the claims of authorship and integrity are universal, although they can be embedded in plural legal expressions, depending on traditions and cultures.

42. The fact that a right of publicity (linked to privacy) is today advocated with renewed emphasis by the U.S. Copyright Office points in that direction (*see Ibid.*, 7).

Chapter 14

Toward an International Common Core of Exceptions and Limitations?

Raquel Xalabarder

Exceptions and Limitations (E&L) are a clear example of "pluralism" in international copyright. Like exclusive rights, E&L remain subject to the principle of national treatment and to *lex loci protectionis* (i.e., Article 5(2) Berne Convention (BC)). Unlike exclusive rights, however, E&L are rarely part of the "conventional minimum" achieved by international copyright instruments. As a general rule, international copyright treaties leave E&L for national laws; however, they include strong reminders of the importance of E&L and their inherent relationship with the exclusive rights (*see* section 14.1 below).

As a result of this plural scenario, acts of exploitation exempted (permitted by law) in one country may differ from those permitted in another country and, sometimes, even lead to the opposite solution (*see* section 14.2 below).

In addition, permitted uses under E&L face a common threat: their weakness in front of Technological Protection Measures (TPM) and contractual terms that may restrict and even prevent their enforcement. No universal consensus exists as to the very nature of E&L: whether they are public policy or, instead, remain subject to private ordering. This issue, too, may have different solutions under different national laws (*see* section 14.3 below).

E&L are an integral part of the exclusive rights granted to authors. National differences (regarding their existence and scope) create legal uncertainty and unpredictable results, reinforcing—unnecessarily—the role of licensing and ultimately trumping the very public interests that E&L are meant to safeguard. Excessive pluralism in E&L upsets the internal balance of copyright laws and ultimately delegitimizes the whole system.

This is also predictable within harmonized scenarios, such as the internal market of the European Union (EU). The EU copyright Directives have traditionally done very little to harmonize E&L. Nevertheless, the recently approved Directive on Copyright in the Digital Single Market[1] (CDSM Directive) may be seen as an inflection point toward a higher uniformity of E&L within the EU. After all, rights granted to authors cannot be properly enforced without also enforcing E&L to these rights—especially so, but not only in digital and online markets.

Thus, as we walk toward a more uniform, universal protection of exclusive rights under copyright, we should also aim at more uniform E&L at international level (*see* section 14.4 below).

14.1 E&L IN INTERNATIONAL COPYRIGHT TREATIES

Intellectual property (IP)—like any other property right—is limited. Within copyright, these limits are mainly secured through E&L,[2] which safeguard public policy objectives and often fundamental rights, such as freedom of expression, access to information, etc.

Over the years, international copyright treaties have done little to secure E&L.

Copyright and related rights treaties aim at securing protection of foreign authors at an international level—that is, beyond their "countries of origin" (ex Article 4 of the Berne Convention). This is achieved by combining a "minimum of rights" granted to all Union authors in Union countries other than their countries of origin with the application of the national law of the country of protection (*lex loci protectionis*—ex Article 5(2) of the Berne Convention). This approach has been followed by all international instruments for the protection of copyright and related rights.

There is no "minimum of E&L" secured by international treaties. With the notable exceptions of Article 10(1) of the Berne Convention and the 2013 Marrakesh Treaty,[3] E&L are not uniform under international copyright instruments and remain a matter of plural national laws. Nevertheless,

1. Directive (EU) 2019/790 of the European Parliament and of the Council of 17 April 2019 on copyright and related rights in the Digital Single Market and amending Directives 96/9/EC and 2001/29/EC (Apr. 17, 2019) Official Journal L 130, 17.5.2019, pp. 92-125.
2. Other "internal" limits may be found in the very definition of work (not everything is protected under copyright), the scope of exclusive rights and, of course, in the term of protection.
3. Marrakesh Treaty to Facilitate Access to Published Works for Persons Who Are Blind, Visually Impaired or Otherwise Print Disabled (Jun. 27, 2013), UNTS I-54134.

international treaties do include some strong reminders of the importance of E&L and their inherent relationship with exclusive rights.

14.1.1 Berne Convention

The Berne Convention[4] provides for several E&L, either for free or subject to equitable remuneration.

Exceptions provided for free include the following: Article 2bis(2) regarding public speeches; Article 10(1) regarding quotations; Article 10(2) for teaching purposes; Article 10bis(1) for press uses; Article 10bis(2) for the reporting of current events; and Article 11bis(3) regarding ephemeral recordings by broadcasting organizations.

Subject to equitable remuneration, limitations are provided for in Article 13(1) regarding the recording of musical works and Article 11bis(2) regarding broadcasting and cable retransmission.

In addition, two other provisions are fundamental to complete the picture of exempted uses under the Berne Convention. One of them is expressly enshrined in Article 9(2) of the Berne Convention: the so-called three-step test (adopted at the Stockholm Conference 1967). The other one is to be found in the documents of the Brussels Conference (1948): the "Minor Reservations" doctrine. Both provisions have something in common: they resulted from failed attempts to secure within the Berne Convention a list of exceptions to the newly introduced rights of reproduction and public performance, respectively.

14.1.1.1 Article 10(1) of the Berne Convention: Quotations

According to Article 10(1) BC:

> It shall be permissible to make quotations from a work which has already been lawfully available to the public, provided that their making is compatible with fair practice, and their extent does not exceed that justified by the purpose, including quotations from newspaper articles and periodicals in the form of press summaries.

Quotations were first introduced in the 1928 Rome Act, with the following language:

> analyses or short textual quotations of published literary works for the purposes of criticism, polemical discussion or teaching.

The current language, revised at the Stockholm Conference (1967), is not restricted to any specific uses because it was concluded that no list could ever hope to be exhaustive.

4. Berne Convention for the Protection of Literary and Artistic Works (Sep. 9, 1886), S. Treaty Doc. No. 99-27.

Silence regarding the affected rights must be read in favor of any acts of exploitation, including translations.[5]

The quotation exception applies to all kinds of works (provided they have been "lawfully made available to the public"), without any limitation as to the amount that may be quoted. Of course, the term "quotation" itself already suggests some restriction ("that the thing quoted is a part of a greater whole"),[6] but it was preferred to leave the length of the quotation as a matter to be determined in *casu*, "to the extent justified by the purpose."[7] Notice, also, that the quotation exception is neither restricted in terms of beneficiaries nor of technology.

Article 10(1) of the Berne Convention does not require remuneration, but nothing prevents Member States from doing so—which "should more readily justify the requirement of compatibility with fair practice than would a free use."[8]

Quotations are allowed under Article 10(1) of the Berne Convention to the extent that they are compatible with fair practice.[9] Accordingly, its assessment requires taking into account not only the copyright interests involved in the exempted use but also any other interests, including general public benefits, in terms of culture and society, market efficiency, etc.

The same conclusion would result under the three-step test[10] since it is comparable to the standard rule of being "compatible with fair practice."[11] Furthermore, being a mandatory limitation, compliance with the three-step

5. *See* Sam Ricketson. *WIPO Study on Limitations and Exceptions of Copyright and Related Rights in the Digital Environment* 12 (WIPO, 2003), https://www.wipo.int/edocs/mdocs/copyright/en/sccr_9/sccr_9_7.pdf (accessed Jun. 1, 2019)*; See also* Sam Ricketson & Jane C. Ginsburg, *The Berne Convention for the Protection of Literary and Artistic Works: 1886-1986,* §13.83-87 (2nd ed., Oxford University Press, 2006). Aligned with this conclusion *see*, Tunis Model Law on Copyright (July-August 1976), s. 7 expressly allows (under all the listed exceptions) the use of works "*either in the original language or in translation.*"
6. *See* Ricketson (n. 5), 12.
7. *Ibid. See* Ricketson & Ginsburg (n. 5), §13.42.
8. *See* Ricketson & Ginsburg (n. 5) 786, §13.41.
9. This reference was meant to imply that "the use in question can only be accepted after an objective appreciation" *see* Ricketson & Ginsburg (n. 5), §13.41.
10. Within a strictly Berne Convention perspective, Art. 10(1) of the Berne Convention remains unaffected by the original three-step test in Art. 9(2) of the Berne Convention. Under the WCT, compliance with the *three-step test* seems to be imposed by Art. 10(2) WCT "*when applying the Berne Convention*"; Nevertheless, it was expressly agreed that "Article 10(2) neither reduces nor extends the scope of applicability of the limitations and exceptions permitted by the Berne Convention."
11. *See* Ricketson & Ginsburg (n. 5), §13.110. Like the reference to "fair practice," the three-step test is a tool meant to ensure a correct balance between the private and public interests involved in each case. *See* also Declaration: A Balanced Interpretation of the Three-step test in Copyright Law; Available at: https://www.ip.mpg.de/en/research/research-news/a-balanced-interpretation-of-the-three-step-test-in-copyright-law.html.

test could never result in a restriction of the scope exempted under Article 10(1) of the Berne Convention or in a derogation of its mandatory nature.

Yet, the most interesting feature of Article 10(1) of the Berne Convention is its mandatory nature.

As acknowledged by Ricketson, Article 10(1) of the Berne Convention is:

> the one Berne exception that comes closest to embodying a "user right" to make quotations.[12]

Bently and Aplin refer to it as "mandatory fair use," explaining that it was consciously adopted in Stockholm, after formal rejection of a proposal to make it "optional," like other E&L.[13]

Being an imperative restriction to the authors' rights, Member States cannot reduce its extent in favor of Union authors and works.[14] As Ricketson explains:

> it will be contrary to the Convention for national legislation to provide protection in a case where this has been specifically prohibited. In the same way that there is a principle of minimum of protection that operates under article 19 in favor of Union authors, so (it can be argued) there is a corresponding principle of maximum protection to be implied in those few cases where the Convention limits or excludes protection.[15]

Ficsor prefers another explanation: the compulsory nature of Article 10(1) of the Berne Convention is not so much an exception to the principle of minimum protection granted under the Berne Convention but rather:

> it follows from a basic human freedom—the freedom of speech and criticism—that is justified and necessary to allow free quotations in appropriate cases.[16]

---

12. *See*Ricketson & Ginsburg (n. 5), §13.41.
13. *See* Lionel Bently &Tanya Aplin, *Whatever Became og Global, Mandatory, Fair Use? A Case Study in Dysfunctional Pluralism*, University of Cambridge Faculty of Law Research Paper No. 34/2018, https://ssrn.com/abstract=3119041 (accessed Jun. 1, 2019); *See also* Tanya Aplin & Lionel Bently, *Displacing the Dominance of the Three-Step Test: The Role of Global, Mandatory Fair Use*, University of Cambridge Faculty of Law Research Paper No. 33/2018, https://ssrn.com/abstract=3119056 (accessed Jun. 1, 2019).
14. As with all other Berne Convention provisions, its effectiveness is restricted to works claiming protection under the Convention (*ex* Art. 5.1 of the Berne Convention: in countries of the Union other than the country of origin). Any national quotation exception that is more restrictive than Art. 10(1) of the Berne Convention would only be applicable to purely domestic scenarios of copyright protection. Instead, any domestic quotation exception broader in scope than what is exempted under Art. 10(1) Berne Convention should still apply to foreign works and authors, as a result from the Berne Convention principle of national treatment (Berne Convention, Art. 5(1)).
15. *See* Ricketson & Ginsburg (n. 5), §§6.110-111.
16. *See* Mihály Ficsor, *The Law of Copyright and I Internet, The 1996 WIPO Treaties, Their Interpretation and Implementation* §5.12 (Oxford University Press, 2002).

Be it as an internal restriction of the minimum of protection granted by the Berne Convention or as an external obligation (*via* human rights protection), Berne Union States are obliged—when granting protection to foreign Union nationals and their works under the Berne Convention—to allow quotations, also online, at least with the scope permitted in Article 10(1) of the Berne Convention and regardless of the scope of the quotation limitation in their national laws.

14.1.1.2 Article 10(2) of the Berne Convention: Illustration for Teaching

Instead, most other E&L in the Berne Convention are not mandatory for Union States. Article 10(2) may serve as an example.

The teaching exception in the Berne Convention may be traced back to its very origins. Article 8 of the Berne Act of 1886 reserved to national legislation:

> the liberty of extracting portions from literary or artistic works for use in publications destined for educational or scientific purposes, or for chrestomathies.

The Brussels Act of 1948 modified the matter reserved to national law under Article 10(2) as:

> the right to include excerpts from literary or artistic works in educational or scientific publications.

The 1976 Stockholm Revision provided its current wording.[17] According to Article 10(2):

> It shall be a matter for legislation in the countries of the Union, and for special agreements existing or to be concluded between them, to permit the utilization, to the extent justified by the purpose, of literary or artistic works by way of illustration in publications, broadcasts or sound or visual recordings for teaching, provided such utilization is compatible with fair practice.

It is an open, flexible and technology-neutral exception that leads us to consider the specificities (nature and amount of work, technology, purposes, institution) of each scenario in order to find in *casu* the right balance between the public interest (education) and that of the author.

---

17. The proposal of a minor amendment (which only affected the English text) to replace "excerpts" with "borrowings" (because it was thought to correspond better to the French text "*émprunts*") opened an important debate that resulted in current Art. 10(2); *see* WIPO, *Reports on the Work of the Five Main Committees of the Intellectual Property Conference of Stockholm 1967,* §93-94 (WIPO Publication 309(E), 1976).

Nothing is said in Article 10(2) of the Berne Convention as to remuneration. Member States are free to implement it either as a free exception, as a remunerated limitation, or as a combination of both.

Unlike the minimum mandatory scope of Article 10(1) of the Berne Convention, Article 10(2) simply sets the outer limits within which an exception for teaching purposes may be carried out by national laws.[18] In short, the exempted use of works for teaching purposes remains a matter of pluralism.

14.1.1.3 The Doctrine of "Minor Reservations" (Brussels, 1948)

A formal declaration made in the Final Report of the Brussels Conference states that minor reservations (E&L) to the right of public performance (communication to the public) existing in national laws are in conformity with the Berne Convention:[19]

> making an express mention of the possibility available to national legislation to make what are commonly called minor reservations … . The Delegates of … have all mentioned these limited exemptions allowed for religious ceremonies, military bands and the needs of child and adult education.[20]

In addition, the Brussels Conference noted that these minor reservations should have "a restricted character."[21]

Subsequently, the Stockholm Conference endorsed the validity of the "Minor Reservations" doctrine under the Berne Convention[22] and even conveyed a general scope applicable to other exploitation rights in addition to public performance. According to Article 31(2) of the Vienna Convention on the Law of Treaties of 1969,[23] the "Minor Reservations" doctrine forms part of the context which must inform the interpretation of the Berne Convention.

18. *See* Ricketson & Ginsburg (n. 5), 791, §13.45.
19. It was initially intended as a general provision inserted in the Convention to allow Member States to retain any limitations existing in their national laws, but it was finally rejected by fear that such a provision would "positively incite" those States which had not such exceptions to incorporate them in their laws; *See* Ricketson (n. 5), 34-37. *See* also Ricketson & Ginsburg (n. 5), §13.79.
20. *See* WIPO, *Documents for the Conference of Brussels 1948,* 100 (1951), as reported by Ricketson (n. 5), 34; *See also* Ricketson & Ginsburg (n. 5), §13.80.
21. *See* Ricketson (n. 5), 35; *See* also Ricketson & Ginsburg (n. 5), §13.80.
22. *See* Ricketson & Ginsburg (n. 5), §13.81.
23. Vienna Convention on the Law of Treaties (May 23, 1969), 1155 UNTS 331.

14.1.1.4 Article 9(2) of the Berne Convention: The "Original" Three-Step Test

The so-called three-step test in Article 9(2) of the Berne Convention sets three standard criteria to establish whether national exceptions or limitations to the reproduction right are in conformity with the Berne Convention:

> It shall be a matter for legislation in the countries of the Union to permit the reproduction of such works in certain special cases, provided that such reproduction does not conflict with a normal exploitation of the work and does not unreasonably prejudice the legitimate interests of the author.

The three-step test was introduced at the Stockholm Conference (1967) on account of the newly recognized right of reproduction[24] (Article 9(1) of the Berne Convention). As it happened in Brussels, it was feared that an exhaustive list of limitations to the reproduction right would be very long and always "inadequate, because it could never cover all the special cases existing in national legislation" and might "encourage the adoption of all the exceptions allowed and abolish the right or remuneration."[25]

The test was designed as an enabling tool to guide legislators in Member States, through a cumulative succession of steps, when drafting statutory E&L in national laws.

Article 9(2) of the Berne Convention has now been displaced by subsequent versions of the three-step with subtly revised language that will be examined later.

14.1.2 Rome Convention

The Rome Convention somehow mimics—for performers and phonogram producers—the same E&L provided for authors in the Berne Convention.

Article15(1) of the Rome Convention allows Member States to introduce or maintain national E&L for specific purposes, such as: (1) private use; (2) the reporting of current events; (3) ephemeral fixation by broadcasting organizations, as well as; (4) use for teaching purposes or scientific research.[26]

Additionally, Article 15(2) of the Rome Convention permits the application of the national limitations and exceptions envisaged for copyright (authors' rights):

24. Translation rights must be also implied under Art. 9(2) of the Berne Convention, as well as under other exceptions. *See* Ricketson (n. 5), 37-39. *See also* Ricketson & Ginsburg (n. 5), §§13.83-87.
25. *See* Ricketson & Ginsburg (n. 5), §13.07.
26. In general, *see* Ricketson & Ginsburg (n. 5), §§19.11-16.

> Irrespective of paragraph 1 of this Article, any Contracting State may, in its domestic laws and regulations, provide for the same kinds of limitations with regard to the protection of performers, producers of phonograms and broadcasting organizations, as it provides for, in its domestic laws and regulations, in connection with the protection of copyright in literary and artistic works. However, compulsory licenses may be provided for only to the extent to which they are compatible with this Convention.

This means that despite no mandatory quotation exception, the general clause in Article 15(2) allows Union States to envisage a quotation exception also for neighboring rights.

14.1.3 Tunis Model Copyright Law of 1976

World Intellectual Property Organization's (WIPO's) Tunis Model Law on Copyright for Developing Countries (1976) includes a rather extensive list of E&L, accompanied by commentaries to help interpret them. Under section 7, entitled "Fair use," several uses of lawfully published works are allowed "either in the original language or in translation," such as (i)(a) for the user's own personal and private use, (i)(b) for quotations, (i)(c) by way of illustration for teaching purposes.

Despite being a non-binding "Model Law," several national laws have mirrored its provisions.

14.1.4 TRIPS (1994), WCT/WPPT (1996)

Leaving aside the provisions regarding the three-step test (*see* below), neither the Agreement on Trade-Related Aspects of Intellectual Property Rights (TRIPS)[27] nor the WIPO Copyright Treaty (WCT) (1996)[28] or WIPO Performances and Phonograms Treaty (WPPT) (1996)[29] formulate any specific E&L.

However, both instruments provide strong reminders of the importance of E&L for the protection of copyright. While Article 7 TRIPS obliges States to enforce IP law in a manner "conducive to social and economic welfare and to a balance of rights and obligations," the WCT expressly recognizes in its Preamble:

---

27. Agreement on Trade-Related Aspects of Intellectual Property Rights (Apr. 15, 1994), 1869 UNTS 299 (hereinafter "TRIPS").
28. WIPO Copyright Treaty (Dec. 20, 1996), TRT/WCT/001 (hereinafter "WCT").
29. WIPO Performances and Phonograms Treaty (Dec. 20, 1996), TRT/WPPT/001 (hereinafter "WPPT").

> the need to maintain a balance between the rights of authors and the larger public interest, particularly education, research and access to information, as reflected in the Berne Convention.

14.1.5 The New Three-Step Tests: TRIPS, WCT/WPPT, InfoSoc Directive

At least eight different versions of the so-called three-step test may be found today in four different international treaties.[30] The "original" three-step-test in Article 9(2) BC was later reenacted in Article 13 TRIPS (as well as in Articles 17, 20(2), 30 TRIPS), in Article 10 WCT and Article 16 WPPT, and within the EU, most notably in Article 5.5 Information Society Directive (Infosoc Directive).[31] Each reenactment comes with slight, yet substantial, language modifications, which have been described by some as "the dangerous mutations of the three-step test."[32] Let us examine them.

Article 13 of the TRIPS Agreement reinforced the scope of the Berne Convention test by incorporating slightly modified language[33] applicable to all exclusive rights listed in the Berne Convention and the TRIPS (i.e., not restricted to reproduction):

> Members *shall confine* limitations or exceptions to exclusive rights to certain special cases which do not conflict with a normal exploitation of the work and do not unreasonably prejudice the legitimate interests of the rightholder.

Similarly, the 1996 WCT also extended the Berne Convention three-step test to all rights and all works.[34]

---

30. For a deeper analysis, *see* Andrew Christie & Robin Wright, *A Comparative Analysis of the Three-Step Tests in International Treaties,* 45 International Review of Intellectual Property and Competition Law 409-433 (2014) https://doi.org/10.1007/s40319-014-0202-2.
31. Directive 2001/29/EC of the European Parliament and of the Council, of 22 May 2001, on the harmonization of certain aspects of copyright and related rights in the information society (May 22, 2001) Official Journal L 167, 22/06/2001, pp. 10-19 (hereinafter "InfoSoc Directive").
32. *See* Christophe Geiger, *From Berne to National Law, via the Copyright Directive: The Dangerous Mutations of the Three-Step Test,* 12 European Intellectual Property Review 486 (2007).
33. Reference to the "rightholder" instead of the "author"; the mandatory character ("shall confine") rather than a standard proviso; and ultimately, the fact that, unlike the Berne Convention, the TRIPS Agreement is "enforceable." For a detailed analysis of Art.13 of the TRIPS Agreement and its relation with the Berne Convention, *see* Ricketson & Ginsburg (n. 5), §§13.94-115.
34. Specifically, Art. 10(1) of the WCT extended the language of Art. 9(2) of the Berne Convention to the new granted rights of distribution and rental, communication to the public and making available. The WPPT did the same for performances and phonograms.

Article 10(1) of the WCT enables national legislators to enact E&L:[35]

> Contracting Parties *may, in their national legislation, provide* for limitations of or exceptions to the rights granted to authors of literary and artistic works under this Treaty in certain special cases that do not conflict with a normal exploitation of the work and do not unreasonably prejudice the legitimate interests of the author.

Article 10(2) of the WCT, instead, presents a different flavor of the test:

> Contracting Parties shall, when applying the Berne Convention, confine any limitations of or exceptions to rights provided for therein to certain special cases that do not conflict with a normal exploitation of the work and do not unreasonably prejudice the legitimate interests of the author.

According to the Agreed Statement, "… Article 10(2) neither reduces nor extends the scope of applicability of the limitations and exceptions permitted by the Berne Convention."[36] Yet, its language is closer to Article 13 TRIPS in the sense that instead of an enabling clause (as in Article 9(2) BC and Article 10(1) WCT), they both introduce a "restrictive interpretation" for E&L in national laws.

Similarly, the Article 5.5 EU Directive on Copyright in the InfoSoc Directive formally subjects the list of E&L to a restrictive interpretation rule:

> The E&L provided for in paragraphs 1, 2, 3 and 4 shall only be applied in certain special cases which do not conflict with a normal exploitation of the work or other subject-matter and do not unreasonably prejudice the legitimate interests of the rightholder.

Interestingly, the three-step test had already been somehow introduced into EU *acquis* by two previous Directives: Article 6(3) of the Computer Programs Directive (CPD) (1991)[37] and Article 6(3) of the Database Directive (1996).[38] Both provisions presented the three-step-test as a hermeneutical rule that only includes the last two steps in a disjunctive manner:

> the provisions of this Article may not be interpreted in such a way as to allow its application to be used in a manner which unreasonably

35. *See* Agreed Statement Concerning Art. 10(1) of the WIPO Copyright Treaty, clarifying that such limitations and exceptions may be extended and devised for digital uses and environments.
36. *See* Agreed Statement Concerning Art. 10(2) of the WIPO Copyright Treaty.
37. Directive 2009/24/EC of the European Parliament and of the Council of 23 April 2009 on the legal protection of computer programs (Apr. 23, 2009) Official Journal L 111, 5/5/2009, pp. 16-22—which repealed, replaced and codified the original Directive 91/250/EEC of 14 May 1991.
38. Directive 96/9/EC of the European Parliament and of the Council of 11 March 1996 on the legal protection of databases (Mar. 11, 1996) Official Journal L 77, 27/3/1996, pp. 20-28.

prejudices the rightholder's legitimate interests or conflicts with a normal exploitation of the computer program/database.

In a nutshell, in Ricketson's words:

> originally a test of limited application under Berne, it has now been adopted as a general template for limitations and exceptions under the TRIPS Agreement, the WCT and WPPT. This has been more by accident than by design … .[39]

Over the years, several academic proposals have offered different and alternative readings of the test. Some scholars have proposed a backward reading, where the third step is assessed first and the second and first become irrelevant,[40] while others support an overall, holistic reading of the test, so as to avoid merely "restrictive" interpretations of E&L and to restore its flexible nature as originally designed in Article 9.2 of the Berne Convention.[41] Instead, the test may also be read as conveying a maximum of permitted uses as a "maximalist exception" that operates as a safety net permitting any acts that satisfy the test, even though there is no specific statutory exception for that use.[42] Some academics even propose a reverse reading of the three-step test to assess the full scope of copyright granted to authors: the scope of exclusive rights granted to authors is what the three-step test does not permit (hence, the test as a "positivized" film).[43] And last but not least, at an EU level, the three-steps have also been presented as factors in a "fair use" tool to be used by national courts and legislators.[44] The interpretation and enforcement of the three-step test and of any E&L—remains in the hands of

39. *See,* Ricketson (n. 5), 65.
40. *See,* Christophe Geiger, *Implementing an International Instrument for Interpreting Copyright Limitations and Exceptions,* 40 International Review of Intellectual Property and Competition Law 627 (2009).
41. *See, Declaration: A Balanced Interpretation of the Three-Step Test in Copyright Law,* http://www.ip.mpg.de/ww/en/pub/news/declaration_on_the_three_step_.cfm (accessed Aug. 1, 2009). In fact, some domestic courts are already applying the three-step test as a hermeneutic mechanism to "close" the copyright system and help compensate the lack of flexibility within it (perhaps more acute in *droit d'auteur* than in copyright systems), sometimes resulting in an "extensive" interpretation of the applicable exception.
42. *See* Andrew Christie, *Maximising Permissible Exceptions to Intellectual Property Rights at The Structure of Intellectual Property Law The Structure of Intellectual Property Law: Can One Size Fit All?* 121-135 (Annette Kur & Vytautas Mizaras eds., Edward Elgar, 2011).
43. *See* Daniel Gervais, *(Re)structuring Copyright: A Comprehensive Path to International Copyright Reform* (Edward Elgar, 2017).
44. Martin Senftleben, *The International Three-Step Test: A Model Provision for EC Fair Use Legislation,* 1 Journal of Intellectual Property, Information Technology and Electronic Commerce Law 67, para. 1 (2010); *See also* Christophe Geiger, Daniel Gervais & Martin Senftleben, *The Three-Step Test Revisited: How to Use the Test's Flexibility in National Copyright Law,* 29 American University International Law Review 581 (2014) https://doi.org/10.2139/ssrn.2356619.

national courts.[45] Only time and national courts will tell what the effects of these "accidental" three-step test templates for the international uniformization of E&L will be. Nevertheless, either as an enabling rule to guide national legislators when drafting E&L or as a hermeneutical rule when interpreting E&L as applied to specific cases, there is no doubt that the test has become a universal rule capable of bringing plural national laws closer.

14.1.6 The Marrakesh Treaty for the Visually Impaired (2013)

The Marrakesh Treaty to Facilitate Access to Published Works for Persons Who Are Blind, Visually Impaired, or Otherwise Print Disabled was adopted by the WIPO Member States on June 27, 2013.[46] The Treaty obliges Contracting Parties to provide limitations or exceptions to copyright in order to allow the making and obtaining of accessible format copies (AFC) of works to be used by persons with a print disability and the exchange across borders of lawfully obtained AFC. Contracting Parties are free to implement these two obligations according to their own legal systems and practices.

The Marrakesh Treaty is a singular instrument. First, it is the only international treaty that provides exclusively for mandatory exceptions or limitations rather than providing for minimal exclusive rights. Second, this exception or limitation is mandatory for contracting parties. And third, the Treaty formally overcomes the very principle of territoriality (ex Article 5.2 BC) when permitting that an AFC lawfully obtained in one country may be "exchanged" (exported/imported) to another contracting country. Only time will tell if this Treaty remains a singularity or, instead, the turning point in the manner that international instruments address E&L. So far attempts to continue expanding mandatory E&L through international instruments have not brought any significant results.[47]

The EU played an active role in the negotiation of the Marrakesh Treaty and signed it on April 30, 2014. Its implementation was done by means of

45. *See*, the WTO Panel Report, United States—Section 110(5) of the Copyright Act (2000), https://www.wto.org/english/tratop_e/dispu_e/1234da.pdf (accessed Jun. 1, 2019); The WTO Report may have clarified the terms of reference but did not make the three-step test more predictable, since it is not an authoritative interpretation of the test in the Berne Convention or WCT/WPPT; *See* Jane Ginsburg. *Toward Supranational Copyright Law? The WTO Panel Decision and the "Three-Step Test,"* 187 Revue Internationale du Droit d' Auteur 16 (2001) https://doi.org/10.2139/ssrn.253867.

46. There is no requirement to be a member of any other international copyright treaty to join the Treaty.

47. Since 2009, exceptions and limitations has been an item in the standing agenda of the WIPO's Standing Committee on Copyright and Related Rights (SCCR); *See* https://www.wipo.int/copyright/en/limitations/ (accessed Dec. 1, 2024).

two instruments:[48] a Directive (to introduce the mandatory exception and allow exchange of AFC within the internal market) [Marrakesh Directive] and a Regulation (to govern the exchange of AFC beyond the EU market) [Marrakesh Regulation]. Both instruments must be read together (Recital 2 of the Directive).

Perfectly compatible with the Marrakesh Treaty, the EU legislator made a couple of important choices that are binding for EU Member States when implementing the Directive: to exclude any prior checking of commercial availability before permitting the making and dissemination of AFC and to prohibit imposing this or any additional requirements to allow for the making or exchanging of AFC. Beyond that, EU Member States are free to decide whether (or not) to require compensation for the making of AFC within some harmonized conditions.[49]

14.2 E&L REMAIN A MATTER FOR NATIONAL LAWS AND NATIONAL COURTS

Having seen how international instruments deal with E&L, it can be concluded that E&L remain a matter for national laws. And this may not be

48. Directive (EU) 2017/1564 of the European Parliament and of the Council of 13 September 2017 on certain permitted uses of certain works and other subject matter protected by copyright and related rights for the benefit of persons who are blind, visually impaired or otherwise print-disabled and amending Directive 2001/29/EC on the harmonisation of certain aspects of copyright and related rights in the information society (Sep. 13, 2017) Official Journal L 242, 20/09/2017, pp. 6-13; Regulation (EU) 2017/1563 of the European Parliament and of the Council of 13 September 2017 on the cross-border exchange between the Union and third countries of accessible format copies of certain works and other subject matter protected by copyright and related rights for the benefit of persons who are blind, visually impaired or otherwise print-disabled (Sep. 13, 2017) Official Journal L 242, 20/09/2017, pp. 1-5.
49. Compensation (if required by a Member State) can only be imposed on authorized entities in that country (no compensation should be required for AFC done by beneficiary persons or for AFC "imported" from other countries). Recital (14) of the Directive specifically refers to the criteria to be taken into account to establish the amount of compensation and mandates that no payment should be required when the harm to a rightholder is minimal. The existence of diverging compensations across Member States have never been considered an obstacle to the functioning of the internal market. For instance, differences regarding the compensation for private copying which have been endorsed by the CJEU: *see* Case C-468/08 Commission of the European Communities v. French Republic (2009) ECLI:EU:C:2009:602; Case C-435/12 ACI Adam BV and Others v. Stichting de Thuiskopie and Stichting Onderhandelingen Thuiskopie vergoeding (2014) ECLI: EU:C:2014:254; Joined Cases C-457/11 to C-460/11 Verwertungsgesellschaft Wort (VG Wort) v. Kyocera and Others (C-457/11) and Canon Deutschland GmbH (C-458/11) and Fujitsu Technology Solutions GmbH (C-459/11) and Hewlett-Packard GmbH (C-460/11) v. Verwertungsgesellschaft Wort (VG Wort) (2013) ECLI:EU:C:2013:426; Case C-463/12 Copydan Båndkopi v. Nokia Danmark A/S (2015) ECLI:EU:C:2015:144; Case C-572/13 Hewlett-Packard Belgium SPRL v. Reprobel SCRL (2015) ECLI:EU:C:2015:750.

a bad outcome. National E&L result from a myriad of cultural, economic, market and legal inputs. E&L respond not only to national legal traditions (be it detailed statutory lists, like in the EU, or open fair use defenses, like in the United States of America) but also to specific language and market conditions of each country. After having examined the main differences in the copyright systems in the EU and the USA (*see* section 14.2.1 below), we will present some examples of how different national laws and courts find different solutions to the same problems, especially in digital and online contexts (*see* section 14.2.2 below).

14.2.1 E&L in EU *Acquis*

In the EU, the harmonization of E&L to copyright and related rights has traditionally been done by means of exhaustive lists (*numerus clausus*), which are optional for implementation by Member States; the lists in Article 5.2 and Article 5.3 InfoSoc Directive are the best examples. They include E&L for private copying, reprography, uses in libraries, museums and archives, teaching and research purposes, uses by people with a disability, quotations, public security or official proceedings, public speeches, incidental inclusion, art catalogues, religious celebrations, parody, works located permanently in public places, library uses, etc. Some of these permitted uses are for free; others require compensation, although Member States may choose to require compensation for any of them, especially so as to comply with the three-step test (Article 5.5 InfoSoc Directive).

Before that, the Databases Directive had somehow "harmonized" several E&L[50] by means of an optional list that included reproduction for private use (only of non-electronic databases), uses for teaching or scientific purposes, public security or administrative or judicial procedures, or any other limitations set for "works."

Mandatory exceptions are far less common in the EU *acquis*. According to the CPD, the lawful acquirer of a computer program is allowed to use it for the intended purposes, as well as to make a backup copy and to observe, study and test the functioning of the program; additionally, decompilation (for purposes of achieving interoperability with another program) is also permitted; these E&L were mandatory exceptions imposed uniformly to all

50. Also the Rental and Lending Directive provided for a list of optional E&L to the related rights granted for by it, such as private use, reporting of current events, ephemeral fixations by broadcasting organizations, teaching and research purposes … and any other E&L that may be set for the use of copyrighted works, always subject to compliance with the three-step test; *See* Directive 2006/115/EC of the European Parliament and of the Council of 12 December 2006 on rental right and lending right and on certain rights related to copyright in the field of intellectual property—which repealed and codified Directive Council Directive 92/100/EEC of 19 November 1992 (Dec. 12, 2006) Official Journal L 376, 27/12/2006, pp. 28-35.

Member States. Beyond computer programs, only three general mandatory E&L existed in the EU *acquis:* (1) the temporary copies exception (Article 5.1 InfoSoc Directive); (2) the orphan works exception (Directive 2012/28/EU)[51] and; (3) the exception for thevisually impaired Marrakesh Treaty (Directive 2017/1564).[52]

Mandatory exceptions have considerably increased with the recent "CDSM Directive",[53] which introduced a few mandatory E&L for text- and data- mining (TDM) (Article 3), digital and online teaching (Article 5), preservation of cultural heritage (Article 6) and, when not covered by a collective license, out-of-commerce works (Article 8.2). The CDSM may be the dawn of a new trend in the EU *acquis*, but it certainly confirms the need for a more holistic harmonization of E&L—in addition to harmonizing exclusive rights—in order to build the internal market (at least, the digital market).[54]

This need had already been identified by the Court of Justice of the European Union (CJEU), which used the preliminary rulings submitted by national courts as an opportunity to further harmonize E&L beyond the EU Directives.

The CJEU fully acknowledged the principle of strict interpretation of E&L (as set in the three-step test) but consistently denied it as the only hermeneutical criterion.[55] Instead, the CJEU has turned to several other hermeneutical criteria for the interpretation and application of E&L in national laws. Namely, the CJEU has applied:

- The principle of proportionality, to safeguard *a "fair balance"* between copyright and other fundamental rights and public interests, such as the freedom of expression and information.[56]

---

51. Directive 2012/28/EU of the European Parliament and of the Council of 25 October 2012 on certain permitted uses of orphan works (Oct. 25, 2012) Official Journal L 299, 27/10/2012, pp. 5-12.
52. *See* above (n. 48).
53. Directive 2019/790/EU.
54. The existence of diverging national law solutions, a diversity of licensing practices—or insufficient licensing—across Europe, and the high transaction costs involved in the clearing of rights cause legal uncertainty, market fragmentation and have a negative impact on the internal market.
55. *See,* for instance, Joined Cases C-403/08 and C-429/08 Football Association Premier League Ltd and Others v. QC Leisure and Others (C-403/08) and Karen Murphy v. Media Protection Services Ltd (C-429/08) (2011) ECLI:EU:C:2011:631, paras. 162-163; Case C-201/13 Johan Deckmyn and Vrijheidsfonds VZW v. Helena Vandersteen and Others (2014) ECLI:EU:C:2014:2132, paras. 22-23.
56. *See,* Case C-275/06 Productores de Música de España (Promusicae) v. Telefónica de España SAU (2008) ECLI:EU:C:2008:54; Case C-360/10 SABAM v. Netlog (2012) ECLI:EU:C:2012:85; Case C-70/10 Scarlet Extended SA v. Société belge des auteurs, compositeurs et éditeurs SCRL (SABAM) (2011) ECLI:EU:C:2011:771; Case C-283/11 Sky Österreich GmbH v. Österreichischer Rundfunk (2013) ECLI:EU:C:2013:28; Case

- The principle of interpretation in conformity, to require interpreting EU *acquis* and national laws "in the light of the applicable rules of international law, and in particular those set forth in the Berne Convention"[57] (i.e., Article 10(1) of the Berne Convention); as a result, any domestic provision which is contrary to international obligations or to EU law should be set aside.[58]
- The teleological/functional principle to "enable the effectiveness of the exception ... to be safeguarded and its purpose to be observed."[59]
- And last, but not least, by qualifying the limitations in Article 5 InfoSoc Directive as "autonomous concepts of EU law," that must be uniformly interpreted across the EU and, if necessary, prevail over any dissenting interpretation and/or more restrictive national law provisions.[60]

The CJEU doctrine on E&L[61] has brought further harmonization far beyond the consensus reached in Article 5 InfoSoc Directive.

14.2.2 Fair Use in the USA

The USA Copyright Act (USCA)[62] offers a combination of detailed statutory E&L with the notable fair use defense. Fair use relies on the specific circumstances of the case rather than on *a priori* statutory exempted

C-145/10 Eva Maria Painer v. Standard VerlagsGmbH, Axel Springer AG and others (2011) ECLI:EU:C:2011:798.

57. *See*, Case C-306/05 Sociedad General de Autores y Editores de España (SGAE) v. Rafael Hoteles SA (2006) ECR ECLI:EU:C:2006:764, paras. 35,40,41; Joined Cases C-403/08 and C-429/08 Football Association Premier League Ltd, para. 189; *See also,* InfoSoc Directive, Recital 44.
58. *See*, Case C-145/10 Eva Maria Painer, para. 126; The CJEU refused as irrelevant (para. 136) the requirement in French law that the work is quoted as part of a new literary work: neither Art. 10(1) of the Berne Convention nor Art. 5(3)(d) of the InfoSoc Directive require so and the specific use in that case was not contrary to the three-step test (ex Art. 5(5) InfoSoc Directive) (para. 137).
59. *See,* Case C-145/10 Eva Maria Painer, para. 133; *See also,* Joined Cases C-403/08 and C-429/08 Football Association Premier League Ltd, paras. 162, 163; *See also,* Case C-275/06 Productores de Música de España (Promusicae).
60. Accordingly, the optional nature of the list of E&L in Art. 5(2) and (3) of the InfoSoc Directive is restricted to its "selection," but once an exception has been "selected" by a Member State, the scope of this E&L in the InfoSoc Directive will prevail, if different from national law.
61. *See*, for instance, Case C-201/13 Johan Deckmyn and Vrijheidsfonds: the CJEU assessed the scope of the parody limitation (Art. 5(3)(k) of the InfoSoc Directive) under the teleological/functional criterion (to enable the effectiveness of the limitation) and the proportionality principle (seeking to achieve a fair balance), setting aside the principle of strict interpretation (three-step test) as the only hermeneutical criteria for E&L.
62. Copyright Law of the United States, https://www.copyright.gov/title17/ (accessed Jun. 3, 2019).

scenarios. Fair use is an equitable rule of reason, which can only be examined and decided on the specific facts of each infringing case.

According to section 107 USCA:

> Notwithstanding the provisions of sections 106 and 106A, the fair use of a copyrighted work, including such use by reproduction in copies or phonorecords or by any other means specified by that section, for purposes such as criticism, comment, news reporting, teaching (including multiple copies for classroom use), scholarship, or research, is not an infringement of copyright. In determining whether the use made of a work in any particular case is a fair use the factors to be considered shall include: (1) the purpose and character of the use, including whether such use is of a commercial nature or is for nonprofit educational purposes; (2) the nature of the copyrighted work; (3) the amount and substantiality of the portion used in relation to the copyrighted work as a whole and; (4) the effect of the use upon the potential market for, or value of, the copyrighted work. The fact that a work is unpublished shall not itself bar a finding of fair use if such finding is made upon consideration of all the above factors.

The fair use doctrine was codified for the first time in the 1976 Copyright Act, adopting the set of standards historically developed by courts to balance competing interests in copyright infringement claims. Nothing in section 107 USCA was intended to limit or otherwise alter the scope of the fair use doctrine. Fair use remains a rule of equity[63] and continues to be a critical tool to accommodate copyright in the evolving technological markets.

Fair use is a specific national solution. Other countries may find other solutions, legislative or judicial, to accommodate their copyright laws to evolving technological markets. Let us see some examples.

14.2.3 Search Engines and Thumbnails: *Ius Usus Inocui* and Abuse of Rights

Search engines play a fundamental role in the Internet. Navigation online would be virtually impossible without search engines. From a copyright perspective, their functioning often involves acts of exploitation[64] that have been neither expressly authorized by rightholders nor permitted by law, to the

63. No single factor will determine whether the use is fair or not; all must be weighed together in light of the particular circumstances of each case.
64. Search engines reproduce the content available online before offering any results to searches introduced by users (which, in its turn, enacts another act of reproduction and, perhaps, of making available to the public).

extent that most national laws fail to provide for any exception or limitation for search engines.

In the USA, basic functioning of search engines was cleared from copyright infringement in the early years, when the Ninth Circuit cleared thumbnails of works used in search engines as fair use; *see Perfect 10*[65] and *Arriba Soft.*[66]

It is unlikely that a similar result could be achieved with the EU, since none of the existing limitations or exceptions listed in national copyright laws (or in the EU *acquis*) may formally exempt the operation of search engines. The quotation limitation in Article 5(3)(d) InfoSoc Directive might—if interpreted broadly—exempt the showing of snippets resulting from searches regarding the rights of reproduction and communication to the public and making available online. Yet, it would never allow for the whole copying, indexing and storing of the protected contents, as defined widely under the exclusive right of reproduction in Article 2 InfoSoc Directive. Neither would the temporary copies exception in Article 5(1) suffice to exempt them.[67] Displaying search results might qualify as a temporary and transient act of reproduction in the light of the CJEU rulings in the *Infopaq* case,[68] but—once again—the copying, indexing and storing necessary for the search engine to run is far from being temporary, transient or incidental.

However, the Spanish Supreme Court, in its ruling of April 3, 2013, found a way to exempt the Google search engine from an infringement claim aimed at shutting the service down. After accepting that none of the statutory limitations listed in the Spanish Copyright statute permitted the unauthorized use of fragments of the contents of a personal website through the Google search engine and cache copy service, the Supreme Court found no infringement on the grounds that the copyright owner has an obligation to endure any *ius usus inocui* (harmless uses by third parties) and must abide by the general law principles of good faith and prohibition of abuse of rights (ex Article 7 of the Spanish Civil Code).[69] The Spanish Court was clearly annoyed by the "abusive" claim and turned to general legal principles (and

65. Perfect 10, Inc. v. Amazon.com, Inc., 508 F.3d 1146 (9th Cir. 2007).
66. Kelly v. Arriba Soft Corp., 336 F.3d 811 (9th Cir. 2003).
67. According to Recital 33 of the InfoSoc Directive, this exemption is intended to cover reproductions on Internet routers, reproductions created during web browsing or copies created in Random Access Memory of a computer, copies stored on local caches of computer systems or copies created in proxy servers.
68. Case C-5/08, Infopaq International A/S v. Danske Dagblades Forening (2009) ECLI: EU:C:2009:465, para. 64; the scanning of whole works—within what they called a "data capture process"—for purposes of obtaining extracts qualifies under Art. 5(1) of the InfoSoc Directive; an act is transient "only if its duration is limited to what is necessary for the proper completion of the technological process in question."
69. Raquel Xalabarder, *Spanish Supreme Court Rules in Favour of Google Search Engine … and a Flexible Reading of Copyright Statutes?,* 3 Journal of Intellectual Property, Information Technology and Electronic Commerce 162, para. 1 (2012).

Roman law) to prevent it. In practice, the Spanish result is not far from what would have been achieved under a fair use defence.

14.2.4 TDM: Articles 3 and 4 CDSM

In 2004, Google launched the project "Google Books." The project consists of a massive scanning of books in participating libraries,[70] the storage and indexation of all the digitized contents and the making available to the public "snippets" of these works online through the search engine "Google Books." Users can only view snippets of copyrighted books; the full content is only available (also for downloading) when the work is in the public domain. Therefore, unless a malfunctioning (or hacking) of the database occurs, users cannot download the full contents of works that are not in the public domain.

In 2005, the Authors Guild—the biggest association of writers in the USA—filed a lawsuit against Google.[71] On November 14, 2013, the claim was dismissed on the grounds of fair use, concluding that the unauthorized use of works done in the Google Books search tool is "highly transformative," the project provides "significant public benefits," and it does not harm the market for the original works.[72] The ruling was confirmed on appeal[73] and, in its turn, confirmed by the Supreme Court on April 18, 2016, when denying *certiorari*.[74]

Instead, in the EU, the Google Books project can hardly be formally permitted under any E&L in the EU *acquis*[75] The most visible confirmation comes from France, where several publishers sued Google for copyright infringement (*Les Editions du Seuil)*.[76] In its defence, Google alleged the quotation limitation in the French IP Code. The Court refused it because of the works:

70. The scanning was done in cooperation with several public and private libraries, mainly in the United States. Many more libraries all over Europe and around the world soon followed. Google provided participating libraries with a digital copy of all scanned books in their collections.
71. Shortly after, so did the Association of American Publishers and both actions were consolidated; the publishers and Google reached a private agreement in October 2012 but the Authors Guild carried on with the claim.
72. Authors Guild v. Google Inc., 05 Civ. 8136 (DC) (S.D.N.Y. No. 14, 2013).
73. Authors Guild v. Google Inc., 804 F.3d 202 (2d Cir. 2015).
74. *See*, docket, https://www.supremecourt.gov/search.aspx?filename=/docketfiles/15-849.htm (accessed Jun. 3, 2019).
75. *See*, Raquel Xalabarder, *Google Books and Fair Use: A Tale of Two Copyrights?,* 5 Journal of Intellectual Property, Information Technology and Electronic Commerce 53, para. 1 (2014).
76. *See* TGI Paris, 3e Chambre, Dec. 18, 2009 Jurisdata n. 2009-016553; Google appealed the ruling but started negotiations and over the years settled with all publishers.

are made available to the public in their entirety, even in reduced form, and the randomness of the choice of excerpts displayed denies any informatory purpose as required by article.122-5-3 CPI.[77]

The Google Books project is a notable example of the broader and more powerful digital technology known as TDM, the automated processing, computational analysis or "machine reading" of large volumes of text, sound, image and data to uncover new knowledge or insights or "to generate patterns, trends, correlations" (Article 2.2 CDSM Directive). From a strict copyright perspective, TDM activities will always involve acts of reproduction of any works or protected subject matter that is used to "feed" the algorithm—and, eventually, also of communication to the public, making available and transformation. Failing to be exempted under any E&L in national laws, the need for authorization to conduct TDM activities makes the development of these projects extremely complex and, ultimately, unviable.[78] This is especially dramatic considering that mining is aimed at obtaining information rather than using or exploiting the mined work, per se, "as a work."

For these reasons, Article 3 CDSM Directive introduced a mandatory exception (not compensated) allowing reproduction and extraction of works and data (under a *sui generis* right) made by research institutions to conduct TDM for purposes of "scientific research," provided that they have "lawful access" to the contents (Article 3 CDSM). Article 3 is a uniform exception, with a clear mandatory scope, and all national laws should transpose it in its very exact terms, thus securing its uniform scope across all of the EU.[79] Member States cannot provide any compensation scheme for the copyright owners of the mined works. In other words, Article 3 is a true exception rather than a limitation subject to compensation.

---

77. In addition, the court found an infringement of the moral right of integrity for the display of "random excerpts as torn paper pieces," and dismissed the claim for unfair competition on the grounds of free riding (*parasitisme*) for lack of evidence.
78. TDM projects may face several obstacles, such as contractual restrictions and TPM restricting reproduction and storage of contents, legal uncertainty regarding lawfulness, high transaction costs involved in identifying and negotiating TDM uses. All of them resulting in smaller data sets and poorer quality of results; *See,* Commission Staff Working Document Impact Assessment on the modernisation of EU copyright rules, Accompanying the document Proposal for a Directive of the European Parliament and of the Council on copyright in the Digital Single Market Brussels (Sep. 14, 2016) SWD301 final, §4.3.1 (2016).
79. Rather surprisingly, Spain has implemented Arts. 3 and 4 in a single exception without distinguishing between research uses or other uses for TDM. One single exception to allow TDM, either for scientific research purposes or for other purposes, as long as it has not been opted out by the copyright owner. No special treatment is made for scientific research: a copyright owner in Spain could prohibit the use of any TDM including for scientific research purposes (thus contravening Art. 3 CDSM Directive). Unless revised, the Spanish law may be challenged at some point in front of the CJEU for incorrect transposition of a mandatory and uniform provision (Art. 3).

Furthermore, in order to broaden the possibilities of TDM, a second mandatory exception permits reproductions and extractions of lawfully accessible works and other subject matter for the purposes of TDM, retained for as long as is necessary for the purposes of TDM, provided the TDM use was not expressly reserved by rightholders "in an appropriate manner, such as machine readable means in the case of content made publicly available online" (Article 4 CDSM). While the mandatory exception should be uniformly applied across all EU States, the optional exception will likely result in diverse national solutions.[80]

Beyond strict TDM uses, it remains to be seen how (and how successfully) the TDM provisions in Articles 3 and 4 CDSM will apply to permit, at large, the training of Generative Artificial Intelligence (genAI) systems at large. The prevailing reading among stakeholders seems to be that Article 4 CDSM permits the training of genAI systems unless the copyright owners have "opted out" of it.

At a very first glance, Articles 3 and 4 CDSM are structurally ill-equipped to permit TDM for Artificial Intelligence (AI) training. On the one hand, the definition of TDM in the 2019 CDSM was aimed at gathering data for analytic uses (to extract information, patterns, and knowledge) and far from any machine reading destined to "generate" new content. On the other, Articles 3 and 4 CDSM Directive only refer to "reproduction" (and extractions from databases); these E&L do not concern the right of communication to the public, let alone the right of transformation (which is not harmonized in the EU).[81] But perhaps the most troublesome feature of Article 4, as applied for purposes of AI training, is the feasibility of the express reservation (opt-out) requirement. How can this opt-out reservation be executed and enforced in "an appropriate manner"?

Time will tell (and perhaps also the CJEU) whether or not Article 4 CDSM is applicable—and if so, under which conditions—to govern the use of copyrighted contents to train and exploit genAI systems.

14.3 ENFORCEMENT OF E&L AGAINST TPM AND CONTRACTUAL TERMS

E&L are vulnerable against TPM and contractual terms. This is not so much a result of international obligations, such as the WIPO Treaties of 1996 (*see*

80. Article 4 CDSM opens for Member States the possibility to decide which TDM purposes should be authorized by law and whether to subject it to a compensation.
81. Generative AI systems not only reproduce but often transform the works in their datasets (making derivative works or protected subject matter, such as in a database) and subsequently communicate these transformed outputs to the public, or at least, make them available online.

section 14.3.1 below), but rather of their diverse implementation in national laws (*see* section 14.3.2 below).

International protection of TPM to enforce copyright was first enacted by the WIPO Treaties of 1996.[82]

As we will see, the scope of TPM protection granted under Article 11 WCT was substantially enlarged when these international instruments sieved into the national laws of the USA (Digital Millennium Copyright Act (DMCA), 1998) and the EU (InfoSoc Directive, 2001). Ever since, both the USA and the EU have been geographically expanding their national provisions on the protection of TPM by means of trade agreements with other countries. As a result, rather than the WCT/WPPT provisions on TPM, it is the EU and USA national provisions on TPM, usually known as "WCT/WPPT plus" or "TRIPS plus" standards[83] that are uniformly expanding worldwide.

14.3.1 Article 11 of the WCT

According to Article 11 of the WCT, contracting parties shall provide protection and remedies against the circumvention of effective technological measures used by rights owners to prevent uses of their works which have not been authorized or permitted by law:

> *Article 11—Obligations concerning Technological Measures*
>
> Contracting Parties shall provide adequate legal protection and effective legal remedies against the circumvention of effective technological measures that are used by authors in connection with the exercise of their rights under this Treaty or the Berne Convention and that restrict acts, in respect of their works, which are not authorized by the authors concerned or permitted by law.

In principle, Article 11 of the WCT does not grant authors a new substantive right under copyright; it simply defines a "general framework, describing the outer limits"[84] to allow them to enforce and manage their rights by technical means. In theory, nothing in Article 11 of the WCT is meant to extend the protection of TPM beyond the scope of copyright; hence, the reference to:

82. Both "Internet Treaties" contain parallel provisions regarding TPM: WCT, Art. 11 and WPPT, Art. 18. We will only refer and examine the WCT provisions. In addition, rights management information are protected in WCT, Art. 12 and WPPT, Art. 19. They will not be considered in this chapter.
83. *See*, Xavier Seuba, *The Global Regime for the Enforcement of Intellectual Property Rights* (Cambridge University Press, 2017).
84. *See,* Ricketson & Ginsburg (n. 5), §15.25.

> the exercise of their rights under this Treaty and the Berne Convention and that restrict acts, in respect of their works, which are not authorized by (them) or permitted by law.

Circumvention of a TPM is only prohibited when it controls acts of exploitation that fall within the rightholder's power to authorize. Accordingly:

> if, for example, a work has fallen into the public domain because the term of copyright protection has expired …, any technological measure preventing the reproduction of the work does not benefit from Article 6.[85]

However, while the work is protected, the relationship between TPM and E&L does not come easy.

Protection is granted "against the circumvention" of effective technological measures. Certainly, *effective* protection of TPM may also require prohibiting trafficking acts,[86] in addition to circumventing acts, but this protection will not be *adequate* if it prevents uses which are permitted under copyright laws. Once again, this balancing act remains in the sole hands of national laws and courts.

The Marrakesh Treaty for the Visually Impaired (2013) offered the international legislator another opportunity to deal with the interaction of TPM and E&L. Unfortunately, the issue is only addressed in a very general manner, deferring it—once again—to national laws.

> *Article 7 Obligations Concerning Technological Measures*
>
> Contracting Parties shall take appropriate measures, as necessary, to ensure that when they provide adequate legal protection and effective legal remedies against the circumvention of effective technological measures, this legal protection does not prevent beneficiary persons from enjoying the limitations and exceptions provided for in this Treaty.

---

85. *See*, Thomas Dreier & P. Bernt Hugenholtz, *Concise European Copyright Law* 475 (2nd edn, Kluwer, 2016).

86. Scholars read this reference as a minimum protection, allowing contracting parties to extend this protection beyond circumvention and include other acts, such as "preparatory acts" (manufacturing, importing or distributing circumventing devices) as well as to control "access" to protected works. According to them, "a circumvention only approach appears, therefore, to be insufficient." However, as Ricketson and Ginsburg point out: "the challenge for national laws, then, is to determine how to regulate the creation and dissemination of circumvention devices without effectively cutting off the fair uses that at least some devices, in the right hands would permit"; *See,* Ricketson & Ginsburg (n. 5), §15.20.

14.3.2 National Implementation

It remains to be seen whether the legal protection of TPM granted by these laws is "adequate" to safeguard the effectiveness of any E&L in copyright laws. The USA and EU laws choose different approaches.

14.3.2.1 USCA

Section 1201 USCA[87]—introduced by the DMCA of 1998—prohibits circumvention of any TPM[88] used to control or restrict use of copyrighted works, as well as any trafficking acts (i.e., the manufacturing and distribution of any devices or the provision of any services aimed at circumventing these measures).

In order to ensure that the protection of TPM will not prevent uses permitted under fair use or other statutory E&L, the DMCA distinguishes between access and copying control. For TPM controlling access, acts of circumvention as well as trafficking are prohibited, while for TPM controlling use/copying, only acts of trafficking are prohibited. In other words, circumventing a TPM to entertain a fair use of a copyrighted work is allowed, as long as the user has lawful access to the work; yet, fair use cannot exempt circumventing access-control TPM. In addition, section 1201 USCA provides for a list of specific uses where the circumvention of a TPM controlling access is allowed[89] and for a rule-making process—known as "jailbreaking"—that allows the Librarian of Congress (upon recommendation of the Register of Copyright, based on a public fact-gathering process) to introduce additional exceptions that allow circumvention of access controls in order to accommodate specific permitted uses and reevaluate them every three years.[90]

14.3.2.2 EU *Acquis* and National Implementation

The EU approach is far less consistent than the USA one, being regulated across several scattered provisions adopted over the years.

87. Copyright Protection and Management Systems, http://www.copyright.gov/title17/92chap12.html (accessed Jun. 3, 2019).
88. TPM are defined broadly so as to include access control and use/copy control.
89. *See,* USCA, s. 1201(d) to (j): in favor of nonprofit libraries, archives and educational institutions, for purposes of federal law enforcement activities, for reverse engineering of a computer program, for encryption research, for protecting personal data or identifying information and to prevent minors from accessing material on the internet.
90. Over the years, several exceptions have been added by this rule-making process; *see,* Rule Making Proceedings under s. 1201 of Title 17, https://www.copyright.gov/1201/ (accessed Jun. 3, 2019).

[a] Article 6 InfoSoc Directive

The WIPO 1996 Treaties were implemented by the EU through the InfoSoc Directive (2001). Some of their provisions had already been—to some extent—harmonized under previous directives,[91] but the provisions on TPM were brand new to the European Community (EC) *acquis*—except—as we will see for some "budding" protection of TPM previously provided for in the CPD (1991).

Like in the USA, TPM are broadly defined[92] to control both access and use/copying. Two different kinds of acts are prohibited: circumventing acts, as well as preparatory acts[93] and the provision of services to circumvent TPM.[94] However, unlike section 1201 USCA, the European legislator has chosen not to prohibit all acts of circumvention, but only circumvention that is carried out "with knowledge, or with reasonable grounds to know."[95]

Article 6 InfoSoc Directive is not a mandatory—directly applicable—provision, but rather an obligation imposed on Member States to "provide adequate legal protection against the circumvention" of TPM,

91. This is why InfoSoc Directive, Art. 1(2) "leaves intact and in no way affects" the previous Directives on computer programs, rental and lending, satellite and cable, term of protection and databases.
92. According to Art. 6.3 InfoSoc Directive, the definition of "technological measures" includes "any technology, device or component" designed "to prevent or restrict acts … which are not authorised by the rightholder." TPM may be software technologies but they may also be imbedded in hardware; TPM may be implemented in one device or across a combination of programs and devices, making specific reference to encryption and scrambling technologies, as examples.
93. "manufacture, import, distribution, sale, rental, advertisement for sale or rental or possession for commercial purposes" concerning "devices, products or components."
The protection of TPM granted under the InfoSoc Directive is complemented by Art. 4 of the Conditional Access Directive which prohibits manufacture, distribution, installation, maintenance and commercial promotion or advertising of illicit devices to circumvent conditional access technologies used in the provision of online services for commercial purposes. Since its scope is not restricted to TPM used by copyright owners for the exploitation of copyrighted subject matter, this Directive may offer protection to a wider range of devices and distributors of online contents and services. However, notice that the Conditional Access Directive (Art. 4) does not prohibit the acts of circumvention but only the acts of trafficking with illicit devices. *See* Directive 98/84/EC of the European Parliament and of the Council of 20 November 1998 on the legal protection of services based on, or consisting of, conditional access (Nov. 20, 1998) Official Journal L 320, 28/11/1998, pp. 54-57.
94. Which: (1) are advertised to circumvent TPM; (2) have no other use than to circumvent TPM; or (3) are primarily aimed, "designed, produced, adapted or performed for the purpose of enabling or facilitating circumvention."
95. Instead, in the USA, all acts of circumvention are prohibited by USCA, s. 1201 regardless of any knowledge, awareness or intent to infringe; yet, acts of circumvention in the USA are only prohibited regarding access-control TPM, not use-control TPM (which remains subject to fair use) and courts may reduce sanctions for unaware acts of circumvention. There is no need to formally require knowledge in Art. 6(2) of the InfoSoc Directive, since it has already been implied in the prohibited preparatory activities.

without defining what will be "adequate." As a result, Member States enjoy some flexibility when implementing this obligation to their national laws.[96] In fact, Recital 49 seems to confirm that Article 6.2 InfoSoc Directive only conveys a minimum of mandatory protection and that Member States may provide for a larger scope of protection (for instance, prohibiting the private possession of these circumventing devices, regardless of any commercial purposes). Similarly, the national implementation of Article 6.4 InfoSoc Directive—commonly referred to as "interface" between TPM and E&L, "has led to divergent and potentially inconsistent approaches."[97]

This "interface" consists of several parts.[98] First, in order to secure E&L against TPM preventing acts of circumvention,[99] rightholders should provide "voluntary measures"[100] to beneficiaries (e.g., schools, libraries ...) so that they can benefit from the E&L. In the absence of such voluntary measures taken by rightholders, "within a reasonable period of time" (Recital 51), Member States shall take "appropriate measures" only regarding seven *E&L.*[101] These E&L acquire some sort of "privileged" status, in comparison with the rest. Nevertheless, rather discouragingly, "appropriate measures" adopted by national laws[102] to safeguard these "privileged" E&L tend to simply grant access to mediation or arbitration procedures (usually by a government body) or to general jurisdiction (civil or criminal claims).

As far as private copying (Article 5.2(b) InfoSoc Directive), Member States may (no obligation to do so) take appropriate measures when absent

96. For a comprehensive study on the national implementation of Arts. 6 and 7 of the InfoSoc Directive, *see* Guido Westkamp, *The Implementation of Directive 2001/29/EC in the Member States* 51-78 (Queen Mary University of London, 2007).
97. *See*, Westkamp (n. 96), 70.
98. Diverging opinions were already expressed by the Commission and the Parliament during its legislative proceedings. Simply put, the Parliament favored that TPM should always prevail over exceptions in Art. 5 (beneficiaries should find a way to use the work from a source that is not TPM-protected), while the Commission contended that E&L should prevail and be secured against TPM. The Council came up with a sophisticated (or simply, complicated) solution to balance E&L against prohibited circumvention of TPM.
99. Article 6(4) of the Infosoc Directive only affects circumvention under Art. 6(1), since preparatory acts (as defined under Art. 6(2)) with circumventing devices are always prohibited.
100. Lacking any definition in the Directive, "voluntary measures taken by rightholders" may consist of a specific password or decryption device, a non-TPM-protected copy of the work. According to the InfoSoc Directive, Recital 51, they may consist of "agreements between rightholders and other parties concerned."
101. Member States are only obliged to Art. 5.2: (1) reprography; (2) libraries and alike; (3) broadcasting organizations; (4) hospitals, prisons. And alike, Art. 5.3: (1) illustration for teaching and research purposes; (2) people with a disability; (3) administrative-parliamentary-and-judicial-proceedings.
102. For a table comparing national implementation of the InfoSoc Directive, Art. 6(4), *see* Westkamp (n. 96), 95-101; *See,* Michel Walter & Silke von Lewinski, *European Copyright Law: A Commentary* §11.6.13, 1100-1141 (Oxford University Press, 2010) (Implementation in Member States).

voluntary measures, but rightholders can always restrict (with TPM) the number of copies permitted as a private copy.[103]

Nothing is said regarding the rest of limitations in Article 5 of the InfoSoc Directive;[104] it is unclear whether Member States cannot take appropriate measures to ensure these E&L or whether they may do so. In principle, allowing rightholders to flat override *any* statutory E&L by using TPM would contravene Article 11 WCT: if uses permitted by law can be overridden by TPM (and by contracts), the protection granted is not "adequate."

And last, not least, this "interface" does not apply to works obtained "on agreed contractual terms" by means of interactive on-demand services (Article 6.7 of the InfoSoc Directive); in these instances, contractual terms will prevail over any E&L.[105] As online markets evolve, and bearing in mind that most works and protected contents will be accessible only via licenses and contractual terms, this might mean that the balance struck by E&L in copyright law may soon become de facto irrelevant in digital formats.

Unlike the USCA, the InfoSoc Directive "interface" makes no distinction between access-control and copy-control TPM: in principle, none can be circumvented "knowingly and without authorization."[106] Unlike the USCA, the InfoSoc Directive does not provide for any statutory exemptions to allow circumventing TPM; a few reasons are mentioned in the recitals: research in cryptography (Recital 48 InfoSoc Directive) and the exceptions provided for computer programs (Recital 50 InfoSoc Directive). Member States could certainly enact such exemptions;[107] yet none has done so.[108]

As a result, Article 6.4 InfoSoc Directive fails to properly ensure E&L against the protection of TPM, leaving them in the sole hands of licensing (voluntary agreements with rightholders). The idea that E&L can be adequately secured through licensing is rather naïve, if not utterly misleading: allowing a permitted use to be subject to specific licensing terms and

103. Apparently, only a few countries have made use of this faculty: the Netherlands, the U.K. and Belgium; *See,* Westkamp (n. 96), 72; Walter & Lewinski (n. 102), §11.6.16, fn. 480.

104. Namely, E&L in Art. 5(1) temporary copies (which is mandatory), as well as in Art. 5(3)(c), (d) and (f) to (o).

105. InfoSoc Directive, Recital 53 justifies this exclusion so as to "ensure a secure environment for the provision of interactive on-demand services." To the extent that not all online provisions qualify as "interactive" making available to the public (InfoSoc Directive, Art. 3), the possibility of contracts overriding E&L will not affect all copies obtained "on-line"; push-communications (broadcast, webcast, etc) will remain subject to the difficult balance in Art. 6(4)(1) and (2) of the InfoSoc Directive; *See* Walter & Lewinski (n. 102), §11.6.18.

106. However, not all national laws prohibit circumvention of both TPM, *see* Westkamp (n. 96), 52-53.

107. To a different degree, Finland, Norway, Sweden and UK have enacted exemptions for cryptographic research, *see* Westkamp (n. 96), 60.

108. *See* Westkamp (n. 96), 59.

conditions amounts to deflating the exception or limitation from any public order value.[109]

Similarly, some scholars contend that an exception or limitation is sufficiently secured when its beneficiaries have access to an analogue copy of the work.[110] We are not persuaded. Restricting the effectiveness of E&L to analogue formats will hardly qualify as an "adequate protection" of TPM as required by Article 11 WCT—the more so, as analogue formats become less and less available. Additionally, such reading disregards the Agreed Statement concerning Article 10 WCT that permits "Contracting Parties to carry forward and appropriately extend into the digital environment limitations and exceptions in their national laws which have been considered acceptable under the Berne Convention. Similarly, ... to devise new E&L that are appropriate in the digital network environment."

Last, but not least, in theory, the protection of TPM against circumvention needs to be restricted to copyright-infringing uses. Although only a few formally state so,[111] most European national laws intend to restrict the prohibition of circumvention to copyright-infringing acts.[112] Thus, once the work is in the public domain (and no other rights subsist on it), circumventing a TPM preventing access or copying should not be considered an infringement under Article 6.1 InfoSoc Directive. However, in practice, nothing prevents the use of TPM to control access and use of non-protected works or to prevent permitted uses of protected works, unduly restricting access to public domain and statutorily exempted uses. The international obligations (WCT/WPPT) may be a minimum required for TPM protection against circumvention, but this does not mean that the scope of TPM protection granted by national laws is unlimited.

[b] Article 7 CPD

Article 6 InfoSoc Directive does not apply to computer programs.[113] The enforcement of TPM in computer programs is governed by the CPD, as *lex specialis,* offering a very different picture (maybe because the CPD pre-dated the WCT/WPPT adoption).

Under Article 7 CPD, Member States must provide appropriate remedies against three different acts. The first two deal with "infringing copies":

109. In countries where E&L cannot be contracted out (namely, Belgium, Portugal and Denmark), rightholders *must* provide the means for beneficiaries to use the work regardless of any licensing terms. Instead, in most other countries, "the result will depend on the application of general contract law, and specifically whether restrictions on permitted uses constitute unfair terms." *See* Westkamp (n. 96), 70.
110. *See* Walter & Lewinski (n. 102), §11.6.15.
111. In Germany and Austria, for instance, acts not infringing exclusive rights have been exempted from the definition of TPM; *see* Westkamp (n. 96), 52.
112. *See* Westkamp (n. 96), 57.
113. Article 6 InfoSoc Directive applies to all works and other protected subject matter, as well as to the *sui generis* right on databases, but not to computer programs.

putting infringing copies into circulation and possessing infringing copies for commercial purposes. The third one is the one dealing—albeit indirectly—with TPM:

> putting into circulation, or the possession for commercial purposes of, any means the sole intended purpose of which is to facilitate the unauthorised removal or circumvention of any technical device which may have been applied to protect a computer program.

A comparison of Article 6 InfoSoc Directive and Article 7 CPD identifies some substantial differences:

- The act of circumvention itself is not prohibited for computer programs. This is in sharp contrast with Article 6.1 InfoSoc Directive and Article 11 of the WCT, which require effective remedies against any "acts of circumvention," not only preparatory activities. Article 7.1 CPD could have been amended (or derogated) by the 2009 codified version, so as to adapt it to subsequent international law; it was not.[114] No reference is made to the "possession of infringing copies" in either the InfoSoc Directive (Article 6) or the Enforcement Directive; accordingly, Article 7.1(b) of the CPD offers wider protection against the infringement of copyright in computer programs, despite requiring that the possession is for commercial purposes and with knowledge.[115]
- Article 7 CPD covers "any means," the "sole intended purpose" of which is circumvention: this will exclude means which, in addition to circumventing, may be used for other purposes.[116] It also excludes the provision of circumventing "services" (i.e., the distribution of written instructions which enable the purchaser to install program updates).[117] After all, the reference to "technical device" (used in Article 7 CPD)—which may perfectly apply to software as well as hardware[118]—seems to be more restrictive than the reference to "technological measures" (used in Article 6 InfoSoc Directive).

114. To the extent that "putting into circulation" infringing copies qualifies as an infringement of the exclusive right of distribution, some scholars contend that Art. 7(1)(a) CPD might be overruled by the more detailed provisions of the Enforcement Directive, which require Member States to provide for the measures, procedures and remedies necessary to ensure the enforcement of copyright (and other intellectual property rights), including criminal sanctions; *See* Directive 2009/24/EC of the European Parliament and of the Council of 23 April 2009 on the legal protection of computer programs, Art. 7(1)(a) (Apr. 23, 2009) Official Journal L 111, 5/5/2009, pp. 16-22; Walter & Lewinski (n. 102), §5.7.17.
115. Germany does not require either commercial purpose, or knowledge; *see* Walter & Lewinski (n. 102), 225.
116. *See*, Walter & Lewinski (n. 102), §5.7.28.
117. *See* Dreier & Hugenholtz (n. 85), 269.
118. *See* Walter & Lewinski (n. 102), §5.7.27.

- Despite the protection of TPM afforded under Article 7 CPD being smaller in scope, the interface between TPM and E&L is stronger. E&L to rights in computer programs are comprehensively listed in Articles 5 and 6 CPD.[119] Recital 13 CPD explains that the "acts of loading and running necessary for the use of a copy of a program which has been lawfully acquired, and the act of correction of its errors, may not be prohibited by contract." The other three exceptions (backup copy, reverse engineering and decompilation for interoperability) are formally mandatory and cannot be contracted out.[120] In summary, the "interface" for software is quite different (if not the opposite) from the general "interface" adopted 10 years later in Article 6.4 InfoSoc Directive.[121]

It might be argued that in order to fully comply with Article 11 WCT, the lack of protection under Article 7.1(c) CPD against acts of circumvention could be "filled in" by the wider protection granted under Article 6.1 InfoSoc Directive as well as by Article 6.4 "interface."[122] Apparently, the Commission preferred to stay away from this analogy option and to rely on Members States to adopt "meaningful protection of technological measures regarding computer programs while safeguarding an appropriate balance with E&L to the rights."[123] Most Member States have simply done a *literal* transposition of Article 7 CPD, thus failing to formally prohibit circumvention (cfr. Article 6.1 InfoSoc Directive).[124]

The provisions regarding technological measures and E&L in the original CPD (Directive 91/250/EEC) remained untouched in its codified version (Directive 2009/24/EC). Yet, as digital products evolve, the line separating computer programs from other hybrid digital products—such as videogames and multimedia—blurs, making it harder to avoid the application of both Directives. In fact, the CJEU confirmed so for videogames in the

119. In principle, no additional E&L are applicable to software; *see* Walter & Lewinski (n. 102), §§5.5.51.
120. According to Art. 8.2 CPD, "any contractual provisions contrary to [them] … shall be null and void."
121. Several reasons may explain the different approaches. The development of computer and software markets took place at a very early stage of the development of TPM. Instead, the markets for the exploitation videogames and consoles, music, films and e-books developed fully integrating DRMs. In its turn, the inherently functional nature of computer programs led copyright laws to establish a requirement of interoperability (decompilation) for software and to allow reverse engineering, while the same was not deemed necessary for other works, including videogames.
122. *See* Walter & Lewinski (n. 102), §5.7.32.
123. *See* the Commission Staff Working Paper on the review of the EC legal framework in the field of copyright and related rights (Jul. 19, 2004) SEC(2004)995, p. 9.
124. As a result, circumventing a technical device to enable a legitimate use (any legitimate use) of a computer program would not be, in principle, prohibited.

Nintendo case[125] when restricting the scope of application of the InfoSoc Directive interface in favor of the CPD interface, as far as videogames.

This was not the first time that the CJEU avoided Article 6.4 InfoSoc Directive and turned instead to the specific interfaces provided for in other Directives, safeguarded as *lex specialis*. For instance, in the *UsedSoft* and *VOD* cases,[126] by avoiding the InfoSoc Directive interface and applying instead the Rental and Lending Directive (RLD Directive)[127] and the CPD as *lex specialis*, the court had more leeway to interpret the scope of the exception or limitation for public lending and leverage it against any use of TPM.

[c] Marrakesh and CDSM Directives

In the EU, the Marrakesh Treaty was implemented by means of two instruments: a Directive (to be transposed into national laws) and a Regulation (directly applicable).[128]

Article 3(4) of the Marrakesh Directive integrates the mandatory exception within the general "interface" scheme set in Article 6(4) of the InfoSoc Directive, specifically to its paragraphs 1, 3 and 5 only. In other words, the mandatory exception for the visually impaired is to be included within the list of E&L that enjoy the "special protection" against TPM, and Member States are obliged to secure that TPM will not prevent their effective enjoyment.[129]

---

125. *See* Case C-355/12 Nintendo Co. Ltd and Others v. PC Box Srl and 9Net Srl (2014) ECLI:EU:C:2014:25. The CJEU confirmed that TPM are not absolute and that they can only apply to control (restrict) acts protected under copyright, not beyond it. Furthermore, the CJEU confirmed that when assessing whether the circumvention of a TPM amounts to an infringement, the court needs to take into account the principle of proportionality: "and should not prohibit devices or activities which have a commercially significant purpose or use other than to circumvent the technical protection"; *See, Ibid.,* §30.

126. *See* C-128/11 UsedSoft GmbH v. Oracle International Corp. (2012) ECLI:EU:C:2012:407, the CJEU extended the exhaustion principle beyond the distribution of tangible copies, to copies of a computer program that had been downloaded (hence, made available to the public online); in *VOB* Case C-174/15 Vereniging Openbare Bibliotheken v. Stichting Leenrecht (2016) ECLI:EU:C:2016:856, the CJEU confirmed that e-books could also be subject to public lending by libraries and regardless of any licensing terms and conditions. This later ruling is especially important since e-books are usually downloaded and licensed (not sold, like tangible copies) and, accordingly, under Art. 6.4(7) InfoSoc Directive, the licensing terms and TPM would prevail over any E&L.

127. Under the RLD, Member States may derogate from the exclusive public lending right "provided that at least authors obtain a remuneration for such lending" (Art. 6.1 RLD) and establishing no "interface" rules regarding TPM. *See* Directive 2006/115/EC of the European Parliament and of the Council of 12 December 2006 on rental right and lending right and on certain rights related to copyright in the field of intellectual property (Dec. 12, 2006) Official Journal L 376, 27/12/2006, pp. 28-35.

128. *See* above (n. 48).

129. The Marrakesh Directive includes an amendment (Art. 8) to the general exception in favor of people with a disability provided for in Art. 5(3)(b) of the InfoSoc Directive,

Similarly, according to Article 7 CDSM, the first, third and fifth subparagraphs of Article 6(4) InfoSoc Directive shall apply to the newly introduced mandatory E&L in Articles 3, 4 and 5 CDSM.

Furthermore, both instruments expressly state that uses permitted under the new mandatory exception cannot be overridden by contract.[130] This is very much aligned with the CPD (Article 9.1.2) and the Database Directive[131] (Article 15): both expressly prohibiting that E&L could be overridden by contract.

This seems to be a first step ahead (an improvement) from Article 6(4) InfoSoc Directive, which was not only silent about this issue but formally permitted contractual overriding of E&L when the works have been made available to the public "on agreed contractual terms."

In summary, in the recent Directives, the EU legislator seems to be re-adjusting the interface between TPM and contractual terms.

Nevertheless, as far as the Marrakesh Treaty, there is an inherent inconsistency between, on the one hand, declaring null and void any contractual terms contrary to E&L (i.e., Article 3.4 Marrakesh Directive) and, on the other, prohibiting circumvention of TPM that restrict these permitted uses (i.e., Article 3.5 Marrakesh Directive and Article 6.4 InfoSoc Directive). In order to comply with the obligation in Article 7 Marrakesh Treaty that Countries "take the appropriate measures" to ensure that the legal protection of TPM does not prevent beneficiary persons from enjoying uses permitted by the Treaty, this inconsistency could be overcome by interpreting that the use of TPM amounts to a prohibited contractual overriding.

In summary, both the Marrakesh Directive and Article 7 CDSM Directive could be interpreted to prohibit not only contractual measures but also any TPM that restrict or prevent permitted uses under the Treaty; thus, prevailing over the less-than-optimal solution in Article 6(4) InfoSoc Directive. This appears to be a sensible interpretation of an internationally mandatory exception—not only mandatory for EU Member States but for all Marrakesh Treaty contracting parties.[132]

---

which was already listed in Art.6(4) InfoSoc Directive. It makes perfect sense that both E&L (for people with a visual impairment and for people with a disability) are treated equally.

130. *See*, Marrakesh Directive, Recital (9) and CDSM Directive, Art. 7(1).

131. Directive 96/9/EC of the European Parliament and of the Council of 11 March 1996 on the legal protection of databases (Mar. 11, 1996) Official Journal L 77, 27/3/1996, pp. 20-28.

132. Despite the Marrakesh Treaty did not go as far as to formally protect the exempted uses against contracts, this conclusion is perfectly aligned with the goal and spirit of the Treaty.

14.4 TOWARD A "COMMON CORE" OF E&L?

In the long term, granting uniform international protection of exclusive rights but not of E&L has adverse effects on the functioning of the markets, especially in the field of Digital Rights Management (DRM), causing legal uncertainty and, ultimately, dissonance between law and reality. Strict pluralism of E&L may end up delegitimizing the copyright systems. To avoid this, there may be an opportunity to either reexamine the goodness of the *lex loci protectionis* principle (ex Article 5.2 of the Berne Convention), at least for Internet uses, or even to start examining a further integration of E&L under a common core of exempted uses.

If only for exploratory purposes, let us briefly examine several options.

14.4.1 A Uniform Copyright Code?

A uniform code unifying not only the definitions of work and author and of exclusive rights but also defining E&L is not only a rather unfeasible solution in practice (as proven by international and EU copyright history) but also an undesirable one. E&L are a precious tool for public policy and should remain linked to national culture, markets and, ultimately, national laws.

14.4.2 A Treaty on E&L?

Beyond academic assessments,[133] the adoption of the Marrakesh Treaty seems to have opened up the possibility of adopting international Treaties on the issue of E&L. However, several reasons advise against it. First, because the circumstances of an exception for visually impaired people were rather unique, not only due to the strong and fundamental/human rights considerations it entails (which, after all, may also be shared with other E&L) but also to the fact that this exception had never been formally envisioned in any of the existing international treaties. Most importantly, the "scale economies" introduced by the Treaty when allowing the cross-border "exchange" of AFC obtained is also a very peculiar element of this Treaty. The Marrakesh Treaty positive externalities clearly outweigh any damages caused to the markets of these works.

Furthermore, except where specific circumstances apply, instruments of E&L cannot be separated from the instruments defining the exclusive rights.

133. P. Bernt Hugenholtz & Ruth Okediji, *Conceiving an International Instrument on Limitations and Exceptions to Copyright* Amsterdam Law School Research Paper No. 2012-43; Institute for Information Law Research Paper No. 2012-37, http://dx.doi.org/10.2139/ssrn.2017629 (accessed Jun. 3, 2019).

Exclusive rights and E&L are part of the same token;[134] copyright law is a carefully balanced system that takes into account private and public interests for the ultimate benefit of all. And last but not least, because several examples in the history of copyright prove that any agreement on a list (and scope) of specific E&L to be adopted at an international level is going to fail. The Berne Convention tried and failed twice: in Brussels (for the right of communication to the public) and in Stockholm (for the reproduction right), both leading to the declaration of minor reservations and the three-step test, respectively. Even in the EU, a failed attempt to come up with an exhaustive list of E&L in Articles 5.2 and 5.3 InfoSoc Directive ended up in an exhaustive list of examples which has already proven to be insufficient and disqualified by subsequent instruments on E&L: namely, for orphan works, visually impaired, and the new E&L in the recently adopted Directive on CDSM.

14.4.3 A Common "Fair Use" or Three-Step Test?

Some academic proposals seem to favor the approach, at least within the EU, to adopt a fair use system based on the three-step test criteria (Article 5.5 InfoSoc Directive).[135] The proposal is as attractive as problematic, not only because any "*a posteriori*" test, based on the specific circumstances of the case, offers less predictability and legal certainty than the statutory lists of E&L,[136] but also because courts would need to feel comfortable with it (let us not forget the origins of section 107 of the USCA as a judicial rule of equity).

Perhaps, in many countries, general law principles—such as the abuse of right and good faith—may play a role in the search for equity similar to fair use. This is precisely what the Spanish Supreme Court did in the

134. In fact, the definition of the scope of exclusive right is the first "limitation": if the specific use is not deemed an act of exploitation (as applicable), then there is no need for any E&L. The perfect example of that is the (too) broad definition of the exclusive right of reproduction in Art. 2 of the InfoSoc Directive and its corresponding exception for temporary copies in Art. 5(1) of the InfoSoc Directive.

135. *See,* P. Bernt Hugenholtz & Martin Senftleben, *Fair Use in Europe: In Search of Flexibilities*, https://ssrn.com/abstract=1959554 or http://dx.doi.org/10.2139/ssrn.1959554 (accessed Jun. 3, 2019); Martin Senftleben,*Overprotection and Protection Overlaps in Intellectual Property Law: The Need for Horizontal Fair Use Defences*, at The Structure of Intellectual Property Law The Structure of Intellectual Property Law: Can One Size Fit All? 121-135(Annette Kur & Vytautas Mizaras eds., Edward Elgar, 2011), http://dx.doi.org/10.2139/ssrn.1597123 (accessed Jun. 3, 2019).

136. Despite it is often portrayed as unpredictable, the fair use factors in USCA, s.107 and the amount of caselaw and Fair Use guidelines, that have been issued and agreed upon over the years, offer a valuable ground for predicting fair use v. infringing outcomes. However, the finding of a fair use is only certain when the ruling is out.

Google/Megakini case.[137] Civil court judges would be more prone to apply general legal principles (rooted in their historic legal culture) than rather foreign criteria, such as the USCA fair use[138] or a "three-step test" as an open clause.

Equity—as allowed within the general law principles or under a fair use defence—should not be foreign to copyright law. Yet, it should work as a supplement (not as a substitute) to the E&L statutorily envisioned, which can never hope to be exhaustive and adjusted to evolving markets and technology.

14.4.4 A Common "*De Minimis*" Test?

Another possible uniformization of E&L could be built on a common understanding: uses with minimal significance do not fall within the scope of exclusive rights granted to authors. This principle implicitly exists in most copyright laws and international instruments but has rarely been presented as a specific statutory provision.

The importance of this common principle becomes apparent as the development of technology and markets is constantly questioning the boundaries of copyright and the scope of the exclusive rights granted to authors and copyright owners. At a time of technological change, it would allow some flexibility to help define and adapt the scope of exclusive rights in rapidly evolving markets.[139]

The *de minimis* test would cover, for instance, the incidental use of a work in another work or material,[140] temporary uses which are necessary to enable a lawful use (that has been authorized by the copyright owner or by law),[141] or any other uses which have minimal or no independent economic significance when compared to the normal exploitation of the work.

137. The Spanish Supreme Court concluded that copyright owners must endure *ius usus innocui* (harmless uses done by third parties); *see,* Raquel Xalabarder, *Spanish Supreme Court Rules in Favour of Google Search Engine … and a Flexible Reading of Copyright Statutes?* 3 Journal of Intellectual Property, Information Technology anf Electronic Commerce https://www.jipitec.eu/issues/jipitec-3-2-2012/3445 (accessed Jun. 3, 2019).

138. *See,* Martin Senftleben, *Internet Search Results: A Permisible Quotation?* 235 Revue Internationale du Droit d' Auteur 3 (2013).

139. The CJEU has somehow used a "contact print" of this *de minimis* test when requiring that version of this "*de minimis*" when requiring some economic significance and lucrative purpose to qualify as an infringement of an act of exploitation.

140. This would apply to any use which has minor importance (*de minimis*) in terms of the quantity (amount) and quality (significance) of the part used.

141. This would be especially important in digital contexts, to secure the efficiency of licenses and statutory exceptions. It would include the mandatory exception in Art. 5(1) of Directive 2001/29 (regarding temporary copies) and go beyond it, to cover any other acts of exploitation as long as they are temporary and necessary to enable a lawful (licensed or exempted) use. There is no need for the requirement of "no independent economic

The insignificant uses (*de minimis*) principle is somehow related to the substantiality test used in some countries to identify an infringement,[142] as well as the three-step test (Article 9.2 of the Berne Convention). This "*de minimis*" rule is already embedded in the incidental uses already exempted under Article 5(3)(i) InfoSoc Directive (and under specific national laws) as well as the analogue uses of minor importance already exempted under Article 5(3)(n) InfoSoc Directive.

The *de minimis* principle is often used in connection with the interpretation of E&L, explaining that "exceptions to the rights granted in the relevant articles of the Convention must be concerned with uses of minimal, or no, significance to the author."[143] However, the application of this principle should not be restricted to the interpretation of the statutory E&L; after all, if all exempted uses were indeed *de minimis*, there would be no need for an exception or limitation at all. The scope and aim of a *de minimis* could be precisely to correctly assess the scope of the exclusive rights *a priori*—before any E&L needs being applied—excluding any uses that have a minimal significance from the scope of exclusivity.

The Wittem "European Copyright Code" (Article 5.1)[144] already made a similar proposal, although presented as an exempted use:

> Uses with minimal economic significance. The following uses with minimal economic significance are permitted without authorization, and without remuneration: (1) the making of a back-up copy of a work by a person having a right to use it and insofar as it is necessary for that use; (2) the incidental inclusion of a work in other material; (3) use in connection with the demonstration or repair of equipment, or the reconstruction of an original or a copy of a work.

14.4.5 A Combination of "Strong" Reasons and a Two-Step Test?

Other academic proposals submit a combination of a few strong circumstances that describe, rather than strictly define,[145] areas or reasons that justify exceptions to the exclusive rights. These circumstances would be

---

significance" because any independent economic significance that these temporary uses might have should be already taken into account under the license (charging a higher price, for instance) or exempted (if so) under the limitation.

142. Case law in some countries has also retained the *de minimis* test when considering the existence of infringement, under the so-called substantiality test: when the copying is deemed to be so minor, insubstantial or insignificant that no finding of infringement may derive from it.

143. *See* Ricketson (n. 5), §9.63(1); Ricketson & Ginsburg (n. 5), §13.82.

144. European Copyright Code, https://www.ivir.nl/copyrightcode/introduction/ (accessed Jun. 3, 2019).

145. *See*, Andrew Christie, *Making it Simple: How Copyright Legislation Can Be Simplified,* 6(5) New Zealand Intellectual property Journal 739-790 (2011).

based on fundamental rights, free speech (i.e., quotations and parodies), teaching and research purposes, access to culture, information, disabilities, etc.

The Wittem "European Copyright Code" (2010) described the following permitted uses in Chapter 5—Limitations:

> Article 5.1 Uses with minimal economic significance
> Article 5.2 Uses for the purpose of freedom of expression and information
> Article 5.3 Uses permitted to promote social, political and cultural objectives
> Article 5.4 Uses for the purpose of enhancing competition
> Article 5.5 Further limitations.

Then, upon this list of justified reasons, the two-step test (normal exploitation and legitimate interests) would apply to define the scope or permitted uses (i.e., the "special case") and—where necessary—to require compensation. Under this proposal, exempted uses (and, as a counter part, likely infringements) could be more predictable because regardless of the applicable national law, the justifying circumstances would remain unaltered; only the scope of use permitted and the compensation (if any) might depend on the applicable national law, and respond to the cultural and market differences in each country. It may be a reasonable first step towards a stronger common core of E&L in international copyright law.

Chapter 15

International Fragmentation of Copyright Duration: The Only Place Where the Little Prince and Anne Frank Grow Old

Séverine Dusollier

The time you spend on your rose makes your rose so important
The Little Prince, Saint-Exupéry

The duration of rights in literary and artistic creation, and the key principle of a limited duration, is one of the less contested or discussed principles of international copyright law.[1] The term of copyright is only minimally addressed by international treaties. The Berne Convention imposes a minimum duration of 50 years after the death of the author but leaves the determination of the term to national States.

A more complex picture lurks behind the set of apparently simple rules that could be found at the international level (a limited duration, a minimum of 50 years after the death of the author, and the determination of the duration according to the rule of protection) and hides rather well the failure of international copyright legislation to fix a uniform term of protection throughout the world. As a result, the determination of the end of copyright

1. Sam Ricketson, *The Copyright Term*, 23 International Review of Intellectual Property and Competition Law 753 (1992); To the notable exception of the International Conference of ALAI that convened in Vienna in 2010 around that topic, *see* Michael Walter, *The Duration of Copyright and Related Rights* (ALAI Study Days 2010 Vienna, Medium und Recht Publishing, 2012).

in a specific work and the composition of public domain that is constituted by expiration of protection is almost impossible to decide with certainty or stability.

This chapter aims to expose this complexity and some of its conundrums. It starts by describing how the determination of copyright duration in a work[2] oscillates between the minimum rules laid down by the Berne Convention and the national copyright laws (*see* section 15.1 below). A second part explores other reasons for even more fragmentation by looking at some oddities specific to certain national regimes (*see* section 15.2 below). In the third part, the variability of the copyright duration resulting from repeated term extensions and transitory provisions will be addressed (*see* section 15.3 below).

15.1 THE COPYRIGHT DURATION BETWEEN INTERNATIONAL RULES AND NATIONAL DETERMINATION

15.1.1 The Minimum Rules of the Berne Convention

The rules on duration appear in Articles 7 and 7bis of the Berne Convention.[3]

The most important one is the minimum duration of 50 years after the death of the author that should be provided by the States when applying the Convention.[4] Beyond this threshold, an implicit but key principle is that the term is limited in time. After a determined period of time has elapsed, the work is said to fall into the public domain.

The debates that took place in many countries during the nineteenth century as to the extension of such duration insisted on that point. A limited duration aimed at achieving a balance between proprietary protection and public availability, thus creating two separate domains constituted by the passing of time. The erection of a private property right was only a limited intrusion into the public domain that should stay the rule. J. Ginsburg has shown that this predominance of the public domain was present in the early regimes of literary and artistic property both in France and in the United States (U.S.).[5] In 1774, in *Donaldson v. Beckett,*[6] one of the seminal copyright cases in the United Kingdom (U.K.), the Court of Lords voted in

2. This paper will be limited to copyright and will not address the duration of neighboring or related rights.
3. And are integrated into Trade-Related Aspects of Intellectual Property Rights by its general Art. 9, as well as in the WIPO Copyright Treaty.
4. States can provide for a shorter duration for their domestic works.
5. Jane Ginsburg, *A Tale of Two Copyrights: Literary Property in Revolutionary France and America,* 144 Revue Internationale du Droit d' Auteur (1991) https://doi.org/10.4324/9781315092621-2.
6. 1 English Reports 837 (H.L. 1774).

favor of the principle that copyright should be limited in time, insisting on the public interest in preserving the public domain as the rule.[7]

This principle is perfectly reflected in that oft-quoted declaration of Lord Macaulay in a speech before the English House of Commons in 1841:

> It is good that authors should be remunerated; and the least exceptionable way of remunerating them is by monopoly. Yet monopoly is an evil. For the sake of the good we must submit to the evil; but the evil ought not to last a day longer than is necessary for the purpose of securing the good.[8]

In addition to the determination of this minimal duration, the Berne Convention lays down other rules,[9] some of them being mandatory, such as: (1) a term of 50 years for anonymous and pseudonymous works after the date where the work has been made available to the public (except when the identity of the author is known or later disclosed); (2) the computation of the terms starting at January 1 of the year following the death of the author or the relevant event to be taken into consideration; (3) the calculation of the duration for works of joint authorship from the death of the last surviving coauthor.

Other rules are left at the discretion of the Union States, like the possibility of calculating the protection term of cinematographic works from the date of making available to the public or from the making of the film and providing for a shorter term of a minimum of 25 years for photographic works and works of applied art.

As to the moral right provided for by Article 6bis, the international Convention makes it mandatory to maintain it after the author's death, at least until the expiry of the economic rights, but it authorizes States that, at the time of their accession to Berne Union, did not protect moral rights for longer than the author's lifespan, to keep that rule. Therefore, the duration of moral rights largely varies from perpetuity in some countries to the same duration as economic rights or for the only period corresponding to the author's life.

15.1.2 National Copyright Laws

The final determination of the duration is left to national laws. Therefore, the duration of a copyright in a work, and thus figuring out what is protected and

7. *See also*, Michael Walter, *Historical Perspectives Regarding the Duration of Authors' Rights: Convergence of Term Systems*, at The Duration of Copyright and Related Rights, 15 (ALAI Study Days 2010 Vienna, Medium und Recht Publishing, 2012).
8. Thomas Babington Macaulay, *Macaulay Speeches and Poems* 285 (1874), Speech delivered to the House of Commons on Feb. 5, 1841.
9. For a comment, *see* Sam Ricketson & Jane Ginsburg, *International Copyright and Neighbouring Rights*, n° 9.50 et seq. (Oxford University Press, 2006).

what is in the public domain, shall be a matter for national lawmakers. The length of protection, therefore, varies greatly from one country to another.

Given that the Berne Convention does not impose a uniform rule for the duration of copyright, but only a minimum of 50 years *post mortem auctoris*, each country is free to decide about a longer term or specific rules applying to some cases. And the duration actually diverges quite significantly depending on the country.

The calculation of the duration from the death of the author, which was adopted by the Berne Convention, reflected at the time the growing individualization of copyright and is now used in most national copyright laws. Some traces of the date of publication that were used in the early copyright legislation, such as the Statute of Anne, still subsist, though. The U.S. for instance, relied on the date of publication until the Copyright Term Extension Act of 1998, where it switched to 70 years after the death of the author. Works created before 1978 still largely depend upon their date of publication, as will be seen later on.

As a general rule, the date of publication would also matter when the identification of the author or of the date of her death proves to be impossible, as is the case with anonymous or pseudonymous works or works made for hire where the authorship lies with another person than the creator. Anonymous and pseudonymous works are protected in the European Union (EU) for 70 years after they have been lawfully made available to the public. They are protected for 95 years after publication or 120 years after creation in the U.S. The same duration applies to U.S. works made for hire and the EU admits a similar rule where a Member State provides for particular provisions in respect of collective works or for a legal person to be designated as the rightholder.[10]

For copyright terms based on the author's death, the length of protection also varies. The 50 years or the Berne-minimum standard is less and less of application worldwide, but still prevails in most African and Asian countries. Instead, the life-plus-70-years is becoming the standard and applies in the EU, in States close to the EU,[11] in the U.S. to some extent, in Russia, Australia, Brazil, Israel, in a good part of Latin America,[12] in a few African or Asian States,[13] and was recently adopted in Japan and Canada. This

10. Directive 2006/116/EC of 12 December 2006 on the term of protection of copyright and certain related rights (codified version of the 93/98 Directive), Art. 1(4) (Dec. 12, 2006) Official Journal L 372, 27.12.2006, pp. 12-18.
11. Either geographically (e.g., Andorra, Ukraine, Armenia), or due to integration in the European Economic Area (e.g., Norway, Island, Liechtenstein, Switzerland) or aspiration to adhere to EU (Turkey, Macedonia, Montenegro, Albania, Serbia, Kosovo, Bosnia, Moldova).
12. The duration of 70 years *post mortem auctoris* is applicable in Argentina, Chile, Costa Rica, Dominic Republic, Nicaragua, Paraguay and Peru.
13. Like Singapore, Sri Lanka, Burkina Faso, Madagascar, Mozambique, Nigeria and Senegal.

expansion, from its adoption as a basis for harmonization in 1993 by the EU,[14] propagated along the extension of the EU, the competition in terms pursued by the U.S.,[15] and through bilateral agreements imposed by the European or American trade negotiating forces.[16]

Odd durations might apply in some countries, like life-plus-60-years in India and Venezuela, 75 years in Guatemala and Honduras, 80 years in Columbia or 97 years in Jamaica. The champion is Mexico which protects copyright for 100 years after the death of the author. The works of the great Mexican painter Frida Kahlo, deceased in 1954, have entered the public domain in Europe and most parts of the world in January 2025, or even sooner when a 50 years pma rule applies, but are still protected in her home country until 2055.

Most countries share the rule inspired by the Berne Convention, for calculating the term of joint authorship works from the death of the last surviving coauthor and apply a shorter term for photographs or works of applied art.

15.1.3 The Duration Determined by the Country of Protection

This national determination of copyright term is reinforced by Article 7(8), which provides that:

> in any case, the term shall be governed by the legislation of the country where protection is claimed.

This rule of *lex loci protectionis*, which is inherent to the fundamental principle of territoriality in copyright, also applies to the duration of copyright protection, with some qualifications that will be addressed below.[17]

This geographical variability of copyright duration means that a work of authorship will be protected or not anymore, depending on the country in

---

14. Council Directive 93/98/EEC of 29 October 1993 harmonizing the term of protection of copyright and certain and related rights (Oct. 29, 1993) Official Journal L 290, 24/11/1993, pp. 9-13 (codified by Directive 2006/116/EC).
15. The U.S. extended its term to 70 years in 1998 after the EU harmonization to prevent U.S. works to be less protected on the European market (due to the comparison of terms principle that we will see later on).
16. *See* Rebecca Giblin, *Reimagining Copyright's Duration*, in What If We Could Reimagine Copyright 179 (Rebecca Giblin & Kimberlee Weatherall eds., ANU Press, 2017).
17. The only exception concerns expressions of folklore, by virtue of Art. 15(4)(a) of the Berne Convention:

    > In the case of unpublished works where the identity of the author is unknown, but where there is every ground to presume that he is a national of a country of the Union, it shall be a matter for legislation in that country to designate the competent authority which shall represent the author and shall be entitled to protect and enforce his rights in the countries of the Union.

    This provision deals more with the competent authority to enforce rights in folklore than with the determination of the applicable law, but its rationale at the time of its insertion in the Berne Convention was certainly to ensure that national folklore is protected according to the law of the country of their origin.

which the protection is sought. For instance, works of Virginia Woolf, who killed herself in 1941, have been in the public domain in the EU since January 1, 2012, but might have entered therein at later times in the U.S., where it will depend on the date of publication of each work. Works published before 1930 in the U.S. are in the public domain since January 2025, so *The Voyage Out*, her first novel, that has been published in the U.K. in 1915 and in the U.S. in 1920, is in the public domain in both countries. *Mrs. Dalloway* was published simultaneously in U.S. and U.K. in 1925,[18] which seems to result from a clear intention of Leonard Woolf, her husband and publisher, to avoid copyright problems in the U.S.[19] Its copyright status hence differs in the EU, where the novel belongs to the public domain since 2012, and in the U.S., where its copyright only expired in 2021 (95 years after publication date). The same is true for, her iconic essay, *A Room of one's Own,* that just entered the U.S. public domain in January 2025, after its EU copyright expired already in 2012.

Sometimes, the work falls in the public domain in the U.S. sooner than in Europe due to the former importance of formalities. As an example, the copyright in the film *It's a wonderful life*, by Frank Capra, which was released in 1946, has not been renewed, as imposed by the then applicable law, and expired after a unique term of 28 years, so in 1975. In Europe, the cinematographic work is still protected for 70 years after the death of the last surviving coauthor, who could be one scenarist, Albert Hackett, who died in 1995 (whereas Capra died in 1991), so until the end of 2065. As it was not common to renew copyright in 1940s or 1950s movies, for no new exploitation could be foreseen in the 1970s (just before the advent of VHS and DVD, without mentioning the Internet), most Hollywood golden age movies are in the public domain in the U.S.

That variability can greatly complicate the task of identifying the composition of the public domain, particularly when the exploitation or use of a public domain work is envisaged simultaneously in many countries, as is increasingly the case with online exploitation. Another rule of terms comparison might further complicate the determination.

15.1.4 Comparison of Terms

The Berne principle of determination of duration by the *lex loci protectionis* is somewhat attenuated by recourse to the duration provided for by the country of origin. The last part of the Article 7(8) of Berne states that:

---

18. In the case of works published in the U.S. less than 30 days after publication abroad from 1923 to 1978, the duration rule applicable to U.S. works applies.
19. E.F. Shields, *The American Edition of "Mrs. Dalloway"* 27 Studies in Bibliography 157 (1974).

unless the legislation of that country otherwise provides, the term shall not exceed the term fixed in the country of origin of the work.

Therefore, if the State has not decided otherwise,[20] the determination of the term of protection will endure a comparison of the terms laid down in the country of origin and in the country of protection.

The term-comparison rule will increase the unstable definition of the public domain. It implies a rule of "material reciprocity," favoring the application of a shorter term of protection as fixed in the country of origin of the work. Most countries apply such rule. The EU imposes it on its Member States for works whose country of origin is outside the EU and the author is not an EU national.

To give a concrete example, the duration of the works of the Nobel Prize Rabindranath Tagore (deceased in 1941), whose works were originally published in India (where the term of protection is fixed to 60 years *post mortem auctoris*) shall be considered in France or in U.K. (both countries that apply the rule of the shorter term) to be 60 years after the death of the author, putting aside the application of the normal term of 70 years.[21] His works have thus been in the public domain in the EU since 2002, like in India, hence 10 years before the works of Virginia Woolf or James Joyce, who both died in the same year.

In the U.S. though, where the comparison of terms is not applied, the works of Tagore will be subject to the same rules of duration as U.S. works (complicated, however, by the consideration of conditions of publication in the U.S. after the first publication abroad). Most of his works, having been published before 1923, will also be in the public domain there (and have been since the entry into force of the Copyright Term Extension Act of 1998). In Canada, that does not apply Article 7(8) either; the life-plus-50-years term (in force until recently) is applied to Tagore's works (as the duration in its country of origin is longer), which put them in public domain as early as 1992.[22]

Of course, only his works in their original Bengali language are concerned, the duration of copyright in the translations being determined by the date of death of the translator. Some of Tagore poems have been translated into English by the Indian Nobel Prize himself and would follow the rest of the work in the public domain. From English, André Gide has translated some works into French. Those translations would be in the public

20. For a comprehensive explanation of the rule of term comparison, *see* Ginsburg & Ricketson (n. 9); Stéphanie Choisy, *Le domaine public en droit d'auteur* 117-142 (Litec 2002).
21. The French law reinforces the rule of shorter term by providing that the duration of a work whose author and country of origin is outside of the EU will be that granted in the country of origin without being superior to the term provided in France (*see Code de la Propriété Intellectuelle* (CPI), Art. L.123-12).
22. The extension of duration from 50 to 70 years in Canada does not have the effect of reviving copyright in works for which protection expired prior to 2023.

domain in France, for instance, 70 years after 1951, the year of death of Gide, thus, in 2022, 20 years after the original work.

It should be reminded that the country of origin is mostly determined, according to Article 5 of the Berne Convention, by the place of the first publication of the work and not by the nationality of the creator. A musical work by Rachmaninov, the *n°3 Piano Concerto*, was granted the same duration as French works, as it had been first published in Germany, another EU Member State, and not in Russia.[23] The shorter time of protection (50 years *post mortem auctoris*) that then applied in Russia was not relevant.[24]

Finally, the term provided for in the country of origin should not exceed that of the country of protection, as repeated in Article 7(1) of the EU Term Directive. It entails that a work by a Mexican author, for instance Frida Kahlo, will not be granted the life-plus-100-years term of the Mexican copyright law on EU territory, but only the European duration of 70 years. Conversely, as it seems that the rule of a shorter term does not apply in Mexico, European works will benefit there from the extra-long protection.

A recent example illustrates the intricacies of application of such a rule. The iconic Mickey Mouse entered in the public domain in the U.S. on January 1, 2024, at least in the form it first appeared in the animated movie of 1928, *Steamboat Willie*.[25] In application of the extension of copyright duration enacted by the U.S. in 1998 (that was said to have been fiercely lobbied by Disney company to avoid the coming fall of its famous mouse into the public domain), the copyright in the film and the character expired 95 years after their first publication, i.e., on January 1, 2024.

Immediately, the question arose as to whether Mickey also entered in the public domain on the same date at a global level, including in the EU. The EU rule of 70 years after the death of the last surviving coauthor would have implied that copyright would last until 2042, 70 years after the death of Ub Iwerks, who made most animations of that first movie.[26] However, the application of the rule of shorter term would prevail and impose on Member States to apply the duration as mandated by U.S. law, which is the country of origin of the work.

Some media and copyright scholars have uncovered an intriguing element that might trouble the waters on which Mickey is sailing, at least in Germany. An ancient bilateral treaty between Germany and the United States, from 1892, provides that U.S. citizens enjoy, in Germany, the protection of copyright on the same basis on which such it is granted to

23. Cour d'Appel Paris, 4e Ch., May 22, 2002 (Propriétés Intellectuelles 2003, 47).
24. Rachmaninov died in 1943, which would have put that work in the public domain in France in 1994, should the Russian rule be applied.
25. On all the intricacies of the entrance of this first version Mickey Mouse in the public domain, but probably not of others, *see* Jennifer Jenkins, *Mickey, Disney, and the Public Domain: A 95-year Love Triangle* (2024) https://web.law.duke.edu/cspd/mickey/.
26. The other coauthor being Walt Disney who died in 1966.

German nationals.[27] Article 7(3) of the EU Term Directive[28] allows Member States to retain acquired rights under international agreements despite the application of the rule of the shorter term. The national treatment granted by Germany to U.S. works would then align the duration on that provided for German works. The Federal Court of Justice considered in 2014 that this treaty still applied to U.S. works but was trumped by the intervention of the Universal Convention on Copyright, with the consequence that the copyright in the novel *Tarzan of the Apes* by Edgar Rice Burroughs expired in 2001, i.e., 50 years after the death of the author, and not 70 years as it would be for German works.[29]

That being said, the computation of term of protection resulting from the combination of this ancient treaty, the Universal Convention on Copyright and the Berne Convention in different configurations depending on the work in question, its date of publication and of death of its author, might end up in applying the longer term of 70 years *post mortem auctoris* to U.S. works in Germany (hence somewhat fissuring the EU harmonized rule). Nonetheless, some recent Court of Justice of the European Union (CJEU) decisions could raise some doubts about the extent of the international competence of Member States in copyright matters that would entitle them to derogate by international agreements, even old ones, to the harmonized rules on duration.[30]

In early January 2024, Google still answered to notice-and-take-down requests issued by Disney company to remove Steamboat Willie from YouTube in some EU Member States, including Germany. However, within a few days, and probably due to protests from YouTubers having uploaded transformed versions of the famous film, Disney retracted its claims,[31] and Mickey Mouse is now freely navigating on YouTube waters.

In conclusion on the rule of shorter term, one can say that computing the term of protection will first require knowledge as to whether the country has explicitly derogated from Article 7(8) of the Berne Convention and second to

27. Übereinkommen zwischen dem Reich und den Vereinigten Staaten von Amerika über den gegenseitigen Schutz der Urheberrechte, Jan. 15, 1892, https://de.wikisource.org.
28. "Member States which, on 29 October 1993, in particular pursuant to their international obligations, granted a longer term of protection than that which would result from the provisions of paragraphs 1 and 2 may maintain this protection until the conclusion of international agreements on the term of protection of copyright or related rights."
29. BGH, 26.2.2014, I ZR 49/13 (GRUR Int. 2014, 610).
30. *See* for instance Case C-414/11, Daiichi Sankyo, 18.7.2013, ECLI:EU:C:2013:520 (establishing an exclusive EU competence in all IP matters related to trade, which could include many aspects of copyright if one considers that the TRIPS includes the Berne provisions, as trade-related rules); Case C-265/19, Recorded Artists Actors Performers, 8.9.2020, ECLI:EU:C:2020:677 (though it relates to some specific provisions and does not seem to edict a general rule); Case C-227/23, Kwantum Nederland & Kwantum België, 24.10.24, ECLI:EU:C:2024:914.
31. Matt Binder, *Disney Backs Down from "Steamboat Willie" YouTube Copyright Claim*, https://mashable.com/article/disney-pulls-youtube-steamboat-willie-copyright-claim.

determine the country of origin of the work and the duration applicable in that country in order to compare it with the duration provided by the law of the country where the protection is sought. Consequently, the comparison of terms leads to a further fragmentation of copyright duration. Due to the *lex loci protectionis*, the work is not protected at the same time everywhere in the world. In addition, it might not be protected as domestic work either if the country applies the shorter term. The status of the work will be affected in a twofold way: when traveling abroad, the creation does not normally bring with it the rule of protection of its country of origin but will need to refer to it in some countries of protection. The centrality of the date of death of authors to decide about the duration of copyright is also only partially true, as the date and place of publication of each work will determine their country of origin, which might have an impact on the length of protection.

The example of the decision related to Rachmaninov illustrates this fragmentation of duration within the lifework of a creator. Depending on whether his musical compositions were first published in Russia or Germany or elsewhere, their protection under French copyright law would vary.

Instability and fragmentation combine to provide for an uncertain duration of creations, to the detriment of both users and authors. And this is only made worse by the subsistence, sometimes despite EU harmonization, of national-specific rules.

15.2 MORE REASONS FOR FRAGMENTATION

At this point, your head is spinning, right? Bear with me, as it is far from being over. It seems already complicated, but other legal provisions might make the calculation of copyright duration even more intricate. Some oddities appear here and there in national copyright regimes, justifying a longer term of protection for cultural, historical or economic motives.

15.2.1 War-Related Extensions of Protection Terms

The so-called wartime extensions purport to add some time to the normal duration of copyright in order to compensate for the lack of exploitation suffered during the two World Wars.[32] Such rule namely exists (or existed) in France, Belgium, Austria, Hungary, Japan, Portugal, Italy and Russia.[33]

32. On this topic, *see* Astri M. Lund, *War-Related Extensions of Terms: A Possible Obstacle to Further Approximation of the Duration of Authors' Rights?*, at The Duration of Copyright and Related Rights 170 (ALAI Study Days 2010 Vienna, Medium und Recht Publishing, 2012).

33. Belgium only extended the protection by 10 years for WWI and this law is considered to have been absorbed by the extension to 70 years *post mortem auctoris* by the directive of 1993. War extensions have been abrogated by Austria, Italy, Norway when transposing

For instance, two French laws, in 1919 and 1951, added extra months of protection to works that were not in the public domain when the laws were enacted. The first law added 6 years and 152 days to works published before 1921; the second one added 8 years and 120 days for works published before 1948. That means that a work published before 1921 would be protected for an extra time of almost 15 years.

Besides, if the author died fighting for France, his (or her, but women are largely absent from that list) works enjoy a supplementary term of protection of 30 years. The "authors dead for France" are enumerated in an official list[34] that includes, for instance, the most famous ones, Alain-Fournier, Desnos, Saint-Exupéry and Apollinaire, the only woman being Irène Némirovsky (only added to the list in 2010).[35]

This set of extensions has created much controversy in France, particularly as to whether it was compatible with the term of protection now harmonized throughout the EU.[36] While most EU States had considered that the wartime extensions were absorbed by the new duration of life-plus-70-years and did not apply anymore, some French courts opted for their cumulation. The *Cour de Cassation* partially settled the controversy in 2007 in a case involving a painting by Monet, who died in 1926.[37] The work normally entered into the public domain on January 1, 1997,[38] but the right owners claimed the benefit of the two war extensions and hence protection until 2011. The court refused such extension on the ground that it was covered by the 70 years now imposed by the EU Directive. The only exception, said the court, would result from the application of Article 10(1) of the duration Directive that states that:

> where a term of protection which is longer than the corresponding term provided for by this Directive was already running in a Member State on 1st July 1995, this Directive shall not have the effect of shortening that term of protection in that Member State.

---

the 1993 Directive. Russia extends the protection to 74 years for authors who fought in or worked during the Second World War. In other countries, these extensions were generally absorbed when a longer duration was enacted.

34. Including the authors whose certificate of death indicates that they died for France and authors similarly acknowledged as Dead for France in a government decree.
35. Nemirovsky died in a concentration camp and was neither a soldier or a resistant during the war. But other male authors are in the list without having actually fought for France. As to the absence of women in the list, some female writers have been in the resistance and would merit this distinction but might have been less visible as their male counterparts.
36. Cour d'Appel Paris (n. 23), applying the wartime extensions to works of Gabriel Faure and Camille Saint-Saens.
37. Cour de Cassation (1e civ.), Feb. 27, 2007 (Dalloz 2007, 807).
38. The first term of 50 years *post mortem auctoris* being extended by the directive of 1993, the work still being protected in Germany at the date of entry into force of the directive.

Monet's works were not protected anymore on July 1, 1995, in France, since the duration then applicable was 50 years after the death of the author plus 14 years and 172 days of war extensions (thus 1926 + 50 years + war extensions = copyright expired during 1991). Copyright was restored by the directive to confer Monet's works a protection until 1997, but no longer.

This decision leaves open the possibility of taking the wartime extensions into account, if they triggered a longer-than-70-years *post mortem auctoris* term that would be running upon the entry into force of the directive. Cases for application would be rare though, as the life-plus-70-years would normally be longer than the sum of the then applicable life-plus-50-years term and the 14-years extension. Indeed, the Court of Cassation decision does not result in adding those war extensions to the now applicable term of 70 years, but to compare the former 50 years + wartime extensions to the new duration. However, the term of protection for musical works in France has been extended to 70 years by a legal revision of 1986. As an example, the Bolero by Ravel (date of death, 1937) that was created in 1928, benefits from the Second World War extension and normally sees its copyright expire in April 2016 (1937 + 70 years + extension of 8 years and a few months). On July 1, 1995, date of entry into force of the directive, a longer term of protection than the life-plus-70-years (so until 2008), had started to run and should prevail.[39]

Another possible application of a longer duration could result from the 30-year bonus benefiting works of authors who died for France. One example is Apollinaire, who died in 1918 from the Spanish flu. As he was wounded on the battlefield in 1916, which had weakened him when he got the flu, he was considered "*mort pour la France.*" Therefore, without considering the war extensions, the work of Apollinaire, published before the First World War, should have entered the public domain on January 1, 1969 (50 years after the death of the author, which was the duration at that time). Apollinaire benefited though from an extension of 30 years (as dead for France), 6 years and 152 days [for World War I (WWI)] and 8 years and 120 days [for World War II (WWII)]. His work actually fell in the public domain only on September 29, 2013, which is 95 years after the poet's death. In 1995, when the Term Directive entered into force, this longer duration than the now applicable 70 years *post mortem auctoris* was already running, which allows the subsistence of this extended term according to Article 10(1) of the Term Directive.

The problem arose again for the works of Saint-Exupéry, the famous author of *The Little Prince*. Saint-Exupery disappeared with his plane in the

39. Note that Ravel's heirs have initiated a ltigation against the French CMO for musical works, SACEM, that refused to register the designer of the ballet decors, Benois, as a co-author, which would have the effect of extending the term of protection until 2039. A French court has rejected their claim in June 2024 (Tribunal Judiciaire de Nanterre, Nanterre, 28 juin 2024, N° RG 18/06332), but an appeal has been filed.

Mediterranean Sea in 1944 while he was flying for the allied forces. There was a lot of controversy on the circumstances of his death, with some German soldiers affirming they had shot a plane on that date approximately when he disappeared, but suicide was also sometimes advanced. In 1948, Saint-Exupery was officially recognized as "*mort pour la France*" even though his plane was only found and identified in 2000. His works having all been published between WWI and WWII (*The Little Prince* in 1943), he would enjoy only the second war extension (8 years and 120 days) plus the 30-year extension for his war-related death, which would add 38 years and 4 months. As on July 1, 1995, when the directive entered into force, this new period of 38 years had already started to prolong the then applicable 50-year duration; this extension is maintained and *The Little Prince*, though bitten by the snake, will still be alive until April 2033[40] (and later in the hearts of all lovers of that book).

Nonetheless, due to territoriality of copyright provisions, this extra time will only apply on his French planet, as this work has fallen in the public domain in all countries applying a 50 or 70-year *post mortem auctoris* copyright term. Along with his travels to other planets, *The Little Prince* will lose such benefit. On the occasion of the 2015 Public Domain Day celebration, an event organized in some countries to promote the value of public domain, a Belgian website put online illustrations of Saint-Exupery (that have entered in the public domain in all EU States but France), as well as derivative creations made by children at a workshop on *The Little Prince*, to expose the conundrum of the different durations throughout the EU.[41] A similar French event pointed at the Belgian website and made hyperlinks to the work of Saint-Exupery, to illustrate the peculiar situation in France. In comparison, the uploading of *Le Petit Prince* on a French website was immediately threatened with sanctions by the owners of copyright. A recent referral to the CJEU, that will be developed below, is questioning the cross-border effect of such different durations.

Note that *The Little Prince* is still protected in the U.S., too, as it was published there in 1943,[42] and its copyright was renewed, which makes it protected for 95 years after publication, hence until the end of 2038. And in Mexico, with its 100 years of protection and no application of the rule of comparison of terms, the work will be protected until the end of 2044.

---

40. 1944 + 50 years + 30 years + 8 years +120 days.
41. *Le Petit Prince*—Epub, http://www.saintexupery-domainepublic.be.
42. *Le Petit Prince* was only published in France after the war in 1946 and posthumously; Note also that the translations of the work might be protected longer depending on the date of death of the translator.

15.2.2 The Intriguing Case of *Peter Pan* in U.K. Copyright Law

Another little prince is the marvelous character created by J.M. Barrie in the 1930s, Peter Pan. This child who did not want to grow old has seen his wish granted by the U.K. Copyright Act. Its section 301 contains indeed a very peculiar rule that says:

> The provisions of Schedule 6 have effect for conferring on trustees for the benefit of the Hospital for Sick Children, Great Ormond Street, London, a right to a royalty in respect of the public performance, commercial publication [or communication to the public] of the play "Peter Pan" by Sir James Matthew Barrie, or of any adaptation of that work, notwithstanding that copyright in the work expired on 31st December 1987.

Technically speaking, one could say that this right to remuneration is not an extension of duration of copyright as the text itself recalls that the copyright expired in 1987, i.e., 50 years after the death of J.M. Barrie (or rather in 2007, considering the application of the transitional rule of the 1993 Directive), but a specific right to remuneration that is not even conferred to the heirs of the author but to an institution that does not hold any copyright in the work. In any case, Peter Pan has not completely fallen into the public domain or is now in a fairyland of a singular type of *domaine public payant*.

15.3 THE INSTABILITY OF DURATION DUE TO TERM EXTENSIONS

When lawmakers decide to extend the duration of copyright, they need to choose whether the new rule would have a retroactive effect, being of application to works that have already entered into the public domain but would still be in the conditions of the new duration, or whether only works for which copyright is still running, would be concerned by the legal change.

That question of application in time generally implies intricate transitory provisions that are likely to obscure even further the computation of copyright duration (*see* below section 15.3.1), as the example of persistence of some former duration rules despite the EU harmonization will demonstrate (*see* below section 15.3.2). Transitory provisions could also have the effect of restoring copyright in works that are not copyrighted anymore or even never were (*see* below section 15.3.3), as well as adherence to international treaties could lead to copyright restoration in other countries (*see* below section 15.3.4).

15.3.1 Options in Transitory Provisions

Australia is an example of a non-retroactive application of an extended term. When lengthening the copyright duration in 2005, the Australian lawmaker decided to apply it only to works that were still under protection.[43] Works whose authors died before 1955, hence fallen into the public domain when the new law was enacted, would not regain protection and would still be subject to the former rule of 50 years *post mortem auctoris*. The extended duration of 70 years would only apply to works for which the copyright was still on. Canada opted for the same solution when recently lengthening its copyright duration to 70 years. Such non-retroactivity might look unfair as it subjects authors (or rather their heirs or derivative copyright owners) to different treatment only because they died even a few days before others.

The U.S. has opted for an even more complicated picture, as it piled up different rules of duration without substituting the new ones for the former provisions based on other criteria for calculation. Determining the duration of copyright in the U.S. then requires intermingling different criteria depending on when the work is situated on a timeline and how the term was then calculated.

Indeed, the U.S. Copyright Act provides that works that were published between 1923 and 1963 would still be dependent upon the accomplishment of former formalities of affixing a copyright notice and renewing the copyright.[44] Works that have been published between 1923 and 1989 without a copyright notice are in the public domain;[45] likewise, if they were published with a notice before 1963 without their copyright being renewed. Works published before 1978 with notice and with renewal are protected for 95 years after publication date. After 1978, the term of copyright still relates to the dates of creation and publication with proper notice.

This complex regime hence requires ascertaining whether and when the work has been published or not, whether the formalities have been complied with and whether the copyright was renewed later on.

In the EU, the two directives related to copyright duration, one in 1993 to harmonize the term of copyright to 70 years *post mortem auctoris* and the related rights term to 50 years, the other in 2011 to extend the duration of related rights pertaining to music to 70 years, have adopted different rules. The second directive does not apply the new duration to performances and

---

43. *See* U.S. Free Trade Agreement Implementation Act 2004, s. 131 that has provided for this extended duration:

> The amendments made by this Part apply to copyright in works and other subject-matter that subsists on or after the day on which this item commences.

44. The following analysis was helped by the sheet prepared by Cornell University: Copyright Term and the Public Domain in the United States, https://copyright.cornell.edu/publicdomain.
45. If published between 1978 et 1989, they are in the public domain if they failed to register within five years after publication.

phonograms that were in the public domain at the date of entry into force of the directive.

On the contrary, the major harmonization of 1993 applied to all works and performances, whether they were still protected or not in their Member State of origin before the entry into force of the new rule. The overall objective of harmonization was to avoid fragmented rules that could:

> impede the free movement of goods and freedom to provide services and distort competition in the common market.[46]

The choice for the longer protection in force in some Member States (life-plus-70-years) in order to protect established rights and preserve protection enjoyed by rightholders in the EU[47] entailed that works who benefited from a shorter protection in other States would see it extended. It could often mean that copyright was restored in a work that was in the public domain.

15.3.2 National Provisions Surviving EU Harmonization

Despite the intended harmonization of duration rules, the EU transitory provisions have had another potential effect of leaving intact some existing national provisions.

The main culprit is Article 10(1) of the 1993 Term Directive, which is a major source of discrepancies in the harmonization by providing that:

> where a term of protection which is longer than the corresponding term provided for by this Directive was already running in a Member State on 1 July 1995, this Directive shall not have the effect of shortening that term of protection in that Member State.

We have already seen the impact of this article on the limited preservation of the French wartime extensions. Here are some other consequences of fragmentation of duration of copyright.

The duration of copyright in Spain, in conformity with the EU rules, is 70 years after the death of the author. However, a longer term of 80 years *post mortem auctoris*, that was the duration of the existing law upon the enactment of the EU harmonization, was preserved when transposing the directive for authors dead before December 7, 1987. One example is Antonio Machado (1875-1939), an important Spanish poet, whose works would hence enter in the public domain in Spain only in 2020, whereas it was free of copyright in other Member States as early as 2010, or Jacinto Benavente, another Spanish writer dead in 1954, whose works have entered the EU public domain on January 1, 2025, but will still be protected in Spain until 2035.

46. Directive 2006/116/EC, Recital 3.
47. Directive 2006/116/EC, Recital 10.

CJEU referral and Belgium NL courts decisions can be found in the copyright saga of the Journal of Anne Frank, which unfolded a few years ago and made national provisions pertaining to duration of posthumous works collide with the EU harmonized term.

The explanation of the case requires some preliminary historical background. The *Diary of Anne Frank* was written during WWII when the Frank family was hiding in a house in Amsterdam (*Het achterhuis* in Dutch which gave the original title to the Diary). Two versions of the Diary were written at the time, the second one being a development of the first Diary that the teenager, being aware of the coming victory of the Allies, revised in the hope it would be published after the war. The first version, written from 1942 to 1944, has been designated as Version A. The "re-write," also known as Version B, dates back from 1944 and is based on Version A. Anne Frank also wrote some stories known as the "Storybook."

After a denunciation, the whole family was deported, and Anne Frank died in 1945 in the Bergen Belsen concentration camp, only a few weeks before the camp was liberated.

Her father, Otto Frank, was the only one to come back from the camps. Upon his return, he was given the writings that his friends could find back in their hiding place. He decided to publish the Diary of his daughter. He compiled and selected some parts of Version A, Version B and a minor part of the "Storybook" while omitting some parts. The publication, known as Version C, was published with the title *Het Achterhuis* in 1947 and then published in many languages around the world.

Otto Frank died in 1980 and entrusted the Anne Frank Foundation he had set up in 1963 with the copyright in his and Anne Frank's works. He also bequeathed the original manuscripts of his daughter's work to the Dutch State. It enabled to discover the original writing of Anne Frank, and in 1986, a completely new version of the Diary was published, composed of the original manuscript in its two versions, A and B, including fragments that were not published in 1947.

In the approach of 2016, where the normal duration of 70 years after the death of Anne Frank, the author of the Diary would come to an end, copyright owners tried several strategies to keep control of the work.[48] Two legal arguments were successfully developed. First, version C that had been published by the father was considered a derivative work, of which Otto Frank was the author. Consequently, it was protected 70 years after his death in 1980, hence until 2050. The publication of versions A, B and C in their

48. Beyond arguing that copyright had not expired, the Anne Frank Foundation also registered the name Anne Frank or Diary of Anne Frank as a trademark, which was accepted by the OHMI, (OHMI, 4th Board of Appeal, Aug. 31, 2015, R 2401/2014-4), but not by some national courts. *See:* Cour d'appel de Bruxelles (9ème ch.), Oct. 3, 2013, N°2012/AR/2166. Note that in the aftermath of the Vigeland decision of the EFTA Court (Apr. 6, 2017, E-5/16), it could be argued that registering the *Diary of Anne Frank* as a trademark could be considered to be against *ordre public*.

entirety, with a direct comparison of the fragments as selected, rewritten and published by Otto Frank[49] shows that his intervention was rather extensive. In most cases, he changed the language and structure of his daughter's writing,[50] substituting his own style and way of expressing things without changing the content, the structure or the narration itself. Indeed, far from only editing the text or censoring passages that he found offensive, as it is generally said, he wanted to honor the testimony of his daughter by giving it a more literary form (not seeing much literary talent in her teenage style). Therefore, it could be argued that he made some creative choices and could earn copyright in his own version.

For the original writings that were published in 1986, a specific rule of duration applicable to posthumous works in many EU countries before the harmonization of copyright duration was called upon. In France, the Netherlands and Belgium, to take only a few examples, works published after the death of their author would be granted a term of protection of 50 years after publication. Thereby, the duration would better correspond to the useful life of the work starting in that case only with the publication and not with the death of the author. Such provision could also aim at enticing publication of works after the death of their author by any person in possession of unpublished writings, unperformed music or other types of works, particularly when the copyright would be conferred to the owner of the embodiment of the work, as was the case in Belgium,[51] and not to the author's heirs.[52]

This duration of 50 years *post publicationem* could be longer than the harmonized duration of 70 years *post mortem auctoris,* that replaced it in 1995, at the entry into force of the 1993 Directive. Therefore, Article 10(1) of the directive that protects longer terms of protection that were already running could result in maintaining that former rule. An Amsterdam Court agreed with that longer protection.[53] As the original manuscripts of Anne Frank were only published in 1986, the duration of copyright that was running in 1995 was 50 years after that publication date and should have expired on January 1, 2037. This is a longer duration than the normal term of 70 years after the death of the young woman, which would have expired

49. Harry Paape, G. van Der Stroom & David Barnouw eds., *De Dagboeken van Anne Frank* (Staatsuitgeverij/Bert Bakker, 1986).
50. That analysis is based on the French translation available to us, not on the original Dutch version, which should be the proper material for assessing the originality of the father's rewriting.
51. *See* Belgian Copyright Law, Art. 4:

> The owners of a posthumous work enjoy copyright for 50 years after the day it is published, performed, executed or exhibited (my translation).

52. Frans van Isacker, *De exploitatierechten van de auteur*, n° 69 (Larcier 1963).
53. Rechtbank Amsterdam, Dec. 23, 2015, Anne Frank Fonds v. Anne Frank Stichting, N° C/13/583257/HA (2015).

in 2016, which justifies that it is still in application.[54] Nevertheless, it would not be relevant for parts of Versions A and B published in 1947 or for other stories published in 1949 or 1960, as the copyright term applicable thereto would not extend the new duration provided for by the directive but would have lasted respectively until end of 1997, 1999 or 2010. Any remaining fragment of Anne Frank's works published after 1995 would also be subject to the rule of 70 years *post mortem auctoris.*[55] The Court of Appeal of Antwerpen in Belgium has reached another conclusion and held that the Diary was not protected anymore in Belgium on the ground of a specific interpretation of the former copyright law provision on posthumous works.[56]

As for wartime extensions, the survival of such former national rules and the discrepancy between their judicial interpretation disrupts the harmonization of duration and fragments the constitution of a European public domain. In the *Anne Frank* case, the Hoge Raad of the Netherlands has referred preliminary questions to the CJEU, not on the validity of such national derogations to the harmonized rule of duration, but on their online effect.[57] The Diary has been made available on a Belgium website gathering the original manuscripts of the famous author while preventing, through a geo-blocking measure, users from countries where the work is not yet in the public domain from accessing the text. As no technical measure is ever completely secured and geo-blocking can be circumvented by a VPN, the questions referred to the EU Court relate to the determination of the location of the act of communication and whether such an act of communication can occur in the blocked country, by means of the intervention of the user having recourse to a VPN or other device. It could be regretted that direct questions on the discrepancy of different rules of duration have not been asked to the EU jurisdiction, though it would not be surprising that the CJEU, once again, decides to address a question that it was not requested to answer.

15.3.3 Restoration of Copyright and Copyright Zombies

When harmonizing the term of protection to 70 years *post mortem auctoris*, the EU has opted for the restoration of copyright for works still protected in one country of the Union at the time of the entry into force of the directive.

54. This conclusion might not the same in all countries having this former regime for posthumous works. In Belgium, the transition to 70 years *post mortem auctoris* was achieved a few months (on Aug. 1, 1994 exactly) before the entry into force of the directive, which raises the question of the survival of this regime.
55. Some letters have surfaced in 1998 and were published in 2001. In 2013, a new publication of "The Collected Works" in Dutch consisted of version A, B and D, and other works, as well as yet unpublished letters.
56. Antwerpen, 13.3.2024, 2023/AR/10.
57. Case C-788/24, Anne Frank Fonds.

Consequently, a work in the public domain in one State could see its copyright revived if it was still protected in another Member State.

The European Court of Justice had to deal with such copyright or related rights restorations in two cases. The first one related to rights in phonograms which were restored by the effect of the 1993 Directive, their duration being extended from 30 to 50 years.[58] In its decision, the court clearly stated that:

> application of the terms of protection laid down by the Directive may have the effect, in the Member States which had a shorter term of protection under their legislation, of protecting afresh works or subject-matter which had entered the public domain.[59]

Another case followed 10 years afterward, again with rights in phonograms that had the curious effect of granting a right in recordings that were at no time protected before in the Member State concerned and benefited non-EU rights owners.[60] V.-L. Benabou coined this "renaissance" of rights in previously public domain works or subject matter the "zombies of copyright,"[61] which perfectly qualifies the effect of a copyright restoration law that creates new living creatures amongst the dead. It is not only a revival, she explains, as this mechanism does not only apply to rights that were dead but also to rights that were never born.[62]

In the same vein, a decision of the U.S. Supreme Court refused to consider the public domain as immutable. Whereas one Court of Appeal had qualified the public domain as a "bedrock principle of copyright law" with the consequence that "what is in the public domain should remain there,"[63] the Supreme Court held that:

> Neither the Copyright and Patent Clause nor the First Amendment makes the public domain, in any and all cases, a territory that works may never exit.[64]

This case challenged the constitutionality of a law restoring copyright in foreign works to comply with the adhesion of the U.S. to the Berne

58. Case C-60/98, Butterfly Music Srl v. Carosello Edizioni Musicali e Discograohice Srl, 29.6.2009, ECLI:EU:C:1999:333.
59. *Ibid.,* para. 18.
60. Case C-240/07, Sony Music Entertainment (Germany) GmbH v. Falcon Neue Medien Vertrieb GmbH, 20.1.2009, ECLI:EU:C:2009:19.
61. Her use of the "zombie" terminology was made in her oral intervention at the 2010 ALAI Conference on duration in Vienna but does not unfortunately appear in her written publication, *see* Valérie-Laure Benabou, *Transitional Law and Treatment of Aliens, The European Court of Justice's Judgement in the Sony/Falcon/Dylan Case*, at The Duration of Copyright and Related Rights 215 (ALAI Study Days 2010 Vienna, Medium und Recht Publishing, 2012).
62. *Ibid.*, 218.
63. Golan v. Gonzales, 501 F.3d 1179 (10th Cir. Colo., 2007).
64. Golan v. Holder, 132 S. Ct, 873 (2012).

Convention. Many foreign works were not protected in the U.S. due to either lack of mutual recognition between the U.S. and their country of origin or on the ground that they did not comply with the formalities required by the U.S. Copyright Act. But the ratification of the Berne Convention imposed a change of law to make those works benefit from the protection. The Uruguay Round Agreements Act (URAA), enacted in 1994, achieved that objective by restoring copyright in such works and providing some period of time during which the users of those formerly-in-the-public-domain works get the now-needed copyright clearance. One user, who managed a website with music partitions of classical music, including many foreign works, opposed copyright restoration on the basis of freedom of expression and the limited constitutional mandate conferred to Congress in copyright matters ("to promote the progress of science and the arts"). The Supreme Court upheld the constitutionality of such copyright restorations to comply with international obligations, as it did for term extensions a few years before.[65]

15.3.4 Copyright Restoration Due to Accession to Berne

The last accident in the normal application of duration rules can be found in transitory provisions due to accession to the Berne Union. Article 18(1) of the Berne Convention provides in that case that:

> This Convention shall apply to all works which, at the moment of its coming into force, have not yet fallen into the public domain in the country of origin through the expiry of the term of protection.

Here, the restoration of copyright in works that could have entered in the public domain in their country of origin is not due to a temporal but to a geographical extension of the protection. The application of this provision is limited though, as works whose term of protection has ended will stay in the public domain.

This article explains the need for new adhering countries to the Berne Convention to welcome foreign works that would have been considered before as unprotected for reasons other than the expiration of copyright term, as well the obligation for old Berne members to protect the new Berne members' works. It is a "two-way street," as aptly described by J. Ginsburg.[66] As an illustration of the first consequence of this provision, section 514 of the U.S. URAA of 1994 restores copyright in foreign works that had not complied with formalities and were hence not protected under U.S. copyright, as was mentioned earlier.[67]

---

65. Eldred v. Ashcroft, 537 U.S. 186 (2003).
66. Jane Ginsburg, *The French Cour de Cassation Reconciles Berne Convention Article 18(1) and 5(2),* at The Duration of Copyright and Related Rights 210 (ALAI Study Days 2010 Vienna, Medium und Recht Publishing, 2012).
67. *See* Golan v. Holder, 132 S. Ct 873 (2012), for a legitimation of this restoration.

The second consequence of Article 18(1) of the Berne Convention, leading to a mirror effect of protecting works of a new adhering State in the rest of the Union, was given a broad scope by the French *Cour de Cassation* in a case involving a Howard Hawks' movie, *His Girl Friday*. The film was in the public domain in the U.S. by default of renewal of its copyright. One company sold DVDs of the film in France and sought a declaration that the film was in public domain in its country of origin, which enabled such an exploitation in France. Copyright owners claimed that even if not protected anymore in the U.S., France was obliged under Article 18 of Berne to grant protection to the film.

The Court followed that second position by applying together Article 18(1) and Article 5(2) prohibiting formalities.[68] When the U.S. adhered to the Berne Convention, the film was in the public domain there not by the expiration of duration, said the court, but by the effect of unaccomplished formalities.[69] Such formalities being outlawed by Berne, *His Girl Friday* would have still been protected by the then applicable term of 56 years. This is another example of a "copyright zombie," not protected anymore in its country of origin but regaining a new life in other countries. And the movie escapes the application of the shorter-term rule as it would result in a duration (the 28-year term of protection applicable to the work in the U.S.) below the minimum of life-plus-50-years imposed by the Berne Convention.[70]

15.4 CONCLUSION

Duration is generally presented as a simple rule in copyright law, and despite its national determination, minimum term provided for by the Berne Convention and the harmonization achieved in the EU are signaled as key factors toward uniformity and universalism.

Particularly the EU extension to life-plus-70-years had external effects by inciting other States to align on such standard. The application of the comparison of terms rule in the EU and the measure of material reciprocity it entails was indeed a key motive to extend duration in the U.S. in order to prevent cultural products not benefiting on the EU market from the same duration as EU products. Bilateral agreements have eventually finished the job of imposing the now common EU and U.S. standard on third countries.[71]

68. Cour de Cassation (1e civ.), Dec. 17, 2009, n° 1302.
69. For a critique of the decision, *see* André Lucas, *Propriétés Intellectuelles* 733 (2010).
70. *See* the elegant commentary of Jane Ginsburg on the entanglement of the many rules of Berne Convention in that case; Ginsburg (n. 66) 212-213.
71. Silke von Lewinski, *The Framework of the International Copyright Treaties and Comparative Overview of the Terms Granted in National Law (General Report)*, at The Duration of Copyright and Related Rights 29 (ALAI Study Days 2010 Vienna, Medium und Recht Publishing, 2012).

"Is enough enough?" as Sam Ricketson wondered?[72] If one can, along with this prominent copyright scholar, be puzzled by the continuous lengthening of copyright term, another cause for concern should be the fragmentation it paradoxically maintains around the globe. The term extension, when justified by a harmonization narrative (or a competition one when States outrun each other for longer protections), should normally achieve some uniformization, even upward. Actually, the application of territoriality and its attenuation by the comparison of terms, complex transitory provisions and subsistence of specific national rules contribute to diverse durations for the same work across borders. Such distortions create lack of certainty about the contours of protection and un-protection, copyright and public domain, which can prove troublesome, particularly in the online environment. How can the legal frame for an online exploitation of a work be ascertained if its status would vary from one country to the other, with many elements and a good dose of legal expertise (and definitely some humor) needed to determine diverging and uncertain terms of protection?

With unstable and ever-expanding rules of copyright duration at national level, what place is left for circulation of public domain works, whereas economic studies show the increase of public availability of creations upon their entrance into the public domain?[73]

The blind spot in which duration is left in international copyright law ought to merit further attention. Even if a complete uniformization appears difficult and maybe undesirable, as it would wipe out cultural differences or national public policies or bear the risk of extending the protection again, some simplification could be beneficial. *The Little Prince* took great care of his rose and removed wild weeds to prevent the baobabs from growing and suffocating its little planet. Likewise, international lawmakers could be advised to take more care of the ecology of the copyright system by achieving more balance between protection and public domain and by not letting the first one grow wildly at the detriment of the free space left for creation and access to culture.

72. Sam Ricketson, *Further Approximation (Minimum Term) or Need for Harmonization in the Digital Age?,* at The Duration of Copyright and Related Rights 136 (ALAI Study Days 2010 Vienna, Medium und Recht Publishing, 2012).

73. *See* for instance Paul J. Heald, *Property Rights and the Efficient Exploitation of Copyrighted Works: An Empirical Analysis of Public Domain and Copyrighted Fiction Bestsellers,* 92 Minnesota Law Review 1031 (2008) https://doi.org/10.2139/ssrn.955954; Giblin (n. 16) 187-188.

Chapter 16

Dangers and Challenges of Copyright Law's Segmentation in the Digital Era from a Private International Law Perspective

Paul L.C. Torremans

Copyright is a complex animal. Before we even get to the cross-border level and to private international law,[1] we are already confronted with the different layers of copyright in certain works.[2] One can start with the easy example of a translation of a literary work such as a poem. There is copyright as a literary work in the original poem (as it is hard to see how there will be an "originality" problem with poetry).[3] There is also copyright as a literary work in the translation of the poem, but that does not affect the copyright in the original poem. One will, therefore, need a license from the owner of the copyright in the original poem to make the translation. And one will need another permission and license to communicate the original poem to the public by putting it on one's website alongside the translation. We assume for the purposes of this example that the original poem had not yet been communicated to the public in order to avoid the additional complication of

1. *See* Paul Torremans, *Private International Law Issues on the Internet*, at The Future of Copyright: A European Union and International Perspective 369-396 (I. Stamatoudi ed., Kluwer Law International, 2016); Paul Torremans, *Intellectual Property and Private International Law* (3rd edn, Oxford University Press, 2024).
2. Paul Torremans, *Holyoak and Torremans Intellectual Property Law* 187-188 (9th edn, Oxford University Press, 2019).
3. Case C-5/08, Infopaq International A/S v. Danske Dagblades Forening (2009) ECLI: EU:C:2009:465.

the new public question in scenarios such as the one in which a hypertext link had been used to refer to the original poem.[4] And one can follow up with the additional complication of the case of a movie in the format of a musical. Let us only mention the separate copyrights in the scenario, the lyrics, the music, etc.

Once one moves to the cross-border level, the good old Berne Convention principle of national treatment,[5] which was also taken on board as the guiding principle of the international intellectual property system established by the Trade-Related Aspects of Intellectual Property Rights (TRIPS) Agreement,[6] leads to a further level of complexity, which is generally known as the concept of territoriality.[7] In 1886, the concept may have looked simple and attractive. In the absence of a single international copyright or even full harmonization of national copyright laws or a model law, each country is left with the authority to run its own copyright system, but it has to grant access to it to foreign authors by treating them as if they were national authors. Hence, in the absence of formalities such as registration requirements, parallel and territorially limited national copyrights become the norm for the majority of copyright works. Such a system works well if copyright works are exploited on a country-by-country basis and if works do not cross borders. In the digital age, that is no longer the case, and exploitation takes, almost by definition, place at an international level. Hence, a massive choice of law issue arises. Copyright lawyers, and by extension all intellectual property law experts, tend to forget it, but the standard approach in private international law is to determine the single applicable law to an issue. When it comes to copyright infringement, the majority opinion accepts that the concept of territoriality renders this impossible and leads instead to the country-by-country application of the local copyright law as the *lex loci protectionis*. To take just one example, a European Union (EU) wide unauthorized broadcast of copyright-protected movie will lead to the distributive application of 28 national copyright law when the rightholder objects to the broadcast. And let us then forget, to go back to the example of the musical, that rather than a single rightholder in a single copyright work, there may in practice be multiple rightholders in multiple copyright works.

4. Case C-466/12 Nils Svensson v. Retriever Sverige AB (2014) ECLI:EU:C:2014:76; C-348/13, BestWater International GmbH v. Michael Mebes and Stefan Potsch (2014) ECLI:EU:C:2014:2315.
5. Berne Convention for the Protection of Literary and Artistic Works (Sep. 9, 1886), S. Treaty Doc. No. 99-27, Art. 5(1) (hereinafter "Berne Convention").
6. Agreement on Trade-Related Aspects of Intellectual Property Rights (Apr. 15, 1994), 1869 UNTS 299, Art. 3 (hereinafter "TRIPS").
7. Paul Torremans, *Intellectual Property and Private International Law* (3rd edn, Oxford University Press, 2024), Chapter 12.

Furthermore, copyright consists of a number of exclusive rights. Let us merely take the pair of the right of reproduction and the right of communication to the public as an example. Hypertext link cases are easy in this sense, as they merely raise (difficult) questions regarding the right of communication to the public. But let us simplify the technological aspect slightly while complicating the legal aspects. Let us replace the hypertext link to a photo on a different website with a scenario in which the photo is first downloaded, read, reproduced or copied on a Universal Serial Bus (USB) stick and then uploaded to a different website. The latter raises questions in relation to the right of communication to the public that come on top of the questions relating to the right of reproduction. And as the copying and the uploading may take place in different countries, conflict of laws problems arise, and a different national copyright law or different national copyright laws may apply to each act.[8]

But for copyright experts, there are two separate issues. The later communication to the public does not absorb, let alone erase, the act of reproduction. There are potentially two infringing acts, and for each of them, the court with jurisdiction will have to determine the applicable law and apply it separately to each of the infringing acts. And let us leave the discussion on how a court may have jurisdiction in such a case to one side for now.

Having demonstrated the complexity of matters, the time has come to look at solutions. At an academic level, we have proposed the Conflict of Laws in Intellectual Property (CLIP) principles, primarily focusing on special rules for cases of ubiquitous (copyright) infringement. We will return to these later, but whereas these follow the traditional private international law approach to look for the law with the closest connection to the case through a balancing act weighing various factors, it is proposed to look first of all at a recent approach of the Court of Justice of the European Union (CJEU), that focuses on a single infringing act; it determines the law applicable to that act and then applies that law to all the infringing acts. One therefore skips the determination of the applicable law for the other infringing acts. The question needs to be asked how far the Court want to take this approach, as it may create a revolution in the field of intellectual property.

16.1 *LAND NORDRHEIN-WESTFALEN V. DIRK RENCKHOFF*

At a first glance, case C-161/17 *Land Nordrhein-Westfalen v. Dirk Renckhoff*[9] is yet another case concerning the right of communication to the public.

8. *See* Paul Torremans, *The Law Applicable to Copyright Infringement on the Internet* 43(4) Nederlands Internationaal Privaatrecht 687-695 (2016).
9. C-161/17 Land Nordrhein-Westfalen v. Dirk Renckhoff (2018) ECLI:EU:C:2018:279.

Admittedly, it is a slightly peculiar case and one that differs from cases such as *Svensson* and *GS Media*[10] in that there is no hypertext linking to a copyright work on another site, but instead, a photo has been copied from a site to some kind of support device, before being used on in a digital homework by a pupil, which was then uploaded onto the school website. The question here is whether that act of uploading amounts to a communication to the public.

But the matter is slightly more complex if one looks at the case in a bit more detail. Mr. Renckhoff had taken the original picture of the city of Cordoba. It looks like a standard picture of the city, but there is no doubt that under German law, one way or another, there is copyright in the picture. The pupil had found the picture on the website www.schwarzaufweiss.de of a digital travel-magazine with the same name. Mr. Renckhoff had granted a copyright license to the magazine, but this license merely covered the use of the website for illustration purposes. He argued though that the act of downloading into a support device, such as a hard drive or a USB stick, of his photo of the city of Cordoba constituted, first of all, an unauthorized act of reproduction. One can see why the pupil wanted to illustrate a digital piece of homework for her course of Spanish with a photo of the city of Cordoba and why the school wanted to upload good or nice pieces of student work onto its website, and there might even be a whole debate in there whether some or all of these activities can be covered by educational and other exceptions and limitations, but the starting point remains; there still is an unauthorized act of reproduction and a claim to this point by the photographer.

It is therefore important to note for our current purposes that Mr. Renckhoff complained about two infringing acts. In the first stage, there is an infringement of his right of reproduction, and only in the second stage follows, in his view, an infringement of his right of communication to the public. In this case, both allegedly infringing acts happened in Germany, but one can easily see how, from a private international law perspective, an additional complication arises if the act of reproduction occurs in one country and the act of communication to the public occurs in another country.

It is therefore remarkable to see that the *Bundesgerichtshof* is merely asking the CJEU to clarify the position in relation to the act of communication to the public. Admittedly, there is an interesting question here. Does the absence of a hyperlink matter? In other words, should the Court's hyperlink/communication to the public approach also be applied in cases such as this one, where the hyperlink is replaced by the combination of an act of downloading-reproduction and an act of uploading? And if that is the case,

Advocate-General Campos Sánchez-Bordona delivered his opinion on Apr. 25, 2018, *see* curia.europa.eu.

10. Case C-466/12 Nils Svensson.; Case C-160/15 GS Media BV v. Sanoma Media Netherlands BV and others (2016) ECLI:EU:C:2016:644.

how do the various criteria set out by the Court apply in this somewhat peculiar educational context? But the *Bundesgerichtshof* goes further than that. There is no suggestion that the point of whether or not the downloading amounts to an act of reproduction is *acte claire,* i.e., that no question is needed on this point. Instead, the *Bundesgerichtshof* suggests that one is confronted here with a pattern of behavior by the alleged infringers that needs to be seen as a single act. The act of reproduction is absorbed by the act of communication to the public. It is merely a necessary step to enable the act of communication to the public.

All this cannot have escaped the attention of the Advocate-General, as he mentions specifically that the French government emphasizes the point that there is first and foremost an act of reproduction—by putting the photograph on the school's website without authorization—and that only in a second stage the act of communication to the public enters the scene.[11] Nor does the Advocate-General feel bound by the question of the *Bundesgerichtshof.* He spells out the importance of the case for the daily life of millions of pupils, and he announces that he will therefore also look at other factors that he thinks are useful for the case and for a full answer. That even includes a discussion on the point of whether the photograph, as a standard view of the city of Cordoba, qualifies for copyright protection. But there is no reconsideration of the act of reproduction as a separate infringing act. On the contrary, the matter is disposed of summarily. The Advocate-General merely states without further comment that he considers the approach to see the whole behavior as a single act, in this case, an act of communication to the public, as a correct approach adopted by the *Bundesgerichtshof.* The fact that this flies in the face of decades of copyright tradition is left untouched and not worthy of further elaboration.[12]

Focusing on a single act and, in this case, getting rid of the alleged unauthorized act of reproduction allows the Advocate-General also to suggest that there is no difference in approach between hypertext link cases and cases like this where the hypertext link is replaced by an act of reproduction and an act of uploading.[13] The focus remains then squarely on the question of whether or not there has been an act of communication to the public, irrespective of how the content of the communication to the public

11. C-161/17 Land Nordrhein-Westfalen, ECLI:EU:C:2018:279, para. 49.
12. *Ibid.,* para. 51; One cannot ignore the fact that this works rather well in the light of the Advocate-General's overall conclusion that there is no communication to the public in this kind of circumstances. It leaves schools and pupils free to continue this kind of activity without having to worry about copyright licences. If there had been a separate act of reproduction, such an outcome might have become elusive, as it is hard to see how an exception can cover uploading the whole photograph. And there is nothing by way of factors in the definition of an act of reproduction that could have offered an escape route.
13. The CJEU did not follow the Advocate-General on this point in a decision that focused entirely on the communication to the public point. Case C-161/17 Nordrhein-Westfalen v. Dirk Renckhoff (2018) ECLI:EU:C:2018:634.

has been acquired, and the same factors apply. That point in itself is, of course, worthy of a detailed analysis, but the concept of communication to the public is not our topic here, so we will leave that for another day.[14]

What one sees here is an approach that ignores the fact that the exclusive right of copyright is split up into independent acts, or, if one prefers that word, "rights," such as the right of reproduction or the act of communication to the public. One simplifies the case by merely focusing on a single act. That means, against the background of the copyright reality, that one has to pick one act and focus on a single exclusive right. What is not exactly crystal clear is how one makes that choice. In this case, one could argue that the main damage is created by the act of communication to the public. The act of reproduction could also then be seen as a minor technical step to enable communication to the public. But one could turn that around by saying one should focus on the basic step that enables the whole scenario to unfold. That would then focus on the act of reproduction as without it there could never have been an act of communication to the public. The *Bundesgerichtshof* and the Advocate-General do not set out criteria for their preference for the act of communication to the public. One has the impression that in this case they thought it was an obvious choice and that "*fingerspitzengefühl*"[15] prevailed as a criterion.

The *Renckhoff* case involved a purely domestic German scenario, even if the school's website could be accessed from anywhere in the world. But if we return to our topic of digital copyright in a private international law setting, one does after all reduce the international aspects of the case and thus its level of complexity by focusing on a single act. It may well be that it is easier to localize such a single act, and by all means, once it is done, the conflict of laws rule will lead to the identification of a single law that can then be applied to the whole case. The application of different laws to the different acts depending on where they are located is therefore ruled out.

One could, of course, object that we are maybe paying too much attention to a single opinion of a single Advocate-General in what is after all a rather peculiar set of facts. This could be a one-off case rather than an example of a trend to focus on a single right and a single infringing act. And why are we trying to draw private international law conclusions on the basis of what is and remains essentially a German case? The answer to that is that there is more. The CJEU has already been going down the same path in a case dealing with the unitary design right. That brings us to Wii game consoles and *Nintendo v. BigBen*.

---

14. C-161/17 Land Nordrhein-Westfalen, ECLI:EU:C:2018:279, paras. 89, 90.
15. The concept is hard to translate accurately, but the idea "instinctive feeling" comes close.

16.2 *NINTENDO V. BIGBEN*

There is also a jurisdiction aspect to *Nintendo v. BigBen*,[16] but let us leave that to one side for now and focus on the choice of law aspect.[17] In this case, there was a real private international law aspect, as part of the allegedly infringing activity was carried out in Germany by BigBen Germany, while another part of the allegedly infringing activity was carried out in France by BigBen France.

The starting point for the conflict of laws analysis in relation to a unitary intellectual property right is Article 8(2) Rome II Regulation:

> 2. In the case of a non-contractual obligation arising from an infringement of a unitary Community intellectual property right, the law applicable shall, for any question that is not governed by the relevant Community instrument, be the law of the country in which the act of infringement was committed.[18]

What makes it interesting for our current purposes was the fact that the discussion focused on remedies and therefore touched on a point outside the relevant Community instrument. The CJEU therefore had to decide how one determines, under these circumstances, the law of the country in which the act of infringement was committed.

BigBen had allegedly committed infringing acts in various Member States. According to Nintendo, its German customers could order remote controls and accessories that were compatible with Nintendo's Wii game consoles at BigBen Germany. Those remote controls and accessories were manufactured in France by BigBen France, and they were also delivered to German (and other) customers directly from France. That meant that from a conflict of laws perspective, two solutions were possible in an Article 8(2) Rome II Regulation context. On the one hand, one could opt to determine and apply the applicable law separately to each of the allegedly infringing acts in a distributive manner. That would then lead to German law for the allegedly infringing acts committed in Germany and to French law for the allegedly infringing acts committed in France. On the other hand, one could also analyze the infringing behavior of BigBen in its entirety and identify and apply a single applicable law to the whole of the behavioral pattern, e.g., on

16. Joined Cases C-24/16 and C-25/16 Nintendo Co. Ltd v. BigBen Interactive GmbH and BigBen Interactive SA (2017) ECLI:EU:C:2017:724.
17. *See* Paul Torremans, *Intellectual Property and Private International Law* (3rd edn, Oxford University Press, 2024), Chapter 12; Paul Torremans et al., *European Max Planck Groups on Conflict of Laws in Intellectual Property: The CLIP Principles and Commentary* (Oxford University Press, 2013); *Principles on Conflict of Law in Intellectual Property* (Dec. 1, 2011), Art. 3:601 (hereinafter "CLIP Principles").
18. Regulation (EC) No. 864/2007 of the European Parliament and of the Council of 11 July 2007 on the law applicable to non-contractual obligations (Rome II) (Jul. 11, 2007) Official Journal L 199, 31/07/2007, pp. 40-49.

the basis of the strongest or closest link between the allegedly infringing behavioral pattern and a certain country and its legal system.

The CJEU very clearly rejects the distributive application of different legal systems and applicable laws and prefers the application of a single legal system as applicable law to the whole case. In order to identify and determine that single applicable law, the correct approach, according to the Court, is "to make an overall assessment of that defendant's conduct in order to determine the place where the initial act of infringement at the origin of that conduct was committed or threatened."[19] The connecting factor is therefore the place of the initial infringing act, i.e., the one from which all the other infringing acts flow and without which they would not have occurred. That initial infringing act is determined by looking at the behavior of the defendant in its entirety and by making an overall assessment of that behavior.

The Court argues that such an approach corresponds with the unitary character of the intellectual property right, but there is no suggestion that it flows from it, i.e., that the approach is necessarily limited to unitary rights. On the contrary, the Court refers even more strongly to the fact that the approach strikes a fair balance between the rights of all the parties involved and to the fact that the approach makes matters predictable for the parties, as they can easily determine the applicable law in advance.[20] These two arguments are by no means linked exclusively to unitary rights. They come straight out of the Court's standard approach to private international law, as the reference to the *Homawoo* case proves.[21]

So, how did the approach work out in the Nintendo case? BigBen was relying on electronic commerce and a website that targets consumers in various Member States. On this website, it offered for sale various products that allegedly infringed Nintendo's community design rights. The infringing act is then the offering for sale of the allegedly infringing products, more precisely by putting such an offer on its website. That is the initial infringing act without which the other allegedly infringing acts could not follow. The place where such an infringing act takes place is then the place where the market participant starts the procedure to place the offer for the sale of the allegedly infringing article on its website. That initiating act clearly took place in Germany. It is important to note that the Court refers to the initiating act. That may take place at the company's headquarters while the website is hosted elsewhere. In the Nintendo case, that point did not arise, but the Court made it clear that all subsequent infringing acts, such as the manufacturing activity in France and the supply to customers in all Member States of the allegedly infringing articles from France, are irrelevant for the choice of the

19. Joined Cases C-24/16 and C-25/16 Nintendo Co. Ltd, para. 103.
20. *Ibid.*, paras. 102, 104.
21. Case C-412/10 Deo Antoine Homawoo v. GMF Assurances SA (2011) ECLI:EU:C:2011:747.

applicable law, as they are ancillary and as they flow from the initial infringing act.

One cannot deny that this approach that leads to the application of a single law is attractive as a result of its simplicity and predictability. That is even more so in the context of a unitary intellectual property right, but not exclusively. It also fits in well with the logic of private international law.[22] But in it, there is an inherent tension between, on the one hand, the idea of an overall assessment to identify that infringing act that will lead to the applicable law and, on the other hand, the idea one identifying the initial infringing act. In the Nintendo case, matters were relatively clear and simple. The offer on the website is key. All the other activities are merely filling such offers. It is therefore clear that the initial act dominates and that any overall assessment of the behavior of the defendant will ultimately lead to it. The *Renckhoff* case already shows that the matter is not necessarily so straightforward. The initial act is clearly the act of reproduction. Without it, the photograph can never appear on the website and there can be no (alleged) act of communication to the public. But the overall assessment of the behavior of the defendant will point in the direction of communication to the public. The website was after all a key instrument to share the work of pupils with other pupils, parents and the public at large. The act of reproduction does then become ancillary and is merely there to facilitate communication to the public. So, how crucial is the concept of the initial act? If one is looking for the start of the chain and the overall assessment is merely a tool to establish that all elements form part of the same chain, then Advocate-General Campos Sánchez-Bordon did get it wrong in the *Renckhoff* case. If one is, on the other hand, merely making an overall assessment to determine the key infringing act in the chain that reduces all other infringing acts to ancillary status, then the test becomes more flexible and seems to make more sense in a copyright scenario such as that in the *Renckhoff* case. But it would make the whole test far less predictable and that was after all the major justification for the whole approach. The CJEU undoubtedly has to clarify its approach in the coming months and years.

Be that as it may, there remains a clash with the underlying substantial intellectual property rights and their system. That system works in a completely different manner. There is no necessary link or chain between the various infringing acts. In a legal sense, they are not components of a more complex infringing activity,[23] even if in practice and in fact certain infringing acts often appear together. The intellectual property logic is therefore that one determines the applicable law for each of the allegedly infringing acts,[24]

---

22. Torremans et al. (n. 17); CLIP Principles, Art. 3:601.
23. Paul Torremans, *Holyoak and Torremans Intellectual Property Law* (9th ed., Oxford University Press, 2019), Chapter 15.
24. *See* Paul Torremans, *Intellectual Property and Private International Law* (3rd edn, Oxford University Press, 2024), Chapter 12.

especially if, as was the case in the BigBen group of companies, they are committed by entities with separate legal personalities. Even more worrying from an intellectual property law perspective is the outcome that the rightholder seems to be left with no means of redress in relation to the ancillary acts of infringement if, under the applicable law, there is no liability for the initial (main) infringing act. The *Renckhoff* case does indeed suggest that there will be no liability for the act of reproduction should the Court follow the Advocate-General's suggestion that there is no act of communication to the public. And why should BigBen France get away with blatantly copying the design when manufacturing the allegedly infringing articles in case, for one reason or another, BigBen Germany's offering for sale of the allegedly infringing articles on its website does not amount to an infringing act? A single law maybe, but one should build in a fall-back solution and an alternative choice of applicable law in case the claim for the initial act of infringement fails under the "single" applicable law.

Although that basis of jurisdiction was not used in the Nintendo case, let us return to the aspect of jurisdiction for a second. It is indeed the case that for unitary rights courts can take jurisdiction if they are the court of the place where the infringing act takes place. There is at least an interesting parallelism there with the choice of law approach. It does therefore not come as a surprise that the *Bundesgerichtshof* found plenty of inspiration in the Nintendo case when it dealt with the jurisdiction question in a case concerning EU trademarks.

16.3 *PARFUMMARKEN*[25]

If a parallelism between the approach to jurisdiction and the approach to choice of law looks attractive and may back up the Nintendo approach in relation to choice of law, a more thorough investigation of the approach to jurisdiction imposes itself. It must be clear though that the approach, as currently developed by the courts, has nothing to do with copyright. For now, it is dealing exclusively with unitary rights, i.e., primarily EU trademarks and by extension also Community designs. But as the Nintendo case does not clearly limit the scope of its choice of law approach to unitary rights, the question must at some stage be asked whether the jurisdiction approach could at some stage also be extended to nonunitary rights such as copyright, i.e., could the interpretation of the special unitary rights rules be extended to intellectual property right under the Brussels I Regulation[26] and more

25. BGH, Urt. v. 9.11.2017, I ZR 2016, 164, http://juris.bundesgerichtshof.de/cgi-bin/rechtsprechung/document.py?Gericht=bgh&Art=en&nr=80153&pos=0&anz=1.
26. Council Regulation (EC) No. 44/2001 of 22 December 2000 on jurisdiction and the recognition and enforcement of judgments in civil and commercial matters (Brussels I) (Dec. 22, 2000) Official Journal L 12, 16.1.2001, pp. 1-23.

specifically under its Article 7(2) (the old Article 5(3) dealing with tort jurisdiction)? So, let us look at the rule in relation to EU trademarks and Community designs that infringement jurisdiction is also granted to the courts of the country where the infringing act takes place (and that seems to leave out the place of the damage)[27] and let us do so in a trademark context as it is there that one at present finds the cases. From a purely factual perspective, infringing acts can, of course, take place in more than one Member State, and one will need to set out an approach that applies special rules in those circumstances.

Let us therefore start with Article 9 of the EU Trademark Regulation.[28] A EU Trademark entitles the proprietor of that EU trademark to prevent all third parties not having his consent from using in the course of trade, in relation to goods or services, any sign where the sign is identical with the EU trademark and is used in relation to goods or services which are identical with those for which the EU trademark is registered. That covers, amongst other things, affixing the sign to the goods or to the packaging of those goods, offering the goods, putting them on the market, stocking them for those purposes under the sign, or offering or supplying services thereunder, importing or exporting the goods under the sign and using the sign on business papers and in advertising. It is by no means unrealistic to assume that in a practical case, the defendant performs this combination of infringing acts and is then sued on this basis for infringement on the basis of Article 9 of the Regulation by the holder of the EU Trademark. The problem that arises then from a private international law perspective is that each of these (allegedly) infringing acts can have taken place in a different Member State.

A relatively straightforward scenario unfolded in the *Parfummarken* case[29] that was recently decided by the German *Bundesgerichtshof.* In this case, an Italian company offered perfumes that were protected by trademarks to the German public on a website that was also available in German. Signs that were identical to the registered and protected marks were thus used one way or another in Italy and in Germany, without there being a need for our current purposes to enter into the details of trademark law.

The question that arises, however, is what this means in terms of the jurisdiction of the courts in Germany and Italy when the owner of a trademark wishes to rely on the rule that jurisdiction is given to the court of the place where the infringing act took place or risks to take place. One could in this respect opt for the distributive application of the conflict of law rule

27. *See* Paul Torremans, *Intellectual Property and Private International Law* (3rd edn, Oxford University Press, 2024), Chapter 7.
28. Regulation (EU) 2017/1001 of the European Parliament and of the Council of 14 June 2017 on the European Union trademark (Text with EEA relevance) (Jun. 14, 2017) Official Journal L 154, 16.6.2017, pp. 1-99.
29. BGH, Urt. v. 9.11.2017, I ZR 2016, 164, http://juris.bundesgerichtshof.de/cgi-bin/rechtsprechung/document.py?Gericht=bgh&Art=en&nr=80153&pos=0&anz=1 (accessed Jun. 27, 2019).

to each of the infringing acts, as found in Article 9 of the Trademark Regulation. One would then (separately) determine the court with jurisdiction for each of the infringing acts. But the result could then also be that the German judge would have jurisdiction for certain infringing acts, while the Italian judge would have jurisdiction for other infringing acts. Such a fragmentation of jurisdiction and the fact that what clearly forms a single infringement pattern would be dealt with by different judges is hard to reconcile with the concept of the EU Trademark as a single intellectual property right for the whole of the EU. But that finding can be rebutted by the obvious finding that the owner of a European Trademark will always have the option to bring the whole case in the court of the place of residence or place of business of the defendant or, depending on the circumstances, the court of its own residence or place of business. And it also seems a logical consequence of the fact that Article 9 of the European Trademark Regulation divides the protection offered by the exclusive right into protection against several infringing acts that are each, in their own right, sufficient to lead to a finding of infringement of the European trademark.

Nevertheless, the *Bundesgerichtshof* refuses to apply the conflict rule in a distributive manner. The court argues that one should not make reference to each of the allegedly infringing acts, but instead, one should make an overall assessment of the behavior of the defendant in order to determine where the initial infringing act that forms the basis of the infringing behavior has been carried out or risks to be carried out by the defendant. In the *Parfummarken* case, that meant, according to the *Bundesgerichtshof,* the start of, or the decision to make a start with, the process by which the perfumes that were protected by the trademarks were offered to the public via the defendant's website. But there has to be an active intervention by the defendant (or a risk of active intervention).[30] In this logic, all other allegedly infringing acts are ancillary, and they flow from the setting up of the website on which the perfumes are offered for sale. The starting up of the website is therefore the initial infringing act if one assesses the behavior of the defendant as a whole. The fact that the website is in German,[31] that it is accessible from Germany[32] and that potentially perfumes are delivered to the German public in Germany merely gives rise to allegedly infringing acts that, in the infringing behavior of the defendant as a whole, flow from or follow the setting up of the website. In terms of jurisdiction, one then leaves these allegedly infringing acts to one side and the whole infringing behavior is linked to the place where the initial infringing act took place. That leads to jurisdiction being given to a single court, and in this case, that was the Italian court, as the defendant set up its website in Italy.

30. *Ibid.*, para. 27.
31. *Ibid.*, paras. 17, 29.
32. *Ibid.*, para. 31.

The major advantage of this approach is that one avoids dispersing the jurisdiction over what appears to be a single case and that all grounds of jurisdiction in the EU Trademark Regulation now lead to one court having jurisdiction to handle the whole case. That fits in well with the unitary character of the EU Trademark. There is also no clash with the territoriality principle; as for the EU Trademark, the whole EU is the territorial unit that is to be taken into account.

The *Bundesgerichtshof* turned down the request to refer the matter to the CJEU. One may indeed look at the CJEU's decision in *Coty v. First Note*[33] to derive support for the position taken by the *Bundesgerichtshof*, but one has to be careful in this respect. The *Coty* decision merely rules out reliance on the place of the damage to grant jurisdiction to a court in cases concerned with EU Trademarks. The Court of Justice argued that in such cases, the alternative forum is merely the court of the place where the infringing act took place. Coty does not offer support for the approach to merely rely on the initial infringing act.[34] On that point, doubts remain and the U.K. Court of Appeal decided recently to refer that matter to the CJEU.[35]

16.4 A CRITICAL ANALYSIS

A first question that needs to be addressed is whether the jurisdiction approach that was developed by the CJEU and by the *Bundesgerichtshof* in relation to EU Trademarks in particular, and in relation to unitary rights more generally can be expanded to all intellectual property rights. Admittedly, the special jurisdiction rules for unitary rights do not apply in those circumstances, but Article 7(2) Brussels I Regulation in its first limb also refers to the place where the infringing act takes place.[36] The courts of the country where the infringing act takes place will therefore have jurisdiction, and that jurisdiction extends to the whole case. One would merely have to accept that the second limb of Article 7(2) Brussels I Regulation also applies and may grant jurisdiction to another court on the basis of the damage occurring in the country of that other court. That jurisdiction will be limited to the local damage only, but that aspect can be left to one side for our current purposes. More importantly, this potential other ground for jurisdictions in no way

33. Case C-360/12 Coty Germany GmbH, formerly Coty Prestige Lancaster Group GmbH v. First Note Perfumes NV (2014) ECLI:EU:C:2014:1318.
34. For a highly critical analysis of the *Parfummarken* decision *see* Annette Kur, *Abolishing Infringement Jurisdiction for EU Marks?: The Perfume Marks Decision by the German Federal Court of Justice,* 49 International Review of Intellectual Property and Competition Law 452-465 (2018) https://doi.org/10.1007/s40319-018-0696-0.
35. AMS Neve Ltd and Ors v. Heritage Audio and Anor [2018] EWCA Civ 86, now pending as Case C-172/18.
36. *See* Paul Torremans, *Intellectual Property and Private International Law* (3rd edn, Oxford University Press, 2024), Chapter 5.

affects the ground for jurisdiction found in the first limb of Article 7(2) Brussels I Regulation. Also, for nonunitary intellectual property rights, there is therefore a ground of jurisdiction based on the place where the infringing act takes place. So far so good, but that brings us to the crucial question. Does it make sense to extend the approach advocated by the *Bundesgerichtshof* to these cases as well and to merely rely on the initial infringing act to determine jurisdiction on the basis of the first limb of Article 7(2) Brussels I Regulation? It would of course again have the advantage of bringing the whole case before a single court and to avoid partial jurisdiction to be given to different courts if different infringing acts in the whole infringing behavior of the defendant take place in different countries. In typical CJEU speak, it would enhance predictability. But maybe that is too simplistic as an argument. The real option to bring the whole case in front of a single court is really the one offered by Article 4 Brussels I Regulation, and that option is always on the table. Article 7(2) is supposed to offer an alternative. That alternative moves away from the link with the defendant and focuses on the link between the facts and the jurisdiction, either in terms of infringing act or in terms of damage. That link exists separately for each of the infringing acts if there is more than one, and it makes little sense to merely determine it for the initial act of infringement and then merely assume that the outcome will also suit the other infringing acts. Bringing the whole case in front of a single court is not the aim of Article 7(2) Brussels I Regulation; instead, each infringing act should be dealt with by the court of the country with which it presents the strongest factual link. Offering a second single court solution that will in fact often overlap with the one in Article 4, as the defendant is likely to initiate its allegedly infringing activity in the place where it has its habitual residence or its place of business, makes therefore little sense in the context of the Brussels I Regulation.[37] Tempting as it may seem, on this basis, there is no reason to expand the approach to nonunitary intellectual property rights.

A second question that needs answering is whether it really makes sense to distinguish between the grounds of jurisdiction for unitary intellectual property rights and those found in Article 7(2) Brussels I Regulation. Admittedly, the wording looks different and, as the CJEU pointed out in *Coty v. First Note*,[38] there is no trace of the place of the damage in the jurisdiction grounds for unitary intellectual property rights. But does it matter?[39] Article 7(2) Brussels I Regulation is the "tort" provision and deals with all kinds of traditional tort scenarios. Intellectual property infringement cases come under it, but they are not the standard type of case for which the provision was designed. In the traditional scenario, the tortuous act may take place in

37. Kur (n. 34).
38. Case C-360/12 Coty Germany GmbH.
39. *See* Paul Torremans, *Intellectual Property and Private International Law* (3rd edn, Oxford University Press, 2024), Chapter 8.

one country, and the damage that results from it may take place in another country. In the good old days, private international law textbooks tended to refer to the scenario of a hunter firing his gun on one side of the border and accidentally hitting a hiker on the other side of the border, but one can also think of a factory dumping toxic waste in the river in one country and the polluted water causing damage when use in the next country crossed by the river.[40] It is therefore logical that in providing appropriate jurisdiction links, Article 7(2) Brussels I Regulation refers both to the place of the act that leads to the damage and to the place of the damage. But intellectual property presents a different picture. Intellectual property is based on a territorial system.[41] In that system, there will only be an infringement if the element of damage is also present. Damage is an integral part of the definition of an infringing act.[42] And in a territorial system, there will therefore only be an infringement if both aspects, act and damage, occur in a single jurisdiction.[43] It makes therefore little sense to distinguish between act and damage when it merely comes to intellectual property rights. That then explains why the unitary intellectual property regulations do not refer to both. And when they refer to the place where the infringing act takes place, the "act" refers to the whole infringement, including the aspect of damage. Despite the different language, there should therefore arguably be no difference between the application of the nonunitary and unitary jurisdiction rules when it comes to intellectual property rights. This puts a huge question mark behind the Court of Justice's decision in *Coty v. First Note*.[44] And as this decision is the starting point for the line of argument that eventually leads to the *Parfummarken*[45] decision, it puts at the same time that line of argument in doubt. Sticking to *Coty v. First Note* also has the disadvantage that the alternative ground of jurisdiction that is intended to be provided by this provision will often merely be the same as the general ground linked to the person of the defendant. It is after all the standard scenario that the defendant acts and initiates the infringement in his habitual residence of his place of business. The approach will therefore frustrate the aim of the provision and the intention of the legislator.[46]

---

40. Think Case C-21/76 Handelskwekerij G. J. Bier BV v. Mines de potasse d'Alsace SA (1976) ECR 01735.
41. *See* Paul Torremans, *Intellectual Property and Private International Law* (3rd edn, Oxford University Press, 2024), paras. 12.31, 12.32.
42. *See, e.g.,* Berne Convention, Arts. 9, 5.
43. Paul Torremans, *Questioning the Principles of Territoriality: The Determination of Territorial Mechanisms of Commercialisation,* at Copyright Law: A Handbook of Contemporary Research, Edward Elgar Publishing, Chapter 19 (Paul Torremans ed., 2007).
44. Case C-360/12 Coty Germany GmbH.
45. BGH, Urt. v. 9.11.2017, I ZR 2016, 164, http://juris.bundesgerichtshof.de/cgi-bin/rechtsprechung/document.py?Gericht=bgh&Art=en&nr=80153&pos=0&anz=1.
46. Kur (n. 34).

When the *AMS Neve* case[47] came along, the CJEU clarified that the approach in *Coty Germany* only applies where the defendant is a third party who did not actively participate in the infringement. Then the alternative ground for jurisdiction merely gives jurisdiction to the courts of the Member State where the act giving rise to the alleged infringement occurred and in the presence of active conduct. That can indeed be an alternative ground of jurisdiction if a defendant domiciled in country A puts goods with an allegedly infringing mark on the market in country B. The courts in country B will have jurisdiction, but not in case the right holder wishes to sue an intermediary who merely sold the goods to the defendant in country C.

AMS Neve establishes a new approach for those scenarios where the defendant is alleged to have committed its own infringing act in the forum Member States, the jurisdiction of which is being established. The CJEU here has recourse to the targeting approach to establish the place where the infringement has been committed or threatened. In this particular case, the Court argued that the advertising and offering for sale were directed at the United Kingdom (U.K.) public and could therefore under a targeting approach be localized in the U.K.[48] Activation of the website and the advert is not an alternative, as, on the one hand, the location of the server is hard to determine, and on the other hand, the alleged infringer could locate these acts in its place of domicile and that would take away the idea that Article 125(5) provides an alternative forum.[49] The Court adds that a targeting approach leading to the local jurisdiction of the court of the Member State concerned also leads to a degree of consistency with the *Wintersteiger* approach to national trade mark cases in the courts of the country where the trade mark has been registered. In combination with the fact that Article 125(5) does exclude negative declaration cases that means that multiple proceedings in different jurisdictions can be avoided when the claimant sues both on the basis of its national trade mark and its EU trade mark. The same court will in general have jurisdiction to hear the whole infringement case. That avoids the frequent application of Article 136 that contains a mechanical rule giving preference to the court first seised.[50] There may, on the other hand, be multiple courts that each will have local jurisdiction as a result of the targeting approach. That is fully in line with the role of Article 125(5) to provide an alternative forum that is well-placed to deal with the case from the perspective of its facts. Other considerations apply in a choice of law context,[51] making the application in a jurisdiction context of the single

47. Case C-172/18, AMS Neve Ltd, Barnett Waddingham Trustees, Mark Crabtree v. Heritage Audio SL, Pedro Rodríguez Arribas, ECLI:EU:C:2019:674.
48. *Ibid.*, at paras. 37-42 and 56.
49. *Ibid.,* at paras. 47-53.
50. *Ibid.*, at paras. 56-57.
51. Paul Torremans, *From Nintendo Wii to Perfumes, Driving a BMW Car: A Tale of Transition to the Wrong Kind of Coherence*, at *Transition and Coherence in Intellectual*

connection of the activation of the website, as in the *Nintendo* case,[52] undesirable.[53] A different targeting approach does not then lead to inconsistencies, as the Court rightly remarks.[54]

It is important to bear in mind that in the targeting approach, mere accessibility of the website is not sufficient to establish jurisdiction.[55] Active conduct by the defendant is required,[56] but that conduct does not need to be physical.[57] In the digital age, it can happen entirely online, replacing the traditional idea that the seller or any tangible goods enter the targeted territory. In practice, the active conduct required mirrors the infringing acts in the trade mark regulation, which also enhances consistency, especially when taking into account that the targeting approach also found its way into substantive trade mark law in the *L'Oréal* case.[58] Jurisdiction will only be given to a court in a territory where there is clearly an alleged infringement, and the proximity of the court is to be applauded, even if the targeting approach departs from the rule that the EU trade mark produces its effect throughout the whole area of the EU. But in that sense, Article 125(5) is a statutory exception.[59] In a recent example, it was held that use of an allegedly infringing sign by means of paid referencing on a search engine website which uses a national top-level domain name of a Member State means that the Member State is targeted even if the alleged infringer does not expressly list that Member State as a country in which it supplies its goods.[60]

Property Law: Essays in Honour of Annette Kur (Niklas Bruun, Graeme Dinwoodie, Marianne Levin & Ansgar Ohly eds., 2021) pp. 145-154.

52. Joined Cases C-24/16 and C-25/16, Nintendo Co. Ltd v. BigBen Interactive GmbH, BigBen Interactive SA, ECLI:EU:C:2017:724.
53. Contra: Parfummarken decision of the German Bundesgerichtshof, Annette Kur, *Abolishing Infringement Jurisdiction for EU Marks?: The Perfume Marks Decision by the German Federal Court of Justice,* 49 International Review of Intellectual Property and Competition Law 457 (2018) https://doi.org/10.1007/s40319-018-0696-0.
54. Case C-172/18, AMS Neve Ltd, Barnett Waddingham Trustees, Mark Crabtree v. Heritage Audio SL, Pedro Rodríguez Arribas, ECLI:EU:C:2019:674, at paras. 60-64.
55. A Lopez- Tarruella, *International Jurisdiction in EU Trademark Infringements on the Internet: Is It* Possible to Complicate Things Even Further?, 13(2) Cuadernos de Derecho Transnacional 352-361, at 358 (2021) https://doi.org/10.2139/ssrn.3993862.
56. Case C-172/18, AMS Neve Ltd, Barnett Waddingham Trustees, Mark Crabtree v. Heritage Audio SL, Pedro Rodríguez Arribas, ECLI:EU:C:2019:674, at para. 46.
57. Annette Kur, *Abolishing Infringement Jurisdiction for EU Marks?: The Perfume Marks Decision by the German Federal Court of Justice,* 49 International Review of Intellectual Property and Competition Law 457 (2018) https://doi.org/10.1007/s40319-018-0696-0.
58. Case C-324-/09 L'Oréal SA, Lancôme parfums et beauté & Cie SNC, Laboratoire Garnier & Cie, L'Oréal (UK) Ltd v. eBay International AG and others ECLI:EU:C:2011:474.
59. Lydia Lundstedt, *AMS Neve and Others (C-172/18): Looking for a Greater "Degree of Consistency" Between the Special Jurisdiction Rule for EU Trade Marks and National Trade Marks,* 69(4) GRUR International 355 (2020) https://doi.org/10.1093/grurint/ikaa032.
60. Case C-104/22 Lännen MCE Oy v. Berky GmbH and Senwatec GmbH & Co. KG ECLI:EU:C:2023:343.

A third question is whether there needs to be a parallelism between jurisdiction and choice of law. The *Bundesgerichtshof*[61] attaches a lot of importance to the parallel its approach to jurisdiction is creating with the CJEU's conflict of laws approach in *Nintendo*.[62] By linking both the act initiating the infringement, one is likely to create a situation where the court with jurisdiction will then apply its own law, as the single applicable law in most cases. Attractive as this may seem, one needs to ask the question of whether this really adds anything. It is suggested that it does not. The underlying aims for jurisdiction and choice of law are fundamentally different. Jurisdiction always comes first, and these rules aim to bring the case before a court that is well-placed to deal with the matter. Hence, the reliance on rules that are either linked to the defendant, according to the logic that while the defendant has no choice but to defend itself against the allegations made by the claimant, the balance between the parties is restored by allowing the defendant to play at home in its home court, or to the fact of the case, according to the logic that the court is well-placed to deal easily with the facts and their impact and has the evidence, etc., easily to hand. That is one question, and the jurisdiction rules that deal with it are designed to fulfill the aims behind it. Only once that stage is over and we are in the court with jurisdiction does the choice of law matter arise. We are moving from procedure to substance. Which law will the court with jurisdiction apply to the case? There are likely to be connections with more than one legal system, and the court will need to select the appropriate law.[63] The basic principle for these rules is that one determines the closest connection, i.e., the applicable law will be the law that is most closely connected to the (facts of the) case. The jurisdiction rules will enable the case to be brought before a single court, and the choice of law rules will determine the single law that applies. Having one court and having one applicable law has its value and such an approach is to be encouraged, but different elements determine the outcome in either case and the determination serves different aims. There is, in other words, no added value in having a parallelism between jurisdiction and choice of law.[64] The CJEU seems to agree, as it ignored the approach in its *AMS Neve* decision. That decision clearly confines Nintendo to jurisdiction and the definition of the concept of the country in which the act of infringement was committed.[65]

61. BGH, Urt. v. 9.11.2017, I ZR 2016, 164, http://juris.bundesgerichtshof.de/cgi-bin/rechtsprechung/document.py?Gericht=bgh&Art=en&nr=80153&pos=0&anz=1.
62. Joined Cases C-24/16 and C-25/16 Nintendo Co. Ltd.
63. *See* Paul Torremans, *Intellectual Property and Private International Law* (3rd edn, Oxford University Press, 2024).
64. Kur (n. 34).
65. Case C-172/18, AMS Neve Ltd, Barnett Waddingham Trustees, Mark Crabtree v. Heritage Audio SL, Pedro Rodríguez Arribas, ECLI:EU:C:2019:674, at para. 61.

16.5 CONCLUSION AND SUGGESTION

Focusing merely on a single act of infringement and on the initial act therefore makes little sense. The approach is hard to reconcile with the basic principles of the EU's set of private international law rules and principles. And focusing on a single act is irreconcilable with the fact that copyright is made up of separate rights, such as the right of reproduction and the right of communication to the public. There is simply no rule that can justify that in a case with a heavy focus on communication to the public, such as the *Renckhoff* case, the right of reproduction can simply be brushed under the carpet. There is no reason why there cannot be a remedy for an infringement, and *a fortiori* there is no reason why there cannot be such a remedy if the court decides there is no infringement of the right of communication to the public. Infringement of a separate right, such as the separate right of reproduction, needs to be determined separately in its own right.

The CJEU has not had the opportunity to deal with nonunitary intellectual property cases in a private international law context to any significant extent since *Nintendo*, but it is encouraging to see that in judgments such as *AMS Neve,* the emphasis is clearly put on the fact that unitary rights are subject to special rules, also when it comes to jurisdiction. And where the rules are the same, the approach is different. That became clear recently in multiple defendants' cases concerning an EU trade mark. On that point, only Article 8(1) Brussels I Regulation applies and whilst the court sticks to its *Roche*[66] and *Solvay*[67] approach, it is clear that the requirement of there being the same facts is interpreted much more loosely. How else can one explain that the mere existence of a distribution agreement between independent parties was sufficient?[68] Two different approaches may not be ideal, but at least restriction of the Nintendo approach to unitary right is a step in the right direction. With that encouraging development in mind, it is time to return to the general picture, though.

If *Renckhoff, Nintendo* and *Parfummarken* are therefore not the way forward, how can one arrive at a single court with jurisdiction and a single applicable law?

In terms of jurisdiction, the current Brussels I rules already allow for the case to be brought in a single court. Article 4 does after all exactly that. Article 7(2) offers an alternative, and one should let it do so by taking both the act leading to the damage and the damage into account. It may offer a solution if the aim of the claimant is not to bring the whole case before the

66. Case C-539/03, Roche Nederland BV et al v. Frederick Primus en Milton Goldenberg, ECLI:EU:C:2006:458.
67. Case C-616/10, Solvay SA v. Honeywell Fluorine Products Europe BV, Honeywell Belgium NV, Honeywell Europe NV, ECLI:EU:C:2012:445.
68. Case C-832/21, Beverage City & Lifestyle GmbH, MJ, Beverage City Polska Sp. z o.o.,FE v. Advance Magazine Publishers Inc., ECLI:EU:C:2023:635.

court, but to focus on a specific jurisdiction, if the court of the place of the act leading to the damage is better placed to deal with the case. These are legitimate aims in a private international law context. The real risk is a digital Internet environment is a different one. If mere access to the material from a jurisdiction becomes the criterion, courts in all jurisdictions could become courts of competent jurisdiction. The claimant could then harass the defendant and bring the case to an inconvenient jurisdiction with a flimsy link to the case. One therefore needs to add a *de minimis* rule that stops this by requiring a minimal link with the jurisdiction.

It would lead too far to go into detail here, so let me merely refer to the example in the CLIP Principles:

> In disputes concerned with infringement of an intellectual property right, a person may be sued in the courts of the State where the alleged infringement occurs or may occur, unless the alleged infringer has not acted in that State to initiate or further the infringement and her/his activity cannot reasonably be seen as having been directed to that State.[69]

And one needs a separate rule for the real ubiquitous cases that really see infringement happen worldwide.[70] The CLIP proposal is as follows:

> (1) Subject to paragraph 2, a court whose jurisdiction is based on Article 2:202 shall have jurisdiction in respect of infringements that occur or may occur within the territory of the State in which that court is situated.
> (2) In disputes concerned with infringement carried out through ubiquitous media such as the Internet, the court whose jurisdiction is based on Article 2:202 shall also have jurisdiction in respect of infringements that occur or may occur within the territory of any other State, provided that the activities giving rise to the infringement have no substantial effect in the State, or any of the States, where the infringer is habitually resident and:
> (a) substantial activities in furtherance of the infringement in its entirety have been carried out within the territory of the State in which the court is situated; or
> (b) the harm caused by the infringement in the State where the court is situated is substantial in relation to the infringement in its entirety.[71]

69. CLIP Principles. Art. 2:202; *See* Torremans et al. (n. 17), 69 et seq.
70. *See* Paul Torremans, *Intellectual Property and Private International Law* (3rd edn, Oxford University Press, 2024), Chapter 11.
71. CLIP Principles, Art. 2:203; *See* Torremans et al. (n. 17), 85 et seq.

In terms of conflict of laws, one mirrors that.[72] Territoriality leads in principle to the application of the *lex loci protectionis* on a country-by-country basis. Such a patchwork works well for cases that involve only a limited number of jurisdictions. What one needs to do is, on the one hand, cut out the countries and applicable laws with which there is no real connection, while on the other hand, applying a single law to the really ubiquitous cases. The CLIP Principles propose to do that as follows:

Article 3:601: Basic principle:

> Unless otherwise provided in this Section, the law applicable to the infringement is the law of each State for which protection is sought.
>
> For the purposes of these provisions, "infringement" includes the violation of the intellectual property right, the remedies, as defined in Article 3:605.

Article 3:602: De minimis rule:

> A court applying the law or the laws determined by Article 3:601 shall only find for infringement if the defendant has acted to initiate or further the infringement in the State or the States for which protection is sought, or the activity by which the right is claimed to be infringed has substantial effect within, or is directed to the State or the States for which protection is sought.
>
> The court may exceptionally derogate from that general rule when reasonable under the circumstances of the case.

Article 3:603: Ubiquitous infringement:

> In disputes concerned with infringement carried out through ubiquitous media such as the Internet, the court may apply the law of the State having the closest connection with the infringement if the infringement arguably takes place in every State in which the signals can be received. This rule also applies to existence, duration, limitations and scope to the extent that these questions arise as incidental questions in infringement proceedings.

In determining which State has the closest connection with the infringement, the court shall take all the relevant factors into account, in particular, the following:

(a) the infringer's habitual residence;
(b) the infringer's principal place of business;
(c) the place where substantial activities in furtherance of the infringement in its entirety have been carried out;

72. *See* Paul Torremans, *Intellectual Property and Private International Law* (3rd edn, Oxford University Press, 2024), Chapter 17.

(d) the place where the harm caused by the infringement is substantial in relation to the infringement in its entirety.

Notwithstanding the law applicable pursuant to paragraphs 1 and 2, any party may prove that the rules applying in a State or States covered by the dispute differ from the law applicable to the dispute in aspects which are essential for the decision. The court shall apply the different national laws unless this leads to inconsistent results, in which case the differences shall be taken into account in fashioning the remedy.[73]

Admittedly, this will need to be done separately, e.g., for the right of reproduction and for the right of communication to the public, but in case such as *Renckhoff*, which might be the majority of cases, a single law will apply to the right of reproduction and in ubiquitous case, it might well be the same law as the one applied under the ubiquitous infringement rule.

One may not be able to put all of this into practice without intervention by the legislator, but it is submitted that a flexible approach to the current legal tools can go a long way. And this approach sticks much more closely to the basic principles of copyright law. It is therefore a better way forward than the one that can be derived from the *Renckhoff*, *Nintendo* and *Parfummarken* cases.

73. CLIP Principles, Art. 3:601 to 3:603; *See* Torremans et al. (n. 17), 301 et seq.

Part IV

Gaps in the International Copyright Law *Acquis*

Chapter 17

Authorship in International Copyright Law

Tatiana Eleni Synodinou

The concept of the author constitutes the privileged moment of individualization in the history of ideas, knowledge, literature, philosophy and science.[1]

In literary criticism, the vivid discussions about authorship are closely related to searching for the meaning of the text.[2] In copyright law, the author acts as a focal point around which many copyright rules and concepts are organized.[3] Furthermore, the way the figure of the author is perceived expresses conflicting visions over the identity of copyright law as either a personalist or a utilitarian legal mechanism.

The debates about the position and role of the author are extrapolated due to the lack of a meaningful definition of authorship in national, European and international copyright law. Indeed, like its "twin" concept of originality, the concept of authorship has not traditionally been defined by law.

However, in contrast to the abstract legal concept of originality, which has purposefully remained a legal chameleon so that it can be specified by the courts, the reason for the existing lacunae in the definition of authorship

1. Michel Foucault, *Qu'est-ce qu'un auteur?*, 63(3) Bulletin de la Société française de philosophie 73 (1969).
2. Caio Gagliardi, *The Problem of Authorship in Literary Theory: Deletions, Resumptions and Reviews*, 24(69) Estudos Avançados (2010). For the question of the relationship between copyright and literary authorship, *see*: Brad Sherman & Alain Strowel, *Of Authors and Origins, Essays on Copyright Law* (Clarendon Press 1994).
3. Lionel Bently, *Copyright and the Death of the Author in Literature and Law*, 57(6) The Modern Law Review Limited 973 (1994) https://doi.org/10.1111/j.1468-2230.1994.tb01989.x.

vary and are dependent on the idiosyncrasies of each copyright tradition. In personalist "author's rights" systems, the non-definition of authorship follows naturally from an implied dominant perception of the author as the natural person who has created the work. The dogma of the human author being the creator (the so-called creator doctrine)[4] is obvious, and any attempt to formally consecrate this could be cynically viewed as a way of questioning the sanctity of the rule. In this context, in the rare cases where a legal definition exists, it solemnly declares this manifest principle.

Conversely, in utilitarian copyright systems, such as common law copyright jurisdictions, statutory definitions of authorship[5] and entrepreneurial authorship[6] are used as a legal mechanism to allocate rights.[7] In this context, authorship is an artificial construct[8] for defining the first ownership over the work and is not a real definition of authorship. Consequently, while copyright law might have been built on an image of authorship, it paradoxically serves to grant authors a property right only to enable them to divest themselves of that property. Accordingly, and ironically, the concept of the author needs only to be sustainable for an instant.[9]

This chapter analyzes the main elements of a nascent delimitation of the concept of the author in the international copyright acquis. It is divided into two sections. Section 17.1 will demonstrate that, despite the lack of an official confirmation, a general principle of human intervention as a component of authorship is part of the international copyright acquis. Section 17.2 will examine the thorny relationship between authorship and originality. In this context, the need for a proper, consistent and autonomous definition of the concept of authorship will be defended.

17.1 TOWARD A GENERAL PRINCIPLE OF HUMAN INTERVENTION AS A COMPONENT OF AUTHORSHIP

17.1.1 The Natural Person: Author by Default in the Copyright System

In international copyright law, the concept of the author is at the epicenter of protection under the Berne Convention. Article 1 states, "The countries to

4. According to Jaqueline Seignette, "most modern copyright laws are indeed founded on the basic principle that copyright vests to the 'author' and that the 'author' is the natural person who created the work." This principle is further defined by Seignette as the "creator doctrine." *See*: Jaqueline Seignette, *Challenges to the Creator Doctrine* (Kluwer Law International 1994).
5. *See*, *e.g.*, the U.K. Copyright, Designs and Patents Act 1988, s. 48.
6. *Ibid.*
7. Lionel Bently, Brad Sherman, Dev Ganjee & Phillip Johnson, *Intellectual Property Law* 125 (Oxford University Press 2018).
8. *Ibid.*, 126.
9. Bently (n. 3) at 980, 981.

which this Convention applies constitute a Union for the protection of the rights of authors in their literary and artistic works," while Article 2(6) is more explicit in providing that "This protection shall operate for the benefit of the author and his successors in title."

While the absence of a clearly identified author is not completely alien to copyright law, it appears to be a marginal question. In this context, anonymous works from traditional culture with an uncertain date and origin or indigenous cultural expressions and traditional knowledge are seen as cases that lie outside the scope of copyright law, to which special regimes apply or are to be applied.[10] The Berne Convention has specific provisions covering the term of protection of anonymous works,[11] and a general rule of presumption has also established that the publisher is deemed to represent the author.[12] Furthermore, in the case of unpublished works where the author's identity is unknown, the "folklore rule"[13] provides that where there is every ground to presume that he/she is a national of a European Union (EU) country, it shall be a matter for legislation in that country to designate the competent authority which shall represent the author and be entitled to protect and enforce his/her rights.[14]

However, even though the figure of the author is dominant in copyright law, the issue of the legal nature of the author is not explicitly regulated.[15] Consequently, a key question to which the Convention does not provide a clear answer[16] has been whether the "author" must be a human being or whether legal persons can also be designated as authors according to the copyright traditions of Member States of the Union, which have the leeway to do so.[17]

The question is classical in the sense that it epitomizes the dominant existential dilemma of modern copyright law. According to the natural law approach, which perceives the property of the author as deriving from a theory of personality,[18] the work of the mind is the genuine fruit of the personality of the natural person who has created it. Consequently, it must be defined with reference to the sacred figure of its originator and thus of the

10. Daniela Simone, *Dreaming Authorship: Copyright Law and the Protection of Indigenous Cultural Expressions*, 37(4) European Intellectual Property Law Review 240 (2015).
11. Berne Convention, Art. 7(3).
12. *Ibid.*, Art. 15(3).
13. Jorgen Blomqvist, *Primer on International Copyright and Related Rights* 101 (Edward Elgar 2014).
14. Berne Convention, Art. 15(4).
15. Paul Goldstein & P. Bernt Hugenholtz, *International Copyright: Principles, Law, and Practice* 246 (3rd ed., Oxford University Press, 2013).
16. Blomqvist (n. 13), at 97.
17. Jane C. Ginsburg & Edouard Trepoz, *International Copyright Law: U.S. and E.U. Perspectives, Texts and Cases* 533 (Edward Elgar Publishing 2015).
18. Alina Ng, *Copyright Law and the Progress of Science and the Useful Arts* 18 (Elgar Law, Technology and Society 2011).

creator.[19] In this context, the author can normally only be a natural person, while originality is also inevitably defined with reference to the person of the creator. This approach is dominant in civil law copyright systems, where the emphasis is placed on protecting the work as the expression of a person's creative genius.[20]

Conversely, under Anglo-American copyright law, where justifications of copyright law are based both on the naturalist Lockean labour theory[21] and on utilitarian considerations,[22] the application of copyright law to legal persons too, via a legal regime of deemed authorship, is easily accepted. In light of a perception that "*the author is not more than the maker of what would become copyright*—property,"[23] producers of entrepreneurial works (sound recordings, films, broadcasts) are also called "authors" and enjoy copyright as initial rightholders under the law. The perception of the work is objective, in the sense that the focus is placed on the work and not on the author. Terminologically speaking, copyright law is the right to control the circulation of copies of the work and arises from the existence of a "copy."[24] The prevailing approach is that the work shall be protected by law as an immaterial good, which after its creation, is independent of the author and shall circulate smoothly, regardless of the whims of its originator. In this context, the American doctrine embraces a very broad conception of the author and allows legal persons who are promoters of the work to be authors, since the attribution of this status is deemed useful to the development of the creation of works. Indeed, as Melville and Nimmer pinpoint in relation to United States (U.S.) copyright law, "the primary purpose of copyright is not to reward the author," but is rather to secure "the general benefits derived by the public from the labors of authors."[25]

Therefore, since the "origin" of the work is not important, attributing the legal capacity of authorship to juridical persons who have invested in the production of the works and are capable of ensuring the smooth circulation of works in the market is very well conceivable.[26] Similarly, in the United

19. Frédéric Pollaud Dulian, *Le Droit d'auteur* 48 (Economica 2014).
20. Florence-Marie Piriou, *Légitimité de l'auteur à la propriété intellectuelle*, 196(4) Diogène (2001); Alexandra Bensamoun, *La protection de l'oeuvre de l'esprit par le droit d'auteur: "qui trop embrasse mal étreint*," 44 Recueil Dalloz 2919 (2010).
21. *See,* Edwin C. Hettinger, *Justifying Intellectual Property*, 18 Philosophy & Public Affairs 31, 36, 45 (1989).
22. Orit Fischman Afori, *Human Rights and Copyright: The Introduction of Natural Law Considerations into American Copyright Law*, 14 Fordham Intellectual Property Media & Entertainment Law Journal 497 (2004).
23. Andreas Rahmatian, *Copyright and Creativity: The Making of Property Rights in Creative Works* 43 (Edward Elgar 2011).
24. Jeremy Phillips, *La notion d'"auteur" dans la législation sur le droit d'auteur. Considérations sur la base du droit d'auteur au Royaume-Uni*, 103(1) Le Droit d'auteur 26 (1989).
25. David Nimmer, *Nimmer on Copyright* §1.03[A] (LexisNexis 2003).
26. André Lucas, *L'œuvre de l'esprit: création d'une personne physique ou morale? in*

Kingdom (U.K.), authorship is mainly property, based on a one-dimensional approach to Locke's economic theory of possessive individualism.[27] Historically, the concept of an "author" in the Statute of Anne has to be distinguished from the romantic concept of the "author," and therefore, "authors" are nothing more than "proprietors."[28] In the same vein, entrepreneurial works do not necessarily have human authors,[29] and they will be protected regardless of whether the "author" has employed mental skill, labor or effort in the creation of the work.[30] It is also noteworthy that U.K. legislation has been the first to openly contest the principle of human authorship by extending the conceptual boundaries of "authorship" from legal persons to include computer-generated works, which are defined as being "generated by computer in circumstances such that there is no human author of the work."[31]

In this context, U.K. law has been a precursor for the development of a flexible, transfigured "depersonalized" model of authorship, which is based on rewarding investment and does not have the human essence as a prerequisite.[32]

In international copyright law, the dominant interpretation of the Berne Convention appears to favor the position that the author shall be a natural person,[33] even though some jurisdictions appear to welcome legal persons as well.

Some expressions of this principle are the calculation of the term of copyright protection *post mortem auctoris* (from the death of the natural person of the author) and the recognition of moral rights which aim to secure

---

L'œuvre de l'esprit en question(s), Un exercice de qualification, Actes de colloque, mare & martin 31 (Alexandra Bensamoun, Françoise Labarthe, Agnès Tricoire eds, Collection droit privé & sciences criminelles 2015).

27. Anne Marie Bridy, *Coding Creativity: Copyright and the Artificially Intelligent Author*, 5 Stanford Technology Law Review 1, 4 (2012) https://doi.org/10.31235/osf.io/5ru6m.
28. Hitoshi Sakata, *The Making of the Concept of Authorship in U.K. Copyright Law,* 36 Revue Internationale du Droit d' Auteur 2013.
29. Bently, Sherman, Ganjee & Johnson (n. 7) at 187.
30. *Ibid.*, at 118.
31. Copyright, Designs and Patents Act 1988, s. 178.
32. As Guadamuz notes, besides the U.K., such protection exists only in Ireland, New Zealand, India and Hong Kong. *See*, Andres Guadamuz, *Do Androids Dream of Electric Copyright? Comparative Analysis of Originality in Artificial Intelligence Generated Works*, 2 Intellectual Property Quarterly 169, 175 (2017) https://doi.org/10.1093/oso/9780198870944.003.0008.
33. In favor of such an approach, *see*, Blomqvist (n. 13) at 97; Silke von Lewinski, *International Copyright Law and Policy* §5.84 (Oxford University Press 2008); Sam Ricketson, *The Need for Human Authorship: Australian Developments—Telstra Corp Ltd v Phone Directories Co Pty Ltd,* 34 European Intellectual Property Review 54 (2012); Adolf Dietz, *The Concept of Authorship under the Berne Convention*, 155 Revue Internationale du Droit d' Auteur 3 (1993); *See, e.g.*, Christopher Buccafusco, *A Theory of Copyright Authorship*, 102 Virginia Law Review 1229, 1260 (2016).

elements of the creator's personhood (the author's "honour and reputation").[34] This approach is also consistent with the prevailing natural law justification which inspired the Berne Convention, according to which "copyright law is a natural right which arises—without intermediation of the state—from the very act of 'authorship' itself."[35]

The only exception that can be found in the Berne Convention is the case of cinematographic works,[36] which allow Member States to determine who is the first owner of a cinematographic work. However, this is a rule of allocation of rights (a rule in relation to "first ownership") and should not be confused with the question of authorship. On the contrary, the prerequisite of "*human essence*" is reinforced, since the provision refers to film producers as "makers" rather than "authors."[37] For Jane Ginsburg, "contending that Berne embraces a concept of copyright in which incentive/investment rationales supply the sole justification for exclusive rights, … implies the expulsion of human authors and, given Berne's humanist cast, that would purge copyright of its 'soul'."[38]

This approach is also consistent with the prevailing natural law justification which inspired the Berne Convention, according to which "copyright law is a natural right which arises—without intermediation of the state—from the very act of 'authorship' itself."[39] "The same result can be reached through a fundamental/human rights approach. Both the Universal Declaration of Human Rights and the International Covenant on Economic, Social and Cultural Rights grant human rights to everyone—where everyone practically means humans."[40]

Subsequently, since expressions of the principle of human authorship are already present, albeit sporadically, in European copyright law, a formal consecration of this principle in a future codification of European copyright

34. Berne Convention, 6bis.
35. Martha Woodmansee, *The Romantic Author in Research Handbook on the History of Copyright Law* 63-64 (Isabella Alexander, H. Tomás Gómez-Arostegui eds., Edward Elgar 2016).
36. Berne Convention, Art. 14bis(2)(a).
37. Jane C. Ginsburg, *People Not Machines: Authorship and What It Means in the Berne Convention*, 49(2) International Review of Intellectual Property and Competition Law 131 (2018) https://doi.org/10.1007/s40319-018-0670-x, with reference to Sam Ricketson, *People or Machines: The Berne Convention and the Changing Concept of Authorship*, 16 Columbia-Volunteer Lawyers for the Arts Journal of Law & the Arts 1 (1991).
38. Ginsburg, (n. 37) at 131-135.
39. Woodmansee (n. 35) at 64.
40. Péter Mezei, "*You AIn't Seen Nothing yet*"*: Arguments Against the Protectability of AI-Generated Outputs by Copyright Law in Informational Rights and Informational Wrongs—A Tapestry for Our Times* (Maurizio Borghi & Roger Brownsword eds., Routledge 2023); Luke McDonagh & Plamen Dinev, *Copyright in Works Created by Artificial Intelligence: Between Creativity and Investments,* at The Cambridge Handbook of Investment-Driven Intellectual Property (Patrick Goold and Enrico Bonadio eds., Cambridge University Press 2023).

law would be welcome. In this context, Article 2.1 of the Wittem Group's European Copyright Code provides that "The author of the work is the natural person or group of natural persons who created it."[41]

From a comparative point of view, the principle that the author of the work is primarily a human being also seems to prevail,[42] even though copyright systems based on utilitarian justifications of copyright law accept deemed authorship for legal persons. This differentiation is eminent in common law jurisdictions, where legal persons have easily attributed the status of author, but at the same time, authorship is reserved only for human beings, with the exception of the U.K. provision in relation to computer-generated works. This oxymoron might be partially explained by the historic prevalence in common law jurisdictions of the legal fiction regarding the personality of legal persons,[43] even though the dichotomy between the doctrines of legal fiction and the so-called organic theory has today become a purely doctrinal topic.[44] According to this theory, the acts of the legal person are always deemed to derive from and to be attributed to the natural persons who are behind the corporate body instead of recognizing that the juridical person is a fully autonomous legal personality, as in the organic theory.[45] Extrapolating this legal fiction into copyright law signifies that legal persons can be allocated rights and even *ab initio* ownership, but not the capacity of an author because they are materially incapable of creating anything alone. The work is not the creation of the legal person but a creation

41. The text of the Code is available at: https://www.jipitec.eu/jipitec/article/view/53/49. Accordingly, Bernt Hugenholtz pinpoints in relation to the Wittem Code that is "uncontroversial" to regard the author of a work as the natural person or group of natural persons who created it. *See*, P. Bernt Hugenholtz, *The Wittem Group's European Copyright Code, in Codification of European Copyright Law* 345 (Tatiana Eleni Synodinou ed., Kluwer Law International 2012).
42. Jaqueline Seignette, *Authorship, Copyright Ownership and Works Made on Commission and under Employment in a Century of Dutch Copyright Law: Auteurswet 1912-2012* 119 (Bernt Hugenholtz, Antoon Quaedvlieg & Dirk Visser eds., deLex 2012); In the seminal study on the concept of authorship in comparative copyright law, Jane Ginsburg arrives at the conclusion that the legal systems in the U.S., the U.K., Canada and Australia, as well as in France, Belgium and the Netherlands appear to agree that an author is a human being who exercises subjective judgment in composing the work and who controls its execution. *See*, Jane C. Ginsburg, *The Concept of Authorship in Comparative Copyright Law*, 52 DePaul Law Review 1063 (2003) https://doi.org/10.2139/ssrn.368481. In China, para. 3 of Art. 11 of the 1990 Law declares that citizen who has created a work is the author of the work. As Xinqiang Sun mentions, Chinese Copyright Law, "like most other copyright laws of civil law countries, recognizes only a natural person as the author of a work." *See*, Xinqiang Sun, *Authorship in China (and Beyond): Authorship and Related Issues under the Chinese Copyright Law of 1990*, 54 Houston Law Review 469, 485 (2016).
43. *See*, Derek French, *Mayson, French and Ryan on Company Law* 150-156 (34th edn, Oxford University Press, 2017). *See also:* Maximilian Koessler, *The Person in Imagination or Persona Ficta of the Corporation*, 9 Louisiana Law Review 435 (1949).
44. French (n. 43) at 159-160.
45. *Ibid.*, 150-156.

made by human persons whose rights are attributed to a third party by operation of law. It is noteworthy that breaches of the principle of attributing authorship only to natural persons can be found even in highly humanistic copyright traditions, such as the French one, for example, in the case of the legal fiction[46] of "collective works."

The production of works by entities which could not be considered human beings has from time to time been examined by national courts. Even though these cases may be marginal or peculiar, the courts have consistently affirmed the principle of human authorship. The impossibility or difficulty of designating a human being as the direct originator of the work has been examined in automatic writing cases. Automatic writing is a technique for channeling messages from the spirit world. Since the person who produces psychographic writing claims to be acting only as a transcriber on behalf of a spirit,[47] the central questions are whether such writings are protected by copyright and who is the author of these works. The courts, both in the U.K. and in the U.S., have been reluctant to attribute authorship to non-human entities.[48] In the Naruto (the so-called *Selfie Monkey*) case, claims that copyright could also vest in an animal, and thus in an entity which cannot be legally classified as a human being, have also failed.[49]

As regards computer-generated works, the permanent stance of the U.S. Copyright Office, as formulated in the Compendium of U.S. Copyright Office practices, is that it will register an original work of authorship, provided that the work was created by a human being, and therefore works produced without any contribution from a human author are not entitled to protection.[50] The unwillingness to recognize automated non-human authorship has also been affirmed in Australia, where the courts have emphasized that works

46. *See*, Christophe Caron, *Droit d'auteur et droits voisins* 210 (5th edn, LexisNexis 2017).

47. Bridy (n. 27) at 191; Olivier Laligant, *La veritable condition d' application du droit d' auteur: originalite ou creation?* 52(1) Revue internationale de droit comparé 270 (2000).

48. Cummins v. Bond, 1 Ch. 167 (1927); No. 96 Civ. 4126, 2000 U.S. Dist. LEXIS 10394 (S.D.N.Y. 2000).

49. Naruto v. David John Slater, No. 3:2015cv04324—Document 45 (N.D. Cal. 2016); For an analysis, *see*, Andres Guadamuz, *The Monkey Selfie: Copyright Lessons for Originality in Photographs and Internet Jurisdiction,* 5(1) Internet Policy Review 1 (2016) https://doi.org/10.14763/2016.1.398.

50. *See*, Copyright Office's Compendium II, *§503.03(a)*, *Works Not Originated by a Human Author*, at Shlomit Yanisky-Ravid & Luis Antonio Velez- Hernandez, *Copyrightability of Artworks Produced by Creative Robots and Originality: The Formality-Objective Model,* 19 Minnesota Journal of Law Science & Technology 1, 15 (2018) https://doi.org/10.2139/ssrn.2943778. *See also*: Copyright Registration Guidance: Works Containing Material Generated by Artificial Intelligence, 88 Fed. Reg. 16,190, 16,192 (Mar. 16, 2023) (Whether a work made with artificial intelligence is registerable depends "on the circumstances, particularly how the AI tool operates and how it was used to create the final work").

which were missing a significant human creative input cannot be protected by copyright law.[51]

Nowadays, the development of artificial intelligence (AI) systems capable of producing works that cannot be distinguished from works created by humans ominously defies the privilege of human authorship.

The prerequisite of human creation regarding copyright protection of AI-generated outputs has also been confirmed in the decisions of the U.S. Copyright Board and the subsequent U.S. court decision in the Thaler case. Stephen Thaler created software that uses AI to generate visual art (the "Creativity Machine"). Thaler applied to the U.S. Copyright Office to register copyright in an image generated by this software (the artwork entitled "A Recent Entrance to Paradise"), identifying the "Creativity Machine" as the author of the work. According to his application, the artwork was "autonomously created by a computer algorithm running on a machine." Thaler claimed ownership of the copyright in the artwork as a "work made-for-hire" on the basis that he created the AI tool that had autonomously generated the artwork. The Copyright Office denied Thaler's application, explaining that image lacked "the human authorship necessary to support a copyright claim." Both the Copyright Office and the Copyright Review Board maintained that position in subsequent reconsiderations, confirming that copyright protection does not extend to the creations of non-human entities.

Regarding Thaler's action against the Copyright Office and Shira Perlmutter, in her official capacity as the Register of Copyrights and the Director of the United States Copyright Office,[52] the United States District Court for the District of Columbia confirmed that an artwork generated autonomously by AI alone is not entitled to protection under the U.S. Copyright Act. According to the Court, although copyright is designed to adapt to the times and apply to works created with or involving new forms of technology, human creativity is the *sine qua non* at the core of copyrightability. Copyright has "never stretched so far as to protect works generated by new forms of technology operating absent any guiding human hand. Human authorship is a bedrock requirement of copyright." Having ascertained human authorship as a prerequisite for copyright protection, the Court also admitted that a work generated by a human with the assistance of an AI tool might be protected by copyright law, depending on the degree of human involvement. The decision was confirmed by the U.S. Court of

51. IceTV Pty Ltd v. Nine Network Australia Pty Ltd 239 CLR 458 (2009); Telstra Corporation Ltd v. Phone Directories Co Pty Ltd (2010) 264 ALR 617, affd 194 FCR 142 (2010); Acohs Pty Ltd v. Ucorp Pty Ltd (2010) 86 IPR 492, affd 201 FCR 173 (2012). For an analysis, *see:* Jani McCutcheon, *The Vanishing Author in Computer-Generated Works: A Critical Analysis of Recent Australian Caselaw,* 4 Melbourne University Law Review (2013).
52. Thaler v. Perlmutter, Aug. 18, 2023, in Thaler v. Perlmutter, Case No. 1:22-cv-01564, (D.D.C. 2022).

Appeals on March 18, 2025. The Court notes that as a matter of statutory law, the U.S. Copyright Act requires all work to be authored in the first instance by a human being. Even if the term "author" is not defned in the law, multiple provisions of the statute indicate that authors must be humans. For the Court, "*All of these statutory provisions collectively identify an 'author' as a human being. Machines do not have property, traditional human lifespans, family members, domiciles, nationalities, mentes reae, or signatures. By contrast, reading the Copyright Act to require human authorship comports with the statute's text, structure, and design because humans have all the attributes the Copyright Act treats authors as possessing. The human-authorship requirement, in short, eliminates the need to pound a square peg into a textual round hole by attributing unprecedented and mismatched meanings to common words in the Copyright Act.*"[53]

However, despite the implicit recognition of human authorship in the Berne Convention, the lack of an explicit international acquis on the concept of authorship could lead to pluralist approaches on whether AI-generated outputs can be protected by copyright law. In this context, Chinese courts have already confirmed that AI-generated outputs could be, under certain conditions, protected by copyright law. In *Shenzhen Tencent Computer System Co Ltd v. Shanghai Yingxun Technology Co Ltd (Tencent)*,[54] the Nanshan District Court of Shenzhen ruled that an output generated by an intelligent writing computer software could be protected under Chinese copyright law on the basis of the human creator's selection and arrangement involved in producing the relevant output.[55] Furthermore, in November 2023, the Beijing Internet Court held that there was copyright infringement of an image generated with the use of Stable Diffusion (a text-to-image generative AI model). According to the court, the plaintiff—the user of the AI tool—should be considered the author of the image, given the fact that he made an intellectual achievement justifying copyright protection. Specifically, the plaintiff entered relevant prompts to generate an image that matched the plaintiff's expectations and then further adjusted the prompts based on the preliminary images generated by Stable Diffusion.[56] This

53. Thaler v. Perlmutter, Mar. 18, 2025, Appeal from the United States District Court for the District of Columbia (No. 1:22-cv-01564), No. 23-5233.
54. Yue 0305 Min Chu 14010 (2019).
55. Yong Wan & Hongxuyang Lu, *Copyright Protection for AI-generated Outputs: The Experience from China*, 42 Computer Law & Security Review (2021).
56. Beijing Internet Court, Li v. Liu, (2023) Jing 0491 Min Chu No. 11279 (2023). *See*, Yuqian Wang & Jessie Zhang, *Beijing Internet Court Grants Copyright to AI-Generated Image for the First Time*, Kluwer IP Law (Feb. 2, 2024) https://copyrightblog.kluweriplaw.com/2024/02/02/beijing-internet-court-grants-copyright-to-ai-generated-image-for-the-first-time; Loke-Khoon Tan, James Lau & Harrods Wong, *China: A Landmark Court Ruling on Copyright Protection for AI-generated Works*, Baker McKenzie Global Litigation News (May 8, 2024) https://globallitigationnews.bakermckenzie.com/2024/05/08/china-a-landmark-court-ruling-on-copyright-protection-for-ai-generated-works/.

decision of the Chinese court appears a priori to adopt a more flexible approach regarding what constitutes a human contribution that justifies the recognition of the user of the AI tool as the author compared to the approach of the U.S. Copyright Office guidance, which states that works generated with the use of AI could be protected by copyright law if the "AI contributions are the result of … an author's 'own original mental conception'."[57] However, based on the U.S. Copyright Office's understanding of the technology, "users do not exercise ultimate creative control over how such systems interpret prompts and generate material" and, par consequent, they are not eligible for copyright protection over this content.[58]

In conclusion, the concept of the author as the human being who created the work is a central underlying principle in modern copyright law. Nonetheless, the depersonalization of authorship through the recognition of legal persons as "authors" and the mass production of artworks by sophisticated AI systems undermine the foundations of this principle. Specifically, as regards AI-generated works, the prevalence of the sacred principle of human authorship requires a significant human intervention in the creative process[59] and consequently renders heretical the recognition of authorship without human input, such as in the relevant U.K. legislative provision. The question of human authorship is also linked to the issue of whether authorship implicitly requires an "intention to create." In this case too, the emergence of AI-generated outputs brings to the forefront the lack of a systematic analysis regarding the core, the delimitation and the application of such a requirement.

17.1.2 The Intention to Create: The Emergence of a New Criterion in Copyright Law?

As has been demonstrated, the concept of authorship in copyright law is human-centric in the sense that significant human creative contribution is required in order to recognize the status of author.

Nonetheless, both international copyright law and national copyright laws remain silent on the question of whether there is an implicit requirement that creativity must be intentional or purposive. The main question is whether an essential component of authorship is the fact that the author is conscious

57. Copyright Registration Guidance: Works Containing Material Generated by Artificial Intelligence, A Rule by the Copyright Office, Library of Congress on Mar. 16, 2023, https://www.federalregister.gov/documents/2023/03/16/2023-05321/copyright-registration-guidance-works-containing-material-generated-by-artificial-intelligence.
58. McCarthy Tétrault LLP, *Copyright and Generative AI: Understanding Recent Chinese Court Decisions* (Mar. 17, 2024) https://www.lexology.com/library/detail.aspx?g=d73da3c3-e7ad-4f6f-b7cc-0657bc6a720b.
59. Shlomit Yanisky-Ravid & Xiaoqiong (Jackie) Liu, *When Artificial Intelligence Systems Produce Inventions: The 3A Era and an Alternative Model for Patent Law,* 39 Cardozo Law Review 2215 (2018) https://doi.org/10.2139/ssrn.2931828.

of creating the work, which also implies that the author has the will to create a work[60] and that he/she has a minimum of control over the creative process.[61]

Consciousness of creation seems obvious when the work is the fruit of a human conscience. However, this criterion impedes the recognition of non-humans, such as machines or animals, as authors.

The existence of an intrinsic criterion that creativity must be purposive has been advanced by copyright scholars,[62] while in some instances, it has been implied in case law,[63] mainly in cases where the issue of the protection of sports games was raised. In *NBA v. Motorola*,[64] where the NBA claimed that Motorola had infringed the NBA's copyright over the broadcasting of games, the U.S. Court of Appeals rejected this argument by highlighting the fact that athletes are competitors and do not act by following an underlying script. As the Court noted, "The preparation is as much an expression of hope or faith as a determination of what will actually happen."

In other words, the will to create the work is absent, since the athletes have the will to compete, and they do not act in collaboration and purposively in order not to create a specific work.

Similarly, in *FWS Joint Sports Claimants v. Canada*,[65] the Canadian Federal Court of Appeal upheld the Copyright Board's finding that the magnetism and appeal of sports games derive from unforeseeable occurrences. Despite the degree of planning involved, what happens on the field is dictated by the interaction with the opposing team and it is necessarily unpredictable.

The lack of protection of adversarial sports games (such as football, basketball and volleyball) under copyright law[66] was also acknowledged in

60. Noémie Enser, *Conscience et création en droit d'auteur* 380 (Thése de doctorat, Université Paris-Saclay, 2015).
61. André Lucas, Agnès Lucas-Schloetter & Carine Bernault, *Traité de la propriété littéraire et artistique* 89 (5th edn, LexisNexis 2017). (at 77), no 57.
62. *Ibid.*; F. Pollaud-Dulian, *Le droit d'auteur* 124 §131 (2nd edn, Economica 2014); André Lucas, Jean Devèze & Jean Frayssinet, *Droit de l'informatique et de l'internet* 413 §648 (Puf, Coll. Thémis Droit privé, 2001) Pierre Sirinelli & Ministère de la Culture et de la Francophonie, *Industries culturelles et nouvelles techniques* 61 (La Documentation française, 1994).
63. As Bridy mentions, in the seminal *U.S. Feist* case, the Court quotes the case *Burrow-Giles. See*, Bridy (n. 27) at 8, citing *Feist Publ'ns.*, Inc. v. Rural Tel. Serv. Co., *499 U.S. 340* (1991) (quoting Burrow-Giles Lithographic Co. v. Sarony, 111 U.S. 53, 59-60 (1884)). However, in *Bell,* it was held that unintentional or accidental variations (e.g., "a shock caused by a clap of thunder") may be claimed by an author as his or her own, as long as those variations are more than merely trivial.
64. National Basketball Assoc v. Motorola *INC*, 105 F. 3d 841 (2nd Cir. 1997).
65. FWS Joint Sports Claimants v. Canada (The Copyright Board) 22 IPR 429 (1991).
66. As Viola Elam, notes, "*Adversarial Sports Differ from Choreographed Sports in that the Former Category Places Primary Emphasis on Direct Competition While the Latter Presents a More Essential Artistic Component.*" *See*, Viola Elam, *Sporting Events as*

European copyright law.[67] In the *Football Association Premier League* and *Murphy* rulings,[68] the Court of Justice of the European Union (CJEU) concluded that sports events as such do not qualify as protected subject matter under EU copyright law. As the Court stated, football games cannot be classified as works which are the author's own intellectual creation, since they are subject to rules of the game which leave no room for creative expressive freedom.[69]

While the concept of the will is pervasive in law, especially in the law of contracts and the law of obligations, the "intention to create" has not been expressly established as a criterion for copyright protection to subsist. Certainly, it would be irrational to impose a requirement to investigate the internal will of the author either before or during the creative process in order to attribute the legal capacity of an author to a person. However, authorship necessitates at least a minimum preconception by the author of the general shape of the intellectual form that will be externalized and materialized. In this sense, it is irrelevant whether part of the materialization of the work is deliberately left to chance or is made with the use of technical means, provided that the author exercises a general control over the creative process.

If such a requirement exists, accidental works which are entirely unpredictable cannot be protected under copyright law, while works which have arisen partially due to chance could still be protected. Such an approach has been defended by copyright scholars,[70] while there is a notable exception in U.S. copyright law, where the courts have admitted that even mere "accidental works" are protected.[71]

Furthermore, it would not be possible to recognize machines as the authors of copyright-protected works, even if the dominant prerequisite of "human authorship" were to be disregarded. Machines act on orders and obey rules, and they do not have the consciousness and intellectual awareness that they are creating a work, which is a vector that conveys

---

Dramatic Works in the U.K. Copyright System, 13(1) The Entertainment and Sports Journal (2015) https://doi.org/10.16997/eslj.1.

67. *See*, Thomas Margoni, *The Protection of Sports Events in the EU: Property, Intellectual Property, Unfair Competition and Special Forms of Protection*, 47(4) International Review of Intellectual Property and Competition Law 386 (2016) https://doi.org/10.1007/s40319-016-0475-8.
68. Joined Cases C-403/08 and C-429/08 Football Association Premier League Ltd and Others v. QC Leisure and Others (C-403/08) and Karen Murphy v. Media Protection Services Ltd (C-429/08) (2011) ECLI:EU:C:2011:631.
69. *Ibid.*, para. 98.
70. X. Linant de Bellefonds, *Droits d'auteur et droits voisins* 21 §65 (2nd edn, Dalloz, Coll. 2004); Michel Vivant & Jan Michel Bruguière, *Droit d'auteur et droits voisins* 123 §105 (2nd edn, Dalloz, 2013).
71. Bridy (n. 27) at 8; Ginsburg (n. 37) at 1086 with reference to Judge Frank's description of accidental works in the case Bell v. Catalda, notably images generated by bad eyesight, claps of thunder and frustrated flinging of sponges. *See*, Bell v. Catalda 191 F.2d 99 102, 103 (2d Cir. 1951).

meanings and messages. In the absence of a consciousness of creation, the AI system does not go beyond the stage of reproduction.[72]

If there is significant human intervention, the "intention to create" must be perceived flexibly and objectively as the existence of consciousness and will to produce a work, even if the exact final form of the work was not completely conceived by the author, and part of the materialization of the work has been left to chance. Therefore, it is sufficient that the author has a general, minimum level of control over the creative process.[73]

The exclusion from copyright protection of unpredictable productions which do not directly derive from a human intention to create is crucial not only for sports games but also for AI-generated productions, as the following paragraphs will demonstrate.

17.1.3 The Conundrum of AI Production

The degree of autonomy of AI systems is a factor which depicts the evolution of the machine from a simple computational processing tool to a robust advanced decision-making system. In the present state of the art, autonomous agents are able to generate new forms of expression through the use of software that mimics the configuration of human neural networks. This process is often both automatic and independent of human intervention. AI systems are therefore able to generate works which—if created by humans—would deserve copyright protection.

However, if autonomy is defined as the status whereby an agent is self-governing in the sense that he/she can determine freely how she/he will act, then AI autonomy is a fiction. AI-generated creations, even those which appear unpredictable, are still dependent on the design of the software which is generating the work. In other words, AI agents do not have a free will which can supersede the software creator's choices.

---

72. Alexandre Lourié & Alexis Aulagnier, *Création artistique et intelligence artificielle: de l'art ou du cochon?*, Medium (Nov. 9, 2017) https://medium.com/@lourielexandre/cr%C3%A9ation-artistique-et-intelligence-artificielle-de-lart-ou-du-cochon-728e28402b03.

73. For a conceptual distinction of consciousness to subjective and objective, *see:* Enser (n. 59) at 405 and 415. According to Enser, subjective consciousness refers to the consciousness of the person of his existence, and therefore, the strict application of such a criterion would result in denying the protection to infants, to persons with intellectual handicap and to persons who are under the influence of psychotropic drugs. The concept of objective consciousness may be interpreted as the consciousness to create a work which is protected by copyright law and, also, the consciousness of the specific result of the creative process (the final form of the work) and the control of the creative process. The author rejects the subjective consciousness criterion and holds the opinion that the objective consciousness shall be seen only as an indication for the existence of authorship and not a criterion for the award of copyright protection.

The impossibility of defining a human being as the direct originator of the AI-generated work challenges the justifications and fundamental principles of copyright law and could be seen as the main impediment to including AI-generated works in the existing copyright law framework. Indeed, in the case of AI-generated works, the "author" appears prima facie to be another work, the computer program which acts as the "mind" of the AI system. In this context, the recognition of AI as a legal personality capable of being granted authorship has been advanced by some scholars. It has been argued that in the contemporary world, even if AI today is not a fully autonomous, self-aware, conscious robot with an inner personality experiencing emotions and explaining choices, it must be given authorial rights as a legal person based on its high intelligence and efficiency.[74] Under such an approach, modern justifications for personhood would not be rooted in the unique nature of humans, needing self-expression or subjective will, given that rights have also been granted to non-humans, such as legal corporations. Recognizing the resulting social benefit, legal corporations have been legal entities for hundreds of years, even if they will never reach the point of autonomously acting without the direction of their board of directors, shareholders, etc.[75] In the same context, based on modern justifications, it has been argued that legal personhood must be granted to AI as it is something that can produce intelligent results and that people will benefit from it, usually—but not exclusively—in the economic sense.[76] Indeed, although such an idea was later dropped, the European Parliament adopted a resolution requesting the Commission to consider giving "electronic personalities" to robots in cases where robots render autonomous works.[77] In this context, granting authorship to AI could also enhance social and legal stability through the concept of allocation-attribution.[78]

However, the attribution of legal personality to AI and, par consequent, the recognition of AI authorship should be rejected. Due to their lack of awareness, machines cannot be creative.[79] Furthermore, the recognition of AI as a legal personality and author is difficult to enforce as it requires the "re-construction" of copyright law in all jurisdictions, which—based on

74. Tzipi Zipper, *Mind over Matter: Addressing Challenges of Computer-Generated Works under Copyright Law*, 22(2) Wake Forest Journal of Business and Intellectual Property Law 129 (2022).
75. *Ibid.*
76. *Ibid.*
77. Blaseetta Paul, *Artificial Intelligence and Copyright: An Analysis of Authorship and Works Created by A.I.*, 4(5) International Journal of Law Management & Humanities 2345 (2021).
78. Laetitia Coguic, *Forward Thinking or Right on Time?: A Proposal to Recognize Authorship and Inventorship to Artificial Intelligence*, 8(3) Indonesian Journal of International & Comparative Law 223 (2021).
79. Ana Ramalho, *Will Robots Rule the (Artistic) World? A Proposed Model for the Legal Status of Creations by Artificial Intelligence Systems*, 21(1) Journal of Internet Law 12 (2017) https://doi.org/10.2139/ssrn.2987757.

originality requirements and copyright justifications—all equate the author with a human being.[80] Moreover, a machine does not need to have an incentive for the creation of a work, while granting authorship to AI may disincentivize humans from producing AIs.[81]

Considering their actual capabilities, even the most advanced robots should be treated only as useful tools, helping humans to reach the best result, while the significant human involvement in the creation process of work will not be reduced soon.[82] Human creativity in AI-assisted production may occur in different phases of the creative process: "conception" (design and specifications), "execution" (producing draft versions), and "redaction" (selecting, editing, and finalizing). Although AI has largely replaced human creators in the execution phase, the contribution in the other two stages is purely by humans through the selection of detailed design choices concerning style techniques, materials, etc., in the conception phase and the revision of the final product before publication in the redaction phase.[83] Consequently, such a human contribution is more than enough for the recognition of humans as authors for now and in the near future. In addition, from a practical perspective, it is difficult to imagine a machine being capable of claiming copyright infringement or negotiating and signing transfers or licences of its rights to others.[84]

Consequently, the only way to award copyright protection to AI-generated works would be to attribute the work to a natural person. This could be either the computer programmer who created the software which, in turn, produced the work, or the user of the AI tool.

In terms of recognizing the software engineer as an author, he should be seen as the ultimate cause of the production of the work since he/she will be the one who, through his/her personal creative contribution, will determine how the software reasons and acts. The machine will be considered a simple processor and an executor whose technical or artistic skills cannot be a basis for authorship.

However, this approach appears problematic. The causal link of the work with the software programmer is weak since he/she sets the rules and parameters under which the software operates, but he/she does not define the final form of the work. Since the final expression (the "form") of the work is generated by the machine, attributing authorship to the "planning" or to the "design" conceived by the creator of the software could be seen as a violation

80. *Ibid.*
81. Coguic (n. 77) at 245.
82. *Ibid.*
83. Christophe Geiger, *The Role of Human Creativity in the Copyrightability of Artificial Intelligence-Generated Works*, Jotwell: The Journal of Things We Like (Lots) (2022).
84. Enrico Bonadio & Luke McDonagh, *Artificial Intelligence as Producer and Consumer of Copyright Works: Evaluating the Consequences of Algorithmic Creativity,* 2 Intellectual Property Quarterly 112 (2020).

of the fundamental copyright principle of the dichotomy between idea and expression.

One way to move beyond that impasse would be to promote a redefinition of originality which introduces a concept of "creation by proxy." This presupposes that the act of creation is a complex and multilayered act, which has a dual aspect and cannot be reduced either solely to its immaterial/intellectual aspect or to the materialization/fixation of the work. Since copyright protection is not conditional upon completion of the work, the preparatory forms of the work can also be protected.[85]

This abstraction is not completely unfamiliar with copyright law. In joint authorship cases, national courts have in some instances broadly analyzed the prerequisite of the significant creative input of the potential coauthor in order to recognize as a coauthor a person who was not physically involved in the fixation of the form of the work. In the French case *Renoir v. Guino*,[86] Renoir was considered to be the coauthor of artistic works which were physically created only by Guino, thanks to Renoir's dominant role in relation to the creative choices which defined the final form of the work. Similarly, the courts have attributed the status of joint authors to contributors of a substantial intellectual input that partly shapes the output, even if the contributor was not "pushing the pen."[87]

Nonetheless, in the case of Renoir, the Court has acknowledged that the internal structure and the essence of the work were conceived by Renoir. This is not the case with the software programmer who has created the AI system since the final forms of expression of the works have not been conceived or shaped by him/her. The impossibility of linking the final form of the work with the natural person who is behind the machine has also been affirmed in Australian case law, where it was held that the author's intellectual effort must be directed at the particular form of expression.[88] Accordingly, any intellectual effort which is "too" anterior to the materialization of the final form of the work shall be excluded.[89] In this context, the Toulouse Court of Appeal denied the status of coauthor of a rugby match analysis software program to the person who gave the software programmer an outline and detailed specifications analyzing rugby matches.[90]

In European copyright law, the possibility of protecting the preparatory material of a work as part of the work itself has been officially recognized in

85. Lucas, Lucas-Schloetter & Bernault (n. 61), at 89.
86. Renoir v. Guino, Cour de Cassation, civil 1 (Nov. 13, 1973), D. 1974, Jurisp., p. 533, note C. Colombet.
87. McCutcheon (n. 51) at 937, with reference to: Cala Homes (South) Ltd v. Alfred McAlpine Homes East Ltd *[No 1]* FSR 818, 835 (1995).
88. *Ibid.*, with reference to: IceTV (n. 51) at [54].
89. Jani McCutcheon, *When Sweat Turns to Ice: The Originality Threshold for Compilations Following IceTV and Phone Directories*, 22 Australian Intellectual Property Journal 87, 89-91 (2011) https://doi.org/10.2139/ssrn.2265163.
90. CA Toulouse, 2e ch., JurisData n° 2007-358024 (2007).

the specific case of computer programs. Recital 7 of Directive 2009/24 provides that the term computer program also includes preparatory design work leading to the development of a computer program, provided that the nature of the preparatory work is such that a computer program can result from it at a later stage.[91]

Consequently, the preparatory design material is protected as part of the computer program only if it is a step in the program's development and is reflected in the program.[92] Therefore, material (such as requirement specifications)[93] which is "too" distant from the final form of the program is not protected as part of the work. Similarly, in the *Painer*[94] case, the CJEU recognized, as regards the protection of photographs, that creativity can be expressed in the preparatory phase of taking a photograph.

Indeed, even though creativity might have been expressed in the preparatory stages of the genesis of a work, the creative choices made in the preparatory phase must have shaped the form of the work and must be reflected in it. As demonstrated in section 17.1.2, the "intention to create" prerequisite challenges such an approach since it would require that the "author" of these choices has deliberately contemplated and conceived her/his contribution as being part of the final form of the work and aimed at the creation of that work.

Another possibility would be to attribute authorship to the user of the AI tool. Here, again, as in the case of the software programmer, the question of AI authorship is necessarily tied to the degree and the nature of the involvement of the human user in the creative process and the user's connection with the AI-generated output.

For a significant part of the copyright doctrine, the user appears as a more prominent candidate for being attributed authorship than the software programmer. Indeed, several arguments have been advanced for recognizing the user as the author of the AI-generated output. First, the user often appears to have a closer and more substantial connection with the final output than the software programmer. The user will often be the person who sets the parameters and provides data for the AI in ways that influence the ultimate

91. For the application of this rule *see*, Case C-393/09 Bezpečnostní softwarová asociace—Svaz softwarové ochrany v. Ministerstvo kultury (2010) ECLI:EU:C:2010:816, paras. 38, 39 where the CJEU denied the protection of graphic user interfaces as a form of expression of a computer program, whose reproduction would engender the reproduction of the computer program itself, thus enabling the computer to perform its task.

92. Walter Blocher & Michel M. Walter, *Computer Programs Directive in European Copyright Law, A Commentary* 100, 101 (Michel M. Walter & Silke von Lewinski eds., Oxford University Press 2010).

93. *Ibid.*, 101, no 5.1. 28.

94. Case C-145/10 Eva-Maria Painer v. Standard VerlagsGmbH and Others (2013) ECLI:EU:C:2013:138.

output.[95] This is also reinforced by the fact that the same AI system used by different persons could result in various and different outputs based on the personal choices and creative decisions made by each user.[96]

Copyright law policy could also favor an approach where the user of the AI system is recognized as the author of the output. In this context, attributing authorship to the user would be justified by copyright incentive theories, since denying copyright protection to AI-generated outputs would also deny the incentive of copyright to an increasingly large group of works that are indistinguishable in substance and public value from works created by human beings.[97] The attribution of copyright to users could also provide some additional reward to users who train and instruct the AI-produced outputs.[98] Attributing authorship to the user would also promote the dissemination and exploitation of the AI outputs more efficiently and more responsibly, since a "legally sanctioned monopoly allows the users to use, sell, or distribute the works more efficiently, as well as to be accountable for avoiding infringements and counterfeits."[99]

The use of the AI system would result in granting authorship to the user on the condition that the user's free and creative choices are sufficiently reflected in the AI-generated output. Inversely, if the use of the AI by the user did not entail any creative choices which are reflected in the output, there should be no claim for user authorship. However, machine learning (ML) systems can be instructed and trained to perform complex tasks and produce sophisticated output in ways that the user of the system will not be able to (precisely) preconceive, understand or explain.[100] Indeed, a key problem is that the less precise the input instructions are and the more patterns exist that a human would not have discovered, the less intellectual connection to and

95. Enrico Bonadio & Luke McDonagh, *Artificial Intelligence as Producer and Consumer of Copyright Works: Evaluating the Consequences of Algorithmic Creativity*, 2 Intellectual Property Quarterly 112-137 (2020).

96. Samantha Fink Hedrick, *I Think, Therefore I Create*, 8(2) NYU Journal of Intellectual Property & Entertainment Law 324, 344-346 (2019).

97. Robert C. Denicola, *Ex Machina: Copyright Protection for Computer-Generated Works*, 69 Rutgers University Law Review 251, 284 (2016).

98. William Ralston, *Copyright in Computer-Composed Music: HAL Meets Handel,* 52 Journal of the Copyright Society of the USA 281, 303-304 (2005); Nina Brown, *Artificial l Authors: A Case for Copyright in Computer-Generated Works,* 9 Columbia Science and Technology Law Review 1, 37 (2019).

99. Shlomit Yanisky-Ravid, *Generating Rembrandt: Artificial Intelligence, Copyright, and Accountability in the 3A Era—The Human-like Authors are Already Here: A New Model,* Michigan State Law Review 659, 712 (2017) https://doi.org/10.2139/ssrn.2957722.

100. P. Bernt Hugenholtz & Joao Pedro Quintais, *Copyright and Artificial Creation: Does EU Copyright Law Protect AI-Assisted Output?,* International Review of Intellectual Property and Competition Law 1190-1216, at 1203 (2021) https://doi.org/10.1007/s40319-021-01115-0.

direction of the output by the human exists.[101] Often, the user of the machine could be considered a distant instigator of the AI output but not the origin of the final expressions which will be produced by the machine.

Simple data selection and classification by a human is insufficient to meet the "originality" requirement, but a substantial human intervention to guide the AI system in the creative process must be found.[102] As noted by Bently, Sherman, Gangjee and Johnson, "pre-expressive" contributions seem to be irrelevant under the EU author's own intellectual creation standard that seems "focused on contributions and choices that are directly relevant to the structuring of the expression of the work."[103] In light of this, the AI user's choices might often be considered "skill" (selection or classification of the data that will feed the AI system as a step preceding the creative process) or abstract (not protected ideas) or minimal or insignificant (de minimis) regarding their influence or their reflection on the final expression.

Indeed, through her choices, the user would have possibly guided the type of expression (for instance, painting), the content (for instance, the image of a young woman sitting on a bench), the style (cubism, expressionism, etc.), the method and the techniques of digital creation (color quantization, superpixel segmentation, neural style transfer, etc.). While all these decisions and choices are free and express the intention of the user that the machine generates a work embodying these choices, they will be mainly at an abstract level, or it would be extremely difficult to detect whether their level of precision has been sufficient to shape the main creative elements of the final outputs.

In this context, the "human creative will" requirement would be difficult to meet or prove. Certainly, this would also depend on the specific circumstances of each case, since the level of precision of the human input will vary. For instance, if the user in the post-production phase has creatively edited and formatted the AI output, the link with the output would probably be strong enough, even if some elements of the expression have been produced randomly by the machine. Indeed, while in projects such as "The Next Rembrandt Portrait," important human creative input is required at several stages; this may not be the case for more mundane AI-assisted outputs such as weather forecasts and news reports.[104] As has been demonstrated, the assessment of authorship poses significant challenges or at least requires a creative interpretation or understanding of core principles of copyright law. Since the interpretation and application of these principles is

101. Reto Hilty, Jörg Hoffmann & Stefan Scheuerer, *Intellectual Property Justification for Artificial Intelligence in Artificial Intelligence & Intellectual Property* 54 (Jyh-An Lee, Kung-Chung Liu & Reto Hilty eds., Oxford University Press 2020).

102. Niloufer Selvadurai & Rita Matulionyte, *Reconsidering Creativity: Copyright Protection for Works Generated Using Artificial Intelligence*, 62 Journal of Intellectual Property Law & Practice 536, 539 (2020) https://doi.org/10.1093/jiplp/jpaa062.

103. Bently, Sherman, Gangjee & Johnson (n. 7) at 106.

104. Hugenholtz & Quintais (n. 99) at 1206.

a matter of the competence of national authorities or case law, pluralist approaches will necessarily emerge and prevail, either flexible or not, depending on copyright traditions and idiosyncrasies.

17.2 THE THORNY RELATIONSHIP BETWEEN AUTHORSHIP AND ORIGINALITY

In copyright law, the concepts of authorship and originality appear as the variables of a logic equation, the result of which is copyright protection. As Sam Ricketson has pointed out, it is not possible to consider the concept of the author without asking "author of what?"[105] For Jane Ginsburg, "originality" is synonymous with "authorship."[106] Bently and Sherman have put it more practically. In order to define who the author is, we answer in a way similar to that with which the originality is determined. The person should be able to show that her/his contribution is of the type and extent that is sufficient to confer originality on the work.[107]

The Berne Convention does not expressly state that works have to be original. However, the term "original" appears sporadically in several articles of the Convention, such as in the case of derivative works (Article 2(3)). Furthermore, Article 2(5) secures the protection of collective works on the condition that they are "intellectual creations." As stated in the Guide to the Berne Convention, even if the term "work" is not defined, it is clear from the general tone of the Convention that these works must be "intellectual creations."[108]

On the basis of the above, it has been argued that there is a strong connection between the concept of authorship and the implicit requirement that the author's production must be an intellectual creation, i.e., an "original" work. In light of this approach, the author is the source of originality and the question of authorship cannot be discussed in isolation since the requirement of originality is correlative.[109]

17.2.1 "Authors" and "Creators": Synonymous Terms?

Defining authorship through originality is consistent with the idea that copyright regulation necessarily deals only with protected "works" (i.e.,

105. Sam Ricketson, *The Common Law of Intellectual Property, Essays in Honour of Professor David Vaver* 229 (Hart Publishing 2010).
106. Ginsburg (n. 37) at 1078.
107. Bently, Sherman, Ganjee & Johnson (n. 7) at 126.
108. World Intellectual Property Organisation (WIPO), *Guide to the Berne Convention for the Protection of Literary and Artistic Works (Paris Act, 1971)* 17, para. 2.7 (1978).
109. McCutcheon (n. 51) at 935, with reference to the Australian case Sands & McDougall Pty Ltd v. Robinson 23 CLR 49, 55, 57 (1917) (Isaacs J) (emphasis added).

"intellectual creations") which meet the main prerequisite of copyright law, i.e., originality. In this context, not all creators are authors, since only those human creations which meet copyright law's standards shall be protected. Indeed, "not every actual creation that comes within the scope of copyright-eligible subject matter should in fact be protected by copyright."[110]

In this context, identifying the creator is a question of fact, while identifying the author of an "intellectual creation" presupposes a legal assessment.

Nonetheless, the distinction between authorship and creatorship is not always clear. In national laws with a personalist tradition, the terms "author" and "creator" (defined as the natural person who actually created the work) appear to predominantly coincide. Furthermore, the prerequisite of a work being an "intellectual creation" is mainly understood as setting a standard of authorship based on creativity. On this basis, the author could essentially be defined as the natural person who expressed the necessary degree of creativity in the process of generating the work.

On the contrary, in countries following the Anglo-American copyright tradition, the factual term "creator" does not always coincide with the legal status of "author."[111] Employers and investors (either natural or legal persons) who are not the actual creators are deemed to be authors. In this context, authorship is not synonymous with creatorship but with first copyright ownership.

Making authorship dependent on creativity and, on the contrary, assimilating authorship with first copyright ownership are both concepts that blur the conceptual core of authorship. Defining authorship through originality is a backward approach. A human creation must first have been brought to life and attributed to a person before its originality can be judged. As Seignette notes, even if it seems very logical to assume that the author is the natural person who created the work, this assumption is not always obvious in practice.[112] The creative process might involve a large number of persons with various contributions and roles, while today, more than ever, it might be difficult to identify the direct personal contribution made by a human being to the process of generating the work.

Furthermore, the strong correlation of the concept of authorship with originality could be a reason for the existing gaps in the definition of authorship in international copyright law. Since there is no consensus on the concept of originality (national laws follow either a subjectivist or objectivist standard of originality), the concept of authorship as an international norm is an empty shell with no precise meaning.

---

110. Anthony R. Reese, *What Should Copyright Protect?*, at What If We Could Reimagine Copyright? 134 (Rebecca Giblin & Kimberlee Weatherall eds., Australian National University Press 2017).

111. Seignette (n. 42).

112. Seignette (n. 4) at 58.

17.2.2 Toward a Definition of Authorship Which Does Not Depend on Originality

So, the main question is whether there is an autonomous criterion of authorship that does not inherently depend on originality. As already been mentioned, some general principles seem to apply:

(1) that an author is a human being; and
(2) possibly, an implicit prerequisite of a creative will resulting in the production of the specific form of the work, but not necessarily a will to be an author.

Nevertheless, there is no definition of which acts or contributions ("the type and amount of the contribution") result in qualifying a person as an author.

The epitome of international copyright law, the Berne Convention, does not include a definition of authorship, while any attempt to provide such a definition in later versions of the Convention and related documents has failed.[113] Certainly, some elements could be deduced in places from the wording of Berne provisions. In this context, the reference to "productions," which implies that only works realized or brought into existence,[114] together with the underlying principle of exclusion of the protection of ideas,[115] means that authorship necessarily presupposes that the author's contribution is expressed in concrete form.

Additionally, it could be argued that some aspects of the concept of authorship could be deduced from certain voluntary "omissions" from the Berne Convention, such as the non-inclusion of certain categories of "productions" in the protectable subject matter in Article 2(1). Broadcasts and sound recordings have remained outside Berne because their protection was deemed to be seeking to protect the manufacturer's skill and investment rather than the author's interests.[116]

This exclusion could serve as a basis for various interpretations in relation to the construction of an international standard of authorship. First,

113. Sam Ricketson & Jane C. Ginsburg, *International Copyright and Neighbouring Rights, the Berne Convention and Beyond* (Volume 1) 361 §7.05 (Oxford University Press 2010). The authors refer to the attempt to provide a definition of authorship in the "Model Provisions for Legislation in the Field of Copyright" undertaken by the WIPO and to the inconsistencies of the proposed definitions, which appeared to confuse authorship with copyright ownership.

114. *Ibid.*, at 403, para. 8.03.

115. The Berne Convention implicitly includes that principle since it protects works and not ideas. *See*, Jörg Reinbothe & Silke von Lewinski, *The WIPO Treaties on Copyright: A Commentary on the WCT, the WPPT, and the BTAP* 74, para. 7.2.6 (2nd edn, Oxford University Press 2015). *See also*, Agreement on Trade-Related Aspects of Intellectual Property Rights (Apr. 15, 1994), 1869 UNTS 299 (TRIPS), Art. 9(2); WIPO Copyright Treaty (Dec. 20, 1996) TRT/WCT/001 (WCT), Art. 2.

116. Ricketson & Ginsburg (n. 112) at 505, 508.

the reference to the manufacturer's "skill and investment" is not helpful for the purpose of constructing a definition of authorship which is not based on originality, since the concept of "skill and investment" lies at the heart of the Commonwealth "skill and labour" originality standard. Second, the non-inclusion of certain categories of "productions" in the protectable Berne subject matter makes "entrepreneurial authorship" appear at first sight incompatible with the general spirit of Berne, or at least with its mainstream historical understanding of the concept of author. Could this assumption lead to the conception of an international standard of authorship which prohibits the vesting of authorship in legal persons? Or conversely, could the tolerance of "deemed authorship" mean that the prototype of authorship in Berne is neutral in the sense that the Convention equally promotes both "real authorship" and "deemed authorship" copyright regimes? The answer is in the negative. The underlying prevailing principle of the Convention is that only the natural persons of the creators are "real authors," even if this has not been explicitly stated. Otherwise, the concept of authorship would simply be synonymous with first ownership. This fundamental principle militates against the proliferation of "deemed authorship" regimes within copyright law. It is therefore more favorable to legal mechanisms involving a secondary transfer of exploitation rights from authors to investors.

However, some useful findings may be extracted from the differentiation between "manufacturers" and "authors." Since a work of mind is necessarily an intellectual achievement, its expression in the universe of forms which are perceptible by the human senses is the result of a process involving its externalization in concrete form. In this context, the author shall be deemed the natural person who had the will to create a specific work and expressed this will in the sense that she/he autonomously conceived and probably executed its final form or, in the words of Jane Ginsburg, closely controlled the execution of the work.[117] In this context, the conception of an idea does not amount in itself to authorship, since this contribution is at an abstract level.[118] On the contrary, free and autonomous acting and/or control during the process of concretization of the intellectual form are decisive in terms of qualifying a person as an author. In this sense, creation would be the result of a free intellectual activity, where autonomous, self-governing choices in relation to concretization of the work are made.[119]

The idea that the author has conceived the intellectual form of the work and that she/he freely concretized this form or controlled its concretization excludes manufacturers, processors and persons with mere technical, organizational or financial interventions (such as producers, publishers, typists, stenographers and copy editors) from the concept of authorship, since they do not take part in the conception of the specific intellectual form of the

117. Ginsburg (n. 37) at 1017.

118. Bently, Sherman, Ganjee & Johnson (n. 7) at 127.

119. Bernard Edelman, *La propriété littéraire et artistique* 16 (4th edn, P.U.F. 2008).

work.[120] According to a mainstream perception of authorial contribution, any natural or legal persons who take the initiative, invest in, organize and control the process of manufacturing/producing the media on which works will be first fixed (such as film producers and producers of sound recordings) or provide transmission services for signals which carry works (broadcasting organizations) intervene after the completion of the final intellectual form of the work and they cannot be considered to be authors. In this context, vesting authorship in such persons could be considered an anomaly. Similarly, defining films, sound recordings and broadcasts as "works" is also inconsistent, since, regardless of the question of originality, the concept of a work presupposes an intellectual achievement or contribution, which is non-existent in the process of recording or transmitting signals or financing/organizing/controlling the fixation and dissemination of tangible media or, more broadly, the communication of works to the public.

In most cases, the protection of such persons would be based on their investment and skill in the process of production or transmission of "real works" produced by "real authors," even though the protection granted is much broader, as films,[121] sound recordings[122] and broadcasts[123] do not require the existence of "real works" which are being fixed or transmitted. As a result, if a video recorder or tape recorder is turned on and left on a table, the resulting film or sound recording will be protected.[124]

In conclusion, leaving aside the question of originality, in the absence of a multiplicity of contributors, it would be fairly straightforward to define who the creator of a work is. However, there will still be some cases where it would be difficult to define the creator, such as in relation to AI-generated works[125] (no human author, no creative will), works generated by animals[126] (no human author, no creative will), sports games[127] (no creative will) or purely accidental works (no creative will), except in the U.S.[128]

120. This is also reflected in case law. For example, in the U.S. case Community for Creative Non-Violence v. Reid, 490 U.S. 730 (1989), it was held that "[a]s a general rule, the author is the party who actually creates the work, that is, the person who translates an idea into a fixed, tangible expression entitled to copyright protection."
121. For example, in the U.K., a film is defined as a recording on any medium from which a moving image may be produced by any means (Copyright, Designs and Patents Act 1988, s. 5B (1)).
122. Copyright, Designs and Patens Act 1988, s. 5A(1).
123. *Ibid.*, s. 6(1).
124. Bently, Sherman, Ganjee & Johnson (n. 7), at 118.
125. Lucas, Lucas-Schloetter & Bernault (n. 61) at 172, no. 148; Jacques Larrieu, *Le robot et le droit d'auteur* in Mélanges André Lucas 474 (LexisNexis 2014).
126. Copyright scholars unanimously reject animal authorship. *See,* Vivant & Bruguière (n. 69) at 120, 121 §102; Caron, (n. 46) at no 48; Lucas (n. 26) at 172, no 148.
127. Lucas (n. 26) at 77 no. 57.
128. Ginsburg (n. 37) at 1951.

17.3 CONCLUSION

The mythical figure of the author is omnipresent in modern copyright law. There is no definition of authorship in international copyright law. Pluralism is an absolute norm.

Similarly, with respect to the question of originality, the concept of authorship has not been crystallized in a specific legal mold, so as to be flexible and to reflect new ways of creative activity. National laws have their own doctrines regarding authorship. But in a digitally interconnected world, the various concepts of authorship act as communicating vessels as cultural and economic interactions grow.

Today, investors and legal persons have an increasingly significant role with regard to the ownership and administration of the author's rights. The day has come where machines claim to be creators and the producers of those machines claim to be authors.

The elaboration of a common understanding of authorship, which respects the human-centered approach of Berne, but also takes into account new contexts of creation and practical needs, is necessary.

Otherwise, the emblematic figure of the author will just remain a shadow.

Chapter 18

Nonoriginal Databases and Works of Applied Art as Nonharmonized Matter in International Copyright Law: What Lessons Can Be Learned?

Estelle Derclaye

18.1 PROS AND CONS OF UNIVERSALISM

18.1.1 The Negative Aspects

Universalism entails three main negative aspects. Adopting a universal norm in an international intellectual property treaty is unfair if the parties are not all in the same or at least similar situation, i.e., when they are not at the same level of development.[1] This has been shown throughout history. Countries refused to join the Berne Convention in the nineteenth[2] century as they were still developing, and the Convention's norms at that time were not adapted to

1. *See, e.g.*, for designs, Anna Kingsbury, *International Harmonisation of Designs Law: The Case for Diversity*, 32(8) European Intellectual Property Review 382, 385 (2010).
2. Berne Convention for the Protection of Literary and Artistic Works (Sep. 9, 1886), S. Treaty Doc. No. 99-27.

them.[3] A more recent example is the Trade-Related Aspects of Intellectual Property Rights (TRIPS)[4] agreement, which was tailored to this particular issue with more flexibility in the rules and long periods of adaptation so that developing countries could implement the agreement later than developed countries. As G. Dinwoodie and R. Dreyfuss note in the abstract of the first chapter of their book on TRIPS, which is a synopsis of the book's argument, "[b]ecause countries with different economic and cultural conditions will need to adopt different approaches to intellectual property, a one-size-fits-all code is undesirable."[5] Nevertheless, TRIPS has added many rules where no flexibility exists, and that is the case also for copyright (e.g., computer programs must be treated as literary works (Article 10(1)) and the enforcement rules, including criminal remedies for copyright infringement at a commercial scale (Articles 41-61)).

This universalism's flaw leads to the linked problem of power in the international negotiations for such intellectual property agreements and not only international ones (i.e., where all nations are invited to the negotiating table) but also simple multilateral ones such as free trade agreements (FTAs). If such power is unbalanced, the universal rules agreed upon even by parties at different stages of development end up favoring a certain vision of intellectual property/copyright, which suit those in power better. These rules may or may not be suited to particular countries or regions. The universal here is therefore universal because it is imposed and not consensual (when it is consensual, everyone agrees that this rule should be universal because it is good for all, whatever his or her position is). The concept of universality of a norm should be that all subjects of the norm should be treated in the same way if they are in the same situation. However, the concept of universality as enshrined in an agreement where negotiating power is unequal may result in a universal rule, which is not really universal in the sense just described above. A classical objection to this is that, in TRIPS and FTAs, which cover many other trade sectors than intellectual property and are not stand-alone agreements like the other copyright conventions, countries may have obtained other trade advantages and only entered the agreement on that basis, so that the imbalance in relation to intellectual property rights/copyright is compensated by favorable rules in other trade sectors. That said, the recent increase in multilateral and bilateral treaties between countries had led to the development of (generally) increased copyright protection outside of the international arena (e.g., more rights, longer duration). So, where countries

3. *See* Sam Ricketson & Jane Ginsburg, *International Copyright and Neighbouring Rights, the Berne Convention and Beyond* 882, no. 14.02 (2nd edn, Oxford University Press, 2005).
4. Agreement on Trade-Related Aspects of Intellectual Property Rights (Apr. 15, 1994), 1869 UNTS 299.
5. Graeme B. Dinwoodie & Rochelle C. Dreyfuss, *A Neofederalist Vision of TRIPS: The Resilience of the International Intellectual Property Regime* (Oxford University Press, 2012).

bound by these rules have to return to the international negotiating table, they are bound by rules which they cannot ignore. This movement thus leads to an ever-increasing amount of protection nationally with effects at international level.

A second problem with universal rules is that once they are enshrined in a treaty, they are extremely hard to change owing to requiring unanimity;[6] so, therefore, enshrining them there too early or without enough experience is a double edge. It is therefore very important to be cautious about which rules to include in the minimum standards and how to phrase them. This problem is also linked to the issue of power in negotiations mentioned above.

A third issue is that of courts. At international level, it is the World Trade Organization (WTO) panels. Even if their decisions are only binding on the parties, in other words, there is no doctrine of precedent; the reports constitute a basis for other panels to consider in similar disputes.[7] Because treaties are very hard to change, such courts are in fact the "de facto" legislatures when issues are unclear in the law. There is so far not much case law at WTO level in the field of copyright.[8] Suffice it to give the example of the Court of Justice of the European Union (CJEU), which deals, among others, with issues arising from the copyright *acquis* (now 11 directives and one regulation). The CJEU copyright case law in that area has been criticized for its inconsistency (owed mainly to its lack of specialist judges) and/or its judicial activism, namely its bias toward harmonization in the name of the importance of the single market.[9] If more copyright disputes come before the WTO panels, some of these issues, or others, could occur as well, if not prevented, in advance.

Finally, universal rules prevent countries from being laboratories and experiments with different rules. Such experiments are beneficial as they allow to compare the strengths and weaknesses of different rules over time, allowing therefore to pick the most adequate rule after this period of experimentation.

---

6. *See, e.g.,* Berne Convention, Art. 27(3) Berne Convention.
7. *See* https://www.wto.org/english/tratop_e/dispu_e/disp_settlement_cbt_e/c7s1p1_e.htm (accessed Jan. 3, 2024) and *Japan—Taxes on alcoholic beverages*, Appellate Body Report 1/11/1996, WT/DS8/AB/R WT/DS11/AB/R, 34.
8. Only two disputes have so far involving copyright law namely United States—Section 110(5) of U.S. Copyright Act, Panel Report, 15/6/2000, WT/DS160/R, available at https://www.wto.org/english/tratop_e/dispu_e/cases_e/ds160_e.htm (accessed Jan. 3, 2024) and *China—Measures Affecting the Protection and Enforcement of Intellectual Property Rights*, 26/1/2009, WT/DS362/R, available at https://www.wto.org/english/tratop_e/dispu_e/cases_e/ds362_e.htm (accessed Jan. 3, 2024).
9. For an empirical analysis of this claim, *see* Marcella Favale, Martin Kretschmer & Paul Torremans, *Is there an EU Copyright Jurisprudence? An Empirical Analysis of the Workings of the European Court of Justice,* 79(1) Modern Law Review 31-75 (2016) https://doi.org/10.1111/1468-2230.12166. A recent example of judicial activism is the Kwantum case, *see* below.

18.1.2 The Positive Aspects

However, universalism has positive aspects. First, it imposes the same rules, so no longer minimum rules. This creates a level playing field for all parties, namely countries and stakeholders. As we said above, though, it is only a level playing field if all the countries are more or less at the same level of development. Second, private international law vanishes as all parties have the same norms. Universal rules replace national laws with a single international law, making conflict of laws redundant. Third, universal rules also help international trade; they create a single market without borders, like that we have in the European Union (EU).[10] As the rules are the same for all countries, there is no need to change products to comply with other countries' different rules to enter those countries' markets. Last but not least, having universal rules brings countries and stakeholders together: they have agreed to adopt the same rules, and they literally "speak the same language," this brings them together rather than apart. A good illustration is the EU, where most citizens feel part of something common, shared, bigger, and in short they have a common identity.

All in all, universal copyright rules lower costs and increase efficiency, legal certainty,[11] understandability and mutual understanding, cohesiveness, in addition to enabling a smoother trade.

As we have noted above, universalism is probably best achieved through international conventions. This is because, with multilateral agreements such as some FTAs, one party generally has more power than the other and thus sometimes manages to impose imbalanced norms. With international conventions, the power of all countries is reduced. That said, some multilateral efforts, such as those of the EU, where countries have more or less equal bargaining power, could serve as models.[12]

18.2 SPECIFIC EXAMPLES

18.2.1 Nonoriginal Databases

As is known, the database sui generis right (further referred to as "database right") is a pure EU creation. It protects the substantial investment in collecting, verifying or presenting data into a database. Thus, it complements

---

10. Bernt Hugenholtz, *Is Harmonization a Good Thing? The Case of the Copyright Acquis*, at The Europeanization of Intellectual Property Law, Towards a European Legal Methodology 72 (Justine Pila & Ansgar Ohly eds., Oxford University Press, 2013), listing the advantages of adopting a copyright regulation in the EU.
11. *Ibid.*, 72.
12. One such initiative, though not at state level, is that of the Wittem group, a group of academics from all over the EU, which drafted a copyright code, available at https://www.ivir.nl/copyrightcode/european-copyright-code/ (accessed Jan. 3, 2024).

database copyright, which protects a database's structure (the intellectual creation of selecting and arranging the data).[13] The EU at the end of the 1980s saw the advent of digitization as both an opportunity and a threat, an opportunity to grow the data industry and a threat from other competitors, mainly the United States of America (USA). Therefore, it decided to adopt a specific right to incentivize the creation of databases. The right is enshrined in the so-called Database Directive.[14] The Database Directive harmonizes database copyright and creates a new database right. The latter is meant to replace the old sweat of the brow British and Irish copyright and the continental slavish imitation unfair competition tort that covered collections of data. The right had to be implemented into national law by January 1, 1998, now over 20 years ago. Database copyright did not attract considerable debate as it was not changing Member States national laws much, if at all, except for the United Kingdom (U.K.) and Ireland. The EU tried to push its creation into the international arena and, along with the World Intellectual Property Organization (WIPO) Internet treaties of 1996, was tagged a database treaty which in the end never saw the light of day, owing mainly to American opposition. Over the same period and up to 2004, the United States (U.S.) also toyed with the idea of adopting a special right protecting database contents. Many bills were introduced in Congress but all were in the end rejected.[15]

The failure of the right in the U.S. and internationally was not surprising as the database right attracted a lot of criticism in the literature on both sides of the Atlantic and also down under.[16] The major issue was that it would risk creating an intellectual property right on data, an anathema in intellectual property law. Not the least because the right could potentially be renewed forever, and the exceptions were few and narrow.

13. Such copyright protection exists at international level in Art. 5 of the WIPO Copyright Treaty.
14. Directive 96/9/EC of the European Parliament and of the Council of 11 March 1996 on the legal protection of databases, Arts. 7-15, Official Journal L 77, 27.3.1996, pp. 20-28. On the Database Directive and especially the database right, *see, e.g.*, Jens Gaster, *Der Rechtschutz von Databanken* (Carl Heymanns, 1999); Viola Bensinger, *Sui generis Schutz für Databanken, die EG-Datenbank Richtlinie vor dem Hintergrund des nordischen Rechts* (Beck, 1999); Matthias Leistner, *Der Rechtsschutz von Datenbanken im deutschen und europäischen Recht, Eine Untersuchung zur Rechtlinie 96/9/EG und zu ihrer Umsetzung in das deutsche Urheberechtsgesetz* (Beck, 2000); Mark Davison, *The Legal Protection of Databases* (Cambridge University Press, 2003); Anne-Marie Beunen, *Protection for Databases: The European Database Directive and Its Effects in the Netherlands, France and the United Kingdom* (University of Leiden, 2007); Estelle Derclaye, *The Legal Protection of Databases, A Comparative Analysis* (Elgar, 2008).
15. For an account, *see* Davison (n. 18); Jonathan Band & Makoto Kono, *The Database Protection Debate in the 106th Congress* 62 Ohio State Law Journal 689 (2001).
16. Jerry Reichman & Pam Samuelson, *Intellectual Property Rights in Data?*, 50 Vanderbilt Law Review 52-166 (1997), Bernt Hugenholtz, *De Databankrichtlijn Eindelijk Aanvaard: Een Zeer Kritisch Commentaar,* 4 Computerrecht 131 (1996); Leistner (n. 18); Davison (n. 18).

So, taking stock after almost 30 years, what has happened? There has been a fair amount of case law. National courts first struggled to interpret the sui generis right properly, and some referred decisions to the CJEU for answers. The EU case law is now rich in 11 decisions on the sui generis right.[17] Whereas this case law has clarified the right to some extent, many questions remain unanswered as the CJEU has not been asked to rule on them yet or has not fully clarified some of the notions it was asked to rule on. For instance, the notion of substantial investment is still unclear, and no one knows whether this is a low or high level. The same goes for the notion of a substantial part. Even if the court declared that investing in creating data does not trigger the database right,[18] separating investments between creating and collecting data is often hard to do.[19] Also, the court did not pronounce itself on the status of recorded data (such as meteorological, traffic data, patient's health data and more generally sensor-generated or machine-generated data). The maker of a database which the directive ill-defines[20] has been transposed in vastly different and opposing ways in the Member States.[21] Despite this, the CJEU has not had a case referred to on the notion, leaving the law in a very chaotic state. Those are the major sticking points, but the list goes on.

Since 1998, the European Commission has commissioned two studies in order to evaluate the directive, in conformity with Article 16(3) of the directive, one in 2003[22] and the other in 2018.[23] The first study is a purely

---

17. Case C-338/02 Fixtures Marketing Ltd v. Svenska Spel (2004) ECLI:EU:C:2004:696; Case C-46/02 Fixtures Marketing Ltd v. Oy Veikkaus (2004) ECLI:EU:C:2004:694; Case C-444/02 Fixtures Marketing Ltd v. Organismos Prognostikon Agonon Podosfairou (2004) ECLI:EU:C:2004:697; Case C-203/02 The British Horseracing Board v. William Hill Organisation (2004) ECLI:EU:C:2004:695; Case C-304/07 Directmedia Publishing v. Albert-Ludwigs-Universität Freiburg (2008) ECLI:EU:C:2008:552; Case C-545/07 Apis-Hristovich EOOD v. Lakorda AD (2009) ECLI:EU:C:2009:132; Case C-604/10 Football Dataco v. Yahoo UK! (2012) ECLI:EU:C:2012:115; Case C-202/12 Innoweb v. Wegener ICT Media BV, Wegener Mediaventions (2013) ECLI:EU:C:2013:850; Case C-490/14 Freistaat Bayern v. Verlag Esterbauer (2015) ECLI:EU:C:2015:735 and Case C-30/14 PR Aviation v. Ryanair (2015) ECLI:EU:C:2015:10; Case C-762/19 CV-Online Latvia (2021) ECLI:EU:C:2021:434.
18. *See* the *Fixtures Marketing* and *British Horseracing Board* cases (n. 21).
19. As results many replies to the public consultation organized by the European Commission and the workshop organized to support the study evaluating the Database Directive commissioned by the European Commission in 2017. *See Study in Support of the Evaluation of the Database Directive*, https://ec.europa.eu/digital-single-market/en/news/study-support-evaluation-database-directive (accessed Jan. 3, 2024).
20. It does not even deserve an article in itself but is pithily considered only in one recital (Recital 41).
21. Michal Koščík & Matěj Myška, *Database Authorship and Ownership of Sui Generis Database Rights in Data-Driven Research,* 31(1) International Review of Law, Computers & Technology 43 (2017) https://doi.org/10.1080/13600869.2017.1275119. *See also Study in Support of the Evaluation of the Database Directive* (n. 23), 45-49.
22. Nauta Dutilh, *The Implementation and Application of Directive 96/9/EC on the Legal Protection of Databases*, Study Contract ETD/2001/B5-3001/E/72, Final Report, 2003.

legal evaluation of the directive and its implementation and uses questionnaires. The second study has an economic and legal analysis, complemented by a survey and a workshop. In 2005, the Commission based its economic evaluation on the Gale directory of databases, an incomplete source, to draw the conclusion that the impact of the database right on the protection of databases was unproven.[24] In 2018, the second study concluded that it is not impossible to obtain economic data on the database sector apart from the Gale directory and found that the economic evidence on the effects of the sui generis right is inconclusive. In other words, it is unclear that it has incentivized the production of databases in the EU compared to elsewhere in the world. The views of the different stakeholders (database producers and users) who responded to the public consultation, the survey and attended the workshop in 2017 are overall polarized on most issues. The producers want the status quo or more rights (mainly that the database right extends to created and recorded data), while the users want more exceptions or even an abolition of the database right, claiming that the right has added a new layer above copyright and one of complexity and uncertainty.

That said, the database right has so-called EU added-value; namely, the directive creates a harmonized framework applicable throughout the EU. This is the view across the board namely both from the producers' and users' points of view and also in the literature.[25] It has some of the advantages of universal rules described above, namely that the same rules apply all over the EU, leading to easier licenses and lower costs, despite the fuzziness of some of its notions. That said, as the database right is only harmonized (directive) as opposed to unified (regulation), it is still territorial.

Thirty years on, has the database right been adopted elsewhere? South Korea has a right very similar to the database right; though it lasts five years (compared to the EU database right's 15 years term), like the database right, it is also renewable if a new substantial investment is made.[26] Article 108 of the Mexican Copyright Act provides that nonoriginal databases are protected for five years. But no other provision gives details about the right. The EU

---

23. *Study in Support of the Evaluation of the Database Directive* (n. 23). Technically the Commission should issue such reports every three years. *See* Art. 16(3).
24. DG Internal Market and Services Working Paper, First evaluation of directive 96/6/EC on the legal protection of databases, 5, 18-23 (Brussels, 2005).
25. On this issue, *see ibid.* Section 6, Importance of a legal protection of databases at the European level, and the Evaluation Report of the European Commission based on the study available at https://digital-strategy.ec.europa.eu/en/library/staff-working-document-and-executive-summary-evaluation-directive-969ec-legal-protection-databases (accessed Mar. 18, 2025).
26. Copyright Act, Law. 432 of Jan. 28, 1957, as amended by Act no. 9625 of Apr. 22, 2009, Chapter 4, Arts. 91-98. FTA, Art. 10.2 which the EU concluded with South Korea, ratified in 2015 and has been in force since Jul. 1, 2016 does not impose the adoption of a database right http://publications.europa.eu/resource/cellar/a2fb2aa6-c85d-4223-9880-403cc5c1daa2.0022.03/DOC_1 (accessed Jan. 3, 2024) but it may be because the right was already in the South Korean Copyright Act.

has successfully exported the sui generis right in the European Economic Area (EEA) (Liechtenstein, Norway and Iceland) as well as some associated states such as Turkey[27] and Albania,[28] though not in Belarus and Ukraine.[29] Apart from that, the EU has not been successful at exporting the right through FTAs. For instance, there is no provision in the Canada Comprehensive Economic and Trade Agreement (CETA), the EU-Japan Agreement, the Singapore Trade and Investment Agreements, the Mercosur,[30] or the EU-New Zealand Trade Agreements.[31] The Australia and India Trade Agreements, which are being negotiated, do not include the right either.[32]

Therefore, the database right has spread beyond the EEA and some associated states, though its effectiveness is far from proven, its scope is arguably too broad and many of its notions are far from clear.

In conclusion, the experience of the database right shows that in some cases, in those where a new intellectual property right is adopted, it is better to be pluralist. This enables the country/region that decides to have a new rule to experiment with it and to learn about its impact so that if the experiment is inconclusive or has a negative impact, the right is not adopted at international level. In the case of the database right, since the right has not proven to have an economic impact or at best has a mixed impact in terms of its legal notions, it is wise not to adopt it at international level before more economic evidence is available and the notions are clearer. In conclusion, this shows that it is unwise to adopt new rules outright universally, i.e., via an international convention. Proper testing is required.

18.2.2 Works of Applied Art

The second topic is copyright's protection of works of applied art or, in other words, the copyright/design interface.[33] Contrary to the database right, the

---

27. *See* additional Art. 8 of the Turkish Copyright Act of 1951, which was introduced in the act on Mar. 3, 2004. The act provides for the database right in the same terms as in the EU with the same duration but does not provide for exceptions.
28. Law 35/2016, Arts. 119-126 (the Albanian Copyright Act).
29. For the list of agreements agreed or being negotiated by the EU, *see* https://policy.trade.ec.europa.eu/eu-trade-relationships-country-and-region/negotiations-and-agreements_en (accessed Mar. 18, 2025).
30. https://policy.trade.ec.europa.eu/eu-trade-relationships-country-and-region/countries-and-regions/mercosur/eu-mercosur-agreement_en (accessed Mar. 18, 2025).
31. https://policy.trade.ec.europa.eu/eu-trade-relationships-country-and-region/countries-and-regions/new-zealand/eu-new-zealand-agreement/text-agreement_en (accessed Mar. 18, 2025).
32. https://policy.trade.ec.europa.eu/eu-trade-relationships-country-and-region/countries-and-regions/australia/eu-australia-agreement_en and https://policy.trade.ec.europa.eu/eu-trade-relationships-country-and-region/countries-and-regions/india/eu-india-agreement/documents_en (accessed Mar. 18, 2025).
33. On this issue, *see* Estelle Derclaye (eds.), *The Copyright/Design Interface, Past, Present and Future* (Cambridge University Press, 2018).

issue is as old as copyright and design laws are, and countries have adopted different rules for centuries to decide whether either copyright or a sui generis design right or both should protect works of applied art. The international conventions have still not succeeded in harmonizing this issue. Article 2(7) of the Berne Convention provides that:

> Subject to the provisions of article 7(4) of this Convention, it shall be a matter for legislation in the countries of the Union to determine the extent of the application of their laws to works of applied art and industrial designs and models, as well as the conditions under which such works, designs and models shall be protected. Works protected in the country of origin solely as designs and models shall be entitled in another country of the Union only to such special protection as is granted in that country to designs and models; however, if no such special protection is granted in that country, such works shall be protected as artistic works.

The said Article 7(4) further provides that:

> It shall be a matter for legislation in the countries of the Union to determine the term of protection of photographic works and that of works of applied art in so far as they are protected as artistic works; however, this term shall last at least until the end of a period of twenty-five years from the making of such a work.

So, the choice as to whether a work of applied art is protectable by copyright is left to countries, and if a country protects them by copyright, then the term must not be shorter than 25 years from the making of the work. The TRIPS agreement does not touch the issue. The current situation at international level has not moved an iota.[34] In October 2024, the Court of Justice handed down its decision in Case C-227/23 (Kwantum), further harmonizing one aspect of the copyright/design interface in the sense that it held that Member States do not have the possibility to apply the criterion of material reciprocity laid down in the second sentence of Article 2(7) of the Berne Convention in respect of a work of applied art the country of origin of which is a third country and the author of which is a national of a third country. The judgment thus takes away the autonomy of Member States on this aspect.

34. David Stone, Elisabeth Siew Kuan Ng & Graeme Dinwoodie, *Editorial*, *Singapore Designs Conference Special Issue,* 13(4) Journal of Intellectual Property Law & Practice 251-252 (2018) https://doi.org/10.1093/jiplp/jpy026 ("attempts at the WIPO Standing Committee on Trademarks, Industrial Designs and Geographical Indications (SCT) to agree a harmonisation treaty for designs have foundered, if not quite yet sunk. The draft text of the treaty is cautious, and does not attempt to change national substantive law on designs").

Even the EU has failed. Article 17 of the Design Directive[35] leaves the copyright/design interface untouched:

> A design protected by a design right registered in or in respect of a Member State in accordance with this Directive shall also be eligible for protection under the law of copyright of that State as from the date on which the design was created or fixed in any form. The extent to which, and the conditions under which, such a protection is conferred, including the level of originality required, shall be determined by each Member State.[36]

As a result, over the years, countries have used many criteria to determine if a work of applied art should be protected by copyright law, namely the requirement of originality, with mixed results.[37] If a country's design act was very strict (strict novelty requirement and thorough examination like in patent law, or the term of protection was very short), it was not used, but authors reverted to copyright, or in some cases to unfair competition. In that case, courts in some countries lowered their requirements of originality to accommodate such works with the effect that the term of protection was far longer and far more protective than via the registered design regime. This state of affairs protected functional works too much and for too long. Some countries having such strict requirements did, however, not do that, so valuable works of art were, and sometimes still are (e.g., Japan), very (too) hard to protect both under copyright and design law. So, at the other extreme, worthy works are denied any intellectual property protection. A few criteria to determine whether a work of applied art was worthy of copyright protection emerged as "winners" in the sense of most used over time across countries—artistic merit,[38] separation between art and function[39] and number of copies made of the work.[40] Copyright laws shun

35. Directive 98/71/EC of the European Parliament and of the Council of 13 October 1998 on the legal protection of designs, Official Journal L 289, 28/10/1998, pp. 28-35.
36. The EU has not gone further in FTAs. *See, e.g.*, Art. 20.25 of the CETA; Art. 10.28 of the EU-Singapore Trade and Investment Agreements.
37. For a list, *see* Estelle Derclaye, *A Model Copyright/Design Interface: Not an Impossible and Undesirable Task?*, at The Copyright/Design Interface, Past, Present and Future 421,439 (Estelle Derclaye ed., Cambridge University Press, 2018).
38. *See, e.g.*, the German case law at least since 1965, s. 4(1)(c) U.K. Copyright Act and corresponding case law (mainly George Hensher v. Restawhile Upholstery [1976] AC 64) and Art. 1(4) Italian Copyright Act.
39. The former version of the 1941 Italian Copyright Act stated until 2001: "if their artistic value is distinct from the industrial character of the product with which they are associated." Section 101 of U.S. Copyright Act protects "works of artistic craftsmanship," but copyright covers the design of a useful article "only if, and only to the extent that, such design incorporates pictorial, graphic, or sculptural features that can be identified separately from, and are capable of existing independently of, the utilitarian aspects of the article."
40. Such as under s. 52 of the U.K. Copyright Act before its repeal by the Enterprise and Regulatory Reform Act 2013.

artistic merit for other copyright works because it is unfair to whoever decides the work is worthy, be it the judge, the experts or the public, as tastes change over time. Separation between art and function is either too harsh (copyright can almost never protect a functional work in three dimensions)[41] or impossible to determine because the tests used are not easily applicable in practice.[42] Arguably, the best criterion, i.e., objective, least unworkable and with most legal certainty and thus least unfair, is that of the number of copies. After a number of copies (to be determined by the legislature) have been sold by the author of the work of applied art, its copyright protection should cease after a shorter period of time than the usual copyright term (an option the Berne Convention provides in its Article 7(4)).

Where pluralism has been going on for so long and legal experiments have yielded results so that one criterion emerges as the best, and there is no cultural diversity problem,[43] adopting a universal rule is warranted, from both a legal and economic point of view, for the reasons stated in section 18.1.2 relating to the advantages of having a universal rule. Retaining the status quo at international level as we are now is admittedly just down to a stubborn refusal to address the obvious based on erroneous or political beliefs. Such state of affairs impacts designers and users alike negatively. Time is more than ripe to adopt universal rules on this topic. Incidentally, the CJEU had to solve this issue in the *Cofemel* case, a case relating to clothes and referred by the Portuguese Supreme Court.[44] Adopting the same criterion for all works, including works of applied art, the EU finally has a harmonized rule for the protection of works of applied art, bringing the EU experiment to an end. The proposed recast Design Directive and Design Regulation codify this case law: "A design protected by a design right registered in or in respect of a Member State in accordance with this Directive shall also be

41. Such as in Italy before 2001.
42. Such as in the USA. For a history, *see* Jane Ginsburg, *Courts Have Twisted Themselves into Knots (and the Tangled Knots Remain Tangled): US Copyright Protection for Applied Art after Star Athletica,* at The Copyright/Design Interface, Past, Present and Future 297 (Estelle Derclaye ed., Cambridge University Press, 2018), and the decision of the U.S. Supreme Court in Star Athletica v. Varsity Brands, 197 L. Ed. 2d 354 (2017).
43. Namely when adopting a single rule would not reduce legitimate cultural diversity. Cultural diversity is one of the main reasons why copyright exceptions are not harmonized fully at EU level and the principle of subsidiarity fully applies. On this, *see* Ansgar Ohly, *Concluding Remarks, Postmodernism and Beyond,* at The Europeanization of Intellectual Property Law, Towards a European Legal Methodology 255, 259-260 (Justine Pila & Ansgar Ohly eds., Oxford University Press, 2013).
44. Case C-683/17, Cofemel—Sociedade de Vestuário SA v. G-Star Raw CV (2019) ECLI:EU:C:2019:721. For a comment, *see* Tito Rendas, *Copyright Protection of Designs in the EU: How Many Originality Standards Is Too Many?,* 13(6) Journal of Intellectual Property Law and Practice 439 (2018) https://doi.org/10.1093/jiplp/jpy037; European Copyright Society, Opinion of the European Copyright Society in relation to the pending reference before the CJEU in Cofemel v. G-Star Raw, C-683/17, https://europeancopyrightsocietydotorg.files.wordpress.com/2018/11/ecs-opinion-cofemel_final_signed.pdf (accessed Jan. 3, 2024).

eligible for protection by under the law of copyright as from the date on which the design was created or fixed in any form provided that the requirements of Union copyright law are met."[45] Thus, the new instruments (which have been adopted in 2024 and should be published in the official journal late in 2024 or early 2025) simply codify the case law of the CJEU. However, national courts are still "resisting" or misinterpreting the CJEU's now-old *Cofemel* precedent,[46] which it further elaborated in *Brompton,*[47] so much so that two more references are pending before it.[48]

18.3 CONCLUSION

Pluralism is mandated if cultural diversity requires it. Pluralism is good from a historical perspective. When a new problem arises, it is better that countries/regions adopt different rules to see which one(s) work best. Universalism is good ex post facto once these legal experiments have been conducted and little if any controversy remains on the rules to adopt. Learning from the database right's so far "failed experiment," it would have been best for the EU to have waited before adopting a publisher's right,[49] as the German and Spanish legal experiments are inconclusive or at least it is too early to tell what their impact is.[50] Going back in time, it is very arguable that the protection of computer programs by copyright has also been a failed experiment and one that we now may live to regret as it is well enshrined at international level.[51] At least because copyright lasts so long and programs

45. *See* Art. 23 of the new text of the directive and 96 of the new regulation, COM/2022/667 final and COM(2022) 666 final.
46. Estelle Derclaye, *The Status of Three-Dimensional Functional Works post-Cofemel. An Empirical Analysis of the Member States' Case Law*, at Kreation, Innovation, Märkte: Creation, Innovation, Markets, Festschrift Reto Hilty (C. Geiger, T. Jaeger, A. Peukert & F. Thouvenin eds., Springer 2024, pp. 121-138).
47. Case C-833/18, SI and Brompton Bicycle Ltd v. Chedech/Get2Get (2020) ECLI: EU:C:2020:461.
48. Cases C-580/23 (MIO) and C-795/23 (konektra).
49. A publisher's right is embodied in the directive on copyright in the digital single market Directive (EU) 2019/790 of the European Parliament and of the Council of 17 April 2019 on copyright and related rights in the digital single market and amending Directives 96/9/EC and 2001/29/EC, OJ L 130, 17.5.2019, pp. 92-125(accessed Jan. 3, 2024). *See* letter signed by numerous academics specialists in intellectual property law opposing the right, https://www.ivir.nl/academics-against-press-publishers-right (accessed Jan. 3, 2024).
50. *Ibid.*
51. WIPO Copyright Treaty, Art. 4; TRIPS, Art. 10.1. There have been numerous litigations around the world in relation to the anticompetitive effects copyright has granted to computer programs, some of the most prominent ones being United States v. Microsoft Corporation, 253 F.3d 34 (D.C. Cir. 2001) and Case T-201/04 Microsoft Corp. v. Commission of the European Communities (2007) ECLI:EU:T:2007:289.

are already well-protected thanks to their secrecy.[52] In a similar vein, the EU is wise to have put on hold a data producer's right (protecting data as such as opposed to databases), taking advice from numerous voices that it is too early to legislate on this issue.[53] The countries currently negotiating trade agreements with the EU would be well-advised to resist adopting the database right, at least in its current form. They could, collectively if they are so inclined, even push the EU to revise the right by refusing to adopt it. Of course, this will depend on their clout. Hence why, it is always better, as stated above, to harmonize or unify the law at international level rather than in multilateral treaties outside of the aegis of the United Nations.

---

52. Pamela Samuelson, Randall Davis, Mitchell D. Kapor & Jerome Reichman, *A Manifesto Concerning the Legal Protection of Computer Programs,* 94 Columbia Law Review 2308 (1994) https://doi.org/10.2307/1123142.
53. *See* esp. Osborne Clarke LLP, *Legal Study on the Ownership and Access to Data*, Final Report for DG Connect (2016) https://publications.europa.eu/en/publication-detail/-/publication/d0bec895-b603-11e6-9e3c-01aa75ed71a1 (accessed Jan. 3, 2024); P. Bernt Hugenholtz, *Against "Data Property,"* at Kritika: Essays on Intellectual Property, 48-71 (H. Ullrich, P. Drahos & G. Ghidini eds., Elgar, 2018).

Chapter 19

Copyright Contract Law

Agnès Lucas-Schloetter

Demands for authors and performers to get a fairer share of the economic success of their works and performances are becoming louder. In the music industry, studies have shown that artists receive a very small slice of the "streaming pie."[1] Since creative people are popular and their income is often very low, proposals to enhance their economic situation—under the motto "artists must be fairly remunerated"—usually receive significant support. There is indeed consensus that authors and performers should be adequately rewarded for their creative contribution, but not on how to do so. One means to achieve this goal is to provide for a stronger, author-protective, copyright contract law.

Copyright contract law is hereinafter referred to in the narrow sense as "primary"[2] copyright contract law, which includes a body of mandatory rules aiming at protecting authors and performers in their contractual relationships with publishers and producers. Thus, its scope of application covers only "upstream" or "first-level" contracts by which copyright in works and performances is assigned or licensed by authors or performers themselves. Rights administration agreements between authors and collecting societies, as well as sublicenses and "downstream" contracts with end users, are therefore excluded. As a matter of fact, primary copyright contract law is

1. *See* Emmanuel Legrand, *Study on the Place and the Role of Authors and Composers in the European Music Streaming Market* 27 (September 2022) according to which songwriters and composers receive approximately 10% and recording artists 16.5% of the streaming revenue.
2. Adolf Dietz, *Das primäre Urhebervertragsrecht in der Bundesrepublik Deutschland und in den anderen Mitgliedstaaten der Europäischen Gemeinschaft* (Schweitzer, 1984).

based upon the assumption that authors and performers are the weaker contracting parties to the contracts made for the exploitation of their works and performances, similar to consumers in Business-to-Consumers contracts.[3] It rests on the rationale that freedom of contract is illusory when contracting parties have grossly disproportionate bargaining power and that statutory provisions are needed to restore the balance.

However, this basic premise is not undisputed and is in fact completely alien to some jurisdictions. Copyright contract law is, like the moral right, an issue, which is typically influenced by the division between civil law and common law countries. Whereas civil law (especially the European continental) countries have a long tradition of mandatory limitations of freedom of contract in favor of authors, common law jurisdictions are more reluctant to provide for such author-protective rules,[4] with the exception of reversion rights.[5]

International copyright conventions do not provide for author-protective rules in contractual matters. They usually protect copyright owners without distinguishing between authors as initial rightholders and their successors in title as "derivative" rightholders.[6] At European level, however, copyright contract law has been harmonized by Directive 2019/790 of April 17, 2019 (CDSM Directive).[7] This is all the more remarkable since copyright contracts had so far always been regarded as an area of law that could not be harmonized and therefore had to be left to the Member States.[8] In fact, it appears that authors and performers need support in two respects:

3. But with the difference that creative people and their contractual partners are in the same boat as they have a common interest in the successful exploitation of the work or performance.
4. Jack Black, *Authors' Rights and the UK Law of Copyright Contracts: A Case of Practical Evolution?,* at Urheberrecht im Informationszeitalter 557-570 (Ulrich Loewenheim ed., FS Nordemann Beck, 2004); Jane C. Ginsburg, *Authors' Transfer and License Contracts under U.S. Copyright Law,* at Research Handbook on Intellectual Property Licensing 3-28 (Jacques de Werra ed., Edward Elgar, 2013); Jane C. Ginsburg, *Authors' Remuneration: Reforms to Wish for,* at Reforming Intellectual Property 125-138 (Gustavo Ghidini & Valeria Falce, eds., Edward Elgar, 2022).
5. Lionel Bently & Jane C. Ginsburg, *"The Sole Right ... Shall Return to the Authors": Anglo-American Authors' Reversion Rights from the Statute of Anne to Contemporary U.S. Copyright* 25 Berkeley Technology Law Journal 1475 (2011).
6. Giuseppina D'Agostino, *Contract Lex Rex: Towards Copyright Contract's Lex Specialis,* at Intellectual Property and General Legal Principles. Is Intellectual Property a Lex Specialis? 9 (Graeme Dinwoodie ed., Edward Elgar, 2015).
7. Chapter 3 of Title IV of the Directive is entitled "Fair remuneration in exploitation contracts of authors and performers" and includes six provisions dealing with copyright contract law. *See* European Copyright Society, *Comment of the ESC on Arts 18 to 22 DSM-D,* 11 Journal of Intellectual Property, Information Technology and Electronic Commerce Law (2020) 132; Ted Shapiro, *Remuneration Provisions in the DSM Copyright Directive and the Audiovisual Industry in the EU: The Elusive Quest for Fairness,* 42(12) European Intellectual Property Review 778 (2020).
8. Lucie Guibault, *Relationship Between Copyright and Contract Law,* at Research Handbook on the Future of EU Copyright 526 (Estelle Derclaye ed., Edward Elgar, 2009).

to control the scope of copyright assignments and license agreements on the one hand (section 19.1) and to negotiate appropriate remuneration on the other hand (section 19.2). A strong copyright contract law also requires certain enforcement mechanisms (section 19.3 below).

19.1 THE SCOPE OF COPYRIGHT ASSIGNMENTS AND LICENSES

19.1.1 The Rights Granted

Authors and performers first retain some control over the exploitation of their works or performances on the basis of their moral rights, which are always designated as nontransferable in all jurisdictions recognizing them. Economic rights,[9] however, may be either assigned or licensed. As a rule, there are hardly any limits to the design freedom of the contracting parties. Three instruments can, however, be used to protect authors: first, the interpretation rule *in dubio pro auctore* according to which, in the event of ambiguities, the transfer only covers those rights which are expressly mentioned in the contract. Second, the obligation of specification according to which copyright contracts must expressly indicate which rights are granted, for which types of use, geographical scope, duration and in return for which remuneration. Finally, special provisions for contracts on future works and/or future types of use may also be considered. In particular, a prohibition of copyright assignments or licenses in respect of as yet unknown types of use, as some continental European legal systems know it, could be contemplated at European Union (EU) level. Such a rule, which prevents authors from divesting rights the value of which they cannot yet estimate, has not, however, been included in the Directive on Copyright in the Digital Single Market.

19.1.2 The Duration

In many areas of the media and culture industry, authors and performers are called upon to transfer their entire rights for the whole duration of the statutory copyright, with the consequence that the long term of copyright protection actually only benefits their contractual partners. Such a practice of "stockpiling of rights" is questionable as these extensive assignments or licenses often exceed the needs of the publisher or producer who does not make any use of all rights he has been granted. Thus, some derogation from the basic principle of binding force of contractual agreements (*pacta sunt*

9. Or all copyright in those countries that do not provide for moral rights.

servanda) could be considered, which would allow authors to renegotiate or terminate such contracts under certain circumstances.[10]

19.1.2.1 Termination of the Contract Due to Insufficient Exploitation

Prior to the adoption of the CDSM Directive, some EU Member States provided for a statutory reversion right in case the publisher or producer did not exploit the work or performance for which he had been granted the copyright. However, this right of withdrawal for insufficient exploitation has proven rather ineffective in practice, as it could only be exercised if the lack of exploitation had seriously harmed the legitimate interests of the author or performer,[11] which is difficult to prove in practice.

A statutory termination right need not be admittedly expressly stated where the publisher or producer has a duty to exploit the work or performance for which he has been granted the copyright, as is the case in most EU Member States for publishing contracts. Failure to fulfill this obligation constitutes nonperformance and gives rise to a claim for breach of contract, which, however, must be asserted in court.[12] One means of improving the contractual position of authors and performers might be to introduce a duty to exploit each right granted for each type of use. Rather than a statutory duty, the breach of which would trigger an automatic reversion of the rights to the author or performer, it could be designed as a "use it or lose it" clause that would have to be enforced before the courts.

EU Member States introduced such a clause when transposing Article 22 of the CDSM Directive. This provision provides for a "right of revocation" whereby an author or a performer who has licensed or transferred his rights in his work or performance may revoke the licence or transfer in whole or in part if the work or performance is not exploited. However, this revocation mechanism may be excluded if the work contains contributions from several authors or performers, as is the case, for example,

10. *See, e.g.,* Directive 2019/790 on Copyright in the Digital Single Market, Recital 80: "When authors and performers license or transfer their rights, they expect their work or performance to be exploited. However, it could be the case that works or performances that have been licensed or transferred are not exploited at all. Where those rights have been transferred on an exclusive basis, authors and performers cannot turn to another partner to exploit their works or performances. In such a case, and after a reasonable period of time has elapsed, authors and performers should be able to benefit from a mechanism for the revocation of rights allowing them to transfer or license their rights to another person."

11. *See, e.g.,* s. 41 of the German Copyright Act (UrhG) as it read prior to the transposition of the CDSM Directive, according to which the author also had to compensate his contracting partner for any harm the revocation may cause him.

12. In France, however, Art. L.132-17-2 of the Code de la propriété intellectuelle (CPI) provides for an automatic termination of the publishing contract in case the publisher fails to publish the work within a certain time or to reissue a book that has gone out of print.

with audiovisual works, and specific provisions may be laid down to take account of the specificities of different sectors and different types of works and performances.[13]

19.1.2.2 Termination of the Contract Irrespective of Failure to Exploit

In addition to reversion for insufficient exploitation, authors and performers could also be granted the right to terminate a copyright contract after a specific period of time. This termination right would not be subject to any conditions and could be exercised without having to compensate the contracting party for losses incurred. In the course of the reform of German copyright contract law, the legislature had contemplated introducing such a mechanism but ultimately lacked the necessary courage.[14] Instead, section 40a of the German Copyright Act allows an author who has granted an exclusive license for a period of more than 10 years against a lump sum payment to otherwise exploit his work at the end of that period, with the first licensee retaining a non-exclusive license for the remaining term of the original grant. Although the CDSM Directive has not adopted this approach, as the right of revocation provided for in Article 22 applies only in the event that the work or performance is not exploited, consideration could be given, in Europe too, to introducing a termination right based on the United States (U.S.) model irrespective of any lack of exploitation.[15] This nonwaivable reversion right, which in principle takes effect 35 years after the copyright assignment or license,[16] does not apply to the important category of works made for hire but otherwise enables authors to regain control over the exploitation of their works.[17]

19.2 THE REMUNERATION OF AUTHORS

The central concern of primary copyright contract law is to ensure that authors and performers receive a fair share of the proceeds from the exploitation of their works and performances. However, according to a

---

13. Ula Furgal, *Interpreting EU Reversion Rights: Why "Use-It-or-Lose-It" Should Be the Guiding Principle,* 43(5) European Intellectual Property Review 283 (2021).
14. Agnès Lucas-Schloetter, *Das neue Urhebervertragsrecht* Gewerblicher Rechtsschutz und Urheberrecht 235, 238 (2017).
15. *See also* Copyright Act of Canada, s. 14(1) (transfers made after Jun. 4, 1921, automatically revert to the author's estate 25 years after his death).
16. If the contract was concluded after Jan. 1, 1978; U.S. Copyright Act of 1976, s. 203; U.S. Copyright Act of 1976, s. 304(c)(d): For agreements made before this date, the reversion right can be exercised 56 years after the "copyright registration."
17. Paul Goldstein, *Paternalism and Autonomy in Copyright Contracts,* at Intellectual Property in the New Millennium: Essays in Honour of William R. Cornish 261 (David Vaver & Lionel Bently eds., Cambridge University Press, 2004).

general principle of contract law, parties to a contract are free to negotiate the price of a good or service. Mandatory rules restricting contractual freedom can therefore be contemplated in order to compensate for the structural imbalance in bargaining power between authors and performers on the one hand and publishers and producers on the other. Various mechanisms of both individual and collective copyright laws are available for this purpose.

19.2.1 Individual Copyright Contract Law

19.2.1.1 *Ex Ante* Mechanisms

A first solution to improve the bargaining power of authors and performers is to impose—as was already the case prior to the CDSM Directive in some EU Member States such as France, Belgium, Greece,[18] Italy, Portugal[19] and Spain—that their remuneration be proportional to the revenues derived from the exploitation of their works or performances.[20] Thus, authors are, as a matter of principle, to receive royalties rather than a lump sum payment. Another solution can be to require that the remuneration of authors and performers be fair. It is the solution in Germany[21] and the Netherlands[22] where, as a general rule, copyright contracts are to stipulate an appropriate remuneration for assignments of rights or grant of licenses. Such a general fairness requirement regarding the remuneration of authors does not, however, constitute a mere statement of general policy without any concrete and effective enforcement mechanism. If the remuneration agreed between the contracting parties is not adequate, the contract must be amended. The claim to adequate remuneration is a contractual one, which is, however,

18. In Greece, the percentage of the income from exploitation to be received by authors is sometimes statutory determined. *See, e.g.,* Law 2121/1993 (Greek Copyright Act), s. 33 about publishing contracts, according to which, after the sale of the first 1,000 copies of a certain work, the percentage cannot be less than 10%.
19. According to Código de Direito de Autor e dos Direitos Conexos (1985) (Portuguese Copyright Code), s. 91(3), the author is entitled to a royalty of 25% of the proceeds of each copy, unless otherwise agreed in the publishing contract.
20. Depending on the countries, the rule of proportional remuneration, which applied only to authors and not to performers, applied to all contracts or only to some specific ones and to all categories of works or only to some of them.
21. UhrG, s. 32.
22. Auteurswet, s. 25c. On the reform *see* Bernt Hugenholtz, *Regulating Creator's Contracts under the DSM Directive. What We Can Learn from the Dutch,* Nordiskt Immateriellt Rättsskydd 467 (2022) https://doi.org/10.1093/oso/9780198850427.003.0003; Berndt Hugenholtz, *Towards Author's Paradise: The New Dutch Act on Authors' Contracts,* at Liber Amicorum Jan Rosén 397 (2016); Thomas Dysart, *Author-Protective Rules and Alternative Licences: A Review of the Dutch Copyright Contract Act,* 37(9) European Intellectual Property Review 601 (2015).

statutorily enforceable, with courts being given the power to adjust the contract.[23]

Article 18 of the CDSM Directive requires that authors and performers receive "appropriate and proportionate remuneration" when they license or transfer their exclusive rights for the exploitation of their works or performances. EU Member States enjoy considerable discretion in transposing this provision and may implement the principle of appropriate and proportionate remuneration through different mechanisms, such as collective bargaining[24] or statutory residual remuneration rights.[25] The Directive is silent on how the appropriateness of the remuneration is to be assessed. As regards the proportionate nature of the remuneration, Recital 73 states that it must be related "to the actual or potential value of the licensed or transferred rights, taking into account the author's or performer's contribution to the overall work" or performance, as well as all other circumstances of the case, "such as market practices or the actual exploitation of the work." In rather exceptional circumstances, a lump sum payment may be deemed appropriate. Unfortunately, the rule envisaged in the Draft Directive, according to which "contracts shall specify the remuneration applicable to each mode of exploitation,"[26] was not retained in the final version. Some Member States, like France[27] and Belgium,[28] nevertheless provide that remuneration must be calculated separately for each type of use.

19.2.1.2 *Ex Post* Mechanisms

Many EU Member States[29] provided, prior to the CDSM Directive, for a bestseller clause, i.e., a claim for an additional remuneration in case of a disproportion between the remuneration agreed upon and the later income

23. Agnès Lucas-Schloetter, *The Remuneration of Authors and Performers in Copyright Contract Law* at Research Handbook on Copyright Law 254-272 (Paul Torremans ed., 2nd ed., Edward Elgar, 2017).
24. CDSM Directive, Recital 73.
25. Raquel Xalabarder, *The Principle of Appropriate and Proportionate Remuneration for Authors and Performers in Article 18 Copyright in the Digital Single Market Directive,* 4 Revista para el Análisis del Derecho (InDret) 1 (2020) https://doi.org/10.31009/indret.2020.i4.01. *See*, however, the proceedings brought before the Belgian Constitutional Court (Sep. 26, 2024, n°98/2024: ECLI:BE:GHCC:2024:ARR.098), which referred the matter to the ECJ (Referral C-663/24 *Streamz and Others*, Oct. 9, 2024).
26. Draft Directive on Copyright in the Digital Single Market (P8_TA-PROV(2018)0337), Art. 14 para. 4.
27. CPI, Art. L. 132-25 for audiovisual production contracts and CPI, Art. L. 132-31 for authors of commissioned works used for advertising.
28. Belgian Code of Economic Law, Art. XI.167 §1 para. 4.
29. European Commission, *Impact Assessment on the Modernisation of EU Copyright Rules* Part 3/3, Annex 14 D, 220 (SWD 2016) 301 final listing examples of contracts adjustment mechanisms in at least 13 Member States.

generated from the exploitation of the work or performance.[30] In Germany and the Netherlands, the claim for additional compensation may be brought not only against the author's or performer's contractual counterpart but also against third parties to whom rights have subsequently been granted. This is a very important rule since the substantial revenues and profits generated by the exploitation of works are often not made by the author's contractual partner but by other exploiters in the licensing chain.[31] The issue has been addressed by the German Federal Court in its landmark rulings concerning two successful films, respectively the German classic "Das Boot"[32] and the U.S. blockbuster "Pirates of the Caribbean."[33]

In the meantime, the bestseller clause exists in one form or another in all EU Member States, as they have implemented the contract adjustment mechanism of Article 20 of the CDSM Directive, according to which "authors and performers or their representatives are entitled to claim additional, appropriate and fair remuneration from the party with whom they entered into a contract for the exploitation of their rights, or from the successors in title of such party, when the remuneration originally agreed turns out to be disproportionately low compared to all subsequent relevant revenues derived from the exploitation of the works or performances."

19.2.2 Collective Copyright Contract Law

The greatest challenge of drafting a piece of legislation on copyright contracts is certainly to adequately reflect the specificities of every single sector (publishing, music or audiovisual). As for employment legislation, there is a need for flexibility, which could be addressed by resorting to collective agreements between trade unions and employers' associations, especially to assess the appropriateness of the remuneration. However, in many branches of the creative industry, authors are freelancers to whom collective agreements under labor law do not apply. New models of collective agreements should therefore be developed that address the needs of authors as independent contractors.

30. In Germany, the corrective claim for contractual amendment does not, however, apply if the remuneration has been determined in accordance with common standards on remuneration or in a collective agreement (UhrG, Art. 32a para. 4).

31. Nikolaus Reber, *The "Further Fair Participation" Provision in Art. 32a (2) German Copyright Act: Claims Against a Third-Party Exploiter,* 11(5) Journal of Intellectual Property Law and Practice 382, 383 (2016) https://doi.org/10.1093/jiplp/jpw025.

32. BGH, *Das Boot I* 22.9.2011, Gewerblicher Rechtsschutz und Urheberrecht (GRUR) 2012, 496; BGH, *Das Boot II* 20.2.2020, GRUR 2020, 611; BGH, *Das Boot III* 1.4.2021, GRUR 2021, 955.

33. BGH, Fluch der Karibik 10.5.2012 Gewerblicher Rechtsschutz und Urheberrecht (GRUR) 2012, 1248. For the outcome of the lawsuit, *see* Higher Regional Court Berlin, 1.6.2016 Gewerblicher Rechtsschutz und Urheberrecht, Internationaler Teil (GRUR Int) 2016, 1072-1081, with a comment by Nikolaus Reber.

In Germany, the remuneration of authors and performers is deemed appropriate if it is determined in accordance with so-called common standards of remuneration,[34] which are established by representative organizations of authors or performers, on the one hand, and producers or publishers, on the other hand.[35] In France too, collectively negotiated remuneration agreements may be made mandatory by decree of the Ministry of Culture for all parties concerned within a specific sector.[36] The German experience shows, however, that some coercive measures with regard to the negotiation of such collective agreements are unavoidable. The mechanism of "common standards of remuneration" has proven to be quite ineffective, notably due to the unwillingness of publishers and producers to negotiate such standards.

19.3 ENFORCEMENT OF COPYRIGHT CONTRACT LAW

19.3.1 Reporting Obligations

The majority of Member States provided, prior to the CDSM Directive, for reporting obligations imposed upon contractual partners of authors and performers, either as a general rule or for some types of contracts only.[37] In Germany, a general reporting obligation was introduced as part of the 2016 revision of copyright contract law, which is enforceable not only against the author's or performer's contracting partner[38] but also against third parties to whom the initial contracting partner has granted a license.[39]

The CDSM Directive also addresses the issue of the so-called information asymmetry, meaning that authors and performers do not receive adequate information from their contracting partners especially on the revenues generated by the use of their works or performances. Article 19, entitled "Transparency obligation," requires Member States to ensure that authors and performers receive "up to date, relevant and comprehensive information on the exploitation of their works and performances." The

34. UhrG, s. 32(2).
35. UhrG, s. 36. Common standards of remuneration shall take into account the circumstances of the field to be regulated, especially the structure and size of the exploitation business.
36. CPI Art. L. 132-17-8 (publishing contract), Art. L. 132-25-1 (audiovisual production contract) and Art. L. 132-31 para. 4 CPI (commission contract for advertising purposes). For examples of such extended professional agreements in the audiovisual sector, *see* Pascal Kamina, *Film Copyright in the European Union* 216 (2nd edn, Cambridge University Press, 2016).
37. *See* European Commission, *Impact Assessment on the modernisation of EU Copyright Rules*, Part 3/3, Annex 14, 200 (SWD 2016) 301 final.
38. UhrG, s. 32d.
39. UhrG, s. 32e.

transparency obligation, which takes into account the specificities of each sector, is provided "on a regular basis," by the first contractual counterpart of authors and performers or by the sub-licensees.

19.3.2 Right to Sue

In order to improve the enforcement of the transparency obligation under Article 19 and the contract adjustment mechanism under Article 20, Article 21 of the CDSM Directive provides for a voluntary, alternative dispute resolution procedure. "Member States shall ensure that representative organizations of authors and performers may initiate such procedures at the specific request of one or more authors and performers." The Directive thus addresses the so-called issue of blacklisting, which should be welcomed. Authors are reluctant to initiate legal proceedings against their contracting partners in view of the economic consequences. Freelancers in particular fear being blacklisted and deprived of further contracts.

19.3.3 The Mandatory Nature of Copyright Contract Law

The most protective rules are of no interest to authors and performers if they can be contractually overridden. Copyright contract law should therefore include some mandatory provisions. This is the case at national level in most countries which, prior to the CDSM Directive, already offered some protection to authors and performers in their contractual relations with producers and publishers.[40] However, it is not enough to enact imperative rules on copyright contract law if it is possible to choose another law or another forum[41] that does not follow a comparable approach.[42] The decisive question is therefore how to avoid circumvention of protective national copyright contract law at the international level.

---

40. Clauses that do not comply with the requirements of copyright contract law are, e.g., void in France (André Lucas, Agnès Lucas-Schloetter & Carine Bernault, *Traité de la propriété littéraire et artistique* Nos. 744, 765, 784-787 (5th edn, LexisNexis, 2017)) or unenforceable in Germany (Gernot Schulze, § 32 No. 75, Urheberrechtsgesetz Kommentar (Thomas Dreier/Gernot Schulze eds., 7th ed., Beck 2022)). Section 32a para. 3 of the German Copyright Act expressly provides that claims to additional remuneration on the basis of the bestseller clause may not be renounced.
41. Copyright contract law may be evaded by way of choosing the courts of another forum state.
42. Alexander Peukert, *Protection of Authors and Performing Artists in International Law: Considering the Example of Claims for Equitable Remuneration under German and Italian Copyright Law,* International Review of Intellectual Property and Competition Law 900, 921 (2004).

According to a basic rule of private international law, the law applicable to contractual obligations may be freely chosen by the parties.[43] The free choice of law principle is in practice not very favorable to authors and performers because of the prevailing bargaining power of producers and publishers.[44] However, the freedom of the parties to choose the applicable law is not absolute. First, for certain categories of structurally weaker parties, such as consumers and employees, the parties' choice of law often cannot set aside the protection offered by the mandatory provisions of the law that would have been applicable had the parties not consented to a choice of law.[45] A similar rule protecting authors and performers against disadvantageous choice of law clauses would deserve serious consideration.[46]

Second, copyright contract law may be qualified as rules that override the choice of the parties for another legal system and are of mandatory application. This is the case under German law where section 32b[47] of the Copyright Act declares the claims for equitable remuneration (section 32) and additional remuneration (section 32a) to be internationally mandatory rules that may not be derogated from by stipulation of another applicable law.[48] However, it has been argued in recent times that section 32b would be superseded by the stricter provision of Article 9(1) of the Rome I Regulation

43. *See, e.g.*, Regulation (EC) No. 593/2008 of the European Parliament and of the Council of 17 June 2008 on the law applicable to contractual obligations (Rome I), Art. 3.1 (Jun. 17, 2008), Official Journal L. 177, 4/7/2008, pp. 6-16 (hereinafter "Rome I Regulation"); Volume 1, American Law Institute, *Restatement (Second) of Conflict of Laws*, §186.
44. Paul Katzenberger, *Protection of the Author as the Weaker Party to a Contract under International Copyright Contract Law,* 19 International Review of Intellectual Property and Competition Law 731, 736 (1998).
45. Geert van Calster, *European Private International Law* 215 (2nd edn, Hart Publishing, 2016). For consumers, this is the law of the country where the consumer has his habitual residence (Art. 6(1) Rome I Regulation). For employees, the law of the country in which or, failing that, from which, the employee habitually carries out his work in performance of the contract, Rome I Regulation, Art. 8(2).
46. Lucie Guibault & Bernt Hugenholtz, *Study on the Conditions Applicable to Contracts Relating to Intellectual Property in the European Union* 158 (Brussel: European Commission, 2002). *See* Rome I Regulation, Recital 23. *See* already Katzenberger (n. 44), 739.
47. UhrG, s. 32b(1) overrides an effective choice of foreign law if the contract is most closely connected with Germany. This is the case if the producer is contractually obliged to exploit the work and has its registered office in Germany, or—if the producer is not obliged to use the work—if the author or performer is domiciled in Germany. Section 32b (2) supersedes not only a choice of law clause but also additionally the applicable law in the absence of a party choice of law. Therefore, even if the parties deliberately choose another law than German law and Germany is not the country with the closest connection with the contract, s. 32 and 32a are applicable insofar as substantial use of the work takes place in Germany.
48. Reto Hilty & Alexander Peukert, *"Equitable Remuneration" in Copyright Law: The Amended German Copyright Act as a Trap for the Entertainment Industry in the U.S.?*, 22 Cardozo Arts & Entertainment Law Journal 401, 432 (2004).

on "overriding mandatory rules" and would be no longer applicable.[49] This opinion is not convincing since primary copyright contract law may indeed be regarded as "provisions the respect for which is regarded as crucial by a country for safeguarding its public interests, such as its political, social or economic organization."[50]

---

49. On the discussion, *see* Paul Katzenberger, § 32b No. 7a at Urheberrecht Kommentar (Schricker/Loewenheim eds., 6th ed., Beck, 2020).
50. Rome I Regulation, Art. 9(1). *See* Paul Torremans, *The Duran Duran Case in Private International Law: Copyright, Copyright Contracts and the Question Whether Section 203 U.S. Copyright Act Involves a Form of Reversionary Copyright*, 254 Revue Internationale du Droit d'Auteur 81, 101 (2017).

Part V

Human Rights and International Copyright Law

Chapter 20

Universalism, Pluralism or Isolationism? The Relationship Between Authors' Rights and Creators' Human Rights

Jonathan Griffiths

It is sometimes suggested that authors' rights[1] are protected under international human rights law. This claim is often supported by reference to the "creators' rights"[2] established under Article 27(2) of the Universal Declaration of Human Rights (UDHR)[3] and Article 15(1)(c) of the International Covenant on Economic, Social, and Cultural Rights (ICESCR).[4] Article 27(2) of the UDHR is framed in the following terms.

1. The term "authors' rights" is employed here to describe the rights granted to authors under international and national copyright/authors' rights systems. In this chapter, "authors' rights" and "copyright" are generally employed synonymously.
2. The term "creators' rights" is used here to describe the rights provided to authors under UDHR, Art. 27(2) and ICESCR, Art. 15(1)(c), and equivalent provisions in human rights and constitutional documents. However, there is no settled name for these rights in the commentary on the relevant provisions. *See*, for example, Graeme W. Austin, *Authors' Human Rights & Copyright Policy,* 40(4) Columbia Journal of Law & the Arts 405 (2017) ("authors' human rights"); UN Human Rights Council, Report of the Special Rapporteur in the Field of Cultural Rights, Farida Shaheed, Copyright Policy & the Right to Science & Culture (Dec. 24, 2014) UN Doc A/HRC/28/57 (part of a broader "right to science and culture").
3. Universal Declaration of Human Rights (Dec. 10, 1948) A/RES/217(III) (hereinafter "UDHR").
4. International Covenant on Economic Social and Cultural Rights (Dec. 16, 1966) (hereinafter "ICESCR").

> Everyone has the right to the protection of the moral and material interests resulting from any scientific, literary or artistic production of which he is the author.[5]

If authors' rights, as established in international copyright law, were indeed human rights, claims to the universalism of copyright norms would be significantly reinforced as, in addition to the obligations imposed by international agreements such as the Berne Convention and Agreement on Trade-Related Aspects of Intellectual Property Rights (TRIPS),[6] states would assume duties to protect authors under human rights instruments. Such duties would not be limited by an author's nationality, as is currently the case under international copyright agreements. Individual creators might, in certain circumstances, be entitled to bring proceedings directly against states for failure to comply with their obligations to protect creators' rights.[7] The concept of "creators' rights" in human rights law might also be expected to play an important role in shaping policy at international and national levels, as an important element within a pluralist international *acquis*.[8]

Is it true, then, that the authors' rights protected under copyright laws are synonymous with the creators' rights protected in human rights law and, if not, what is the relationship between the two sets of rights? These are the questions explored in this chapter. Section 20.1 outlines the claim that authors' rights are protected as human rights. It not only focuses on the creators' rights protected under Article 27(2), UDHR and Article 15(1)(c), ICESCR but also touches on arguments that authors' rights are encompassed within other generally recognized human rights, such as the right of freedom of expression and the right of property. The chapter then moves on to examine the scope of creators' rights within international human rights law (section 20.2), doing so by reference to the reports of the United Nations (UN) Committee of Economic, Social & Cultural Rights[9] and the UN Human Rights Committee's Special Rapporteur in the field of cultural rights.[10] These

5. *See* s. 20.1 *infra* for the text of Art. 15(1)(c).
6. Agreement on Trade-Related Aspects of Intellectual Property Rights (Apr. 15, 1994), 1869 UNTS 299.
7. Individual communications to the Committee on Economic, Social & Cultural Rights alleging violation of the ICESCR can be made against state parties which have ratified the Optional Protocol to the International Covenant on Economic, Social and Cultural Rights (Dec. 10, 2008), A/RES/63/117; to date, only a relatively small minority of states have ratified the Optional Protocol; *see*, https://www.ohchr.org/EN/HRBodies/CESCR/Pages/CESCRIndex.aspx (accessed Jun. 10, 2019).
8. For discussion of the potential of such a pluralist copyright *acquis, see* Graeme W. Austin, *Authors' Human Rights & Copyright Policy,* 40(4) Columbia Journal of Law & the Arts 405 (2017); Henning Grosse Ruse-Khan, *The Protection of Intellectual Property in International Law* (Oxford University Press, 2016); Graeme B. Dinwoodie & Rochelle C. Dreyfuss, *A Neofederalist Vision of TRIPS* (Oxford University Press, 2012).
9. *See* s. 20.2.2 *infra.*
10. *See* s. 20.2.3 *infra.*

reports emphasize significant distinctions between authors' rights and creators' rights and, as a consequence, challenge the universalist claim that human rights law provides fundamental reinforcement for the norms established in copyright law.

Section 20.3 seeks to establish the known contours of the relationship between authors' rights and creators' rights. It suggests that, while the copyright system as a whole is clearly not underpinned by creators' rights, there are aspects of the system which appear to be closely connected with human rights norms. Similarly, there are features of copyright law, at international and national levels, which sit uneasily with the obligations assumed by states under Article 27(2) of the UDHR and Article 15(1)(c) of the ICESCR. The chapter concludes by arguing that there is a significant (if unresolved) relationship between authors' rights and creators' rights, but that we currently do not have a mutually supportive, pluralist copyright *acquis* in which the latter plays a fully recognized role. As a matter of politics and doctrine, the two systems operate in relative isolation from one another. This situation is unlikely to change until, at the very least, the scope and effect of creators' rights are defined in greater detail. The means through which such clarification might be achieved are considered.

While creators' rights have received relatively little scholarly attention in the past, commentators have increasingly begun to turn to them as a potential antidote to the law's perceived failure: (i) to protect individual authors' rights adequately, and (ii) to balance copyright with competing interests.[11] This chapter seeks to contribute to this work by examining the nature of the relationship between the two forms of legal claim and, in particular, by asking whether aspects of the law of authors' rights are required, or precluded, by international human rights law.

20.1 AUTHORS' RIGHTS AS HUMAN RIGHTS

Human rights arguments have frequently been advanced by *users* of copyright works.[12] Increasingly, however, authors and other rightholders have sought to rely on human, or fundamental, rights in support of claims

11. *See* s. 20.3 *infra*.
12. Indeed, the first recital in the preamble to the Marrakesh Treaty to Facilitate Access to Published Works for Persons who are Blind, Visually Impaired or otherwise Print Disabled (Jun. 27, 2013) states: "Recalling the principles of non-discrimination, equal opportunity, accessibility and full and effective participation and inclusion in society, proclaimed in the Universal Declaration of Human Rights and the United Nations Convention on the Rights of Persons with Disabilities." For discussion of the relationship between the Marrakesh Treaty and the protection of human rights, *see* Lida Ayoubi, *Human Rights Principles in the WIPO Marrakesh Treaty: Driving Change in Copyright Law from Within,* 9 Queen Mary Journal of Intellectual Property 282 (2019) https://doi.org/10.4337/qmjip.2019.03.03.

relating to works or other subject matter. Sometimes such arguments are made in general terms, without linkage to specific rights recognized under international human rights instruments or under national constitutions.[13] There is a clear relationship between such general claims and the universalist rationales of international copyright law.[14] The Berne Convention, established with the intention of providing borderless rights for authors, has itself been described as a form of human rights document.[15] Arguments premised upon specific rights granted under international human rights law, or equivalent regional or national constitutional instruments, have also been made. In a European context, property is the most obviously relevant right in this regard.[16] Authors' claims to be entitled to rely on the right of property have received particular support from the inclusion of a "right of intellectual property" in the European Union's (EU's) Charter of Fundamental Rights.[17] In several Judgments of the Court of Justice, Article 17(2) has served to anchor the interests of authors and other rightholders within a framework of "fair balance"[18] and provided a bulwark against unjustified interference with authors' rights by national legislators.[19] However, the right to property has significant limitations from the perspective of creators or those deriving rights from creators. It does not specifically require the recognition of, or support for, creativity. Rather, it provides a general guarantee of established legal entitlements (including the authors' rights provided by law) against expropriation and other unjustified interference. Thus, for example, the right of property will not support an author's claim to a form of legal protection which is not already recognized in positive law.[20]

---

13. For an example of such an enquiry, *see* Michel Vivant, *Authors' Rights, Human Rights*, 174 Revue Internationale du Droit d' Auteur 60 (1997).
14. For a discussion of the universalist foundations of authors' rights, *see* Jane C. Ginsburg, *From Hypatia to Victor Hugo to Larry and Sergey: All the World's Knowledge and Universal Authors' Rights,* 22 British Academy Review 39 (2013) https://doi.org/10.5871/bacad/9780197265666.003.0004.
15. *See* Berne Union Assembly, Solemn Declaration Commemorating the Centenary of the Berne Convention (Jun. 27, 1986), as reproduced in Copyright 373 (1986).
16. For detailed discussion, Caterina Sganga, *Propertizing European Copyright* (Edward Elgar, 2018). In national law, *see*, for example, Ronan Kennedy, *Was It Author's Rights All the Time?: Copyright as a Constitutional Right in Ireland,* 33 Dublin University Law Journal 253 (2011).
17. Charter of Fundamental Rights of the European Union, Official Journal C 326, 26/10/2012, pp. 391-407, Art. 17(2); this provision simply confirms that intellectual property is covered by the Charter's general guarantee of property rights (Art. 17(1)); *see*, Case C-70/10 Scarlet Extended v. SABAM (2011) EU:C:2011:771, para. 43.; Case C-314/12 UPC Telekabel v. Constantin Film Verleih GmbH (2014) EU:C:2014:192, para. 61.
18. *See*, for example, Case C-160/17, GS Media BV v. Sanoma Media Netherlands BV (2016) EU:C:2016:644.
19. *See*, Case C-277/10 Luksan v. Van der Let (2012) EU:C:2012:65.
20. For a discussion of the limitations of the right of property in this regard, *see* Alexander Peukert, *The Fundamental Right to (Intellectual) Property and the Discretion of the*

Given the limitations of the fundamental right of property, it is not surprising that attempts have also been made to establish a human rights foundation for authorship on other rights protected under international and domestic bills of rights. Thus, for example, the description of copyright law as the "engine of free expression"[21] is often repeated and attempts are sometimes made to argue that authors' rights reflect the right to freedom of expression as a matter of theory.[22] These have, however, had little effect in substantive doctrine, where the argument that freedom of expression encompasses a justiciable right not to speak, or a right not to speak in particular terms, has not had significant practical impact.[23] Similarly, while the rights of privacy and dignity have played a role in copyright law in some jurisdictions,[24] their influence has not been felt more generally.

The most likely foundation for the argument that creators are protected in human rights law therefore remains the creators' rights protected under Article 27(2) of the UDHR and Article 15(1)(c) of the ICESCR. The text of the former was set out in the introduction to this chapter above. Article 15(1)(c), which is based on Article 27(2), provides that:

> The States Parties to the present Covenant recognize the right of everyone: ... (c) To benefit from the protection of the moral and material interests resulting from any scientific, literary or artistic production of which he is the author.[25]

Legislature, at Research Handbook on Human Rights and Intellectual Property 132 (Christophe Geiger ed., Edward Elgar, 2015).

21. Harper & Row v. Nation Enterprises 471 U.S. 539, 558 (1985).
22. *See*, for example, L. Kim Treiger-Bar-Am, *The Moral Right of Integrity: A Freedom of Integrity,* 2 New Directions in Copyright Law 128 (Fiona Macmillan ed., Edward Elgar, 2006); for analysis of the claim that copyright is "the engine of free expression," *see* Neil W. Netanel, *Copyright's Paradox* 81-108 (Oxford University Press, 2008).
23. Although, for the acceptance of a comparable example based on the freedom of thought, conscience and religion under the EU Charter of Fundamental Rights (Art. 10), *see* the Opinion of Advocate General Szpunar in Case C-516/17 Spiegel Online GmbH v. Volker Beck (2019) EU:C:2019:16, para. 79. *See* also Christophe Geiger and Elena Izyumenko, *Designing a Freedom of Expression-Compliant Framework for Moral Rights in the EU: Challenges & Proposals* 292-314 (Ysolde Gendreau, ed., Edward Elgar, 2023).
24. For discussion, *see* Josef Drexl, *Constitutional Protection of Authors' Moral Rights in the European Union,* at Human Rights & Private Law: Privacy as Autonomy 159-176 (Katja S. Ziegler ed., Hart Publishing, 2007).
25. Article 15(1) as a whole provides that:

    > The States Parties to the present Covenant recognize the right of everyone:
    >
    > (a) to take part in cultural life;
    > (b) to enjoy the benefits of scientific progress and its applications;
    > (c) to benefit from the protection of the moral and material interests resulting from any scientific, literary or artistic production of which he is the author.

    Limitations imposed on the rights granted under the ICESCR are permissible, as long as certain general conditions are satisfied, *see* ICESCR, Art. 4. Article 15(2)-(4) reinforces the rights establish under Article 15(1) by requiring states (i) to take necessary steps for the conservation, development and diffusion of science and culture (Article 15(2)); (ii) to respect the freedom

Article 15(1)(c) appears alongside two other "cultural rights": (i) a right to take part in cultural life,[26] and (ii) a right to enjoy the benefits of scientific[27] progress and its applications.[28] The latter right has come to be referred to as the "right to science"[29] and, after a long period of obscurity,[30] has enjoyed more attention recently, as a consequence of the publication of the Committee on Economic, Social and Cultural Rights' (CESCR's) *General Comment 25 on the Right to Enjoy the Benefits of Scientific Progress*[31] and of increased pressure for "open science."[32]

While the UDHR is not directly enforceable,[33] there is an enforcement mechanism for the rights protected under the ICESCR. Contracting states are obliged periodically to report on the measures that they have taken to comply with the Convention and, where a state has ratified the Optional Protocol to the ICESCR, there is a right of individual petition to the CESCR. The obligations imposed by economic, social and cultural rights, such as

indispensable for scientific research and creative activity (Article 15(3)); and (iii) to recognize the benefits to be derived from the encouragement and development of international contacts and co-operation in the scientific and cultural fields (Article 15(4)).

26. *See* Committee on Economic, Social & Cultural Rights, *General Comment No. 21: Right of Everyone to Take Part in Cultural Life (Article 15, para. (1)(a), of the International Covenant on Economic, Social & Cultural Rights)* (2009), E/C. 12/GC/21, Dec. 24, 2009.
27. Science includes social science, *see* United Nations, Economic and Social Council, Committee on Economic, Social and Cultural Rights, *General Comment No. 25 (2020) on Science and Economic, Social and Cultural Rights (Article 15(1)(b), (2), (3) and (4) of the International Convention on Economic, Social & Cultural Rights)* (Apr. 30, 2020), E/C.12/GC/25, §5.
28. For discussion of the relationship between cultural rights and intellectual property more generally, *see* Caterina Sganga, *Right to Culture and Copyright: Participation and Access*, at Research Handbook on Human Rights and Intellectual Property 560-576 (C. Geiger ed., Edward Elgar, 2015).
29. However, General Comment No. 25 describes the relevant protected right as: "the right to participate in and to enjoy the benefits of Scientific Progress and its Applications."
30. *See* Sebastian Porsdam Mann, Helle Porsdam, & Yvonne Donders, *"Sleeping Beauty": The Right to Science as a Global Ethical Discourse,* 42 Human Rights Quarterly 332 (2020).
31. United Nations, Economic and Social Council, Committee on Economic, Social and Cultural Rights, *General Comment No. 25 (2020) on Science and Economic, Social and Cultural Rights (Article 15(1)(b), (2), (3) and (4) of the International Convention on Economic, Social & Cultural Rights)* (Apr. 30, 2020), E/C.12/GC/25.
32. *See* Helle Porsdam & Sebastian Porsdam Mann eds, *The Right to Science: Then and Now* (Cambridge University Press, 2022); Aurora Plomer, *Patents, Human Rights and Access to Science* (Edward Elgar, 2015).
33. Although it has been suggested that the UDHR has the force of customary international law, *see* Roberta Rosenthal Kwall, *The Soul of Creativity: Forging a Moral Rights Law for the United States* 133 (Stanford University Press, 2010); Peter Yu, *Reconceptualizing Intellectual Property Interests in a Human Rights Framework,* 40 University of California at Davis Law Review 1039, 1046 (2007).

Article 15(1)(c), are not equivalent to the civil and political rights protected under "first generation" human rights instruments such as the International Covenant on Civil and Political Rights or the European Convention on Human Rights, under which state parties are required immediately to satisfy all protected rights.[34] By contrast, it is recognized that a state's ability to satisfy economic, social and cultural rights depends, to an extent, on its resources. Accordingly, the ICESCR generally imposes an obligation upon states to realize rights such as the creators' rights established under Article 15(1)(c) progressively.[35] However, even within this looser enforcement framework, protected rights establish certain "core obligations," by which contracting parties are immediately bound. States are also prohibited from interfering with protected rights by taking "retrogressive measures" on issues covered by the protected rights.

Against this background, claims have been made that Article 27(2) and Article 15(1)(c) entrench and support the rights of authors under national and international copyright law. Thus, for example, in its submission to the Human Rights Council's Special Rapporteur in the field of cultural rights in 2014, the International Publishers Association wrote that:

> Copyright (understood as encompassing both economic and moral rights) is a concretisation of the human rights of creators: their freedom [...] to create science, their freedom of expression ... It is our view that human rights and intellectual property rights are not only compatible, but also mutually supportive and interdependent.[36]

It is not only lobbyists who have stressed the close relationship between authors' rights and creators' rights. In her pioneering work on the legislative history of creators' rights, Chapman described Article 27(2) and Article 15(1)(c) as giving rise to a "human right to intellectual property."[37] Bécourt has also argued that the "Universal Declaration considers copyright to be a human right in itself, within the more general context of the right to

---

34. However, *see* the discussion of "core obligations" in s. 20.2.2.
35. For a brief summary of the obligations imposed, *see* Committee on Economic, Social & Cultural Rights, *Human Rights & Intellectual Property: Statement by the Committee on Economic, Social & Cultural Rights*, para. 11 (Dec. 14, 2001) E/C.12/2001/15. For a more detailed review of the institutional context of the relationship between intellectual property law and international human rights, *see* Laurence R. Helfer & Graeme W. Austin, *Human Rights & Intellectual Property* 1-89 (Cambridge University Press, 2011).
36. Jens Bammel, *Consultation on the Impact of Intellectual Property Regimes on the Enjoyment of the Right to Science and Culture* (Sep. 15, 2014), https://www.ohchr.org/Documents/Issues/CulturalRights/ConsultationIntelectualproperty/International%20Publishers%20Association.pdf (accessed Jun. 13, 2019).
37. *See*, for example, Audrey R. Chapman, *The Human Rights Implications of Intellectual Property Protection,* 5(4) Journal of International Economic Law 861, 866 (2002) https://doi.org/10.1093/jiel/5.4.861.

culture"[38] and Dietz and Françon have written that "… to attack copyright is to attack a human right, the highest and most venerable form of legal protection of human activity."[39] More recently, Minero has noted that at the "international level, copyright is considered a fundamental or human right in Art 27 of the Universal Declaration of HR."[40]

Thus, there appears to be a widely held view that the creators' rights protected under the international human rights system map closely to the authors' rights established in international and national copyright law. In its strongest form, this view suggests that the international human rights system provides a "right to copyright." In the following section of this chapter, this equation between authors' rights and creators' rights is evaluated. In order to establish whether it is justified, it is first necessary to understand how creators' rights are conceived in international human rights law.

20.2 CREATORS' RIGHTS AS HUMAN RIGHTS

In referring to creators' "moral and material interests," the texts of Article 27(2) and Article 15(1)(c) indicate some form of relationship with positive copyright law. These two forms of interest appear, at first sight, to correlate the two forms of right—moral and economic—generally granted under authors' rights instruments. However, those texts provide no further guidance on the interpretation of these rights. The national reports submitted to the CESCR are equally unhelpful. Generally, to the extent that they cover cultural rights, they tend to focus on access to culture and science, rather than the interests protected under Article 15(1)(c).[41] Similarly, no substantial jurisprudence has been established through decisions on individual petitions

38. Daniel Bécourt, *Copyright and Human Rights,* XXXII(3) Copyright Bulletin 13, 14 (1998).
39. Adolph Dietz & André Françon, *Copyright as a Human Right,* XXXII(3) Copyright Bulletin 7, 8 (1998).
40. Gemma Minero, *Intellectual Property Rights & Human Rights: Coinciding and Cooperating* at Intellectual Property Law & Human Rights 163-184, 169 (Paul Torremans ed., 3rd ed., Wolters Kluwer, 2015); *see also* Paul Goldstein & Bernt Hugenholtz, *International Copyright: Principles, Law & Practice* 23 (3rd ed., Oxford University Press, 2013) 23; Jorgen Blomqvist, *Primer on International Copyright and Related Rights* 17 (Edward Elgar, 2014); Paul L.C. Torremans, *Is Copyright a Human Right?,* 2007 Michigan State Law Review 271-291 (2007).
41. The National Reports to the Committee on Economic, Social & Cultural Rights are available at: https://www.ohchr.org/en/treaty-bodies/cescr. One exception to the general trend is provided by the 2022 periodic report submitted to the Committee on Economic & Social Rights by the Russian Federation, which notes accession to international intellectual property treaties. *See* Committee on Economic, Social & Cultural Rights, Seventh periodic report submitted by the Russian Federation under Arts. 16 and 17 of the Covenant, Nov. 16, 2022, §§ 307-313.

brought under Article 15(1)(c) under the Optional Protocol. In such circumstances, it is necessary to seek normative guidance elsewhere. Might the *travaux préparatoires* clarify the scope and effect of creators' rights?

20.2.1 Travaux Préparatoires

The circumstances in which both Article 27(2) of the UDHR and Article 15(1)(c) of the ICESCR were negotiated have been studied in detail.[42] The literature on the *travaux* reveals that the motives for the incorporation of these provisions in international human rights law were mixed.[43] It also demonstrates that their inclusion was controversial.[44] Article 27(2) was a disputed addition during the drafting of the UDHR and there was no automatic carryover of that provision into the ICESCR. Some states which promoted the inclusion of creators' rights in international human rights law were clearly motivated by a desire to strengthen international copyright law[45] and, in particular, some seem to have been keen to bolster the patchy protection available for moral rights at an international level.[46] There is also evidence that some states wanted to influence the ongoing negotiation of international copyright agreements.[47] However, there was also considerable resistance to the inclusion of creators' rights in international human rights law on the grounds that creators' rights were not human rights[48] or that the issues raised by authors' rights were simply too complex to be resolved within a human rights framework and were better handled in the domain of

---

42. *See*, for example, Johannes Morsink, *The Universal Declaration of Human Rights: Origins, Drafting and Intent* 217-222 (Philadelphia: University of Philadelphia Press, 1999); Audrey Chapman, *Approaching Intellectual Property as a Human Right: Obligations Related to Article 15(1)(c),* 35 Copyright Bulletin 4, 10-13(2001); Maria Green, *Drafting History of the Article 15(1)(c) of the International Covenant* (Oct. 9, 2000) UN Doc E/C.12/2001/15; Ruse-Khan (n. 8) 8.5, 8.10 (Oxford University Press, 2016); Yu (n. 33), 1039; Ragnar Adalsteinsson & Páll Thórhallson, *Article 27* at The Universal Declaration of Human Rights: A Common Standard of Achievement 577-580 (Gudmundur Alfredsson & Asbjorn Eide eds., Brill, 1999); Aurora Plomer, *IP Rights & Human Rights: What History Tells us and Why it Matters,* at The Right to Science: Then and Now (Helle Porsdam & Sebastian Porsdam Mann eds., Cambridge University Press, 2022) 54-75.
43. *See*, for example, Ruse-Khan (n. 8), §8.07; Yu (n. 33), 1050.
44. Ruse-Khan (n. 8), 805; Yu (n. 33), 1054; Kwall (n. 33), 134; *see also*, UN Human Rights Council, Report of the Special Rapporteur in the Field of Cultural Rights, Farida Shaheed, Copyright Policy & the Right to Science & Culture, para. 30 (Dec. 24, 2014) UN Doc A/HRC/28/57.
45. Morsink (n. 42), 221.
46. Yu (n. 33), 1039, 1081-1083.
47. *See* Chapman (n. 42), 4, 10.
48. Morsink (n. 42), 221.

international copyright law.[49] Furthermore, a number of states noted that creators' rights, as ultimately agreed, had to be read alongside both: (i) other elements of Article 27 and Article 15 guaranteeing access to culture,[50] and (ii) the rights protected under other Articles of the Convention.[51]

Thus, the *travaux* clearly demonstrate that creators' rights have a historical connection with the structures of international and domestic authors' rights law, but do not provide an exact explanation of the nature of this relationship.[52] However, further sources of interpretative guidance on Article 27(2) and Article 15(1)(c) have subsequently become available. Two UN human rights bodies, the CESCR and the Human Rights Council have sought to clarify the nature and scope of creators' rights. In 2006, the CESCR issued "General Comment No. 17: The Right of Everyone to Benefit from the Protection of the Moral and Material Interests Resulting from Any Scientific, Literary or Artistic Production of which He is the Author"[53] and, in 2014, the United Nations' Human Rights Council's Special Rapporteur in the field of cultural rights published her report on *Copyright Policy and the Right to Science and Culture*.[54] Together, these offer important guidance on the interpretation of creators' rights and have been described as an "emerging jurisprudence" on these rights.[55] It is to these documents that we now turn.

20.2.2 General Comment No. 17 of the CESCR

By the 1990s, the negotiation of new international intellectual property agreements (TRIPS, in particular) had given rise to disquiet in some quarters. Many argued that the ratcheting-up of intellectual property protection (including copyright) under such agreements threatened important public interests, including access to medicines and education. In this climate of challenge to international norm-setting in intellectual property law, the CESCR decided that further clarification of the concept of creators' rights in

49. Green (n. 42), 8.
50. For discussion of the importance of balancing the various rights protected under Art. 15(1), *see* Lea Shaver & Caterina Sganga, *The Right to Take Part in Cultural Life: On Copyright & Human Rights,* 27 Wisconsin International Law Journal 637-662 (2010) https://doi.org/10.31228/osf.io/6xv8h; Chapman (n. 42), 4, 13; Ruse-Khan (n. 8), §8.10.
51. Adalsteinsson & Thórhallson (n. 42), 575-596, 580.
52. Indeed, some scholars have argued strongly that the *travaux* do not support a precise equation between creators' rights and authors' rights, as protected in international copyright law, because creators' rights must be viewed in the broader context of Art. 27 and Art. 15 and the human instruments more generally. *See*, for example, Plomer (n. 42).
53. Committee on Economic, Social & Cultural Rights, *General Comment No 17: The Right of Everyone to Benefit from the Protection of the Moral and Material Interests Resulting from Any Scientific, Literary or Artistic Production of Which He Is the Author* (Jan. 12, 2006) UN Doc E/C12/GC/17 (General Comment 17).
54. UN Doc A/HRC/28/57 (n. 2).
55. Austin (n. 8), 405, 418.

international human rights law was required. A "preliminary contribution" was made in the Statement on *Human Rights & Intellectual Property* (2001 Statement), which aimed to identify key human rights principles deriving from Article 15(1)(c) of the ICESCR and, in particular, to distinguish those principles from those applicable in intellectual property law.[56] The 2001 Statement notes that the realms of trade, finance and investment are not exempt from the requirements of international human rights law and calls upon bodies such as the World Intellectual Property Organization and the World Trade Organization to take appropriate account of the rights protected under the ICESCR.[57] It distinguishes emphatically between human rights (such as creators' rights), which are described as "fundamental as they derive from the human person as such," and intellectual property rights, which it describes as instrumental policy tools.[58] It also stresses the importance of nondiscrimination and the consequent need to pay particular attention to the most disadvantaged and marginalized individuals and groups in society, at national and international levels. In general terms, the 2001 Statement notes the need to maintain a balance between the two competing aspects of Article 15 of the ICESCR:

> On the one hand, Article 15.1 (a) and (b) recognizes the right of everyone to take part in cultural life and to enjoy the benefits of scientific progress and its applications. On the other hand, Article 15.1 (c) recognizes the right of everyone to benefit from the protection of the moral and material interests resulting from any scientific, literary or artistic production of which he or she is the author. When adopting and reviewing intellectual property systems, States should bear in mind the need to strike a balance between those concurrent Covenant provisions.[59]

Furthermore, it notes that state parties to the ICESCR are not only under a duty progressively to realize the right protected under Article 15(1)(c), but also come under certain obligations that have immediate effect under that provision, including "core obligations."[60]

The CESCR followed up the 2001 Statement with more detailed interpretative guidance on creators' rights in "General Comment No 17: The Right of Everyone to Benefit from the Protection of the Moral and Material Interests Resulting from Any Scientific, Literary or Artistic Production of

56. Committee on Economic, Social & Cultural Rights, *Human Rights & Intellectual Property: Statement by the Committee on Economic, Social & Cultural Rights* (Dec. 14, 2001) E/C.12/2001/15 (2001 Statement); for discussion, *see* Chapman (n. 37), 861.
57. 2001 Statement, §§3, 9; it also declares that all those affected by intellectual property regimes should be entitled to participate in decision-making processes in an active and informed manner.
58. *Ibid.*, §6.
59. *Ibid.*, §17.
60. *Ibid.*, §11.

which He is the Author" (General Comment 17).[61] This document, which has been referred to as a "key point of reference for analysis of the normative content of Article 15(1)(c),"[62] restates the general principles set out in the 2001 Statement. In particular, it reiterates the distinction between creators' rights, which are inherent to human beings and intellectual property rights, which are instrumental policy tools[63] and notes again that creators' rights must be balanced against other important human rights and public interests.[64] Additionally, it provides detail on the normative content of Article 15(1)(c), noting, for example, that creators' rights are granted to natural persons (including groups of natural persons)[65] and that legal entities, while recognized as proprietors of rights in intellectual property law, are not covered by Article 15(1)(c).[66] Concerning the nature of the cultural productions covered by creators' rights, General Comment 17 explains that "any scientific, literary or artistic production" is a broader category than the "literary and artistic works" protected under the Berne Convention[67] and encompasses "scientific publications and innovations, including knowledge, innovations and practices of indigenous and local communities" and "performances and oral traditions."[68]

By reference to Article 27(2) of the UDHR,[69] General Comment 17 identifies the "moral interests" of authors as a particularly important aspect of the creators' rights established under Article 15(1)(c). It suggests that these interests, which include both an attribution and an integrity right, are defined in a manner which aligns them closely with the moral rights guaranteed under the Berne Convention.[70] At the same time, it goes out of its way to distinguish the concept of "material interests" from international copyright norms, particularly in relation to the duration and extent of protection:

---

61. General Comment 17; for discussion, *see* Hans M. Haugen, *General Comment No. 17 on "Author's Rights,"* 10(1) Journal of World Intellectual Property 53 (2007) https://doi.org/10.1111/j.1422-2213.2007.00314.x; Laurence R. Helfer, *Toward a Human Rights Framework for IP University of California,* 40 Davis Law Review 971 (2007); Graeme W. Austin & Amy G. Zavidow, *Copyright Law Reform Through a Human Rights Lens,* at Intellectual Property Law & Human Rights 303-333 (Paul Torremans ed., 3rd edn., Kluwer, 2015).
62. Helfer & Austin (n. 35), 172; although it has been noted that the 2001 Statement and the General Comment are interpretative, rather than binding. *See* Helfer (n. 61), 988; Ruse-Khan (n. 8), §8.12.
63. General Comment 17, §1.
64. *Ibid.*, 35.
65. *Ibid.*, §§8, 32; the rights of indigenous persons are a particular issue of concern for the Committee.
66. *Ibid.*, 7, 8.
67. *See*, Berne Convention for the Protection of Literary and Artistic Works (Jul. 24, 1971), TRT/BERNE/002, Art. 2.
68. General Comment 17, §9.
69. *Ibid.*, 12.
70. *Ibid.*, 13.

> The term of protection of material interests under [A]rticle 15, paragraph 1(c), need not extend over the entire lifespan of an author. Rather, the purpose of enabling authors to enjoy an adequate standard of living can also be achieved through one-time payments or by vesting an author, for a limited period of time, with the exclusive right to exploit his scientific, literary or artistic production.[71]

According to General Comment 17, state parties to the ICESCR are obliged to ensure that remedies for violation of creators' moral and material interests are available, accessible and efficient.[72] They must also make sure that access to such remedies is provided in a nondiscriminatory manner and that particular attention is paid to the interests of disadvantaged and marginalized groups.[73] Any limitations on the rights of authors must pursue a legitimate aim and must be proportionate (in line with ICESCR, Article 4)[74] and may be accompanied by an obligation to provide compensation to authors.[75]

In addition to this outline of the standards of protection required under Article 15(1)(c), General Comment 17 elaborates on the nature of the obligations placed upon state parties. As noted in the previous section of this chapter, in line with other economic, social and cultural rights protected under international human rights instruments, creators' rights are subject to an obligation of progressive realization. Such obligations are sensitive to the resource constraints of individual states. Within this framework, states have duties to respect, protect and fulfill creators' rights.[76] The duty to *respect* precludes states from infringing the moral interests of creators and from unjustifiably infringing their material interests.[77] The obligation to *protect* those interests encompasses a duty to safeguard creators against third parties, including a duty to ensure compensation for unlicensed use. The obligation to *fulfill* the requirements of Article 15(1)(c) requires states to maintain judicial, administrative or other appropriate remedies for creators, to facilitate the formation of professional and other associations representing the moral and material interests of authors and to promote the involvement of creators in decision-making on policies having an impact on their interests.[78]

General Comment 17 also confirms that Article 15(1)(c) imposes certain immediately effective obligations, including a prohibition on measures that reduce the existing level of protection available to authors without

71. *Ibid.*, 16; however, protection must be effective, §10.
72. *Ibid.*, 18.
73. *Ibid.*, 19.
74. *Ibid.*, 22-23. It has been noted that the proportionality standard applicable may be more exacting than the equivalent doctrine in international copyright law (the so-called three-step test). *See*, for example, Austin & Zavidow (n. 61), 303-333, 320-321.
75. General Comment 17, §24.
76. For discussion in this context, *see* Shaver & Sganga (n. 50), 637-662.
77. *Ibid.*, 30.
78. *Ibid.*, 34.

particular justification[79] and a duty to satisfy certain current "core obligations," which are set out in the following terms:[80]

(a) To take legislative and other necessary steps to ensure the effective protection of the moral and material interests of authors.
(b) To protect the rights of authors to be recognized as the creators of their scientific, literary and artistic productions and to object to any distortion, mutilation or other modification of, or other derogatory action in relation to, their productions that would be prejudicial to their honor or reputation.
(c) To respect and protect the basic material interests of authors resulting from their scientific, literary or artistic productions, which are necessary to enable those authors to enjoy an adequate standard of living.
(d) To ensure equal access, particularly for authors belonging to disadvantaged and marginalized groups, to administrative, judicial or other appropriate remedies enabling authors to seek and obtain redress in case their moral and material interests have been infringed.
(e) To strike an adequate balance between the effective protection of the moral and material interests of authors and States Parties' obligations in relation to the rights to food, health and education, as well as the rights to take part in cultural life and to enjoy the benefits of scientific progress and its applications, or any other right recognized in the Covenant.

It is noteworthy that, while the terminology employed to describe the core obligation to protect the *moral* interests of attribution and integrity aligns closely with the text of Article 6bis, Berne Convention, the equivalent obligation to respect and protect the material interests of authors is more qualified, as it is limited to "basic" material interests, being those which are "necessary to enable those authors to enjoy an adequate standard of living."

Although General Comment 17 has been criticized as lacking ambition,[81] it takes a valuable first step in tracing broad principles for the interpretation of the creators' rights protected in international human rights law. Overall, as has been demonstrated, it tends to emphasize the distinctions between those rights and the interests protected by international and national copyright law.

79. *Ibid.*, Art. 27 (retrogressive measures).
80. *Ibid.*, 39.
81. For criticism on this basis, *see* Ruth L. Okediji, *Does Intellectual Property Need Human Rights?,* 50 New York University Journal of Law & Politics (2018) 1-67; Saleh Al-Sharieh, *Toward a Human Rights Method for Measuring International Copyright Law's Compliance with International Human Rights Law*, 32 Utrecht Journal of International & European Law (2016) 5-26 https://doi.org/10.5334/ujiel.233.

20.2.3 Report of the Special Rapporteur in the Field of Cultural Rights, 2014

Following a 2009 Resolution, the United Nations Human Rights Council appointed Farida Shaheed, as an "independent expert in the field of cultural rights."[82] In 2012, the title of "Special Rapporteur in the field of cultural rights" was conferred upon her and the period of her mandate was extended.[83] In the course of this mandate, Shaheed produced 10 linked reports on various aspects of the cultural rights protected under the international human rights *acquis*.[84] In December 2014, she issued her "Copyright Policy and the Right to Science and Culture" report,[85] which was intended to provide further clarification of the relationship between authors' rights and the creators' rights protected under the UDHR and the ICESCR. The terminology employed in her report is significant. Shaheed describes the rights set out in Article 27 of the UDHR and Article 15(1) of the ICESCR collectively as the "right to science and culture." This concept encompasses both aspects of those rights: on the one hand, the right to take part in cultural life and to enjoy the benefits of scientific progress and its applications,[86] and, on the other, the right of authors to the protection of the moral and material interests resulting from their scientific, literary or artistic productions.[87] The choice of terminology emphasizes the linked nature of the different elements

82. United Nations, Human Rights Council, Resolution 10/23 (Mar. 26, 2009).
83. The mandate was extended and Farida Shaheed served in the role until 2015, *see* https://www.ohchr.org/EN/Issues/CulturalRights/Pages/MandateInfo.aspx (accessed Jun. 14, 2019).
84. For reflection on the mandate and reports, *see* Farid Shaheed, *The United Nations Cultural Rights Mandate: Reflections on the Significance and Challenges,* at Negotiating Cultural Rights 21 (Lucky Belder & Helle Porsdam eds., Edward Elgar, 2017); Farid Shaheed, *Introductory Remarks by the Special Rapporteur,* at Intellectual Property & Access to Science 19-20 (Christophe Geiger ed., CEIPI/ICTSD, 2016); Mylene Bidault, *Intellectual Property Policies & the Right to Science and Culture: The Work of the Special Rapporteur in Context,* at Intellectual Property & Access to Science 21-29 (Christopher Geiger ed., CEIPI/ICTSD, 2016); Lea Shaver, *Intellectual Property & the Right to Science and Culture: The Reports of the Special Rapporteur in the Field of Cultural Rights,* at Intellectual Property & Access to Science 30-41 (Christopher Geiger ed., CEIPI/ICTSD, 2016). *See also* UN Human Rights Council, Report of the Special Rapporteur in the Field of Cultural Rights, Farida Shaheed, The Right to Enjoy the Benefits of Scientific Progress and its Applications (May 14, 2012) UN Doc A/HRC/20/26.
85. A/HRC/28/57 (n. 2); the Special Rapporteur also produced a subsequent report on patent law and cultural rights, *see* UN Human Rights Council, Report of the Special Rapporteur in the Field of Cultural Rights, Farida Shaheed, Patent Policy & the Right to Science & Culture (Aug. 4, 2015) UN Doc A/HRC/70/279.
86. *See* UDHR, Art. 27(2); ICESCR, Art. 15(1)(a), (b).
87. UDHR, Art. 27(1); ICESCR, Art. 15(1)(c); Shaver's academic work influenced the Special Rapporteur's choice of terminology (Lea Shaver, *The Right to Science & Culture,* 1 Wisconsin Law Review 121-184 (2010)) https://doi.org/10.31228/osf.io/cax7k; *see* Shaver (n. 84), 30-41, 31.

of the "right to science and culture" and, in so doing distinguishes this right yet more clearly from the rights granted under intellectual property laws. The aspect of the right to science and culture which has been referred to above as "creators' rights" (i.e., the rights protected under Article 27(2) of the UDHR and Article 15(1)(c) of the ICESCR) is described as the right to "protection of authorship."[88]

While building on the conclusions of General Comment 17,[89] the Special Rapporteur explores the relationship between creators' rights and copyright in a more detailed and discursive manner than the earlier document. Having explained the "dual aspects of cultural participation and protection of authorship,"[90] she emphasizes concerns about inequity and lack of transparency in the making of international copyright law, forcefully reiterating the distinction between creators' rights and authors' rights made in General Comment 17:

> It is sometimes claimed that intellectual property rights are human rights or that [Art 15(1)(c)] recognizes a human right to protection of intellectual property along the lines set out by the TRIPS Agreement and other intellectual property treaties. The Committee on Economic, Social and Cultural Rights has stressed that this equation is false and misleading. Some elements of intellectual property protection are indeed required—or at least strongly encouraged—by reference to the right to science and culture. Other elements of contemporary intellectual property laws go beyond what the right to protection of authorship requires, and may even be incompatible with the right to science and culture.[91]

Again, the fact that creators' rights exist for the benefit of human beings, rather than corporate entities, is underlined.[92] On this basis, it is suggested that such rights are aligned with the personality-based, "moral rights" philosophy of civil law states such as France and Germany.[93] The "moral interests" protected under Article 27(2) of the UDHR and Article 15(1)(c) are explicitly identified with the rights required under Article 6bis of

88. A/HRC/28/57 (n. 2), §§26-29.
89. *Ibid.*, 12.
90. *Ibid.*, §9.
91. *Ibid.*, §26 (footnotes omitted). For an even more strongly worded assertion of the distinction between the two rights, *see* Fiona Macmillan, *Copyright Policy and the Right to Science and Culture: Report 2014 (A/HRC/28/57)* at Negotiating Cultural Rights 181-198 (Lucky Belder & Helle Porsdam eds., Edward Elgar, 2017).
92. *Ibid.*, §§27, 28; again, the rights of indigenous persons are emphasized §§55-59, 114-118.
93. *Ibid.*, §33. This is a tendency which had also been identified by others, *see* Francois Dessemontet, *Copyright & Human Rights,* at Intellectual Property & Information Law: Essays in Honour of Hermann Cohen 113 (Jan J.C. Kabel & Gerard J.H.M. Mom eds., Kluwer, 1998) (the UDHR and the ICESCR said to "mark the apex of the French vision of literary and artistic property, as opposed to the Anglo-American 'mercantilist' view ensconced in TRIPS" at 114).

the Berne Convention.[94] However, in keeping with the dual conception of the right to science and culture, such "moral interests" are also considered potentially to cover the interest in the creative reuse of others' works, such as in parody.[95]

In the case of material interests, the Special Rapporteur identifies the problem of power in the relationship between human authors and the corporate bodies with whom authors enter into contractual arrangements.[96] She suggests that the introduction of author-protective rules, such as unwaivable "reversion rights," *droit de suite* and statutory licensing, where these do not already exist, might serve to address this problem.[97] She also emphasizes that the introduction of exceptions and limitations, coupled with a right to remuneration, might satisfy the dual aspects of the right to science and culture in a nuanced manner.[98] At the same time, it is made very clear that authors' material interests may be protected by means other than copyright; for example, through minimum wage protections, collective bargaining and the adoption of policies promoting the cultural sector and the right to science and culture.[99] By comparison with the lengthy term of protection required under national and international copyright laws, it is suggested that creators' material interests may be satisfied through relatively short-term measures.[100]

Shaheed also states that copyright exceptions and limitations may play a valuable role in securing the "cultural participation" aspect of the right to science and culture (supporting, for example, follow-on creativity, education, access to works for people with a disability and translation into nondominant languages), while also providing authors with income through statutory compensation mechanisms.[101] Without being entirely prescriptive, she floats a number of potential developments that might serve the right to science and culture in this area, including the introduction of flexible, fair use-type limitations[102] and mandatory limitations[103] in national laws and the negotiation of further Marrakesh-like treaties relating to libraries, archives and education at international level.[104] She also suggests, that open licensing systems, and support for those systems by public bodies, have considerable

---

94. *Ibid.*, §35.
95. *Ibid.*, §§36-39.
96. *Ibid.*, §§40-43.
97. *Ibid.*, §§44-47; on the potential role that termination rights might play in supporting creators' rights, *see also* Austin (n. 8), 405.
98. *Ibid.*, §48.
99. *Ibid.*, §49.
100. *Ibid.*, §50, drawing explicitly on General Comment 17 here (*see* General Comment 17, §16).
101. *Ibid.*, §§71-72.
102. *Ibid.*, §73.
103. *Ibid.*, §74.
104. *Ibid.*, §76.

potential to assist in satisfying state obligations under the right to science and culture.[105]

Human rights have important procedural aspects. The Special Rapporteur provides a number of examples of procedural initiatives which might bring copyright law and the right to science and culture into closer alignment.[106] She advocates more transparent, participatory copyright law-making processes, the application of human rights assessment processes to legislation and the adoption of human rights-compliant canons of legal interpretation.[107] Measures to combat infringement in a digital environment, such as criminal sanctions and website blocking, should not be adopted where they would have a disproportionate impact on other human rights such as the right to freedom of expression.[108]

20.2.4 General Comment No. 25 of the CESCR

In 2020, the CESCR issued a further General Comment (*General comment No. 25 (2020) on science and economic, social and cultural rights (Article 15(1)(b), (2), (3) & (4) of the International Covenant on Economic, Social & Cultural Rights)*).[109] This focuses primarily on the right of everyone to enjoy the benefits of scientific progress and its applications.[110] However, in so doing, it touches on the relationship between the rights protected under Articles 15(1)(b) and 15(1)(c). In doing so, it questions the role of copyright, and other intellectual property rights, in restricting access to scientific literature for low-income researchers, especially in developing countries:

> States should take appropriate measures to foster the positive effects of intellectual property on the right to participate in and to enjoy the benefits of scientific progress and its applications, while at the same time avoiding its possible negative effects … . States should make every effort, in their national regulations and in international agreements on intellectual property, to guarantee the social dimensions of intellectual property, in accordance with the international human rights obligations they have undertaken … A balance must be reached between intellectual property and the open access and sharing of scientific knowledge and its applications, especially those linked to the realization of other economic, social and cultural rights, such as the rights to health,

105. *Ibid.*, §§77-84.
106. *Ibid.*, §§85-89.
107. *Ibid.*, §§90-97.
108. *Ibid.*, §51.
109. E/C.12/GC/25, Apr. 30, 2020. For further discussion of the Report, *see* Helle Porsdam & Sebastian Porsdam Mann eds, *The Right to Science: Then and Now* (Cambridge University Press, 2022).
110. *Ibid.*, §3.

> education and food. The Committee reiterates that ultimately intellectual property is a social product and has a social function and consequently, States parties have a duty to prevent unreasonably high costs for access to … schoolbooks and learning materials from undermining the rights of large segments of the population to health, food and education.[111]

In this passage, we can see that the Committee is building on the foundation established by General Comment 17 and the Special Rapporteur's report. It emphasizes that intellectual property is only to be protected to the extent that it serves social purposes and begins to flesh out more specific State obligations in the sphere of scientific literature.

20.3 UNIVERSALISM, PLURALISM OR ISOLATIONISM? AUTHORS' RIGHTS AND CREATORS' RIGHTS

What do these assessments of the meaning of creators' rights within the human rights community tell us about the relationship between these rights and the law of authors' rights? First, it is very clear that any argument that creators' rights underpin and justify the copyright system as it currently stands is misconceived. Claims, by lobbyists or others, that creators' rights give rise to a straightforward "right to copyright" are simply wrong.[112] Nevertheless, even though General Comment 17 and the Special Rapporteur go out of their way to highlight the fact that creators' rights cannot be *equated* with authors' rights, there is clearly a link between the rights protected under the positive law of the copyright system and those protected under Article 27(2) of the UDHR and Article 15(1)(c) of the ICESCR. This is apparent from the text of those provisions, from the historical records of their negotiation and from General Comment 17 and the report of the Special Rapporteur[113] However, the exact nature of this link remains lightly sketched.

In these circumstances, can it be said that any aspects of the legal system for the protection of authors' rights are *required* under international human rights law?[114] Conversely, are any features of the existing system

111. *Ibid.*, § 62.
112. *Ibid.*, §26; any such claim is "false and misleading."
113. Shaver notes that the Report of the Special Rapporteur suggests a need to reform, rather than abandon, the current rules of copyright law (*see* Shaver (n. 84), 30-41, 34).
114. The Special Rapporteur suggests that some aspects of copyright protection are required, or at least strongly encouraged (*see* her report at §26). However, she does not specify *which* aspects these are. Restrictively interpreted, this statement may only refer to moral rights, but it is far from certain that it is so limited.

inconsistent with creators' rights, as conceived within the UN's human rights bodies?[115]

In considering the first of these questions, the strongest claim can be made for copyright's system of moral rights.[116] There is a clear linkage between the "moral interests" referred to in the human rights instruments and the moral rights required under the Berne Convention and protected in most countries' authors' rights laws. The desire to influence the broader adoption of positive moral rights protection was an instrumental factor at the time of the negotiations leading to the adoption of creators' rights in the UDHR and the ICESCR. Both General Comment 17 and Farida Shaheed's report connect the "moral interests" protected by creators' rights with the rights of attribution and integrity required under the Berne Convention. Almost invariably, moral rights are granted to *human* authors, who are the beneficiaries of creators' rights, rather than to corporate rightholders, whom Article 27(2) and Article 15(1)(c) do not protect. Beyond this, however, the human rights documents do not provide precise guidance on the shape that national moral rights regimes should take. It is not clear, for example, whether the author-centric focus of creators' rights militates in favor of a more generous approach to moral rights than that adopted in many common law jurisdictions, requiring legal protection against unauthorized divulgation of a work or a broader concept of infringement under the integrity right.[117] Nevertheless, in this area, it seems possible to discern the outline requirements of the obligation to protect creators' rights, and it seems reasonable to argue that creators' rights underpin the interests protected typically by integrity and attribution rights in national copyright laws. Accordingly, it may be arguable that a state that provides no, or only weak, moral rights protection fails to comply with its obligation to protect creators' rights under international human rights law.[118] Equally, a state that curtails its protections for authors' moral interests may be regarded as violating creators' rights through the taking of retrogressive measures.

---

115. There is disagreement as to the relative hierarchy of international norms, including international human rights norms (*see* Ruse-Khan (n. 8), [8.93]-[8.94]); consequently, human rights obligations may not, in any event, prevail over rules deriving from international copyright law.
116. *See* Kwall (n. 33); Michel Vivant, *Authors' Rights, Human Rights,* 174 Revue Internationale du Droit d' Auteur 60 (1997).
117. These possibilities are floated by Austin & Zavidow; *see* Austin & Zavidow (n. 61), 303-333, 331.
118. The United States (U.S.) has no comprehensive system of moral rights protection and the statutory moral rights provided for authors in the United Kingdom are undermined by serious limitations (including the possibility of waiver). The possibility that there might be an incompatibility in this respect between the international human rights law's requirement to protect creators' rights and a legal system such as that of the United States has been noted by commentators. *See*, for example Yu (n. 33), 1039, 1082-1083. Any conflict is hypothetical because, while the U.S. has signed the ICESCR, it has not ratified the Convention. U.K.?.

In the case of creators' *material* interests, the picture is much less certain. It can be suggested that there is a connection between the existing structures of positive authors' rights law and creators' rights in international human rights law. The detailed references to substantive copyright law in General Comment 17 and in the Special Rapporteur's report imply that states may secure the material interests of creators through an appropriately calibrated law of authors' rights, as long as that body of rules is applied in a balanced and nondiscriminatory manner.[119] Indeed, it appears to be assumed that this is the method that states will generally employ to protect creators' rights. However, unlike the reference to "moral interests," there is no obvious terminological link between the texts of Article 27(2) of the UDHR and Article 15(1)(c) of the ICESCR and the exclusive rights provided to creators under the international law of authors' rights. Indeed, the fact that a neutral description ("material interests") was chosen in this context is itself significant in marking a distinction from the established authors' rights regime. As noted above, both General Comment 17 and the report of the Special Rapporteur emphasize that states are entitled to protect creators' material interests by mechanisms other than exclusive rights, such as welfare systems. There is thus little in the human rights materials that dictate the detailed scope of authors' exclusive rights, as long as effective support for creators' material interests is provided and as long as this support is balanced with protection for competing rights.[120]

It is also important to consider whether the *procedural* requirements of Article 27(2) and Article 15(1)(c) might have an impact in the copyright context. General Comment 17 makes it clear that, whatever its form, the legal protection of the moral and material interests of creators must be effective[121] and must be applied in a nondiscriminatory manner,[122] with particular regard paid to the interests of disadvantaged persons.[123] It has been suggested that these requirements cast doubt on the formal preconditions for protection that form an important element of the current international system for the protection of authors' rights.[124] From a human rights perspective, the fact that the protection of a copyright work depends to some extent on the nationality of its author seems difficult to justify. For example, in the United Kingdom,

119. For discussion of potential situations in which the application of such rules might apply in a discriminatory manner, *see* Helfer & Austin (n. 35), 199-211.
120. For discussion of the potential impact of Art. 15, ICESCR more generally on intellectual property law, *see* Caterina Sganga, *Right to Culture and Copyright: Participation and Access*, at Research Handbook on Human Rights and Intellectual Property (C. Geiger ed., Edward Elgar, 2015), 560-576.
121. General Comment 17, §10, 18, 31, 32, 34.
122. *Ibid.*, §[19]-[21].
123. *Ibid.*, §20, 34, 39, 46; A/HRC/28/57 (n. 2), §66. For a suggested example of a situation in which a copyright system may not adequately protect the rights of disadvantaged creators, *see* Austin (n. 8), 405, 423.
124. *See* Helfer & Austin (n. 35), 206-210.

an Iranian author may not be able to exercise her authorial rights in a manner that supports her moral and material interests while an Australian Swedish or Chilean author would be able to do so in comparable circumstances. It seems unlikely that the creators' rights of the Iranian author are adequately protected under such a system.[125] Similarly, while international copyright law generally prohibits contracting states from discriminating against the nationals of other contracting parties, it does not prohibit discrimination against a state's own nationals. Again, it appears difficult to justify the potential consequences of this rule from a human rights perspective.[126]

Against this background, commentators have sought to interpret the potential impact of a human rights approach, or perspective, on copyright law and policy.[127] Generally, this has involved viewing the rights covered by section 27(2) and section 15(1)(c) within the context of a recalibrated balance between creators' interests and the rights of access to science and culture provided under section 27(1) and section 15, more generally. It has been suggested that the adoption of such an approach may require, for example: (i) greater attention to be devoted to the interests of users, particularly vulnerable users;[128] (ii) the adoption of state-fostered open science and open publishing models;[129] (iii) the curtailment of the term of copyright protection;[130] and (iv) the abandonment of doctrines that pre-set the balance of interests in rightholders' favour, such as the "three-step test."[131] More radically, and more critically, some have argued that true recognition of a "human rights approach" would require a complete rethink of the existing models for reconciling the interests of users and rightholders within copyright law, with much greater preference being given to the interests of vulnerable users.[132] However, the traffic is not all in one

125. Cf. Blomqvist (n. 40), 17.

126. *See* Helfer & Austin (n. 35), 209-210; Blomqvist (n. 40), 17.

127. *See,* for example, Audrey Chapman, *A Human Rights Perspective on Intellectual Property, Scientific Progress, and Access to the Benefits of Science,* at World Intellectual Property Organisation/Office of the United Nations High Commissioner for Human Rights, IPO/OHCHR, Intellectual Property and Human Rights, A Panel Discussion to Commemorate the 50th Anniversary of the Universal Declaration of Human Rights (WIPO, 1999) 127-168; Peter K. Yu, *Reconceptualizing Intellectual Property Interests in a Human Rights Framework,* 40 U.C. Davis Law Review 1039 (2007).

128. *See*, for example, Okediji (n. 81).

129. *See*, for example, Klaus D. Beiter, *Reforming Copyright or Toward Another Science? A More Human Rights-Oriented Approach under the REBSPA in Constructing a "Right to Research" for Scholarly Publishing,* 48 Brooklyn Journal of International Law 88 (2022).

130. *See* Saleh Al-Sharieh, *Toward a Human Rights Method for Measuring International Copyright Law's Compliance with International Human Rights Law*, 32 Utrecht Journal of International & European Law 18-19 (2016) https://doi.org/10.5334/ujiel.233.

131. *See,* for example, Lida Ayoubi, *Human Rights Principles in the WIPO Marrakesh Treaty: Driving Change in Copyright Law from Within,* 9 Queen Mary Journal of Intellectual Property 282, 292 (2019) https://doi.org/10.2139/ssrn.3333489.

132. *See*, for example, Okediji (n. 81).

direction. It has also been argued that, in order to comply with their obligation to secure creators' rights, states must take a *stricter* approach to exceptions and limitations to the narrowly drawn, core rights of human creators than is mandated under the three-step step.[133]

20.4 CONCLUSION

This chapter has sought to examine the nature of the relationship between authors' rights, as established under international, regional and national copyright laws, and the creators' rights protected under international human rights law. In particular, it has considered whether the two regimes support one another and/or whether there are aspects of the current copyright system which are difficult to reconcile with creators' rights. It has been demonstrated that, while the precise relationship between these two bodies of rules remains incompletely worked out, it is possible to discern the general direction in which a whole-hearted recognition of creators would be likely to lead copyright law. A "human rights approach" would favor a human author-centric system of authors' rights that provides significant space for the public interest in access to culture and follow-on creativity. It would also protect all authors without discrimination.

Nevertheless, within this overall picture, there are few policy outcomes which are clearly dictated, or precluded, by international human rights law. The substantive requirements of Article 27(2) of the UDHR and Article 15(1)(c) of the ICESCR are not yet sufficiently clearly defined to support such detailed claims. For this reason, many of the copyright reform proposals advanced on the supposed foundation of creators' rights (including some of the Special Rapporteur's more detailed suggestions) have a speculative quality. If creator's rights are to assume a more fully integrated influence on the legal structures protecting authors in future, their content will need to be plotted more closely and agreed upon more widely. Many states have constitutional rights that draw specifically on Article 27(2) of the UDHR and Article 15(1)(c) of the ICESCR. Over time, jurisprudence on those provisions may help to flesh out the potential application of creators' rights in specific situations.[134] While national reports to the CESCR currently tend to

---

133. *See* (n. 34).
134. For a discussion of these provisions, *see* Christopher Geiger, *Reconceptualizing the Constitutional Dimension of Intellectual Property* at Intellectual Property Law & Human Rights 115, 129-130 (Paul Torremans ed., 3rd edn., Kluwer, 2015); Christopher Geiger, *Implementing Intellectual Property Provisions in Human Rights Instruments: Towards a New Social Contract for the Protection of Intangibles,* at Research Handbook on Human Rights & Intellectual Property 661, 674-675 (Christopher Geiger ed., Edward Elgar, 2015); Adolf Dietz, *Constitutional and Quasi-Constitutional Clauses for the Justification of Authors' Rights (Copyright): From Past to Future,* at Exploring the Sources of Copyright: Proceedings of the ALAI Congress 2005 55 (AFPIDA, 2007); ALAI

say little about concrete measures required to fulfil Article 15(1)(c), this may change in future. Similarly, responses to individual complaints under the Additional Protocol may begin to provide further guidance on the scope and requirements of international human rights law in this area. Human rights bodies may themselves produce more detailed sets of indicators or benchmarks on the requirements for compliance with creators' rights.

Of course, the gulf between the human rights system's protection of creators' rights, on the one hand, and copyright law, on the other, is not purely doctrinal. There are important political and institutional impediments to the further integration of the two legal regimes. The response to the Special Rapporteur's report on "Copyright Policy and the Right to Science and Culture" demonstrates this.[135] Shaheed's challenging stance was welcomed by some.[136] However, it was met with hostility by groups representing rightholders and by states that have historically dominated the policymaking arena in intellectual property law[137] and the report itself appears to have had little actual impact on the institutions within which copyright policy is determined. Overall, it is difficult to escape the sense that, at the moment, authors' rights and creators' rights still occupy relatively distinct institutional spheres. The mainstream literature on authors' rights has next to nothing to say about creators' rights, even where such discussion might have been expected.[138] If a more pluralist international copyright *acquis* is ever to be established, a shared, and more fully realized, understanding of the requirements of creators' rights as international human rights will have to be developed. The political environment required for such a *rapprochement* seems a long way off at the moment. However, if that situation were to change, it is already possible to discern an outline of the direction in which a whole-hearted endorsement of creators' rights would be likely to take international copyright law.

Proceedings 2005. For particular examples of the operation of such provisions, *see* Martin Husovec, *Tank Man Hits the Constitutional Court*, http://copyrightblog.kluweriplaw.com/2015/04/06/tank-man-hits-the-constitutional-court/ (accessed Jun. 14, 2019); Maximiliano Marzetti, *Community Right to Access Unpublished Work Trumps Moral Rights of Heir, Argentine Court Says*.

135. For discussions of the response, *see* Bidault (n. 84), 21-29, 26-27; Shaver (n. 84), 30-41, 40-41.

136. *See*, for example, Macmillan (n. 91), 181-198.

137. *See*, for example, Keith Harper, *Statement of US Ambassador to the Human Rights Council*, https://geneva.usmission.gov/2015/03/11/human-rights-council-dialogue-with-special-rapporteurs-item-3/ (accessed Jun. 14, 2019). *See also* Monika Emert, *EU Copyright Review Divisive; French MEP Says UN Expert Lacks Balance*; Bidault (n. 84), 26-27; Shaver (n. 84), 40-41. Farida Shaheed & Andrew Mazibrada *On the Right to Science as a Cultural Human Right,* at The Right to Science: Then and Now (Helle Porsdam & Sebastian Porsdam Mann eds, Cambridge University Press, 2022) 107-123.

138. *See*, for example, Jane Ginsburg, *The Most Moral of Rights: The Right to Be Recognized as the Author of One's Work* Columbia Public Law Research Paper No. 14-517, https://papers.ssrn.com/sol3/papers.cfm?abstract_id=2806316 (accessed Jun. 14, 2019).

Chapter 21

Access to Works Protected by Copyright Law

Philippe Jougleux

Both civil law and common law traditions recognize the numerus clausus principle in property law. According to this principle, the number of basic forms of property is finite, and in civil and common law systems alike, the principle places the ability to make changes to the property system solely with the legislature.[1]

Ownership is perceived as the totality of powers that can be exercised over, and benefits that can be derived from, property. The right is therefore described as absolute, and *ipso facto,* unitary.[2] In traditional theory, ownership expresses itself in various elements, such as the *usus* (right to use), *fructus* (the right to enjoy) and *abusus* (the right to dispose), which are described in Roman law and are commonly used to describe the characteristics of property.

There is an obvious analogy between the principle of numerus clausus in property law, which limits the number of types of rights that are recognized as property rights, and the limitative description of the rightholder's prerogative in copyright law. The generally unitary concept of property, which is mostly adhered to in civil law countries, explains this idea in the most accurate way, even if imperfectly,[3] as it explains that all forms of property (movable, immovable, intangible) are governed in the same way.

1. Yun-chien Chang & Henry E. Smith, *The Numerus Clausus Principle, Property Customs, and the Emergence of New Property Forms,* 100 Iowa Law Review 2275 (2015).
2. Barbara Pierre, *Classification of Property and Conceptions of Ownership in Civil and Common Law,* 28(2) Revue générale de droit 235 (1997), https://doi.org/10.7202/1035639ar (accessed May 27, 2019).
3. Andreas Rahmatian, *Copyright and Creativity: The Making of Property Rights in Creative Works* 24 (Edward Elgar, 2011).

However, it is a matter of discussion whether or not copyright law recognizes a similar numerus clausus principle.[4] Nevertheless, the various economic prerogatives that are included in copyright law have to be recognized by the legislator and included in the closed list of economic exclusive rights of the author or other rightholder. As has been stated in the United Kingdom, for instance, copyright law is traditionally "a creature of statute."[5]

However, some scholars propose that copyright law be perceived as a social construct[6] and consequently that the sphere of application of the regime is influenced by the public's perception. This means that even if copyright law is governed by the concept of unitary ownership and the numerus clausus of rights, these rights have to be interpreted in a way that corresponds to the needs and expectations of society.[7] Characteristically, Christophe Geiger explained that:

> The inclusion of intellectual property within the protection of property at the constitutional level is important because it expands the social function of property to intellectual property.[8]

Therefore, by applying the theoretical framework of the unitarian concept of property to copyright law, some conclusions can be drawn. As usus is the right to use a thing, we could consider that the right of communication to the public, the rental right and more indirectly the right of reproduction refer to the *usus*. *Fructus* is the right to the fruits produced by or derived from a thing without diminution of the thing's substance. In this category, we could include the distribution right (first resale), as it does not concern the direct use of the intangible good, but only its commercialization. Since *abusus* is the right to dispose of a thing, it covers the contractual law of copyright and the possibility of transferring economic rights. Therefore,

---

4. Christina Mulligan, *A Numerous Clausus Principle for Intellectual Property* 80 Tennesse Law Review 235 (2013), https://digitalcommons.law.uga.edu/fac_artchop/912 (accessed May 27, 2019) https://doi.org/10.2139/ssrn.2017023.
5. Ronan Deazley, *Rethinking Copyright: History, Theory, Language* 69 (Edward Elgar Publishing, 2006).
6. Matthew Rimmer, *A Creature of Statute: Copyright Law and Legal Formalism* 13(2) Entertainment Law Review 31 (2002).
7. Alexander Peukert, *The Fundamental Right to (Intellectual) Property and the Discretion of the Legislature,* at Research Handbook on Human Rights and Intellectual Property 132 (Christophe Geiger ed., Edward Elgar, 2015); Jonathan Griffiths & Luke McDonagh, *Fundamental Rights and European IP Law: The Case of Art. 17(2) of the EU Charter,* at Constructing European Intellectual Property: Achievements and New Perspectives 75 (Christophe Geiger ed., Edward Elgar, 2013); Christophe Geiger, *The Social Function of Intellectual Property Rights, or How Ethics Can Influence the Shape and Use of IP Law,* at Intellectual Property Law: Methods and Perspectives 153 (Graeme Dinwoodie ed., Edward Elgar, 2013).
8. Christophe Geiger, *Copyright as an Access Right: Securing Cultural Participation Through the Protection of Creators' Interests,* at What if We Could Reimagine Copyright? 87 (Rebecca Giblin & Kimberlee Weatherall eds., ANU Press, 2017).

most of the economic rights are perceived through the prism of usus but can the concept of usus legitimize other rightholder prerogatives? The concept of use has recently emerged in copyright law through the creation of the notion of the "lawful user." Within the framework of this chapter, however, the term "access" will be used instead, as it encompasses all of the problems related to the digital environment.

The practical impossibility of controlling use rendered this question largely academic in the past. How can an author's right to control access be recognized when no technology exists to enforce it? The digital revolution and specifically the emergence of Digital Rights Management (DRM) technology have opened wide the Pandora's box of the rightholders' control over use of the digital work. This had mainly been described as the author's right to control access. Nowadays, a second digital revolution is unfolding: a revolution consisting not only of digitalization but also dematerialization, which is characterized by a massive transfer of content to the cloud. The core function of online copyright law is therefore becoming linked to one fundamental question: who controls the access? The shift to cloud computing has de facto placed the work beyond the control of the user.[9] The right of access is not explicitly recognized by legislation. Three different directions therefore have to be explored: is the right implicitly recognized by national legislators or by an international convention? Is the right recognized by the courts in an act of judicial activism based on the interpretation of existing economic rights? Is *de lege ferenda* useful or even productive for helping copyright law recognize a right of access? While the first two questions refer to an analysis of the existing economic right conferred by copyright law (section 21.1), the last one highlights the potential risk of the incompatibility of a possible right to control access with the emerging category of users' rights and specifically with the debated user's right to obtain access (section 21.2).

21.1 THE RIGHTHOLDER'S RIGHT TO CONTROL ACCESS: THE CONTROVERSIAL QUESTION OF ITS EXISTENCE

21.1.1 Origins and Legal Basis of the Right to Access

It could be asserted that the doctrinal debate around the right to access dates from the beginning of the new millennium. Two main factors contributed to the emergence of the discussion at that time. First, in the United States of America (USA), the *LA Times v. Free Republic decision*[10] in 1997 was read

9. Niva Elkin-Koren, *The New Frontiers of User Rights*, 32 American University International Law Review 1 (2016).
10. LA Times v. Free Republic, 98 CV 7840 (1998); LA Times v. Free Republic, 00-57211.

as a first jurisprudential recognition of a right to access. In this case, a small online site republished and archived newspaper articles from the Washington Post and other newspapers. While the case apparently concerned the right of reproduction, the court did indeed state that plaintiffs have the "right to control" access to their articles.

Second, with the new millennium there emerged a discussion related to the much-discussed issue of DRM. These are tools incorporated into the work that can prevent it from being copied or even deny access to it after a certain period of time or a given number of uses. With the legal protection for these technical measures introduced by the 2001/29 Directive on Copyright in the Information Society (now known as the "InfoSoc Directive"),[11] rightholders acquired the technical and legal means to control the use of a digital work, even if this involved enforcing copyright law on the private premises of the user of a protected work. The European legislation was specifically seen and commented on as giving "de facto copyright holders the possibility of controlling access and use of copyright works beyond their exclusive rights."[12] It was even stated that "a right to control the availability of access to a work is a fundamentally new right that is qualitatively different and additional to the rights that have traditionally been associated with copyright."[13]

However, the doctrine soon concluded that it was far too premature to recognize a new and autonomous right to control access,[14] and following the flurry of activity accompanying the arrival of the new millennium, the discussions related to the right to access quickly dried up. First, leaving aside the jurisprudential innovations in the United States (U.S.), and the issue of DRM analyzed above, there is still no express legal basis (neither from the World Intellectual Property Organization, nor in the Agreement on Trade-Related Aspects of Intellectual Property (TRIPS),[15] nor in the Berne Convention)[16] to support the idea of a new economic right under copyright law. Second, the new right to access would greatly diverge from the other rights since it only applies in the digital environment. The recognition of

11. Directive 2001/29/EC of the European Parliament and of the Council of 22 May 2001 on the harmonization of certain aspects of copyright and related rights in the information society, Art. 6, 22 May 2001, Official Journal L 167, 22/06/2001 pp. 0010-0019 (hereinafter the "InfoSoc Directive").
12. Marcella Favale, *The Right of Access in Digital Copyright: Right of the Owner or Right of the User?,* 15(1) The Journal of World Intellectual Property 1-25 (2012) https://doi.org/10.1111/j.1747-1796.2011.00433.x.
13. Gregory Lastowka, *Free Access and the Future of Copyright,* 27 Rutgers Computer & Technology Law Journal 293 (2001) https://doi.org/10.2139/ssrn.913989.
14. Thomas P. Heide, *Copyright in the EU and U.S.: What "Access-Right"?,* 48(3) Journal of the Copyright Society of the USA (2001) https://doi.org/10.2139/ssrn.270861.
15. Agreement on Trade-Related Aspects of Intellectual Property Rights (Apr. 15, 1994), 1869 UNTS 299.
16. Berne Convention for the Protection of Literary and Artistic Works (Sep. 9, 1886), S. Treaty Doc. No. 99-27.

such a right would suppose a dichotomy of copyright law into two subcategories: traditional copyright law and digital copyright law. It can also be argued that the recognition of such a right by the European legislator would jeopardize the ongoing efforts to reach uniform and harmonized rules of copyright law at international level.

21.1.2 The Indirect Right to Control Access Through Other Economic Prerogatives: Jurisprudential Developments

This lack of explicit recognition by the legislator has not led, however, to a final conclusion of this discussion. The right to control access did not completely disappear from the debate and, on the contrary, it can be argued that this right has received de facto recognition, while it is implicit in the broad jurisprudential interpretation of the existing rights by the case law of the Court of Justice of the European Union (CJEU). The two main economic rights conferred by copyright are affected by this evolution: the right of reproduction and the right of communication to the public.

First, the right of reproduction as defined broadly by the InfoSoc Directive concerns every kind of reproduction, even those that are temporary, partial or indirect. Therefore, de facto, every instance of digital access to a protected work falls within the scope of the right of reproduction, in the sense that even browsing online content or viewing streamed content implies a form of temporary downloading. The digital era has provided the author with the means to control access to the work by reference to his/her oldest economic prerogative: the right to reproduction.[17] In order to avoid the absurd situation where all Internet activities are covered by the broad right of reproduction, a new mandatory exception has been inserted into the InfoSoc Directive,[18] which exempts temporary acts of reproduction. However, in light of the CJEU's case law forged from the *ACI Adam* case,[19] exceptions to economic rights can only be invoked in the case of a lawful user. Indeed, principles of civil law inherited from Roman law provide, in general, that the law does not protect those who consciously place themselves outside of its protection (*ex turpi causa* principle). Therefore, if mere online access to the protected work is not—at least implicitly—granted by the rightholder, access to the work will infringe his or her right of reproduction, even if the temporary copy exception of Article 5 would normally cover the act. Characteristic of this situation is the CJEU's *Kodi box* case.[20] While, in the

17. Séverine Dusollier, *Incidences et réalité d'un droit de contrôler l'accès en droit européen, Le Droit d'auteur: un contrôle de l accès aux œuvres?,* 18 Cahier du CRID (2000).
18. InfoSoc Directive, Art. 5(1).
19. Case C-435/12 ACI Adam BV and Others v. Stichting de Thuiskopie and Stichting Onderhandelingen Thuiskopie vergoeding (2014) ECLI:EU:C:2014:254.
20. Case C-527/15 Stichting Brein v. Jack Frederik Wullems (2017) ECLI:EU:C: 2017:300.

light of the landmark *Svensson* case,[21] the CJEU was in no doubt that the act of selling smart TV devices with embedded settings that help the device to connect to servers full of pirated content is in itself an act of communication to the public, the court continued its reasoning by explaining that the use of such a device to access content is also illegal, as the temporary reproduction exception cannot apply.

The *VCAST* case[22] is also noteworthy in this context. The CJEU decided that the users of a broadcast digital recording mechanism cannot invoke the private copy exception in order to justify access to content hosted in the cloud by the recording service. Given that the same content can be accessed by various users who have subscribed to the service, the issue has to be dealt with not only as a question of the right of reproduction but also from the perspective of the right of communication to the public. This means that even in cases where online access is permitted by an exception to the right of reproduction, the issue of access has to be examined in conjunction with the right of communication to the public.

Nevertheless, the right of communication to the public has evolved significantly in the digital sphere and nowadays greatly interferes with the user's freedom of access to work. It can be argued that the right to online communication to the public is now defined in Europe as a right to control access to online content. This evolution was to be anticipated, as the definition provided in Article 3 of the InfoSoc Directive referred to:

> the making available to the public of their works in such a way that members of the public may access them from a place and at a time individually chosen by them.

The landmark cases of *Svensson/GS Media*[23] built on this idea. Hyperlinks constitute the digital means of offering access to online content. The right of communication to the public presupposes an act of communication and, depending on the situation, a "new" public. In *Svensson*, the CJEU accepted that hyperlinks constitute an act of communication in their own right, while in *GS Media*, the CJEU added that consciously creating access to illegal content means that a new public is reached (and subsequently created a presumption of knowledge of the illegality of the content, in the case of professional users).

As a consequence, offering access to online content without permission is illegal. Also, this principle has to be seen as technologically neutral: the technological means used (a simple hyperlink, as in the *Svensson* case, an embedded hyperlink to a photograph, as in the *GS Media* case, or device settings or torrent keys, as in subsequent cases) does not interfere with this

21. Case C-466/12 Nils Svensson v. Retriever Sverige AB (2014) ECLI:EU:C:2014:76.
22. Case C-265/16 VCAST v. RTI SpA (2017) ECLI:EU:C:2017:913.
23. Case C-160/15 GS Media v. Sanoma Media Netherlands BV et al. (2016) ECLI:EU:C:2016:644.

logic. In the *Reha Training* judgment,[24] the CJEU literally explained that to apply the right of communication to the public, a communication to the public is not de facto needed. The court emphasizes the notion of position action in order to facilitate access to the protected work. What is covered, therefore, is access.[25]

Consequently, a right that is traditionally defined as the combination of an act of communication and a public is so broadly interpreted that, in fact, on the one hand, an act of communication does not really need to occur and, on the other hand, the public, analyzed *in abstracto* as a probability,[26] may not really exist. It is, therefore, easy to conclude that the right of communication to the public in the digital environment has implicitly evolved into a new kind of economic right, where the rightholder has managed to secure control over access to digital work.

In conclusion, it is perceived, at least in the digital environment, whether online or otherwise, that access to a protected work is nowadays clearly regulated as a new prerogative of the rightholder. However, it should be borne in mind that copyright law is founded on a balance of interests and this de facto extension of the rightholder's prerogatives finds its counterbalance in the parallel emergence of a theory of the public freedom to have access to the work.

21.1.3 The Contemporary Doctrinal Approach on the Right to Control Access

As analyzed above (21.1.1), the doctrine was first hostile to the idea that online copyright law has shifted from traditional economic rights to a new right to control access. Nonetheless, the reality of this shift gradually became clear, and this was reflected in various doctrinal works this past decade.

A first wave of authors commented on the legislative reforms in the USA (the 1998 Digital Millennium Copyright Act (DMCA)). Most notably, *Ginsburg* argued in 2000 that it demonstrated a shift toward the development

24. Case C-117/15 Reha Training Gesellschaft für Sport- und Unfallrehabilitation mbH v. Gesellschaft für musikalische Aufführungs- und mechanische Vervielfältigungsrechte eV (GEMA) (2016) ECLI:EU:C:2016:379.
25. *See*, para. 36 of the judgment: "Furthermore, as is apparent from Article 3(1) of Directive 2001/29, for there to be an 'act of communication', it is sufficient, in particular, that a work is made available to a public in such a way that the persons forming that public may access it, irrespective of whether they avail themselves of that opportunity (*see* the judgment of 13 February 2014, Svensson and Others, C-466/12, EU:C:2014:76, paragraph 19 and the case law cited)."
26. *See,* Case C-306/05 Sociedad General de Autores y Editores de España (SGAE) v. Rafael Hoteles SA (2006) ECLI:EU:C:2006:764.

of an access right,[27] even if it was also commented on as the "postmodern symbol" of a contemporary copyright deconstruction.[28]

Although *Ginsburg's* theory of a new economic right of control of access has been based on the legislative developments in the USA, it is at its core conceptual, and, therefore, may apply to European Union (EU) copyright law as well. In 2012, Favale argued that while copyright law does not expressly grant a right of access, technological protection measures have given copyright holders de facto control over access, which needs to be balanced against users' rights.[29]

In Europe, *Geiger* developed and adapted this theory to the European landscape in 2016.[30] In 2024, through a collaboration between *Geiger* and *Jütte*,[31] a complete model that balances the right to control access and the users' right to access is proposed.

It can be concluded that part of the doctrine has fully encompassed this notion of the right to control access. It must be highlighted, however, that all reflections on this concept are accompanied by a correlative analysis of the rise of a new user's right: the right to obtain access to the work.

21.2 THROUGH A USER'S RIGHT TO OBTAIN ACCESS?

21.2.1 ACCESS TO THE INFORMATION INCLUDED IN THE WORK AND ACCESS TO THE WORK ITSELF

Digital copyright law can nowadays be seen as a battle between rightholders and users over the issue of access.[32] It should be borne in mind that in a certain sense, the theory of public access to a protected work, also known as the user's right to obtain access, is in fact older than its counterpart, namely the rightholder's right to control access. Indeed, the distinction between idea

27. Jane C. Ginsburg, *From Having Copies to Experiencing Works: The Development of an Access Right in U.S. Copyright Law* at U.S. Intellectual Property: Law and Policy (Hugh Hansen, ed., Sweet & Maxwell, 2000).
28. Thomas Hoeren, *Copyright Dilemma: Access Right as a Postmodern Symbol of Copyright Deconstruction?* at Digital Rights Management. Lecture Notes in Computer Science, Vol. 2770 (Eberhard Becker, Willms Buhse, Dirk Günnewig, Niels Rump, eds., Springer, Berlin, Heidelberg, 2003) https://doi.org/10.1007/10941270_34.
29. Marcella Favale, *The Right of Access in Digital Copyright: Right of the Owner or Right of the User?* (Jan. 2, 2012) (n. 12).
30. Christophe Geiger, *Copyright as an Access Right: Securing Cultural Participation Through the Protection of Creators' Interests,* at What if We Could Reimagine Copyright (n. 8).
31. Christophe Geiger, Bernd Justin Jütte, *Copyright as an Access Right: Concretizing Positive Obligations for Rightholders to Ensure the Exercise of User Rights. Independent Expert Study for Communia* (June 2024).
32. Zohar Efroni, *Access-Right: The Future of Digital Copyright Law* (Oxford University Press, 2011).

and expression, often perceived as a philosophical foundation stone of copyright law, ensures that the user can acquire access to all information, news, data and equations included in the protected work.[33] This has been forcefully reaffirmed because, in the view of the European Commission, free movement of knowledge is to be considered the fifth EU freedom, as confirmed by the adoption of the Regulation on the free flow of nonpersonal data.[34]

Therefore, access to the information included in the work was never to be challenged. However, in practice, the importance of this right is sometimes put into perspective due to the exponential rise of informational works claiming the protection of copyright law. The introduction of two new copyright law exceptions in the new Directive on copyright in the Digital Single Market,[35] known as "content and data mining" exceptions, should be enough to reestablish this principle in all its force. The text and data mining exceptions, which have acquired much importance in the era of artificial intelligence, can be analyzed not only as a protective measure for the general principle of non-protection of ideas but also as the recognition of a user's right to access the works.[36] Specifically, by adding through Article 3 (and to some extent through Article 4 for commercial purposes) an exception allowing data mining of protected work in free access, the European legislator implicitly enforces the notion that the free access, once lawfully obtained, cannot be restrained. In other words, in this case, the user's freedom of access becomes a right, a positive obligation on the rightholder to refrain from challenging the access.

More generally, it is worth mentioning that the Directive includes a section entitled "measures to improve licensing practices and ensure wider access to content." This section refers to the use of out-of-commerce works

---

33. This principle has also been recognized by the CJEU in relation to software in the Cases C-393/09 Bezpečnostní softwarová asociace—Svaz softwarové ochrany v. Ministerstvo kultury (2010) ECLI:EU:C:2010:816 and C-406/10 SAS Institute Inc.v. World Programming Ltd (2012) ECLI:EU:C:2012:259. For an analysis of the latter, *see*: Tatiana Synodinou, *Descripting the Code: CJEU SAS v. World Programming,* Kluwer Copyright Blog, http://copyrightblog.kluweriplaw.com/2012/05/07/decrypting-the-code-cjeu-sas-vs-world-programming/ (accessed May 27, 2019).
34. Regulation (EU) 2018/1807 of the European Parliament and of the Council of 14 November 2018 on a framework for the free flow of nonpersonal data in the European Union (Text with EEA relevance), PE/53/2018/REV/1, ELI: http://data.europa.eu/eli/reg/2018/1807/oj.
35. Directive (EU) 2019/790 of the European Parliament and of the Council of 17 April 2019 on copyright and related rights in the Digital Single Market and amending Directives 96/9/EC and 2001/29/EC (Apr. 17, 2019) Official Journal L 130, 17/5/2019, pp. 92-125.
36. Christophe Geiger, Giancarlo Frosio & Oleksandr Bulayenko, *The Exception for Text and Data Mining (TDM) in the Proposed Directive on Copyright in the Digital Single Market: Legal Aspects, Policy Department for Citizens' Rights and Constitutional Affairs European Parliament*, http://www.europarl.europa.eu/RegData/etudes/IDAN/2018/604941/IPOL_IDA(2018)604941_EN.pdf (accessed May 27, 2019).

by cultural heritage institutions and cross-border uses, two measures that also protect the user's access to the work in some circumstances.

At the same time, the controversial issue of DRM examined above has been dealt with by the courts in both the USA and Europe. In the USA, the landmark *Lexmark*[37] decision ensures free access to software mechanisms, as it was ruled that circumvention of Lexmark's ink cartridge authentication process does not violate the DMCA. Likewise, in Europe, the case of *Nintendo v. PC Box*[38] stated that "it is necessary to examine the purpose of devices provided for the circumvention of protection measures, taking account, according to the circumstances at issue, of the use which third parties actually make of them." In both cases, the idea is not to transform the insertion of DRM into an absolute right to control access, which would not recognize any fair access to the protected work when the activities or devices have a commercially significant purpose other than infringement of copyright. It has been commented in the U.S. case that "[t]he rhetoric of Chamberlain makes it clear that the court believed copyright law, in general, actually grants some rights to the public, among which is the right to access a work," even if this right is not a statutory one, but a contractual one, by reference to the general principle of implicit terms.[39]

These questions (the free access to information as a principle or as an exception through the data mining exception, the abuse of DRM) are only part of a larger discussion related to the contemporary emergence of users' rights. For instance, the user may have access to the software mechanisms for interoperability reasons. He or she may ask for their access to the work to continue and remain, even if the principle of territoriality forbids it, by using their new right to portability.[40] Indeed, Article 3(1) of the Regulation on cross-border portability states that:

> The provider of an online content service provided against payment of money shall enable a subscriber who is temporarily present in a Member State to access and use the online content service in the same manner as in the Member State of residence, including by providing access to the same content, on the same range and number of devices, for the same number of users and with the same range of functionalities.

The same evolution appears in other domains, such as access to protected work for the benefit of persons who are blind or visually

37. Lexmark International, Inc. v. Static Control Components, Inc., 387 F.3d 522 (2004).
38. Case C-355/12 Nintendo and Others v. PC Box Srl and 9Net Srl (2014) ECLI:EU:C:2014:25.
39. Zohar Efroni, *A Momentary Lapse of Reason: Digital Copyright, the DMCA and a Dose of Common Sense,* 28 Columbia-Volunteer Lawyers for the Arts Journal of Law & the Arts 249 (2005).
40. Regulation (EU) 2017/1128 of the European Parliament and of the Council of 14 June 2017 on cross-border portability of online content services in the internal market (Jun. 14, 2017) Official Journal L 168, 30/6/2017, pp. 1-11.

impaired.[41] As has been commented in relation to this evolution, the growth of technology permits inaccessible works to become accessible, with the subsequent imperative not to create discrimination in the access granted to them.[42]

These innovations complete a recognized system of exceptions that provide the user with some critical freedoms. Private copying, educational exceptions and quotations all protect a right to obtain access in one way or another. However, a new approach is appearing, for instance in the orphan works framework,[43] which directly bases its justification on the user's right to obtain access. The movement toward open access responds to a similar logic.[44] Academic works funded by public resources are already affected by this issue in some countries that oblige the author to publish them in an open-access server, de facto neutralizing the prerogatives of the rightholder to a significant extent. Applying the Hohfeldian model, it is, however, only fair to underline that exceptions grant only privileges and not rights to the users.[45]

21.2.2 The Influence of Human Rights on Protecting Freedom of Access

While in the past copyright law was restricted by the use of general interest exceptions or practical considerations, an increasing number of references to human rights are being made in order to justify a limitation of copyright law prerogatives. This new human rights approach to copyright law includes, of course, the notion that copyright law itself is a human right. Therefore, "the

---

41. Directive (EU) 2017/1564 of the European Parliament and of the Council of 13 September 2017 on certain permitted uses of certain works and other subject matter protected by copyright and related rights for the benefit of persons who are blind, visually impaired or otherwise print-disabled and amending Directive 2001/29/EC on the harmonisation of certain aspects of copyright and related rights in the information society (Sep. 13, 2017) Official Journal L 242, 20/9/2017, pp. 6-13.
42. Mary Bertlesman, *The Fight for Accessible Formats: Technology as a Catalyst for a World Effort to Improve Accessibility Domestically,* 27 Syracuse Science & Technology Law Report 26 (2012).
43. Carine Bernault, *Accès à la connaissance et droit d'auteur. Mélanges en l'honneur du professeur André Lucas* 830 (Lexis Nexis, 2014).
44. Farida Shaheed, *Copyright Policy and the Right to Science and Culture,* Report of the Special Rapporteur in the Field of Cultural Rights, A/HRC/28/57 (2014), https://www.ohchr.org/EN/HRBodies/HRC/RegularSessions/Session28/Documents/A_HRC_28_57_ENG.doc (accessed May 27, 2019). The Special Rapporteur directly suggests that "[p]ublic and private universities and public research agencies should adopt policies to promote open access to published research, materials, and data on an open and equitable basis, especially through the adoption of Creative Commons licenses" (para. 113). Report from Farida Shaheed, who is a "Special Rapporteur" in the area of "cultural rights."
45. Zohar Efroni, *Towards a Doctrine of "Fair Access" in Copyright: The Federal Circuit's Accord,* 46 IDEA ® The Journal of the Franklin Pierce Center for Intellectual Property 99 (2005).

right of everyone to take part in cultural life"[46] is put forward as an opposing argument that aims to circumvent copyright law based on the principle of establishing a balance of interests between equal human rights. Interestingly, this evolution was foreseen and in some cases advocated by a large part of the doctrine during the past decade. The volume of works related to the relationship between copyright law and human rights from eminent authors such as *Hugenholtz*,[47] *Geiger*,[48] *Torremans*,[49] or *Griffiths and Suthersanen*,[50] for instance, shows the contemporary emergence of a new, more user-friendly doctrine of copyright law, which protects the right to obtain access.[51] Indeed, it cannot be ignored that the current shift of online copyright law toward a right to control access has provoked a subsequent crisis regarding the user's freedom to access culture.[52]

The *Renckhoff*[53] case is characteristic both of the contemporary extension of the right to control access and of the associated effort to contain it on the basis of logical constraints, in order to protect free access. In this case, the legality of the reproduction by a schoolgirl of a photograph of the city of Cordoba is discussed. The student had found the photograph on a tourism website and included it in a presentation for her class (which her teacher uploaded onto the website). The photographer had given the website a license for the photo. The CJEU comments that this is not a case of access to the work and therefore *Svensson/GS Media* case law is not relevant, as the teacher did not try to access the photograph posted on the city of Cordoba's website but instead committed a distinct act of reproduction of the protected work, which led to a communication to the public. The court's reasoning in fact confirms the trend analyzed above in relation to the creation of a right to control access because one determinative criterion in finding a copyright

46. International Covenant on Economic Social and Cultural Right, Art. 15(1)(a), Dec. 16, 1966.
47. P. Bernt Hugenholtz, *Copyright and Freedom of Expression in Europe,* at Innovation Policy in an Information Age (R. Cooper et al. eds., Oxford University Press, 2001).
48. Christophe Geiger, *Research Handbook on Human Rights and Intellectual Property* (Edward Elgar, 2015).
49. Paul Torremans, *Copyright and Human Rights: Freedom of Expression, Intellectual Property, Privacy* (Kluwer, 2004).
50. Jonathan Griffiths & Uma Suthersanen, *Copyright and Free Speech, Comparative and International Analyses* (Oxford University Press, 2005).
51. Christoph Graber, *Copyright and Access: A Human Rights Perspective,* at Digital Rights Management: The End of Collecting Societies (Christoph Beat Graber, eds., Bern: Staempfli Publishers, 2005), https://ssrn.com/abstract=1617892 (accessed May 27, 2019).
52. Karen Walsh, Andrea Wallace, Mathilde Pavis, Natalie Olszowy, James Griffin & Naomi Hawkins, *Intellectual Property Rights and Access in Crisis*, 52 International Review of Intellectual Property and Competition Law 379-416 (2021) https://doi.org/10.1007/s40319-021-01041-1.
53. Case C-161/17 Land Nordrhein-Westfalen v. Renckhoff (2018) ECLI:EU:C:2018:634.

infringement was the fact that the rightholder de facto lost control over the protected work as soon as it was uploaded elsewhere.[54]

The conclusions of the Advocate General (AG)[55] were very different from the somehow orthodox position adopted by the CJEU: his thoughts merit a mention for their originality, even though they failed to convince the court in this case. First, he stated that in the case of not-for-profit use, the burden of proof that the protected work was not deemed to be accessed lay with the author, not the user. He laid down two conditions associated with this new idea: (1) those who act without a profit-making intention do not usually act with full knowledge of the consequences of their behavior; and (2) the work communicated by the user was already lawfully and freely accessible on another website. In this way, he aims to move the current status quo of online access toward a broader freedom for the user. Second, the AG made a very interesting reference in paragraph 79 to both the right to education and the right to information, explaining that limiting the use of most information available online could affect these issues.

This is not the first time that such a reference has been made. For instance, both in *Luksan*[56] (protection of property) and *Deckmyn*[57] (principle of nondiscrimination) the court referred to human rights (as included in the Charter of Fundamental Rights of the European Union) in a copyright law situation. However, it demonstrates a clear trend toward the adoption of a human rights perspective in copyright law, a position that is certainly recognized by the European Court of Human Rights (ECtHR), as this court established in 2013, in two rulings, that copyright law is subject to legal scrutiny as an interference with the freedom of expression.[58] Even if the CJEU is still somewhat reluctant to open the closed list of exceptions and to accept human rights as an external limitation to copyright law, the AG is exercising real pressure on the courts to accept this new perspective.

To the conclusion on the *Renckhoff* case, it is only fit to add the conclusions on the *Funke Medien NRW* case (also known as the *Afghanistan Papers* case)[59] and the conclusions on the *Pelham* case (the *Metall auf Metall*

54. On para. 28 of the decision, the court accepts the argument of "the communication of a work by means not of a hyperlink, but by a new posting on a different website from that on which it was initially communicated with the consent of the copyright holder, should be treated as a 'new communication to the public', in particular, having regard to the fact that, as a result of the making available of the photograph once again, the copyright holder is no longer in a position to exercise his power of control over the initial communication of that work."
55. Case C-161/17, Land Nordrhein-Westfalen v. Renckhoff (2018) ECLI:EU:C:2018:279.
56. Case C-277/10 Martin Luksan v. Petrus van der Let (2012) ECLI:EU:C:2012:65.
57. Case C-201/13 Johan Deckmyn and Vrijheidsfonds VZW v. Helena Vandersteen and Others (2014) ECLI:EU:C:2014:2132.
58. Ashby Donald and Others v. France, No. 36769/08 (ECtHR Jan. 10, 2013); Neij and Sunde Kolmisoppi v. Sweden ["The Pirate Bay"] No. 40397/12 (ECtHR Feb. 13, 2013).
59. Case C-469/17 Funke Medien NRW GmbH v. Federal Republic of Germany (2018) EU:C:2018:870.

case), in order to further elaborate on this evolution. It has not gone unnoticed by scholars that AG Szpunar, specifically, is pushing toward an admission of this human rights approach.[60] In the conclusion on the *Afghanistan Papers*, the AG explained that the CJEU should adopt a similar approach to that used by the ECtHR (paragraph 42 of the Opinion) and accepted that freedom of expression may delimit copyright law in some circumstances (with a wide margin of discretion). This case clearly concerns access, as the German government aims to prevent access to confidential information held in military reports, on the legal basis of its copyright rights over the report. While the AG implicitly refers to the famous dualist theory to define copyright law,[61] he chooses to give precedence to the right to obtain access over the right to control access.

In the Opinion of AG Szpunar in the *Spiegel Online* case,[62] an analogous, albeit more restrictive[63] interpretative stance was followed in relation to the possibility of limiting copyright protection on the basis of fundamental rights. For the AG, the balancing of copyright protection with other fundamental rights belongs to the competence of the legislator and not the courts. However, he still considers that such an external limitation is possible "in exceptional cases," specifying that this is in particular the case when the "essence of a fundamental right" is at stake.[64]

60. Christophe Geiger & Elena Izyumenko, *Freedom of Expression as an External Limitation to Copyright Law in the EU: The Advocate General of the CJEU Shows the Way*, Center for International Intellectual Property Studies Research Paper No. 2018-12, SSRN Electronic Journal (2018) https://doi.org/10.2139/ssrn.3293735.
61. Case C-469/17 Funke MedienNRW GmbH v. Federal Republic of Germany (2018) ECLI:EU:C:2018:870, para. 58: "Copyright has two main objectives. The first is to protect the personal relationship between the author and his work as his intellectual creation and therefore, in a sense, an emanation of his personality. This primarily involves the area of moral rights. The second objective is to enable authors to exploit their works economically and thus earn an income from their creative endeavours. This involves the area of property rights, subject to harmonisation at EU level. In order for a restriction on freedom of expression flowing from copyright to be characterised as necessary, it must meet those two objectives. However, it seems to me that the protection by copyright of military reports such as those at issue in the main proceedings meets neither."
62. Case C-516/17 Spiegel Online GmbH v. Volker Beck (2019) ECLI:EU:C:2019:16.
63. Christophe Geiger & Elena Izyumenko, *Freedom of Expression as an External Limitation to Copyright Law in the EU: The Advocate General of the CJEU Shows the Way* 41(3) European Intellectual Property Review 131 (2019) https://doi.org/10.2139/ssrn.3293735; Centre for International Intellectual Property Studies (CEIPI) Research Paper N° 2018-12, https://ssrn.com/abstract=3293735 or http://dx.doi.org/10.2139/ssrn.3293735 (accessed Jun. 28, 2019).
64. For an analysis of the Opinion, *see*: Part I, Synodinou T., *Mirror, Mirror, Tell Me, Is the Copyright Law Fair and Balanced? Reflection on AG's Conclusions on the Spiegel Online Case* (2019), http://copyrightblog.kluweriplaw.com/ (accessed May 27, 2019); Part II, Synodinou T., *Mirror, Mirror, Tell Me, Is the Copyright Law Fair and Balanced? Reflection on AG's Conclusions on the Spiegel Online Case* (2019), http://copyrightblog.kluweriplaw.com/ (accessed May 27, 2019).

In the opinion published on *Metall auf Metall*,[65] which is about the legality of sound sampling, however, the AG has found that copyright law should prevail over other fundamental rights.[66] Using the principle of proportionality, the AG concluded that in this case, freedom of the arts and freedom of expression should yield to copyright law's prerogatives. The tone here is much more restrictive, as the AG on the one hand recognizes that copyright law is the outcome of a balancing of interests between various human rights, but on the other hand, considers that this balance is achieved by using tools intrinsic only to copyright law.[67] In this context, the prestigious European Copyright Society published an opinion[68] and characteristically found that "the right to access creative expression," as encompassed in freedom of creative expression under both Articles 11 and 13 of the Charter, should "weigh heavily in the balance."

This evolution aims to complete the traditional right/exceptions balance of copyright law, which is seen as flawed since the famous three-step test method of interpreting exceptions is used only as a shield in favor of the author, despite scholars' calls for reassessment.[69] The human rights perspective therefore offers more flexibility (at the price of greater uncertainty) than the classic rights/exceptions approach in balancing the author's private interest and the users' general interest as regards access to the work. It is of note that not only did these three cases have in common the audacious conclusions of the AG but also that they share some similarities in terms of their facts. The use of photography by the schoolgirl for her essay, access to military reports by a journalist and sound sampling for the purpose of

65. Case C-476/17, Pelham and Others v. Ralf Hütter, Florian Schneider-Esleben (2018) ECLI:EU:C:2018:1002.
66. The act is defined by the Advocate General as taking an extract of a phonogram for the purpose of using it in another phonogram.
67. Case C-476/17, Pelham and Others v. Ralf Hütter, Florian Schneider-Esleben (2018) ECLI:EU:C:2018:1002, para. 90 "Copyright and related rights, inasmuch as they establish a rightholders' monopoly over intellectual or artistic property such as works, phonograms etc., are likely to restrict the exercise of certain fundamental rights, in particular, the freedom of expression and the freedom of the arts. In addition, intellectual property is itself protected as a fundamental right to property. It is therefore necessary to strike a balance between those rights, none of which are, in principle, superior to the others. (47) So far as concerns copyright, copyright law itself achieves this through the provision of a number of limitations and exceptions. The purpose of those limitations and exceptions is to strike a fair balance between, on the one hand, the rights and interests of rightholders of copyright and related rights and, on the other, various other public or private rights, including the protection of fundamental rights."
68. Opinion of the European Copyright Society in relation to the pending reference before the CJEU in Case C-476/17, Hutter v. Pelham, 2018, https://europeancopyrightsociety.org/portfolio/opinion-on-reference-to-cjeu-in-case-c-476-17-hutter-v-pelham/ (accessed Jan. 31, 2019).
69. Christophe Geiger, Jonathan Griffiths & Reto Hilty, *Towards a Balanced Interpretation of the "Three-Step Test,"* 1(2) Journal of Intellectual Property, Information Technology and Electronic Commerce (2010).

creating new music have in common the fact that in each case, the user does not immediately interfere with the economic exploitation of the protected work. At the same time, they all concern a use of the work. Traditional copyright law principles cannot provide an answer for these digital uses of a protected work that sweep away the boundary between public and private spheres. Appealing to a human rights perspective, in order to arbitrate between the two antagonistic notions of access protection and freedom to access, is therefore mandatory.

It should be noted that in this context, strictly speaking, and following a Hohfeldian analysis of legal concepts, the use of supra legislative regulations to protect a user's access does not confer a "right" but a "liberty" on the user. This leads the court to a conservative interpretation of the three-step test, as for instance in the famous French case of *Mulholland Drive*.[70] Establishing real users' rights that can be enforced in court would be a positive step toward incorporation into copyright law of human rights considerations.[71] This means a legislative intervention in order to make exceptions mandatory and to prevent contractual mechanisms from overriding them.

On July 29, 2019, the CJEU delivered its ruling on these cases (*Afghanistan Papers*, *Metall auf Metall* and *Spiegel Online*). The Court clearly and strongly rejected the position that fundamental rights can justify exceptions or limitations beyond those in Article 5(3) of the Information Society Directive. However, the CJEU left the door open for an analysis of copyright protection, which is indirectly influenced by a human rights perspective.

Characteristically, the Court considered in the *Spiegel Online* case that, in striking the balance which is incumbent on a national court between the exclusive rights of the author on the one hand, and the rights of the users of protected subject matter on the other hand, "a national court must, having regard to all the circumstances of the case before it, rely on an interpretation of those provisions which, whilst consistent with their wording and safeguarding their effectiveness, fully adheres to the fundamental rights enshrined in the Charter of Fundamental Rights of the European Union." Therefore, while the right of the user to obtain access to a copyright-protected work cannot be directly based on freedom of expression, the existing available exceptions—such as data mining, private copy, quotation, use of a protected work for the purposes of reporting current events, and uses by persons with disabilities—have to be interpreted in light of freedom of expression in a way to ensure the effective protection of the users' freedom.

70. Cour de Cassation, civil 1, Jun. 19, 2008, M. Perquin, UFC Que choisir c/ Soc. Universal Pictures Vidéo France et a.
71. Christophe Geiger, *Copyright as an Access Right: Securing Cultural Participation Through the Protection of Creators' Interests at What if We Could Reimagine Copyright?* 94 (Rebecca Giblin, Kimberlee Weatherall eds., ANU Press, 2017).

Furthermore, in the same case, the Court also emphasized that the "exceptions or limitations do themselves confer rights on the users of works,"[72] departing from the traditional concept of users' freedom of access and adopting on the contrary the modern concept of copyright users' rights.[73]

21.2.3 The Right to Interoperability as a Technical Counterpart of a User's Right to Obtain Access

While the concept of the right to obtain access has advanced mostly in legal research, it could be argued that it empirically arose hidden behind another concept of more technical content: the right to interoperability. Indeed, interoperability must be understood as the ability to have access to content, a service, or a device, in a way that is independent from the control of the provider of the content or service or the manufacturer of the device.

The concept of interoperability has received more attention in the age of "metaverses" as a meta-principle that applies to various fields of law.[74] The notion exists in copyright law through the exception of reverse engineering of software[75] and also in the data mining exception. It is present in European Internet law,[76] in personal data protection,[77] and even in consumer law. Indeed, interoperability is nowadays included in the list of subjective obligations of conformity of the digital content or service, together with the requirements of quantity, quality and compatibility.[78] Furthermore, Article 16

72. Paragraph 70 of the decision.
73. Tatiana Eleni Synodinou. *Lawfulness for Users in European Copyright Law: Acquis and Perspectives*, 10 Journal of Intellectual Property, Information Technology and Electronic Commerce 20 (2019).
74. Marc Bourreau, Jan Krämer, Miriam Buiten. *Interoperability in Digital Markets. Report for the Centre on Regulation in Europe* (CERRE, 2022). Available at: https://cerre.eu/wp-content/uploads/2022/03/220321_CERRE_Report_Interoperability-in-Digital-Markets_FINAL.pdf.
75. Article 6 of the Directive 2009/24/EC of the European Parliament and of the Council of 23 April 2009 on the legal protection of computer programs (Codified version) (Text with EEA relevance), OJ L 111, 5.5.2009, pp. 16-22, ELI: http://data.europa.eu/eli/dir/2009/24/oj.
76. Articles 1 and 39 of the Electronic Communication Code, Directive (EU) 2018/1972 of the European Parliament and of the Council of 11 December 2018 establishing the European Electronic Communications Code (Recast). OJ L 321, 17/12/2018, pp. 36-214, ELI: http://data.europa.eu/eli/dir/2018/1972/oj.
77. Article 18 of the Regulation (EU) 2016/679 of the European Parliament and of the Council of 27 April 2016 on the protection of natural persons with regard to the processing of personal data and on the free movement of such data, and repealing Directive 95/46/EC (General Data Protection Regulation). OJ L 119, 4.5.2016, pp. 1-88. ELI: http://data.europa.eu/eli/reg/2016/679/oj.
78. Article 7(a) of the Directive "digital content." Directive (EU) 2019/770 of the European Parliament and of the Council of 20 May 2019 on certain aspects concerning contracts for the supply of digital content and digital services, ELI: http://data.europa.eu/eli/dir/2019/770/oj.

of Directive 2019/770 created for the consumer a new right to portability of their nonpersonal data, which has indirect but substantial consequences on copyright law. At its core, this right allows the user to keep access to the content created on an online platform in case of termination of the contract, on the condition that the content must have an autonomous existence and an independent economic value from the digital service.

Therefore, interoperability presents itself as a specific user's right to obtain access to the work, in specific situations. Most of these situations are defined legislatively, but the essential facilities theory should also be mentioned here, as it plays a substantial role in extending the scope of the right to obtain access.

This theory initially belonged to competition law and can be described as the obligation to license a product when it is absolutely needed for a competitor to enter a market.[79] However, the European Court of Justice applied it to copyright law in the seminal cases *Maggil*[80] and *IMS Health.*[81] It does not automatically mean that monopolistic situations due to the existence of intellectual property rights are by themselves problematic: it is the specific way the rights are exercised that must be analyzed (*see* the *Renault* and *Volvo* cases).[82]

The Microsoft case,[83] in this context, is of the utmost importance, as the Court explicitly considered that the application of the essential facilities theory involves a right to interoperability. The Court explained that four steps are required for a compulsory licensing mechanism to be applied: (i) the refusal to provide interoperability information relates to a product or service indispensable to the exercise of a particular activity on a neighboring market; (ii) the refusal is of such a kind as to exclude any effective competition on that neighboring market; (iii) the refusal prevents the appearance of a new product for which there is potential consumer demand; and (iv) once it is established that such circumstances are present, the refusal by the holder of a dominant position to grant a license may infringe Article 82 EC unless the refusal is objectively justified.

---

79. Rooijen Ashwin van, *The Software Interface Between Copyright and Competition Law: A Legal Analysis of Interoperability in Computer Program* (Wolters Kluwer, 2010).
80. ECJ, cases C-241/91 P and C-242/91 P, Radio Telefis Eireann (RTE) and Independent Television Publications Ltd (ITP) v. Commission of the European Communities, (1995), ECLI:EU:C:1995:98.
81. ECJ, case C-418/01, IMS Health GmbH & Co. OHG v. NDC Health GmbH & Co. KG, (2004), ECLI:EU:C:2004:257.
82. ECJ, case C-53/87, CICRA v. Renault, [1988] ECR 6039. C-238/87, Volvo AB v. Eric Veng,(UK) Ltd [1988] ECR 6211.
83. ECJ, case T-201/04, Microsoft Corp. v. Commission of the European Communities, (2007), ECLI:EU:T:2007:289.

21.3 CONCLUSION

To summarize, three main arguments work in favor of the right to control access: the scope of the rightholder's prerogative; the possibility of inserting DRMs into digital assets; and the extension of the economic prerogative in the online environment in order to cover access. It is remarkable that each of these three arguments faces a counterargument in favor of the right to obtain access: the content-mining exception encounters the idea of access control, and the case law that emphasizes human rights puts into perspective both DRM protection and the current broad interpretation of online economic rights.

It would be simplistic to conclude from this that access has become a new battlefield in a struggle between proponents of a strong copyright law and activists arguing in favor of more user-friendly mechanisms. Instead, it shows that ultimately, a compromise could be reached between these two positions, with the ultimate goal of achieving a fair balance of rights. In other words, paradoxically, the right to control access and the right to obtain access do not cancel each other out. Each has its own objective application and can therefore coexist with the other. However, even if the majority of scholars would agree on the principle of copyright law as the outcome of a balancing of rights, a number of fundamental issues remain as regards whether this balancing can be achieved by using intrinsic elements of copyright law only or whether recourse to external limitations is unavoidable. Future clarifications from the CJEU on this point are expected. In particular, Christophe Geiger has already emphasized this dynamic between protection and free access and demonstrated that in any case, it forms part of copyright law policy.[84] In conclusion, to focus only on controlling access or obtaining access, and omitting its counterpart, would not represent fair treatment for the mechanisms of copyright law and for the universal principle on which it is founded, i.e., a balance of interests.

84. Christophe Geiger, *The Future of Copyright in Europe: Striking a Fair Balance Between Protection and Access to Information*/L'avenir du droit d'auteur en Europe: Vers un juste équilibre entre protection et accès à l'information, Report for the Committee on Culture, Science and Education—Parliamentary Assembly, Council of Europe, Strasbourg, July 2009 (Revised and updated in October 2009), www.ceipi.edu (short version published in French in: 48 La Semaine Juridique, Ed G. 50-57; extended version published in English in: 14(1) Intellectual Property Quarterly 1-14 (2010)).

Chapter 22

Universal Measures in the Service of Global Challenges: Proportionality, Blocking Orders, and Online Intermediaries as Hybrid Bodies

Orit Fischman Afori[*]

Much has been written about the understanding that copyright law encapsulates a complicated balance of interests: On one hand are the interests of copyright owners, often perceived as "property rights," and on the other the public's interest in access to protected materials, identified as part of "freedom of expression." In the past few decades, copyright law has been facing a severe crisis, intensified by the digital online environment. Copyright law is accused of not promoting a "fair" and "balanced" regime, and of being inefficient, in utilitarian terms. It is blamed for serving rightholders' interests while neglecting the vast public interest.[1]

---

* This chapter is based on a lecture presented at the conference on Pluralism or Universalism in International Copyright Law, held at the University of Cyprus in May 2018. Some of the ideas expressed here were also discussed in a previous article of mine: Orit Fischman Afori, *Proportionality: A New Mega Standard in European Copyright Law,* 45(8) International Review if Intellectual Property and Competition Law 889-914 (2014) https://doi.org/10.1007/s40319-014-0272-1. I thank the participants of the conference for their valuable comments.

1. *See*, for example: Jessica Litman, *The Politics of Intellectual Property*, 27 Cardozo Arts & Entertainment Law Journal 313 (2009); William Patry, *Moral Panics and the Copyright Wars* 1-41 (2009).

Accordingly, contemporary scholarly writings propose various ways to ease the crisis. For instance, excessive discourse is devoted to the exceptions and limitations to rights, as a vehicle for promoting fairness. Yet, rights and exceptions are subject to the strict regime of international intellectual property law.[2] Therefore, this discourse has to a significant extent reached a dead end.[3] This chapter belongs to a recent line of writings exploring an alternative path on which a gradual process is overtaking the copyright discourse, and which is of the constitutionalization of copyright law.

A concrete case study for operating this alternative path concerns the role of online intermediaries, such as Internet service providers (ISPs), search engines, and other online platforms like social media and video-sharing platforms. One of the most prominent challenges facing current copyright law is mass infringing activity on the Internet. Since enforcing copyright against direct online infringers is not feasible, current copyright law perceives the various online intermediaries as gatekeepers and imposes obligations on them to take down or block access to infringing content. A prominent means for addressing online infringements that has been used since the 2010s is the granting of site-blocking orders by courts. Another significant means is the obligation adopted in 2019 in Article 17 to the European Union (EU) Directive on Copyright in the Digital Single Market (CDSM Directive), according to which online platforms can be held liable for unauthorized copyrighted content uploaded by users unless they demonstrate that they have made "best efforts" to obtain authorization for such activity or have taken specific measures to prevent the uploading of infringing content.[4]

The obligations imposed on online intermediaries as gatekeepers have raised many policy-oriented questions. First, it should be asked what the legal basis is for imposing obligations upon online intermediaries that are aimed at promoting another party's welfare or even broad social values. It should be borne in mind that these intermediaries are private bodies seeking to maximize profit. In this regard, a proposition to perceive online intermediaries as hybrid private/public bodies would be presented in this chapter.[5]

2. The restrictions on exceptions to copyright are imposed by the Berne Convention for the Protection of Literary and Artistic Works (Jul. 24, 1971), TRT/BERNE/002, Art. 9(2); Agreement on Trade-Related Aspects of Intellectual Property Rights (Apr. 15, 1994), 1869 UNTS 299, s. 13.
3. Reto M. Hilty, Cop*yright Law and the Information Society: Neglected Adjustments and Their Consequences*, 38 International Review of Intellectual Property and Competition Law 135 (2007).
4. Directive (EU) 2019/790 of the European Parliament and of the Council of 17 April 2019 on copyright and related rights in the Digital Single Market and amending Directives 96/9/EC and 2001/29/EC, 2019 O.J. (L 130) (DCDSM).
5. For an extended discussion of online intermediaries as hybrid bodies, *see* Orit Fischman Afori, *Online Rulers as Hybrid Bodies: The Case of Infringing Content Monitoring*, 23 University Of Pennsylvania Journal Of Constitutional Law, 121 (2021).

Acknowledging this hybrid status may make it possible to require compliance with some core public law principles.

Furthermore, site-blocking orders are a remedy. The powerful alternative path for easing the current copyright crisis is operated, *inter alia*, through the remedies granted. Remedies are left to the discretion of national courts and are crafted on a case-by-case basis; therefore, they may play a major role in realizing a de facto fair, balanced, and more efficient copyright law.[6] The main argument presented in this chapter is that one of the most outstanding legal principles used within the remedial framework for balancing these conflicting constitutional interests is the principle of proportionality.

Proportionality functions as a universal notion, vesting discretion in the judiciary to craft the final legal solution pragmatically. It is an open standard, similar to reasonableness; however, it is specifically tailored to enable courts to strike a proper balance between competing constitutional values or human rights involved in a certain and particular case.[7] In that regard, the appeal of the measure of proportionality to current copyright law reflects both the emergence of human rights issues in this area of private law and the need for a new powerful, acceptable, and universal measure that would facilitate the promotion of new solutions for current challenges in copyright law.

A few prominent examples can demonstrate the use of the universal measure of proportionality as a basic prism for evaluating the legitimacy of granting site-blocking orders. The Court of Justice of the European Union (CJEU) handed down several landmark decisions, marking the opening of the constitutional era of copyright law. Then, British High Court decisions, handed down by Justice Richard Arnold, further elaborated the measure of proportionality into a concrete set of considerations that should be evaluated in the case of any site-blocking order. The argument presented here is that despite the great potential of leveraging the notion of proportionality into a policy-oriented measure, this line of decisions transforms judicial discretion into a procedural-technical tool. Finally, a snapshot outside Europe, along with a short description of the new Israeli legislation, codifying the British High Court's "checklist" of considerations, will be presented. All these examples together demonstrate the potential of the new constitutional phase of copyright law, which is facing global challenges to be solved by universal measures.

The concluding remark focuses on the important role that online intermediaries can play in the new constitutional phase of copyright law. As

6. This idea was explored in a previous article of mine: Orit Fischman Afori, *Flexible Remedies as a Means to Counteract Failures in Copyright Law*, 29 Cardozo Arts & Entertainment Law Journal 1 (2011).
7. For the various functions of the notion of proportionality in EU law, *see*: Evelyn Ellis, *The Principle of Proportionality in the Law of Europe* (Hart Publishing, 1999). Particularly *see* David Feldman, *Proportionality and the Human Rights Act 1998*, at The Principle of Proportionality in the Law of Europe 116, 127 (Evelyn Ellis ed., Hart Publishing, 1999).

agents not only for copyright enforcement but also for voicing the vast public interest, online intermediaries are key players in the free flow of content in the online environment. If not only the judiciary would stress the importance of a proportionate remedy but also the online intermediaries themselves, the constitutional standard of proportionality may be leveraged to promote a more balanced copyright law that acknowledges users' rights and the public interest in online access to content. Because they function as a technological "intermediary," their legal status should reflect their complicated task in serving all stakeholders, copyright holders as well as users. Therefore, online intermediaries should be proactive not only in mitigating copyright infringement but also in preserving the free flow of legitimate content online.

22.1 THE GLOBAL CHALLENGES OF COPYRIGHT LAW

The impact of the digital environment on copyright law is immense. Digital technology has changed the way copyrighted works are created, consumed, and disseminated.[8] Moreover, digital technology has changed the way copyright is infringed upon and enforced.[9] In 1998, the Digital Millennium Copyright Act was enacted in the United States (U.S.) to accommodate copyright law to digital technologies.[10] However, after two decades, questions have been raised on whether the legal mechanisms introduced by it (such as the "notice & takedown" and "safe harbor" rules) are still relevant.[11]

One of the most prominent challenges copyright law needs to face is the online infringing activity conducted by certain operators on some Internet platforms, such as websites that allow illegal downloads of copyrighted movies or even their illegal streaming (i.e., online illegal broadcasting). Acting against the primary infringers in these cases, whether it regards the operator of the infringing Internet sites or even the end users, has proven to

8. *See*, for example: Craig Joyce, Marshall Leaffer, Peter Jaszi & Tyler Ochoa, *Copyright Law* (6th edn, LexisNexis, 2016).
9. *Ibid.*; One of the most prominent scholars, describing the general impact of digital technology on law enforcement and compliance, is Lessig, *see*: Lawrence Lessig, *Code: Version 2.0* (2006), http://codev2.cc/download+remix/Lessig-Codev2.pdf (May 13, 2019). For the stance that though copyright law basics are still valid, it still should be profoundly revised to adapt copyright enforcement to digital technologies, *see*: Alden Abbott, Adam Mossof, Kristen Osenga, Brian O' Shaughnessy & Mark Schultz, *Creativity and Innovation Unchained: Why Copyright Law Must Be Updated for the Digital Age by Simplifying It* (The Regulatory Transparency Project of the Federalist Society, 2017), https://regproject.org/wp-content/uploads/RTP-Intellectual-Property-Working-Group-Paper-Copyright.pdf (accessed May 12, 2019).
10. Digital Millennium Copyright Act, Pub. L. 105-304, 112 Stat. 2860 (1998); 17 USC §512.
11. For the view that the Digital Millennium Copyright Act does not work *see* Abbott, Mossof, Osenga, Shaughnessy & Schultz (n. 9).

be heavy-handed and ineffective.[12] Direct infringers tend to use anonymity to avoid legal liability; infringing site operators tend to frequently change their Internet address.[13] In addition, although the infringing acts are conducted on a global scale, court orders are limited to the jurisdiction of the courts. The court's limited ability to govern acts outside its jurisdiction stands at the heart of the seminal Canadian Supreme Court decision, handed down in 2017, in the case of *Google Inc. v. Equustek Solutions Inc.*, upholding an order according to which Google should index all websites that sell goods violating a Canadian company's trade secrets worldwide.[14]

In light of the lack of feasibility to police direct copyright infringement in the online environment, the legal spotlight is turned on online intermediaries, particularly ISPs and key online platforms such as search engines (Google), video-sharing platforms (YouTube), and social media networks (Facebook). Online intermediaries may serve as gatekeepers, since they have the technological ability to block access, on various technological levels, to content, websites or addresses.[15] Search engines may remove results and links to specific content sources. Therefore, although online intermediaries are non-infringing third parties that should not be held directly liable, their technological ability nevertheless makes them accountable.[16]

Imposing accountability, and thereby a certain degree of liability, on online intermediaries involves various considerations: from the exact technological measure expected to be used, through the tailoring of legal obligation of a noninvolved third party, to the major question of the collateral effect on various freedoms and basic rights of both intermediaries and end users.[17] The acknowledgment of the courts' authority to grant a site-blocking order, which is an equitable injunction, imposing on online intermediaries to try and reduce the volume of illegal online activity requires in-depth, policy-oriented discussion on the balance between the interests of competing fundamental rights. In other words, site-blocking orders have inevitably taken copyright law discourse into the sphere of public law, and eventually the next phase of copyright constitutional discourse.

---

12. Christophe Geiger & Elena Izyumenko, *The Role of Human Rights in Copyright Enforcement Online,* 32 American University International Review 43, 44 (2016) https://doi.org/10.2139/ssrn.2805572.
13. *Ibid.*
14. Google Inc. v. Equustek Solutions Inc., SCC 34 (2017).
15. David Lindsay, *Website Blocking Injunctions to Prevent Copyright Infringement: Proportionality and Effectiveness,* 40 University of New South Wales Law Journal 1507 (2017) https://doi.org/10.53637/qkaw8800.
16. Martin Husovec, *Injunctions Against Intermediaries in the European Union* (Cambridge University Press, 2017).
17. Niva Elkin-Koren & Maayan Perel, *Guarding the Guardians: Content Moderation by Online Intermediaries and the Rule of Law,* at Oxford Handbook of Intermediary Liability Online 669 (Giancarlo Frosio ed., Oxford University Press, 2020); *See also* the article of Matthias Leistner, *Intermediary Liability in a Global World*, published herewith.

22.2 ONLINE INTERMEDIARIES AS HYBRID PRIVATE/PUBLIC BODIES

Online intermediaries are private bodies, usually incorporated as companies, and thereby they are motivated by profits. These business entities are governed by private law principles, even if their shares are publicly offered. The imposition of social duties on online intermediaries, due to their technical ability to serve as gatekeepers against illegal acts, raises questions about imposing public law principles on private bodies, at least to a certain extent. Exploring the issue of hybrid private/public entities falls outside of the scope of this chapter. However, the legal acknowledgment that major online intermediaries are accountable to public values such as the rule of law, prevention of illegal acts, and other social goals, and therefore are subject to legal obligations to promote these goals leads to the broader question of their legal status as hybrid private/public bodies.[18]

Moreover, site-blocking orders involve the interests of both sides: copyright owners' interests and the vast public interest in free access to the Internet as part of freedom of speech.[19] Yet, online intermediaries, particularly ISPs, are often caught between the two sides while having no concrete stance. In some cases, ISPs are simply indifferent on the matter, and the site-blocking order is granted on an ex parte basis, namely with only the representative of the copyright owner in attendance, or with no true objection or discussion.[20] The problem is clear: The public's voice is not heard in these cases, and therefore the final decision may be one-sided. Since online intermediaries are a much-needed party for carrying out the order—even if they are a non-infringing third party—certain duties and obligations for serving both rightsholders and users should rise. While copyright owners are well represented as the party filing the plea, it leaves online intermediaries, particularly ISPs, as key players, the only ones who may represent the public's voice. In other words, site-blocking orders may entail the imposition of an obligation on a private body to represent the public interest.

18. Fischman Afori (n. 5). For the expanding concept of accountability *see*: Richard Mulgan, *"Accountability": An-Ever-Expanding Concept?,* 78 Public Administration Review 555 (2000) https://doi.org/10.1111/1467-9299.00218. For similar views, proposing to impose some public law principles upon private bodies operating social network sites such as Facebook, due to the impact on users' basic human rights, *see:* Noa Mor, *No Longer Private: On Human Rights and The Public Facet of Social Network Sites,* 47 Hofstra Law Review 651 (2018); For the view that private law fiduciary duties should be applied to some of the Internet platforms *see:* Jack M. Balkin, *Information Fiduciaries and the First Amendment*, 49 UC Davis Law Review 1183, 1205 (2016).

19. The UN has declared Internet access as a human right and part of the freedom of speech, *see* Report of the Human Rights Council on its 17th session (May 16, 2011), A/HRC/17/2.

20. For a comparative survey of "secondary liability" imposed on online intermediaries and their stance in the various jurisdictions *see*: Graeme B. Dinwoodie, *Secondary Liability of Internet Service Providers* (Springer, 2017).

The dichotomy between private and public laws has blurred over the past few decades, and it is now accepted that the two should not be viewed as totally separate legal areas.[21] There are various models for the application of public law norms to private parties: direct or indirect application of norms and application through statutes or judicial decisions.[22] For example, according to the doctrine of hybrid bodies, private entities that control public resources or the supply of a basic social need are in a nexus to governmental service or fulfill a public function, or whose function may promote a certain social value under necessity may be to some extent subject to public or administrative law norms.[23] In the United Kingdom (U.K.), the doctrine of hybrid bodies is codified under the Human Rights Act,[24] whereas in other countries it is applied according to court-made rules.[25]

The line between private and public is particularly blurred in the online environment.[26] In the early days of the Internet, private actors in the market were notably able to control public access to information; therefore, it was

21. Morton J. Horwitz, *The History of the Public/Private Distinction,* 130 University Pennsylvania Law Review 1423 (1982) https://doi.org/10.2307/3311976; Aharon Barak, *Constitutional Human Rights and Private Law,* 3 Review of Constitutional Studies 218, 220-221, 241 onwards (1996) https://doi.org/10.5040/9781472559197.ch-002 (describing Israeli law and other jurisdictions models for imposing public law obligations duties between private parties); Dawn Oliver, *What, if Any, Public-Private Divides Exist in English Law*, at The Public-Private Law Divide: Potential For Transformation, 1, 13-15 (Matthias Ruffert, ed., 2009); Sabino Cassese, *New Paths for Administrative Law: A Manifesto,* 10(3) International Journal of Constitutional Law 603, 607 (2012) https://doi.org/10.1093/icon/mos038.
22. *See*: Barak (n. 21), 241 onwards; Jody Freeman, *Private Parties, Public Functions and the New Administrative Law,* 52 Administrative Law Review 813 (2000) https://doi.org/10.4324/9781315183770-18.
23. Barak (n. 21), 220-221; Oliver (n. 21), at 13-15; Fischman Afori (n. 5), at 150-161.
24. Human Rights Act 1998, c.42 § 6(1) (U.K.) proclaiming that "it is unlawful for a public authority to act in a way which is incompatible with a Convention right" and § 6(3) proclaiming "In this section 'public authority' includes—(a) a court or tribunal, and (b) any person certain of whose functions are functions of a public nature."
25. Fischman Afori (n. 5), at 159-161, 163-164. *See*, for example, the evolving application of the doctrine in German law: Peter E. Quint, *Free Speech and Private Law in German Constitutional Theory*, 48 Maryland Law Review 247 (1989); Jacco Bomhoff, *Luth's 50th Anniversary: Some Comparative Observations on the German Foundations of Judicial Balancing*, 9 German Law Journal 121, 124 (2008) https://doi.org/10.1017/s2071832200006349; The Frankfurt Airport ("Fraport") case BVerfG, Judgement of the First Senate of Feb. 22, 2011—1 BvR699/06, English translation available at https://www.bundesverfassungsgericht.de/SharedDocs/Entscheidungen/EN/2011/02/rs20110222_1bvr069906en.html; Livia Fenger & Helena Lindemann, *The FRAPORT Case of the First Senate of the German Federal Constitutional Court and Its Public Forum Doctrine: Case Note*, 15 German Law Journal 1105 (2014) https://doi.org/10.1017/s2071832200019283.
26. *See* Mor (n. 18), 698-699 (Referring to a similar issue of social networks accountability, *see* Sandvig v. Sessions, 315 F. Supp. 3d 1, 12 (D.D.C. 2018)).

proposed to impose upon them public law obligations.[27] Major online intermediaries fall into one of the categories within which imposing some public law duties may be justified: They supply access to information, a basic need that fulfills the right to freedom of speech; their position allows them to control the flow of both legal and illegal information over the Internet, and they are thus a necessary agent for promoting social values; and, as explained above, their position turns them into the major or even sole agent able to represent the public interest.[28] These characteristics may justify imposing certain public law obligations and duties over relevant online intermediaries.[29] To date, the courts have rejected the view that large online intermediaries should be perceived as hybrid bodies.[30] Nevertheless, a significant development in that regard is the landmark EU enactment of the Digital Services Act (DSA) in 2022, which addresses general practices that should be followed by the main online platforms, aimed at ensuring a safe and accountable online environment.[31] The DSA, therefore, has adopted the position that the main online platforms should be obligated to function as gatekeepers for the public good.

The imposition of public law obligations on private entities should be accompanied by public law doctrines and measures. If we want online intermediaries to be held accountable for online infringements and serve as public good gatekeepers, the constitutional discourse along with its concepts should be introduced into private copyright law. This understanding serves as the background for the function of the notion of proportionality in current copyright law, as further explored below.

---

27. *See:* Henry H. Perritt, *Towards a Hybrid Regulatory Scheme for the Internet*, 215 (University of Chicago Legal Forum 2001).
28. Fischman Afori (n. 5), at 123, 127; Daphne Keller, Hoo*ver Inst., Who Do You Sue? State and Platform Hybrid Power Over Online Speech,* 11-13 (Aegis Series Paper No. 1902) (2019); Kate Klonick, *The New Governors: The People, Rules, and Processes Governing Online Speech*, 131 Harvard Law Review 1598, 1664 (2018).
29. For a similar view *see:* Ira Steven Nathenson, *Super-Intermediaries, Code, Human Rights*, 8 Intercultural Human Rights Law Review 19, 149-156 (2013) (proposing the application of "Digital Due Process" on online intermediaries); K. Sabeel Rahman, *The New Utilities: Private Power, Social Infrastructure, and the Revival of the Public Utility Concept*, 39 Cardozo Law Review 1621, 1668-1670 (2018) (proposing to perceive online platforms as public utilities).
30. *See,* e.g., Richardson v. Facebook & Richardson v. Google, [2015] EWHC 3154, at para. 63 (QB) (holding that "Facebook does not act 'in the public interest' in the relevant sense, nor can it conceivably be described as performing 'functions of a public nature'").
31. Regulation (EU) 2022/1925 of the European Parliament and of the Council of 14 September 2022, on contestable and fair markets in the digital sector and amending Directives (EU) 2019/1937 and (EU) 2020/1828 (Digital Markets Act) (DSA).

22.3 THE UNIVERSAL MEASURE OF PROPORTIONALITY

Proportionality is a fundamental principle of universal constitutional law; however, it has no single accepted meaning.[32] The legal notion of proportionality was developed extensively in German public law, beginning in the nineteenth century, and it reflected a general transition from a discourse of concepts (or doctrines) to a discourse of interests.[33] The German approach to proportionality extended to other European countries, from where it spread to numerous non-European jurisdictions, with the exception of the U.S.,[34] by way of "legal transplantation."[35]

The modern notion of "proportionality" encapsulates the understanding that constitutional rights are relative and not absolute and should therefore be balanced against each other on a case-by-case basis.[36] The proportionality measure, therefore, is used to limit constitutional rights.[37] The term "proportionality" in the constitutional sense reflects careful reasoning and rational thinking.[38] Yet in European constitutional law, it has developed into a more concrete four-factor test, consisting of:

> proper purpose, rational connection, necessary means, and a proper relation between the benefit gained by realizing the proper purpose and the harm caused to the constitutional right.[39]

The last component is also referred to as the "proportionality *stricto sensu*," also known as "balancing."[40] In fact, current global constitutional law is diagnosed as being in its "age of balancing,"[41] since the notion of

---

32. Grant Huscroft, Bradley W. Miller & Gregoire Webber, *Introduction,* at Proportionality and the Rule of Law: Rights Justification Reasoning 2 (Grant Huscroft, Bradley W. Miller & Gregoire Webber eds., CUP, 2014).
33. Aharon Barak, *Proportionality: Constitutional Rights and Their Limitations* 17 (Cambridge University Press, 2012). *See also:* Orit Fischman Afori, *Proportionality: A New Mega Standard in European Copyright Law,* 45(8) International Review of Intellectual Property and Competition Law 889, 895 (2014) https://doi.org/10.1007/s40319-014-0272-1.
34. Barak (n. 21), 180-183; Moshe Cohen-Eliya & Iddo Porat, *Proportionality and Constitutional Culture* 14-15 (Cambridge University Press, 2013).
35. Barak (n. 21), 180; Matthias Klatt & Moritz Meister, *The Constitutional Structure of Proportionality* 2 (Oxford University Press 2012).
36. Barak (n. 21), 131.
37. *Ibid.,* 131-133.
38. *Ibid.,* 175-176.
39. *Ibid.,* 131. *See also,* Klatt & Meister (n. 35), 8.
40. Takis Tridimas, *The General Principles of EU Law* 90-93 (Oxford EU Law Library, 2000).
41. *See* T. Alexander Aleinikoff, *Constitutional Law in the Age of Balancing,* 96 Yale Law Journal 943 (1987) https://doi.org/10.2307/796529; Klatt & Meister (n. 35), 1.

proportionality is used by European courts, while the notion of balancing is used by U.S. courts to describe roughly similar judicial tools.[42]

Along with its constitutional function, the notion of proportionality is gradually turning into a moral principle, reflecting the "logicality," "rationality," or "reasonability" embedded in the court's inherent judicial capacity. In its metaphoric sense, proportionality denotes the judiciary's prerogative to craft the final legal solution according to the rule of law.[43] Timothy Endicott further proposed to understand the function of the notion of proportionality as an element shifting the authority to craft the law from the legislature to the court, since:

> in some instances leaving matters to the discretion of judges is less arbitrary than trying to remove that discretion through the imposition of rules that are themselves arbitrary.[44]

It was even explained by some scholars that:

> it is no exaggeration to claim that proportionality has overtaken rights as the orienting idea in contemporary human rights law and scholarship.[45]

Thus, proportionality reflects universal values, which explains its spread on a global scale.[46]

22.4 PROPORTIONALITY AS A TOOL FOR BALANCING SITE-BLOCKING ORDERS IN COPYRIGHT LAW

Site-blocking orders, to some extent, symbolize the current challenges of copyright law in the online environment: They reflect the urgent need of rightholders to fight the fast spread of infringing content in the online environment; it reflects the need to protect users' rights and freedoms; and it challenges the boundaries of court-vested authority to grant remedies. The

42. *See* Eric Engle, *The Rights Orchestra: Proportionality, Balancing, and Viking,* 17 New England Journal International & Competition Law 87, 97 (2011). *See also,* Cohen-Eliya & Porat (n. 34), 10-11.
43. *See*, Timothy Endicott, *Proportionality and Incommensurability,* at Proportionality and the Rule of Law: Rights, Justification, Reasoning 311 (Grant Huscroft, Bradley W. Miller & Gregoire Webber eds., Cambridge University Press, 2014); *See also,* Martin Luteran, *The Lost Meaning of Proportionality,* at Proportionality and the Rule of Law: Rights, Justification, Reasoning 21 (Grant Huscroft, Bradley W. Miller & Gregoire Webber eds., Cambridge University Press, 2014) (proposing to reconstruct the proportionality test in a way that focuses on ends and means rather than balancing).
44. *See* Endicott (n. 43), 320; *See also*, Huscroft, Miller & Webber (n. 32), 1, 14.
45. Huscroft, Miller & Webber (n. 32).
46. *Ibid.; See also,* Cohen-Eliya & Porat (n. 34).

popularity of site-blocking orders is growing on a global scale.[47] Blocking orders have been granted, occasionally extensively, mainly in European countries, including Austria, Belgium, Denmark, Finland, France, Italy, Ireland, and the U.K.[48] Outside Europe, blocking orders are granted, for instance, in Australia,[49] New Zealand,[50] and Israel,[51] and were approved by the Canadian Supreme Court in the aforementioned case of *Google Inc. v. Equustek Solutions Inc.*[52] This case could have signaled the start of a tendency to grant global injunctions, although no additional "*Equustek* injunctions" were granted[53] but only site-blocking orders, limited to the territory of Canada.[54]

Surprisingly, and despite the American "safe harbors" regime, in a case decided in 2017 by the Virginia district court, *ACS v. Sci-Hub*,[55] the court granted an order to block access to a site operated from outside the U.S. that provided access to unlicensed scientific materials. This decision could have signaled a shift in the attitude of the judiciary toward website blocking in the U.S. as well[56] but these orders have not proliferated in the U.S. Nevertheless, occasionally site-blocking orders are granted in the U.S., such as the order granted in 2022 against a site operated from outside the U.S. that provided access to unlicensed films.[57]

Site-blocking orders, being an equitable injunctive relief, by their nature are subject to the discretion of the courts.[58] Court decisions in various jurisdictions have stressed different considerations concerning the application of the court's discretion. In jurisdictions where there is no explicit

---

47. Giancarlo Frosio & Oleksandr Bulayenko, *Study on Dynamic Blocking Injunctions in the European Union: IPR Enforcement Case-Law Collection* (2021), available at https://papers.ssrn.com/sol3/papers.cfm?abstract_id=3807277.
48. Husovec (n. 16); Frosio & Bulayenko (n. 47), pp. 59-62.
49. Australian Copyright Act 1968, s. 115A authorizes injunctions against intermediaries; *See also* Lindsay (n. 15), 1524 onwards (describing recent Australian court decisions granting site-blocking orders).
50. New Zealand Copyright Act 1994, s. 122p.; Graeme W. Austin, *Legislating for Site-Blocking Orders* (Jan. 1, 2023). (2023) New Zealand Universities Law Review, Available at SSRN: https://ssrn.com/abstract=4393233.
51. Israeli Copyright Act 2007, s. 53A authorizes injunctions against intermediaries.
52. Google Inc. v. Equustek Solutions Inc.
53. Michael Geist, *The Equustek Effect: A Canadian Perspective on Global Takedown Orders,* at The Age of the Internet: Oxford Handbook of Online Intermediary Liability, 709 (Giancarlo Frosio ed. 2020).
54. *See, for example*, Rogers Media Inc. v. John Doe 1, 2022 FC 775.
55. ACS v. Sci-Hub, Civil Action No. 1:17cv0726.
56. *See* Maayan Perel, *Digital Remedies*, 35 Berkley Technology Law Journal 1 (2020).
57. United King Film Distribution Ltd. v. Does 1-10 d/b/a Israel.tv (S.D.N.Y. 21-CV-11024-AJN-RWL) (Apr. 26, 2022). In an *amicus* filed in this case, it was argued the U.S. courts have no authority to grant broad site-blocking orders; *see* https://www.eff.org/document/amicus-brief-behalf-cloudflare.
58. For the general equitable nature of injunctions *see* Owen M. Fiss & Doug Rendleman, *Injunction* 104-108 (University Casebook Series, 1984).

authorization by the legislature to grant injunctions against non-infringing intermediaries, the court may focus on its vested authority to grant such an order. This was the case, for instance, in the British decision of *Cartier v. British Sky Broadcasting*,[59] stating the vested authority of the court to grant a blocking order in case of trademark infringement, since there is no explicit authorization for such remedy in British trademark law, in contrast to British copyright law.[60] This was the opening reasoning of the Canadian Supreme Court decision in *Google Inc. v. Equustek Solutions Inc.* as well; Justice Rosaline Abella delivered the opinion of the majority and began by noting that injunctions are court orders that are equitable in nature and that they should, therefore, promote fairness and justice. Courts have wide discretion to grant injunctions, making them a "flexible and drastic remedy."[61]

Yet, in jurisdictions where site-blocking orders are authorized by specific legislation or governed by specific legislative norms, the focal point of the decision turns from the mere legitimacy of granting the order to its specific terms and conditions. The discussion of the terms and conditions of the blocking order is usually governed by the umbrella principle of proportionality.

As to European law, the notion of proportionality was introduced into the legislative norm through the framework of remedies acknowledged by two key directives. The first is the Directive on Harmonization of Certain Aspects of Copyright and Related Rights in the Information Society (Directive 2001/29/EC) ("Information Society Directive"), which states that the:

> measures, sanctions, and remedies against infringements of intellectual property rights should not only be effective but also "proportionate."

The second is the Directive on the Enforcement of Intellectual Property Rights (Directive 2004/48/EC) ("Enforcement Directive"), which states:

> Those measures, procedures, and remedies shall also be effective, proportionate, and dissuasive and shall be applied in such a manner as to avoid the creation of barriers to legitimate trade and to provide safeguards against their abuse.

These two directives made it clear that any discussion on the terms of a blocking order would be drilled down into an elaboration of the measure of proportionality. Accordingly, as we will describe in the next two sections, the CJEU and the British High Court took the next move by explaining and interpreting the measure of proportionality in the specific context.

---

59. Cartier International and others v. British Sky Broadcasting and others, EWHC 3794 (2014) (Ch); 1 All ER 949 (2015). Upheld on appeal EWCA Civ 658 (2016).
60. Site-blocking orders are authorized by British Copyright, Designs and Patent Act (1988) (CDPA), s. 97A. Introduced by the Copyright and Related Rights Regulations 2003 (U.K.) SI 2003/2498, Reg. 27.
61. Google Inc. v. Equustek Solutions Inc., para. 23.

22.4.1 CJEU Decisions

The CJEU made the first move in realizing the proportionality measure as a remedial vehicle designed by the Directives. To begin with, in 2006 the CJEU handed down its first comprehensive decision in the case of *Promusicae*,[62] stressing the role of "proportionality" within the intellectual property arena. The guidance given to national courts was clear:

> When the Directives are applied on a national level, it is important to ensure that the interpretation adopted does not conflict with other general principles of EU law, headed by the principle of proportionality.[63]

Following the *Promusicae* case, the focal point of any copyright/remedies discourse would now be on the standard of proportionality.

In a long series of decisions, the CJEU has developed, step-by-step, the new standard. As a major milestone in 2011, the CJEU handed down two decisions, discussing the legality of a Belgian decision and ordering an ISP to block access to certain infringing Internet websites—the *SABAM* cases.[64] In relying on the *Promusicae* holding, the CJEU further developed the rule, by refining the proportionality measurement as an internal constitutional benchmark. The court held that:

> national authorities and courts must strike a fair balance between the protection of copyright and the protection of the fundamental rights of individuals who are affected by such measures. Accordingly, in circumstances such as those in the main proceedings, national authorities and courts must, in particular, strike a fair balance between the protection of the intellectual property right enjoyed by copyright holders and that of the freedom to conduct a business enjoyed by operators such as ISPs.[65]

The final conclusion was that the Belgian decision was not proportionate, and therefore the blocking order was rejected. The importance of this decision lies not only in the CJEU statement that site-blocking orders raise various interests that should be balanced one against the other but also in the specification that copyright owners' interests stand vis-à-vis the private bodies' newly framed right to conduct their business freely.

Another significant decision was handed down in March 2014: The CJEU laid down another brick in elaborating the notion of proportionality in

62. Case C-275/06 Productores de Música de España (Promusicae) v. Telefónica de España SAU (2008) ECLI:EU:C:2008:54.
63. *See Ibid.*, para. 70.
64. Case C-70/10 Scarlet Extended SA v. Société Belge des Auteurs, Compositeurs et éditeurs SCRL (SABAM) (2011) ECLI:EU:C:2011:771 (Scarlet Extended case); Case C-360/10 SABAM v. Netlog (2012) ECLI:EU:C:2012:85.
65. *See*, Case C-70/10 Scarlet Extended SA v. Société Belge des Auteurs, Compositeurs et éditeurs SCRL (SABAM), paras. 45-46.

copyright law, this time discussing an Austrian site-blocking order in the *Telekabel* case.[66] The court stressed the conflict between copyright and the freedom to conduct a business, which was concretized as a right of:

> any business to be able to freely use, within the limits of its liability for its own acts, the economic, technical, and financial resources available to it.[67]

Yet, this time the blocking order was approved since the ISP was given leeway with respect to how it should be applied—namely in a manner that would minimize the harm done to and costs borne by the ISP. More specifically, the court held that an injunction that leaves it to the ISP to determine its means does not seem to infringe the freedom of an ISP since such an injunction enables the ISP to choose the measures best adapted to its resources and abilities and is therefore proportionate. This decision thus translated the measure of proportionality into procedural safeguards aiming to support the position of both the ISP and Internet users.[68] The *Telekabel* decision left a great deal of uncertainty in its wake, both concerning the means that would meet the "effectiveness" requirement and the actual scope of Internet users' rights.[69] Later CJEU rulings, reinforcing the *Telekabel* decision, were not of much avail. For example, in the *McFadden* ruling, handed down in 2016, the CJEU noted that copyright holders may seek injunctions forcing online intermediaries to prevent third infringements by parties as long as such remedy respects the balance of the conflicting interests at stake.[70] Yet, no clear clarification was offered as to how such balance should be achieved. Nevertheless, all the evolving CJEU decisions inevitably take European copyright law to its constitutional phase, where the granting of site-blocking orders requires evaluation of the potential conflict with human rights, first and foremost, freedom of expression.[71]

22.4.2 British High Court of Justice Decisions

Already in 2003, the British legislature enacted a specially tailored clause authorizing the grant of a site-blocking order against a non-infringing ISP,

---

66. Case C-314/12 UPC Telekabel Wien v. Constantin Film Verleih (2014) ECLI:EU:C:2014:192.
67. *See*, *Ibid.*, para. 49.
68. Tatiana-Eleni Synodinou, *Intermediaries' Liability for Online Copyright Infringement in the EU: Evolutions and Confusions*, 31 Computer Law & Security Review 57, 60 (2015) https://doi.org/10.1016/j.clsr.2014.11.010.
69. *Ibid.*, 61.
70. Case C-484/14 Tobias McFadden v. Sony Music Entertainment Germany Gmbh (2016) EU:C: 2016:689.
71. Christophe Geiger & Elena Izyumenko, *Blocking Orders: Assessing Tensions with Human Rights*, at The Age Of the Internet: Oxford Handbook Of Online Intermediary Liability, 566 (Giancarlo Frosio ed., 2020).

under certain conditions. Article 97A of the Copyright, Designs and Patents Act (CDPA)[72] states the following:

97A Injunctions against service providers

(1) The High Court (in Scotland, the Court of Session) shall have power to grant an injunction against a service provider, where that service provider has actual knowledge of another person using their service to infringe copyright.

(2) In determining whether a service provider has actual knowledge for the purpose of this section, a court shall take into account all matters which appear to it in the particular circumstances to be relevant and, amongst other things, shall have regard to—

(a) whether a service provider has received a notice through a means of contact made available in accordance with regulation 6(1)(c) of the Electronic Commerce (EC Directive) Regulations 2002 (SI 2002/2013); and

(b) the extent to which any notice includes—

(i) the full name and address of the sender of the notice;

(ii) details of the infringement in question.

(3) In this section "service provider" has the meaning given to it by regulation 2 of the Electronic Commerce (EC Directive) Regulations 2002.

It is evident that the British legislature has focused on the ISP's actual knowledge as a precondition for granting an injunction. Yet, the scope of the provision is very wide, and no guidance is given to the court as to the set of considerations that should be taken into account while issuing an order.[73] Following the use of such broad language, British courts naturally turned to the norms set by the Directives, as interpreted by the CJEU. The outcome is that Article 97A of the CDPA serves as the general framework for introducing the entire constitutional balancing mechanism, encapsulated within the standard of proportionality, into copyright law.

More specifically, it was Justice Arnold who opened the door to the new standard of proportionality in British copyright cases. In a long series of decisions, commencing in 2011, he gradually implemented and developed the proportionality test. In all these cases, the remedies served only as the gateway to introducing the proportionality test, which was further elaborated in order to strike a balance between the competing human rights involved. Therefore, the impact of the proportionality test was not limited to the

72. Copyright, Designs and Patents Act 1988.

73. Althaf Marsoof, *The Blocking Injunction: A Critical Review of Its Implementation in the United Kingdom, Within the Legal Framework of the European Union,* 46 International Review of Intellectual Property and Competition Law 632 (2015) https://doi.org/10.1007/s40319-015-0379-z.

remedies but rather affected the substantive questions of copyright limits. The clear line in all these decisions is that the grant of the remedies should be inspected very carefully and should be tailored to each case, according to the potential harm to various constitutional rights.

In July 2011, the decision of *Twentieth Century Fox Film Corporation and Others v. British Telecommunications plc* (*Fox, BT*) was handed down.[74] Fox pleaded for a site-blocking order, claiming injury to its property rights by illegal downloading. BT claimed that the grant of a site-blocking order would injure their subscribers' right to receive information, which is part of freedom of speech. Justice Arnold opened his decision by stressing the need to strike a balance between two competing human rights: property rights and freedom of information, both protected under the EU Charter. Thereafter, Justice Arnold analyzed the constitutional conflict reflected within this copyright case and eventually determined that the grant of the order under the circumstances is proportionate.

A further decision was handed down in 2012, in the case of *Golden Eye*.[75] This case concerned the need to balance copyright against the right to privacy since the ISP was asked to disclose details of customers who had allegedly infringed copyright. Justice Arnold looked closely at the specific terms of the order that was granted and discussed every condition through the prism of the proportionality or balancing test. The *Golden Eye* ruling elaborated the proportionality test by using the benchmarks of "necessity" and "efficiency," as are often used in constitutional law discourse.

The next decision concerning site-blocking orders was handed down in 2013, in the *EMI Records* case.[76] Once again, the conflict between copyright and freedom of expression was at stake. Justice Arnold held that every order should be inspected by courts, *ab initio*, since "the proportionality of a blocking order is bound to be a context-sensitive question"[77] and should therefore be considered only on a case-by-case basis. This last decision is a reminder that the proportionality measure is a remedial tool, aimed at promoting pragmatic results in each case, and therefore should be always open to courts for reconsideration.

This line of decisions is expanding, and each decision further elaborates the function of the measure of proportionality as a balancing remedial tool. For example, a decision handed down in 2017 in the *Premier League* case[78] expounded the idea that a blocking order could be granted for a very limited

74. Twentieth Century Fox Film Corporation and others v. British Telecommunications plc EWHC 1981 (Ch) [2011]; EWHC 1981 (Ch) (2011); 1 All ER 806 (2012).
75. Golden Eye (International) Ltd and others v. Telefonica UK Ltd, EWHC 723 (Ch) (2012).
76. EMI Records Ltd and others v. British Sky Broadcasting Ltd and others, EWHC 379 (Ch) (2013).
77. *See*, EMI Records Ltd and others v. British Sky Broadcasting Ltd and others, paras. 95-99.
78. Football Association Premier League v. British Telecommunications EWHC 480 Ch (2017).

time, as part of the concrete balance of interests at stake, which involved live broadcasting.

Summarizing the entire body of decisions handed down by Justice Arnold leads to the conclusion that for an injunction to be granted, it should meet the following parameters: necessary, effective, dissuasive, not unduly costly or complicated, avoiding barriers to legitimate trade, striking a fair balance between the fundamental rights engaged, proportionate, and safeguarded against abuse.[79] Out of all these factors, proportionality is the key one, since all other considerations feed into the proportionality analysis. Yet, Justice Arnold's approach suffers from certain drawbacks, similar to the ones of the *Telekabel* decision.[80] While the notion of proportionality aims to allow the judiciary to craft the legal outcome according to basic values of reasonableness, logicality, and the general idea of balancing fundamental rights, it is transformed into a set of technical and procedural safeguards. It is therefore not surprising that at the end of the day Justice Arnold granted the blocking orders in all cases decided by him. Procedural safeguards may always be designed de jure, but not necessarily applied de facto.

22.4.3 Outside Europe: Israeli Legislation

Outside Europe, the new Israeli legislation could serve as an interesting case study. While lower courts disagreed as to their vested authority to grant a blocking order against non-infringing ISPs,[81] in January 2019 the Israeli Knesset (Parliament) enacted a very detailed clause on the matter: Article 53A to the Copyright Act 2007.[82] In a nutshell, this Article could be perceived as a detailed codification of Justice Arnold's legacy into the Israeli Copyright Act.

To begin with, explicit authorization is given to the court to issue a blocking order against an ISP to block the entire source of content or part of it, if the court is convinced that a substantial part of the content thereof is infringing.[83] The standing to plea for such an order is given to the copyright owner or an exclusive licensee only.[84] The general framework already uses the open standard of "substantial part," acknowledged in copyright law. This standard aims to filter out sites that are mostly legal. In the explanatory part

79. *See* Cartier International and others v. British Sky Broadcasting and others EWHC 3794 (Ch) (2014).
80. *See also*, Marsoof (n. 73).
81. *See* two contradicting decisions: N.M.C. United Entertainment v. Bloomberg CC 33227/11/13, handed down May 2015(acknowledging court's power to grant blocking order); ZYRA (Copyright in the Internet) v. John Doe CC 37039/05/15, handed down July 2015 (asking the legislature to regulate blocking orders).
82. Copyright Act (Amendment 5), S.H. 2777 p. 187, approved by the Parliament on Jan. 9, 2019.
83. Israeli Copyright Act (2007), Art. 53A(3).
84. *Ibid.*, Art. 53A(2).

of the Bill, it was clarified that the requirement of substantiality should be interpreted as a qualitative measure and not in a technical-quantitative way.[85]

Moreover, the Article specifies that within the order granted, the court shall order the ISP to take reasonable measures to block the site, in its entirety or in part, by terms and conditions designed by the court to an extent no greater than required, to prevent harm to the copyright owner or exclusive licensee under the circumstances.[86] The order shall include, *inter alia*: the details of the site to be blocked, instructions as to the scope of the access blocking, and the period of access blocking.[87] The court is furthermore instructed to consider, *inter alia*, the following considerations: the severity of infringement; the necessity of the order; the effectiveness of available alternative remedies; the injury to access to other Internet sites; the injury to the privacy of Internet users; and the impact on the public if access is blocked, or if the order is rejected.[88] In the explanatory part of the Bill, it was clarified that all these measures aim to ensure that the grant of blocking orders would be proportionate, namely applied with reasonable measures to an extent no greater than required.[89]

This last explanatory sentence made it clear to any Israeli court that we are entering the field of public law, and more specifically the constitutional zone. Two key signs point to the entrance to such a zone. The first is the term "proportionality," which is a highly developed notion in Israeli constitutional law, used to balance competing constitutional rights.[90] The second sign is the phrase "*to an extent no greater than required*," which is taken from Israel's Basic Laws, such as the one on Human Dignity and Liberty, according to which:

> there shall be no violation of rights under this Basic Law except by a law befitting the values of the State of Israel, enacted for a proper purpose, and to an extent no greater than is required.[91]

This phrase is used in Israeli adjudication as another face of the measure of proportionality.

As for the problem of public awareness to the grant of a blocking order, the Israeli Copyright Act imposes an obligation on the ISP to post a notice on the blocked site, providing information about the order granted and specifying the procedural details of the court decision (as long as it is

85. Copyright Act Bill—H.H. 1164 (Amendment 5) (Nov. 1, 2017).
86. Israeli Copyright Act (2007), Art. 53A(3).
87. *Ibid.*
88. *Ibid.*, Art. 53A(4).
89. Copyright Act Bill—H.H. 1164 (Amendment 5) (Nov. 1, 2017).
90. This notion was developed in Israeli law by former Chief Justice Barak, who is perceived as one of the leading scholars on the matter, *see*: Endicott (n. 43); *See also*, Barak (n. 21).
91. Israeli Basic Law: Human Dignity and Liberty, 1992. S.H. 150 amended 1994 S.H. 90, Art. 8. This phrase appears also at the Israeli Basic Law: Freedom of Occupation, 1994, Art. 4.

possible to post such a notice).[92] Moreover, any person is entitled to ask to cancel or change the order.[93] This last clause aims to enable various Nongovernmental Organizations, representing users' rights or the public's digital rights, to join the legal procedure as a party and not only by submitting an amicus.

It remains to be seen whether the codification of the constitutional safeguards into Israeli law will shift the courts' approach from a technical-procedural measure, as demonstrated by both the *Telekabel* decision on the European level and Justice Arnold's legacy in the U.K., to a more principle-based reasoning.[94]

22.5 BACK TO THEORY: UNIVERSAL SOLUTIONS FOR GLOBAL CONSTITUTIONAL CONFLICTS IN COPYRIGHT LAW

The gradual intrusion of human rights discourse into the realm of copyright law has been explored by many scholars. The first period of scholarly work identified human rights interests, headed by freedom of speech, nested in copyright law.[95] The following stage focused on the various internal vehicles incorporated into copyright law, headed by exceptions and limitations, which would allow for the implementation of the balance of competing human rights.[96] This chapter belongs to the third phase of scholarly works, identifying a major leap, or at least a potential one, according to which copyright law should be placed in the heart of the constitutional sphere.[97]

As explained above, the move to copyright law's constitutional phase has taken place due to several reasons, including the constraints to craft more flexible exceptions and limitations to copyright due to international law obligations and the evolution of the online environment that has introduced new challenges to copyright law.[98] While the basic constitutional conflicts in

---

92. Israeli Copyright Act (2007), Art. 53A(9)(a).
93. *Ibid.*, Art. 53A(9)(b).
94. Thus far, a series of decisions handed down by the District Court had no reasoning at all or minimal reasoning; *See*, ZYRA (Copyright in the Internet) v. John Doe.
95. *See*, for example: Christophe Geiger, *Fundamental Rights, a Safeguard for the Coherence of Intellectual Property Law*?, 35 International Review of Intellectual Property and Competition Law 268 (2004).
96. *See*, for example, Bernt Hugenholtz & Martin R.F. Senftleben, *Fair Use in Europe in Search of Flexibilities* 6-9 (2011); Martin Senftleben, *Copyright, Limitations and the Three-Step Test* (Kluwer, 2004).
97. *See*, for example, Jonathan Griffiths, *Constitutionalising or Harmonising?: The Court of Justice, the Right to Property and European Copyright Law*, 38 European Law Review 65 (2013); Christophe Geiger & Elena Izyumenko, *The Role of Human Rights in Copyright Enforcement Online: Elaborating a Legal Framework for Website Blocking*, 32 American University International Law Review 43 (2016) https://doi.org/10.2139/ssrn.2805572.
98. *See supra* s. 22.2.

copyright law—between copyright owners' interests and users' freedom of speech—are already acknowledged, the solving mechanisms are constantly developing. Synthesizing the development described above with respect to the introduction of the measure of proportionality into copyright law raises several insights that should be further explored.

First, we should bear in mind that the measure of proportionality is operated with respect to remedies granted in case of copyright infringement. This development reflects the rise of the remedial era, recognizing that remedies are the flipside of the coin of rights. Rights and remedies are interconnected, and remedies are an effective vehicle for promoting policy considerations.[99] Particularly in intellectual property law, which leaves remedies to domestic governance, the remedial path enjoys amplified potential for serving as a means for reconciliation. The recent CJEU decisions and Justice Arnold's legacy explored above reinforce the understanding that proportionality is not simply a tool for calibrating remedies, but rather the court shapes the scope of rights—of both copyright owners and users—through the specific design of the remedy at stake.[100]

Taking this last insight one step further means that through the measure of proportionality, courts may redesign copyright law, yet in this current phase of copyright law, in light of the human rights conflict. In other words, the balance of human rights at stake should be the underlying leading principle of crafting the concrete rule. Whereas thus far the balance of the conflicting human rights has lagged behind the design of the concrete norm, the use of the measure of proportionality may turn over the order of considerations, in the sense that first the proper balance of conflicting human rights would be weighed, and only then would the concrete solution be sought. Applying such analysis would denote a full constitutionalization of copyright law.[101]

Moreover, the current challenges of copyright law are global. There is no difference between the conflicting human rights involved in various jurisdictions nor in the proper solutions. The online environment has made copyright law conflicts truly international. The dominance of Google's

99. As to the role of remedies in crafting rights *see*, Guido Calabresi & A. Douglas Melamed, *Property Rules, Liability Rules, and Inalienability: One View of the Cathedral*, 85 Harvard Law Review 1089 (1972) https://doi.org/10.2307/1340059; *See also*, Steve Hedley, *Remedies: The Key to the Common Law System*?, at The Law of Remedies: New Directions in the Common Law 305, 314 (Jeff Berryman & Rick Bigwood eds., Irwin Law, 2010); Orit Fischman Afori, *Flexible Remedies as a Means to Counteract Failures in Copyright Law*, 29 Cardoxo Arts & Entertainment Law Journal 1 (2011).

100. The best example for such insight is the CJEU decision in the *SABAM* cases. While inspecting the legality of a blocking order, the court has developed a new protected right to conduct a business freely, *see* (nn. 52-53).

101. For the constitutional balancing *stricto sensu* mechanism, in which the relevant human rights are scaled first and only then the solution is crafted, *see*, Aharon Barak, *Proportionality and Principled Balancing*, 4 Law & Ethics of Human Rights 1, 7-14 (2010) https://doi.org/10.2202/1938-2545.1041.

search engine reflects this phenomenon best, and the Canadian Supreme Court decision in the case of *Google Inc. v. Equustek Solutions Inc.*,[102] granting a global injunction, reflects a wish for a global solution. In light of this development, the universalism of the notion of proportionality is significant. Proportionality reflects the common thread in aspirations of courts, wherever they are; it means the vested power of courts to seek reasonable, pragmatic, and fair legal outcomes. The universal character of this emerging standard, which is spreading on a global scale, may function as the starting point for developing a global copyright law, based on human rights principles.

Against these utopic views stand current trends of recent case law, which have taken the measure of proportionality to a procedural-technical level. Proportionality has been transformed into a legal "checklist" that functions as a "placeholder" for judicial discretion. Therefore, to fulfill proportionality's promise for constitutionalizing copyright law, another profound legal move is needed. Acknowledging online intermediaries as hybrid bodies, namely private entities that are to a certain extent subject to public law norms, may serve such a goal. Various universal administrative rules may apply in such cases,[103] headed by the core duty of accountability to the public interest.[104] Online intermediaries would be prevented from being indifferent to users' rights since an obligation to maintain the public interest would be imposed upon them; the accountability of private entities would mean liability for both sides—that of copyright owners and users—and would therefore entail a duty of care to ensure a proportionate and reasoned concrete outcome.[105] The landmark EU enactment of the DSA takes a significant step in this direction, imposing a far-reaching obligation on online intermediaries, acknowledged as gatekeepers for the benefit of the public interest.

Furthermore, one of the most important administrative duties is that of authorities to provide a (full) reasoning.[106] The underlying rationale is that

102. Google Inc. v. Equustek Solutions Inc.

103. For the position that there are some common principles of universal administrative law, *see*, Benedict Kingsbury, Nico Krisch & Stewart B. Richard, *The Emergence of Global Administrative Law,* 68 Law and Contemporary Problems 15 (2005). *See also* Orit Fischman Afori, *Taking Global Administrative Law One Step Ahead: Online Giants and the Digital Democratic Sphere*, International Journal of Constitutional Law, (2022) https://doi.org/10.2139/ssrn.3874915.

104. For an analysis of the basic European common administrative agencies' duties, *see*, Diana-Urania Galetta, Herwig C. H. Hofmann, Oriol Mir Puigpelat & Jacques Ziller, *The General Principles of EU Administrative Procedural Law* (2015), http://www.europarl.europa.eu/supporting-analyses (accessed May 14, 2019).

105. Fischman Afori (n. 5), at 150-161.

106. The reason-giving requirement applies to state authorities under U.S. law, *see* 5 USC §§500-596 (2012). A similar administrative rule applies in the EU, *see,* Case C-222/86 Union nationale des entraîneurs et cadres techniques professionnels du football (Unectef) v. Georges Heylens and others (1987) ECLI:EU:C:1987:442, para. 15. *See*

state authorities should make deliberative, nonarbitrary, and coherent decisions.[107] Imposing such a duty on online intermediaries would force them to present their position in court and avoid the undesirable phenomenon of blocking orders granted on an ex parte basis,[108] with no consideration of the consequences of such order for the public interest. It is hoped that the obligation of reasoning would ban the automatic granting of site-blocking orders and would further promote more policy- and principle-oriented decisions rather than procedural-technical ones.

Acknowledging online intermediaries as hybrid bodies thus may ensure that the universal measure of proportionality would function more optimally as a means to ease constitutional conflicts in global copyright law.

22.6 CONCLUSIONS

Current copyright law is inevitably driven into its constitutional phase on a global scale. Now, the battlefield has shifted to a new constitutional mode of operation. While the constitutional phase has the potential to make a leap forward in the development of the law, some trends reducing the discourse into a procedural-technical one may prevent such a move.

This chapter explored the great potential of the measure of proportionality as a tool for promoting a better equilibrium of interests in the online environment through the framework of remedies. It proposes a legal framework for introducing public law principles into private copyright law by acknowledging online intermediaries as hybrid bodies that should be held accountable not only for preventing online infringements but for protecting public freedoms as well.

---

also, Jarrod Hepburn, *The Duty to Give Reasons for Administrative Decisions in International Law,* 61(3) International & Comparative Law Quarterly 641 (2012) https://doi.org/10.1017/s0020589312000309; Carol Harlow, *Global Administrative Law: The Quest for Principles and Values,* 17 European Journal of International Law 187 (2006) https://doi.org/10.1093/ejil/chi158.

107. Martin Shapiro, *The Giving Reasons Requirement,* 1992 University of Chicago Legal Forum 179 (1992).

108. It should be noted that U.S. Administrative Procedure Act (APA), s. 557 forbids ex parte contact by agency officials with any interested party in formal rulemaking or adjudication. *See* APA §5(c), 5 USC §557(dXl) (1994).

Table of Cases

EU Case Law, Requests for Preliminary Rulings and Opinions

French Case law

German Case law

UK Case Law

US Case Law

Canadian Case Law

ECHR Case Law

Other Jurisdictions

Index

INFORMATION LAW SERIES

1. Egbert J. Dommering & P. Bernt Hugenholtz, *Protecting Works of Fact: Copyright, Freedom of Expression and Information Law,* 1991 (ISBN 90-654-4567-6).
2. Willem F. Korthals Altes, Egbert J. Dommering, P. Bernt Hugenholtz & Jan J.C. Kabel, *Information Law Towards the 21st Century,* 1992 (ISBN 90-654-4627-3).
3. Jacqueline M.B. Seignette, *Challenges to the Creator Doctrine: Authorship, Copyright Ownership and the Exploitation of Creative Works in the Netherlands, Germany and The United States,* 1994 (ISBN 90-654-4876-4).
4. P. Bernt Hugenholtz, *The Future of Copyright in a Digital Environment, Proceedings of the Royal Academy Colloquium,* 1996 (ISBN 90-411-0267-1).
5. Julius C.S. Pinckaers, *From Privacy Toward a New Intellectual Property Right in Persona,* 1996 (ISBN 90-411-0355-4).
6. Jan J.C. Kabel & Gerard J.H.M. Mom, *Intellectual Property and Information Law: Essays in Honour of Herman Cohen Jehoram,* 1998 (ISBN 90-411-9702-8).
7. Ysolde Gendreau, Axel Nordemann & Rainer Oesch, *Copyright and Photographs: An International Survey,* 1999 (ISBN 90-411-9722-2).
8. P. Bernt Hugenholtz, *Copyright and Electronic Commerce: Legal Aspects of Electronic Copyright Management,* 2000 (ISBN 90-411-9785-0).
9. Lucie M.C.R. Guibault, *Copyright Limitations and Contracts: An Analysis of the Contractual Overridability of Limitations on Copyright,* 2002 (ISBN 90-411-9867-9).
10. Lee A. Bygrave, *Data Protection Law: Approaching its Rationale, Logic and Limits,* 2002 (ISBN 90-411-9870-9).
11. Niva Elkin-Koren & Neil Weinstock Netanel, *The Commodification of Information,* 2002 (ISBN 90-411-9876-8).
12. Mireille M.M. van Eechoud, *Choice of Law in Copyright and Related Rights: Alternatives to the Lex Protectionis,* 2003 (ISBN 90-411-2071-8).
13. Martin Senftleben, *Copyright, Limitations and the Three-Step Test: An Analysis of the Three-Step Test in International and EC Copyright Law,* 2004 (ISBN 90-411-2267-2).
14. Paul L.C. Torremans, *Copyright and Human Rights: Freedom of Expression – Intellectual Property – Privacy,* 2004 (ISBN 90-411-2278-8).
15. Natali Helberger, *Controlling Access to Content: Regulating Conditional Access in Digital Broadcasting,* 2005 (ISBN 90-411-2345-8).
16. Lucie M.C.R. Guibault & P. Bernt Hugenholtz, *The Future of the Public Domain: Identifying the Commons in Information Law,* 2006 (ISBN 978-90-411-2435-7).

17. Irini Katsirea, *Public Broadcasting and European Law: A Comparative Examination of Public Service Obligations in Six Member States,* 2008 (ISBN 978-90-411-2500-2).
18. Paul L.C. Torremans, *Intellectual Property and Human Rights: Enhanced Edition of Copyright and Human Rights,* 2008 (ISBN 978-90-411-2653-5).
19. Mireille van Eechoud, P. Bernt Hugenholtz, Stef van Gompel, Lucie Guibault & Natali Helberger, *Harmonizing European Copyright Law: The Challenges of Better Lawmaking,* 2009 (ISBN 978-90-411-3130-0).
20. Ashwin van Rooijen, *The Software Interface between Copyright and Competition Law: A Legal Analysis of Interoperability in Computer Programs,* 2010 (ISBN 978-90-411-3193-5).
21. Irini A. Stamatoudi, *Copyright Enforcement and the Internet,* 2010 (ISBN 978-90-411-3346-5).
22. Wolfgang Sakulin, *Trademark Protection and Freedom of Expression: An Inquiry into the Conflict between Trademark Rights and Freedom of Expression under European Law,* 2011 (ISBN 978-90-411-3415-8).
23. Stef van Gompel, *Formalities in Copyright Law: An Analysis of their History, Rationales and Possible Future,* 2011 (ISBN 978-90-411-3418-9).
24. Nadezhda Purtova, *Property Rights in Personal Data: A European Perspective,* 2012 (ISBN 978-90-411-3802-6).
25. Brad Sherman & Leanne Wiseman, *Copyright and the Challenge of the New,* 2012 (ISBN 978-90-411-3669-5).
26. Ewa Komorek, *Media Pluralism and European Law*, 2012 (ISBN 978-90-411-3894-1).
27. Joris van Hoboken, *Search Engine Freedom: On the Implications of the Right to Freedom of Expression for the Legal Governance of Web Search Engines,* 2012 (ISBN 978-90-411-4128-6).
28. Natali Helberger, Lucie Guibault, Marco Loos, Chantal Mak, Lodewijk Pessers & Bart van der Sloot, *Digital Consumers and the Law: Towards a Cohesive European Framework*, 2012 (ISBN 978-90-411-4049-4).
29. Tatiana-Eleni Synodinou, *Codification of European Copyright Law: Challenges and Perspectives,* 2012 (ISBN 978-90-411-4145-3).
30. Heather Ann Forrest, *Protection of Geographic Names in International Law and Domain Name System Policy*, Second Edition, 2017 (ISBN 978-90-411-8839-7).
31. Sari Depreeuw, *The Variable Scope of the Exclusive Economic Rights in Copyright*, 2014 (ISBN 978-90-411-4915-2).
32. Vikrant Narayan Vasudeva, *Open Source Software and Intellectual Property Rights*, 2014 (ISBN 978-90-411-5228-2).
33. Frederik J. Zuiderveen Borgesius, *Improving Privacy Protection in the Area of Behavioural Targeting*, 2015 (ISBN 978-90-411-5990-8).
34. Paul L.C. Torremans, *Intellectual Property Law and Human Rights*, Fourth Edition, 2020 (ISBN 978-94-035-1304-1).

35. Irini A. Stamatoudi, *New Developments in EU and International Copyright Law*, 2016 (ISBN 978-90-411-5991-5).
36. Lodewijk W.P. Pessers, *The Inventiveness Requirement in Patent Law: An Exploration of Its Foundations and Functioning*, 2016 (ISBN 978-90-411-6731-6).
37. Susy Frankel & Daniel Gervais, *The Internet and the Emerging Importance of New Forms of Intellectual Property*, 2016 (ISBN 978-90-411-6789-7).
38. Axel M. Arnbak, *Securing Private Communications: Protecting Private Communications Security in EU Law – Fundamental Rights, Functional Value Chains, and Market Incentives*, 2016 (ISBN 978-90-411-6737-8).
39. Christina Angelopoulos, *European Intermediary Liability in Copyright: A Tort-Based Analysis*, 2017 (ISBN 978-90-411-6835-1).
40. João Pedro Quintais, *Copyright in the Age of Online Access: Alternative Compensation Systems in EU Law*, 2017 (ISBN 978-90-411-8667-6).
41. P. Bernt Hugenholtz, *Copyright Reconstructed: Rethinking Copyright's Economic Rights in a Time of Highly Dynamic Technological and Economic Change*, 2018 (ISBN 978-90-411-9103-8).
42. Manon Oostveen, *Protecting Individuals Against the Negative Impact of Big Data: Potential and Limitations of the Privacy and Data Protection Law Approach*, 2018 (ISBN 978-94-035-0131-4).
43. Tatiana Eleni Synodinou (ed.), *Pluralism or Universalism in International Copyright Law*, Second Edition, 2025 (ISBN 978-94-035-2688-1).
44. Martin Senftleben, *The Copyright/Trademark Interface: How the Expansion of Trademark Protection Is Stifling Cultural Creativity*, 2021 (ISBN 978-94-035-2370-5).
45. Tito Rendas, *Exceptions in EU Copyright Law: In Search of a Balance Between Flexibility and Legal Certainty*, 2021 (ISBN 978-94-035-2395-8).
46. Martin Senftleben, Joost Poort, Mireille van Eechoud, Stef van Gompel & Natalie Helberger (eds), *Intellectual Property and Sports: Essays in Honour of P. Bernt Hugenholtz*, 2021 (ISBN 978-94-035-3733-7).
47. Marijn Sax, *Between Empowerment and Manipulation: The Ethics and Regulation of For-Profit Health Apps*, 2021 (ISBN 978-94-035-3791-7).
48. Thomas Tombal, *Imposing Data Sharing among Private Actors: A Tale of Evolving Balances*, 2022 (ISBN 978-94-035-4160-0).

www.ingramcontent.com/pod-product-compliance
Lightning Source LLC
LaVergne TN
LVHW020003031026
849161LV00023B/865